This is a volume in

THE UNIVERSITY OF MICHIGAN HISTORY OF THE MODERN WORLD

Upon completion, the series will consist of the following volumes:

The United States to 1865 *by Michael Kraus*

The United States since 1865 *by Foster Rhea Dulles*

Canada: A Modern History *by John Bartlet Brebner*

Latin America: A Modern History *by J. Fred Rippy*

Great Britain to 1688: A Modern History *by Maurice Ashley*

Great Britain since 1688: A Modern History *by K. B. Smellie*

France: A Modern History *by Albert Guérard*

Germany: A Modern History *by Marshall Dill, Jr.*

Italy: A Modern History *by Denis Mack Smith*

Russia and the Soviet Union: A Modern History *by Warren B. Walsh*

The Near East: A Modern History *by William Yale*

The Far East: A Modern History *by Nathaniel Peffer*

India: A Modern History *by Percival Spear*

The Southwest Pacific to 1900: A Modern History *by C. Hartley Grattan*

The Southwest Pacific since 1900: A Modern History *by C. Hartley Grattan*

Spain: A Modern History *by Rhea Marsh Smith*

Eastern Europe: A Modern History *by John Erickson*

Africa: A Modern History *by Robin Hallett*

THE NEAR EAST

A Modern History

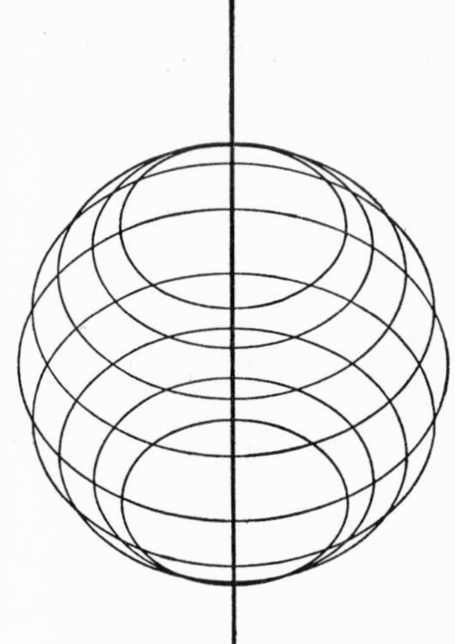

The University of Michigan History of the Modern World

Edited by Allan Nevins and Howard M. Ehrmann

THE NEAR EAST

A Modern History

BY WILLIAM YALE

NEW EDITION
REVISED AND ENLARGED

Ann Arbor : The University of Michigan Press

Library of Congress Catalog Card No. 68-29269
Published in the United States of America by
The University of Michigan Press
Designed by George Lenox
United Kingdom agent: The Cresset Press
Manufactured in the United States of America by
Vail-Ballou Press, Inc., Binghamton, New York

TO EDITH HANNA YALE

For whom this book was written
and but for whom it would not
have been written.

Contents

MAPS

THE NEAR EAST

A Modern History

CHAPTER I

Historical Foundations

The history of the Near East is that of a geographical area and its varied peoples, not that of any single nation. In modern times, down to 1918, the story centers around the Ottoman Empire; then, after World War I, it deals principally with the evolution of new nations—Iraq, Israel, Jordan, Lebanon, Syria, Saudi Arabia, Turkey, and Egypt.

Although this strategically situated region was subjected to invasion and conquest by many peoples from both Asia and Europe, the rich indigenous cultures of the Near East throughout most of its history had a strongly civilizing effect upon the surrounding barbarians and on alien invaders and conquerors. It is only in recent times that the impact of foreign nations and cultures has become of greater significance to the Near East than that of Near Eastern culture upon the West. This reversal of the role formerly played by the Near East is one of the most notable features of its recent and contemporary history.

۞ EAST IS EAST AND WEST IS WEST?

At the dawn of recorded history, many of the fundamental patterns of western civilization had been developed in Egypt, Mesopotamia, and Palestine. Here most of the basic social institutions of the West, as well as the ethical and philosophical concepts of its peoples, found their beginnings. But although East and West possess this common heritage, so many divergences have grown up between them in their respective ways of life and thought that Westerners, upon their first contact with the peoples of the Near East, find them strange and incomprehensible. The instinctive Occidental response was stated most effectively by Rudyard Kipling: "East is East and West is West and never the twain shall meet." Happily, the absurdity of this idea has been demonstrated by the successful bridging of the gap by many notable Europeans and by the countless thousands of inconspicuous Oriental immigrants to both

Europe and the Americas who have completely assimilated western culture. East and West "can meet" when there is mutual understanding, sympathy, and good will.

The principal causes of the difference between the peoples of the Near East and those of the West are historical in nature. The westerner lives in the complex society of an industrial era. The Near Easterner has not fully emerged from the Middle Ages. His ideas and institutions are largely those of a remote past now quite beyond the ken of the westerner, who must cross this historical gulf if he wishes to comprehend the contemporary Near East.

Throughout centuries of time the geography and climate of the Near East have been determining factors with respect to cultural as well as economic and political developments. In the river valleys of the Nile and of the Tigris and Euphrates, where intensive agriculture was possible for primitive people, industrious peasants created the wealth essential to the growth of urban centers. There industry and commerce flourished, producing accumulations which made possible the evolution of civilized life on a high cultural level for a small minority, the owning and controlling classes.

❁ ANCIENT INDUSTRIES AND TRADE ROUTES

In early times the Near East became a center of industrial and mercantile activity as well as of agricultural production. The peasant cultivators supplied the manufacturing and trading cities with food; the skilled craftsmen made products for markets near and far. Commerce developed at first along the river highways and then on the caravan and sea routes to more distant lands. The cities of the Near East became the foci of trade routes reaching far into Europe, Asia, and Africa. North and south, east and west, merchandise was carried along the rivers, across the deserts and steppes, and over the seas. Through Central Asia ran the great caravan routes to China. By way of the Aegean, the Straits (the Dardanelles, the Marmora Sea, and the Bosporus), and the Black Sea men found easy water passage to the rivers of Eastern Europe, which gave access to the great Eurasian plain stretching from the Urals to the Vosges Mountains. The Red Sea and the Persian Gulf furnished highways to East Africa and to India. The Mediterranean made trade possible with North Africa and southwestern Europe. Active local caravan routes which traversed Anatolia, Syria, Palestine, and Arabia provided connecting links in this intercontinental transportation system. For many centuries the Near East, as a nexus of trade routes, enjoyed a most favorable geographical position for economic prosperity.

Connected with these geographic features, which contributed so greatly to the welfare and cultural progress of the Near East, were certain disadvantages. The caravan and sea routes became avenues of invasion accessible to the Indo-European nomads from the north and to the Turkish and Mongolian nomads from the east. The caravan routes crossed arid and semiarid lands suitable only for wandering tribes, who were ever a threat to the trade routes and the agrarian and urban population. The great wealth of the Near Eastern cities was a constant temptation to invasion by "barbarian" nomads, as well as by predatory civilized states.

SECURITY AND THE STRUGGLE FOR POWER

To maintain law, order, and security, the cornerstones of prosperity and culture in the Near East, centers of political power arose in the valleys of the Nile, the Tigris, and the Euphrates. The Egyptians evolved a national state, and the Sumerians city states, but eventually in both Egypt and Mesopotamia empires were organized, which strove in vain to achieve domination of the Near East. The wars between these imperial states tended to undermine the security necessary to economic well-being.

It was not until the sixth century B.C. that political integration of western Asia was achieved by the Persians. Having secured control of the southern and eastern land and water routes, the Persians with their satellites, the Egyptians and the Phoenicians, attempted to wrest from the Greeks the northern and western trade routes. The conflicts which followed are known to us as the Persian Wars. This inconclusive struggle, which left the Persians in control of most of western Asia and the terminals of the Asiatic trade routes while the Greeks retained domination of the Aegean and Mediterranean sea lanes, created an unstable situation, which was unsatisfactory to the ruling classes in both the Persian Empire and the Greek city states.

Ostensibly, the Greeks were fighting for Hellenism and the Hellenic way of life against the "barbarian" Persians. The struggle had the superficial appearance of a conflict between the political individualism of the competitive Greek city states and the political totalitarianism of the multinational Persian Empire. The actual stakes were the control of the Near East, with its rich centers of industrial production and its intercontinental trade routes. The impasse was resolved 148 years later by Alexander the Great in 331 B.C. After bringing the Greek city states under subjection, he rapidly conquered Egypt and destroyed the Persian Empire, in an endeavor to create an imperial state embracing all the Near East, plus Iran and Central Asia.

This temporary political unification was soon terminated by the struggles for power among Alexander's successors. From the death of Alexander in 323 B.C. until its conquest by the Romans nearly 200 years later, the Near East was the victim of the rivalries of the Ptolemaic rulers of Egypt, the Seleucids of Asia Minor, and the Antonids of Macedonia. The inconclusive conflicts between these dynastic families and the remaining Greek city states were brought to an end eventually when the Roman Republic became the ruler of the eastern as well as the western Mediterranean with the adjacent hinterlands.

The resulting political and economic integration brought prosperity to the Near East under the Pax Romana. By the third century A.D., however, growing disorders within the Roman Empire and the rise in Persia of the new Sassanid dynasty (226–651) challenged Roman control of the eastern trade routes and threatened to undermine the political security and economic prosperity of the Near East. As a result of the declining importance of Italy in comparison with the economic wealth of the Near East, Emperor Constantine I in 325 decided to build his capital on the Bosporus near the site of the ancient Greek city of Byzantium. This new city, the first Christian city, which Constantine named New Rome, came to be called Constantinople. From this political and administrative center the Roman emperors and their successors the Byzantine emperors were able for more than a thousand years to hold in check the Persian Sassanids, to cope with the Teutonic, Slavic, and Turanian invaders, and to prevent the Arab Moslems from conquering Anatolia.

After the division of the Roman Empire into two parts in 395, the Christian emperors of Constantinople ruled over the greater part of the Near East until their power was challenged in the seventh century by the Moslem Arabs who swept out of Arabia conquering all of southwest Asia and Egypt. From the time of the defeat of the Byzantine armies in Syria in 642 until the capture of Constantinople in 1453, the Near East became the principal battlefield of the struggle between Christianity and Islam.

THE ADVENT OF ISLAM AND THE ARABS

The rulers of the Eastern Roman Empire were faced by a major crisis after the "fall of Rome" in 476. In addition to the burdens and dangers created by the invasions of Teutonic, Slavic, and Mongolian tribes, who overran the Balkans, interrupting trade along the principal river routes of eastern Europe and southern Russia, the rulers of Constantinople were faced with a prolonged economic depression resulting from the rapid decline of the West. The political disintegration of the Western Roman Empire had brought in its train social decay and economic collapse. Western European markets for the manufactured goods of Asia Minor were practically destroyed. Commerce came to a standstill. In the sixth century Justinian, Emperor of the East, made vigorous attempts to regain control of the western regions which were so important economically to the Near East. His successes in the West were partial and proved to be of a temporary nature, for his western policies undermined his power in the Near East.

By the seventh century the Byzantine Empire had also fallen into a weakened condition. In the north Asiatic nomads had disrupted the trade in the Black Sea area, in the Balkans the Slavs and Bulgars were a constant menace, and in Syria and Palestine the Persian Sassanids were a continuing threat. Heavy taxation, loss of income, and general poverty naturally produced great popular discontent. In the southern part of the empire, loyalty to the Byzantine government dropped to a low ebb. For there had developed in both Egypt and in Syria a nascent spirit of nationalism due in part to the linguistic and cultural differences which separated the Egyptians and the Syrians from their Greek rulers at Constantinople. These divergences were further augmented by the religious schisms which had rent the Christians of the Near East. Coupled with economic discontent these cultural and religious quarrels created a situation that prepared the way for the invasion of the Byzantine Empire by the fierce Moslem fighters of the Arabian Peninsula.

In the latter part of the sixth century and the beginning of the seventh, a religious and a political revolution occurred in Arabia, where the nomadic tribes and petty states of Arabia were brought under the political control of the merchants of Mecca by Mohammed. This gifted prophet based his new religion on the concept of one god, Allah, to whom mankind should submit in a universal society, Dar-al-Islam. After Mohammed's death, his successors, the early caliphs of Islam, led hosts of Arab pastoral nomads, inspired with religious zeal and inflamed by the hope of loot, to the conquest of western Asia. The Byzantine Empire was able to retain its control over Anatolia and the Balkans, but the Persian Empire was destroyed and its people brought within the fold of Islam.

The early Moslem leaders sprang from the commercial oligarchy of Mecca. They were merchants who had become religious and military leaders. Having acquired the rich and productive area of southwestern

Asia with armies composed, for the most part, of Arabian nomads, these merchant-warriors proceeded to organize it politically so as to ensure the order and security essential to economic prosperity. Using well-trained military forces to extend their conquests, the leaders of Islam protected the landowners and their peasants against raids and pillage by the Bedawi, the nomads of Arabia, and enforced security along the trade routes upon which the city craftsmen and merchants depended. Religious fervor and economic interest led to further expansion both east and west. Moslem armies extended their conquests north and east of Persia (Iran); moving westward from Egypt they swept across North Africa, conquered Spain, and crossed the Pyrenees into France, where they were halted by Charles Martel at the battle of Tours in 732, just one hundred years after the death of Mohammed.

These conquests gave the Arabs control of the network of trade routes converging on the Near East. Moslem merchants rapidly exploited this favorable political situation, extending their commercial activities east and west by land and sea. Arabs soon dominated the trade routes to India and the East Indies and to the coast of East Africa. Arab businessmen established branches in distant Canton and carried their operations north of the Caucasus and the Caspian Sea to the Volga and the Don and west of the Balkans to southern Italy and Spain. Reaping so rich a harvest, the southern part of the Near East flourished and gave birth to a new culture, that of Islam.

The Arabs, however, failed in one quarter. They were barred from control of the northern trade routes so long as they were unable to drive the Byzantine armies out of Anatolia and to capture Constantinople. The Byzantine Empire continued, until the seizure of Anatolia by Turkish tribes in the eleventh century, to hold a dominant position in the northern part of the Near East, and to profit from the trade routes to Eastern Europe via the Danube and the rivers of southern Russia.

The most enduring results of the Arab conquests, so far as the Near East is concerned, were neither economic nor political; they were cultural and social. A large percentage of the peoples of the Near East became Moslem. The faith of Islam spread across Egypt and North Africa to Spain, to India, to the East Indies, and to China, where even today the Chinese Moslems play a significant political role. The Asiatic nomads, Turanian and Mongol, Turk and Tatar, who overran southern Russia and the Near East, eventually became Moslem. Islamic theology, law, ethics, social institutions, and customs became dominant throughout the Near East. Islam established a pattern of life which created an almost unbridgeable gulf between the Christian minorities and the

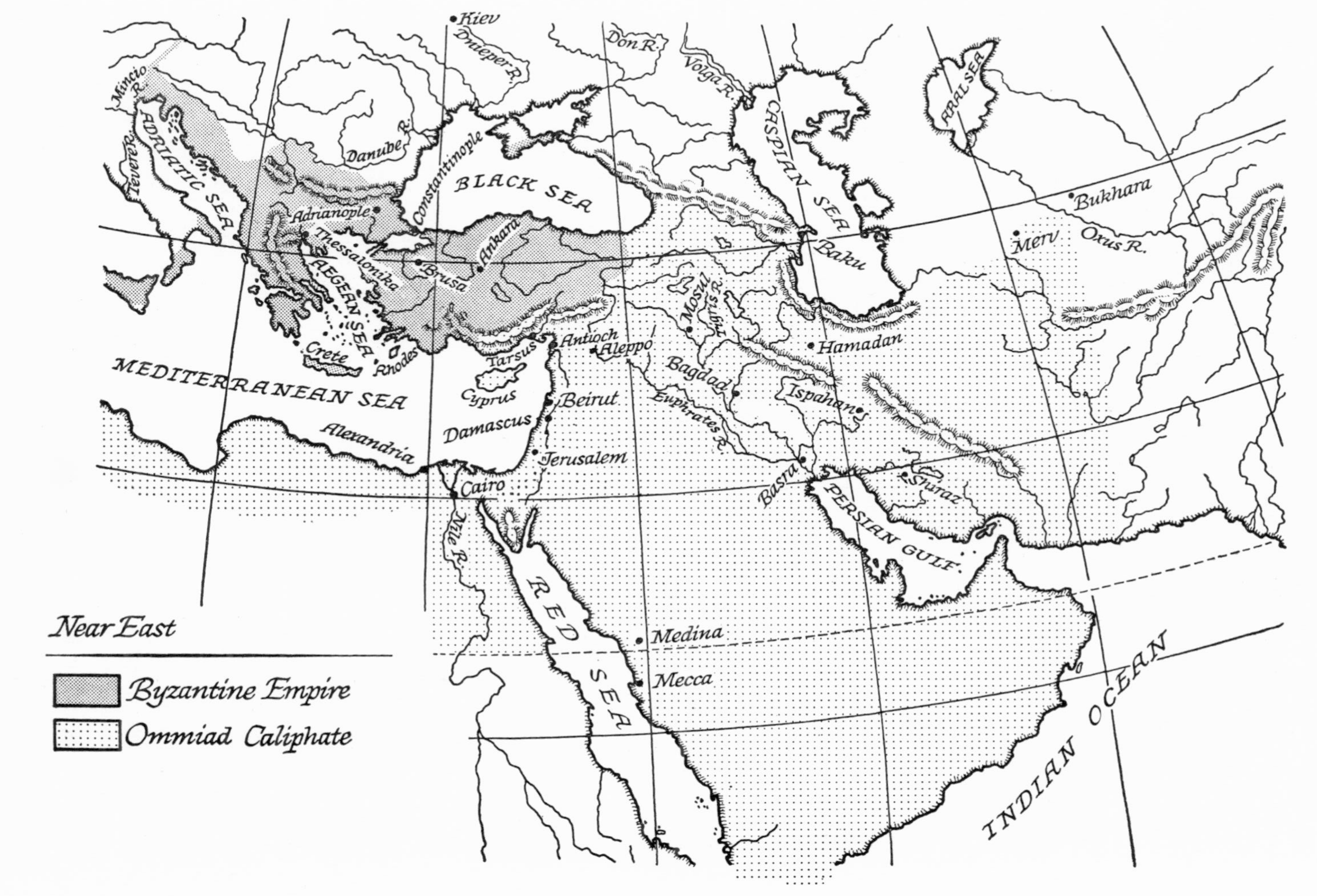
Near East
Byzantine Empire
Ommiad Caliphate
Kiev
Dnieper R.
Don R.
Volga R.
Mincio R.
Tevere R.
ADRIATIC SEA
Danube R.
Constantinople
BLACK SEA
CASPIAN SEA
ARAL SEA
Bukhara
Merv
Oxus R.
Baku
Adrianople
Thessalonika
AEGEAN SEA
Brusa
Ankara
Crete
Rhodes
Tarsus
Antioch
Aleppo
Mosul
Tigris R.
Hamadan
MEDITERRANEAN SEA
Cyprus
Beirut
Damascus
Alexandria
Jerusalem
Bagdad
Euphrates R.
Ispahan
Basra
Shiraz
PERSIAN GULF
Cairo
Nile R.
RED SEA
Medina
Mecca
INDIAN OCEAN

Moslem majorities; a gulf that exists down to the present time. The sharp divergence between the culture of Europe and that of the Near East was due in large measure to the advent of Islam.

The Arab Moslems, however, never succeeded in imposing either a political or cultural unity upon the Near East. The northern part of western Asia remained Christian, under Byzantine control, until the eleventh century. The establishment of the Scandinavian Varangians at Kiev in the ninth century and their organization of the first Russian state, which controlled the river trade route from the Black Sea to the Baltic, favored the expansion of Constantinople's trade, and in part compensated the Byzantine Empire economically for its losses in the south to the Arabs. The Near East, in consequence, remained divided between two political and economic rivals, whose struggle for power was further embittered by religious antagonisms. An uneasy equilibrium between the Christian and Moslem states was maintained until the invasions of the Turkish tribal nomads from central Asia.

The offensive power of the Arabs was greatly lessened during the eighth century by internal dynastic struggles. The Ommiad caliphs of Damascus were overthrown in 750 and a capital was set up at Bagdad in 762. Although this new Abbasid caliphate endured until it was destroyed in 1258 by the Tatars, its rulers were unable to retain control of the sprawling Moslem empire. Islamic Spain refused to acknowledge the Abbasid caliphs; Moslem Egypt asserted its independence in the tenth century and established the rival Fatimite caliphate. After an era of great prosperity and political power in the early part of the ninth century during the time of Harun al Rashid, the Abbasid caliphate grew so weak that, in order to maintain its control over the Arab lands of western Asia, it was obliged to employ mercenary troops recruited from a nomadic Turanian tribe known as the Seljuk Turks.

In the tenth century the Abbasid rulers came to be little more than puppets of the Seljuk Turks. By the eleventh century Turkish tribes were moving into the eastern part of Asia Minor in increasingly large numbers. The Byzantine army sent against them was defeated at the battle of Manzikert in 1071. The train of events which followed this Turkish victory makes it loom up as one of the most decisive contests in the long history of the Near East from the Arab victory over Byzantine forces at the battle of the Yarmuk in 636 to the British defeat of the Ottoman armies in Palestine and Syria in 1918. Whereas the battle of Yarmuk assured the triumph of Islam in the southwest, the Turkish victory at Manzikert foreshadowed dominance of the Moslem religion and culture in eastern Asia Minor.

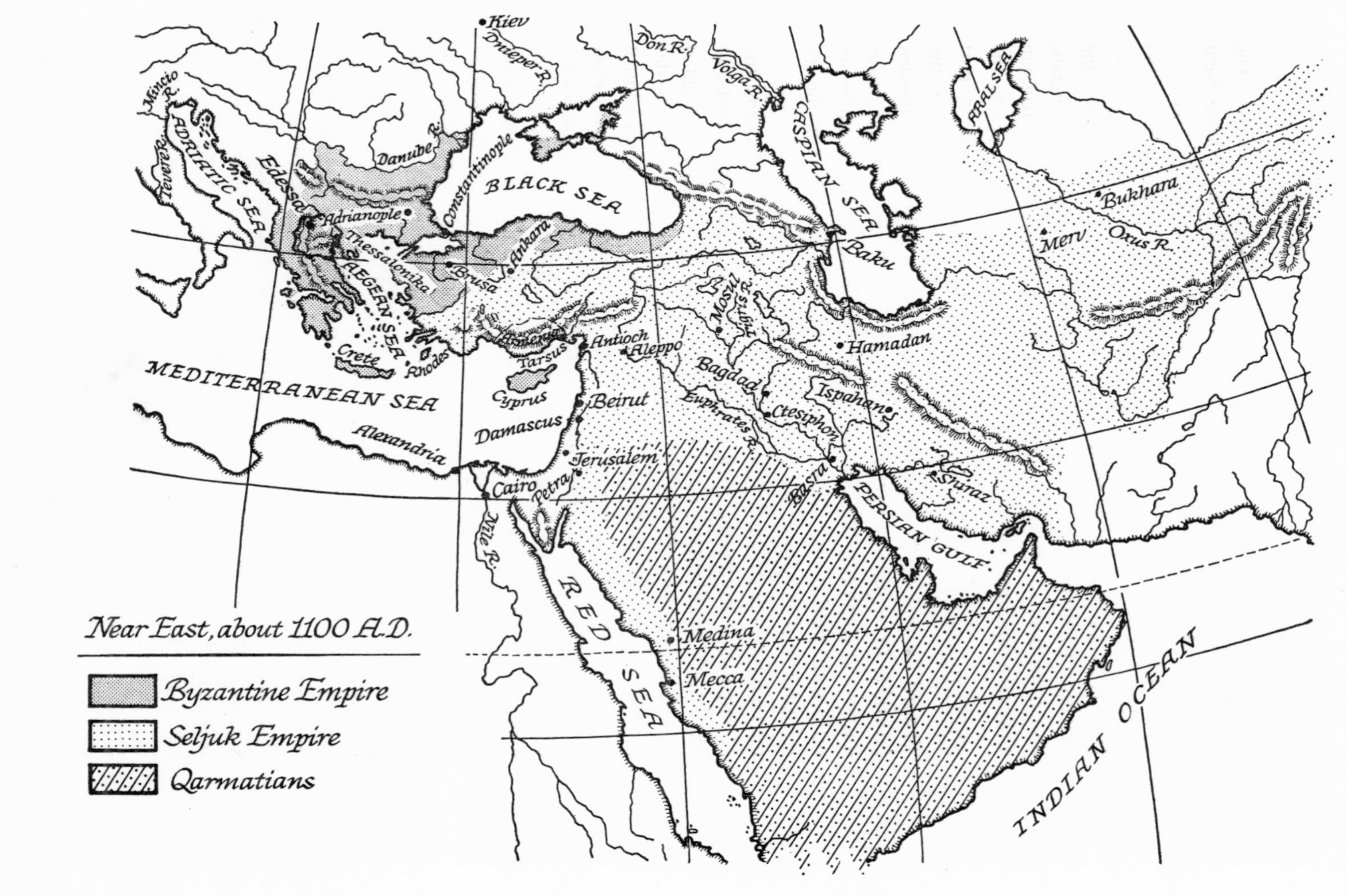
Kiev
Dnieper R.
Don R.
Volga R.
Mincio R.
Tevere R.
ADRIATIC SEA
Edessa
Danube R.
Constantinople
BLACK SEA
CASPIAN SEA
ARAL SEA
Bukhara
Merv
Oxus R.
Baku
Adrianople
Thessalonika
AEGEAN SEA
Brusa
Ankara
Mosul
Tigris R.
Hamadan
Armenia
Antioch
Aleppo
Tarsus
Crete
Rhodes
MEDITERRANEAN SEA
Cyprus
Beirut
Bagdad
Ispahan
Euphrates R.
Ctesiphon
Damascus
Alexandria
Jerusalem
Cairo
Petra
Basra
Shiraz
PERSIAN GULF
Nile R.
RED SEA
Medina
Mecca
INDIAN OCEAN
Near East, about 1100 A.D.
Byzantine Empire
Seljuk Empire
Qarmatians

The Seljuk Turks became the masters of eastern and central Asia Minor, where they organized a Moslem Turkish state which marks the beginning of the extension of Islamic culture to the northern part of the Near East. Threatened by the expansion of Turkish Moslem power to the west, the Byzantine Emperor Alexius I appealed to Pope Urban II in 1094 for military aid from the West against the infidel Turks. This request for help precipitated the Crusades, which in the long run proved disastrous both to the Byzantine Empire and to the survival of Christianity as a dominant culture in the Near East.

CRUSADERS, TURKS, AND TATARS

Toward the end of the eleventh century, conditions in Europe became favorable for expansion to the east. In Italy, where urban centers of industry and commerce had developed, the merchants, bankers, and shipowners of Venice and Genoa were seeking to extend their economic activities in Asia Minor. As increasing production and expanding commerce forced the ruling classes of these Italian city states along the road of imperialist expansion, they sought naval and commercial bases in the eastern Mediterranean and in the Black Sea. Meanwhile in western and central Europe, the political and economic structure remained still predominantly feudal. The basis of wealth and power lay principally in the ownership of land and serfs. Existing methods of agriculture, however, did not provide adequately for the increasing population, which could not be absorbed by the medieval towns, their commerce and industry as yet being insufficiently developed. Political unrest and social discontent grew bitter among the nobles, the peasants, and the townsmen. The times favored agrarian as well as commercial expansion at a moment in history when psychological forces, aroused by the rivalry between Mohammedanism and Christianity, supplied the emotional and ideological drive for the Crusades.

During the two hundred years of the Crusades, the Near East was repeatedly overrun from both Europe and Asia. The weakness of the Byzantine rulers and the Abbasid caliphs alike left western Asia unable to cope with the European and Asiatic invaders. All semblance of political unity was shattered. Power was divided and subdivided among rulers in constant conflict with one another; European feudal nobles in Palestine and Syria, at Constantinople, and in the Balkans; the Mamelukes of Egypt, the Byzantine rulers, the Abbasids of Bagdad, the Atabegs in northern Syria and Mesopotamia; and the Turks in Asia Minor. In addition, western Asia was overrun and pillaged by the Tatars from distant Mongolia.

It seems amazing that civilization survived these two hundred years of turmoil and devastation from 1094 to 1294, for the cultures that had been protected by those bitter rivals, the Byzantine emperors and the Abbasid caliphs, suffered a succession of the most grievous blows. The Fourth Crusade, financed by the merchant-bankers of Venice, was directed against the Byzantine Empire. In 1204 the European Crusaders captured the Christian city of Constantinople, drove out the Byzantine rulers, and divided the European provinces into fiefs of a feudal state known as the "Latin Empire of Romania." The expelled Byzantine officials fled to Asia Minor, where in restricted territories they maintained the fiction of an imperial state until their return to Constantinople in 1261. This blow to the commerce, industry, and economic prosperity of the Byzantine realm was a disaster for the Near East, which was worsened by the Tatar invasions of Russia and Eastern Europe that were equally calamitous for Kievan Russia. The capture and destruction of Kiev in 1240 by the Mongols destroyed the Kievan state and terminated the long-established and lucrative trade between Constantinople and Russia. The Seljuk empire in Anatolia, which had reached a high level of prosperity during the early decades of the thirteenth century also was brought under the tutelage of the Mongol khans.[1] These nomads from Mongolia destroyed the political security achieved by the Seljuk Turks and intensified the economic confusion resulting from the Tatar conquest of southern Russia.

In southwestern Asia the Crusaders opened the doors of eastern trade to the Italian merchants. In spite of the intermittent warfare between Christians and Moslems in Syria, Palestine, and Egypt, a close commercial relationship developed between Christian merchants of the Italian city states and the Moslem traders of the Arab lands. While the Christians secured control of the Mediterranean shipping routes the Arabs continued to dominate both land and water routes from southwestern Asia to India and China. In the Arab countries of the Near East, the Crusades thus fostered trade and brought increased prosperity to the mercantile classes. The disaster which really overwhelmed the Mesopotamian area (Iraq) in the thirteenth century was the Tatar devastation in 1258 under Hulagu, who destroyed the system of irrigation, razed the city of Bagdad, and put an end to the Abbasid caliphate.

At the opening of the fourteenth century, no state was strong enough to give order and security to the Near East, which lay in a condition of political chaos. The Byzantine rulers, re-established at Constantinople in 1261, retained only a precarious grip on parts of the Balkan Peninsula, where they were constantly threatened by Serbs and Bulgars and the

Venetians, and a limited foothold in northwest Asia Minor. The greater part of the Anatolian Peninsula was divided into petty Turkish feudal states, none of which was able to extend its power over the whole. Turkish Atabegs ruled the Syrian Desert and Mesopotamia. The Egyptian sultans, who held Palestine and part of Syria, attempted to gain control of southern Asia Minor. The Italian states and the Crusading orders were rivals in seeking control of the islands and trade routes of the eastern Mediterranean and the Aegean.

Stretching across the Near East in the north was the vast Mongol empire of the Tatars, who controlled the Eurasian plain from Poland to Mongolia. The northern caravan routes between Europe and Asia were in the hands of the Tatars. Constantinople had lost the trade of both the Russian rivers and the Asiatic land routes.

Neither Moslem nor Christian, Arab nor Greek, European nor Asiatic Mongol had been able to master the Near East and to achieve that political integration essential to the security and economic well-being of its peoples. In one of the lesser Turkish principalities of western Asia Minor, however, there was gestating that force which, in the next one hundred and fifty years, was to bring the entire Near East, the Balkan Peninsula, Egypt, and to some extent most of North Africa under centralized political control.

CHAPTER II

The Ottoman Turks

Among the many Turanian tribes which, beginning in the tenth century, had been moving westward into Asia Minor from their original homeland in that part of Central Asia known as Turkestan, was a clan which had settled in northwestern Anatolia bordering on the Asiatic territories of the Byzantine Empire. According to Turkish legends, the leader of a band of Turks, named Ertoghrul, aided Seljuk Sultan Ala ed-Din in defeating a Tatar army in 1251, and as a reward for his services Ertoghrul and his followers were granted lands in northwestern Asia Minor.

❁ CONQUESTS AND EXPANSION

Osman (Othman), a Turkish tribal leader in northwestern Anatolia, by legend the son of Ertoghrul, won a series of victories during the first quarter of the fourteenth century over the Byzantines in the region of Nicaea and extended his possessions to the Marmora and Bosporus. Osman became the founder of a dynasty after which the Ottoman Empire and the Ottoman Turks were named.

Orkhan (1326–59), Osman's son, established the first capital of the Ottomans at Brusa in Asia Minor after its capture from the Byzantine rulers in 1326. Under his leadership the Turks crossed the Dardanelles in 1345 and began their conquests in Eastern Europe. Later, Sultan Murad I (1360–89) and Sultan Bayazid (1389–1402) extended and consolidated the control of the Ottoman Turks in the Balkans, where in 1366 Adrianople became the new capital of the Turkish Empire. The Turks thus were established in Europe as a power which the West would have to contend with for nearly six hundred years.

Employing the material and human resources of the Balkans now at their disposal, the Ottoman rulers shortly gained control over the

Turkish principalities in Asia Minor; doing this despite the incursions of the Tatars under Tamerlane, who defeated the Ottoman forces at Ankara in 1402, taking the Sultan Bayazid prisoner. One great prize still remained to be seized. During the following fifty years, the Ottomans, although weakened by internal dynastic struggles following the death of Bayazid, were able by effective organization of their imperial possessions in the Balkans and Asia Minor to capture Constantinople in 1453. Thus, Sultan Mohammed II, the conqueror (1451–81), and his descendants became the heirs of the Greek emperors, and the Ottoman Empire the successor of the Byzantine state.

Holding possession of Constantinople, and controlling most of the Balkans and much of Asia Minor, the Ottoman sultans, within a short period conquered the Near East, Egypt, the Balkans, and part of Hungary. Their control extended even to North Africa and the western Mediterranean. For the first time since the collapse of the Roman Empire, a thousand years earlier, the Near East was brought under a state whose dominion extended far to the west in both north and south. With a strong government capable of maintaining order and security along the intercontinental trade routes from Europe across western Asia to the Middle and Far East, conditions in the early sixteenth century were seemingly favorable to the renewal of economic prosperity and the flowering of a great new Near Eastern culture. The feeble and decadent Byzantine Empire had perished; the petty warring Turkish states of Anatolia, Mesopotamia, and Syria had been eliminated; and Egypt's futile attempts to gain control of Asia Minor had been terminated by the Turkish conquest. The disorganizing political rivalry and activities in the Near East of the Italian city states were checkmated. The turbulent Christian peoples of the Balkans, with their unceasing strife, had been brought under the suzerainty of a powerful centralized state. The vigorous Turkish people, whose leaders had shown considerable capacity to organize and administer an expanding empire, had become political masters of the Near East in both Asia and in Europe.

Unfortunately for the peoples of the Near East, instead of an era of increasing economic prosperity and advancing civilization, a period of progressive economic decline, political deterioration, and cultural stagnation if not decadence followed the sixteenth century. A close analysis of the causes of this degeneration under the rule of the Ottomans is beyond the scope of this volume. A summary examination, however, of some of the contributing factors is useful to an understand-

NEAR EAST

about 1300

approximate boundaries

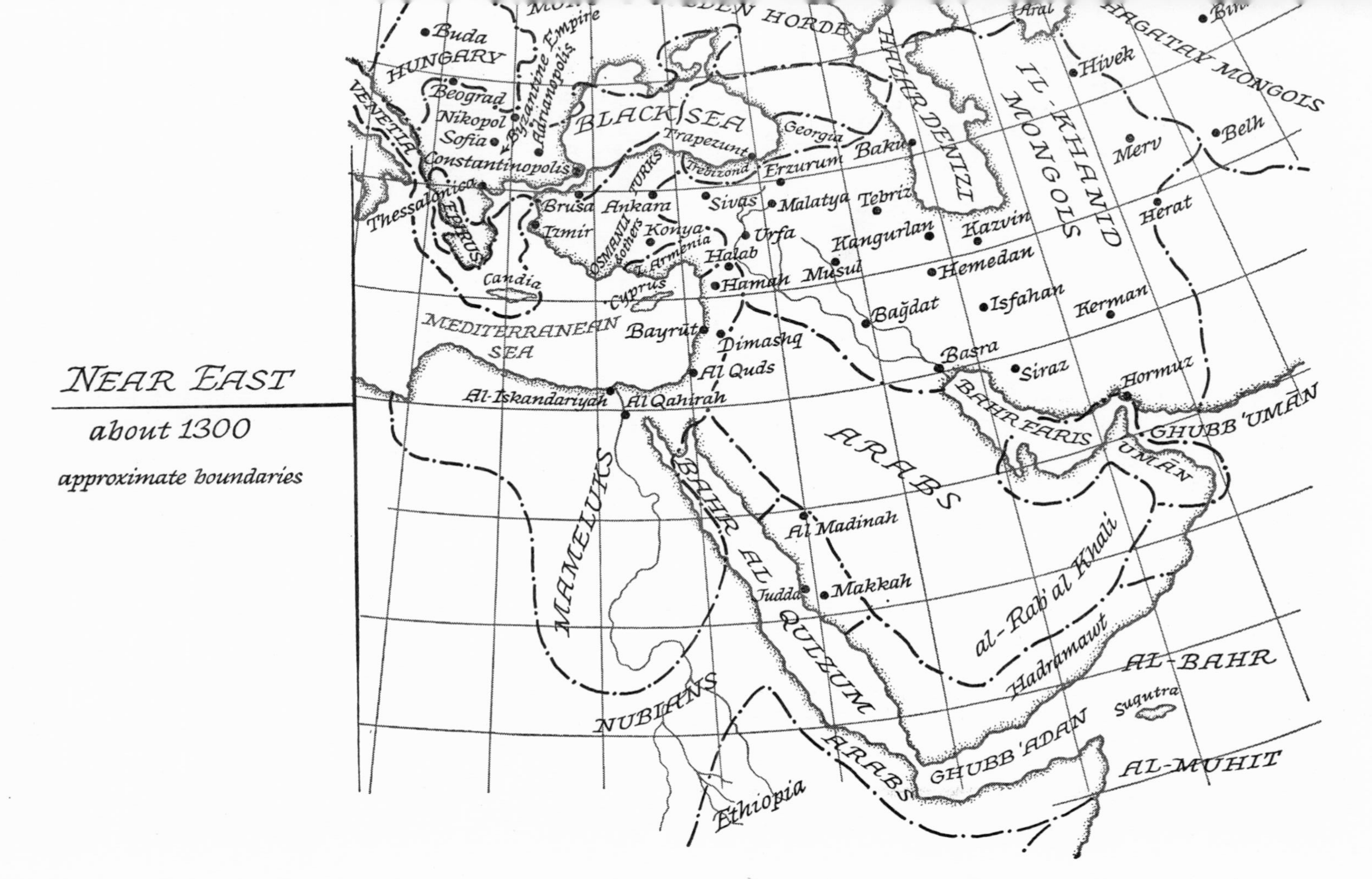

ing of the history and major problems of the Near East in recent and contemporary times.

TURKISH CULTURE

The invasions of Anatolia and the Arab lands of western Asia by the Seljuk and other Turkish tribes in the eleventh century, the wars between the Turks and the European Crusaders, and the Mongol-Tatar invasions of Europe, which began in the thirteenth century, gave rise to the idea in Europe during the fourteenth and fifteenth centuries that the Ottoman Turks were wild, untutored nomads from central Asia. The idea has been perpetuated to modern times and has been the basis for the interpretations of Ottoman history presented by some western writers.

The Turks in southern Russia, the Balkans, and Anatolia are descendants of the Turanian pastoral nomads from central Asia, many of the Turanian tribes having successively moved westward over a period of several centuries. Among the first of the western Turks to organize a strong and extensive state were the Seljuks, who founded their empire in Anatolia during the eleventh century. They had become Moslem from their close contact with the Persians and Arabs, by whom the whole culture of the Seljuks was greatly affected. These Turks had been established in Asia Minor for nearly three hundred years before the Ottoman Turks crossed over into Europe and commenced their conquest of the Balkans. Although there were still Turkish nomads in Asia Minor in the fourteenth century, the bulk of the Anatolian population were peasants. Anatolia also had a numerous and prosperous urban population, a considerable proportion of which was Turkish. Under the rule of the Seljuks and their successors, there flourished many important caravan and commercial cities with well-developed industries.[1]

The Ottoman Turks cannot be compared to the Tatars who, coming from Mongolia as pastoral nomads, overran the Russian Kievan state in the thirteenth century, or to the Tatars under Tamerlane who raided and pillaged Anatolia in the fifteenth century. During three centuries of rule in western Asia, the Turkish upper classes had developed an urban culture which was comparable with, if not superior to, that in Eastern Europe and the Balkans and not inferior to that of Europe in the fifteenth century. Europeans and their American descendants nevertheless, have not as yet completely freed their minds of those historic prejudices regarding the Turks which arose out of ignorance, ideological differences, and war.

OTTOMAN INSTITUTIONS [2]

When the Ottoman Turks became the rulers of a vast empire in Europe, Asia, and Africa, many of their older institutions were greatly modified, while some of those of the Byzantine Empire were adopted. Culturally, the heritage of the Ottomans was Islamic, Persian, and Arab; politically, it was Moslem and Byzantine.

The Moslem Institution.—The Ottoman state was, and remained throughout its history, a theocracy. The fundamental law, known as the Sheriat, was based on the Koran. The courts and judiciary were Moslem, and a vast bureaucracy, known as the Moslem Institution, controlled the legal and judicial system of the empire. At the head of this body of learned Moslems, the ulemas, trained in the sacred law and steeped in ancient Arab scholasticism, was a hierarchy, both religious and legal, composed of the cadis (Moslem judges) and muftis (Moslem jurists with the authority of superior judges). The chief of this numerous and powerful Moslem Institution was the Grand Mufti at Constantinople, with the title of Sheikh of Islam. As any law or official act of the Ottoman sultans or of their ministers could be declared contrary to the Sheriat by the Sheikh of Islam, he and the ulemas had a powerful instrument of control over the government.

The mosques, the schools, the courts, and the great Moslem religious orders known as the dervishes, were all knit closely with the ulemas, and every phase of Moslem life in the empire was influenced by them. Bound by an orthodox interpretation of a dogmatic body of religious law, the Ottoman Moslem society was profoundly conservative with respect to its social and political institutions, and vigorously reactionary in confronting proposals for reform or for basic change.

The Millet *system.*—The Islamic organizations, such as the Moslem Institution and the dervish brotherhoods, were not the only elements which were conservative and reactionary. As Christians could not be compelled to submit to the Sheriat or made subject to Islamic religious courts, the Ottoman government created the *Millet* system in order to bring the Christian and Jewish subjects within the framework of the imperial government. In conformity with Arab tradition and Byzantine practice with respect to foreigners, the Ottoman sultans granted their non-Moslem subjects a limited autonomy under the chief ecclesiastical leaders of the different religious sects. All members of the Orthodox Church, whether Albanian, Arab, Bulgar, Rumanian, or Greek by nationality, were subject to the Greek Orthodox patriarch of Constantinople. The members of the Gregorian Armenian Church were subject to the Armenian patriarch. All the other non-Moslem religious groups were likewise subject to the jurisdiction of their chief ecclesiastical officers. The *Millet* system conferred extensive powers upon the clergy, which made it possible for the priesthood to exert a strong influence over their lay communities.

The Moslem Institution and the *Millet* system strengthened throughout the Ottoman Empire, among Moslems and Christians alike, the grip of conservative and reactionary religious leaders; and it did this at the very time when in Europe the "tyranny of the supernatural" and the power of the priesthood were being challenged as a result of the Renaissance and the Reformation. The Turkish ruling class, living by exploiting both Moslems and Christians, could not repudiate the authority of the Ulemas upon whose support their power depended. The Christian middle class—merchants and professional men—dependent upon their priests for protection against rapacious Turkish officials, could not play the role of their counterparts in the Italian city states and in the national states of western Europe by promoting an intellectual and religious revolt against the clergy. The Christian priests in turn depended upon the sultan's government for the enforcement of the judgments of those ecclesiastical courts which had jurisdiction over the Christians and for the maintenance of the vested interests of the clergy.

The Ottoman system of government and social organization placed almost insurmountable obstacles in the pathway of progress. Christian as well as Moslem obscurantism was responsible to a considerable degree for the failure of the Near East to keep abreast of the rapid developments in western Europe.

The Janissaries.—Two notable institutions created by the Ottoman sultans were the military organization of the Janissaries and the civil service, which has been aptly called the "Ruling Institution" by Professor Lybyer. These institutions evolved from the practice by the Ottoman leaders in Anatolia of employing captured prisoners as mercenary troops. Later on, during the conquest of the Balkans, the Turks, with the religious sanction of the grand mufti, took as tribute from the Christian population a percentage of the male children. These became the "slaves" of the sultan. Completely severed from their Christian families, these children were brought up as Moslems and imbued with religious devotion to Islam and loyalty to the sultan. The more able were enrolled in the palace corps of pages and trained to become administrators and officials in the state bureaucracy, the Ruling Institution. The remainder were given a military education and became members of the famous Janissary corps, recognized in the fifteenth and sixteenth centuries as the best trained and most effective soldiers of Europe.

With a military force and a bureaucracy thus recruited from the non-Turkish and non-Moslem subjects, the earlier Ottoman sultans secured effective control over the empire. This they were able to maintain until the forces of corruption inherent in a military state based essentially on exploitation undermined the integrity of the Ruling Institution and changed basically the structure of the Janissary organization.

The Janissaries were closely associated with the religious order of the Bektash Dervishes, whose agha, or chief, held a commission as colonel in the Janissary organization. Dervishes were attached to all the military units of the Janissaries in their barracks and to the troops in the field. Thus the Janissaries closely affiliated with the Moslem Institution of ulemas, muftis, and cadis acquired elements of political power which threatened that of the sultans.

Growing weakness of the sultans in the seventeenth century resulted in the granting of more privileges to the Janissaries, whose officers became a class exempted from the burdens of taxation which even the Moslem population bore. Although Janissaries held a very special position in the empire and their officers had many opportunities to enrich themselves, the rank and file frequently found themselves without pay when the government was in financial difficulties. Gradually, the very structure of Janissary organization was changed. Because of the opportunities open to the officers, many Turks sought to have their children enrolled in the Janissary corps, and by the last quarter of the seventeenth century the Janissaries ceased to be recruited from Christian families. Meanwhile, many ill-paid Janissary privates engaged in crafts and commercial activities, becoming prominent in so-called "corporations," which were comparable to the craft and merchant guilds of medieval Europe. This military organization holding a specially privileged position closely allied with a powerful religious brotherhood, eventually became intimately associated with important economic organizations. It thus grew to be a potent instrument of political power. The Janissaries, by riots, and mutinies, forced the sultans to dismiss members of the Divan and grand viziers, and even deposed sultans. While it was frequently described by historians as a Praetorian Guard, the Janissary corps, through its affiliations with other Ottoman institutions, had wider alliances than any mere body of mercenary troops.

The growing corruption of the Janissary corps undermined the military power of the Ottoman Empire and exposed it to foreign invasion. It threatened the very existence of orderly government. Not until 1826 was its power broken and the Ottoman state freed from this dangerous incubus. It was only when the ulemas and the members of the Ruling Institution had come to understand its threat to the very existence of the state that Sultan Mahmoud II was able to obtain their consent to the destruction of the Janissary corps.

The Ruling Institution.—The early Ottoman sultans had created an effective administrative bureaucracy in which promotion was based upon service, training, experience, and ability. This rule of advancement grade by grade to high ranking positions in the government was broken by Sultan Suleiman, the Magnificent (1520–66), who appointed to the post of grand vizier a favorite who held only the lowly position of master of the court pages. In fact, Suleiman I not only generally disregarded the rule of precedence in appointment to office, but permitted his favorites to acquire huge fortunes by the sale of places and privileges. These practices, which were enlarged by Suleiman's successors, undermined the integrity and efficiency of the "Ruling Institution," spreading corruption throughout the whole empire. The buying of offices and favors became a common practice, so highly organized that both Ottoman moneylenders and foreign merchant-bankers financed the operations of the office-seekers. The burden of these corrupt practices fell principally upon the peasant and urban workers, both Moslem and Christian subjects of the sultan.

The imperial harem.—Directly connected with the growth of this corruption among the administrative bureaucracy was the Ottoman institution of the imperial harem. Shut up in the sultans' palaces lived a separate community of women, slaves, eunuchs, the court pages, and other members of the imperial household. The successors of Suleiman I retired from active affairs of state and became puppets of the harem. Deprived of any effective education, associating with ignorant slaves and eunuchs, debauched by innumerable concubines, the Ottoman autocrats retained only the power of appointment and dismissal of officials. For nearly seventy years during the reigns of eight sultans—from 1578 to 1656—the women of the harem practically ruled the empire through their favorites, appointed to high office by sultans who were dominated by some one of the rival cliques. Greedy and avaricious, the members of the harem sapped the wealth of the government and of the empire. Moral and financial corruption spread throughout the "Ruling Institution," the "Moslem Institution," and the Janissary corps.

Although corruption reached its apex in the Ottoman Empire by the first quarter of the eighteenth century and was never thoroughly eliminated, it was neither peculiarly Turkish nor Moslem. Corruption is a social phenomenon observable both in the past and present, prevalent in monarchies and republics, empires and kingdoms, autocracies and democracies, wherever the organization of society favors the exploitation of the many by the few. The nature and evolution of the Ottoman state fostered corruption at the top, which spread throughout all its members. There is a Turkish proverb which aptly describes this condition of affairs: "The fish begins to stink at the head." Until its dissolution following World War I, this putrefaction at the center of the Ottoman Empire afflicted the entire Near East for more than three hundred years.

The Capitulations.—Another Ottoman institution, adopted from Arab and Byzantine practices, which at first served the interests of the Ottoman state and was advantageous to its peoples but which later became an instrument of foreign exploitation, was that of the Capitulations.

Constantinople, like other cities of the Near East, was a manufacturing, commercial, and entrepôt center, whose economic life depended upon its export, import, and transit trade. It was, consequently, imperative to encourage foreign traders and shippers. This was recognized by the Turks following their capture of Constantinople, when rights and privileges were granted by the sultan to the merchants of the Italian city states. In the next century, at a time when French trade was expanding in the Near East and when Francis I of France and Sultan Suleiman were at war with the Habsburg Emperor Charles V, a treaty of amity and commerce was signed between France and the Ottoman Empire in 1535. This treaty was the base upon which the capitulatory system, as it existed down to the twentieth century, was evolved. As it and subsequent agreements were drafted in the form of chapters, or *capitularies,* the special rights and privileges, including those of extraterritoriality whereby foreigners were exempt from the jurisdiction of Ottoman courts and from many forms of taxation, thus got their special name. As time went on, many other non-Moslem states acquired capitulatory rights and privileges, which were augmented with the growing weakness of the Ottoman government and the increasing power of the western states. The expansion of the political and economic activities of western states in the Near East, resulted in the growth of foreign groups in the Ottoman Empire whose rights and privileges increasingly encroached upon the sovereignty of the sultans' government.

The feudal land system.—The feudal system of land grants and landholding in the Ottoman Empire differed very considerably from that of central and western Europe, resembling rather that of the Russian Muscovite state. One striking difference was that the Turkish system did not create an hereditary landed aristocracy. It was patterned after the system evolved by the Seljuk Turks at a much earlier date, and was similar to that of the Byzantine Empire. The existence of a feudal society within the framework of a centralized imperial state, with large urban centers and a mercantile economic order operating on the basis of a money economy, necessarily developed a feudal system different from that of western Europe, where urban society and a money economy had practically vanished after the fall of the Roman Empire of the West.

Instead of being granted land titles as feudal fiefs, the Turkish military and civilian leaders were awarded the right to the taxes of given territorial areas. These grants were made as recompense for services, and carried the obligation to furnish armed forces at the call of the sultan. Feudal troops so raised were called the spahis, and formed an important part of the standing army of the Ottoman Empire. In the earlier period, feudal grants were made to men of proven military ability; however, corruption at the court resulted in conferring these feudal grants upon favorites, courtiers, and eunuchs of the harem, and they were bought and sold as were government positions. The system of military feudalism then became as sadly permeated with corruption as were the Ruling Institution and the Moslem Institution.

DECLINE OF OTTOMAN POWER

These typically Ottoman institutions, which at first contributed to the strength of the Empire later became causes of its weakness and decline.

The economic and social factors.—Throughout most of its history the economy of the Near East had been based upon its nomads, peasants, craftsmen, and merchants whose activities and prosperity are interdependent. The pastoral nomads, who live in the extensive semiarid regions of western Asia, supply not only meat, wool, and hides but also the main means of transportation, camels and horses. Across their lands run the principal lines of communications, the local and intercontinental caravan routes. The economic welfare of the nomads is dependent upon the rural and urban markets for their products. The bulk of the Near Eastern population is made up of peasants, whose prosperity is dependent upon security from marauding nomads and robbers and undisturbed access to urban markets along the caravan routes. The craftsmen and merchants of the towns and cities can prosper only when law and order prevail and when food and merchandise can flow freely and securely along the domestic and foreign trade routes. The prosperity of the entire population depends upon a strong and efficient government whose power could only be maintained by meeting the needs of its subjects.

The most favorable political condition for the economic prosperity of the Near East was one of unity under a government capable of maintaining order, removing local obstacles to trade, keeping the routes open, and maintaining relations with neighboring states which would foster commerce. The Ottoman Turks achieved the political unity of the Near East and secured a considerable measure of control over the important trade routes to east and west, north and south. During much of the long period of their rule they maintained domestic law and order and protected the Asiatic parts of the Empire from invasion and pillage. Yet despite conditions seemingly so favorable to economic prosperity, the period of the Ottoman rule was marked by economic stagnation and consequent cultural decline. The causes of this decline lie, in part, within the Ottoman Empire, and in part far beyond the Near East. Whereas it might be reasonable to hold the Ottoman system and the Turkish ruling classes responsible for the domestic factors, it would be unfair to blame them for foreign circumstances quite beyond their control.

It is customary in the West to think of the Turks as looters and exploiters, who destroyed flourishing societies and oppressed non-Turkish people, mostly industrious and worthy Christians. This is a very distorted and unrealistic conception of the Ottoman Empire and the Near East under Turkish rule. The great bulk of the Moslem population, especially in Asia Minor who were workers, peasants in the villages and skilled and unskilled laborers in the cities, were as ruthlessly exploited by the Turkish ruling classes as were the Christians. Those who have seen the Turkish villages of Anatolia and the Arab villages of Syria and Palestine, and compared them with Christian villages in eastern Thrace and western Asia, would agree that the standard of living of the Moslem Turkish and Arab peasants was far from superior to that of the Christian peasants. Ottoman exploitation was irrespective of race, religion, or nationality.

The Turkish ruling classes were composed largely of military, bureaucratic, and religious elements, many of whom were large land owners under a system of feudal grants. The ruling classes in the Ottoman Empire were not exclusively Turkish by race, they included Arabs, Kurds, Egyptians, and Albanians, Bulgarians, Slavs, and other Balkan peoples who had accepted Islam. Among the exploiters of the Ottoman Empire, who must also be included as members of the ruling classes if only within the framework of their respective millets, were the higher clergy and Christian middle class groups who accumulated wealth by usury, speculating in essential commodities, and other devices.

All of these elements, to a greater or lesser degree, profited from the "Ottoman system," exploited the Moslem and Christian masses, and contributed to the economic decline and widespread poverty. The Ottoman military, governmental, and religious institutions were means by which the Ottoman ruling classes could control and exploit the diverse subjects of the sultans.

Widespread corruption.—When corruption permeated the sultan's court, penetrated the bureaucracy (the Ruling Institution), undermined the integrity of the ulemas (the Moslem Institution), and pervaded the armed forces, the Ottoman ruling classes became more completely parasitical, and grew incapable of performing those functions essential to the welfare of the peoples of the Near East. Wars were frequent, domestic order was not maintained, caravan routes were no longer safe, roads and bridges were not repaired, public works and services fell into disrepair. In a world which was rapidly changing during and after the sixteenth century, the Ottoman ruling classes had become an anachronism, which could be eliminated only by revolution.

The corruption and decline of Ottoman institutions, while probably inherent in the very nature of the Ottoman Empire, were intensified and hastened by the developments in western Europe. New conditions created by the economic and intellectual revolutions of the West, were making a state based on military, feudal, and religious exploitation nonviable in competition with the new type of state evolved under modern capitalism.

The Ottoman Turks captured Constantinople and conquered the Asiatic Near East, Egypt, and North Africa at the beginning of an era during which events in Europe were undermining some of the economic foundations of the Near Eastern economy. The Commercial Revolution, whether defined in the narrower sense as the shift of world trade from the inland seas to the oceanic highways, or in its wider meaning, as the development of the technics of modern capitalism in banking, finance, and corporate organization, had an unfavorable effect upon the economy of the Near East.

The loss of trade routes.—The exploration and development of an all-water oceanic route to India, the East Indies, and China destroyed the Italian-Arab monopoly of trade with these eastern markets. Trans-Asiatic trade by caravan on the land routes could not compete with the new oceanic trade. The age-old intercontinental routes languished, and commerce along them dwindled to local proportions. The discovery of the American continents and their colonization, together with the great flow of gold and silver to Europe, vastly stimulated the economic activities of western Europe. Manufacturing centers rapidly developed there.

The centers of finance, commerce, and industry shifted from the city states of Italy and the imperial German cities of the Holy Roman Empire to the national states of western Europe, Portugal, Spain, Holland, France, and England.

World trade bypassed the Near East. Its manufactures no longer commanded the same position in the European markets as formerly. The caravan cities ceased to be service stations along flourishing highways of commerce; transit and entrepôt trade declined; markets for products of Near Eastern industry shrank. The economic and social results were considerable. All four aspects of the socio-economic life of many regions of western Asia were adversely affected. The nomads lost important sources of income in the lessening demand for camels and the tribute from caravan routes. The commercial and industrial depression in the cities, resulting eventually in serious loss of population, undermined agriculture dependent upon the urban markets. Widespread economic and social dislocations resulted. The Near East was not the only area to suffer, for the Italian states were unable, either economically or politically, to compete with the growing power of the western national states. Italy, the victim of the invading armies of Spain and France, suffered a decline from which it did not begin to recover until the middle of the nineteenth century. Central Europe also was eclipsed and experienced an economic decline from which it, too, did not fully recover until after the Napoleonic wars.

Intellectual stagnation.—The Ottoman Empire was ill constituted to cope with the extraordinary new developments in Europe. Europeans were rapidly freeing themselves from the restrictions of theological dogmas and the unsound premises of supernaturalism. The "Age of Reason" and of "Enlightenment" was dawning, and modern science and scientific methods were at the threshold. Education was beginning to be freed from the dead hand of religion. The new system of modern capitalism was making possible a vast extension of commerce and an increase of production. Under these impulsions, the centralized national state was acquiring growing unity and power. Medieval military organizations were being replaced by royal and national armies. Europe was in the process of revolutionary change in all aspects of its life—intellectual, economic, political, and social.

These changes in Europe were generating new forces at a time when the Ottoman system was in a state of decline. Ottoman society, both Moslem and Christian, was dominated by obscurantist religious leaders who molded the intellectual life and controlled the educational systems, and who had a powerful influence in all branches of the government.

The military organization, once the most efficient in Europe, was in a serious state of decay. The economic system remained static, employing age-old methods of organization, finance, and commerce. No new incentives for investment in productive enterprise appeared comparable to those in western Europe, and a considerable portion of capital wealth under the Ottoman system was accumulating in the hands of parasitical classes, who neither cared nor knew how to use it for productive purposes.

The middle classes of western Europe, which engaged in every sort of economic enterprise supported by the mercantilist policies of their governments were a dynamic force energizing all phases of European society. The Ottoman bourgeoisie, on the other hand, was split into various groups, national and religious. The Turkish middle class was very largely made up of officials and professional men in the government bureaucracies. The non-Moslem bourgeois class, composed of Greeks, Armenians and Jews, was for the most part engaged in moneylending, commerce, and handicraft industry. In the Ottoman theocratic state, the inferior position of Christians and Jews made it impossible for a non-Moslem capitalist class to play the important role of the middle class in Europe. The Ottoman Empire was run by and for the sultans' court, the civilian officials, the ulemas, and the military men. Intellectually, economically, and politically, it had ceased to be able to compete effectively even with backward Russia, which under Peter the Great, by the end of the seventeenth century, had begun efforts at modernization.

A realization of the growing power of the Christian states of Europe was forced upon the Turkish leaders by the financial difficulties of the government, by military defeats with losses of territory, and mounting disorders throughout the Empire. Confronted with dangers at home and abroad, the government attempted to meet the situation with reforms and then with revolutionary changes. These attempts to adapt the Ottoman system to the developments taking place in the rest of the world continued down to the end of the Empire in the twentieth century. They met with partial success, but ended in ultimate failure. If the Turks had been able to solve the problems of a multi-national state, the Near East might not today, under the impact of nationalistic and imperialistic forces, be divided into small competing political and economic units, incapable of defending themselves, the puppets of the "Great Powers."

Attempted reforms.—In the western world, the significance of the changes which have been taking place during the past one hundred and fifty years are little understood. So rapid has been the advance that only those over fifty can recall from personal experience the horse-and-buggy

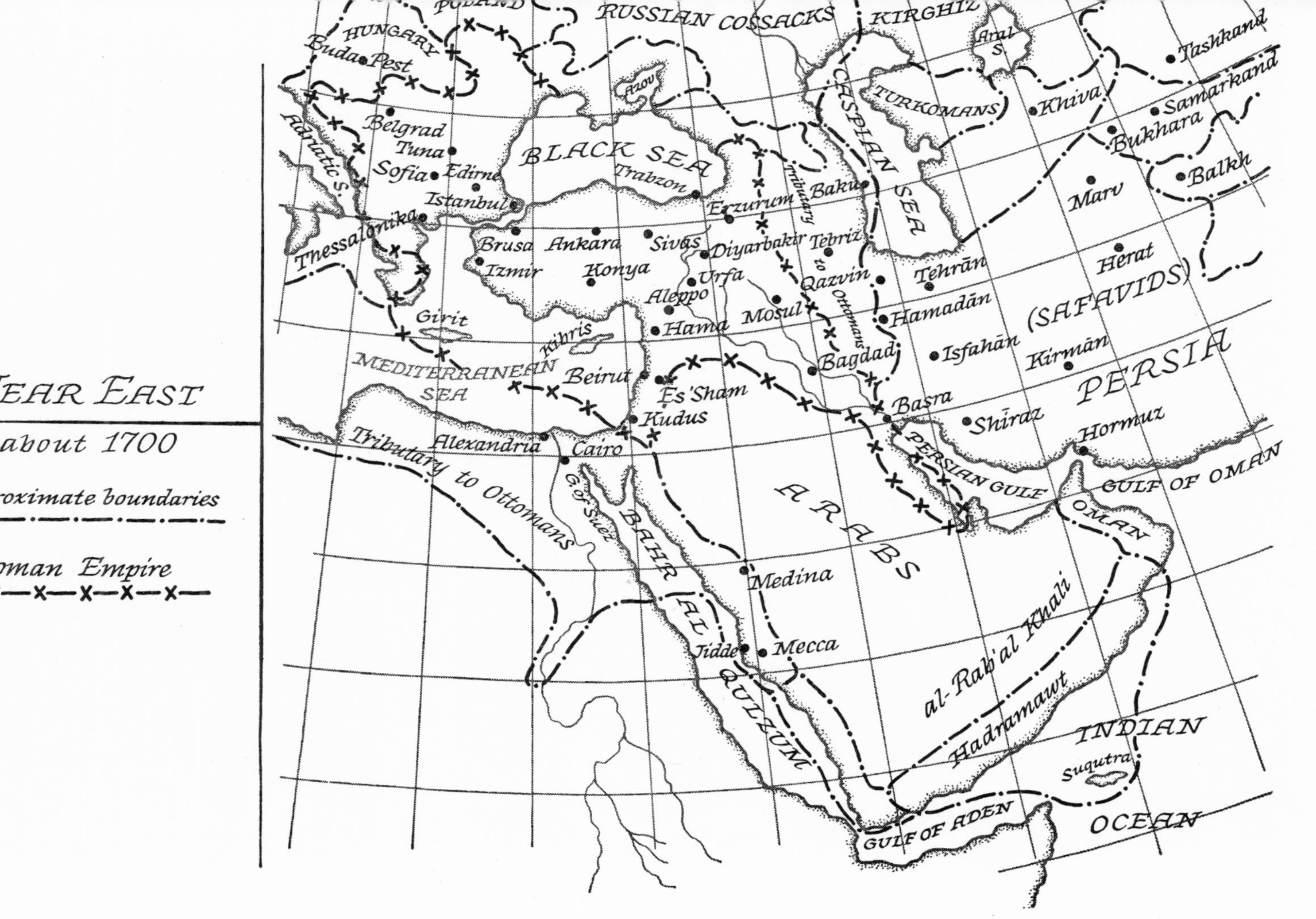

NEAR EAST
about 1700
approximate boundaries
Ottoman Empire
POLAND
HUNGARY
Buda
Pest
Belgrad
Tuna
Sofia
Edirne
Istanbul
Thessalonika
Adriatic S.
RUSSIAN COSSACKS
KIRGHIZ
Azov
BLACK SEA
Trabzon
Erzurum
Tributary
Baku
CASPIAN SEA
TURKOMANS
Aral S
Khiva
Bukhara
Samarkand
Tashkand
Balkh
Marv
Herat
Brusa
Ankara
Sivas
Diyarbakir
Tebriz
Izmir
Konya
Urfa
Aleppo
Mosul
Qazvin
to Ottomans
Tehrān
Hamadān
(SAFAVIDS)
Girit
Kibris
Hama
MEDITERRANEAN SEA
Beirut
Es'Sham
Kudus
Bagdad
Isfahān
Kirmān
PERSIA
Basra
Shiraz
Hormuz
Alexandria
Cairo
Tributary to Ottomans
G. of Suez
BAHR AL QULZUM
ARABS
PERSIAN GULF
GULF OF OMAN
OMAN
Medina
Mecca
Jidde
al-Rab'al Khali
Hadramawt
INDIAN
OCEAN
Suqutra
GULF OF ADEN

age before automobiles, movies, airplanes, and radios. The rapidity of change in Europe and the Americas tends to create an impression of slowness in the Near East. Actually, the transformation of a medieval society by a process of modernization only started in the Near East at the beginning of the nineteenth century. Since then fundamental social, economic, and political changes have taken place at an accelerated pace. Changes have not been uniform, however, throughout the area. In 1957 the life in the peasant villages—Turkish and Arab—differs little from that of the early nineteenth century. The nomads live now as they have lived for centuries past, except in limited areas where the development of oil resources and the centers of the modern systems of motor and air transport are making possible a new way of life for the pastoral tribesmen. Many areas are still far from any mode of transportation but that provided by caravans, and there life remains untouched in any significant degree by the modern world.

Figuratively speaking, in 1800 the Near East was a thousand leagues behind the West. But by 1957, in spite of the increasing rate of speed at which western civilization had traveled during the nineteenth and first half of the twentieth centuries, the Near East was less than fifty leagues behind the West. In 1850, after nearly two hundred years of conflict, the United States was still in the process of destroying or "civilizing" the American nomads. In the Near East, the nomadic way of life continues, and, of course, the nomads are still alive.

In America all men were declared to be free and equal by the Declaration of Independence in 1776; however, slavery continued in the United States until 1864, and as yet in 1957, Negroes do not enjoy complete equality with non-Negroes. In 1839 and again in 1856, the Ottoman government proclaimed the equality of all Ottoman subjects irrespective of religion or sect. Nevertheless, the non-Moslems in the Near East in 1918 did not enjoy fully the paper privileges conferred upon them by the Ottoman government by the Tanzimat during the reign of Abdul Medjid (1839–61) and later by the constitutions of 1876 and 1909. The great European Powers did not, of course, evince the same interest in the American Negro as they did in the Christian minorities in the Near East; nor did they attempt to exert upon the United States those pressures they brought to bear upon the Ottoman government to live up to its reform pronouncements.

In considering the process of reform and revolutionary change in the Ottoman Empire and the Near East, a more accurate perspective may be achieved by comparing the historical realities of both East and West.

The so-called "reform" movements in the Ottoman Empire, before the last quarter of the eighteenth century and previous to the Treaty of Kainardji (1774) with Russia, which was greatly to the disadvantage of the Turks, were attempts to eliminate abuses and corruption. In a sense, they were reactionary movements in that they were aimed at restoring and revitalizing institutions of an earlier period of Ottoman history. The "reform" movements of the seventeenth and eighteenth centuries were not efforts to modify ancient Ottoman institutions to meet the needs of new and different conditions, domestic and foreign.

Sultan Murad IV temporarily broke the power of the harem and reasserted the control of the monarch over officials and soldiers. The famous Kuprulu grand viziers, who ruled the Empire for most of the period 1656–1702, eliminated for a time some of the worst corruption and abuses. Nothing, however, was done to destroy the fundamental causes of Ottoman decadence. How ineffective these "reforms" were in ridding the Turks of ills which beset their empire may be judged from *The Book of Counsel for Viziers and Governors* by Sari Mehmed Pasha.[3] This Turkish official, who had served his government for nearly fifty years and had reached the high post of secretary of the treasury, was dismissed and imprisoned while governor of Salonika under charges of oppression, and was beheaded for treason by order of Sultan Achmed III during whose reign the old abuses again flourished.

CHAPTER III

The Turkish Awakening, 1820-1910

Toward the end of the eighteenth century, internal disorders which threatened the dismemberment of the empire, and military weakness, which had resulted in loss of territories in Europe, made Ottoman leaders realize that changes were essential if the state were to survive. Sultan Mustafa III (1757–74) was convinced that western ways would have to be adopted. Selim III, Sultan from 1789 to 1807, planned army reforms and opened military schools to train Turkish officers in European methods. Although he was deposed by mutinous Janissaries, an increasing number of Turkish officers awakened to the necessity of drastic reforms.

The process of change in the former Ottoman Empire takes on added interest because factors which compelled the Ottoman leaders in the nineteenth century to initiate changes as well as those which caused others to oppose change exist today in several of the Near Eastern states.

THE EARLY REFORM MOVEMENT

In striking contrast with historical developments in the Near East, revolutionary changes in Europe from the Middle Ages down to the present time resulted from conditions in Europe itself, due to economic progress in methods of production and distribution which altered the social structure and brought about a transfer of political power from one group to another. In the Ottoman Empire, no such basic changes in the economic system took place until late in the nineteenth century when western economic methods were introduced. The medieval system in Europe was in the process of transformation from the fifteenth century on, and only vestigial forms of feudalism continued to exist in western Europe by the eighteenth century. On the contrary, in the Near East medievalism prevailed until the nineteenth and in some areas till the twentieth century.

Reform from the top.—The economic developments in western Europe resulted in the evolution of a strong and wealthy middle class which broke the power of the feudal nobles and overthrew the old regime. In the Ottoman Empire reform and revolutionary movements began at the top with the sultans and enlightened members of the "Ruling Institution," officials, and officers. In Europe, the new institutions were indigenous; they were the result of a long process of social evolution in adaptation to a changing economic order whereas in the Near East pressure from without was a principal factor in forcing changes. The new methods and institutions introduced in the Ottoman Empire were of alien origin and in several instances were ill adapted to the social and economic conditions existing in the Near East.

While new political and social institutions may be imposed temporarily by ruthless force, they will prove to be unsuitable adaptations unless measures are taken to bring about corresponding changes in the economic system. A society that remains primarily pastoral and agrarian cannot have forced upon it the institutions of a modern industrial order. The frustrations of the Turkish reformers of the nineteenth century were due to this fact.

The Turkish reformers and revolutionists discovered that it was impossible to implement throughout the Ottoman Empire the methods and institutions borrowed from Europe. Few Europeans had any understanding of the difficulties which confronted this small enlightened group among the Turks. These reformers had to contend with the opposition of powerful tribal chieftains, of rich "feudal" land owners, and of an obscurantist clergy. It was only under the threat of internal disorder and foreign aggression that the Ottoman rulers were forced to undertake the modernization of their military establishment. In the Near East, modernization was begun by the sultans of Turkey and by that remarkable viceroy of Egypt, Mohammed Ali, who employed all the instruments of autocracy to force revolutionary changes on their reluctant peoples. In the twentieth century Mustafa Kemal Pasha in Turkey, Ibn Saud in Arabia, and Colonel Nasser in Egypt continue the process of their Ottoman predecessors.

The reforming sultans.—Sultan Mahmoud II (1808–39) realized that he could not introduce western reforms until he had broken the power of the Janissaries, who had risen in revolt and deposed his reforming uncle, Sultan Selim III (1789–1807). Without the support of the Sheik-ul-Islam and leading ulemas, Sultan Mahmoud could not have destroyed the Janissaries. The religious leaders of the Ottoman Empire were more inclined to favor the modernization of the Turkish military forces because of the growing menace of foreign intervention, due to the Greek revolt, and because of the military successes of Mohammed Ali, the viceroy of Egypt with troops well trained by French officers. Consequently, when in 1826, the Janissaries mutinied, Mahmoud, with the approval of the ulemas, ordered his new troops to attack them. The power of the Janissaries was broken; those who were not killed were disbanded, and this ancient military order was outlawed throughout the empire. The door to military and civil reform was now open to Mahmoud and his reformist ministers.

The Tanzimat, 1826–76.—The reign of Mahmoud II brought to an end the medieval period of Ottoman history and introduced the era of reform, from 1826 to 1876, called Tanzimat by the Turks. Although Mahmoud's innovations did not eliminate many medieval aspects of life in the Near East they nevertheless did prepare the way for the modernization of the Ottoman Empire. It was during the reign of Mahmoud's sons, Abdul Medjid (1839–61) and Abdul Aziz (1861–76) that able and enlightened grand viziers introduced important changes in the decrepit Ottoman system of government.

On coming to the throne in 1839, Abdul Medjid issued the Imperial Rescript of the Rose Chamber, known as the *Hatti-Sherif* of Gul-Khane. If its comprehensive reforms had been fully carried out, they would have revolutionized the Ottoman state and Ottoman society. The most revolutionary change introduced by the Hatti Sherif of Gul-Khane was the recognition by the Ottoman government of the equality of all its subjects irrespective of "religion or sect" under the new dispensation of Sultan Abdul Medjid. It was impossible for the Sultan's government to carry out the full intent of the Hatti-Sherif of 1839 against the opposition of the Moslems who considered all unbelievers—Christians, Jews and Pagans—to be inferiors without the rights of the "Faithful." For such had always been the status of non-Moslems under Islamic and Ottoman law. An imperial decree could not change the attitude of mind of the Moslems of the Empire any more than an amendment to the Constitution of the United States has been able to make fully effective the political and civil rights of the Negroes in those states and even in the federal District of Columbia where political and economic power continues to reside in the hands of those who are opposed to the granting of such equality.

It is of significant interest to note that the impetus back of the reform and revolutionary movements was due, only in part, to internal conditions which threatened the dismemberment. Much of it resulted from pressure on the Ottoman government by one or more of the "Great

Powers" acting individually or jointly. The necessity for changes and the willingness of the ulemas to accept the reforms of Sultan Mahmoud II were due to the situation in Greece and in Serbia, and to the repercussion of these events in Europe.

Impact of French Revolution.—The Ottoman government was confronted by new problems created by the French Revolution of 1789 and the Napoleonic Wars which affected profoundly the Near East. The democratic ideals and nationalistic fervor of the French revolutionaries fired the hopes in the Balkans of Christian subjects of the sultan. Ottoman forces were unable at first to cope with uprisings in Serbia and in Greece. The massacre of Moslems by Serbs and Greeks was ignored by Europeans, but the ruthless retaliation by the Turks aroused deep indignation among the frustrated romantic liberals of Europe. At a time when the Ottoman government was initiating reformist and revolutionary changes, Europe in the throes of reaction under the driving force of Metternich, was waging "cold" and "hot" wars in the name of the Holy Alliance and for the maintenance of European and Christian civilization against liberalism, nationalism, and democracy. In the 1820's, reaction was triumphant in France, Spain, Austria, Russia, and throughout Italy. In England, under a military prime minister, the British were governed by reactionary conservatives. Liberals and nationalists, unable to make their views prevail at home, burned with ardor for the Christian revolutionists in the Ottoman Empire. The savagery and brutality of the struggling Christians were ignored, and the barbarism of the Turks was anathematized. Liberals urged action by their governments and demanded intervention in Turkey.

European governments, which were opposed to liberalism and democracy in their own countries, gave self-righteous support to revolution against the Ottoman government, which was attempting to bring about revolutionary and reformist changes in the Near East. The intervention of the Great Powers in the internal affairs of the Ottoman Empire at the time of the Greek revolution marks a turning point in its relationships with the western Powers.

Since the beginning of the nineteenth century, the Near East has felt continuously the impact of the West. Down to the present western ideas and ideologies, western literature, science, and education have had an ever-increasing effect upon the people of the Near East. Even now their economic life is still in the process of being revolutionized by the introduction of western methods. Political changes and developments were very definitely the result of western intervention and influence.

The growing influence of Europe upon the Turkish "reform" movement is evident in the imperial rescript of 1856, known as the *Hatti-Humayun,* which reaffirmed the equality of all Ottoman subjects and specifically stated the disabilities to be eliminated and the rights and privileges granted to non-Moslems. The *Hatti-Humayun* was issued at the close of the Crimean War, in which Turkey, allied with France and Great Britain, had defeated Russia. It was a concession made to European liberalism on the eve of the Congress of Paris of 1856 to obtain official recognition of the Ottoman Empire as a member of the Concert of Europe in the Treaty of Paris.

Nature of the reforms and revolutionary movements.—The Turkish intellectual awakening during the nineteenth century with its counterparts in the political reform and revolutionary movements was of imperial rather than national import with significant influence upon the non-Turkish parts of the Empire. Turkish intellectuals and reformers until the revolution of 1908 provided leadership to non-Turkish elements throughout the Near East. They stimulated the Moslem Arabs and created conditions favorable to the growth of Arab liberalism.

The process of modernization in the Ottoman Empire was profoundly affected by the rapidly changing conditions in Europe and the western world throughout the nineteenth century when the West itself was experiencing the most revolutionary changes in its long history. Before European peoples had satisfactorily adjusted their ideas and their political and social institutions to the conditions resulting from the Commercial Revolution and from the amazing developments of commercial capitalism, they were caught in the thralls of the swiftly moving Industrial Revolution. This kept western society in a perpetual state of turmoil which had repercussions in all parts of the world. So rapidly were economic and social conditions revolutionized that increasingly great strains were placed upon the political machinery and the social institutions of the western nations. Before eighteenth-century political ideas had received full acceptance and effective implementation in Europe there had already arisen the philosophy of socialism and the dynamic political movement of Marxism. Intellectually, Europe was suffering from disturbances analogous to the disagreeable ills of overeating, indigestion, and faulty elimination. Before being rid of some waste products of Hebraic, Hellenic, Roman, and medieval thinking, the intellectuals swallowed huge amounts of eighteenth- and early nineteenth-century liberalism and had had forced upon them new psychological and sociological theories and the dialectical materialism of Marxism.

The vast amount of energy generated in the West by the Industrial Revolution and its sociological and psychological concomitants had a shattering effect upon the whole structure of the Ottoman Near East. In less than a century, the old multi-national theocratic state was destroyed and many of the age-old social and religious institutions were undermined. Under political pressure from the European nations and the spell of western ideas, the Turkish reformers of the nineteenth century attempted to do in the Near East in a few short decades what had been accomplished in Europe as the result of centuries of development. While the Turkish intelligentsia were absorbing and propounding the ideas of French Encyclopedists and American revolutionists of the eighteenth century, western Europe was proceeding from liberalism to Utopian and Christian Socialism, anarchism, syndicalism, and Marxism.

Comparative Rate of Progress of the West and of the Near East

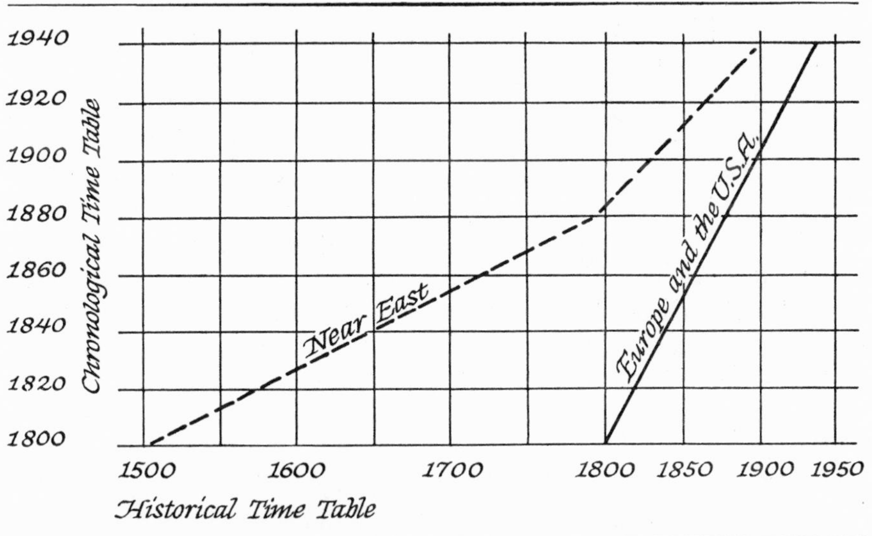

In 1800 Near Eastern culture was comparable to that of Europe in 1500.
In 1880 Near Eastern culture had emerged from medievalism.
By 1940 Near Eastern culture was rapidly being modernized.

Unfortunately, there has been no thorough analysis of the influence of western political and social philosophies and movements upon the various peoples in the Near East. Whereas historians and others have traced the impact of western thought and movements upon developments in Russia from the time of Peter the Great to Lenin, no one has undertaken to write an adequate account of the somewhat similar process that went on in the Near East. Until accurate studies have been made, only broad generalizations with regard to this interesting and important phenomenon are possible.

Successive generations of enlightened Turks, from the latter part of the eighteenth and through the nineteenth century, were greatly influenced by western political ideas and profoundly impressed by European institutions. Lacking previous acquaintance with European thought, literature, and history, these Turkish intellectuals avidly absorbed the provocative and stimulating ideas of the French Encyclopedists of the eighteenth century. Even as late as 1877, the great Turkish reformer and statesman, Midhat Pasha was quoting Montesquieu (1689–1755) as an authority on the difficulties of creating a constitution.[1]

When one stops to recall that until after 1848 most of Europe was under the control of reactionary governments which opposed constitutionalism, denied their subjects representative institutions and civil liberties, and that the owning and controlling classes throughout Europe repudiated the ideas of the eighteenth century *philosophes* as being dangerously revolutionary at a time when the intellectual leaders of the new proletariat class were formulating their communist philosophy, it is not surprising that the Young Turks, as they came to be called, were subject to the influence of a variety of political philosophies and movements.

The most important of these with respect to the Turkish reformers were the ideas of French revolutionary thinkers of the eighteenth century and of the early nineteenth-century liberals. The political, social, and economic thinking of the French Physiocrats and Encyclopedists had long previous to the French Revolution spread to most parts of Europe, even penetrating those strongholds of autocracy—Austria, Prussia, and Russia—all close neighbors of the Ottoman Empire. The famous "Enlightened Despots" of these nations—Maria Theresa, Frederick the Great, and Catherine II—toying with these revolutionary ideas, applied the techniques of autocratic and centralized government to increase their political and military power and began to threaten the existence of their weaker rivals, Poland and Turkey. The first partition of Poland in 1772 by these three great powers of eastern Europe was a warning to the Turks. Two years later, the humiliating Treaty of Kainardji terminated the Russian-Turkish War of 1768–74 on terms very unfavorable to the Turks who lost the Crimea and other Tatar-Turkish territories north of the Black Sea and who surrendered a measure of their sovereignty through the grant to Russia of rather nebulous rights concerning the protection of the Orthodox Christian subjects of the sultan. The Turkish leaders began to realize that drastic changes in the Ottoman system must be made if the empire were to survive.

Before it was possible to initiate reforms, the Ottoman Empire became embroiled in a war with Austria and Russia during the years between 1789 and 1792 and then entangled in the French revolutionary and subsequent Napoleonic wars. The conquest of Egypt and the invasion of Palestine by Napoleon in 1798–99 began the struggle between the western powers for control of the Near East.

The tumultuous torrent of events that engulfed Europe from the last quarter of the eighteenth through the first quarter of the nineteenth century had important repercussions upon the Ottoman Empire. The octopus of western imperialism began to extend the probing of its prehensile tentacles to strategic areas of the Near East. The revolutionary ideas of liberalism and nationalism were sweeping through the Christian minorities in European Turkey, where the Balkan peoples were deeply stirred by the French Revolution, with its thrilling slogans of liberty, fraternity, and equality. Confronted with the threat of internal collapse and revolutionary movements of the subject minorities and with partition by foreign foes, the more enlightened Turks, aware of the military weakness and inferiority of the Ottoman armies, recognized the compelling necessity for change. They turned to the West in search of those ideas and institutions which might solve their problems.

An interesting dualism runs through the entire Turkish reform and revolutionary movements during both the nineteenth and twentieth centuries. Although those Turks who were aware of the grave threat to the very existence of the Ottoman Empire realized that something drastic had to be done, they were not wholly in agreement as to what should be done. The idealists, enamored of western liberalism and convinced of the efficacy of constitutional government and civil liberties, believed these would prove a panacea for the ills which beset Ottoman society. The realists cared little or nothing for constitutionalism, civil liberties, and other liberal objectives. They wished only to regain the former power of the Ottoman Empire while retaining the historic privileges and authority of the sultan and the Turkish ruling classes. The former desired to change the Ottoman Empire into a nineteenth-century political democracy, the latter wished to restore the virility of a senile theocratic autocracy. The showdown between these two groups took place between 1876 and 1883 in the dramatic and tragic struggle between the great leader of the Turkish reform movement, Midhat Pasha, and the last of the Ottoman autocrats, Sultan Abdul Hamid II.

The proponents of the Tanzimat reforms advocated political and social changes in conformity with ideas of western liberalism. Such fundamental changes in the whole structure of the Ottoman system could not be carried out without eliminating the privileges of the most powerful elements of the Turkish ruling classes. An understanding by the Turkish reformers of the significance of the triumph of the Metternich system from 1815 to 1848 in Europe might have warned them that the vested interests of the palace and dynasty with support in both the "Ruling Institution" and the "Moslem Institution" would employ every possible means of preventing the adoption of liberal institutions. A small fragment of the upper classes could not, lacking wide support among the middle and lower classes, impose revolutionary changes against the determined opposition of the privileged classes, lay and ecclesiastical. This was no more possible in the Ottoman Empire in 1876 at the time of the promulgation by Abdul Hamid II of the first Ottoman constitution than it was in the German Confederation during 1848, or in the Russian Empire by the liberal friends of Tsar Alexander I during the first decade of the nineteenth century.

Eventually, the head of the Ottoman dynasty, Abdul Hamid II, as the Habsburgs, Hohenzollerns, and Romanovs had before him, discovered that it was impossible to carry out basic revolutionary changes without the destruction of those privileged elements of the ruling classes upon which the power of the monarchy and dynasty depended.

The failure of the Turkish reformers to achieve political and social reform in the Ottoman Empire may be attributed in part to the fact that the liberal institutions they attempted to introduce were unsuitable adaptations to the conditions then existing in the Ottoman Empire. Midhat Pasha's son somewhat vehemently denies this thesis. The fact, however, remains that the Ottoman Empire was of vast extent, lacked adequate means of transportation, and most of its inhabitants were illiterate. Its economic system was backward and unable to support the bulk of its inhabitants much above subsistence level. Its people were living on several different levels of social organization—tribal, village, and urban—and were divided into groups differing with respect to religion, race, nationality, and language. Until fundamental economic and cultural changes were brought about, it was quite idealistic to think that representative government based on the ideas of western liberalism could function satisfactorily or even long endure in such a state.

It is interesting to note that in our times there is a tendency in the political democracies of the West to think that democracy can be created by fiat just as the Turkish reformers and some of their European supporters in the nineteenth century believed that liberal institutions could be made to function in the Ottoman Empire by imperial decrees obtained from pliable though reluctant sultans.

The western critics of the ineptitudes of the Turkish reformers, often accusing them of insincerity and hypocrisy, lacked historical perspective and an understanding of the magnitude of the task which was undertaken by the Turkish liberals. In most of Europe, liberal institutions did not exist and liberal ideas were ruthlessly suppressed until after 1848. Even the revolutions of that year failed in many parts of Europe to attain the goals of the liberals. The impatient western liberals questioned the integrity of the Turkish reformers, although it was not until the 1860's that serfdom was abolished in Tsarist Russia and slavery in the United States. The Industrial Revolution in the West was so profoundly changing the economic and social structure of European society that a considerable percentage of the new industrial wage-earning class turned to socialistic ideas before the ruling classes in many parts of Europe had accepted liberal ideas and introduced liberal institutions. It is somewhat astonishing that in less than four decades (1839–76) a reform and revolutionary movement in Turkey grew sufficiently influential to force upon so reactionary a ruler as Abdul Hamid II the granting of a constitution in 1876.

This is more remarkable in view of the fact that the tempo of economical change in the Near East throughout most of the nineteenth century was not comparable to the acceleration of economic change in the West. Antiquated methods of agriculture, handicraft industry, age-old methods of business and banking continued to prevail throughout most of the Ottoman Empire. The great majority of the people lived much as their ancestors had in medieval times. There were no fundamental economic and social changes, like those taking place in the West, to stimulate and give form to mass revolutionary movements directed against the ancient ways of thinking and the old Islamic institutions. Only a small segment of the literate upper-class Turks were stirred to action by western ideas and culture. This was most especially true of the Turks and other Moslems. Among the Christian subjects of the sultan, western ideas of liberalism and nationalism spread far more widely, especially in the Balkans.

French revolutionary ideas began to ferment among the Yugoslavs and Greeks before the end of the eighteenth century, when the armies of the French Republic reached Italy and the Dalmatian coast. The discontents of the Christian subject people began to coalesce around the concepts of nationalism and freedom. The Christian peasants of the

Balkans, exploited by Moslem, Turkish, and non-Turkish, landowners, oppressed by a corrupt Ottoman government, harassed by fanatical Janissary troops, and held in the grip of the venal Phanariot Greek Orthodox clergy centered at Constantinople, found in nationalism a weapon to defend themselves from the oppressors. The spread of nationalism among the Balkan Christians, then among the Armenians, later among the Arabs, Christian and Moslem alike, and finally among the Turks, foreshadowed the disintegration of the Ottoman Empire as definitely as similar movements prepared the way for the dissolution of the Austrian-Hungarian Dual Monarchy.

A striking feature of the reform and revolutionary movements in the Near East during the nineteenth century is that among the Christian peoples revolutionary movements received wide support from all classes, while among the Turks and Arab Moslems with exception of Arabi's revolt in Egypt, the masses remained either apathetic to the reform movement, or, when incited by reactionary elements, violently resented the innovations introduced by the Turkish reformers. The Christian minorities adopted the ideas of western liberalism in their struggles to free themselves from Ottoman rule; the Turkish intellectuals turned to western ideas with the hope of reviving their waning power and for the purpose of checking the disintegration and of preventing the partition of the Ottoman Empire. These political movements among Christian minorities and the Turks with their contradictory objectives were clearly incompatible, even though not recognized so at the time.

The Ottoman proponents of western liberalism appear not to have understood the basic contradiction between the maintenance of the Moslem monopoly of power and adoption of liberal institutions in a multi-national state with diverse religious groups. Islam had been a powerful instrument in establishing the empire and in maintaining the political power of the Turks, but it had failed as a solvent of the diverse nationalistic and religious cultures of the Near East. Liberalism and nationalism undermined the very foundations of the theocratic Ottoman Empire. Secularization and representative government, with equality of rights irrespective of race, religion, and national culture, would have terminated inevitably Turkish domination. The realization of liberalism's much cherished ideal of national independence eventually resulted in the disintegration of the Ottoman Empire. The older Turkish liberals strove to prevent this disintegration; their successors, the Turkish nationalists, abolished the sultanate with rejoicing.

The impossibility of implementing the Tanzimat reforms and the constitution of 1876 was due most immediately to the opposition of the reactionary elements among the Turkish ruling classes, but more fundamentally to the fact that liberal institutions could have no real foundations in the Near East until changes in its economic system increased the number and power of the middle class or created a modern industrial wage-earning class. As long as the peasantry and nonindustrialized urban workers remained poverty stricken and illiterate and the middle or mercantile middle class subordinate to the landowning, bureaucratic, and ulema oligarchy, liberal democracy could, and can now, become little more than a façade behind which minority groups with vested interests would continue the age-old struggle to wield the political instruments of power.

The reformist element among the upper-class Turks could eliminate some of the corruption and abuses of the Ottoman administration, but they could not change its fundamental structure without defeating their own aims. The pre-Tanzimat reformers were successful in destroying the Janissaries and in laying the foundations of a modernized army. The Tanzimat reformers in the period from 1839 to 1856 succeeded in part in lessening the influence of the Seraglio and in modernizing the machinery of state and thus eliminated some of the grosser forms of corruption and maladministration. They also obtained from the palace imperial declarations of basic rights in the Hatti Sherif (1839) and the Hatti-Humayun (1856) of Sultan Abdul Medjid.

Midhat Pasha, the last of the great reformers, succeeded in persuading the reluctant Abdul Hamid to promulgate the constitution of 1876. This was the zenith of the Turkish reform movement. On becoming sultan, Abdul Hamid soon used his autocratic power to shelve the constitution, eliminate the reformers, and destroy the reform movement. For thirty-two years, the Ottoman Empire was ruled by a sultan who enforced by every means at his disposal a ruthless despotism.

Although the Turkish reformers did not achieve their aims and although it is probable that their well-intended reforms rather increased than diminished the nationalist and separatist movements among the Christian minorities and rather aggravated than ameliorated the tensions between Moslems and Christians, nevertheless, the political reform movement made possible for almost forty years the uninterrupted development of the Turkish intellectual revolution. It was the intellectual revolution which eventually made Abdul Hamid's tragic reactionary policy utterly futile.

Using the crisis created by the Russian-Turkish War of 1877–78 as an excuse, the new sultan dismissed the recently assembled parliament, and to all practical purposes, abrogated the constitution he had just sanctioned. Abdul Hamid and his supporters were certain that political reforms would lead to the destruction of the Ottoman Empire, while, on the other hand, the liberal reformers were convinced that an unregenerate Empire would soon succumb to its internal enemies and its foreign foes. The reformers had been defeated by the reactionaries, who were unwilling to undertake the modernization of the Ottoman Empire and left it too weak to cope with internal revolt and foreign assault. In the struggle between the reformers and the reactionaries, the Turkish intellectual revolution grew and spread preparing the foundations for the present day Turkish Republic, which was made possible by the intellectual awakening among the Turkish elite during the nineteenth century.

THE INTELLECTUAL AWAKENING

Many of the misconceptions concerning the Near East arise from a lack of historical knowledge and perspective, particularly with respect to the differences of the historical evolution of Europe and of the Near East.

At the time when the intellectual revolution in Europe, which had been gestating in the womb of the Middle Ages, was flowering in the Renaissance, the Ottoman Turks were conquering the Balkans and the Asiatic Near East. During the period when Europe was in revolt against medievalism, the Near East was crystallizing and stabilizing its medieval culture. The conquest of Constantinople did not result in the birth of a new culture or the revival of an ancient one. Without entering into the dispute with respect to the influence of Byzantine culture on the Turks recently provoked by the Turkish historian Kupruluzade Mehmed Fuad,[2] who claims that Ottoman institutions owe little or nothing to the Byzantines, it may be said that the culture of the upper-class Turks remained essentially Seljukian Turkish, which was based on the Persian and Arab Moslem culture. The conquest by the Ottoman Turks had only a slight effect upon the medieval culture of the Arab Moslems and Christians. When Turkish became the official and predominant language in Anatolia and in European Turkey, the Christian minorities there seemingly were more affected by the culture of the Turks than these were by Byzantine culture.

The Byzantine culture then in a condition of decadence did not quicken the intellectual life of the Turks nor create that fermentation of ideas which was taking place contemporaneously in Europe. In the Near East a revival of vigorous intellectual life did not begin until the nineteenth century.

The intellectual awakening in the Near East which has been going on continuously since the opening of the nineteenth century is a process consisting of a series of bewilderingly complex phenomena. One hundred and fifty years ago in the greater part of the Near East most of its inhabitants were living in a medieval world. The villages, towns, and cities, the political and social institutions, and the means and methods of production and distribution were little different from those of the Middle Ages. The boundaries of knowledge hardly extended beyond those of the fourteenth century. The ideas and postulates of ancient and medieval times were accepted without challenge. In almost every phase of human life and activity, the Near East in 1800 was approximately a half a millennium behind Europe and the rest of the western world.

Penetration of European culture.—Its medley of peoples—Arabs, Armenians, Egyptians, Greeks, Slavs, and Turks—began early in the nineteenth century to feel increasingly the impact of the modern western world. Their contacts with western ideas and institutions were infinitely varied. Western culture reached the Near East through a variety of mediums: American, Austrian, British, French, German, and Russian. There was no uniformity of cultural diffusion in all parts of the Ottoman Empire and among all segments of its varied peoples. In the urban centers of Egypt, in many parts of the Balkans, at Constantinople, Smyrna, and Beirut, intercourse with the West was far more frequent and intimate than in the hinterland of Anatolia and of the Arab lands of Asia. The contact of the peasants and nomads in the Asiatic parts of the Ottoman Empire with the western world was practically nil.

Western ideas, manners, customs, and dress tended to be adopted more rapidly by Christians of the middle class in the urban centers than by the Moslems. Nevertheless, this alien culture of western and Christian origin began to spread among educated Moslems. Foreign missionaries in their schools and colleges; foreign businessmen introducing modern goods, services, and methods contributed to the dissemination of western culture. Young men of the upper classes went to Europe to complete their education. Foreign tutors and governesses were employed by wealthy families. A privileged elite became acquainted with European culture in its many diverse phases.

Members of this group, who belonged to many of the different peoples of the Ottoman Empire, propagated western culture within their own communities. They formed centers of revolt against the backwardness, the ignorance, and the obscurantism which prevailed in the Near East. They became protagonists of the "new knowledge." They sought to destroy the old and to introduce the new. With satire and ridicule they attacked the old regime. By the translation of western literature and scientific books and by the publication of magazines and pamphlets they endeavored to introduce others to western thought and knowledge. In the Near East they performed a function somewhat similar to that of the intellectual leaders of the Renaissance in Europe in the fifteenth century.

No adequate study has been made of the varied processes by which the intellectual quickening in the Near East during the nineteenth century produced an Arab renaissance, a revival of Hellenism, a rebirth of the varied Slavic cultures in the Balkans, a revitalizing of the ancient Armenian culture, and the intellectual awakening of the Turks.

The dominant position of the Turks in the Ottoman Empire gave to the Turkish intellectual revolution a wider significance than that of a Turkish national renaissance. Because the Turks were Moslems and because of their prestige, the Turkish renaissance was felt throughout the Near East, particularly among the non-Turkish Moslems. The Turkish intellectual awakening consequently had greater significance than that of the other national groups in the Ottoman Empire.

The Turkish intellectual revolution.—Before discussing the revolution which took place in the nineteenth century in the intellectual life of the Turks, it seems necessary to call attention to the fact that among western authors who have written about the Ottoman Empire and the Turks, there are several who completely ignore the cultural achievements of the Turks and some who deny the existence of any Turkish culture. The profound divergence of views about the Turks is clearly evident in the works of Sir Edwin Pears, a popular British author well known in England and the United States for his books on Constantinople and Turkey, and in the works of E. J. W. Gibb, a renowned British scholar, little known to the British and American public, who was a life-long student of Turkish literature. In the second edition (1912), of *Turkey and Its People* (p. 7), Sir Edwin Pears writes as follows: "All the distinction that the Turks have ever gained has been in war. They have produced no art and no architecture, though they have destroyed much. They have given to the world no literature, science, or philosophy. In all such matters, they were inferior to the races they conquered." [3] In the editor's Preface of the fifth volume (1907), of *A History of Ottoman Poetry,* by E. J. W. Gibb, Edward G. Browne wrote as follows: "Whatever else may be alleged against the Ottoman Turks, it can never again be asserted by the candid and impartial reader that they are, or ever have been, since their first appearance on the stage of history in the thirteenth century, indifferent to literature." [4]

To those unfamiliar with the deep-seated prejudices which color the opinions and judgments of many of the writers on the Near East and its peoples, it is rather disconcerting to discover such contradictory points of view concerning matters about which facts are clearly available. Much of western literature on the Near East is affected by the emotions and ideological biases of its authors. Many Christians cannot write dispassionately about Moslems. Many westerners who have lived and traveled in the Near East tend to be pro-Arab, or pro-Armenian, or pro-Greek, or pro-Jewish, or pro-Turkish, while at the same time being anti many things. Mark Sykes and T. E. Lawrence did not have a decent word for the Armenians. Lawrence's observations regarding Arabs of the Syrian cities lacked any reasonable degree of objectivity because of his romantic admiration of the Arab nomad.

Clearly, one cannot write about a Turkish intellectual awakening and renaissance and trace the changes in Turkish literature without asserting that the Turks had a distinctive culture.

The Turkish intellectual revolution had many phases, its most interesting one, perhaps, was that in the field of language and literature. The old language of the Ottoman Turks had borrowed extensively from both the Persian and the Arabic. Because the vast majority of the Turks were illiterate, the written language—the same was and still is true of Arabic—came to differ greatly from the spoken language. There was a similar divergence between the written and the unwritten literature. The former became that of upper-class Turks at the court and in the higher administrative circles of the government; the latter was that of the peasants and the uneducated urban workers.

The old Ottoman literature, which is the more important of the three main branches of Turkish written literature, was not a national literature of the people. It evolved from the thirteenth century on, first as a religious literature of the theological schools and as a feudal literature of the nobles, and then as a court literature. The religious element borrowed heavily from Arabic, the "sacred" language of Islam; the nobles and the sultan's entourage aped the Persians, adopting Persian metaphors, imagery, and both poetical vocabulary and themes. The court literature became completely divorced from the life of the Turkish people. In fact, it developed into an esoteric literature which only the initiated could understand. From the more robust epic and chivalric literature of the thirteenth and fourteenth centuries, it degenerated into erotic and bacchic gentility as the life of the seraglio became increasingly decadent. The language of officialdom became stilted and pompous. Eventually, the written literature and the language of the court and government became devoid of life and vigor.

It was this condition of affairs which stirred the Turkish literati of the early nineteenth century to revolt. The deep cleavage between the literature and culture of the upper classes and the Turkish masses created a cultural schizophrenia which profoundly affected those Turkish intellectuals who revolted against the old culture and the court literature.

The intellectual backwardness of the Turks until the revolt in the nineteenth century is more understandable when due consideration is given to the fact that it was not until 1727 that the imperial Ottoman government sanctioned the printing of books. A government printing press was established in 1728 against the will of theologians, scholars, and scribes. The opposition of these groups with their vested interests (in the eighteenth century a folio manuscript unilluminated cost from $150 to $175, and a Koran in the famous Nessik calligraphy cost $1,000) was overcome when Sultan Ahmed III (1703–30) was able to obtain a *fetva* from the Sheik of Islam declaring printing was not contrary to the Sheria. The official printing press nevertheless was looked upon as a dangerous beast. It was placed under special guard and four official censors were appointed to supervise its publications. In the thirty-year period, from 1727 to 1756, only eighteen works, consisting of twenty-five volumes, with a total of 16,500 copies, had been published. From 1756 to 1783 the printing press was completely neglected, and the printing office not re-established until 1784. The catalog of publications by the official and only Turkish printing press in the Ottoman Empire lists only eighty works, consisting of ninety-one volumes, between 1727 and 1828. During that one-hundred-year period, not one book of a literary nature was printed.

Under such conditions, literature could not flourish and writers were unable to break the bonds of the old court literature. Early in the nineteenth century, new developments created a situation which made possible the intellectual and literary revolt of the educated Turks. The founding by Mohammed Ali in Egypt of the Boulak Printing Press in 1821, publishing books in Arabic, Persian, and Turkish had a vitalizing effect throughout the Near East. After the founding of a Turkish newspaper in Egypt in 1828, there was established at Constantinople in 1831, under governmental auspices, the first Turkish newspaper. Despite the opposition of foreign diplomats, who attempted to prevent the publication of newspapers, their number began to increase after 1825, when a French journal was founded at Smyrna. In the 1830's and 1840's, several newspapers in French and Turkish were published by foreigners. In 1860 the first nonsubsidized, nongovernmental Turkish newspaper owned and controlled by Turks was founded. This journal, called *The Interpreter of Conditions* (*Terjumani Ahual*) was established by Shinassi, who soon founded another paper, *The Tablet of Opinion* (*Tasviri-*

Efkiar). The Turkish novelist Kemal Bey joined Shinassi in his newspaper work. These two Turks were the leaders of the intellectual and literary revolution and of the Tanzimat political reform movement. They were among those who in 1862 organized the Young Turk Party.

The leaders of Turkish awakening.—The appearance of newspapers in French and Turkish, as well as in Armenian, Bulgarian, and Greek greatly stimulated intellectual curiosity and activity. By 1876 there were forty-seven newspapers published in Constantinople alone. Of these, thirteen were in Turkish. The circle of readers widened beyond that of governmental officials. The newspapers and magazines helped to develop a reading public. The intellectual revolutionists used these new instruments of publicity, which for the most part escaped control by the government and private reactionary interests until the reign of Abdul Hamid II (1876–1909), to educate their readers. In the 1860's three comparatively young Turkish writers and publishers shaped the rapidly developing intellectual revolution. The journalist Shinassi published a volume of translations from the French poets; Namiq Kemal Bey set about to transform the somewhat stilted and inadequate Turkish prose into a literary instrument capable of dealing effectively and forcefully with modern ideas and science; Ebu-z-Ziya established a publishing house, Ebu-z-Ziya's Librairi, which published translations of foreign books, a Turkish dictionary, and a popular magazine containing articles on scientific, social, and other modern developments in the western world.

Although this intellectual revolution in the middle nineteenth century was confined to a comparatively small percentage of the Turkish people, its breadth and scope are of significant importance. Against the strongly intrenched forces of reaction in a society sunk in the depths of ignorance, religious bigotry, and cultural obscurantism, a mere handful of Turkish intellectuals successfully undertook the enlightenment of their people. The crucial and determining years of the struggle were from 1859 to 1879, when the foundations for the modernization of Turkey were firmly laid. Of these two decades, E. J. W. Gibb the distinguished English authority on Ottoman literature and Turkish poetry wrote: "In 1859 the Turks were still practically a medieval community, in 1879 they had become a modern nation." [5]

In poetry there was an almost complete break with the past. The modern Turkish poets abandoned the old poetry and the foundations upon which it rested: the system of rhyming, the verse forms, metaphors, similes, and themes which had largely been borrowed from Persian poetry. In prose writing the stilted and pompous language of the court and the administrative bureaucracy was discarded and Turkish prose developed a new virility and power. Following the era of the Tanzimat reforms when Turkish intellectuals were shaping the new language and literature, the second generation of Turkish literary revolutionists turned largely to French literature of the last quarter of the nineteenth century, and in subject matter and style borrowed heavily from contemporary French writers. This so-called "New Literature" was actually no closer to the Turkish people as a whole than was the court literature which was so greatly despised by the moderns. Much of the Turkish literature of this period was morbid, introspective, and had what the Europeans used to call *fin de siècle* weariness. The Turkish writers, suffering under the oppression and repression of the tyrannous regime of Abdul Hamid, reflected in their writing the frustrations of an intelligentsia sensing their own futility under the Hamidian despotism. A similar phenomenon occurred in Tsarist Russia during the reign of Nicholas I.

Younger writers toward the end of the century reacted against this spirit of dejection and turned away from Europe under the impulse of Turkish nationalism and Turanian racialism. The intellectuals sought out and studied the unwritten and popular literature of the people. The poetry, legends, and fables of the Turkish peasants were collected; tales of Nasreddin Hodja became fashionable among the literati. The peoples' drama, Orta Ognu and Karagöz, was patronized and eulogized by the upper classes. Turkish literature was becoming nationalistic.

It was this nationalistic literary movement, among the forerunners of which was the well-known Turkish woman writer, Halidé Edib (who has written several books in English), which eventually under the Republic led to the purging of Persian and Arabic words from the Turkish language and the discarding of the Arabic script.

Abdul Hamid, during his long reign (1876–1909), did everything in his power to destroy both the political "reform" movement and the intellectual revolution. For long it appeared, superficially at least, that he was successful. Parliament was dismissed, the constitution discarded, the reformist leaders executed or driven into exile, the press enchained by a repressive censorship, and the ignorant masses aroused against the intellectual rebels by reactionary leaders spurred on by the sultan and his palace entourage. It seemed as if the new spirit in Turkey which had little support among the masses, who were materially and spiritually still living in the Middle Ages, would be completely extinguished.

Despite the tyranny of Abdul Hamid enforced by a legion of spies and secret agents, the time had passed when the reading public would not be able to distinguish between the directness and simplicity of the new prose of Shinassi, Kemal, Ebu-z-Ziya, and the stupid, verbose pomposity that was imposed upon the newspapers by the Hamidian government.

The following quotations from Turkish newspapers are typical of the bureaucratic jargon of the 1870's.

> His Imperial Majesty, whose person abounds in sacred qualities and whose chief imperial desires are directed to the end of raising the necessaries of war to the most supreme degree of perfection in order to safeguard the sacred rights of his Sublime Empire, has made to the many acts and efforts, he, as our great and sublime benefactor, has been putting forth since the beginning of the present war, for bringing the military equipment up to a degree satisfactory to his august mind, one more addition, in deigning to issue an imperial order (the orders of the august holder of the Crown are always full of kindness and generosity) to the effect that the imperial yacht, called "Stamboul," which is in the personal service of our august Majesty, whose person abounds in lofty qualities, should be equipped with cannon and be added to the imperial navy. Measures to this effect have been taken accordingly.[6]

> As soon as the magnanimous Padishah, Sultan of Sultans Commander of the Lands and the Seas, Protector of Letters and Sciences had condescended so far as to deign to take note of the fire which burst out yesterday in the Hassan Pasha quarter of Bechiktache had assumed disturbing proportions in his paternal solicitude, the omnipotent Sovereign of whom the sun's rays are a halo. The Shadow of God on Earth whose sole care is to watch over by day and by night the well being and tranquility of all the inhabitants of the universe, deigned order the plague to cease its ravages and on the moment the fire was extinguished.[7]

In contrast to the above examples of journalistic pomposity Mustafa Kemal's famous six-day speech to the Second Congress of the People's Party in October 1927 is striking evidence of the nature and vigor of the intellectual and literary revolution initiated by a small group of Turkish leaders in the nineteenth century.

CHAPTER IV

The Anatomy of Power Politics

It is quite impossible to write about the Ottoman Empire during the past and present century without using the terms imperialism, imperialistic, imperialist, etc. So varied are the connotations of these terms, it is essential to define briefly the word imperialism. This is all the more necessary in the present century when a certain opprobrium is attached to imperialism in all its forms. In the Great Power conflict in the Near East two principal contestants, the U.S.A. and the U.S.S.R., accuse one another of imperialism and imperialistic actions and designs. These accusations differ only in terminology from those made by the various European Powers and Turkey during the nineteenth century. The accusations and terminology are essentially for public consumption and are often used by diplomats, statesmen, and others for propaganda purposes.

IMPERIALISM

In so far as it is possible, the word imperialism and its derivatives will be employed objectively without implications of approval or of opprobrium. Imperialism will be used to mean the extension of political, economic, or psychological power and control—direct or indirect—of the government of one nation, or of private individuals and corporate entities of one nation, with or without governmental support, over another nation or people irrespective of whether such extension of power be beneficent or injurious to those over whom it is exerted.[1]

From the time of the invasion of Egypt by the French under Napoleon in 1798–99, the various great states of Europe, individually, in groups of two or more, and collectively as the Concert of European Powers, expanded their political influence, their economic interests, and their psychological activities—missionary, educational, journalistic, and cultural—throughout the Near East. In all of these fields of activity there was intensive competition even when joint or co-operative action was taken. Every phase of life in the Near East has been affected significantly by the expansion of European and western imperialisms; in consequence, the historical developments there are incomprehensible without an understanding of the role imperialism has played and continues to play in the lives of Near Eastern peoples.

Until the founding of the German Empire in 1871, Austria, France, Great Britain, and Russia were the chief imperialist competitors for power with respect to the Ottoman Empire. It was only during the last quarter of the nineteenth century and in the twentieth that Italy and Germany developed important imperialistic interests in the Near East.

The Habsburgs and the Ottoman.—The Habsburg rulers of the Austrian-Hungarian Dual Monarchy, as well as the people of Austria and Hungary, had fought and dealt with the Ottoman Turks since the fourteenth century. Vienna had twice been besieged by the Turks who had overrun and ruled a considerable part of Hungary. With the aid of Poles and Hungarians, the Habsburgs had checked the Moslem invasion of Europe and became the spearhead of Christian counterattack in the Balkans whose inhabitants remained predominantly Christian under Ottoman rule.

During the nineteenth century, political and economic forces in the Habsburg Empire tended to stimulate expansion in the Balkans. Control of the Danube River, occupation of the eastern coast of the Adriatic Sea, and an outlet to the Aegean at Salonika were not altogether unreasonable ambitions of Austrian-Hungarian statesmen. Geographical location gave many advantages to the Habsburgs. These, however, were offset by very serious disadvantages. The rulers and ruling classes of the Habsburg Empire were Austrian Germans and Hungarian Magyars, while the bulk of the Balkan Christian subjects of the sultan were Serbs, Romanians, Bulgars, and Greeks who had little in common with Teutons and Magyars and much with Slavic Russia. Austrians and Hungarians were Roman Catholics; most of the Christians of the Balkans were members of the Orthodox Church. Furthermore, the rising tide of nineteenth-century nationalism became a stumbling block to Habsburg expansion eastward where Russia, as prospective heir to the sultan's European territories, was a formidable competitor.

The Russians and the Turks.—The contact of Russians with Turanian Turkish tribes is older and much more continuous than that of any of the other European peoples. From the tenth century to the twentieth, from the time of Kievan Russia through that of medieval Muscovy, and of imperial tsarist Russia to that of the Union of the Soviet Socialist Republics (U.S.S.R.), the Russian people and their rulers have had to deal with many different Turkish groups. The Turanian Turkish tribes who are thought to have originated in that part of Central Asia known as Turkestan, like many nomadic peoples, under certain conditions migrated en masse. The steppes of southern and southeastern Russia offered a magnificent grazing land and an open highway to the pastoral nomads of Asia. Between the tenth and thirteenth centuries, the Cuman Turks fought with the Kievan Russians for the control of those extensive grasslands lying north of the Black Sea. The Tatar invasion and conquest in the thirteenth century ended for the time being the conflict between Russians and Turks. When the Tatars, however, became Moslems, the sharp distinction between Tatar Mongols and Turanian Turks tended to disappear. The breakup of the famous Golden Horde resulted in a minor Tatar horde holding possession of the Crimea and the regions bordering on the north shore of the Black Sea. These groups of Tatars and Turks came under the control of the Ottoman government and their lands were considered part of the Turkish Empire.

In the sixteenth century, when the Ottoman Empire was at the peak of its power, the Black Sea was practically a Turkish lake. The Turks, thus, controlled the outlets of all the great river highways of eastern Europe and southern Russia—the Danube, the Pruth, the Dniester, the Bug, the Dnieper, and the Don.

When power was being consolidated at Moscow under Ivan the Great and Ivan the Terrible and later, after 1613, under the Romanovs, the possession of all outlets to the south by the Ottoman Turks became intolerable to the Russians. With the growing power of the Russian state, the tsars, rulers over this vast land-locked hinterland, sought control of outlets to the sea. The political and economic urge to do so was fortified by historical tradition and national pride because the Russian princes of Kiev had ruled from the Danube to the Volga. These lands which once had been Christian were in the seventeenth century controlled by Moslems.

Since the reign of Peter the Great, the Russian government has striven to secure access to the Mediterranean. In the eighteenth century, the Turks were forced to relinquish their somewhat tenuous control over the Crimea and other territories north of the Black Sea. Under the pressure of defeat by the Russians in the last quarter of the eighteenth century, the sultans also lost effective control over the principalities of Wallachia and Moldavia, which later joined to form the independent state of Romania. This Russian drive to the south has always been opposed by the Turks, sometimes aided by Austria, England, France, or Germany, and at the present time by the United States. Each in turn has considered Russian expansion to the Aegean and Adriatic a menace to its imperialistic interests in the Near East. Each has persuaded its people that Russian expansion was a grave danger to its national security. Russian policy, tsarist or Communist, has been directed at obtaining, as a minimum, security from attack via the Balkans and through the Straits and, as a maximum, domination of the Balkans and possession of Constantinople and control of the Bosporus, the Marmora Sea, and the Dardanelles.

By the end of the seventeenth century, following the failure of the Turks to capture Vienna in 1683 and their loss to the Habsburgs by the Treaty of Karlowitz in 1699 of Hungary and Transylvania, the Turks ceased to be a menace to Russia and the Russians became a constant threat to the Ottoman Empire. In 1774 under the Treaty of Kuchuk Kainardji, Russia acquired control over the mouths of the Bug and the Dnieper rivers and over the outlet of the Don and the Straits of Kerch. The sultan surrendered his nominal suzerainty over the Turks and Tatars of the Crimea and Azov regions and granted Russian representatives the right to confer with the Ottoman ruler concerning matters pertaining to his Orthodox subjects. This treaty prepared the way for future Russian advance in the Balkans and opened the door to increasing Russian interference in the internal affairs of the Ottoman Empire, ostensibly on behalf of the Ottoman Christians.

Russian claims to a dominant position in the Near East, particularly in the Balkans and in respect to the Straits, have greater logical validity than those of her European competitors, Austria, England, and France. The tsars maintained that they were political and spiritual heirs of the Christian Byzantine Emperors. The Russian Orthodox Church considered itself to be the protector of the Orthodox Christians throughout the Ottoman Empire. Looking upon themselves as the big brothers of all Slavs, the Russians fostered the pan-Slavic ideal in the Balkans. The Yugo-slavs are Slavs by race and culture, the Bulgars are Slavic by language and culture, the Romanians are largely Slavic by race, though they claim to be the descendants of Roman military colonists, and though their language is derived from ancient Latin. The events of history convinced the Russians that control of the Straits by others was a constant political threat and an economic menace to Russia. Whoever holds the strategic waterway from the Aegean to the Black Sea possesses the key to the most important doorway of the great Eurasian plain. The English historian Gibbon, in his famous *Decline and Fall of the Roman Empire,* postulates that he who controls the seas will eventually control the land. The corollary of this Gibbonesque postulate is that he who controls the hinterland lacks security unless he acquires possession of its outlets and control over adjacent seas. These are some of the main factors in Russia's imperialistic expansion in the Near East at the expense of the Ottoman Empire.

Until the nineteenth century the Greek Orthodox patriarch of Constantinople was the officially recognized head of all the Orthodox Christian subjects of the sultan. The patriarch and his priestly bureaucracy were known as the Phanariots because the ecclesiastical see was located in the Phanar (lighthouse) district of Constantinople on the southern shore of the Golden Horn. Under the Millet system the Phanariots exploited ruthlessly the non-Greek Christians of the Orthodox faith. This tyranny was resisted by the Romanian, Bulgarian, and Serbian laity and clergy whose demands for autocephalous churches were intensified by the rise of nationalism among the Balkan Orthodox Christians. In this struggle against the Phanariots by the national churches Russia took the side of the Slavs. The creation of an independent Greek kingdom in 1832 and the adoption of a Pan-Slavic policy by the tsar's government—it is of interest to note that Pan-Slavism was first advocated in Russia by a Bulgarian intellectual—made Russian propaganda in the Balkans definitely pro-Slavic if not actually anti-Greek. Eventually, when imperially minded Greeks began to talk about the revival of the Byzantine Empire, Russian imperialists came to regard the Greeks as potential competitors for the possession of Constantinople.

Russia and her rivals.—The Ottoman Turks as an obstacle to Russian expansion might have been eliminated by the superior military power of the Muscovites if it had not been for Austria's opposition to Russia's advance in the Balkans, British determination to keep the Russian out of Constantinople, and France's zealous interest in acting as the protector of the Catholic subjects of the sultan. During the first half of the nineteenth century these three dominant European powers held Russian imperialist expansion to the south in check by their support of the Ottoman Empire.

Previous to the nineteenth century, Austria and Russia had a certain degree of mutuality of interest in protecting the Balkan Christians and in their wars against the Turks; but after 1800, as the achievement of their respective imperialistic ambitions appeared nearer of attainment, they found less frequent grounds for co-operation and more for conflict. Throughout the last century British opposition to Russia was consistently maintained, although Tsar Nicholas I proposed an Anglo-Russian partition of the Ottoman Empire. Interestingly enough, England in the nineteenth century managed to get possession of most of what Russia offered and succeeded in preventing Russia from obtaining what she desired. France and Russia remained at odds with one another until the last decade of the nineteenth century, when the Franco-Russian Dual Alliance was signed. In the 1880's, the newly formed German Empire began its drive to the Near East, which the Germans called their *Drang nach Osten,* that eventually made Germany a determined opponent to Russian designs on Constantinople. It is a curious fact that all the principal powers of Europe, individually and at times collectively, opposed and blocked the one nation which had the most rational if not justifiable claim to Constantinople and the Straits, with the exception, of course, of the Ottoman Empire itself.

French interests in the Near East.—The interest and claims of France in the Near East go back to the era of the Crusades, when French kings and nobles played an important role in the wars between Moslems and Christians. During the reign of Francis I in the sixteenth century, France was the first of the great national states of Europe to negotiate commercial treaties with the Ottoman sultan, treaties which became the basis for the capitulations granted to the western non-Moslem nations.

There was a wide and varied base for nineteenth century French imperialism in the Near East. Marseilles the great Mediterranean port of France has throughout history, since the heyday of the Greek city states in the fifth century B.C., been an important factor in the commerce and shipping between Europe and the Near East. In modern times French commercial, financial, and shipping interests particularly in Lyons and Marseilles have had important economic stakes in the eastern Mediterranean and at Constantinople. These interests increased significantly during the nineteenth century after the construction of the Suez Canal by Ferdinand de Lesseps, largely financed by the French. Considerable amounts of French capital were invested in the Ottoman Empire in loans to the Ottoman Government and in the construction of railroads and other public works in Anatolia, Syria, and Palestine. The cultivation of silk worms in Turkey and Syria was of special interest to French textile manufacturers. French shipowners, bankers, merchants, industrialists, and investors took a lively interest in Near Eastern affairs. A variety of organizations—economic, cultural, and social—were constantly alert to anything that might be injurious to French interests in the eastern Mediterranean and actively supported France's Near Eastern policies.

With the treaty of 1535 negotiated during the reigns of Francis I and Suleiman the Magnificent, France acquired special rights in the Ottoman Empire. France, which became the leading Catholic nation in Europe under the Bourbons, assumed, partly on the basis of historical precedents and partly on the basis of juridical rights under treaties with both sultans and popes, the role of protector of Catholic Christians, clergy and property in the Ottoman Empire. Despite the separation of church and state after the establishment of the Third French Republic in 1875, the French government gave unhesitating encouragement and support to French Catholic missions, hospitals, and educational institutions in the Near East. These rights, obligations, and privileges of the French Government with respect to religious matters became a major French interest in the Ottoman Empire and one of the important factors in French cultural and political imperialism.

During the nineteenth century, the French language became the second language of all educated people in the Near East—Moslem, Christian, and Jewish. French culture became the dominant foreign culture throughout the Ottoman Empire.

France's rivals.—The French considered Egypt, even after the British occupation in 1882, and also Palestine, Lebanon, and Syria as special spheres of political interest and significance to France and jealously watched any encroachment upon these areas by any other European power. From the time of Napoleon's ill-fated expedition to Egypt up to contemporary times, the French and British have been acrimonious rivals in the Near East. The bitterness of this rivalry was clearly evident during both world wars. Whenever Russia and later Germany appeared to threaten both French and British interests, however, these two unrelenting competitors joined forces in co-operative efforts to check a common rival in the Near East. Following their acrimonious disputes of the 1840's over the invasion of Syria by the armies of Mohammed Ali, Pasha of Egypt, France and England became military allies during the Crimean War of 1855 against Russia.

These manifold interests were the instruments of French imperialistic power in the Near East, and to protect and extend these interests had been the mainsprings of French policy with regard to the Ottoman Empire throughout the nineteenth century.

Britain's imperial stake in the Ottoman Empire.—British imperialistic interests in the Near East were more definitely political and economic than cultural. Britain's major imperial stake was India; consequently, its security and that of the routes thereto played a predominant role in shaping British policy with respect to the Ottoman Empire and exerted a powerful influence on British relations with Britain's competitors in the Near East. The Napoleonic wars made the British acutely aware of the grave threat to Britain's position in India inherent in the extension to any part of the Near East of the political power of any other European state.

In Mesopotamia (Iraq) and along the entire coast of Arabia, the British consolidated their political and economic position in order to control the Persian Gulf and the Red Sea almost to the exclusion of all European competitors. Until Germany's bid for power in the Near East, Great Britain's two most formidable rivals were France and Russia, the former in the southern part, the latter principally in the northern. In Egypt and the Sudan, in Palestine and Syria, the British watched vigilantly and anxiously every move by France to extend French influence and took steps to block the French whenever British interests appeared seriously threatened. At Constantinople, British representatives followed Russian diplomatic maneuvers and took steps to counter those which might lead to increasing Russian influence over the Ottoman government or to the dismemberment of the Turkish Empire.

The British did not hesitate to co-operate with Russia to check France or to join the French in checkmating the Russians. The keystone, however, of British Near Eastern policy was the maintenance of the sovereignty and independence of the Ottoman Empire. Nevertheless, Britain did not find the taking of Egypt and Cyprus from the Turks at all incompatible with her policy of preventing France and Russia from acquiring control over other vital and strategic parts of the sultan's territories.

British economic interests.—In the field of economics the British for centuries had developed commercial relations in the Persian Gulf region, along the Tigris and Euphrates, and in Persia (Iran). During the nineteenth century, mercantile activities in these areas were greatly increased. British companies opened up commercial communications with both Mesopotamia and Persia, British naval forces eliminated age-old piracy in the Persian Gulf, and through the government of India the British negotiated treaties of an exclusive nature with the Arab rulers of the sheikdoms along the eastern and southern coasts of Arabia.

Several factors resulted in a very great increase in Great Britain's economic interests in Egypt. Of these, cotton was one of the most important. The results of Mohammed Ali's introduction of cotton raising in Egypt during the first quarter of the nineteenth century are truly amazing. Since England was the most important center of the production of cotton textiles, British manufacturers were immediately interested in the cultivation of cotton in Egypt. The American Civil War, which cut off Britain's supply of American cotton and threatened to cripple the British textile industry, further stimulated British interest in Egypt. Later, in the United States the destruction by the boll weevil of long staple Sea Island cotton, so indispensable to the manufacture of fine cotton goods, and the development of the world-famous long staple Sakellaridis cotton in Egypt resulted in greatly augmenting the cultivation, ginning, and shipping of Egyptian cotton. A vast nexus of British economic interests was tied into the Egyptian cotton business. A great amount of capital went into extensive irrigation works and land cultivation, the building of railroads, and the construction of warehouses, cotton gins, and port facilities. All of these directly or indirectly augmented British economic interests in Egypt. British banks financed cotton shipments; British companies insured cotton cargoes; British steamship companies established a monopoly of the shipment of cotton to England, to Europe, and to the United States.

The completion of the Suez Canal in 1869, control of which was acquired by the British government in 1875, through purchase of the shares held by the impecunious Khedive of Egypt, Ismail Pasha, opened up a new and direct route to India. Thus, the southeastern Mediterranean, its islands, the lands bordering on it, and the adjacent seas became of much greater concern to the British. Nine years after the opening of the Suez Canal the British acquired control of Cyprus, and Britain's Prime Minister Disraeli, fearing that the Russian-Turkish Treaty of San Stefano would result in the Russians gaining control of the Straits, threatened to go to war if the tsar's government refused to accept a revision of the treaty insisted upon by the Concert of European Powers at Berlin in 1878. It was only thirteen years after the completion of the new canal that British military forces occupied Egypt to put down a rebellion which jeopardized the large foreign investments in Egypt and the French and British loans to the Egyptian government.

In Syria where British economic interests were less important than those of the French, and in Lebanon where the powerful Maronites (Roman Catholics) were French protégés, the British, as a means of counterbalancing French influence there, gave their support to the Druzes, a heretical Moslem sect who were bitter enemies of the Maronites.

The interaction of the rival and competitive imperialism of Austria, England, France, and Russia in the Balkans and the Near East shaped the foreign policy of the Ottoman government, affected Turkish domestic policy, and had important repercussions on the relations between the various national and religious groups in all parts of the Ottoman Empire.

The interplay of foreign interests resulted in increasing encroachments on Turkish sovereignty and the intervention in Ottoman affairs of the European powers, acting sometimes individually and at other times collectively as the Concert of Europe. The foreign and internal affairs of the Turkish Empire were bedeviled by the impact of the West upon the Near East.

CHAPTER V

Foreign Affairs and Domestic Crises

The foreign affairs of the Ottoman Empire in the nineteenth century became so increasingly entangled with its domestic troubles, both political and financial, that it is almost impossible to deal with them separately.

The reforms of Sultan Mahmoud II (1808–39), who destroyed the Janissaries in 1826, were related to domestic political situations and to foreign complications. The principal domestic situations which confronted Sultan Mahmoud were the Wahhabi revolt in Arabia, the confused state of affairs in Egypt resulting from Napoleon's invasion, the Serbian revolt, and the Greek revolution.

THE WAHHABIS AND IBN SAUD

In 1810 Olivier de Coraricez, former member of Napoleon's Egyptian commission of sciences, in his book *The History of the Wahhabis,* wrote: "These Arabs (the Wahhabis) appear destined to play a great role in history." A contemporary writer might be more cautious about predicting the role which the present Wahhabite Kingdom of Saudi Arabia may play in the future of the Near East, but he would have no hesitancy in affirming that in the first quarter of the nineteenth century, as in the first half of the present century, the Wahhabis have had an important effect upon historical developments in the Near East. The Wahhabite conquest of a large part of Arabia in the first decade of the last century resulted in the invasion and conquest of Arabia by Mohammed Ali, then Viceroy of Egypt. This Egyptian occupation of Arabia from 1812–13 to 1840, under a ruler who was looked upon as a protégé of France, made the British Government realize the strategic significance of the Arabian peninsula and caused the British to take immediate steps to forestall any European competitor from securing footholds there. A hundred years later, the Wahhabite King Abdul Aziz Ibn Saud, by granting a concession for the development of petroleum deposits in his kingdom to the Standard Oil Company of California, paved the way for the termination of Britain's almost exclusive monopoly of foreign influence in Arabia and the rise of American power in the Near East.

The Wahhabite movement is both religious and political. The founder of the Wahhabite sect was Mohammed Abd al-Wahhab, who after his religious and legal studies at Bagdad returned to Arabia to preach a Moslem puritanism and a revival of the simplicity of early Islam. Abd al-Wahhab insisted that the Koran was the only source of authority; he preached against the adoration of Moslem saints and against the decoration of their tombs by the pilgrims to Mecca and Medina; he assailed the superstitions and miracles which had, like barnacles, attached themselves to Islamic monotheism; and he insisted on a return to the simple and penurious life of the early Moslem leaders. Among Wahhab's early converts was Emir Abdul Aziz Ibn Saud, one of the important local princes of central Arabia.

Wahhabism supported by the political power of Ibn Saud and under the inspired leadership of Wahhab spread between 1770 and 1800 from the Nejd in central Arabia to a considerable portion of the peninsula. With armed forces composed of Wahhabite peasants and nomads Ibn Saud in the first decade of the new century raided the Ottoman vilayets of Syria and Bagdad, captured the Holy Cities of the Hejaz and interrupted the annual Haj (Moslem pilgrimage) to Mecca and Medina.

The Turkish Sultan could not ignore for long this challenge to his sovereign authority. As caliph, he was responsible for the safety of the pilgrims to the holiest shrines of Islam. The Wahhabi occupation of the Hejaz followed by the interruption of the Pilgrimage brought protests from Moslems in all parts of the Islamic world. Action by the Ottoman Sultan was imperative. So feeble was the Turkish government that it could not marshal sufficient forces to attack the Wahhabis nor could it compel the pashas of Syria and Bagdad to carry out the imperial orders to destroy the Wahhabis.

In 1811 Mohammed Ali, Pasha of Egypt, decided to give heed to the Sultan's commands and began to prepare an expedition to Arabia in 1812. By 1818, Mohammed Ali's son, Ibrahim Pasha, captured Daraiya, Ibn Saud's capital in the Nejd, and destroyed the political power of the Wahhabis in Arabia. A little more than one hundred years later Ibn Saud as leader of the Wahhabis captured Mecca and Medina, created the Kingdom of Saudi Arabia and conquered a large part of the Arabian peninsula. He thus became the dominant power there and an important factor in the affairs of the Near East.

MOHAMMED ALI

The founding of the so-called Albanian dynasty of Mohammed Ali in Egypt in the first half of the nineteenth century was the result of a combination of historical factors related to the Ottoman Empire and the rivalry of the European powers. In the latter part of the eighteenth century, Ali Bey, the leader of the Egyptian Mamelukes, called the Sheik ul-Beled, overthrew the Ottoman administration in Egypt and set himself up as an independent ruler. His successor Ibrahim at the time of Napoleon's conquest of Egypt in 1798–99 was the chief sheik of the Mamelukes who had played a dominant role in Egypt from the middle of the thirteenth century.

Destruction of the Mamelukes.—The Mamelukes were the descendants of the slaves of the Arab rulers of Egypt.[1] These slaves, called in Arabic *mamluks,* who were largely of Tatar, Turkish, and Circassian origin, overthrew their masters in 1250 and remained the rulers of Egypt for over two hundred and fifty years, during which time they established themselves as a ruling land-owning oligarchy. After the Turkish conquest of Egypt in 1517 the Mameluke pashas and beys were frequently the actual rulers, since the Ottoman governors were for the most part puppets in the hands of the powerful Mamelukes. Until their liquidation by Mohammed Ali, the Mamelukes during a period of five hundred years remained a race apart from the Egyptians. They formed a caste which had no relations domestic or social with the Egyptian population whom they exploited ruthlessly.

Mohammed Ali's rise to power.—The elimination of the Mamelukes occurred a dozen years after Napoleon Bonaparte left Egypt in 1799 following his withdrawal from Palestine. The power of the Mamelukes was broken by Mohammed Ali. This remarkable man of Persian and Turkish ancestry was born in Kavala and raised in Albania, where his father was an Ottoman official. Without much formal education young Mohammed Ali had become an officer in the Turkish army. He was sent to Egypt as second in command of a small contingent of Albanian troops which formed a part of an Anglo-Turkish force which in 1801 was landed in the Nile Delta to drive out the French contingents left there by Napoleon.

Through a succession of events Mohammed Ali made himself the military master of Egypt and was appointed the sultan's viceroy with the title of Pasha of Egypt. One of his acts of political significance was the dramatic massacre of the Mameluke leaders whose misrule and exploitation of the Egyptian people had by 1800 almost ruined the rich land of Egypt.

The foundations of Mohammed Ali's power rested on his reforms.[2] He set out to restore the economic prosperity of Egypt by encouraging agriculture, industry, and commerce. In his efforts to modernize Egypt he founded the Boulak printing press, hired French officers to train a modern type of army to replace his rapacious Albanian troops, and acquired a considerable naval force. As a result he and his son Ibrahim Pasha played important roles politically in the Near East from 1810 to 1840. It was to this powerful and energetic viceroy of Egypt that Sultan Mahmoud II (1808–39) appealed for help, first against the Wahhabis in Arabia and later against the Greek revolutionists in the Morea.

The Greek revolt.—Three years after the defeat of the Wahhabis in Arabia, revolution broke out in the southern part of the Greek peninsula early in April, 1821. This nationalistic uprising to gain independence began as an agrarian revolt of Christian Greek peasants against their Moslem Greek landowners who were supported by Turkish garrisons. So deep was the hatred of the peasants for their oppressors that, as the revolt spread, there was increasing brutality. Some thirty thousand Moslems, irrespective of age or sex, were slaughtered by the enraged Greek peasants. When beleaguered garrisons surrendered to the revolutionists, they did not live up to the terms of the surrender and proceeded to kill both the Turkish prisoners and Moslem civilians. The reaction to these brutalities of the Greeks created enormous indignation in Constantinople among all classes of Turks. Ruthless reprisals against the Greek population in the Ottoman capital took place with official sanction. Religious and national passions were aroused to such a pitch that Moslem mobs fell upon the Greeks in several cities of the empire.

Sultan Mahmoud II was under great pressure to suppress the rebellion, but from 1821 to 1824 the Turks had little success by land or by sea against the Greek rebels. In desperation the sultan called upon Mohammed Ali for help, promising him the pashaliks of Damascus, Tripoli (Asiatic), Syria, and Crete. During the following two years, 1825 and 1826, Egyptian military and naval forces were sent to Greece and were in the process of successfully stamping out the Greek revolt when the Great Powers of Europe intervened.

The Greek revolt had deeply stirred the liberals of Europe, especially those of England and France. The period of the Greek revolution in the Ottoman Empire was one of deep frustration for the European liberals.

The nationalistic and liberal uprisings throughout Italy and in Spain had been crushed by Austria and France as a result of the decisions of the Concert of European Powers at the congresses of Troppau (1820), Laibach (1822), and Verona in 1822. The Habeas Corpus Act had been suspended in England in 1817 by a reactionary government. In France the ultraroyalist Charles X became king and proceeded to destroy the constitution of 1814–15. In Austria and throughout the German Bund, liberalism and nationalism were ruthlessly suppressed. The Greek revolution gave the pent-up emotions of the European liberals an outlet they availed themselves of with great enthusiasm.

Intervention of the Great Powers.—The Greek Revolution resulted in intervention by the European Powers on a broader scale than in Egypt. The policies pursued by the various Great Powers seem at first glance quite inconsistent. Such seeming contradictions of policy frequently are only so in appearance as becomes obvious on closer observation of the fundamental and determining factors. In the decade between 1820 and 1830, the European Powers were divided on the issue of intervention and nonintervention in the internal affairs of sovereign and independent states. Great Britain opposed the policy of intervention pursued by the members of the Holy Alliance under the leadership of Metternich of Austria. The British government unsuccessfully opposed armed intervention of the Powers in Italy and Spain, but with the support of the United States and the Monroe Doctrine, the British prevented the re-establishment of the Spanish colonial empire in Central and South America. British shipping and mercantile interests actively favored the policy of nonintervention in South America fearing the re-establishment of the old Spanish colonial monopoly. The general policy of opposition to the interventionist policy of Metternich was applauded by the English liberals. The reactionary British government, which did not view with favor the Greek revolution, in response to popular demand felt compelled to intervene. By an agreement with France and Russia known as the Treaty of London (1827) Great Britain hoped to bring about the pacification of Greece without armed intervention. The three Powers insisted upon an armistice between the Greek revolutionists and the Turks and threatened the sultan with armed intervention if he refused to accept their proposals for the autonomy of Greece. On the refusal of the Ottoman government to accede to their demands, the three Powers sent under the command of a British admiral a joint fleet to blockade the Greek coast. This was indeed intervention.

The British government adopted this policy with respect to the Ottoman Empire because it feared that Russia, acting unilaterally, might use the Greek revolution as an excuse to force a war with the Turks. The basic factor determining official British opposition to European intervention in South America and for British support of European intervention in the Near East was, in both cases, the forwarding of British interests. The support of liberal opinion for these two seemingly different policies with respect to intervention was only incidental to the formulation of policy.

Austria took no part in the European intervention in the Near East on behalf of the Greeks. Metternich maintained that the Greek uprising was directed against the legitimate government of the sultan and that a revolution in the Ottoman Empire was a threat to the maintenance of the status quo established by the Congress of Vienna in 1814–15. The Austrian statesman was able to persuade Alexander I of Russia that it was not in the interests of autocracy to aid Greek revolutionists. On his accession to the throne in 1825, however, Nicholas I reversed the policy of his predecessor by active intervention on behalf of the Greeks.

The British policy of joint intervention to restrain Russia failed completely. In the Bay of Navarino, "the guns went off of themselves," or to use contemporary phraseology, the "cold war" against Turkey suddenly became a "hot war," when the joint fleet of England, France, and Russia, contrary to instructions from their respective governments, fired on and destroyed the Turkish and Egyptian navies. Despite this disaster, Sultan Mahmoud II refused to consider the proposals of the three Powers. On the contrary, the Ottoman government demanded that the allies cease their interference with Greek affairs and pay an indemnity for the destruction of Ottoman ships at Navarino. When on receipt of this communication, the ambassadors of the three Powers withdrew from Constantinople, the sultan issued an imperial order calling upon all Moslems to wage a Holy War against the Christians who were bent on destroying Islam. Russia promptly declared war on Turkey.

Defeated in Greece and the Balkans and in eastern Anatolia, the Turks were obliged to sign the Treaty of Adrianople in 1829, which foreshadowed the future loss of the greater part of European Turkey. The autonomy of Serbia was reaffirmed, and Turkish sovereignty over the Romanian principalities of Wallachia and Moldavia became purely nominal; in fact, they were now for all practical purposes Russian protectorates. Greece gained independence in 1830, and Russia secured a foothold at the mouth of the Danube.

In the game of power politics in the Near East, Russia had gained at the expense of both Austria and England. The former had attempted to persuade France and England to join her in a war against Russia in support of Turkey. France, who had a secret understanding with the Russians aimed at British power in the Mediterranean, was unwilling to aid the Turks. It was at this time that France was preparing to occupy Algeria, which once had been a part of the Ottoman Empire and, though virtually independent, still was bound by religious ties to the Turkish caliph. The general situation in Europe in 1830, following revolution in France and in Belgium, and revolutionary uprisings in various other parts of Europe, temporarily diverted the attention of European statesmen from the Near East. The next crisis for the Ottoman government and the European imperialists was, however, soon created by Mohammed Ali, whose actions rapidly embroiled England, France, and Russia.

Egyptian invasion of Syria.—After the withdrawal of Egyptian forces from southern Greece, following the Battle of Navarino, Sultan Mahmoud II refused to grant Mohammed Ali the four pashaliks of Syria promised him. Mohammed Ali promptly decided to seize them by force and in 1831 launched an attack on Syria. Keenly aware of the importance of propaganda, the Egyptian viceroy attempted to convince Moslems he was fighting for Islam against an incompetent caliph, to persuade the Arabs he was delivering them from the rapacious Turkish valis, and to convince the British that his campaigns in Syria and Anatolia were directed at strengthening the Ottoman Empire to enable it to resist Russian encroachment.

The rapid Egyptian conquest of Syria followed by the rout of the Turkish forces at Konia created a panic in Constantinople which precipitated an international crisis. Unable to obtain a promise of naval aid from the British, Sultan Mahmoud II asked Russia to send naval and military forces for the defense of Constantinople. The Russians promptly came to the aid of Turkey, much to the dismay of the British and the French. The government of France, while supporting Mohammed Ali as a counterweight to the British, was quite unwilling to see Turkey under the domination of Russia and so joined England in urging the sultan to rescind his request for Russian military and naval aid. This he did not do, and before the crisis was over, the sultan granted Mohammed Ali five pashaliks and signed the Treaty of Unkiar Skelessi (1833) with Russia previous to the withdrawal of Tsarist troops. This treaty was in the nature of an offensive-defensive alliance which threatened the sovereignty of the Ottoman government by granting Russia the right to send military forces to the Straits whenever internal conditions in Turkey were such as to warrant Russia doing so. Russia also obtained the right to send her warships through the Straits, while a secret clause closed them to all other foreign powers.

Such a settlement could only be of a temporary nature. The Ottoman government was not willing to accept the loss of control over the Syrian pashaliks and that of Adana, nor was it prepared to remain under what approximated Russian tutelage. Mohammed Ali was dissatisfied because he had failed to obtain a hereditary title to Egypt on which he set great store. The Moslem Arabs of Syria were far from content under Egyptian rule; and England, France, and Austria were unwilling to allow Russia to play the dominant role at Constantinople. The arrangements of 1833 proved to be purely transitory and the conflict in Syria soon broke out again in 1839.

From 1833 to 1839, Sultan Mahmoud and Mohammed Ali prepared for war. These two Oriental potentates were striving to reform and modernize the institutions of the territories over which they ruled. Of the two, the Pasha of Egypt had made greater progress and achieved more success than his suzerain, the Sultan of Turkey. Mohammed Ali held Mahmoud in contempt and was convinced that unless he could secure hereditary title to the various pashaliks he governed, all his reforms and innovations would crumble under the misrule of a restored Turkish administration. If it had not been for the interference of the European Powers in 1833 and again in the 1840's, there is little doubt that Mohammed Ali would have had sufficient military power to capture Constantinople. His plans, however, came to naught because the Near East had become one of the principal areas of European power politics, and "the Eastern Question" had assumed a position of major diplomatic importance in the chancelleries of Europe, which it was to retain for the balance of the century.

Mohammed Ali and the Great Powers.—In the spring of 1838 Mohammed Ali informed the Great Powers of his intention to declare his independence of the sultan. Mahmoud, urged on by his minister of war and the Prussian officers, including von Moltke, who later was to become the famous chief of staff of the Prussian army, ordered his forces to cross the Euphrates into Syria. The Egyptian forces under Ibrahim Pasha attacked and completely routed the Turks at the Battle of Nozib in June 1839. A week later the sultan died, and shortly afterwards the Turkish fleet sailed into the harbor of Alexandria and gratuitously surrendered to Mohammed Ali. Shaken by these events, the Ottoman divan was preparing to accede to all of Mohammed Ali's demands when the European Powers intervened. Austria, France, Great Britain, Prussia, and Russia presented a joint note to the Porte advising the Turkish government to take no action without their agreement and co-operation.

This unanimity of action by the Europeans had been achieved as the result of the interplay of many different forces. An examination of some of these is most revealing with regard to European diplomacy in the Near East. Foreign Minister Palmerston's uncritical acceptance of the reports of corrupt British consular officers in Syria and of the somewhat jittery British ambassador at Constantinople resulted in absurd misintepretations of Russian policy. As these reports conformed with Palmerston's prejudices and preconceived notions, he decided upon a pro-Turkish, anti-Egyptian policy. Russia, which contrary to Ambassador Ponsonby's despatch was neither supporting Mohammed Ali nor desirous of taking unilateral action in aid of Turkey under the Treaty of Unkiar Skelessi, welcomed joint action by the Powers. France, which favored the independence of Mohammed Ali and his control of Syria, could not risk a war with the other European Powers. Although popular indignation in Paris was great when the other four Great Powers signed a treaty in 1840 dictating terms to be offered to Mohammed Ali, the French government was obliged to acquiesce in the British attack on the Egyptian forces in Syria and Palestine.

After defeating the Egyptians in the Arab provinces, General Napier sailed to Alexandria, and quite on his own, without diplomatic authorization from the other Powers, signed a convention with Mohammed Ali. This brought to an end the second Turkish-Egyptian war in Syria. The old Albanian officer who had arrived in Egypt as a young man in 1800 became its hereditary ruler practically independent of the Turkish government in 1841, although obliged to renounce his claims to the Cretan and Asiatic pashaliks. The European Powers gave recognition to the changed status of Egypt and of the family of Mohammed Ali; in fact, the Powers had forced the terms of settlement not only on Mohammed Ali but also on the Ottoman government. From this date on, peace in the Near East was no longer dependent upon the Turkish or the Egyptian rulers but upon the great European states.

❁ TROUBLE IN THE LEVANT—SYRIA AND LEBANON

The retirement of the Egyptian forces from Syria in 1840–41 precipitated internal disorders which plagued the new Sultan Abdul Medjid (1839–61) and intensified the friction between Great Britain and France. Mohammed Ali's policy in the Syrian pashaliks, together with Turkish, British, and French intrigues, increased the bitterness between rival religious and social groups among the Arabs. The causes of the violent disturbances and conflicts in Mount Lebanon (then a part of the

Syrian pashaliks) during the 1840's and again in the 1860's lay deep in the religious and social cleavages between the Arabic-speaking peoples of Syria, Palestine, and Mount Lebanon.

The people of the Levant.[3]—Until the advent of hundreds of thousands of Jews in Palestine after 1920 the people of Syria, Lebanon, Jordania, and Palestine were overwhelmingly Arab by culture. Living in a land which for at least three thousand years had been a crossroads of the main Near Eastern highways north-south, and east-west, invaded and conquered innumerable times by aliens, the inhabitants are a mixture of races and peoples. The topography and climate of this bridge between Asia and Africa have fostered diversity and perpetuated differences. Despite their common Arab cultural heritage, the nomads of the desert, the peasants of the coastal and hinterland plains, and the shepherd cultivators of the mountains differ greatly from one another. Cutting across these lines of cleavage were those of religion and sect. Until most recent years an inhabitant of these regions was not known as a Palestinian or a Syrian, but as a member of the tribe he belonged to or by the village, town, or city from which he came, and he was identified by his religion and by the sect to which he belonged. Those who were not Turks, Kurds, Armenians, Ottoman Jews, or foreigners were all recognized as Arabs (ibn Arab: i.e., son of an Arab), whether Moslem or Christian, peasant, nomad, mountaineer, or townsman, and these formed the great majority of the population.

The main religious groups among the Moslems were the orthodox Sunnites; the Shiites, known in Syria as the Metawali (those who befriend Ali), who live principally on the coastal plain and in the great central valley of Syria, called the Bekaa between the Lebanon Mountains and the Anti-Lebanon range along the headwaters of the historically famous Orontes and Leontes rivers; and the Druzes. Among the Christians were the Orthodox members of the so-called Greek Church; the Greek Catholic Melchites, who recognize the authority of the pope and are affiliated with the western Roman Catholic Church; and the Maronites, who also give allegiance to Rome.

Added to the bitterness and friction between Moslems and Christians in the narrow Arab lands bordering on the Mediterranean, were sectarian hatreds between Sunnites, Metawali (Shiites), and Druzes, and between Greek Orthodox, Greek Catholic Melchites, and Maronites. The Ottoman Millet system, by placing power in the hands of the clergy of these various Christian sects, intensified and perpetuated these religious cleavages. During the nineteenth century, indigenous divisions and rivalries were increased by the fact that France became more aggressive in fostering the interests of the Catholics, particularly the Maronites; Russia became far more active in the affairs of the Orthodox; and Great Britain became a particular protagonist of the Druzes and, generally speaking, of the Sunnite Moslems. The various religious groups among the Arabs thus became the tools of the imperialists as they had been the instruments of Turkish domination over the Arabs.

Violence in Lebanon.—The violence in Mount Lebanon and Syria during the nineteenth century centered about the conflict between the Maronites and the Druzes. The Druze "nation" has two main centers: one in Jebel Druze (the Druze Mountain) south of Damascus, a mountainous oasis bordering on both the Syrian desert and the rich agricultural plain of the Hauran; and the other in the mountains of Lebanon. The principal concentration of Maronites is in Mount Lebanon and on the Lebanese coastal plain. The struggle for domination of the Lebanon between the Druzes and the Maronites during the last and the present century has played a significant role in the political history of this Arab sector of the Near East. The strategic location of the Druze centers in Jebel Druze and in Mount Lebanon has made it possible for them to exert very considerable influence during the period of Ottoman rule and since then, both during the period of the French mandate and the establishment of the two Arab republics of Syria and Lebanon.

The ruthlessness of the conflict between Maronites and Druzes during the nineteenth century created an antagonism between the leaders of the two groups so intense that in Egypt during 1917 it was impossible to bring together certain leading Druzes and Maronites for discussion of the future of Lebanon and Syria.

The modern phase of this conflict developed in 1840 as a result, in part, of Mohammed Ali's forced withdrawal and, in part, of British and French imperialistic rivalry. Mohammed Ali, in line with his policy of reform and modernization and conforming to his diplomatic efforts to obtain the goodwill of the Christian Powers of Europe, granted equality of status to the Christians in the Syrian pashaliks. By so doing he antagonized all Moslems, but most especially the reactionary, fanatical elements among the Sunnite ulemas of the Syrian hinterland cities.

When the British bombed the coastal cities and landed forces in Syria and Palestine, the Sunnite Moslems and Druzes were determined to put the Christians in their place. The center of the conflict was in the Lebanon between the Druzes and the Maronites. The conflict was by no means purely a religious one, for it had social and economic aspects. The Druze leaders were feudal chieftains whose power over their peasants was enhanced because tribal loyalty still played an important role among Druzes. The Maronite leaders were landowning priests and laymen and wealthy merchants. Underlying the religious conflict was the economic and political struggle between the ruling classes among the Druzes and Maronites. Furthermore, the war between the Druzes and the Maronites had its international aspect because of British and French rivalry in southwestern Asia.

French and British rivalry in the Levant.—Evidence of the intensity of French feeling with respect to British policy in Syria and the Lebanon during the 1840's is found in a history of the Ottoman Empire by Vicomte de la Jonquière, who wrote as follows: ". . . the English, whose one aim was to ruin French influence in Syria, set about fomenting trouble in the Lebanon in order to get a footing there. They exploited the differences of race, the divergences of religion; they incited the Druzes against the Maronites, Moslems against Christians, and fostered in the Mountain, up to then united, racial antagonisms and religious hatreds." [4] Although one would question the objectivity of the vicomte's statements and judgments, it does seem indicative of Frenchmen's attitude toward British policy in the Near East that in 1914 on the eve of World War I a new edition of La Jonquière's history was published. The opening chapters of T. E. Lawrence's *Seven Pillars of Wisdom* shows an equal distrust of the French and reveals his advocacy in 1915 of a policy to keep the French out of Syria and the Lebanon.

The destruction of Maronite villages and the slaughter of Maronite peasants resulted in European intervention and pressure on the Ottoman government to bring about a settlement that would put an end to the disorders in the Lebanon. The crisis was over by 1845, but the settlement was only of a temporary nature, for hostilities broke out again in 1860 and resulted in armed intervention by the French. Before this occurred, however, the Ottoman Empire, in alliance with England and France, was plunged into a war against Russia.

THE CRIMEAN WAR

The Crimean War of 1854–55 now appears as one of the more stupid and useless of the wars between the major European states. Up to the present time, no one has undertaken to evaluate the suffering entailed, the loss of life caused, and the wealth destroyed as a result of the struggle for power between the ruling classes of the competing national states. When the balance sheet of these wars is finally struck, the suffering and misery inflicted on those innocent bystanders, the peoples of the Near East, should find a conspicuous place.

Underlying causes.—It now seems that the Crimean War would not have occurred if it had not been for the political developments in Europe between 1848 and 1851 and the struggle for power between the great European states. The Near East, with all its varied peoples, had become inextricably involved in the affairs of Europe, and Near Eastern history became a part of European history.

The age-old dispute between the Orthodox clergy and the Catholic ecclesiastics with regard to control over the Church of the Nativity in Bethlehem and the Church of the Holy Sepulchre in Jerusalem would probably never have led to war if it had not been for the complexities of forces and events in Europe at the time. In 1848 revolution had broken out in France. It began as a struggle of the middle class and the new French proletariat against the government of King Louis Philippe; after his overthrow it developed into a bitter struggle between these two classes, the former under the leadership of liberals and the latter of socialists. It was during this revolution in France that the Communist Manifesto of Marx and Engels was issued. The upheaval in France had immediate repercussions throughout most of Europe, with middle-class liberals and nationalists struggling to overthrow the autocracies supported since 1814–15 by the regime of Metternich, the reactionary minister of Austria. In every part of the Austrian Empire, there were liberal nationalistic uprisings among the Italian, the Austrian-German, the Czech, Yugoslavic, and Hungarian subjects of the Austrian Empire.

These revolutionary activities had an effect upon both the Ottoman Empire and Russia. In the Romanian principalities of Moldavia and Wallachia, which were still nominally a part of the sultan's possessions, a revolutionary movement, in contact with the revolutionists in Hungary, got underway. This was considered dangerous by both the sultan and the tsar, whose troops were sent to crush the revolution. With considerable armed forces in the Romanian provinces, the Russians used them as a base for military operations in Hungary to aid the Austrian Emperor, Francis Joseph in putting down the Hungarian revolution. When several of these Hungarian rebels, most notably the famous Hungarian liberal revolutionary leader Louis Kossuth, sought refuge in Turkey, Austria and Russia demanded that they be turned over to the Austrian government. This the sultan with encouragement from the British refused to do. Eventually, the matter was settled, despite the Austrian-Russian threat of war, by a compromise that permitted Kossuth and the other revolutionists to go to the United States. Russian-Turkish differences over the Hungarian refugees and the intervention of Russia in the

Romanian provinces were on the way to being settled when the dispute between the Catholic or Latin clergy, backed by France, and the Orthodox clergy, supported by Russia, reached a crisis. The tsar sent Prince Menschikof to make two demands upon the sultan: first, a settlement of the question of the Holy Places satisfactory to the Orthodox; and second, an acknowledgment that Russia, under the terms of the Treaty of Kutçhuk Kainardji (1774), had the right to protect all Orthodox Christian (approximately 10,000,000) subjects of the sultan.

The refusal of the Ottoman government, encouraged by England and France to resist this latter demand, resulted in the Russian government's announcing its intention of occupying the Romanian principalities. With a Franco-British fleet anchored at the Aegean entrance to the Straits the Turks dared to risk war and ordered the Turkish forces to attack the Russians. The Tsar called upon his people to wage a Holy War in defence of their coreligionists in Turkey. Russian-Turkish hostilities began in 1853; the Anglo-French fleet passed through the Dardanelles, anchored in the Bosporus, and after a Russian attack on the Turkish naval forces at Sinope, the Allied fleet entered the Black Sea, and in 1854 France and England signed a treaty of alliance with Turkey. The Crimean War had begun.

Nicholas' proposals to Britain.—Tsar Nicholas I had in 1853, shortly after the Franco-Russian dispute over the Holy Places, spoken very frankly with the British ambassador at St. Petersburg in an attempt to come to terms with Great Britain. The tsar stated that he had no desire to acquire further territories and that he would not claim possession of Constantinople, though he might be obliged to occupy it and would not tolerate possession of it by the British, but he would make no objection to the British taking Egypt and Crete. The tsar emphasized his obligation to protect the Orthodox Christians of the Ottoman Empire. He said, also, that they (England and Russia) had a very sick man on their hands and that it would be foolish not to make plans in view of his possible demise in the near future. In reporting these conversations to his government, the British ambassador, Sir Hamilton Seymour, interpreted them to mean that Nicholas I had come to the conclusion that the hour for, if not of, the dissolution of the Ottoman Empire had arrived. The reaction of the British government to the tsar's proposal corresponded to the diplomatic pattern, set at an earlier date by Palmerston, of maintaining Turkey in order to contain Russia.

Britain sent back to Constantinople her most successful envoy, Lord Stratford de Redcliffe, who, as Stratford Canning, had long served as the British ambassador to Turkey, where he had acquired so great an influence over the Ottoman viziers that he was called by Turks, the English Sultan. He had been a most potent instrument at Constantinople in forwarding Palmerston's anti-Russian policy. Great Britain, however, could not play the game against Russia single-handed, and consequently sought French support.

Anglo-French accord.—Events in France between 1848 and 1853 greatly favored British policy. A prototype of the twentieth-century fascist dictators had made himself emperor of France. Playing upon the bitter animosities resulting from the bloody struggle in Paris between the proletariat, led by socialists, and the middle class, led by liberals, the adventurer and careerist Louis Napoleon, who was all things unto all men, was elected president of the Second French Republic, which he promptly set about to destroy and replace by the Second French Empire. In his ambitious plans he sought alliance with Great Britain and, urged on by a passionately religious wife, sought to gain the support of the ultraclericals in France by opposing Russia in the Near East, posing as the protagonist of Roman Catholicism as against Russian and Greek Orthodoxy.

Because Nicholas I was an archreactionary and an anathema to European liberals, war against Russia was popular among the French and English liberals. Furthermore, the liberals were partial toward a Turkish government controlled by Turkish Tanzimat reformers. The stage was set for a war to protect a "weak nation" against a "powerful aggressor." Intervention in the Near East had popular support in England and France.

Crimean War—Opposing views.—One may obtain a better understanding of the complexities of Near Eastern problems in relationship to international affairs by noting the varied and frequently contrary interpretations of events given by different historians and other writers. In spite of the fact that the Crimean War took place nearly one hundred years ago, the opinions and judgments with respect to its nature and causes show great variations. The following statements by recent and contemporary historians reveal how greatly their views differ. In the revised edition of *Turkey* by Sir Edward S. Creasy, chapter fifteen was written by Professor W. Harold Claflin of Harvard University. Regarding the Crimean War, Dr. Claflin wrote in 1906: "The evacuation of the Danubian provinces had removed the immediate cause of the war, and the Turks might well feel satisfied with what had been accomplished. But both England and France were now determined to displace Russia from the overruling position she had so long held in Europe, and to cripple if possible her threatening predominance in the East."[5] The

French writer, Vicomte de la Jonquière in his *History of the Ottoman Empire,* stated that "if Turkey dared to run the risk of a war in which there was every indication that she would be completely defeated, it was because she felt supported by France and England whose intervention in her favor was anticipated. Since the Treaty of Unkiar Skelessi, British policy was based on the principle that British interests imperiously demand the maintenance of the Ottoman Empire. The British Cabinet was, however, powerless to protect effectively her anti-Christian client without aid. Against Russia it needed a continental ally with a large military force. Lord Palmerston chose France and reserved for her the honor of sacrificing her gold and blood for the very great benefit of Albion." [6]

In a book published in 1901, entitled *The Ottoman Sultans,* Halil Ganem wrote as follows: "In 1853, a final ultimatum was addressed to the Cabinet of Saint Petersburg by the two Powers now more than ever determined to defend the Ottoman Empire against the unjust aggression of which it was the object." [7] Lord Eversley in his book, *The Turkish Empire,* published in 1917, comments on the conversations of Tsar Nicholas I with the British Ambassador, Sir Hamilton Seymour, as follows: "A more reasonable view may now be taken of the policy of the Emperor Nicholas. Subsequent events have conclusively shown that he was fully justified in describing the Turkish Empire as sick, almost to death, for since then it has lost almost the whole of its dominions in Europe. Russia also has acquired but a very small share of the vast territories that have been taken from it. It is also subject to the reflection that, although the British Government in 1852 disclaimed any wish or intention to join in a scheme of partition of the Ottoman Empire, it has since acquired a considerable part of it, approximating to the offer of the tsar—namely, Egypt, the Sudan, and the island of Cyprus." [8] Needless to say, Lord Eversley wrote this before the Bolshevik revolution in November 1917 and previous to the secret agreement of December 1917 between Clemenceau and Lloyd George with regard to Franco-British invasion of Russia and to French and British spheres of influence there; also, it was before France and England, in accordance with their secret wartime agreements, took over under the League of Nations' mandate system the Arab lands of Iraq, Syria, Lebanon, Transjordan, and Palestine.

Treaty of Paris 1856.—Although the Crimean War, as many writers have observed, did not bring about a solution of the Eastern Question, it does mark a significant turning point in the history of the Ottoman Empire and consequently in that of the Near East. In the treaty of peace drafted at the Congress of Paris in 1856, Turkey was recognized as a member of the community of European nations, her territorial integrity was guaranteed, and the Ottoman government promised to protect its Christian subjects. Despite the fact that in the treaty the Powers disclaimed any intention of intervention on their behalf, actually the Powers used this promise to justify such intervention during the disorders in Lebanon in 1860.

Some diverse results of the Crimean War.—Perhaps the most consequential result of the Crimean War with respect to the Ottoman Empire was the fact that the Turkish government in 1854 for the first time in its history had recourse to foreign countries for loans. The Anglo-French war loans at that time initiated a financial policy that within twenty-five years resulted in the Ottoman Empire's coming for all practical purposes under the economic tutelage of her foreign creditors and losing a considerable measure of her internal sovereignty. The Crimean War prepared the way for the subjection of Turkey to the European Powers, politically and economically.

Seemingly, however, the Turks had come out of the conflict with Russia most satisfactorily: their historic enemy had been badly trounced and forced to submit to a humiliating treaty under which she could neither maintain warships in the Black Sea nor construct fortifications on its shores, their allies were the two most powerful states in Europe, and their country had been accepted as a member of the Concert of European Powers, which guaranteed its integrity; furthermore, the Hatti Humayun of 1856 granting equality and civil rights to non-Moslems had won the support and goodwill of European liberals, few of whom had any real understanding of the situation in the Near East.

The Hatti Humayun, although favored by the Turkish reformers, was bitterly opposed by the rank and file of conservative Moslems, Turks, and Arabs, and by a considerable percentage of Ottoman civilian officials and military officers. It has been well said that Sultan Abdul Medjid and his entourage, in their determination to perpetuate the Ottoman dynasty based on Moslem domination, could not lay the foundations of liberty in the Near East. The projected reforms and the "Holy War" of Russia deeply stirred Moslems throughout the Ottoman Empire, whose rulers were divided into two groups, the Old Turks and the Young Turks. The former were far more numerous and were bent on nullifying the policies of the latter.

The secular and religious leaders of the Old Turks appealed to the fears and religious prejudices of the Moslems, fostering bitterness against the Christians who were the protégées of the hated foreigners. The Tanzimat reforms and foreign intervention on behalf of the Christians, by arousing the antagonism and animosity of the Moslems, actually resulted in worsening the condition of the Christian minorities. Moslems became frightened. Their fears begot intolerance. The rising curve of menace to the Moslem ruling classes caused a corresponding rise in the curve of their intolerance. This in turn intensified the fears and hatreds of the Christian minorities, whose leaders realized that resistance to Turkish and Moslem violence against them might bring European intervention, with the possibility of freedom from Ottoman rule. The Treaty of Paris of 1856 and the proclamation of the Hatti Humayun in the same year created a situation which fostered conflicts between Christians and Moslems.

It would be quite futile, in the space which can be given, to enter into the discussion of who was to blame for the disturbances, uprisings, and massacres in various parts of the Ottoman Empire from 1856 to 1918. There are those who maintain that the Great Powers of Europe, pursuing rival imperialistic aims in the Near East, were mainly responsible for the increasing tension between Moslems and Christians. Others place the blame upon the Turkish government and the Moslems. Still others condemn the Christian minorities and their foreign supporters. Without assuming the functions of an omnipotent judge, one may say that the impact of the dynamic society of the modern Western World, itself in the throes of the industrial revolution, upon an ancient society was destroying the old order before a new one could be established. The revolutionary changes forced upon the Near East by the West threatened a variety of long entrenched vested interests and nurtured a diversity of conflicts that augmented the frequency and intensity of violence. This in turn led to increasing interference in the Ottoman Empire by the European Powers.

Two years after the Congress of Paris, a mob of Moslem pilgrims, urged on by their fanatical religious leaders, attacked the Christians in Jidda, the Arabian port of Mecca, and killed the consular representatives of England and France, whose governments promptly sent a naval contingent to fire on the city, following which the two foreign commanders saw to it that ten persons were executed. There were those in the West who naïvely appeared surprised that this demonstration of naval power did not tend to lessen the fears and hatred of the more passionate Moslems for Christians, native and foreign.

RENEWED VIOLENCE IN LEBANON

The following year (1859) violence was brewing in the Lebanon. The Christian peasants were in revolt against their feudal Maronite chieftains. The Maronite clergy, who were largely of peasant origin, were the instigators of a peasant uprising. Druze feudal nobles, some of whom had Christian peasants on their lands, offered to co-operate with the Maronite landowners in suppressing the peasants. Upon this Druze démarche, the Maronite movement changed from a social and economic struggle into a political and religious one. The Maronite ecclesiastical leaders, convinced that the European states under French leadership would come to their help, began to prepare for war against the Druzes with the fond hope of driving them out of Mount Lebanon. Under their religious leaders, and with the co-operation of Maronite merchants and bankers in Beirut, Maronite bands were organized and armed. As such proceedings could not be kept secret, the Druzes also began preparations for war. During the winter of 1859–60, tension mounted throughout the villages of Lebanon. Inevitably, this situation resulted in sporadic incidents of violence, which led to reprisals typical of people with tribal and feudal traditions.

Open warfare soon broke out. The Druzes, with a population less than a third of that of the Maronites, defeated Maronite forces and captured several of their villages. The situation then got completely out of hand, not only in Lebanon but also throughout Syria. Moslems, Metawali and Sunnites, joined in the conflict against the Christians, who were massacred in the villages and cities, some 6,000 being reported slain in Damascus alone. The Turkish government at Constantinople was unable to control the situation, and the local Ottoman officials either could not or would not. It has been alleged that they encouraged and even connived in the slaughter.

Invoking the Treaty of Paris, the French insisted that the Concert of Europe demand that the Ottoman government live up to its commitments with respect to its Christian subjects. Acting on a proposal by Russia, the Concert authorized France to send an armed force to the Lebanon. A contingent of 12,000 French troops landed in Beirut and proceeded to carry out their mission with the reluctant acquiescence of the Ottoman government. When security was re-established, a Great Power Commission was sent to Beirut to investigate the causes of the troubles, to see that the guilty were punished, and to draft a new political setup for Mount Lebanon.

Although a marked cleavage between the French who supported the Maronites and the British who backed the Druzes soon developed, the European Powers, together with Turkey, drafted in 1861 a protocol for the Lebanon which served the purpose of a constitution from 1864, when it was put into operation, until 1914, when Turkey entered World

War I. The Ottoman government under European pressure, following armed intervention, granted autonomy to Mount Lebanon. The process of imperial dissolution, which had begun in European Turkey during the first quarter of the nineteenth century, commenced in Asiatic Turkey in 1861 with the Lebanese Protocol.

CHAPTER VI

European Intervention and Penetration, 1860-81

From the southwest, where British and French interests crossed, the center of the international conflict which repeatedly embroiled Turkey soon shifted to the northwest where Austrian and Russian interests clashed. As in the Lebanon, violence in the Balkans resulted in European protests and interference and terminated in another Russian-Turkish war.

The political developments and changes that took place in Europe during the decade 1861 to 1871 soon had important effects upon the "Eastern Question" and consequently upon relations between the Ottoman government and the European nations. In 1861, as a result of the War of 1859 between Austria and Sardinia in alliance with France, the Kingdom of Italy came into existence. The new Italian state, with imperialistic ambitions menacing to the Turk in the Balkans and in North Africa, became a member of the Concert of Europe and acquired an interest in the "Eastern Question." After the Austrian-Prussian War of 1866, the Habsburgs were obliged to reorganize their empire by sharing power with the Hungarians and creating the Dual Monarchy of Austria and Hungary. Under a constitution known as the *Ausgleich,* which was in the nature of an alliance between Austrian Germans and Hungarian Magyars, the Romanian and Yugoslav subjects of Emperor and King Francis Joseph found themselves at a great disadvantage. These exploited subjects in the Dual Monarchy became associated with the irredentist movements of Romania and Serbia, thus increasing the complications of the Balkan situation and the "Eastern Question." The Franco-Prussian War of 1870–71 and the founding of the German Empire changed the entire balance of power in Europe and projected into the affairs of the Ottoman Empire a new and powerful state, which before the end of the century began to develop important economic and political interests in the Near East.

These events in Europe had a direct bearing upon the situation in European Turkey between the Christians and the Turks. As elsewhere in the Ottoman Empire, the antagonism of the Old Turks and most Moslems to the Tanzimat reforms and of the reformers to the Christian states of Europe for their increasing intervention intensified the friction and increased the frequency of conflicts between Balkan Moslems and Christians.

The interplay of European rivalries and the intricacies of the diplomacy of the Great Powers during the crises of the 1870's in the Ottoman Empire have been studied in minute detail since World War I as the result of the publication of the archives of the major states of Europe and, in addition, of many memoirs and autobiographies of leading European statesmen and military men. An American historian has written a microscopic account of the first year of the Balkan crisis of 1875 to 1878,[1] and a Yugoslav scholar has published a penetrating analysis of the entire period.[2] Both writers have made significant contributions to an understanding of the factors in the disintegration of Ottoman power in European Turkey at the opening of the last quarter of the nineteenth century.

In view of the fact that the United States is playing the leading role in the Near East, at least in the opinion of our statesmen and politicians, although it may be that it is but the cat's-paw of interested parties who lack the power they formerly had, it is pertinent to examine in some detail what interference in Near Eastern affairs has entailed in the past.

IMPERIALISM AND NATIONALISM IN THE BALKANS

When in the latter part of the eighteenth century, as the result of internal weakness and unsuccessful wars with Austria and Russia, the Turks lost those important areas in the Balkan peninsula north of the Danube and the Save, as well as the territories on the north shore of the Black Sea and in the Caucasus, the idea developed in the minds of European rulers and statesmen that the Ottoman Empire was doomed to ultimate dissolution. As this idea became a conviction, it was inevitable, in view of the political philosophy of the European leaders and the expanding nature of a European economic system, that plans should be cogitated in the foreign offices of the European Powers concerning the disposition of the various parts of the sultan's territories. During the first half of the nineteenth century the Christian peoples of the Balkans also began to think in terms of the collapse of the Ottoman Empire and their political leaders to stake out their claims.

Autonomous Serbia and independent Greece developed strong irredentist interests, respectively, in those parts of European Turkey where there were Yugoslav and Greek subjects of the sultan. The plans of the Balkan politicians for the division of European Turkey came into conflict with each other and with those of the interested European Powers. After 1856 the most serious obstacle to the hopes of the Balkan Christians of gaining their freedom from the Turks was the Treaty of Paris and the policy of the then dominant Powers—Austria, England, and France—to maintain the status quo in the Balkans and the territorial integrity of the Ottoman Empire. England and France contended that the Turkish reformers could solve the internal problems and ameliorate the condition of the Christians. English and French bankers and investors were finding it exceedingly profitable to loan money to the Ottoman government at high interest rates and at a large discount. Protected by the three Great Powers from attack from without, the Turks were given a chance to solve their internal problems, especially those concerning their Christian subjects.

Dominating Europe and the Near East from 1856 to 1870, British and French statesmen, blinded perhaps by their own interests and their fear of Russia, failed to gauge the significance of what was going on in both Europe and the Near East. They seemed not to have grasped the significance of the process of centralization of power in Europe under Prussia, nor to have realized that it would be impossible to exclude Russia from a position in Near Eastern affairs. They appeared also to have ignored the failure of the Turkish reformers.

Sultan Abdul Medjid (1839–61) and his successor Abdul Aziz (1861–76) both proved very weak instruments with which to bring about the transformation of Turkey. Although both supported the Turkish reformers, their extravagance and their surrender to the influence of the harem undermined the power of the few enlightened Turkish political leaders and played into the hands of the reactionary vested interests who aroused the religious fanaticism of the ignorant Moslem masses. Thus the reforms were largely nullified.

Increasing tension in Bosnia and Hercegovina.—The extravagance of the government, the ever-increasing deficit, and the growing pressure of the foreign creditors resulted in augmenting the tax burden on both Moslems and Christians. Tensions and discontents mounted. The Balkan Christians, who for many years had listened to the propaganda of secret nationalist committees advocating freedom from the Turks through planned insurrection, chafed under Turkish exactions and feared growing Moslem fanaticism. By 1870 a crisis was developing in the Ottoman provinces of Bosnia and Hercegovina, in the western part of the Balkans bordering on Austria-Hungary, Montenegro, and Serbia.

There were deep religious and social cleavages among the inhabitants of Bosnia and Hercegovina though they were almost wholly Slavic by race. Out of a total population of approximately 1,200,000, there were nearly 450,000 Moslems and over 750,000 Christians, of whom three-quarters were (Greek) Orthodox and one-quarter (Roman) Catholic. The landowners were for the most part Moslem Yugoslavs, who from the time of the Turkish conquest had as feudal nobles ruthlessly exploited a Christian Yugoslav peasantry. From the time of the introduction of the Tanzimat reforms the provinces had been rent with discord. The local feudal Moslem beys had risen in revolt against the Turks, who did not fully regain control of the provincial government until 1850. Although the Turks brought an end to the feudal system they had to leave power in the hands of the Moslem beys. The Christian peasants were from then on subject to exploitation by fanatical Moslem landowners and by Ottoman officials and taxgatherers. By 1872 Bosnia and Hercegovina were seething with revolt. Following a bad harvest in 1874, sporadic violence between armed Christian peasants and Turkish gendarmes broke out in 1875 into open insurrection which resulted in an international crisis that continued until 1878, nearly precipitating a general European war over Near Eastern affairs.

Bulgarian uprisings.—The whole situation was greatly complicated by the Bulgarian uprising of 1876 and the brutality with which the Turks crushed it. The Bulgarian nationalist and revolutionary movement was later in its development than those of the Greeks and Yugoslavs (Serbs). The Bulgarian renaissance did not begin until the second quarter of the nineteenth century, although there had been in the preceding century an apostle of Bulgarian nationalism whose appeal to the ancient glories of Bulgaria was a forerunner of the Bulgarian revolt against the Greek Phanariot control of the church, against the rising tide of Hellenism, and against economic domination by Greeks. In the beginning, the Bulgarian nationalist movement was directed against the Greeks rather than the Turks. In fact, the Bulgarians as late as 1867 asked Sultan Abdul Aziz to follow the example of Francis Joseph by taking the title of Tsar of Bulgaria and thus bringing into existence a Bulgarian-Turkish dual monarchy. Before the Bulgarian church by an imperial decree of the sultan in 1870 had been freed from control of the Greek patriarch of Constantinople and had become autonomous, the Bulgarians had been influenced by Serbian revolutionary propaganda and Russian Pan-Slavism. After 1870 various elements among the Bulgarians were able to coalesce in a national revolutionary movement for independence from Turkish rule.

Secret revolutionary committees in contact with certain groups in Russia and in Serbia became very active during the 1870's in plotting a revolt against the Turks. The insurrection in Bosnia and Hercegovina of 1875 encouraged the Bulgarian revolutionists to plan for an uprising in 1876. Informed of these plots, the Turks at the first evidence of revolt acted with speed and ruthlessness. Massacres of Bulgarians—men, women, and children—took place. Even to the present day no accurate figures of those slain are available, but undoubtedly there were over ten thousand. Although the British ambassador could view with a certain degree of equanimity the Bulgarian massacres of which he wrote as follows to the British minister of foreign affairs: "We may and must feel indignant at the needless and monstrous severity with which the Bulgarian insurrection was put down, but the necessity which exists for England to prevent changes from occurring here which would be most detrimental to ourselves, is not affected by the question whether it was 10,000 or 20,000 persons who perished in the suppression." This unemotional attitude was not true of a great many people in England, in Russia, and among the Greek, Slavic, and other Christians of the Balkans. Public opinion in Europe was inflamed by the journalistic and other accounts of happenings in Bulgaria. The reaction both in the Balkans and in Europe affected the situation throughout the period of the crisis.

The European Powers and the Balkan crisis.—Prime Minister Disraeli, even with Queen Victoria's active support, could not pursue effectively an anti-Russian pro-Turkish policy against the outburst of popular indignation in England at the action of the Turkish government. It was the strong opposition among key members of his Cabinet which was largely responsible for preventing England from going to war with Russia in 1877–78. The Bulgarian affair served only further to convince the Balkan Christians that Turkish rule was unendurable and that the reforms were illusory. Popular feeling in Russia ran high, and the Russian government was determined that action must be taken to protect the Christian subjects of the sultan.

The League of the Three Emperors, created by Bismarck in 1872 to maintain peace and German supremacy on the Continent, left England in voluntary and France in unwelcome isolation. Austria, Germany, and Russia dominated European affairs, and it was impossible for Great Britain to find an ally to support her in action, under the Treaty of Paris, to restrain the Russians. Although many British statesmen and diplomats held tenaciously to the Palmerston policy of supporting Turkey and of containing Russia, it had become impossible and impractical to do so in 1875.

Germany was uninterested in the Near East. Bismarck was prepared to see the Ottoman Empire partitioned to the advantage of Britain, France, Austria, and Russia if his two allies in the Drei-Kaiserbund would agree on the spoils. The British probably would have been obliged to accept a solution along these lines, as proposed by Bismarck, if it had not been for the conflicting objectives of Austria and Russia.

Failing a complete collapse and partition of the Ottoman Empire, Russia wished to have Bosnia, Hercegovina, and the Bulgarian areas organized as autonomous principalities of the Ottoman Empire on a pattern similar to that created in Lebanon in 1862 and in Crete following a rebellion of the Greek Cretans in 1866. Austria was opposed to such a settlement and supported a policy of reforms. The Austrian-Hungarian government feared Russian influence among the Yugo-slavs and Russian domination of the Balkans. Also, it feared the spread of Serbian nationalism and the incorporation of Bosnia and Hercegovina in the Serbian state. Furthermore, the Austrians and Hungarians were not in agreement with respect to a Balkan policy. The Austrian Germans, backed by the militarists, wanted to annex the two Slavic provinces, while the Hungarians opposed the acquisition of further territory inhabited by Yugo-slavs since they thought this would upset the balance of the national groups in the Dual Monarchy. Andrassy, the foreign minister of Austria-Hungary, himself a Hungarian, was only willing to advocate an annexation of Bosnia and Hercegovina in case of the collapse and partition of the Ottoman Empire. Like England, Austria-Hungary did not favor the partition of Turkey, fearing it would increase the power of Russia in the Near East. The Habsburgs opposed any move by Russia that might lead to her obtaining a foothold on the Adriatic and Aegean, either directly or through satellite Slavic states, and feared any Russian move that might threaten Austria-Hungary's route to Salonika.

France, which had not fully recovered from the effects of the Franco-Prussian War and the civil war of 1871, in which the government had ruthlessly suppressed the French socialists and communists, slaughtering some seventeen thousand of them, was not in a position to play an active part in the crisis that arose from the insurrection of the Bosnians and Hercegovinians and the massacre of some 10,000 to 15,000 Bulgarian Christians. Italy was as yet too feeble even to play the jackal role in the Balkans.

A Europe divided by its competitive imperialistic interests in the Near East and by its power politics on the European continent was utterly unable to deal with the Balkan crisis by effective unity of action. The Balkan Christians—the Greeks, Romanians, Bulgarians and Serbians—divided by their competitive nationalistic aims were not able to achieve unity of action against the Turks. When it appeared that the Bosnian-Hercegovinian revolution would be crushed by the Ottoman forces, Serbia and Montenegro went to war against Turkey. This widening of the crisis did not narrow the gap between the policies of the Great Powers; rather it tended to increase their differences. Thus, when it seemed as if the two Slavic principalities would be badly defeated by the Turks, Russia in April 1877 declared war on Turkey after coming to an understanding with Austria-Hungary but failing to do so with Great Britain.

The English were in a stew. The hue and cry against Russia served the same psychological needs of the people as had the outcries against the Turks because of the Bulgarian massacres. Queen Victoria wrote that "war with Russia is inevitable now or later," and Disraeli encouraged the Turks, assuring them that the destruction of the Ottoman Empire would not be permitted.

The critical situation in the Ottoman Empire.—The internal developments in Turkey in 1876 did not tend to tranquilize the general situation. Sultan Abdul Aziz's preoccupation with the affairs of the harem with its two thousand women and their greedy demands had, as in an earlier century, corrupted the administration, undermined the reformers, and with the aid of local and foreign bankers ruined government finances. Falling under the influence of the reactionaries and Old Turks, the sultan had turned out the reform ministry and appointed as Grand Vizier, Mohammed Nedim, ardently pro-Russian and to some extent the tool of the persuasive General Ignatiev, to whom the Turks accorded the highest encomium for western Machiavellian diplomats by calling this Russian ambassador "the Father of Lies."

Excited by the events in Bosnia and Hercegovina and by the Bulgarian revolt and fearful of a general uprising of the Balkan Christians and of Russian intervention, disparate groups among the Turks turned against the ministry of the pro-Russian Nedim and against Sultan Abdul Aziz. On May 10, 1876, popular demonstrations against Nedim resulted in his demission and the appointment of a new ministry controlled by the great Tanzimat reformers, Hussein Avni and Midhat Pasha. On May 29, conspirators seized and imprisoned Sultan Aziz. On the next day, Murad V, who was deposed two months later after being judged insane, was installed as sultan. On June 4, ex-Sultan Abdul Aziz died under mysterious circumstances and was officially declared to have committed suicide. Eleven days later, one of the devoted members of the deceased sultan's staff smashed his way into the council room of the ministers and in a blind fury against those he thought had murdered his master the caliph, shot down Hussein Auni, Minister of Foreign Affairs, and killed and wounded several other members of the group. To the excited minds of European statesmen, it looked as if the Turkish regime was about to collapse in a state of anarchy.

The reform ministers, however, were the masters of the situation for the time being. They deposed Murad V on August 31 and proclaimed Abdul Hamid II sultan. This reactionary autocrat, who dominated the Ottoman Empire under a rule of terror for over thirty years, began his reign by accepting the liberal reformers, and in December 1876 promulgated the first Turkish constitution. This imperial announcement was carefully timed to coincide with the meeting on the same day of the Conference of Great Powers, which had gathered at Constantinople to determine what should be done about the Balkan Christians, the insurrection in Bosnia and Hercegovina, the Bulgarian situation, and the war with Serbia. The constitution fulfilled the hopes of the Turkish liberals and was an instrument used by Abdul Hamid in an effort to avoid foreign intervention.

Russia decides on war.—These political changes at Constantinople had considerable effect upon the international situation. Russian influence with the Ottoman government was replaced by that of Great Britain, whose political institutions were admired by the Turkish intelligentsia. The British statesmen felt that under the constitutional regime in Turkey they could regain popular support for the policy of maintaining the Ottoman Empire. On the other hand, the Russians realized that the reformist party would oppose their plan of autonomy for the Christian communities in the Balkans and, consequently, became more disposed to settle the matter by war. There followed in January 1877 an Austrian-Russian understanding that gave the Russians a certain degree of assurance that Austria would not join Britain in a war against them.

Throughout the Turkish-Russian War of 1877–78, the Turks were hopeful that England would come to their aid, and the Russians were fearful lest she would. After a desperate and valiant resistance at Plevna, the Turks were defeated and Russian troops reached the very gates of

Constantinople at its famous suburb, San Stefano, where a Russian-Turkish treaty was signed on March 3, 1878.

Again Europe was in a state of jitters and on the verge of war. Disraeli, fearing the possibility of the Russians occupying Constantinople and obtaining control of the peninsula of Gallipoli, which dominates the Dardanelles, threatened both Russia and Turkey. This illustrious British statesman did not have the vision to foresee that only thirty-seven years later the British government would be expending men, ships, and treasure in a futile attempt to dislodge the Turks at Gallipoli in order to get supplies to and wheat and oil from her hard-pressed ally, Russia.

After three months of diplomatic skulduggery by the statesmen of the Great Powers, the English and Russians signed the Protocol of London on May 30, which not only made it possible for the Concert of European Powers to open the Congress of Berlin on June 13, 1878, but prepared the way for England to get the Turkish government to sign the secret Convention of June 4, by which Turkey agreed to allow the British to occupy and administer Cyprus if Russia should at Berlin be allowed to retain Batum, Kars, and Ardahan. The likelihood of this the British were well aware of as in the Protocol of London they had promised the Russians not to oppose clauses of the Treaty of San Stefano ceding these Ottoman territories to Russia.

The Congress of Berlin, 1878.—At the Congress of Berlin, Great Britain, whose people had been aroused to a high degree of jingoism to prepare them for a possible war with Russia as the result of Disraeli's policy of "get tough with the Russians," was with Austria-Hungary's support able to bring about a drastic revision of the Russian-Turkish Treaty of San Stefano. It probably would have been impossible for the Great Powers to have brought about a satisfactory and enduring settlement; the Treaty of Berlin, however, was a multiway compromise, which left so many unsolved problems that most of those concerned evolved plans to circumvent its provisions. The bitterness and friction which it engendered led to repeated bloodshed and massacre throughout the balance of the nineteenth century and during the first two decades of the present one.

This pernicious treaty, which was the product of duplicity and double dealing by the Great Powers, imposed upon Turkey territorial cession in Europe and Asia and political concessions which placed limitations on its sovereignty greater than those of the Treaty of Paris (1856) following the Crimean War. Austria acquired a port on the Adriatic and the right to occupy and administer the Turkish provinces of Bosnia and Hercegovina for an unspecified length of time. Serbia and Montenegro not only received an increase of territory at Turkey's expense but also gained recognition as independent states. Greece obtained a slight rectification of her frontier in Thessaly. Romania, who ceded Bessarabia to Russia and, in compensation, was given the Turkish territory of Dobrudja largely inhabited by Bulgarians, achieved full independence from the Ottoman Empire. The Bulgarians, contrary to the generous treatment accorded under the Treaty of San Stefano, were, from their point of view, badly dealt with at Berlin. The *Great Bulgaria* agreed to under the Russian-Turkish treaty was divided into three parts by the Treaty of Berlin. An autonomous Bulgarian principality north of the Balkan Mountains was set up under nominal Turkish sovereignty; territory directly to the south extending to the Rudolfe Mountains became the autonomous Ottoman province of East Romelia, and the region southward of it, known as Macedonia, remained completely under Turkish control. Great Britain acquired the right to occupy and administer Cyprus, Persia gained a slight increase of territory, and Russia extended her frontiers in the eastern part of Asia Minor to include the important Black Sea port of Batum and the towns of Kars and Ardahan, which are of strategic importance because they lie on the eastern slope of the watershed between Transcaucasia and eastern Anatolia. These two towns, which Bolshevik Russia ceded to Turkey, have taken on considerable significance in the "Cold War" between the U.S.S.R. and the U.S.A. in their jockeying to achieve control of highly strategic areas on the periphery of Russia.

Politically, the Ottoman government reaffirmed previous commitments with respect to treatment of the Christians and assumed new obligations which further limited its sovereign power in Europe and in Asia. Between 1856 and 1878 the Turks had lost to a great extent administrative authority over a large part of European Turkey and limits had been placed on their control of Crete and Lebanon. Furthermore, the Turkish government had agreed to undertake reforms in those areas and provinces of Asia Minor inhabited by Armenians, to report periodically to the Great Powers, and to grant them the right of inspecting the carrying out of reform measures. By the Anglo-Turkish Convention the Turks handed Cyprus to Great Britain in return for a British guarantee to protect Asiatic Turkey from Russian aggression. In order to give the Russians no excuse for intervention the British had prevailed upon the Turks to promise the carrying out of a program of reforms in the Armenian provinces. This arrangement implied a quasi-British protectorate over both Asiatic Turkey and the Armenians.

Abdul Hamid's reaction to the Treaty of Berlin.—The advent of

Abdul Hamid to the throne and the Treaty of Berlin mark a distinct turning point in the history of the Ottoman Empire and of the Near East with respect to European intervention. Abdul Hamid's government had neither the will nor the desire to carry out reforms and fulfill the obligations assumed under the Treaty of Berlin and under previous conventions and treaties. The new sultan was determined not only to free Turkey from European interference but to regain those parts of the Empire which had been lost. He waged a ruthless struggle in Turkey against the Turkish reformers and against Christian minorities, and a stubborn resistance to the European Powers which was carried on by aggressively fostering a Pan-Islamic movement against them. While Abdul Hamid was struggling against Europe on the political level, the grip of the western world on the Near East became increasingly economic. This was largely due to the foreign loan policy followed by the Turkish government between 1855 and 1876, which ended in a crisis that resulted in a wide encroachment upon the internal affairs of the Ottoman Empire by her European creditors.

EUROPE'S FINANCIAL AND ECONOMIC PENETRATION

The economic expansion of Europe in the heyday of its imperialism during the second half of the nineteenth and the first quarter of the twentieth century did not bypass the Near East. The Balkans, Anatolia, the Arab lands of western Asia, and Egypt offered an enticing field for European investors, bankers, merchants, and industrialists. In addition to the raw materials and agricultural products to meet the expanding needs of a Europe which was rapidly being industrialized and urbanized, these regions, which economically were still functioning on a primitive form of capitalism and handicraft production, offered many other attractive opportunities for western profit makers.

In spite of, and to some extent because of, the low purchasing power of its people, the Near East was a market for many kinds of goods produced in the factories of the West with which the handmade products of the East could not compete. This medieval world was largely devoid of modern means of transportation, which then were railroads and streetcars. Its cities lacked most of such modern facilities as sewers, waterworks, paved streets, gas, and electric lighting. Few of them had modern dwellings or commercial and public buildings. The ports and port facilities were primitive. In addition, the Ottoman government felt the compelling necessity of equipping its military and naval forces with modern arms. Governmental loans, contracts for the construction of railroads, tramways, and public works, concessions for mines, other natural resources, and commercial monopolies inevitably created a flow of capital to the Near East. Large investment of capital first began in the form of loans to the Turkish government.

Foreign loans.—Growing contact with the West and the development of modern banks in Constantinople, coupled with the desperate financial needs of the Ottoman government, resulted in the negotiation of a foreign loan in 1854. This was an unheard of innovation in the finances of the Turkish Empire. Through the centuries, Ottoman sultans had employed many devices to meet their deficits. Depreciation of currency, expropriation of wealth, and borrowing from native money lenders and from foreign merchants living in Turkey had all been used to fill the gap between expenses and revenues. Never before 1854, however, had any Ottoman government had recourse to foreign loans.

The first two loans were essentially to meet the current expenses of the Crimean War. The second loan of 1855 was jointly guaranteed by the British and French governments. The door to foreign borrowing having once been opened to cope with a national crisis, loan followed loan during a period of twenty years. By 1875, on the eve of another war with Russia, the foreign debt of the Ottoman government amounted to approximately a billion dollars. The loans had been negotiated with private bankers at discount rates some of which were higher than 55 per cent, several in the low fifties and forties, with only a few at a discount of twenty or less. The minimum interest rate for the foreign loans from 1854 to 1876 varied from 7 per cent to 12 per cent. The annual interest and amortization on the foreign debt amounted approximately to $60,000,000 in 1874, while realizable revenues of the Empire amounted to only about $80,000,000. Most of the loans during this score of years were made to meet mounting budgetary deficits. Under such circumstances eventual bankruptcy was inevitable. By the autumn of 1875, at the beginning of the political crisis in the Balkans, the Ottoman government had scraped the bottom of the barrel. Revenues were insufficient to meet current expenses and debt service payments. Grand Vizier Nedim announced a current deficit of over $22,000,000, and an imperial decree cut interest rates in half for a period of five years. In the early spring of the next year, the Ottoman government completely suspended interest and amortizing payments for an indefinite period. This suspension of debt service continued until a settlement was made between the bond holders and the Turkish government in December 1881.

For twenty years Turkey had been on a financial "binge," which, while it lasted, had been highly profitable to the sultan and his entourage, to the local bankers, and to the financiers and investors of Europe. To the people of Turkey it had brought increasing misery, since they had to suffer exploitation not only at the hands of their own rulers but also by foreigners. The double burden was a crushing one. Only a very small fraction of the borrowed capital was employed to increase the economic resources of the empire. The total nominal amount of the foreign loans from 1854 to 1874 was approximately $1,000,000,000. It was upon this amount that interest and amortizing payments were being made until 1875. The actual total sums received by the Ottoman government from these loans amounted to approximately $600,000,000. The people of Turkey were being mulcted of nearly $400,000,000 by financial hocus-pocus. In addition, their own rulers were wasting public funds in useless extravagance. The economic and financial situation had become untenable, its liquidation had become inevitable, an escape from this situation by revolution was impossible for the exploited peoples.

Forceful resistance to European intervention was beyond the power of the Ottoman government. The Egyptians learned this lesson between 1875 and 1883, when the extravagance of Khedive Ismail first led to the impoverishment of the fellaheen and the sale to England of his Suez Canal shares, then to the inability of the Egyptian government to meet the interest charges on loans from the European bankers, resulting in the establishment by the British and French governments of the Dual Control in 1879 over Egyptian finances. When Arabi's revolution broke out against both the Khedive and the foreign interventionists, the British landed forces in the Nile Valley in 1882, rapidly crushed the revolution, and remained in occupation as the real masters of Egypt. Abdul Hamid shrewdly avoided the errors of the Egyptian khedives by negotiating a settlement directly with the representatives of the foreign bondholders, thus avoiding the political complications which led to the invasion and occupation of Egypt.

After the suspension of interest and amortization payments on its foreign loans in the spring of 1876, the Ottoman government waged an unsuccessful war with Russia, suffered losses of territory, and had imposed on it a war indemnity to Russia of approximately $160,000,000. The European bondholders, unable to obtain any satisfaction from the Congress of Berlin, carried on private negotiations with the Turks. By the end of 1881 an agreement was reached that proved advantageous in many ways to the Ottoman government and to the bondholders.

Council of Administration of the Ottoman Public Debt.—In December 1881, Sultan Abdul Hamid promulgated the extraordinary and important Decree of Muharrem, which provided for the setting up of the

Council of Administration of the Ottoman Public Debt. This remarkable organization was composed of an Englishman representing English and Dutch bondholders, a Frenchman, a German, an Austrian, and an Italian, representing the bondholders of their respective countries, and in addition a representative of Ottoman bondholders, and of the Imperial Ottoman Bank. Very wide powers were conferred upon the Council of Administration, which had autonomous control over its own administrative organization, although it and its personnel functioned as a part of the Ottoman governmental bureaucracy. The Council controlled directly certain important tax revenues—namely, the salt monopoly, the stamp tax, taxes on wines and liquors, the fisheries, and silk production and manufacture in certain parts of the Empire. Assigned to it was the tobacco monoply, which it farmed out to a syndicate known as the Tobacco Régie, composed of private European banking houses. Revenues from other sources were assigned to the Council for the payment of the debt services.

This organization representing private bondholders developed extensive control over many phases of the economic life of the Ottoman Empire. It attempted to modernize the production of silk, it brought foreign specialists to study the fishing industry, it undertook to check infections and pests attacking the vineyards. It established branches in all important centers throughout the Empire. Its agent, the Tobacco Régie, controlled most phases of the tobacco industry: the production of tobacco, the export, import, and sale of most of the tobacco products and tobacco, and the manufacture of cigarettes. The Council controlled, of course, all payment on the public debt and matters pertaining to the loans.

The Decree of Muharrem of 1881 set the terms for debt payments. Most of the foreign loans were scaled down from their face value to, or below, the actual sums received by the Ottoman government. The loans between 1858 and 1874 which had a face value of approximately $1,090,000,000 were reduced to approximately $570,000,000. The total indebtedness which by 1881 had risen to about one and one quarter billion dollars was reduced to approximately $700,000,000, not including the Russian indemnity.

This settlement and the competent manner in which the Council of Administration of the Ottoman Public Debt handled its affairs restored Turkish credit in the European money markets and encouraged European capitalists and entrepreneurs to extend further credit to the Turkish government and to undertake large capital investments in the Ottoman

Empire. The peoples of Turkey from this time began, if only to a small extent, to share in the benefits from the flow of European capital to the Near East. Modernization through economic development penetrated more deeply and at an accelerated rate into many parts of western Asia with the building of roads and railroads and the distributions of modern industrial made goods. The ancient foundations of social and economic life and ancient ways of living and thinking began to be undermined. The West was unconsciously preparing the Near East for revolution, which even now has not as yet been consummated except in part.

CHAPTER VII

Abdul Hamid—The Last Ottoman Autocrat, 1876-1909

۞ SOCIAL CHANGES—NATURE AND RATE

It is typical of our times to think of the historical processes of social change in terms of the biological cycle of birth, growth, and death, and of the seasonal cycle of spring, summer, autumn, and winter. Consequently, it has become customary to speak of the birth of a new order and the death of the old order in dealing with social change. As pain and suffering are associated by human beings with birth (it is questionable whether other animals do so), it seems logical to attribute the violence which sometimes accompanies social change to the birth of the new and the death of the old. It is most convenient to do this because it saves the writer and the reader the hard labor of analysis. It is doubtful whether any society or social order is ever static. Variations in the rate of change tend to give the impression of great stability to some and of instability to others. Social change is a normal phenomenon of human society. It is the process of social evolution. When this process brings about basic changes in the social order, in the political structure, in the economic system of production and distribution and in the ways of living and thinking, it has reached the point of revolutionary change. It is the nature of the change which makes it revolutionary. Whether changes occur slowly or rapidly, legally or illegally, peacefully or violently, they are revolutionary only if they are basic changes. The nature of the change alone determines whether or not it be revolutionary.

During the reign of Abdul Hamid the evolutionary process of change had reached among certain elements of the various diverse national and religious groups a revolutionary stage, as it had in several phases of the ways of living and of thinking of an increasing percentage of the sultan's subjects. The time element in change had a dual aspect in the Near East.

Changes which in western Europe had taken place over a period of several generations, were occurring in Turkey during one generation. The adjustments which a single generation was called upon to make created serious individual and group maladjustments which found their expression in resistance to modernization. Despite this rapidity of change in the Ottoman Empire, its tempo was slower than the rate of change in the western world; consequently, new and powerful impulsions for further changes were constantly impinging upon the Near East. Before adjustments to a new order of life had been achieved, more fundamental adjustments were necessary. As the nature of the changes became more and more revolutionary, the intensity and spread of maladjustment grew greater throughout the Near East. The mounting maladjustments developed not only revolutionary demands for a new social order but also counterrevolutionary demands for the restoration of the old order. In the Ottoman world, the Young Turks were the revolutionists; the Old Turks, whose leader was Sultan Abdul Hamid II, were the counterrevolutionists.

ABDUL HAMID

Abdul Hamid's birth and upbringing.—Abdul Hamid was both biologically and psychologically the product of the old order. He was the son of a slave dancing girl of the household of Sultan Abdul Medjid's sister. His mother, who was said to be a Circassian, was also reputed to be a converted Armenian. Ugly rumors originating in the palace and spreading far beyond its walls gave currency to an unsubstantiated story that Abdul Hamid's father was an Armenian cook named Tablakiar Nichan. It is alleged that when Abdul Medjid was informed of the birth of a second son, his first question was "by which woman?" In view of the many women in his harem, this was quite a normal question. A week went by before the sultan acknowledged the baby boy as his son. The gossip of the palace was that Abdul Medjid closely questioned the baby's mother, Faiché, who reminded him that conception had taken place in the bath of the Seraglio.[1]

Whether or not Abdul Hamid was the son of Sultan Abdul Medjid is now a question of slight importance. It is significant, however, that the future ruler of Turkey was conceived and born within a palace system typical of the old historical Ottoman world and of the ancient Orient of deified absolute monarchs. Not only by birth was Abdul Hamid a product of the old order but by education and training. During his youth, from childhood to manhood, his life was spent within the walls of the harem, where he grew up among slaves, females, and eunuchs, for the most part uneducated, grossly superstitious, venal, predatory, and fanatically religious.

Abdul Hamid's mother died of tuberculosis at the age of twenty-six, seven years after his birth; his father, Abdul Medjid also died of consumption when he was thirty-nine. His uncle, Sultan Aziz, was deposed, and shortly thereafter either committed suicide or was murdered. His half brother Sultan Murad V was officially declared mentally deranged and consequently deposed. Feigning liberal ideas and expressing his support of a constitution, Abdul Hamid became Sultan of Turkey on the understanding, given in writing by him, that should his brother recover his sanity, Abdul Hamid would relinquish his title to the throne.

Although Abdul Hamid was of slight stature and sickly constitution, he did not succumb to the enervating and debauching environment of the palace. To survive and overcome the intrigues of the sultan's household, the young prince developed a ruthless will to power, conditioned by fear and hatred. Although he became the victim of his own prejudices, fears, and hatreds, he was not a weakling to become the tool of the palace women or the instrument of his ministers. From 1876 until the revolution of 1908, he remained the autocrat, the master of the Ottoman Empire. Abdul Hamid himself recognized that he was the product of his early environment and upbringing. He is quoted as saying that Allah knows that every man is the product of circumstances which determine the orientation of his life, and he is above all the product of his education.[2]

Abdul Hamid's personality.—His personal strength rested on his cunning, his shrewdness, his ruthlessness, and his industry with respect to all things which concerned the security of his life and his position. The political power of Abdul Hamid resided in the support given him by the reactionary and counterrevolutionary groups among the Moslem subjects of the Empire, who looked upon him as their leader against the Young Turks, against the non-Moslems, against the hated unbelievers of the western Christian powers. The forces of reaction and counterrevolution were solidly arrayed behind Sultan Abdul Hamid II. His weakness lay in the very nature of his supporters. The ignorant, the bigoted, the fanatical clustered around him. From them he chose his most trusted advisers. The swiftly moving currents of the modern world were in the process of sweeping into the limbo all that these men stood for. So powerful and all enveloping was the process of social evolution, speeded up by the unremitting pressure of the western world, that Abdul Hamid and his minions actually only gave the appearance of restraining and retarding the process of change. In fact, the last great Ottoman autocrat found himself obliged to permit and even encourage changes which undermined still further the foundations of the old order.

Were it not for the fact that Abdul Hamid was an autocrat who, in so far as it was possible for one man to do so, directed the internal and foreign policy of the Ottoman Empire, this sultan's personality would be of interest only as a case in psychiatry. Because Turkey was under his personal rule from 1876 to 1908, the personality of Abdul Hamid is of historical importance.

From earliest infancy Abdul Hamid experienced a feeling of insecurity due, at first, to the anomalous position of his mother and the distinct coolness of his father toward him, later intensified by the mysterious death of his uncle, Sultan Abdul Aziz, and by the alleged insanity and deposition of his brother Murad V. The intrigues of the palace, coupled with the gossip concerning his parentage, instilled in him a deep sense of distrust and an abiding fear which grew to be an all pervasive obsession. Less highly developed but nonetheless significant was his feeling of inferiority which was not solely personal, for it concerned both the Turks as a people and the Moslems as a religious group. His hatreds were the offspring of insecurity, distrust, fear, and inferiority. Not unrelated to them were his antipathies and his loyalties.

Abdul Hamid feared and hated the Young Turk reformers, whose leaders he exterminated or drove into exile and harried with his innumerable spies. He hated Europeans and Christians and spoke of the poisonous civilization of Europe. He feared and hated England and said the English were to be more feared than any other nation. Above all, however, he hated the Armenians upon whom he wreaked his vengeance, for the stories about his Armenian parentage rankled in his mind. He resented the constant admonitions and advice he received from European statesmen and their governments. He was bitterly indignant at foreign interference in the internal affairs of the Ottoman Empire.

His belief in and devotion to Islam were profound. These were the counterpart of his contempt for and hatred of Christianity. He placed loyalty to Islam and the Moslem caliph above Turkish patriotism and loyalty to the Ottoman sultan. His international policy of Pan-Islamism was a product of his loyalties and his hatreds. He was revolted at the idea of millions of Moslems under the rule of the hated giaours—the English, the French, and the Dutch. He preached the union of all Moslems under the rule of their caliph and dreamed of a Jihad (Holy War) against the Christian nations. The thought of himself as the caliph of hundreds of millions of the faithful mitigated his sense of inferiority in relation to the great Christian Powers of the West. Abdul Hamid's policy of indigenous progress within the Ottoman Empire, progress of Moslem origin, and his opposition to the introduction of western and Christian innovations as advocated by the Young Turks' program of reforms sprang from his hatred of the civilization of Christian Europe and his love for Islam. In discussing Moslem fanaticism, he praised it as an expression of that love of the noble religion of Mohammed which had made the Ottomans great. Throughout his entire reign these facets of Abdul Hamid's personality affected his personal and official actions and reactions.

Abdul Hamid was so greatly hated by all enlightened Turks, by the Armenians, Bulgars, Greeks, and other Ottoman Christians, and by the liberals and humanitarians in the West that few of his contemporaries have been able to write objectively or dispassionately of him and his reign. Furthermore, nineteenth-century writers thought in terms of the humane and beneficent civilization of the Christian West; they had not experienced two world wars, the first commencing with an assassination at Sarajevo, and the second ending with the destruction of Hiroshima by an atom bomb. Who now, having participated in these world conflicts, would dare to cast a stone at Abdul Hamid for the massacre of a few thousand resulting from the pursuit of policies based on his ideologies?

Domestic and foreign problems confronting the sultan.—When in 1876 Abdul Hamid came to the throne, the Ottoman government was confronted by formidable problems, domestic and foreign. In 1875 Turkey was in the throes of a political and a financial crisis which had far-reaching international complications. Revolt had broken out in Bosnia and Hercegovina, and the Turkish government facing financial collapse had stopped payments in part on its foreign loans. In 1876 a political *coup d'état* had deposed Sultan Abdul Aziz, the continuing financial crisis forced a complete suspension of debt payments, an attempted uprising among the Bulgars had resulted in massacres, which together with the outbreak of war with Serbia and Montenegro, brought foreign intervention. It was in the midst of this turmoil in 1876 that Abdul Hamid became sultan.

Faced with the gathering of a conference of the Great Powers at Constantinople, Abdul Hamid was persuaded to grant a constitution in order to forestall intervention by the Powers. Rejecting the proposals of the conference, Abdul Hamid soon found himself at war with Russia in 1877. Two years after his accession to the throne, the new sultan was forced to sign a humiliating treaty with Russia and then to accept the dictates of the Concert of Europe gathered at Berlin. Turkey was bankrupt. It owed a huge debt to European investors; it had lost control over the larger part of the Balkan provinces, over Cyprus, and had lost territory in Asia Minor to Russia, and, furthermore, had agreed to introduce reforms in the so-called Armenian vilayets. Such was the situation inherited by Abdul Hamid.

Policies of Abdul Hamid.—Assuming personal control over the government of Turkey, Abdul Hamid began to shape the internal and foreign policies of the empire. These were so inextricably interwoven that they cannot be dealt with separately. Following the Congress and Treaty of Berlin in 1878, the most pressing problem confronting the new sultan was financial. It was imperative that a settlement with foreign creditors be arrived at in order to forestall the possibility of official intervention by foreign governments on behalf of their nationals. Foreign bondholders lacking any legal means of enforcing their claims against a sovereign state created an organization to exert pressure on their respective governments. The complete suspension of debt payments in 1876 could not continue indefinitely. Until the debt question was settled, Turkey could not expect to borrow in European money centers, nor could it be free from the threat of foreign intervention. Developments in Egypt indicated what might occur in Turkey unless Abdul Hamid's government acted promptly. In Egypt the extravagance of Khedive Ismail had resulted in the Egyptian government's being unable to meet service on the loans made by British and French bankers. These had been able to exert sufficient power to persuade their respective governments to intervene in Egypt, and in the spring of 1879 an Anglo-French dual control over Egyptian finances was established.

The fate of Egypt was avoided by the Ottoman government's coming to an arrangement with private representatives of the foreign bondholders in December 1881, made official by the famous decree of Muharrem. Whereas this settlement eliminated control of the finances of the Ottoman Empire by the governments of the Great Powers, it gave a large measure of control to a commission which represented private foreign investors. The decree of Muharrem opened the financial markets of Europe to the Ottoman government and likewise opened the doors of the Ottoman Near East to the capitalists of the West. Abdul Hamid had succeeded in escaping the fate of his vassal, the khedive of Egypt. By preparing the way for the flow of foreign private capital into Turkish industry, public works, and railroads, he was fostering the revolutionary changes which would in due course of time destroy the old regime of which he was the protagonist. Consequently, his struggle against the Young Turks and "the reform movement," which in reality was revolutionary, eventually proved to be completely futile.

When it is recalled that most of the leading statesmen in Europe during the years between 1814–15 at the Congress of Vienna and the revolutions of 1848 were unable to grasp the historical significance of the movements of their times, it is not astonishing that Abdul Hamid failed to understand the inevitableness of revolutionary change in the Near East, which had already begun. In both cases during the period of revolutionary change, the retention of power by counterrevolutionists resulted in repression, persecution, and violence.

❁ MODERNIZATION UNDER ABDUL HAMID

Although money lending in the form of loans had been one phase of western penetration of the Near East, it was far less instrumental in bringing about change than the investment of capital in railroad construction, in the modernization of Near Eastern cities, and in the petroleum resources of Iraq and Saudi Arabia.

Railroad building.—As in Europe and the United States, railroad building offered a most enticing field of investment for surplus capital. The construction of railroads in the Asiatic Near East was a sequential and logical outgrowth of railroad construction in eastern Europe and the Balkans. The competitive nature of European capitalism and of the European state system inevitably led to a political and economic struggle for railroad concessions from the Ottoman government. The geographic location of the Near East made the building of railroads a matter of strategic military concern to the European Powers. The Russians were not disposed to allow the grant of railroad concessions to other European nations in eastern Anatolia near the Russian frontier. The British looked with anxiety at the prospect of a concession to the Germans for a railroad from Constantinople to the Persian Gulf.

Previous to World War I the Ottoman Government, England, France and Germany had engaged in railroad construction in the Asiatic part of the Ottoman Empire. In Palestine there were the single track narrow gauge railroad from Jaffa to Jerusalem, and a branch of the Ottoman-built Damascus-Medina-Hejaz railroad from Haifa to Deraa. In Lebanon and Syria there were French-constructed lines connecting Beirut with Damascus and Aleppo, and a branch line from Homs to the port of Tripoli.

In Asia Minor the first railroads were built in the Smyrna (Izmir) area to develop the hinterland of the great Aegean port. One runs southeast through Aidin to Egerdir, one from Smyrna east to Afiun Karahissar where it joins the Anatolian and Bagdad lines, and one north via Magnesia to Panderma on the Marmora Sea. A short line was built to serve the Cilician Plain and its three cities, Mersin, Tarsus, and Adana. The main Anatolian line runs from Haidar Pasha on the Bosporus to Eski-Shehr where it branches, one line going to Angora (Ankara) and the other to Konia via Afiun Karahissar. The line from Haidar Pasha to Konia became part of the famous Berlin-Bagdad railroad which was only partly constructed when World War I began.

Railroads in Turkey, with the exception of the Ottoman built Hejaz railroad, were undertaken on a concession basis under the authority of imperial irades. Many factors militated against a rationally planned railroad transportation system in the Asiatic part of the Ottoman Empire. Turkish officials knew little about the engineering and economics of railroad construction and operation. Furthermore, there was considerable graft in the granting of concessions. The Turks had no capital for investment and had no way of tapping local capital resources. The Ottoman government gave consideration to its own military and political requirements with respect to railroad construction, and it was obliged to manipulate the rival European states from which capital could be obtained. The competitors, each pursuing his own economic, political, and military aims, blocked the construction of an integrated and unified railroad transportation system.

In spite of all the obstacles, it was during the reign of Abdul Hamid that the foundations of the railroad systems of the Near East were laid. Abdul Hamid granted concessions for the extension of Smyrna-Aidin railroad and the Smyrna-Kassaba railroad. In 1888 he granted a concession for the construction of the Anatolian railroad—Haidar Pasha to Angora (Ankara) and later to Konia. In the Arab provinces he gave concessions for the building of the French lines in Palestine, Lebanon, and Syria. With considerable initiative he undertook the financing and construction of the Hejaz railroad from Damascus to Medina with a branch via Deraa to the Palestinian port of Haifa. Most important of all he granted to the Germans a concession to build a railroad to Bagdad. After 1908 the Young Turks continued Abdul Hamid's policy and on the eve of World War I granted concessions to the French for railroad construction to link the Black Sea littoral with the eastern Anatolian provinces and to connect with extensions to the north and northeast of the Bagdad line which would have joined northern Syria and Mesopotamia by rail with the eastern provinces in Anatolia.

The Near East was beginning to reconstruct trade routes, which had fallen into decay during the centuries since Vasco da Gama had discovered the Cape of Good Hope route to the Orient. If the old trade of by-gone days could not be revived, at least the railroads would give access to the interior and by providing an outlet for the produce and products of the hinterland, encourage the economic development of the villages and towns of the interior of Asia Minor and of the Arab lands. For the first time in generations the hinterlands of the Near East were being brought in contact with the outer world. The Near Eastern Rip van Winkle was slowly awakening after a sleep of nearly five hundred years. An area, which had once been, for a period of several thousand years, the highway of world commerce and intercourse and which for the past half a millennium had become a stagnant backwater, was being brought into the full current of world affairs.

A considerable price was paid for this transition. The transportation system had been distorted in many cases by a guarantee of a minimum revenue per kilometre. Because of this guarantee railroad lines in some regions tended to be like the Meander River without its topographical justification. Military reasons also affected the route of railroad lines to their economic disadvantage. Rights to mineral and other resources along the railroad were granted to the concessionaires. It would demand, however, much closer study to determine whether the Near Eastern people paid more extortionately for their transportation system than did the people of the more advanced countries of North America.

The competition of the western capitalists and western nations for railroad concessions in the Near East was paralleled and in some minor ways connected with concessions for petroleum. Under the Bagdad railroad concession the Germans, who had been excluded almost entirely from gaining ownership of oil fields, hoped they might get control of part of the rich oil deposits of northern Mesopotamia. A settlement of this issue between the Germans and the British just previous to World War I brought the Germans into the intense worldwide competitive struggle between American oil interests and those of the British, Dutch, and their affiliates.

The process of modernization, which had been going on in the Near East since the French Revolution and Napoleon's invasion of Egypt and Palestine, was in several ways speeded up by World War I. The most striking example of this was the overrunning of Palestine, Lebanon, Syria and Transjordan with motor cars and motor trucks of the invading armies. The building of roads and the construction of railroads during the war were a continuation of developments which began in the reign of Abdul Hamid and which were a part of the evolution of the capitalist economy of the West.

FAILURE OF ABDUL HAMID'S POLICIES

In both his domestic and foreign policies, Abdul Hamid failed because he lacked an understanding and grasp of the forces in play throughout his empire affecting both Christians and Moslems. During the nineteenth century, liberalism in a variety of forms was stirring the people of Egypt and western Asia, as well as the Turks of Constantinople and the Christian peoples of the Balkans. Liberalism in its many manifestations was opposed to all that Abdul Hamid sought to maintain.

In the great center of Moslem learning at Azhar University at Cairo, Sheikh Jemaleddin, a Moslem from Afghanistan, had become the leader of a liberal group who believed that absolutism as practiced by the sultan of Turkey, the khedive of Egypt, the shah of Persia (Iran), and lesser Islamic potentates was contrary to the spirit of Islam, which was essentially republican, and inculcated the belief that government should be based on law and on public approval. The evolution of this political theory in the leading Moslem theological school bears a resemblance to the development of the ideas of nineteenth-century liberals which grew out of the Social Contract theory promulgated by John Locke in England during the seventeenth century and popularized on the continent by Jean Jacques Rousseau in the eighteenth century. At the very time when Abdul Hamid was appealing to all the most reactionary elements in Islam to rise against their Christian rulers and rally round their caliph-sultan and when a fanatical Moslem leader named Mohammed Ahmed, born a year after Abdul Hamid under conditions far less luxurious than the seraglio on the Bosporus but as representative of an ancient order of things, at the head of the revolutionary masses in the Sudan proclaimed himself Mahdi (the coming Islamic Messiah) and after driving out the Egyptians was establishing a barbarous and devastating tyranny, a liberal group of theological students at Cairo was challenging the religious foundations of autocracy!

Abdul Hamid attempted to fight the encroachments of the Western Powers upon the practically defenseless Moslems of Africa and the Near and Middle East with the antique weapons of religious fanaticism. While the autocrats adopted anachronistic methods to dam the flood tide of imperialism, the people were forging the nineteenth-century tool of nationalism to fight the imperialists. In less than three-quarters of a century since Abdul Hamid began his futile struggle against the Great Powers of Europe the people of the Near East have very largely freed themselves from the political imperialism of the Ottoman Turks and of the European governments.

Reactionary and repressive policies.—Abdul Hamid was determined to do away with the liberal constitution, the representative assembly, and the liberal reformers. The Russian-Turkish War gave him the excuse to shelve the constitution and to dismiss the assembly. The old regime provided a variety of ways to eliminate the leading liberals. "Liquidation" is not a modern device, either on a retail or a wholesale scale, nor historically is it any more Asiatic than European. Abdul Hamid was well versed in the ancient practices. Removal from office, exile, judicial proceedings, character assassination, imprisonment, suicide, unobtrusive murder—these were the age-old methods effectively employed by Abdul Hamid to rid himself of Midhat Pasha and other leading Young Turks. To control the rank and file and to crush the movement, the sultan developed an all pervading spy system so that when two or three were gathered together in the name of liberalism, one at least would be a Hamidian spy or *agent provocateur*. The press was so effectively controlled by official censorship that any journalistic or literary outlet was denied to the reformists and revolutionaries. Abdul Hamid's Turkish version of an F.B.I. was efficient in a variety of ways. It supplied him with more reports than he could read. It kept him in a constant state of jitters. It was a highway to promotion and pay for the unscrupulous informer. It created complete distrust, fear, and hatred of the government. It compelled people to organize secretly and eventually to create an underground political movement which broke Abdul Hamid's system of terrorism and espionage in 1908 and deposed him in 1909.

Diplomatic maneuvers.—Abdul Hamid was sufficiently astute to realize the Great Powers were essentially competing political and economic units whose rivalries he might play upon. Political developments in Europe tended to favor this policy of dividing the Powers in order that he might rule unrestrained in Turkey during most of his reign. France and England remained rivals until the creation of the Entente Cordiale of 1904, when England consented to France's having a free hand in Morocco in exchange for a free hand in Egypt. Russia and England remained competitors for power in the Near and Middle East until 1907, when they arrived at a mutually satisfactory arrangement for the exploitation of Persia (Iran), which then appeared to foreshadow its ultimate partition. Germany had become the most threatening rival of Great Britain and had developed a very active interest in the economic resources of the Near East.

Abdul Hamid's miscalculations and blunders in dealing with the European states were due in part to ignorance and to fear of England, as well as to his hatred of all great powers ruling over Moslems—Britain, France,

Holland, and Russia. Abdul Hamid's animosity toward the British was whetted by loss of Cyprus, by the implied right under the Treaty of Berlin granted them to protect the Armenians, and finally by their occupation of Egypt in 1882.

After the British and French had decided in 1879 arbitrarily without any basis under international law to demand that Khedive Ismail abdicate in favor of his son Tewfik, Abdul Hamid was obliged to act against his will with unaccustomed celerity to depose Ismail and recognize Tewfik as his successor. To Abdul Hamid this action which forestalled a similar act by the detested British appeared as a diplomatic triumph. By such trivia were diplomats accustomed to assuage their wounded vanity. This simulacrum of power gave Abdul Hamid the idea a few years later that he could challenge the British in Egypt.

Events in North Africa and Egypt increased Abdul Hamid's hatred of the Christian Powers of Europe. In 1881 the French invaded and occupied Tunis, thus placing another Moslem country under Christian control. In Egypt a crisis arose shortly after the deposition of Ismail. His successor, Tewfik, was too weak a ruler to cope with the rising complications. The discontented official class resented the Anglo-French dual control over Egyptian finances; the large fellaheen population was bitter against the foreign moneylenders to whom these peasants were indebted. A small group of intellectual liberals wished to do away with absolute monarchy, and there existed a growing antagonism in the army between the ranking Turkish-Circassian officers and the Egyptians.

The Egyptian crisis.—The ruling class in Egypt was made up of *Turkish-Circassians,* who spoke Turkish, and looked with contempt on the native Egyptians, most particularly on the fellaheen. The rank and file of the army was made up of Egyptians, as was also the corps of noncommissioned and junior officers. In recent years a few officers of fellah origin had found favor at the khedivial court and had been promoted to higher ranks and placed in command of troops at the palace and in Cairo. This intensified the friction between the Turko-Circassians and the Arabic-speaking Egyptians. The leader of the discontented Egyptian officers, Colonel, and later Pasha, Arabi, the son of a village sheik and small landowning fellah, before entering the army studied theology at al-Azhar University, where he had come into contact with the liberal movement among the ecclesiastical students. The professional and class struggle between the Turko-Circassians and the Egyptian officers soon developed into a political struggle to oust the ruling caste from the government and to establish a constitutional monarchy with a representative assembly. Arabi became a national hero who gained almost universal support from Egyptians. The national movement, which was in the process of gestation, was composed of a variety of elements. In some ways it was a peasant movement against an alien ruling class and against foreign moneylenders. In other respects, it was a nationalistic movement against foreign intervention and the privileged foreign population, largely Greek. It had elements of religious antagonism of Moslem against Christian. There was also a streak of democratic liberalism opposing the khedivial autocracy.

Such a movement in Egypt could not develop very far before it created serious international complications. The British and French governments, acting as lackeys for the powerful financial interests which had made extensive loans to the khedives, had only recently imposed dual control over Egyptian finances and by diplomatic maneuvers deposed spendthrift Ismail. Neither the British nor the French government was in a mood to allow a nascent Egyptian nationalist movement led by an "untutored" Egyptian fellah, Arabi, to spoil the brew they were industriously cooking. Franco-British agents could readily bend the new Khedive to their will but not Arabi Pasha.

Arabi's revolt had repercussions in the capitals of all the Great Powers and at Constantinople. Britain was bent on intervention, but hesitated to act alone. The British had to consider Abdul Hamid, who was, after all, the suzerain of Egypt, and they had to consider the reactions of the various other European nations. A conference of the European Powers met at Constantinople. The humbuggery of international diplomacy began. In France the ministry of the dynamic Gambetta had fallen and the new cabinet realized that the French voters were not enthusiastic about further adventures after the seizure of Tunis, nor was the French government anxious to have Turkish troops in Egypt even though it was distant from its new Moslem protectorate. Abdul Hamid was confronted with a series of dilemmas. He had no liking for an Egyptian revolutionary who demanded a constitution. He was well aware, however, that Arabi was looked upon not only as a national leader but also as the defender of Islam against the Christian Powers of the West. The sultan abhorred the idea of a British invasion of Egypt, which ignored his sovereign rights, but he disliked even more the sending of Turkish troops under British command to crush an Egyptian movement which opposed foreign control and intervention.

Events in Egypt forestalled all international negotiations and behind-the-curtain arrangements. Under the tension and excitement throughout Egypt on June 11, 1882, a riot broke out in the polyglot city of Alexandria. A Maltese British subject got in a row with an Egyptian donkey boy, who was stabbed to death. Egyptian Moslems running to his aid attacked the Maltese and other foreign Christians, whose coreligionists began firing from their windows. Some hundred odd indigenous non-Egyptian Christians were killed before order was re-established. In Europe, but particularly in England, the Alexandrian riot was portrayed as a violent outbreak of religious fanaticism and the prelude to wholesale massacres. The United States Consul General Forman at Cairo in his book *Egypt and Its Betrayal* [3] claims the British press grossly misrepresented the whole affair. Wilfrid S. Blunt,[4] a British supporter and backer of Arabi Pasha, states that the English financial controller, Sir Auckland Colvin, was a regular correspondent of the influential *Pall Mall Gazette,* and that he inspired the *Times* (London) correspondent on all important diplomatic matters. He also asserts that both Reuter and Havas received $5,000 a year each from the Anglo-French Financial Control. Blunt was convinced that the exaggerated and inaccurate reports in the British press of the Alexandria riot were due to official manipulation "of the organs of public news." British and French warships were sent to Alexandria and an international conference was held at the Turkish capital. While Abdul Hamid delayed his decision whether to accept or reject Britain's proposal to send a Turkish force to accompany a British invasion of Egypt, the British fleet bombarded Alexandria on July 10, 1882, and sent a landing force into the burning seaport. This action was followed by an invasion of Egypt of the British from Port Said and Suez and by a triumphal entry of the British forces into Cairo after a complete rout of Arabi's army at Tel-el Kebir on September 13, 1882.

British occupation of Egypt.—The British were now in sole control of Egypt, but they were in no way free from either local difficulties or foreign interference. Despite the fact that France and Italy had both refused to participate in the invasion of Egypt and the other Powers had shown no interest in doing so, each of the Powers maintained a lively interest in the settlement of the Egyptian affair and each enjoyed capitulatory rights there. Although Abdul Hamid had refused to send troops to Egypt, he was still its suzerain and was the caliph of the Moslem world, and the British thought some arrangement with him was desirable, the more so because British statesmen had said very definitely that their occupation of Egypt was only temporary.

To the complexities and problems of Egypt itself were added those of the Sudan. The Mahdi not only had become the master of the Sudan but threatened Egypt itself. A Britisher, William Hicks, had been appointed by the Egyptian government commander-in-chief of the Egyptian forces operating against the Mahdi in the Sudan. In 1883 General Hicks's expeditionary force was completely annihilated by the dervishes of the Mahdi. The only hope of holding the Sudan lay in obtaining British and Turkish, or British troops. There was a frightful stew in governmental circles in London, because the Liberals under the aged Gladstone did not want England drawn into an adventurous intervention in the region of the Upper Nile, while the Conservatives were blaming the government for vacillation and inconsistency. To add to the confusion, the Egyptian government wanted to ask Sultan Abdul Hamid for aid. The upshot of these contradictions in policymaking was the ill-fated expedition of General Gordon to the Sudan. It reached Khartoum only to be completely destroyed by the triumphant forces of the Mahdi, which captured Khartoum in January 1885.

By the summer of that year of disaster in the Sudan, the British government began special negotiations with Abdul Hamid in the hope of finding some solution of the manifold difficulties with which it was confronted as a result of the occupation of Egypt. Lacking an understanding of the real nature of the revolution in the Sudan and failing to realize that the Turks and the sultan were as much anathema to the Mahdi as were the Christians, the British Foreign Office was under the illusion that Abdul Hamid as caliph might "contribute materially to the establishment of settled order and good government" in the Egyptian Sudan.[5] Sir Henry Wolff, a "lame-duck" Conservative parliamentary candidate, was sent on a special mission to negotiate a convention with the Ottoman government with respect to Egypt. At first, he made surprising progress considering the dilatoriness of the Sublime Porte. Nine weeks after his arrival at Constantinople, he secured the signature of the Ottoman minister for foreign affairs to a preliminary convention which set forth the topics to be discussed and provided for sending special commissioners of Great Britain and Turkey to Egypt. From then on, progress was slow, for it was not until the spring of 1887 that a second convention was signed at the sultan's capital. This agreement to which Abdul Hamid had given his consent stirred up a hornet's nest of the European Powers. Both the French and the Russian governments informed the sultan that they would not adhere to such an agreement. Protocols attached to the Convention proposed a readjustment of capitulatory rights of foreigners, while the main part of the agreement provided for the withdrawal of British troops by 1890, unless internal or external conditions proved threatening and further authorized the re-entry of British troops if the situation in Egypt should warrant it.

Menacing international complications.—Although the occupation forces were to be both British and Turkish, Abdul Hamid, after receiving protests from the French and Russians, delayed giving his final and definite approval to the Convention. He came to the conclusion, whether or not as the result of intimations from the French and Russians is not known, that if he agreed to the terms proposed by the British, particularly the right of re-entry, he might find himself confronted by a situation in Lebanon that would result in France insisting on the right of again sending troops to occupy both Lebanon and Syria. He was well aware of the fact that the Maronites in Mount Lebanon, with or without foreign encouragement, were capable of creating disturbances which would give the French an excuse to claim the right of re-entry. Furthermore, in view of conditions in the six vilayets (provinces) with an Armenian population where no reforms as stipulated in the Treaty of Berlin had been introduced and where Abdul Hamid was soon to begin his policy of extermination, the sultan hesitated to sign a Convention with England which might give Russia the excuse to assert her right to reoccupy those territories in eastern Anatolia which had been conquered by Russian troops during the war of 1877–78. Abdul Hamid knew very well that by the Treaty of San Stefano Russian troops were to remain in the occupied areas until effective reforms had been introduced. The sultan was aware of the fact that it was only due to British pressure that this clause in the San Stefano Treaty had not been included in the Treaty of Berlin. If the sultan should agree to a temporary British occupation of Egypt and grant the right of re-entry in case of internal disturbances or foreign threat, he knew that he might give the Russians a justifiable claim to reoccupy eastern Anatolia.

In a quandary, Abdul Hamid, as was his habit, kept putting off his decision until Lord Salisbury, the British Prime Minister, grew impatient and recalled his special commissioner, Sir Drummond Wolff. After a year, when the sultan came to the conclusion that it had been a mistake not to accept the Convention, it was too late. When the Turkish ambassador at London, acting under instructions from Constantinople, attempted to reopen negotiations about Egypt on the basis of the Wolff Convention he was curtly told by Salisbury that the matter was closed. From this time until November 1914 the suzerainty of the sultan remained a diplomatic fiction, although Egypt paid to the Turkish government annual tribute, which, of course, was allocated to the payment of debt service on some of the Ottoman loans. Egypt in reality had become a British protectorate, though nominally an autonomous khediviate of the Ottoman Empire.

Abdul Hamid continued to foster Pan-Islamic intrigues in Egypt and to assist the Egyptian nationalists who soon were to begin their campaign of "Egypt for the Egyptians" under the leadership of Kemal Pasha. Twice Abdul Hamid attempted to modify the frontiers of Egypt by changes in the Turko-Egyptian boundaries in the peninsula of Sinai, but he never attempted overtly to challenge Britain's position in Egypt. Though Britain's rape of Egypt rankled in his mind, he soon found himself deeply engaged in other affairs, among which the Armenian question was of prime significance.

CHAPTER VIII

Abdul Hamid and the Armenians

❁ THE ARMENIANS

The old regime in the Ottoman Empire, becoming increasingly unsuitably adapted to the conditions developing in the last quarter of the nineteenth century, created maladjustments that confronted Abdul Hamid with problems for which he and his government had no acceptable solutions. Of these, the *Armenian Question* was an old one in the Near East, far older even than the Ottoman Empire. Recent developments there, however, had created some new aspects to it.

Quarreling sectarians and their European sponsors.—The Jesuit missionaries from Rome had by 1700 converted a considerable number of Armenians to Catholicism and organized the United Armenian Church, which recognized the primacy of the Pope. This created much agitation among the Armenians in Constantinople, the majority of whom were of the old Gregorian Church. From 1707 to 1759 there were riots in the city between Catholic and Gregorian Armenians almost every year. Interference by Sultan Mustapha III settled matters for over fifty years. Then, during the Greek revolution in 1828, when Turkish indignation at the massacre of Moslems by the Christian Greek revolutionists gave rise to the rumor that all the Christians were planning to rise against the Moslems, the Armenians set on foot a rumor that their sectarian rivals were conspiring against the sultan.[1] Official arrests and unofficial massacres resulting from this unscrupulous intrigue were terminated by Sultan Mahmoud II, who recognized in 1830 the Armenian Catholics as a separate religious community. This was of considerable significance, because it gave the French, as the protectors of Catholic Christians in the Ottoman Empire, an added interest in Armenian matters.

It was at this time that American Protestant missionaries became actively interested in the Near East, and, finding missionary work among

Moslems unprofitable, they established missions and schools among the Armenians and other Christians. As a result of their efforts, there grew up a Christian Protestant community in Turkey in which Great Britain assumed a solicitous political interest and through the activities of Ambassador Lord Stratford de Redcliffe, obtained official recognition of the independence of the Protestant community in 1850 from Sultan Abdul Medjid. Russia, as a result of the war of 1877–78, had acquired from Turkey territories in the region of Kars and Erivan, which included the seat of the chief Armenian ecclesiastic, the Gregorian Catholicos of Etchmiadzin, which augmented Russia's interest in Turkish Armenia. In addition to these separate interests of three of the European Powers, all the Great Powers had acquired a collective obligation with respect to the Armenians by article 61 of the Treaty of Berlin (1878), which read as follows: "The Sublime Porte undertakes to carry out without further delay the improvements and reforms demanded by local requirements in the provinces inhabited by the Armenians and to guarantee their security against the Circassians and Kurds. It will periodically make known the steps taken to this effect to the Powers who will superintend their application." This general obligation assumed by the Ottoman government was in some respects supplementary to the special obligation assumed by Abdul Hamid in the Anglo-Turkish Convention with regard to Cyprus, the first article of which reads as follows: "His Imperial Majesty the Sultan, promises to England to introduce necessary reforms, to be agreed upon later between the two Powers, into the government and for the protection of the Christians and other subjects of the Porte in these territories (Armenia). . . ."

These interests of the Great Powers, with the obligations of the Ottoman government, together with the growing strength of an Armenian nationalistic revolutionary movement, not unsimilar to such movements among the Balkan subjects of the sultan, would, sooner or later, have compelled Abdul Hamid to deal with the age-old problem of Armenians, in their relations with Kurds and other marauding nomads.

Strategic nature of eastern Anatolia.—The eastern part of Asia Minor and its people have always been a problem to the rulers of western Anatolia. The northeastern extremity of the Ottoman Empire is a bastion of lofty mountain ranges and high valleys. To the north of it lies the Transcaucasian Valley between Batum on the Black Sea and Baku on the Caspian; to the south, its highlands give way to the plains of Syria and Mesopotamia (Iraq). Eastern Asia Minor, despite the rugged nature of its terrain, was a highway for the invasion of central, western, and southern Anatolia. From the plain of Cilicia the anti-Taurus mountain ranges strike northward to Kaisarieh and northeastward to the mountains of Armenia at Erzeroum, which extend southward to the mountain ranges of northern and western Persia. Mountains are the sources of rivers, and in these highlands are the head waters of both the Euphrates and the Tigris.

Through the centuries, commerce flowed along the caravan routes through this mountainous wilderness. From the Persian Gulf, one trade route ran via Bagdad and Mosul to Diyarbakir and across the anti-Taurus either via Harput to Sivas and thence north to the Black Sea at Sinope or west to Constantinople, or via Malatia to Kaisarieh. Sivas was an entrepôt on the crossroads of Asia Minor with access to the north, the west, and to Cilicia in the south. Another route from Ormuz on the Persian Gulf coast of Iran went to Ispahan and via Hamadan to Tabriz and Erzeroum, where it connected with routes leading to the Caspian near Baku and to the Black Sea at Trebizond.

Politically and economically, the highlands of northeastern Asia Minor have throughout history been of vital importance to all the powerful neighboring states. The Sumerian city states of the Tigris and Euphrates Valley were subject to invasions from the mountains to the north and east, as well as from the desert. The Assyrians, the ancient Persians, the Greeks under Alexander, the Romans, the Parthians, the Abbassid caliphs, the Byzantine emperors, and Seljuks in ancient and medieval times have been concerned with the control of these highlands. In modern times the Ottoman Turks and the Russians have fought for the control of parts of this strategic area.

Armenians and Kurds.—Into the high fertile valleys and pasture lands of this mountainous tableland, a great variety of peoples have penetrated. Of all the many invading nomads and conquering armies during four thousand years of history who have penetrated this region, two groups, the Armenians and the Kurds have throughout the centuries maintained their identity and remain in the twentieth century as national groups with distinctive cultural, if not always distinctive biological, characteristics. There still is much uncertainty even among the anthropologists with respect to the racial heritage of these two peoples. Both speak a language which is Indo-European. The supposition is that both peoples were off-shoots of the Indo-European-speaking nomads who in early historic times roamed the grasslands of the central Eurasian plains, differing in biological origin from the Turanians, Turkomen, and Mongol Tatars who ranged the pasture lands of central and northeastern Asia before they erupted into the Eurasian plain and Asia Minor.

Both Armenian and Kurdish nationalists maintain that their national origins go back to the time of the Sumerian city states before the reign of Hammurabi in 1900 (*c*) B.C. Despite the ebb and flow of imperialistic conquerors, these mountain peoples were able to maintain themselves and their peculiar cultural characteristics. The Armenians occupied the northern area, but spread westward to the Anatolian plateau in the neighborhood of Sivas and to the Taurus and anti-Taurus mountains bordering on Cilicia and Syria, and also northeastward in the direction of Transcaucasia. The Kurds established themselves in the north central part of the highlands, in the northern part of Mesopotamia, and in the Zagros Mountains of western Persia. For the most part, the Armenians became peasant cultivators and urban craftsmen and merchants, while the Kurds remained seminomads organized on a tribal basis.

The Armenians become Christians, the Kurds Moslems.—These different ways of life led to continual conflicts between Armenians and Kurds. Throughout the entire history of Asia and much of that of the Eurasian plain, the unremitting conflict between townsmen and peasants on the one hand and the shepherd nomads on the other has been a constant factor and remains so still in various parts of the Near East. The asperity of the Armenian-Kurdish age-old conflicts was greatly augmented by ideological differences that were the result of historical events. Christian missionaries reached the Armenian townsmen and villagers and converted them about 300 A.D. As later in the case of the Slavic and Bulgarian barbarian invaders in the Balkans and of the Slavic tribes in Russia, a native alphabet was invented, and the Greek Bible was translated by a famous priest named Mesrob. This created a distinctly new aspect of Armenian culture which enabled them to preserve their cultural and national identity throughout the coming vicissitudes during the next fifteen hundred years. Christian Armenians were persecuted by their overlords the Persian followers of Zoroaster. Off in the eastern highlands of western Asia among peoples who were pagans and close neighbors of the Persians, the Armenian Christians were isolated from the main body of Christianity.

This isolation was very greatly intensified as the result of the lying propaganda of a handful of zealots. Strangely enough, a lie in 451 A.D. has affected the destinies of the Armenian people down to the present time. When the Monophysite doctrine was condemned as a heresy by the Council of Chalcedon in the year 451, two of its protagonists, Eutyches, who had been excommunicated, and Dioscorus, who was deposed, in their determination to nullify in Asia Minor the effects of the Council's decision, despatched scores of their followers to spread the news that whereas the Greeks had repudiated Monophysite doctrine, the

Latins had accepted it.[2] Before truth could catch up with falsehood in the mountains of eastern Anatolia, the Armenian clergy and people had committed themselves to this heresy, and forty years later a synod of the Armenian clergy, although it repudiated Eutyches, rejected the Council of Chalcedon in 451.[3] This act eventually resulted in a deep cleavage between the Armenian Gregorian Church and both the Catholic Church and the Greek Orthodox Church. This cleavage increased the isolation of the Armenians from the rest of the Christian world. Catholics and Orthodox, whether Greek or Russian, looked upon the Gregorian Armenians as heretics. As the power of Russia grew and her influence in Near Eastern affairs increased, the lack of sympathy for the Armenians in St. Petersburg was unfortunate for the Armenian people.

The Arab Moslem conquests in the Near East enveloped the Kurdish neighbors of the Armenians, and the Kurds became Moslems. From the seventh century on, this small community of Armenian Christian peasants, craftsmen, merchants, and moneylenders lived in constant conflict with Kurdish Moslem nomadic cattlemen. As long as the Armenians were permitted to bear arms, they were able to hold their own in dealings with the Kurds.

TURKS AND ARMENIANS

The Turanian invasions of Asia Minor had by the eleventh century scattered the Armenians over a wider area, particularly in the anti-Taurus, northern Syria, and Cilicia, where they created a kingdom known as "Little Armenia." This dispersion placed them athwart the route which the First Crusade was to follow from Constantinople to Jerusalem. Quite naturally the Armenians took part in the Crusades on the side of the Christians from Europe, which intensified the bitterness between the Armenians and their Moslem neighbors, Kurds, Turks, Persians, and Circassians.

The conquests of the Ottoman Turks upon the fall of the Byzantine Empire created a new situation for the Armenian people after the opening of the sixteenth century. A powerful Moslem state now ruled over the strategic highlands of eastern Asia Minor. Its Christian subjects were recognized and accepted minorities under the Millet system, but in the eastern provinces as in the Balkans, they had an inferior status to that of the Moslems. Turkish power penetrated into the highland valleys and towns, but never effectively controlled the mountain ranges with their pasture lands. The Armenians were readily brought under the administrative control of the Turks, while their hereditary foes the Kurds were able to retain much of their local independence. Furthermore, the Armenians were disarmed and not permitted to serve in the armed forces of the Ottoman government, while the Kurds retained their arms and supplied important contingents to the Turkish army.

Security under the early Ottoman sultan.—As long as the Ottoman Empire remained strong and its government efficient, the position of the Armenians despite their defenceless condition was not altogether intolerable. In many ways, it seems surprising that so alien a minority with respect to religion, language, culture, and social patterns, not only survived but prospered under Ottoman rule. They suffered from frequent raids of the nomadic Kurds, the Kurdish tribal nobles acquired title over much of the land that Armenian peasants tilled, extracting from them as goodly a share of the fruits of their labors as has been the custom of land-owning nobles since time immemorial; government officials exacted taxes and perquisites from the prosperous Armenian merchants and moneylenders, who themselves by more intricate and subtle means had acquired wealth from others. How in the name of Allah could noble Kurdish tribal leaders, respected Ottoman officials, honored Armenian prelates, and industrious Armenian merchants and bankers be expected to be able to live far better than the common herd if they did not have the means of taking wealth away from others? Was not this the proper function of government? As long as its rule was strong, laws were enforced, order was reasonably well preserved, and commerce flowed unimpeded along the caravan routes; the Armenian upper-classes lived reasonably well, both lay and clerical; the Armenian artisans made a living, and Armenian peasants lived as most of the peasants of Europe during the Middle Ages—slightly better than their domestic animals. Under such conditions, troubles in the highlands never reached such proportions as during the reign of Abdul Hamid and the rule of the Young Turks.

Changing conditions in the nineteenth century.—By the nineteenth century, conditions had greatly changed. The Ottoman Empire was in an advanced stage of decline. Commerce and handicraft industry were in a state of stagnation throughout much of the hinterland of Turkey. Roads and bridges had fallen into decay. Many of the famous caravan routes of Asia Minor, which in both ancient and medieval times had carried a considerable volume of trade, became little more than mule tracks and mountain trails. Large tracts of land had been abandoned and remained uncultivated. Marauders and bandits pillaged at will the peasants and the traveling merchants. Imperial and local officials were inefficient, weak, and venal. The sultans were not the masters of themselves, their harems, nor of their empire. Ignorance, poverty, and corruption reigned in Turkey, which was beset on all sides by the aggressive imperialist states of Europe. The putrefying members of its body politic were attracting the vultures to the dying empire during the reign of Sultan Abdul Medjid and Sultan Abdul Aziz. When Abdul Hamid came to the throne, he tried futilely to check the disease and to checkmate the attendant vultures. His attempts to do so, based upon ignorance of the modern world and upon age-old obscurantism, tended to foster the diseased conditions and to augment the ills of the state and the suffering of all its peoples. Among these, the Armenians perhaps paid the highest price in human misery and blood.

Revolutionary ferment among the Armenians.—Revitalizing forces, however, were flowing into the Near East from the West. In due course, the news that in France the peasants had broken the shackles of their landowning nobility, that the middle class had overthrown autocracy, and later that the workers of the world had created an "International" to achieve social democracy reached the Near East. American missionaries and schools brought to the people the knowledge of a far distant country whose people had revolted against their tyrannical rulers and organized a republic based on the equality of man and dedicated to liberty. These revolutionary ideas were fermenting in the Near East throughout the nineteenth century and were giving rise to revolutionary movements which the espionage system, the increasing despotism, and the ruthless repressions of Abdul Hamid could not destroy.

The Armenians were not immune from the revolutionary movements among the Balkan Christians and the Young Turks. The Tanzimat movement had awakened their hopes and stimulated their leaders, especially among the Armenians in Constantinople.

During the reigns of Abdul Medjid and Abdul Aziz when the Young Turk Reformers dominated the Sublime Porte, a revolutionary struggle was going on within the Armenian community in Constantinople. In this city, his new Turkish capital, Sultan Mohammed the conqueror settled many Armenians in the second half of the fifteenth century. This Armenian community grew in numbers and greatly prospered during the early centuries of Ottoman rule. The Patriarch of Constantinople, although he was not the ecclesiastical head of the Armenian Church, was the religious and civil chief executive of the Armenian millet (nation) throughout the Ottoman Empire, and consequently Constantinople was the religious and civil administrative center of the Turkish Armenians. Around this nexus of power developed a numerous Armenian community. Armenian merchants and financiers waxed wealthy, and Armenian professional men held high office in the Ottoman government. The Armenian community of Constantinople had sharp class distinctions. A small rich and politically powerful group, called the *Amira,* the princes, acquired control over the entire community, lay and ecclesiastical, which they used to their own profit.[4] Through bribery and other influences they prevailed upon the sultan to appoint whomever they chose as patriarch. The patriarchate, in fact, became a tool of the Amira. Rivalry developed within this tight little oligarchy of some few score Armenian families. The wealthy merchants and moneylenders, known as the *sarrafs,* were rivals of the politically influential Armenian officials of the Ottoman government. A further division among these Armenian magnates developed in the eighteenth century when some of them became Catholics. This oligarchy, however, retained its control over the clergy and the Armenian tradesmen and artisans of the Turkish capital until the time of the Turkish reforms of the Tanzimat.

The Hatti-Sherif of Gul-Khane proclaimed in 1839 by Sultan Abdul Medjid gave the Armenian tradesmen and craftsmen, in a struggle over the control of the Armenian National College at Scutari, an opportunity to attempt to acquire power in the affairs of the Armenian millet. After various vicissitudes in their struggle against the Armenian magnates an Ecclesiastical and a Civil Council were established on a basis which gave effective representation to the people. After the granting in 1856 of the Hatti Humayun, the Armenians obtained a constitution in 1860 which introduced a large measure of democratic procedure into the religious and civil organization of the Armenian community.

ARMENIANS AND THE GREAT POWERS

Both the Crimean War and the Russian-Turkish War of 1877–78 had directly affected the Armenian people who lived on both sides of the Russian-Turkish frontier. Russian invasion of and military operations in the eastern highlands had resulted in Turkish reprisals against Armenians; consequently, they were rejoiced by the Treaty of San Stefano which provided for Russian military occupation until the Ottoman government introduced stipulated reforms.

When the Congress of Berlin met, a special Armenian delegation sent by the Armenian National Assembly presented a project proposing an autonomous Armenia under a governor general appointed by the Ottoman government with assent of the Great Powers. It is hardly necessary to call attention to the fact that such presumption on the part of the Armenians was viewed with intense disfavor by Abdul Hamid and irritated Moslem Turks and Kurds who were smarting under humiliating defeats and the loss of much of their empire in Europe and some territories in Asia, as well as the island of Cyprus.

Under British pressure, the Berlin Congress substituted for article 16 of the Treaty of San Stefano, which contained some assurance that Turkey would be obliged to introduce and implement effective reforms in the so-called Armenian provinces, the weasel worded article 61 of the Treaty of Berlin. The project of the Armenian delegation was given no consideration. So bitter was the disappointment of the Armenian leaders that Patriarch Nerses Varjabedian, in a formal protest to the Powers, said: "The Armenian delegation will return to the East carrying with it the lesson that without struggle and without insurrection nothing can be obtained."

The Europeans engaged in their century-old competitive conflict for power and absorbed in their own national and imperial ambitions gave little heed to Patriarch Nerses' warning. The contrary was true in the Near East where Abdul Hamid and the Moslem leaders could but read in the words of the Armenian ecclesiastic an open threat of revolution, and where the Armenian people looked upon this declaration of their chief religious leader in Turkey as sanction and encouragement to revolutionary activities. These began within two years after the signing of the Treaty of Berlin and were fostered by Turkish persecution following the evacuation of the Russian troops.

Revolutionary ideas from Europe.—Several Armenian revolutionary societies and organizations sprang up in the decade following the Congress of Berlin.[5] The first of these was organized at Erzeroum in 1880 under the name of the Defenders of the Fatherland. It was broken up by the Turkish government in 1882 with arrest of numerous persons which terminated in their trial as political offenders. This not only served to arouse the Armenians but it deeply concerned the Turks and particularly Abdul Hamid and his entourage. Here was definite evidence of a rising danger to the Ottoman state in eastern Asia Minor from a movement similar to those which had resulted in the loss of Ottoman territories of vast extent in the Balkans. The inevitable response of an autocrat or of any tyrannical government to such a revolutionary movement is to crush it, ruthlessly if necessary. Such action was certain to have popular support from most of the Moslems whose religious leaders would hasten to point out the dangers of revolution against the Padishah.

A few years later in 1885 at Van, a local Armenian political society called Armenakan was organized to help the people prepare for a revolutionary struggle against the Turks. In 1887 a new and far more significant and widespread movement began among the Armenians. Over sixty-odd years ago, Marxist socialism reached the Near East in both Russian and Turkish Armenia. The Hunchagian Party was an Armenian counterpart of the social democratic parties of Europe. Its aim was to create an independent Armenian socialist republic which would include both Russian and Turkish Armenia. The socialist organization made a very considerable appeal to the Armenians and grew rapidly for nearly ten years. It disseminated among the Armenian people in the Near East ideas of the Marxian socialists. At a time when social democracy in Europe was splitting up into factions over Bernstein Revisionism which concerned largely the question as to whether socialism should be achieved by "evolution" through co-operation with the bourgeois class or by "revolution" through the class struggle, and when the Russian Social Democratic Party was on the verge of the split into right-wing Mensheviks and left-wing Bolsheviks, the Armenian socialist party, Hunchagian began to lose some of its influence and support as a result of internal factional disputes.

From 1890 on an attempt was made to bring all the diverse Armenian revolutionary groups into one organization. To accomplish this purpose, there was organized the Armenian revolutionary federation known as the Dashnaktzoutun. This was essentially a nationalistic organization with socialistic objectives which adopted terroristic methods similar to those of the Russian Social Revolutionary Party. The substantial and wealthy Armenian middle class for the most part supported the Ramgavar, the Armenian Democratic Liberal Party, which corresponded to the Russian Constitutional Democrats, whose leader was Professor Paul Miliukov. The Ramgavar favored an autonomous Armenia within the framework of the Ottoman Empire to be attained by constitutional rather than revolutionary means.

ABDUL HAMID'S ARMENIAN POLICY

With a ubiquitous spy system maintaining agents and *agents provocateurs* omnipresent in every social group and in every part of his domains, Abdul Hamid was undoubtedly kept well informed of the extensive and intensive revolutionary activities among the Armenians. These activities, until recently, have been overlooked by some Armenian writers and their European and American sympathizers. Most certainly the Armenians had excellent reasons for planning revolution to overthrow the existing order in Turkey and Russia. In the 1950's it is unnecessary to stress the fact that in both the East and the West it is the practice for established governments, with the enthusiastic support of all those who favor the existing social order, to use every necessary means to suppress and exterminate revolutionary movements and revolutionists even to extending such conservative activities far beyond the frontiers of the state.

Revolutionists, it is expected, shall pay the price in loss of freedom and even of life itself, if security of the state be threatened. Such was the attitude of Abdul Hamid towards the Armenian revolutionists.

He had no intention of granting self-government or autonomy to the Armenians. He was determined to prevent the rise of a Christian nationalist movement in Asiatic Turkey that might result in the loss of full sovereignty of the sultan's government over its subjects and territories in areas so strategically located as the Armenian provinces. He objected to any interference in the internal affairs of the empire in the Anatolian provinces. He avoided fulfillment of the meager obligations of article 61 of the Treaty of Berlin. By devious and dilatory methods, he effectively evaded the half-hearted attempts of the Powers to force his compliance with treaty obligations. Their collective note of 1880 insisting upon suitable reforms received no satisfactory reply from the Porte.

In the 1880's the Great Powers were too deeply concerned with their own domestic and imperialist affairs to give much heed to the Armenians, whose sufferings were soon to reach a crisis in the massacres of 1894 and 1895. In 1881 France seized Tunis whose occupation by a Christian country was annoying to the Moslems and irritating to Abdul Hamid. In 1882 Great Britain occupied Egypt and thus swallowed, overestimating its future capacity of digestion, another part of the sultan's dominions. Under Bismarck, Germany was reforging her hegemony of the continent by the Dual Alliance with Austria in 1879, the revival of the Three Emperors League in 1881, and the creation of the Triple Alliance between Germany, Austria, and Italy in 1882. The Russian autocracy was haunted by the fear of revolution. Alexander II, who had emancipated the serfs, was assassinated by *Liberal* revolutionists, and his successor, Alexander III, began his reactionary reign in 1881 with no sympathy for revolutionists at home or abroad. In the new German Empire, the government of Bismarck had abandoned its "War of Civilization" against the Catholics to take up its struggle against the Marxist socialists and their political organ, the Social Democratic Party. Austria-Hungary was troubled with nationalist parties, as well as with those of the Social Democrats. In fact, the ruling classes and their governments in Europe were not in a mood to sympathize deeply with the revolutionary aims of the Armenians. Britain in the eighties was seeking the assistance and co-operation of Abdul Hamid in suppressing a peoples' revolution in Egypt. Consequently, during a critical decade between 1885 and 1895 Abdul Hamid had almost a free hand in dealing with the Armenians.

Massacres and other atrocities.—While there is no question with regard to the ruthless and cruel atrocities of the Armenian massacres of 1894 and 1895, the fog of propaganda created by Armenians and their European and American sympathizers has so obscured the facts that even today it is difficult to disentangle the true from the false. A frightful tragedy took place. It could not have occurred if the Ottoman government had desired to make determined efforts to prevent the massacres. Abdul Hamid has been accused of deliberately provoking disturbances in the eastern vilayets and of employing massacre as a means of solving a social problem. He gave encouragement to the Kurds and organized Kurdish military forces known as the Hamidieh, which as pets of the sultan, escaped from the discipline of Turkish officers who came to hate them. Abdul Hamid's spies encouraged rumors and fostered lies which aroused the fears and hatreds of Armenians and Kurds against each other. Ottoman officials and troops took no steps to prevent the massacres and are said to have participated in them.

A decadent society ruled over by a corrupt and inefficient government controlled by a sovereign who was dominated by fear, hatred, and reactionary obscurantism was in the process of rapid revolutionary change, which stirred men's deepest passions whether they were the protagonists of the old or of the new order. Added to the confused and multiple contradictions of Near Eastern society were the ancient religious antagonisms between Moslems and Christians and the old feud between Armenians and Kurds. A more balanced perspective of these events is possible if one calls to mind the "slaughter by hanging, crucifixion, decapitation, and drowning" of 100,000 Paulician Christian heretics by the Christian Empress Theodora of the Byzantine Empire or in more recent times the slaughter of 6,000,000 Jews in the heart of Christian Europe.

The Liberals of Europe thundered imprecations upon the head of Abdul Hamid, who was called the Great Assassin and the Red Sultan, but the administration of the public debt went on collecting taxes to pay the interest and amortizement installments to the European bondholders, and concession hunters continued their pursuit of lucrative investments. Some Armenian revolutionists in 1896 thought by striking at the heart of European financial interests in Turkey Europe would surely be compelled to intervene. Their seizure of the Ottoman Bank, from which they were evacuated unharmed, proved to be a fiasco, but their rash act was followed by what appeared to be an organized massacre of the Armenians in the city which lasted over a period of three days.

Violence against the Armenians came to an end before the year 1896 closed. The number of Armenians—men, women, and children—

slaughtered or killed as the result of exposure and starvations is variously estimated from 350,000 to 400,000 out of a total population estimated by the Armenian patriarchate to have been 2,660,000 and by the Ottoman Government only 1,100,000.[6] During the high tide of violence, the Great Powers in 1895 sent two memorable notes to the sultan. One in the spring contained a project for reforms, the second in the autumn in the form of a collective verbal note from the British, French, and Russian ambassadors to Said Pasha expressed confidence in the sultan's determination to implement a program of reforms that in diplomatic lingo meant that they expected Abdul Hamid to fulfill his promises.

Failure of the Powers to intervene.—The Powers succeeded in obtaining from the sultan's government only an acceptance on paper of the reform project presented to it by them. Abdul Hamid acted on the well-founded judgment that the Concert of Europe and the Powers because of their rival interests would not intervene in the Armenian affair. In fact, the political developments in Europe and in the Far East were such as to make collective action unlikely.

Kaiser Wilhelm courts Sultan Abdul Hamid.—In Germany, Kaiser Wilhelm II came to the throne in 1888. He was a man of his times, who, despite his Hohenzollern and Prussian traditions, was more in sympathy and in closer touch with the new and powerful elements of the German ruling classes, the industrialists, the financiers, the shipping, and foreign trade magnates, than with the landowning Junker aristocracy. The young kaiser was an ardent supporter of imperialism, economic and political. The rapidly growing German merchant marine had his endorsement. His naval policy was soon to result in a naval race between Germany and England. Wilhelm II considered the Near East to be a special field for German financial and economic expansion. A year after his accession to the throne, he visited Abdul Hamid at Yildiz Palace and endeavored to persuade him to grant the Germans extensive economic concessions in Asiatic Turkey. The sultan looked upon him as a friend and Germany as a counterweight to the other European Powers. To the scandal of the Liberals in Europe, the Kaiser made an extensive visit to the Ottoman Empire in 1898 shortly after the Armenian massacres and in one of his characteristically flamboyant speeches, at the tomb of Saladin at Damascus, proclaimed himself to be a friend of Abdul Hamid the Caliph and of the three hundred million Moslems.

The youthful ruler of Germany disembarrassed himself of the aging Iron Chancellor Bismarck, whose intricate system of alliances to assure peace and security collapsed and was soon superseded by an alliance system that divided Europe into two armed camps, each feverishly preparing for war. Bismarck had negotiated a secret treaty with Russia in 1887 known as the Reinsurance Treaty, which eliminated the possibility of an alliance between France and Russia that would have exposed Germany to the possibility of a war on two fronts. Kaiser Wilhelm II made no attempt to renew this alliance when it lapsed in 1890. The Kaiser's political advisers knew that Austrian and Russian interests and ambitions in the Balkans were irreconcilable, and they thought Bismarck's secret agreement with Russia might disrupt the Dual Alliance between Austria and Germany. The new German capitalists and industrialists were not pleased by the growing industrial development in Russia to which the tsar's government gave encouragement by tariffs for "infant industries." As a maneuver in this Russian-German economic dispute, the Berlin money markets were temporarily closed to Russian loans. The French were not slow in taking advantage of this situation to find a means of escaping from the isolation which Bismarck's foreign policy had imposed upon them. In 1894 France and Russia had entered a military alliance, four years after Kaiser Wilhelm II had dismissed Bismarck!

Russia otherwise occupied.—This diplomatic reversal soon changed the entire complexion of power relationships in Europe and had worldwide implications of great significance in the Near East, as in the Far East. Temporarily frustrated in her Balkan policy by the other Great Powers at Berlin in 1878 and during the succeeding decade, Russia turned her attention to the Far East, and by 1892 had begun the construction of the Siberian railroad. This eastward drive of Russia was contemporaneous with Japanese expansion to the west in Korea and China.

Japan in 1853 and 1854 had her doors forced open and was obliged to abandon her century-old policy of complete isolation at the point of naval guns on American warships under Commodore Perry. To save themselves from intervention and exploitation by the western world, the Japanese ruling classes rapidly learned western techniques and adopted the western economic system. The results were surprising to the diplomats, quite unnecessarily so, it would seem. Forty years after the "opening of Japan," the same complex forces which were driving the western world along the bloody but exciting and profit-making road of imperialism compelled the Japanese to do likewise. With respect to Japan, the forces making for expansion were even more imperative than those operating in Europe and the United States. The Japanese had to import most of the essential raw products for modern industry, food for factory workers, and fuel. To do so, world markets had to be secured for Japanese goods. Shortly thereafter, Japanese accumulations of capital required foreign fields for investment. In 1894 Japan began her first imperialistic war against China. This was only fifty-two years after England had ended successfully her Opium War to open up China and had obtained possession of Hong Kong.

This Japanese victory over the Chinese made Japan a dangerous competitor of Russia in Korea and Manchuria. Consequently, Russian preoccupation with the Far East from the early 1890's until after the Russian-Japanese War of 1904–5 precluded pursuit by the tsar's government of an adventurous policy in eastern Asia Minor over the Armenian question.

France and Britain hesitate to intervene.—When France's Russian ally became embroiled with Japan in the Far East, those shaping French policy in the Near East had to take into consideration their ally's preoccupation in the Far East. With the rapid development of German interests in the Ottoman Empire, France had two formidable competitors there—England and Germany. Matters reached a crisis in Franco-British relations in 1898 over the control of the Sudan when General Kitchener found Captain J. B. Marchand at Fashoda and arbitrarily ordered him to haul down the French flag. For a time, it was touch and go as to whether France and England would go to war. Not until a secret deal was arranged with regard to the French in Morocco and the British in Egypt and after the creation in 1904 of the Anglo-French entente known at the *Entente Cordiale* did France begin to regain greater freedom of action in international affairs. The increasing expansion of German economic interests in Asia Minor made it dangerous for France to adopt openly a policy unfriendly to the Turkish government. French leaders realized that the collapse and partition of Turkey might result in Germany obtaining part of Asia Minor and thus naval bases in the Mediterranean. Consequently, France followed a cautious policy in dealing with Abdul Hamid.

Not until *the Alliance System* had fully crystallized and when the division in Europe had led to war in 1914, were the allies—England, France and Russia—able to agree upon the partition of the Ottoman Empire. Although Abdul Hamid was unable to forestall intervention in Crete, Macedonia, Thrace, and later in Albania before World War I, he retained a free hand in the Asiatic provinces for fifteen years.

CHAPTER IX

Trouble in Crete and the Balkans

In all parts of his empire, Abdul Hamid had inherited problems with deep historical roots for the causes of which he in no way was responsible but for which he did not find a solution or even a satisfactory working compromise.

❁ THE CRETAN QUESTION [1]

The Cretan situation confronted him from the beginning of his reign in 1877–78 with repeated insurrections and European intervention. There were disorders and uprisings in the late 1880's, a revolution from 1894 to 1897 resulting in the occupation of Crete by the European Powers during the Graeco-Turkish War, and a nationalist uprising in 1905, which eventually culminated in the union of Crete with Greece. The affairs of the island of Crete were entangled with the politics of Greece, with the Greek irredenta movement in other islands of the Aegean and in Asia Minor, and with Graeco-Turkish relations. Because of its strategic position and because the question of what should be done about Crete was tied up with the policy of the maintenance of the political integrity of the Ottoman Empire, Cretan matters were considered to be of concern to the Concert of European Powers.

Historical background.—Nearly two thousand years B.C., when Crete was the principal center of Minoan civilization, its geographical position in relation to shipping routes east and west in the Mediterranean and north and south in the Aegean was one of political and economic importance. Throughout history, it has remained strategically significant, even though at times its importance has been slight. The German invasion and conquest of Crete from the air in 1941 demonstrated in our own times the continuing value of the island to those who gain control of it. In the realm of power politics, whether it was ten, a hundred, a thousand, or four thousand years ago, Crete was one of the pawns of those who sought to control the Near East.

Differences in religion and mores perpetuated by rival priesthoods since 823, when the island was conquered by the Arabs, have bedeviled relations between the Cretans themselves and between Cretans and outsiders. As early as 64 A.D., the Cretans were converted from paganism to Christianity. When the Moslem Arabs took Crete from the Byzantine rulers toward the end of the first quarter of the ninth century, its inhabitants, who were then members of the Eastern, or Orthodox Church, became converted to Islam. More than a century later, in 961, the Byzantines under Nicephorus Phocas, with his Kievan Varangian mercenaries, reconquered the island which they ruled until the impecunious Frankish crusading nobles at the suggestion of their Venetian creditors captured Constantinople and allocated various parts of the Byzantine Empire as feudal principalities to its western looters. Crete was assigned to the Italian Marquis de Montferrat, who, in 1204, promptly disposed of it to Venice for territories in the Balkans with sufficient income to compensate him for the loss of an island which would have necessitated his acquiring at great expense a navy for its defence.

The Cretans underwent from the first century A.D. to the Turkish conquest in the seventeenth century, a variety of religious experiences which left an indelible imprint on their history. From the communal and somewhat socialistic Christian ecclesia of the first century, they gradually became communicants of the sophisticated Orthodox Church, with its icons, incense, music, and elaborate ritual, which the Moslems looked on as a form of paganism. In the ninth and tenth centuries for a period of more than a hundred and twenty-five years, the Cretans remained faithful followers of Mohammed, to become again for a stretch of nearly two hundred and fifty years good Greek Orthodox Christians. At the beginning of the thirteenth century, the Venetians brought with them to the island, the Latin Church and its ubiquitous clergy. The Orthodox Cretans did not, however, embrace Catholicism with the same degree of willingness with which they had accepted Islam.

The Republic of Venice also brought thousands of Italian colonists as agrarian settlers to assist the Venetian officials in holding in check their unruly Cretan subjects. The Italian colonists, however, were no more enthusiastic about their Venetian feudal nobles than were the native Cretans. Greek Orthodoxy as well as the Greek language survived the Venetian occupation of more than four hundred and fifty years. When in 1669 the Venetians ceded Crete to the Turks, the Cretans were Greek-speaking Christians and for the most part Greek Orthodox.

As in the case of the Balkan Greeks and Slavs, numerous members of the Greek Cretan upper-class accepted Islam and enjoyed the numerous advantages which were the rights of all Moslems in the Ottoman Empire. The Turkish conquest of Crete resulted in the development of a Greek-speaking Cretan Moslem exploiting class of landowners, officials, and ulemas, and the exploited Greek-speaking Cretan Christians, merchants, peasants, craftsmen, and shepherds.

Interest of the European Powers in Cretan affairs.—By the opening years of the nineteenth century, Crete became of interest to the European imperialists. In 1806, when Napoleon was toying with the idea of partitioning the Ottoman Empire between Austria, France, and Russia, he earmarked Crete for France. Nothing came of these plans; nevertheless, the successive revolts in Crete, from those in the 1820's to the revolution of 1905, increasingly concerned all the Great Powers. In 1853, on the eve of the Crimean War and only three years before a long and serious uprising in Crete, Tsar Nicholas I informally proposed to the British ambassador at St. Petersburg that England take over Crete, as well as Egypt, to protect British imperial routes to India through the eastern Mediterranean and across the Asiatic Near East.

Cretans react to the Greek revolution.—When the Greek revolution broke out on the mainland in 1821, the population of Crete was approximately 290,000, of whom 160,000 were Moslems and 130,000 were Christians; the overwhelming majority of these were Greek-speaking Cretans. The Moslem Cretan beys, with their Janissaries, had practically nullified the power of the Turkish vali (governor) and ruled in a ruthless and arbitrary manner over the Christian Cretans. The Hellenic revival among the Balkan Greeks and their struggle against the Turks stirred the Christian Cretans to rise against their overlords. It was during this period of anarchy in Crete between 1821 and 1829, which was accompanied by violence and insurrection, that Sultan Mahmoud II destroyed the Janissaries at Constantinople. Osman Pasha, the Turkish vali of Crete, in ridding the island of the local Janissaries, employed tactics similar to those used by Mohammed Ali against the Mamelukes in Egypt. He invited the leading Cretan Moslem beys to a consultation and then had them set upon by his Albanian troops and by Cretan Christians whom he had armed for this purpose.

Relations between Christian and Moslem Cretans were not significantly bettered by this action of the vali, but he did re-establish order! During this period, Egyptian naval forces, which were aiding Sultan Mahmoud in his attempts to crush the Greek Revolution in southern and central

Greece, anchored in the Cretan harbor of Suda Bay. Egyptian troops were landed and a firman of the sultan made Crete for all practical purposes part of the pashalik of Egypt. In 1832, Crete was officially allotted to Mohammed Ali. As in Syria, he put Christians on a basis of equality under the law with Moslems, which did not at all please the Cretan Moslems. He also introduced his state monopolies and taxation system, which did not please Cretan merchants, craftsmen, and peasants. Consequently, there was much unrest in Crete by 1840, when Mohammed Ali was forced to relinquish his control of the island to the sultan.

Although discontented with Egyptian rule, the Christian Cretans had no desire to exchange it for that of the Turks. Greek irredentism and Pan-Hellenism won a warm response from many of the Christian Cretans who ardently sought annexation to Greece. Actually, Athens, the capital of the recently created Greek kingdom, had become a center of Greek irredentism which menaced the Ottoman Empire and the Turks in Macedonia, in the Aegean Islands, and even to some extent in western Anatolia. Uprisings in Crete, whatever might be their nature and cause, received the sympathy and support of Greeks in Egypt, in the Islands, in Asia Minor, in the Balkans, and, of course, in Greece itself. In the same way that Italian and Yugoslav irredentism centering in Rome and Belgrade became a constant irritation and potential menace to the Austrian-Hungarian Dual Monarchy, so Pan-Hellenism and Greek irredentism emanating from Athens angered and frightened the Turks. Many of the nineteenth century romantic liberals seemingly did not grasp the fact that a privileged ruling class, whether the Austrian-Magyar aristocrats or the Moslem Turkish bureaucrats, military men, and ulemas would not surrender to others without a struggle, violent if necessary, those rights and special privileges which were the very basis of their wealth and power. The question was wider and deeper than programs of reforms and administrative efficiency. Nationalism was gnawing at the roots of Ottoman imperialism in the nineteenth as it also was beginning to do in the Asiatic empires of England, France, and Holland with amazing results by the middle of the twentieth century.

Uncertainty about the future.—Throughout the nineteenth century, there was no agreement among the Powers nor among the Cretans, even Cretan Christians, regarding the future of Crete. Generally speaking, Russian policy favored autonomy; French policy, which was far from being constant, wanted annexation to Greece; while the British, except during the 1880's, when English agents in Crete advocated a British protectorate, held to the principle of the maintenance of the political and territorial integrity of the Ottomans and insisted upon the retention of Turkish sovereignty over Crete. The Cretan Christians were divided into two parties, the *Conservatives* who favored autonomy under the sultan, and the *Liberals* who demanded annexation to Greece.

While there is no doubt that the economic and social struggle for power between the Cretan landed aristocracy and the Christian Cretans was one of the basic factors in the numerous insurrections, it is clear that Greek nationalism encouraged by the Greek government and the conviction by the Cretan nationalists that the European Powers could be prevailed upon to intervene on their behalf had much to do with the continuing revolutionary movement in Crete.

During the ascendency of the Young Turk reformers of the Tanzimat period from 1841 to 1876, the Turkish liberals in the Ottoman government seem to have sincerely desired to effect reforms in Crete which would allay the grievances of the Christian Cretans. As elsewhere, however, in Turkey the desire to bring about liberal reforms frequently did not conform with the will to do so, which had to operate through the officials and officers of a bureaucracy who neither favored nor understood the ideas of liberalism. Furthermore, the Cretan insurrectionists were more deeply concerned about nationalism than about liberalism. How incompatible these two may become was not so evident in the nineteenth century as it became in the twentieth with the rise of fascism. Nationalism and self-determination were fundamental tenets of liberalism of the last century. Pan-Hellenism swept across the ranks of the liberals in the West like a storm, and any manifestation of Greek patriotism would fan the ardor of European liberals.

The discontent of Cretan Christians under the unsatisfactory Turkish vali, who failed to carry out the Hatti Humayun of 1856, broke out in open insurrection between 1856 and 1858. The insurrectionists thought that the Great Powers, after imposing their will upon Russia at the Congress of Paris following the Crimean War, would intervene in Crete to see that the Tanzimat reforms were carried out by the Turkish government. The local situation was aggravated by the reconversion to Christianity, which was bitterly resented by Turks and Moslems, of many Cretans who were Moslems only nominally. The uprising was brought to an end in 1858 with the issuance of a firman by the sultan making concessions to the demands of the insurgents.

Insurrections.—Gradually, the Christian Cretans were undermining the political and economic position of the Moslem Cretans. It was to be expected that the latter would not accept this loss of power and position without using what means they had at their disposition to prevent it.

The Turkish government and the Turkish officials were the only external force to which they could turn for support. Quite naturally, the Turkish military and civil officials tended to sympathize with the Cretan Moslem aristocracy in its struggle with the Cretan Christian traders, money-lenders, workers, and peasants. The degree to which firmans granting reforms were implemented depended upon the Turkish officials. The discrepancy between promises and actions was in part the cause of that discontent which, fostered by Pan-Hellenic nationalism and with the hope of foreign assistance, resulted in insurrection. Uprisings beginning in 1866 terminated in new concessions and another firman by 1868. The Balkan revolutions, defeat of Turkey by Russia in 1877–78, and the Treaty of Berlin deeply stirred the hopes of the Cretans and were stimuli for another insurrection ending in still further concessions embodied in the Convention of Halepa of 1878, which modified the Organic Law of 1868 that had made the position of the Christians in Crete more favorable than in any of the other provinces of the Ottoman Empire.

Notwithstanding these concessions to the Christian Cretans, Abdul Hamid was soon troubled again by them. Unrest continued in Crete throughout the 1880's, stimulated by Greek acquisition of Thessaly in 1881 and by Bulgarian annexation of eastern Rumelia in 1885. In retaliation for an insurrection in 1889 the sultan took away some of the rights granted by the Convention of Halepa. The repressive measures of the Turkish vali, the conflicts between Christians and Moslem Cretans, the latter aided by Turkish soldiery, together with the news that the Powers at last were planning intervention in Asia Minor on behalf of the Armenians, brought about another insurrection lasting from 1894 to 1896. Many Christian noncombatants evacuated to Greece aroused the Greek people. A Greek expeditionary force accompanied by units of the Greek navy sailed from Piraeus for Crete with orders from King George of Greece to drive out the Turks.

Intervention by the Great Powers.—This action by the Greek government in 1897 brought about intervention by three of the Great Powers. British, French, and Russian fleets anchored in Cretan harbors but did not bring an end to the Cretan conflicts. The Greek government under pressure from its excited citizens went to war with Turkey in April 1897, but soon suffered serious defeats at the hands of a Turkish army, which had been trained and modernized by German officers. If it had not been for European interference between Greece and Turkey, the Turks would have imposed a harsh treaty on the Greeks who had so ill advisedly gone to war against a superior military power. The war left the Cretan question still unsettled.

The killing of a handful of British soldiers by Turkish forces in Crete led to swift action by the Powers. Abdul Hamid was ordered to withdraw immediately all Turkish troops and civil officials from the island. Having by this act assumed responsibility for Crete, the Powers found considerable difficulty in reaching an agreement about its future government. A provisional regime was set up in August 1898, until a definitive settlement could be decided upon. In November, the post of high commissioner was offered to Prince George of Greece. Crete became an autonomous principality governed by the son of the King of Greece, but remained under the nominal suzerainty of the sultan. As a leader of the Cretan Liberal Party and the outstanding protagonist of annexation to Greece, a young man named Eleutherios Venizelos, who later played a commanding role in the alliance of the Balkan States against Turkey in 1912 and brought Greece into World War I on the side of the Allies, obtained his political, military, and diplomatic education in the rough and tumble politics of Crete.

For all practical purposes, Abdul Hamid had lost another of his provinces, his efforts to crush revolution and to prevent European intervention had failed. With the exception of his victory over the Greek army, he was not much more fortunate in the Balkans, where the Bulgarians had regained part of what they had lost by the revision of the Treaty of San Stefano and where trouble was brewing in Albania and Macedonia.

THE TURBULENT BALKANS

The European part of the Ottoman Empire in 1878 consisted of the following: the provinces of Bosnia and Herzegovina, which under the terms of the Treaty of Berlin were occupied and administered by Austria-Hungary, the autonomous principality of Bulgaria, the autonomous province of Eastern Rumelia under Turkish suzerainty, and an extensive area stretching from the Black and Marmora seas to the Adriatic, known as Rumelia. Rumelia was subdivided into regions: Kossovo in the northwest, Albania on the Adriatic, Epirus and Thessaly on the northern frontier of Greece, Macedonia, lying south of Kossovo and east of Albania with the two important river valleys of the Vardar and the Struma and the port of Salonika, and finally Thrace, with its rolling plains leading to Constantinople, the Straits, and the Black Sea.

Balkan unrest and rival European imperialisms.—This entire area was seething with political and social unrest, intensified by religious and nationalistic rivalries, and by international imperialistic intrigues. The mixed population of European Turkey made any satisfactory territorial partition of it unacceptable to the various Balkan national groups. The strategic importance of it rendered any division of it unacceptable to the European Powers, each of which had plans for securing control over parts of it.

A glance at the varied interests of the Great Powers in European Turkey throws some light on the complexity of problems which confronted Abdul Hamid in the administration of his European territories. Austria-Hungary with a large Yugoslavian minority, augmented by the occupation of Bosnia-Herzegovina in 1878 (in 1908 annexed by the Habsburgs) feared the influence of Serbian nationalism on its Slavic subjects and opposed Serbia's territorial expansion in the Balkans toward the Adriatic and Aegean seas. Furthermore, Russia's Pan-Slavic policy and support of Serbian nationalism appeared to the Dual Monarchy as an added menace to Habsburg interests. Germany, Austria's ally, with her expanding interests in the Near East opposed territorial changes in the Balkans which might threaten her main line of communications with Constantinople. The construction of the Balkan railways and the soon to be projected Berlin to Bagdad railroad greatly increased German interests in the Balkans. Italy, which became a member of the Triple Alliance of Germany, Austria-Hungary, and Italy in 1882, likewise developed imperialistic ambitions in the Turkish Balkan possessions. The Italian rulers looked upon Albania as a possible future protectorate, and they, too, dreamed of securing control of Salonika. Russia looked upon Serbian expansion as a means of blocking Austrian expansion in the Balkans and of checking the German drive to the Near East. To Russia, Bulgaria and Eastern Rumelia appeared like stepping stones to the plains of Thrace and thence to Constantinople. France and England had no direct strategic interest in the Turkish Balkans, but both favored the maintenance of the territorial integrity of the Ottoman Empire, France largely because of her heavy investments there, and England because she was unwilling to tolerate the Russians' securing free access to the Mediterranean.

Greek, Serbian and Bulgarian irredentisms.—Greece, Serbia, and Bulgaria all had irredentist ambitions with respect to the Turkish Balkans. The population of Epirus and Thessaly was for the most part Greek; there were some Greeks and Greek Orthodox Albanians in southern Albania. Greeks were scattered through southern Macedonia and in Thrace. A considerable portion of the population of Kossovo was Serbian and many Serbs were scattered throughout northern and central Macedonia. Serbia, as a land-locked country, sought an outlet to the sea, definitely so on the Adriatic and hopefully so at Salonika. Furthermore, the Serbians looked upon the Austrian-occupied Turkish provinces of Bosnia and Herzegovina as Serbian irredenta. The Bulgarians in the principality sought union with those in Eastern Rumelia, and this they achieved a few years after the Congress of Berlin. Thrace had a considerable Bulgarian population and Bulgarians were scattered throughout much of Macedonia; consequently, both of these areas were Bulgarian irredenta. To add further to this complex population situation, there were scattered throughout the European portion of the Ottoman Empire in 1878 a very considerable Moslem population who were Turks, or considered themselves as Turks.

Abdul Hamid's dilemma.—The problem, which more than any other threatened Ottoman sovereignty, concerned the Balkan tinderbox. Throughout the period of his personal rule, from 1878 to the Young Turk revolution of 1908, during thirty years, Abdul Hamid conserved the major part of his European possessions. His losses indeed were trifling. He was obliged to concede Thessaly to Greece in 1881; however, he would have regained part of it in the Graeco-Turkish War of 1897 with his German-trained troops had it not been for the intervention of the Great Powers who came to the rescue of Greece. Although he lost the autonomous province of Eastern Rumelia, which was annexed to the principality of Bulgaria in 1885, this autonomous principality was still under the sovereignty of the sultan.

This success in holding his European Balkan possessions was not so much due to skillful statesmanship and diplomacy of Abdul Hamid as to the rivalry of the Great Powers and the antagonism between the Greeks, the Serbs, and the Bulgarians. In fact, his failure to effect reforms and to establish a just and efficient administration in the various parts of Rumelia resulted in increasing European intervention and prepared the way for the loss of most of European Turkey between 1908 and 1913.

THE MACEDONIAN PROBLEM

Throughout history the Balkan Peninsula has been a battleground for all those who sought to gain control of so strategic an area. The Ottoman sultans found it to be an unending problem. In modern times since the the Balkan wars of 1912 and 1913 down to the present it has been a focal spot of the rivalries of the great world Powers. From 1914 to 1918 the Balkans became one of the important strategic areas where the Allies and the Central Powers battled for control. Between World Wars I and II, Macedonians carried on active propaganda against the peace settlement, as the Bulgars also did for its revision. In World War

II, a three-cornered struggle for control of the Balkans between the Axis Powers, Great Britain with her ally Greece, and neutral Russia, eventually led to the German invasion of the Soviet Union. Germany's strategic plans called for an assault on the Near Eastern life lines of the British Empire, with Greece and Crete as two of the bases for the eastward advance of the Axis Powers. In 1941 the German military leaders realized that it would be necessary to eliminate the 2,000-mile flank from the Baltic almost to the Aegean, along which were strung the Russian armies, before the Balkans could be used for further extension of German power eastward. Once more the geographic importance of the Balkans in the world struggle for power was demonstrated. Again, shortly after World War II, this area developed into a "hot spot" in the "cold war" between the United States and Soviet Russia. Washington, instead of Vienna, Berlin, Rome, Paris, and London, became the western center of Balkan diplomacy and intrigue.

The historical heritage.—In the very heart of the Balkans lies Macedonia. To a very large degree, its geographic and topographic features have determined the history of its varied peoples in modern as in ancient times. From north to south, Macedonia is crossed by three rivers whose headwaters lie in the rugged mountainous watershed between these river valleys and the Danube and between the Aegean and Black Sea. The most important of these is the Vardar River, whose gentle valley and broad plains provide an easy route from Salonika, near its mouth on the Aegean, through western Macedonia to the valley of the Danube. By this route Serbia and the countries of central Europe have ready access to Macedonia, which is also open to invasion from the lower valley of the Danube and from Thrace.

Serbs, Greeks, and Bulgarians have in past centuries ruled over much of Macedonia. All three peoples during the last hundred years have laid claims to parts of it. Although its people are varied in race, language, religion, and nationality, the greater number are by language and culture Bulgars. In modern times, those who call themselves Bulgars are of a mixed race of people.

Originally, the Bulgars were Mongoloid nomads from Asia. A segment of the Bulgar tribes, separated from the other Bulgars who occupied the middle Volga, were swept south of the Danube by the great migrations set in motion by the Huns in the fourth century. There in the lower Danube Valley their descendants have remained from then till now. The Huns set in motion not only Bulgar and Teutonic tribes but great bodies of Slavic tribes. Of these, those now called Yugoslavs and Macedonian Bulgars were driven into the Balkans. The Asiatic Bulgars in the lower Danube and most of the Slavs in the Balkans were Christianized by the Eastern or Orthodox Church. The famous missionaries Cyril and Methodius translated the Greek Bible and prayers into Bulgarian, a Slavic language, different from but resembling closely the Serbian language. The Mongoloid Bulgars lost their Asiatic language and primitive religion. They adopted a Slavic language and accepted Christianity in 864. Their conquest of a large part of the Balkans and practically all of Macedonia resulted in their language and Christian culture being absorbed by most of the Slavs in Macedonia, who came thus to be called Bulgars.

Before the Turkish conquest of the Balkans, there had been long struggles between the Bulgars and the Byzantine Greeks. The first Bulgar state was organized in the last quarter of the seventh century. In the ninth century, following their conversion to Christianity, the Bulgars extended their power over a large area in the Balkans at the expense of the Byzantine Empire. They submitted to Byzantine rule in the eleventh century after defeat by both Byzantine and Kievan forces. In the twelfth and thirteenth centuries the Bulgars re-established a short-lived empire. Their rule, despite Byzantine, Greek, and later Serbian conquest, left the imprint of Bulgarian language and culture on many of the Slavs of Macedonia.

The Ottoman conquests in the fourteenth and fifteenth centuries created new relationships among the Balkan peoples. The Turkish rulers distinguished between their non-Moslem subjects on the basis of religion and not of nationality or national culture. Most of the Christians of the Balkans were of the Orthodox Church. Consequently, when Mohammed II, the conqueror of Constantinople, officially organized his subjects into millets (nations) the Greek patriarch of Constantinople became the ecclesiastical and civil head of the Orthodox in the Balkans.

Bulgarian culture suffered a serious decline under the millet system because all education for Christian Bulgarians was under the Orthodox clergy control by the Greek prelates. The Bulgarians under the double yoke of Turks and Phanariote Greeks were reduced to a low cultural level. If it had not been for the fact that the Macedonian peasants clung to the Bulgarian language, Bulgarian culture might have perished. Two factors led to the revival of Bulgarian culture and nationalism. The birth of neo-Hellenism among the Greeks in the eighteenth and the rise of Greek nationalism in the nineteenth century sharply differentiated the Bulgarian-speaking Macedonians from Greek Macedonians. In addition, under the Tanzimat reforms the Bulgars were granted the right to organize their own church and to choose their own clergy. This right first granted in 1839 and reaffirmed in 1856 made it possible for the Bulgars in Macedonia to oppose the Greek clergy. The cultural renaissance, which then began, became closely affiliated with the growth of Bulgarian nationalism.

Macedonia a battleground of rival Balkan nationalisms.—Macedonia after 1878 became a battleground of the emerging Balkan peoples. Rivalry between them was accentuated by the conviction that the Turks would eventually be driven out. The Macedonian Bulgars were in a revolutionary mood because of the onerous Turkish administration under Abdul Hamid, and because they were angry and disheartened by the scrapping of the Treaty of San Stefano. Unable to unite with Bulgaria, they demanded autonomy. The Greeks and Serbs were as greatly opposed to this as were the Turks, nor were the Powers in favor of it.

On the union of the Principality of Bulgaria and the autonomous province of Eastern Rumelia in 1885, tension mounted in Macedonia and throughout the Balkans. Only seven years after the Congress of Berlin the untenable territorial settlement in the Balkans, which ran counter to national aspirations and had been forced upon the Powers by Austria-Hungary and England in order to contain Russia, proved abortive. Flouting the wishes of Russia, which in 1885 was opposed to the greater Bulgaria she had proposed in 1878, the people of Eastern Rumelia revolted and invited the Prince of Bulgaria to rule over them. He marched his troops across the boundaries of the autonomous province and proclaimed its union with Bulgaria. Abdul Hamid did not dare risk war with any of the Powers. Russia would not have tolerated a Turkish invasion of Bulgaria; England had reversed her position and now looked with favor on the union; Austria was agreeable to it, and the other Powers stood aside. Only Serbia challenged this Bulgarian infringement of the terms of the Treaty of Berlin. The Serbs, claiming this change in the *status quo* in the Balkans was a menace to the security of Serbia, declared war on Bulgaria. The Serbian armies were defeated quickly by the Bulgarian forces, which then began an invasion of Serbia. The Bulgars, however, felt obliged to promptly make peace when Austria-Hungary interfered.

The Macedonian question was left unsettled and its problems greatly augmented. All parties knew that a successful insurrection in Macedonia against the Turks, unless it brought outside intervention, would result in the union of Macedonia and Bulgaria. This was an intolerable thought to Abdul Hamid and just as unacceptable to the Greeks and the

Serbs. Nor did either Austria or Germany look with favor on the further expansion of Bulgaria in Macedonia. Austrians did not want the Vardar Valley route to Salonika taken over by the Bulgars and the Germans did not want a larger Bulgaria to control the Balkan route to Constantinople and the only route to the Asiatic Near East, which the Germans might hope to control.

The question as to which nationality predominated in Macedonia was and remains a much disputed one.[2] It is complicated by unreliable data and by interpretations of what constitutes nationality in Macedonia. Bulgarian scholars and writers,[3] who claim the Macedonian population is largely Bulgar, define as Macedonian Bulgars those whose language is Bulgar and who consider themselves Bulgar whether they be Catholic, Protestant, Bulgarian Orthodox, Greek Orthodox, or Moslems. The Greeks claim as Hellenes all those Macedonians who are Orthodox as well as those who recognize the Phaniariote patriarch at Constantinople. The Serbs, who, before 1878, looked upon the Macedonian Slavs as Bulgars, now consider them to be Yugoslavs who lost their Serbian culture and language because of former Bulgarian domination.

Religious and political agitation grew increasingly in Macedonia after 1885. Active propaganda was carried on by Serbian and Greek agents, while the Macedonian Bulgars plotted revolution. Inter-Christian violence often took place, as well as violence between Turks and Macedonia Bulgars. The half-hearted attempts to introduce promised reforms did not quiet the situation. Abdul Hamid knew no effective way except ruthlessness to deal with the problem. This, he knew, would sooner or later bring European intervention. He cunningly played off the Balkan states one against the other and used diplomacy with the European Powers, hoping their rivalries and interests would prevent effective action by them. This policy had its limits, and the increasing agitation among the Liberals of Europe for intervention led in 1903 to European agreement to police Macedonia.

Macedonian reforms.—No serious effort was made by the Ottoman government to introduce reforms in European Turkey in accordance with the stipulations of the Treaty of Berlin. An international commission set up to draft reforms based on the organic law of Crete of 1868 drew up in the summer of 1880 what was in the nature of a basic charter for Balkan provinces, known as "the Law of the Vilayets of European Turkey." After considerable delay, Abdul Hamid refused his sanction to it. For a variety of reasons concerning principally their own interests, the Great Powers accepted the sultan's decision without taking any action. Left to its own devices, the Ottoman government did nothing to alleviate the conditions in Macedonia. Corrupt and rapacious administrators, an onerous taxation system, venal judges, arbitrary requisitions, poorly paid soldiers who turned to pillage and brigandage as a means of living—all these added to the centuries-old exploitation of a Christian peasantry by Moslem feudal landowners and to the recently fostered antagonism between Serbs, Greeks, and Bulgars created an intolerable situation in Macedonia.

Lawless rebels, called komitajis, infested Macedonia. The hand of every man was against his neighbor: Moslem village against Christian village; Greek against Bulgarian; Bulgarian against Serb. Macedonia became a festering sore, not only in the body politic of Turkey, but in Europe as a whole. The Liberals of Europe, already aroused by the massacres of the Armenians in Asiatic Turkey, began agitation for reform in European Turkey. Abdul Hamid resorted in 1896 to his dubious but often temporarily successful diplomacy of issuing an imperial decree for reforms in European Turkey which he did not have the capacity, and probably lacked the will, to carry out.

By an agreement between Austria-Hungary and Russia the sultan was spared for seven years more from any impelling external necessity to do anything. Neither of these two Powers was ready for any territorial or political changes in the Balkans at this time. Austria's ally, Germany, wanted no interference in Turkish affairs inimical to the Turks; consequently, the government of the Dual Monarchy could not expect any support from Berlin. Russia was not anxious to bring her ally, France, into the Balkan affair lest the French give support to Britain. In order to sidetrack action by any of the other Great Powers, Austria and Russia signed the Act of 1897 by which they undertook, reciprocally, to allow no territorial changes in the Balkans. This agreement had a double-barreled action: it assured the sultan that he need not fear European intervention, and it gave notice to the Macedonian Christians that they could not expect help from the Great Powers. As the Bulgarian writer, P. D. Draganof well expresses it, the "agreement of 1897 was mischievous." [4]

Every aspect of the situation continued to grow worse. Before the end of 1902, it was clear that a crisis would soon be reached. The European governments were warned in that year by their Balkan agents that an uprising was impending. The chancellories of Europe were agog with proposals for action by the Powers. Alerted by his innumerable agents, Abdul Hamid before the end of the year issued "Instructions Concerning the Vilayets of European Turkey," created two commissions to deal with the situation, and appointed Hilmi Pasha Inspector General of the three Macedonian vilayets. Early in February 1903, Austria-Hungary and Russia sent to the Porte a joint program of reforms worked out at Vienna in December. Events, however, were moving faster than diplomacy. Insurrection of the Macedonian Bulgars had begun and violence was increasing. Europe was shocked by the outrages at Salonika and demands for intervention mounted.

In an attempt to forestall general intervention, the Austrians and Russians, after a meeting at Murzsteg of Emperor Francis Joseph and Emperor Nicholas II in the autumn of 1903, drafted the Murzsteg Reform Program which was sent to the Porte in October and reluctantly accepted by Abdul Hamid. Great Britain, her hands now free following the successful conclusion of the Boer War, began to take an active part in the Macedonian affair and brought about modifications of the Murzsteg plan. Abdul Hamid found himself obliged to permit and to tolerate European intervention in territories not far distant from his capital.

An Austrian and a Russian Civil Adviser were attached to the staff of Inspector General Hilmi Pasha. A new gendarmerie was organized by the Ottoman government and placed under an Italian general, who had attached to his headquarters an Austrian, an Italian, a Russian, a French, a British, and a German officer. Foreign officers and a small number of soldiers were attached to the Turkish gendarmerie of Macedonia; Austrians in the north, Italians in the west along the Albanian border, Russians in the central part, French and British in the eastern portions. The Germans discreetly refrained from sending any troops. Financial reforms were to be carried out by four foreign financial advisers representing Britain, France, Germany, and Italy.

Macedonians were burdened with more than 4,000 of the new gendarmes in addition to Turkish military forces varying from 50,000 to 80,000, to local municipal police and the sultan's imperial secret police. All to no purpose. The Murzsteg reforms, which proposed a repartition of administrative districts and a more regular grouping of the various races, envenomed the relations between the Greeks, the Serbs, and the Bulgars within and outside of Macedonia. The Turkish government effectively avoided carrying out the proposed reforms. As a British member of Parliament and correspondent of the London *Morning Post* wrote in 1908: "The reforms are a farce." [5]

Abdul Hamid again had succeeded in avoiding basic changes in his empire and had been skillful enough to nullify European plans for reform largely due to the rivalry and competition of the European Powers in their worldwide struggle for imperial advantage. He could not, however, escape the nemesis which was taking final shape among the Turkish officers in the Macedonian city of Salonika and would soon overtake him and his whole ancient regime in the Turkish Revolution of 1908 and 1909.

CHAPTER X

Abdul Hamid and Zionism

۞ THE OTTOMANS AND THE JEWS

Among the Ottoman subjects of Abdul Hamid were some quarter of a million Jews, slightly over half of whom were scattered in Asiatic and the balance in European Turkey. The Ottoman Jews had been no source of trouble to the Turkish government. No national movement similar to those of the Balkan Christians and the Armenians had deepened the gulf of sectarian differences and awakened bitter antagonisms between Jews and Turks. The millet system provided a reasonably satisfactory *modus vivendi* between Moslem and Jew. In fact, the Islamic world during the Middle Ages and the Ottoman Empire after 1453 had been places of refuge for the Jews of Europe persecuted by fanatical Christians. Many of the Jews expelled from Spain in 1492 by Ferdinand and Isabella fled to Turkey.

At the height of its power the Ottoman Empire probably had a much larger Jewish population than it did during the time of Abdul Hamid II. In 1881 Rumania had an estimated Jewish population of 265,000, and it is probable that the two provinces of Moldavia and Wallachia when they were still under Ottoman rule had had a considerable Jewish population. There were sizable Jewish groups in Egypt and North Africa.

Abdul Hamid's difficulties in dealing with Jews grew out of foreign complications. Three categories of Jews raised problems for the Ottoman government: Jews who were subjects of foreign countries but who were or became residents in the Ottoman Empire, claiming privileges under the capitulations, Jews who came to Palestine as colonists and retained relationships with their country of origin, and Jews who were foreigners residing outside of the Ottoman Empire but who were passionately interested in Palestine because they had become Zionists.

Abdul Hamid seems to have distinguished clearly between Ottoman Jews and Zionists. When the founder of political Zionism, Theodor Herzl, tried to obtain from the sultan the right of Jews to colonize Palestine, Abdul Hamid came to the conclusion that Zionist colonies there would create still another nationalist minority seeking independence via the road of autonomy and home rule and be likely to appeal to foreign Christian nations for aid in the achievement of its aims.

❀ THE HISTORICAL BACKGROUND

The ferment in world Jewry during the nineteenth century although it had no significant immediate effect upon the Near East became a very highly important factor in the twentieth century. The rapid spread of Jewish political nationalism in the twentieth century with its influence upon international affairs is one of the amazing phenomena of our contemporary world. A combination of factors operating within and upon the Jews of Europe and those European Jews who had migrated overseas, culminated in the creation in Palestine in 1948 of the Jewish state of Israel.

The Jews of Christian Europe had during the Middle Ages sunk to a cultural level far below that of the Roman Empire and of the Arab Caliphate. Like some extraneous and irritating substance in an oyster shell, European Jewry in the matrix of the still barbarous world of medieval Christendom had been enclosed within the ghettoes of the European towns. Complete isolation, however, was not possible, and constant irritation resulting from contact between the indigenous majority and the alien minority repeatedly resulted in cruel persecution. The cultural and religious life of European Jewry tended to stagnate. Education declined, many of the rabbinate were poorly trained, ritual had become stereotyped and sterile, the masses were sunk in ignorance. Bigotry and fanaticism were as prevalent among the Jewish rabbinate as among the Christian clergy. Although in the seventeenth century individual Jews, like Baruch Spinoza, shook off the medieval obscurantism of the clergy, as did an increasing number of Christians, the European Jews as a whole were deeply embedded in the dark life of the ghetto.

Even in their isolation, however, the Jews were not unaffected by the stirrings of life in European Christendom from the Renaissance through the Reformation to the eighteenth-century Age of Enlightenment. The real awakening and struggle, however, for freedom against rabbinical orthodoxy did not begin till after the French Revolution and did not make much headway until the nineteenth century.

The French Revolution by recognizing Jews as citizens on a basis of equality with Christians initiated a process which gradually spread to all of Europe and changed the life of European Jewry and relationships between Jews and Christians. The bulk of European Jewry, in fact of world Jewry, lived in Central and Eastern Europe, the largest concentrations of Jews being in Russia (including Russian Poland), Rumania, and the Austrian Empire (including Austrian Poland).

The Reform movement and Antimessianism.—The awakening and revolt against Talmudic medievalism began among the Jews in the various states of the German Confederation, which was created in 1815 by the Congress of Vienna. The Reform movement launched among the German Jewish congregations spread westward and acquired a large following among the Jews in the United States. Among the main points at issue between the Orthodox Jews and the Reform Jews, which have had a direct bearing upon the Near East, were those concerning Messianism and the restoration of the Jewish state in Palestine. The German and American leaders of the Jewish Reform movement gave a very different interpretation of Messianism than that of the Orthodox rabbinate and repudiated the idea of a return to Palestine. Orthodox Jewry believed in a personal Messiah who would lead the Jews back to the Promised Land and re-establish the Jewish state in Palestine. The ideas of the reformers may best be presented in statements made by them and adopted by representative conferences.[1] A conference of Jewish Reform leaders held in Philadelphia in 1869 issued a public statement, the first paragraph of which reads as follows: "The Messianic aim of Israel is not the restoration of the old Jewish state under a descendant of David, involving a second separation from the nations of the earth, but the union of all the children of God in the confession of the unity of God, so as to realize the unity of all rational creatures and their call to moral sanctification."

The Pittsburgh Conference of Jewish Reform leaders held in 1885 adopted a declaration of principles, the fifth paragraph of which reads as follows: "We recognize in the modern era of universal culture of heart and intellect, the approaching of the realization of Israel's great Messianic hope for the establishment of the Kingdom of Truth, justice and peace among men. We consider ourselves no longer a nation but a religious community and therefore expect neither a return to Palestine, nor a sacrificial worship under the sons of Aaron, nor the restoration of any of the laws concerning the Jewish state."

These declarations were made by men who had neither a prophetic nor a dialectical vision of the age of violence and conflict towards which the social order of the western world was rushing. They did not conceive of the barbarisms which would be unchained in 1914 and would spread with ever-increasing violence, cruelty, and hatred to the era of the atomic and hydrogen bombs. The Reform Jews were battling in the nineteenth century against the obscurantism of medieval Jewry. They did not foresee a future conflict with the combined forces of orthodox historical Jewish nationalism and materialistic Jewish nationalism over the return to Palestine and the re-creation of a Jewish state there.

Distribution of European Jews.—As Abdul Hamid to some extent understood, the distribution of world Jewry was a factor with respect to Jewish colonization in Palestine which the Ottoman government needed to consider before a decision was reached with regard to Theodor Herzl's proposals.

It is estimated that the Jewish population of the world in 1891 was approximately 9,500,000 of whom nearly 7,750,000 were in Europe. The greater part of the European Jews were Russian subjects living in ghettoes under conditions not far different from those of the Middle Ages. At that time over half of the Jews of the world in such countries as Russia and Rumania were discriminated against politically, socially, and economically. From time to time these Jewish communities were subject to outbursts of Christian fanaticism fanned by government encouragement into flaming pogroms. The bulk of eastern European Jewry, like the masses of the Christian population, lived in a condition bordering on poverty. Orthodoxy prevailed for the most part, though Marxian socialism was making considerable progress among Austrian, Hungarian, Polish, and Russian Jews as among the German Jews. Indeed, the Jewish Socialist Bund became a powerful force among eastern European Jews. Later, immigration to America firmly established the Jewish Bund in the United States.

To millions of these eastern European Jews, Palestine was the Promised Land to which someday the Messiah would lead them back and there the Jews would rebuild Jehovah's Temple and re-create the Jewish state. To most of them this was a Utopian dream. Misery and persecution under the Russian tsars stimulated immigration to the countries of central and western Europe and to the Americas. During the last decade of the nineteenth century and the first part of the twentieth, there were large migrations to the west, which later proved of uttermost significance to the Near East.

Early colonies in Palestine and the birth of modern Zionism.—Other than the "escapist" emigrants from Russia and Rumania there were those ardent apostles of a return to Palestine who sought spiritual as well as material salvation in going to the Promised Land. The Russian pogroms of 1881 and 1882 had widespread repercussions throughout world Jewry and also in Christian circles. In Russia, Jewish groups known as the *Lovers of Zion,* Hoveve Zion, began to plan for the establishment of colonies in Palestine. Some of the Russian Jewish intellectuals, who were opposed to Jewish Orthodoxy and believed in the ideas of the Reform Jews and the emancipation of Russian Jews, turned in the face of existing conditions to the ancient idea of a return to Palestine. Among these was the Russian doctor, Leo Pinsker, who first launched the modern concept of political Zionism in a pamphlet written in German, entitled *Auto-Emancipation.* Uprooted Russian Jews, fleeing from the terror of persecution, awakened the sympathies of wealthy western Jews and stirred the imaginations of humanitarian Christians, both of which groups began thinking in terms of Jewish colonization of Palestine and other localities.

The trek to Palestine from Russia of Hoveve Zion settlers resulting in the establishment of a few Jewish colonies on the coastal plain aroused Abdul Hamid to action. The Ottoman government issued a law in June 1882 making it illegal for Jews to enter Palestine. Despite these official restrictions, the Hoveve Zion colonization movement and migration to the Promised Land continued for a decade with the connivance of corrupt Ottoman officials. The colonies, however, soon got into financial difficulties and one after another were taken under the charitable auspices of Baron Edmond de Rothschild. Dr. Pinsker became discouraged with the narrow vision of the leaders of the Lovers of Zion and died. The methods of colonization were ruthlessly attacked by Ahad Ha-am in a pamphlet called, "Not This Is the Way." The Turkish government became more energetic in enforcing its restrictions on Jewish immigration to Palestine.

Excluded from Palestine, Jews flock to U.S.A.—Return to the Promised Land held out little hope to the Jewish masses in Russia, who preferred the fleshpots of the United States to the lot of charity-supported colonists in Palestine. Abdul Hamid's decision during the last quarter of the nineteenth century to close the doors of Palestine to Jewish settlers bore strange fruit in the first half of the twentieth. Denied access to Palestine, the flow of Jewish migration turned to the United States. In 1891 the estimated Jewish population of the United States was 750,000, by 1909 it had increased by more than a million, by 1917—the year of the Balfour Declaration which promised the Jews a national home in Palestine—it amounted to about 2,500,000, and in 1948, when President Truman recognized the new state of Israel, there were over 4,500,000 Jews in the United States. Those Russian Jews who had been forbidden to enter Palestine by Abdul Hamid and their descendants and friends have been able, by using the United States government as a fulcrum, to pry open the doors of Palestine and erect there the Jewish state of Israel. This probably would never have been accomplished had it not been for the driving force of Jewish nationalism generated by Zionism.

While the oppressed of Judea in eastern Europe were nursing the age-old dream of ultimate return to Palestine and were fleeing for refuge to the United States, the elite of central and western Europe were sadly learning that political and civil emancipation was not a passkey to social acceptance. Freed from the ancient restrictions, western Jews with boundless energy plunged into the multifold life of the rapidly expanding activities of the modern world. In a wide diversity of fields, Jews won positions of pre-eminence: in the arts, the professions, politics, business, finance, and industry.

Many of these able and successful Jews, failing to realize that while the Christian bourgeoisie had broken the monopoly of political and economic power formerly held by the old aristocrats, it had not broken down the social barriers between the landed aristocracy and the middle class, also suffered from social discrimination. In addition to the haughty attitude of the upper classes towards the "new men" was added the age-old curse of anti-Semitism. The emergence within the social organisms of Europe of an energetic, dynamic, and successful Jewish bourgeoisie aroused antagonisms against the Jews in every level of European and even American society.

The rise of anti-Semitism in Austria-Hungary, in Germany, and in France during the last quarter of the nineteenth century, coupled with the pogroms in Russia, led certain of the emancipated Jewish intellectuals, who had largely abandoned Orthodoxy and viewed with equanimity ultimate assimilation, to believe that the only solution of the *Jewish Question* was the creation of a Jewish state. Many of the outstanding leaders of western Jewry were ardent liberals and accepted nationalism as a fundamental tenet of their political creed. In the early ardor of the first flush of emancipation, they had become passionate German, French, English, and Italian patriots. Among them, were those who, tasting the bitterness of anti-Semitism, lost all hope of universal Messianism. To them Jewish nationalism and a Jewish state made a tremendously powerful ideological and emotional appeal which was to become the dynamic source of Zionist power over the minds and emotions of a large proportion of world Jewry in the next twenty-five years.

Class structure among the Jews.—Needless to say, the Jews were an inseparable part of the world and times in which they lived. Freed from the ghettoes and pales in most of Europe the Jews became more definitely an integral part of European society and were more potently affected by the social forces and intellectual currents which were seething in the western world during the nineteenth century. The class structure of the Jewish world was in the same process of revolutionary change as was the European gentile society. There developed a Jewish proletariat of wage-earning workers; a petty Jewish bourgeoisie of "butchers, bakers, and candlestick makers," that is, of storekeepers, small merchants, and craftsmen; a middle Jewish bourgeoisie of well-to-do business and professional men; a *haut* bourgeoisie of wealthy great merchants, industrialists, and financiers; and, finally, an elite of artists, writers, and other intellectuals. Each of these strata of Jewish society was increasingly in closer contact with the corresponding stratum of the gentile world. Jews contributed to and took from the general stock of ideas of the wider social group of which they were a part.

The various groups in Jewish society were swept by nineteenth century romanticism, humanitarianism, liberalism, nationalism, and socialism. The middle Jewish bourgeoisie, in the main, became liberals and nationalists of the country in which they were citizens; some of the Jewish intellectuals and proletariat became Marxian socialists and active labor leaders. Both of these groups were opponents of Jewish nationalism: the liberal reformers looked upon the idea of a return to Palestine as a form of rabbinical obscurantism which had no significance in the modern world of progress; the Jewish Marxists considered Jewish nationalism and the Zionist movement as a bourgeois capitalistic manifestation. The Jewish Marxists were convinced that anti-Semitism was one of the inevitable evils of capitalism which would pass away with its overthrow. Other Jewish groups were in complete disagreement with both of these points of view.

A large percentage of the Jewish people of all classes remained orthodox in the field of religion and both loyal and devoted to the ancient ideas with regard to a messianic restoration to Palestine. Some of the less orthodox and more free-thinking liberals and intelligentsia, personally humiliated by anti-Semitic experiences, indignant at the wave of anti-Semitism sweeping Europe, and aghast at the pogroms in Russia, did not envisage anti-Semitism as a phase of the maladjustments of the existing social order. They became convinced that the real cause of anti-Semitism, which they called the *Jewish Question,* was Jewish statelessness, and that only when a national Jewish state came into existence would anti-Semitism cease to exist. This idea, which had its roots in nineteenth-century romanticism and liberalism, fitted well with the orthodox belief and traditions and with the need of Eastern Jewry to escape from the persecution of the tsarist government and from the intolerable economic and social conditions under which they lived. Modern Zionism had fertile ground, alive with the essential bacteria of fermenting ideologies and social discontents, in which to germinate and grow, as did the fierce nationalism of Italian and German fascism after World War I.

EMERGENCE OF POLITICAL ZIONISM

Theodor Herzl becomes a Zionist.—The creator of modern Zionism, in whose lifetime the discontents of disillusioned western Jews were joined with the misery of eastern Jewry, and both with the old Judaic national and religious traditions and beliefs, was Theodor Herzl—a brilliant Austrian Jewish intellectual and journalist. Born in Budapest in 1860, at eighteen years of age he entered the University of Vienna. Although enrolled as a law student, he began to write and sought to become a great author. His literary successes finally won for him in 1891 the much coveted post of Paris correspondent of the most distinguished Vienna newspaper, *Wiener Neue Freie Presse.*

It was during the time that Herzl was a newspaperman in Paris that anti-Semitism in France resulted in a public scandal which received world-wide publicity. Anti-Semitism began to spread in France after the Franco-Prussian War of 1870–71. For nearly two decades France was in a continual state of social and political ferment. The collapse of the Second French Empire precipitated a short but bitter civil war between the proletariat led by Marxists and the French middle class. The ruthless brutality with which the new middle class revolutionary government put down the revolutionists, which was comparable to the contemporary ruthlessness of the Turks in dealing with nationalistic revolutionists in Armenia, Crete, and Macedonia, created bitter animosities in France which continue to the present time. The French middle class did not, however, obtain secure control of France until 1885, and was in a state of constant struggle against the old aristocracy, the Royalists, who largely controlled the army and war department, and their loyal supporters, the clericals, who received encouragement from the papacy.

These social maladjustments and contradictions in a nation which had so recently suffered a humiliating military defeat and occupation created a psychological condition among the French people receptive to theories of racial superiority like those of Gobineau and his ilk, and to anti-Semitism not unconnected with them. In 1885 the violent fascist-like anti-Semite, Edouard Drumond, published his book, *Jewish France.* It attacked the French Jews as an alien people who were exploiting the capitalist economic system in order to destroy the Christian middle class. This diatribe against the Jews received considerable publicity throughout France, and Drumond's book was widely sold. The ideas and emotions of many Frenchmen of different classes were being conditioned toward believing that the Jews were responsible for the causes of their discontents. The ground was being prepared for the perpetration of a most contemptible fraud—the accusation, trial, and condemnation of Captain Dreyfus, which, because it so deeply moved Theodor Herzl, has had a determining effect upon developments in the Near East which now embroil the whole world. Little did the aristocratic officers of the French army understand how their dishonesty and wickedness designed to protect the interests of their own caste would be one of the determining factors in shaping future events in the Near East in a manner unfavorable to France.

"Der Judenstaat."—A French officer, who was a member of one of the oldest and most widely known of the aristocratic families of Europe, Major Charles Esterhazy, sold secret plans of the French General Staff to the German government. To cover up the treason of one member of their caste, top brass in the French military establishment, accused Captain Alfred Dreyfus, a Jew, of this heinous crime. He was brought to trial in 1894, declared guilty, publicly degraded, and sent to a penal colony. The French government was implicated in this vile business, which wide segments of the French public applauded. Happily, it may be recorded to the honor of the French people and government that after a courageous struggle by French liberals the fraud was exposed and Dreyfus fully cleared of any guilt. In the meanwhile, Herzl, who had covered the trial for his Vienna paper, conceived the idea of a Jewish state, later embodied in his famous book, *Der Judenstaat* (*The Jewish State*), as the only solution of the problem of the Jews.

In the very prime of his manhood, Theodor Herzl, with passionate zeal, threw all of his ability and energy into the Zionist movement to create a Jewish state in Palestine if possible, elsewhere if necessary. The Jewish masses in their misery, profoundly obsessed with the idea of Messianism, though unwilling to agree to a Jewish state except in Palestine, found in Herzl a leader. His books, his activities among the leading European Jewish financiers, his dramatic negotiations with Abdul Hamid and prominent political leaders of the Great Powers, made him the focus of various Zionist movements.

Negotiation with Abdul Hamid.—Herzl's plans and schemes were brought to the attention of Abdul Hamid in an amazing interview with the Ottoman despot in 1901. This ardent Austrian Jewish nationalist showed no more compunction in telling Abdul Hamid of his devotion to him because he was so good to the Jews than did the German Emperor Wilhelm II, the imperialist, in calling Abdul Hamid his friend. Both men acting within the framework of their own ideologies were seeking what they conceived to be the interests of their chosen people. The oppression and suffering of the Ottoman Christian minorities were matters not to be recalled when favors from Abdul Hamid were being sought in order to achieve national aims. Theodor Herzl and Kaiser Wilhelm II followed a pattern which had long been set by the statesmen of all the Great Powers of Europe.

In his interviews with and communications to Abdul Hamid, Herzl made two astounding proposals. The first was that Herzl would, through a syndicate of Jewish bankers, refund the Turkish foreign debt and free the Turks from the economic tutelage of the Great Powers; the second proposal was that the sultan grant a charter to a Jewish land company for agricultural development and Jewish colonization. In the midst of loan negotiations with the French, Abdul Hamid employed with Herzl his time-tried methods of delay, postponement, and of playing both ends against the middle in order to get better terms from the French. Abdul Hamid said that he had always been the friend of the Jews, and he was willing to permit scattered settlements of Jews in Anatolia if such Jewish immigrants became Ottoman citizens, renounced their former citizenship, and on condition that their former rulers officially recognized the cancellation of previous citizenship. Abdul Hamid, however, had no intention of allowing mass Jewish immigration and colonization. He was well aware of the aims and purposes of the Zionists, who had recently held the first World Zionist Congress at Basle, Switzerland, in the summer of 1897.

The World Zionist Congress and the W.Z.O.—The program that was adopted by the first World Zionist Congress opened with the following sentence: "The aim of Zionism is to create for the Jewish people a publicly, legally assured home in Palestine." [2] Only the politically illiterate, during the next fifty years, among whom Abdul Hamid cannot be listed, took these words at their face value. The phrase, a "Jewish Homeland," was accepted by the Congress as a compromise, as a necessary euphemism, to meet the political exigencies of the times, when it was absolutely inexpedient, if not actually dangerous, to use the phrase a "Jewish state." One of the members of the Congress who opposed the term "Jewish Homeland" said that the program omitted the leading principle of Zionism—that the Jews wished to be a nation. The proceedings of the Congress clearly show that the real aim of Zionism was the achievement of a national state and that the phrase "publicly, legally assured" home in Palestine was adopted, to use the words of the famous Zionist leader Dr. Max Nordau, "in the interest of opportunism." An old and wily ruler like Abdul Hamid was not to be deceived by such political subterfuges. He knew that publicly meant internationally. He understood what that signified from past experience. He was certain the inhabitants of an autonomous Jewish National Home in Palestine under the sponsorship of the Concert of European Powers would seek sovereignty and independence. Would the Jews act differently from the Greeks, the Serbs, the Bulgars, the Cretans, the Armenians, and the Macedonians?

Herzl's diplomatic maneuvers came to naught. Abdul Hamid would not and did not give his consent to a *Jewish Homeland in Palestine* or to any of the other colonization plans proposed by the Austrian journalist. The British were unwilling because of the anticipated opposition of Cypriot Greeks and Turks to grant the Jews the right to establish themselves in Cyprus, which Herzl proposed in order to create a base from which the Jews might eventually cross over into Palestine. The suggestion that the Khedive should permit Jewish settlement in the barren eastern frontier lands of Egypt at El 'Arish in Sinai, close to the southern boundary of Palestine, did not materialize. The bulk of the Zionists refused to accept a British offer to the Jews of a place of settlement in Kenya, East Africa. It became increasingly evident that the Zionists would not consider any other place of settlement than Palestine, and it was their firm determination to create eventually a Jewish state there. Within a period of little more than half a century after the first World Zionist Congress at Basle in 1897, the Zionists set up the Jewish state of Israel in Palestine.

Although Theodor Herzl failed to achieve his aims, the Zionist movement, responding to the stimulus of his leadership, laid the foundations during the last decade of the nineteenth century and the first of the twentieth of a world-wide organization which attained in 1948 its primary objective. The First Zionist Congress created a permanent international Zionist Executive Committee to carry out the resolutions of the Congress, to transact Zionist business, and to prepare for the next World Zionist Congress. A proposal to create a Jewish National Fund was referred to a committee for report to the next Congress, which assembled in 1898. During the ten years between Herzl's writing *Der Judenstaat* and his death, six Zionist World congresses had been held, a permanent World Zionist Organization had been created, a Jewish National Fund established, and a Jewish Colonial Trust founded. All the basically essential organizational machinery had been created for a world movement, which was to accomplish those ends which Abdul Hamid foresaw and futilely endeavored to prevent. Zionism was another one of those nationalistic movements and forces which Abdul Hamid could not cope with in ways which would do more than temporarily check their ultimate realization.

۞ PALESTINE, A FOCUS OF WORLD INTEREST

The rise of Zionism took place at a time when the Great Powers of Europe were developing a lively interest in the Holy Land. Christendom rather suddenly became deeply concerned about the Near East. Protestant sects, particularly American and British, established missionary posts, schools, and colleges throughout the Ottoman Empire in the Balkans, in distant Armenia, and in Syria, Palestine, and Egypt. Catholic monastic orders long-established in the Near East increased activities and extended their missionary and educational work. The Russian Orthodox Church acquired extensive properties in Palestine and built churches and hospices to serve the flow of Russian pilgrims to the Holy Land. German Lutheranism with the encouragement of Kaiser Wilhelm II after 1890 pursued a similar pattern. A magnificent site on the Mount of Olives was purchased on which an imposing hospice was constructed.

These religious activities took on a nationalistic coloration which added national rivalries to the existing sectarian differences. The Holy Land, particularly the city of Jerusalem became a center of competing Christian sects and rival national interests closely allied to them. The Holy City was rapidly embellished with ecclesiastical edifices which were as much monuments to national pride as to religious ardor.

Better steamship facilities and the building of a railroad by the French from Jaffa to Jerusalem made pilgrimages to the Holy Land increasingly popular. From all over the Christian world more pilgrims every year flocked to Palestine to visit the sacred shrines at Jerusalem, Bethlehem, and Nazareth. The Holy Land was becoming a center of interest for the Christian world at a time when world Jewry revived its interest in the Promised Land.

Few of the thousands of pilgrims and tourists who visited Palestine in the decades which preceded World War I learned much about Zionism and Jewish hopes. But the chancellories of Europe, the diplomatic and consular officers of the great Powers, and the foreign priests and missionaries became increasingly aware of the Zionist movement. Foreign governmental agencies of those countries which had influential Jewish citizens and subjects interested in Jewish colonization in Palestine found it part of their routine duties to deal with problems concerning the Palestinian interests of their Jewish nationals. British, French, and German Jewish educational and charitable institutions in Palestine were considered as national interests to be aided and encouraged.

The foreign missionaries and priests who came into close touch with the Arabs tended to look upon Jewish colonization and the Zionist movement first with skepticism and then with dislike. These foreign pastors and priests reflected in part Arab fears and in part opposition to a competing religious group.

As time went on many Protestant missionaries became bitterly opposed to the establishment of a Jewish National Home in the Holy Land. This was not so, however, among the Protestant Christian churches in the homelands of the missionaries, where many of the Protestant clergy and laity thought of the return of the Jews to Palestine as a fulfillment of Biblical prophesies. Such was not the case in Rome where the papacy, with perhaps a clearer perspective on world affairs, was far from being sympathetic to the Zionist movement.

Interest in and increasing travel to the Near East were not confined to Palestine. As facilities for travel were improved more Europeans and Americans visited the Near East. Likewise, more Near Easterners visited Europe. Both of these factors made Turks and Arabs more aware of the backwardness of the Ottoman Empire. The contrast between the facilities, the luxuries, and the freedoms which existed in the West and conditions existing in the Near East intensified the determination of enlightened Arabs and Turks to rid themselves of the intolerable regime of Abdul Hamid. As the Near East was drawn more and more into the orbit of the western world the ferment of revolution grew more intense.

The inability of the Hamidian regime to deal with the problem of the Balkans, the Armenian question, or even with the Zionist movement intensified opposition to the Ottoman autocrat. The inefficiency, corruption, and tyranny of Abdul Hamid's government were reaching a degree that was becoming unbearable. They fostered a revolutionary movement in the Ottoman Empire which culminated in the Young Turk revolution of 1908 and in an Arab nationalist movement which was to come into a head on collision with Zionism. Injustice and discrimination against Jews in the western world and against the Arabs in the Ottoman Empire helped to create violent and passionate national movements among Jews and Arabs which now breed fear and hatred in the Near East.

CHAPTER XI

The Young Turk Revolution of 1908

The *coup d'état* in July 1908 by the Young Turks under the direction of the Committee of Union and Progress, which compelled Abdul Hamid to issue a decree putting into operation the "Midhat" constitution of 1876, was a new stage in the revolutionary process that had begun in Turkey seventy years earlier and had made considerable headway, politically and intellectually, between 1839 and 1876 during the era of the Tanzimat reformers. The new direction taken by the revolutionary movement from 1908 to 1918 affected significantly subsequent events which led to the more profoundly revolutionary changes brought about in Turkey after World War I under the leadership of Mustafa Kemal (Ataturk), who was one of the Committee of Union and Progress before and after 1908.

THE REVOLUTIONARY MOVEMENT

Like many of the revolutionary movements in modern history, the revolutionary movement in the Ottoman Empire, which ended the autocratic rule of Abdul Hamid, was the result of complex and frequently contradictory forces. The unbearable despotism of the Hamidian regime, the violent internal conflicts between the various religious and national groups, the deepening misery of the people, and the increasing menace of disintegration or partition by the Great Powers brought together men of diverse views and aims in a movement to overthrow autocracy. European history in the nineteenth and twentieth centuries provides many examples of the tendency of diverse and antagonistic groups to combine in united efforts to overthrow a domestic or foreign tyranny and later, when their primary objective had been achieved, to break apart and engage in an internecine struggle for power. Such proved to be the case in respect to the Turkish Revolution of 1908. Several foreign observers, as well as Ottoman subjects, however, were so enthused by the success of the Young Turks that they believed a new dawn, a political millennium, had arrived in which the far from lionlike Turk would lie down with the none too lamblike Christian minorities. The keen chief Dragoman of the British Embassy at Constantinople, G. H. Fitzmaurice,[1] sensed the difficulties which lay ahead. A month after the *coup d'état* of the Young Turks, Fitzmaurice in a private note dated August 25, 1908, to W. G. Tyrrell, a senior clerk in the British Foreign Office and at the time Private Secretary to the British Foreign Minister, Sir Edward Grey, wrote about the events in July as follows: "The die is cast and one must hope for the best, but the task of fusing and welding into one common Ottoman nationality the mosaic of creeds, nationalities and tongues that go to make up the Ottoman Empire will require iron determination and will tax the energies of the stoutest of hearts."

Diverse aims of the revolutionists.—The 1908 revolution was essentially Turkish, although other Moslem groups, Jews, and some Christians participated in it to a limited extent. Among the Turkish revolutionists and among that wider group of Turks who sympathized with their aims to terminate the despotism of Abdul Hamid and to bring about a regeneration of the Ottoman Empire, to end foreign intervention and aggression, and to put a stop to civil war, were men of very different views and aims. The profoundly religious Turks, whose opposition to Abdul Hamid was in no small measure due to the decline of and threat to Islam, had little in common with those free-thinking, atheistically inclined members of the Committee of Union and Progress (C.U.P.) who had become the directing brains of the Young Turk party.

Another division among the Turks was that between those who were proponents of Ottomanism and those who were Turkish Nationalists. The former group believed in the maintenance of the Ottoman Empire as a multinational state in which all citizens irrespective of race, nationality, and creed would be equal and loyal Ottomans. Although the members of this group professed allegiance to this liberal democratic concept, it is questionable how many Turks of this school of thought were prepared actually to accept the full implications of their political philosophy. This should be quite comprehensible to Americans who failed to see for over a half century the basic contradiction between Negro slavery and both the Declaration of Independence and the Constitution of the United States. The other Turkish group had been much affected by the pseudo-racial and nationalistic doctrines so popular in the western world during the last quarter of the nineteenth century. Following the familiar pattern of nationalism, Turkish intellectuals and nationalists turned to the historic past of the Ottoman Turks for inspiration. Turkish history, Turkish folklore, Turkish unwritten literature, the "pure" Turkish language of pre-Ottoman times became subjects of absorbing interest.

Upon the basis of this new form of Turkish nationalism was built the strange superstructure of Pan-Turanianism which became the rage in some Turkish circles. The Ottoman Turks were but an offshoot of the Turanian race; Turkish culture was essentially Turanian; there existed cultural, historic, and racial bonds between all Turanians, whether they were in the Ottoman Empire, in Russia, or in China. Through racialism, some of the Turkish nationalists were nursing the idea of Pan-Turanianism as a new basis for Turkish imperialism to replace that of Pan-Islamism and Ottomanism. Fantastic as this may seem, it was no more so than the Aryan myth fostered by those American, English, French, and German writers who believed in racialism and race superiority. This new obscurantism of a small fragment of the Turkish people, which made little impression upon the illiterate Turkish masses, sprang from fallacious ideas propagated in the West, where they received widespread acceptance among the unenlightened literates of the more "progressive" states of the western world in which political democracy had not been fully conducive to intellectual enlightenment. The complete break between those Turks who believed in Ottomanism and those who believed in nationalism did not occur until after the collapse of the Ottoman Empire following World War I.

Another interesting and important division among the Turks who opposed Abdul Hamid was between those who favored a highly centralized government and those who advocated *decentralization,* a euphemism for autonomy, which among the Young Turk leaders had fallen into disrepute because it had become associated with foreign intervention in and dismemberment of the Ottoman Empire. The cleavage between the Young Turk Party and the Liberal Union Party was increased by their variant views with regard to centralization and decentralization. Long since, the Russian ambassador at Constantinople in the period from 1864 to 1877 had observed that the Ottoman government had the choice of either *l'autonomie ou l'anatomie.* The Liberal Unionists believed autonomy of national minority groups absolutely necessary to the preservation of the Empire, while the dominant faction of the Committee of Union and Progress was convinced that decentralization would result in both *l'autonomie et l'anatomie.*

Since there were but few Zionists among the Ottoman Jews and since Turkish nationalists had shown no indication of the anti-Semitism typical of the Christian people of the West during this period, there was no occasion for conflict between the Jews of the Near East and the new regime in Turkey, in fact Jews played an important role in the C.U.P. This could not be said of the various Christian nationalistic groups. Bordering on Turkey were the independent Christian states of Greece and Serbia and the autonomous principality of Bulgaria. The rulers and the people of these nations considered the Greeks, Serbs, and Bulgars in Macedonia and Thrace as future subjects and the areas they inhabited as national irredenta to be annexed to the homeland eventually. Although the Bulgarian-Macedonian Comitadji might and did co-operate temporarily with the Young Turks, such co-operation did not long continue. The Armenian massacres in Cilicia of 1909 and the wholesale massacres and deportations of Armenians by the Turks during World War I are effective testimony to the incompatibility of Armenian and Turkish nationalists, although Armenian revolutionary leaders associated themselves with the Young Turks in 1908. The Greek subjects of the Sultan were too deeply imbued with Hellenism to become enthusiastic and loyal Ottoman subjects. Even among the Moslem Arabs, Albanians, and Kurds nationalism was developing cleavages in the Ottoman Moslem society that would soon become active.

The universal detestation of the Hamidian regime brought together without "fusing and welding into one common Ottoman nationality the mosaic of creeds nationalities and tongues that go to make up the Ottoman Empire," the diverse groups who wished to overthrow the despotism of Abdul Hamid. The Young Turks provided the leadership, organization, and armed manpower by which this was accomplished.

Revolutionists in exile create an organization.—Many Turkish liberals and other opponents of the Hamidian regime had fled to Europe as a place of refuge, as had many of the Russian revolutionary leaders. Switzerland was one of the favorite places of asylum for revolutionaries: nationalists, liberals, socialists, and anarchists of many different nations. It was at Geneva that Turkish exiles organized in 1891 the Ottoman Committee of Union and Progress. In Europe, as well as in the Ottoman Empire, these Turkish revolutionists had to operate secretly.

They had the choice of patterning their secret organization on that of many different European revolutionary groups, for Europeans suffering for nearly forty years during the reactionary regime of the Metternich era under oppressive autocratic governments had perfected highly the technique of secret revolutionary activities and of revolutionary organization. The earlier Jacobin and Italian Carbonari movements, the Irish Fenian Society, Giuseppe Mazzini's and Giuseppe Garibaldi's Young Italy movement, the various socialist revolutionary groups, including Russian Social Democratic Mensheviks and Bolsheviks, and the anarchists provided examples of secret revolutionary methods. The Turks adopted, however, none of these, but patterned their revolutionary organization upon that of European Freemasonry, which had been closely associated with middle-class, liberal, and nationalist revolutionary movements. The Committee of Union and Progress as organized at Salonika in 1906 became a "secret society to a large extent modelled on Freemasonry." [2]

Headquarters of the Ottoman Committee of Union and Progress was soon established at Paris, where a Young Turk newspaper, *Mechveret,* was published. It was, of course, essential to carry on revolutionary propaganda in Turkey and to create a revolutionary organization there. Initial operations began in Macedonia in 1906, where a Committee of Liberty had been created which was amalgamated with the Ottoman Committee of Union and Progress soon after the C.U.P. was established in Salonika. The ubiquitous Hamidian spy system obliged the Turkish revolutionists to organize themselves along the most secret lines. Acceptance and initiation of new members was on an individual basis. Each revolutionist was permitted to know only the members of his own cell of five members. The organization of the C.U.P. spread rapidly throughout both European and Asiatic Turkey, most especially among Turkish military officers, civilian officials, and other Turkish professional men.

Planning the uprising.—The secret central executive committee of the C.U.P. began to plan in terms of an uprising in 1909 when they thought the movement would be sufficiently strong to seize power. The domestic situation and the developments taking place in foreign affairs forced the hands of the C.U.P. leaders, who decided in June 1908 to raise the standard of revolt.

During 1907 and the early months of 1908 a very considerable change had taken place in the relationship of the Great Powers that was of serious import to the Ottoman Empire. In 1907 England and Russia, having settled their outstanding differences, signed an Anglo-Russian agreement which created the Triple Entente. Europe was now divided into two armed camps preparing for the war which came in 1914. Having agreed to the partition of Persia (Iran) into a British, a

Russian, and a neutral zone, the British and Russian governments began to explore the possibility of reconciling their policies with respect to Macedonia. The development of a common policy by England and Russia brought to an end the co-operation of Austria-Hungary and Russia in Balkan affairs.

European intrigues precipitate the revolution.—Realizing the significance of the Anglo-Russian alignment of 1907 the Austrians promptly obtained from the Ottoman government a concession to build a railroad from Sarajevo in Bosnia through the Turkish sandjak of Novibazaar to connect with a Turkish line to Salonika. Novibazaar was a strategic area in the Balkans which, as a northwestern extension of Macedonia, formed a narrow corridor between Serbia and Montenegro, leading to the Austrian occupied Turkish provinces of Bosnia and Herzegovina. By the Treaty of Berlin, Austria-Hungary was permitted to maintain a garrison in the Novibazaar corridor alongside the Turkish garrison, thus effectively shutting Serbia off from access to the Adriatic as Macedonia did to the Aegean. Political and territorial union of the two Serbian kingdoms, Montenegro and Serbia, was quite impossible as long as Austria dominated Novibazaar.

The granting of this railroad concession to Austria-Hungary gave the Austrians and the Germans control of an important highway to the Aegean at Salonika. The Triple Entente was greatly perturbed by this maneuver of the Teutonic allies. As a counter maneuver Serbia with full Russian backing demanded that the Ottoman government grant a concession to Serbia to build a railroad which would connect the Danube via Serbia and Macedonia with a port on the Adriatic in Montenegro. Negotiations between England and Russia over the Macedonian reforms were speeded up and a visit of King Edward VII to Tsar Nicholas II at Reval was planned for March 1908 to cement the entente between the two countries following the Anglo-Russian agreement. The Reval meeting appeared ominous not only to the Austrians and Germans but also to the Turks, who feared that plans were being made which would result in the loss of Macedonia to Turkey.

Added to these fears of the ardently patriotic Young Turks and the members of the C.U.P. was the action of Abdul Hamid, whose spies had informed him of the widespread growth of a revolutionary movement in Macedonia centering at Salonika. As a consequence of this information, the sultan sent a commission to Salonika to investigate the situation. Under such compulsion, the Executive Committee of the C.U.P. decided upon an uprising in June 1908.

REVOLUTION AND COUNTERREVOLUTION

With a rapidity that was astonishing to European officials and diplomats, who had no idea of the strength and extent of the Turkish revolutionary movement, the Young Turks gained control of the greater part of Macedonia, receiving support from both the Albanian Moslem and the Bulgarian Macedonian bands. With the army corps at both Adrianople and Salonika backing the C.U.P., its leaders sent an ultimatum to Abdul Hamid on July 23, 1908, demanding the restoration of the constitution of 1876. The troops from Macedonia under their Young Turk officers marched on Constantinople. The wily sultan knew that the game was lost, at least temporarily, and promptly on July 24 issued an irade restoring the constitution and authorizing elections to the second parliament in Turkish history.

The ministry was dismissed and an interim cabinet appointed to function until the meeting of Parliament in December. As most of the members of the C.U.P. had had no experience in administration, the Young Turks were obliged to depend upon Turks with governmental training and service for work in the cabinet, the central bureaucracy, and in the provincial administration. The executive committee of the C.U.P. nevertheless did not relinquish its control, and thus a secret society whose membership was not known to the public actually ruled Turkey. Youssouf Fehmi, a devoutly religious Turk, who was violently prejudiced against Freemasonry, which he visualized as a secret society wishing to extend its domination over all the world, became a bitter opponent of the Young Turks and the C.U.P. Despite his decidedly biased opinions and judgments, Fehmi accurately described the controlling group of the C.U.P. as being composed of some thirty odd "directors" supported by about three hundred influential members. Of this group, Fehmi wrote in 1911, "It is they who govern the Ottoman Empire. They make and unmake cabinets, imposing their will on senators, deputies, the press, the high Moslem clergy of Constantinople, and even on the Sultan." [3] As an example of the use of arbitrary power by the C.U.P., Fehmi quotes from the *Oriental Advertiser* of Constantinople of September 3, 1908, as follows:

A Circular of the Central Committee of Union and Progress

The central Ottoman Committee of Union and Progress of Salonika sends us, as to all the press, a telegram as follows:

We recommend to you to write nothing which could injure Ottoman union or could injure the sentiments of the diverse nationalities of the Empire. The press ought not to publish articles attacking the honor of the men in power. It should abstain absolutely from speaking of questions related to Egypt, Bosnia, and the privileged provinces. Should they do so, those who write or cause to have written such articles will be considered as traitors to the fatherland. We call this to their attention for the first and last time.

Three British writers who closely followed the Young Turk Revolution and were well acquainted with some of the leaders of the C.U.P., in their books on the situation in Turkey in 1908 and 1909, give examples of the power of the Committee of Union and Progress. Charles Roden Buxton, who dedicated his book, *Turkey in Revolution,* published in 1909, "to the Ottoman Committee of Union and Progress A Tribute of Admiration," wrote of the power of the C.U.P. from July 24 to December 17, 1908 as follows: "They had placed a Government in power. They now controlled its actions." [4]

E. F. Knight, who had many friends among the members of the C.U.P., wrote of it in his book, *The Awakening of Turkey,* published in 1909, as follows:

It was recognized that, far from losing its *raison d'être* with the opening of Parliament, the Young Turk organization would be needed more than ever for the protection of the country and would have to continue its existence, with the army behind it as heretofore, for a long while to come.

The Young Turks, therefore, apparently deemed it more necessary than ever that strict secrecy be observed as to whom their real leaders were.[5]

G. F. Abbott, who showed more skepticism about the Young Turks than his two compatriots, wrote in his book *Turkey in Transition,* published in 1909, of the C.U.P.:

Despotism was dead, but it did not follow that democracy had been born. The Revolution had transferred the government of the Empire from the hands of the Sultan to the hands of a Cabinet, which derived its power from the men that had created it—the Committee of Union and Progress, a revolutionary association with the military forces of the Empire at its back. This association had already given ample proofs of its omnipotence.

The Committee was the real ruler of Turkey. But was its rule a desirable rule? Was it not a semi-secret and irresponsible society incompatible with free and representative institutions?

In other words, the victory of the Committee, while dealing a mortal blow at despotism, had at the same time dealt a severe blow at Constitutionalism.[6]

In his annual report for 1908, dated February 22, 1909, to the Foreign Office, the British Ambassador Sir G. Lowther wrote of the Committee of Union and Progress as follows:

That occult body, the Committee, has from the first worked with great mystery.

Parliament met on the 17th December, a ceremony surrounded by every show of satisfaction and harmony. But, contrary to general expectation, the Committee, which as a secret body is forbidden by the Constitution, maintained its existence and influence, and its organs planned a determined attack on the Government.

Mr. G. H. Fitzmaurice, Chief Dragoman of the British Embassy at Constantinople wrote privately to Mr. Tyrrell on January 11, 1909, as follows:

> The elections were safely tided over and, though there were fearful blemishes in the way of anti-Christian jerrymandering, quite contrary to the newly proclaimed principle of Equality, it seemed best to condone such imperfections, though really they constituted gross abuses of power by the omnipotent "Committee" which had replaced Yildiz and was gradually assuming its despotic methods.

These contemporary comments on, and estimates of, the power and activities of the C.U.P. have been given in some detail because various events, domestic and foreign, between 1909 and 1913 resulted in a dictatorship of a handful of men who, operating through the C.U.P., ruled Turkey throughout World War I in a manner as arbitrary, ruthless, and despotic as that of Abdul Hamid. The organizational machinery that made this possible was created by the Young Turks previous to the revolution of 1908.

Theoretically, it might have been anticipated in the summer of 1908 that in a period of widespread discontent arising from mounting maladjustments a revolutionary group, which had seized power by a military *coup d'état* would be obliged to resort to dictatorship to accomplish its aims if there were large and important segments of Ottoman society who were opposed to the proposed changes.

Temporary fraternization of Moslems, Jews, and Christians.—For many the realities of the situation throughout the Ottoman Near East were obscured by the manifestations of goodwill and brotherhood between the members of the antagonistic religious and nationalistic groups. The psychological reaction to the termination of the intolerable despotism of Abdul Hamid was stirringly emotional. Openly and spontaneously in the streets of the Turkish cities Moslems and Christians embraced; Moslem hodjas and Christian priests walked arm in arm and drove through the crowds seated side by side in open carriages; Macedonian Bulgars and Greeks fraternized artlessly as did Armenians and Kurds. Deputations of Moslems, led by hodjas, somewhat ostentatiously drove to the Armenian cemeteries to decorate the graves of the Armenians who had perished in the massacres in Constantinople more than ten years before. It is hardly surprising that hopeful, wishful people thought the millennium had arrived and that they failed to see that the ideas seething in the minds of the Young Turks would result only seven years later in a wholesale attempt to eliminate the Armenians.

The people of all the diverse groups were expressing the deepest feelings of humanity suffering from oppression and exploitation without realizing how profoundly in conflict were their feelings with the ideas inculcated in them from childhood by their hodjas and priests and by their social, economic, and political leaders. The dominant classes among the various groups did not let the masses enjoy for long their naive and exuberant fraternization with their fellowmen of different religion and nationality. Soon after the restoration of the constitution, those to whose interest it was to do so were fanning the embers of age-old prejudices, fears, and hatreds. The Young Turk Revolution of 1908 was organized and directed by a small section of the upper-class Turks. Their first successes were applauded by the masses, not because these had revolted against the ancient ideas and customs, but because they were happy to be free from the Hamidian tyranny which had so greatly augmented their miseries.

Revolution foreshadows the future.—Reactionaries of various types began to be active. The old Hamidian camarilla of palace favorites and former officials and the host of Abdul Hamid's spies began to plot the overthrow of the new regime despite the vigilance of the C.U.P. The devoutly religious Moslems who hated and feared the free-thinking leaders of the Young Turks resented the introduction of western ideas and customs. The Liberal Union was opposed to the secret and dominating methods used by the C.U.P. The Armenians were indignant at the renewal of Kurdish raids and pillage, which the new government did nothing effective to check. Macedonian Bulgars, Greeks, and Turks recommenced their struggle for dominance. Several of the tribal chieftains and the theocratic princes in Arabia denounced the Young Turks as no better than unbelievers. The leaders of the emergent Arab nationalist movement were becoming increasingly distrustful of the Young Turks.

It was perhaps inevitable that the C.U.P. would use its power during the elections to the Chamber of Deputies to make sure of obtaining a majority pledged to their reform program and to manipulate election machinery in a way which favored Turkish at the expense of Christian and non-Turkish Moslem representation in both Asiatic and European Turkey. Before the new Parliament met in December 1908, it was beginning to be evident that the Young Turk Party and its directive organism, the C.U.P., were not representative of the Ottoman Christians, of the Albanians, of the Moslem Arabs and Kurds, nor even of the majority of Turks. It was a revolutionary Turkish minority, who were able to retain power only by arbitrary means and eventually by setting up a dictatorship.

During this interim period of ten years between 1908 and 1918, when the C.U.P. controlled the Ottoman Empire, future revolutionary developments in the Near East were foreshadowed by certain incidents and events in 1908 and 1909 despite reactionary manifestations. The emancipation of Turkish women, which was fully accomplished under the Turkish republican regime, received considerable impetus when, following the *coup d'état* of July 24, 1908, some Turkish women discarded the veil, organized a women's club, and took part in political demonstrations. Limited as were the activities of a small group of progressive Turkish women, they were more prophetic of the future than the fanatical reaction against them, such as mobs demonstrating threateningly outside the Women's Club of Constantinople, or such incidents as the assault and maltreatment in the streets of unveiled Turkish women. The reaction against greater freedom of Moslem women was so strong, even in 1913 and 1914 when the C.U.P. dictatorship was at its height, that Turkish women caught unveiled or talking in public to men were arrested and sent, as if in exile, to Anatolia.

The growing nationalism of the Turks at the expense of Ottomanism, the movement to purify the Turkish language, and the attempt to force all schools, whether Arab, Armenian, Bulgar, or Greek, whether foreign or Ottoman, to employ the Turkish language were harbingers of the future Nationalist Turkey. The Arab intellectual renaissance, during Abdul Hamid's reign, had begun to show some evidences of political nationalism. It was, however, the treatment of the Arabic movement by the Young Turks in 1909 that drove Arab nationalists into underground revolutionary organizations that prepared the way for the Arab Revolt during World War I. The Young Turks' opposition to foreign intervention and to the special privileges of foreigners under the Capitulations, which the Ottoman government renounced during World War I, was a portent of the repudiation by the Turkish nationalists under Mustafa Kemal of the Treaty of Sèvres, forced upon the Ottoman government by the victorious Allies in 1920. Few were the contemporary observers who correctly interpreted the omens in the Near East during 1908 and 1909.

The counter revolution of 1909.—During the autumn of 1908 and the winter of 1909, following the meeting in December of the newly elected Chamber of Deputies, there developed increasing opposition to the Committee of Union and Progress among members of the Young Turk Party and among nonparty deputies, both Turks and Christians. The members of the Liberal Union were bitter enemies of the C.U.P. The Liberal Union grew out of the *League of Administrative Decentralization and of Private Initiative* founded by Prince Sabaheddine, the brother-in-law of Abdul Hamid, who became the leader of the Liberal Union and as a refugee in Paris was one of the outstanding Young Turks. The Liberal Unionists insisted that the C.U.P. had abandoned Liberal principles and was attempting to create a dictatorship as despotic as that of Abdul Hamid. Minority organizations of Albanians, Armenians, Bulgars, Circassians, Greeks, and Kurds, disillusioned by the nationalistic tendencies of the C.U.P. and its discrimination against them in the elections to the Chamber of Deputies, began to gravitate toward the Liberal Union because of its program of decentralization. Devout Moslems and many of the ulemas who were antagonized by the free-thinking and atheistic tendencies among some of the C.U.P. members, organized the League of Mohammed in defense of Islam and the Sheriat. These groups were not political reactionaries and, for the most part, supported the Constitution. There were, however, numerous reactionaries who wished to restore the old regime and who joined those who opposed the C.U.P. The reactionaries were hodjas and softas, students in the Moslem ecclesiastical schools, ousted members of the Hamidian regime, and illiterate officers promoted from the ranks by Abdul Hamid who had been dismissed and replaced by Young Turk officers from the military schools.

The situation was reaching a crisis in March 1909, when one of the leading opponents of the C.U.P., Hassan Fehmi, an Albanian, editor of the opposition newspaper *Serbesti,* was murdered in the streets of Constantinople. Those opposed to the C.U.P. decided upon action, and a plot to overthrow the government and designed to break the power of the C.U.P. was put into operation. The revolt, which began in the early hours of April 13, 1909, seems to have been carefully planned in advance. Before daylight soldiers started demonstrations, and mutiny spread to many of the military units in Constantinople, the mutineers crying "Long live our Padishah, long live the Sheriat." Marching to the Yildiz Palace of Abdul Hamid, they cheered the Sultan and demanded the strict enforcement of the Sheriat, the dismissal of the ministry, and the disbanding of the Committee of Union and Progress. These demands corresponded closely to the aims of the different groups who were opposed to the C.U.P. During the evening of April 13 the Sultan granted amnesty to the mutineers. On the whole, this *coup d'état* against the C.U.P. was carried out in two days with very little violence or bloodshed in Constantinople. There were a few accidental deaths from random gunfire, some scores of officers were killed by the troops. There was no looting nor pillaging in the capital. The ministry was dismissed, and on April 15, 1909, Tewfik Pasha was appointed Grand Vizier by a decree of the Sultan, which on the insistence of Tewfik, included a statement that the constitution was one foundation stone of the Ottoman government, the other being the Sheriat. A new cabinet was rapidly appointed and order was fully re-established. The C.U.P. offices and those of the committee's newspapers were looted and the Women's Club closed. C.U.P. officers and officials were either in hiding or had fled.

The situation in the Anatolian provinces was not kept under such effective control. Conflicts between Armenians and Kurds, with the renewal of Kurdish raids, took place in the eastern vilayets. Turkish Moslems fell upon the Armenians in Mersina and in the other towns in Cilicia and northern Syria. The situation developed into a massacre of Armenians.

The C.U.P. regains control.—For a few days it looked as if the power of the C.U.P. had been completely broken. This was an illusion. Committee members acted quickly and effectively. The British Ambassador at Constantinople reported on April 26 to Sir Edward Grey that the supporters of the C.U.P. had successfully misrepresented throughout the Empire by "a bare-faced distortion of the truth" a party movement as a "deep laid scheme of the reactionaries to abolish the Constitution." So effective were their activities that both the Anatolian and Macedonian provinces rallied to the support of the C.U.P. By April 16 troops loyal to this committee were entraining at Salonika for Constantinople. Three days later Macedonian units were at San Stefano in the suburbs of the capital. On April 24 the military forces of the C.U.P. under the command of Shevket Pasha entered and took possession of Constantinople. On April 27 the Sheikh-ul-Islam issued a *fetva* to the effect that it was legal under the Sheriat to depose the Sultan. Upon the receipt of this the National Assembly voted unanimously to depose Abdul Hamid. Mohammed V was proclaimed Sultan. The C.U.P. was completely master of the situation and acted with considerable ruthlessness against its chief opponents, irrespective of whether they were liberals or reactionaries.

In Turkish history the overthrow of the C.U.P. government in mid-April 1909 is known as the Counterrevolution. Although this has become a historically accepted term, it is questionable whether it accurately describes this short-lived *coup d'état*. The preponderant element in the leadership of the movement seems to have been composed of those who supported the constitution and opposed the C.U.P. oligarchy rather than of reactionaries who were the real counterrevolutionists. As political scientists and historians have neglected to define accurately the terms they use in describing social phenomena, it is impossible to find terms which exactly describe this temporary seizure of power by the opponents of the Committee of Union and Progress. To the C.U.P. it was "counterrevolution"; to the Union Liberals, it was a revolutionary movement against what they considered to be the counterrevolutionary despotism of the C.U.P.

FOREIGN COMPLICATIONS AND REACTIONS

The Turkish Revolution of July 1908 set in motion, like a chain reaction, a succession of foreign complications which did not come to an end until the destruction of the Ottoman Empire and the replacement of the Young Turks by the Turkish Nationalists. One of the driving motives of the C.U.P. was to preserve the Empire from disintegration with the added hope of regaining control over areas which were only nominally under the suzerainty of the sultan. These aims and hopes, coupled with the establishment of a parliament with elected representatives from Ottoman provinces, had almost immediate repercussions in Austria, Russia, Bulgaria, Greece, Serbia, and Egypt, which were not ignored in England, France, and Germany.

Austria annexes Bosnia and Herzegovina.—Occupying and administrating the Turkish provinces of Bosnia and Herzegovina since 1878, the Austria-Hungary government could not overlook the threat to its control of these provinces inherent in the new Turkish regime. The Austrians knew that it would be necessary to annex them promptly. This could not be done without risking war unless an agreement was reached with Russia. The Tsar's Minister of Foreign Affairs, Izvolsky, made a secret agreement with Austria-Hungary permitting the annexation of Bosnia and Herzegovina in exchange for a promise that the Austrians would back a Russian démarche to open the Straits to Russian warships. Assured of Russia's consent, the Austro-Hungarian government promptly announced its annexation of the two provinces, agreeing, however, to evacuate the strategic sandjak of Novibazaar.

There was great indignation in Turkey, and a boycott of Austrian goods and merchants was inaugurated. Interesting enough, in view of the discarding of the fez (tarboush) by the Turks in the Turkish Republic, was the wearing of caps by some of the patriotic Turks in 1908 instead of fezzes because these were made in Austria. The excitement in Turkey and the anti-Austrian boycotts soon died down under instructions from the C.U.P. when a settlement was made with the Austrian government which provided for the payment of a sizable sum to the Ottoman government which was badly in need of funds.

Russia was indignant with Austria because her precipitate action precluded the possibility of the Russians preparing the necessary diplomatic maneuvers to obtain the consent of the Concert of European Powers to the opening of the Straits. England and France, who seven years later were to agree to give Russia both Constantinople and the Straits, and who were to spend much blood and treasure in vain attempts to open a route to Russia through the Dardanelles, were unwilling to make any concessions to their ally in 1908. Izvolsky was discredited. He had agreed to Austria's taking the two Turkish provinces without having obtained a *quid pro quo* for Russia. He lost his job as Foreign Minister and was sent to Paris as Ambassador, where as an implacable enemy of Austria-Hungary he worked diligently for war between the Triple Entente and the Triple Alliance. Historians have considered him to be one among those most responsible for the outbreak of World War I.

Serbs prepare for war, Bulgars and Cretans declare their independence.—In Belgrade the Serbs were at fever heat against Austria-Hungary because of the annexation of two Balkan provinces which were almost entirely inhabited by Yugoslavs. Only the restraining hand of Russia, which was not prepared for war and did not expect to be so until 1917, kept Serbia from sending Austria-Hungary an ultimatum. Instead, the Serbs endeavored to negotiate an agreement with Turkey which would compensate them for the change in the status quo in the Balkans. The Young Turks toyed with the idea of regaining absolute sovereignty over the autonomous principality of Bulgaria which the Grand Vizier had spoken of as a vassal state. To forestall any such attempt by the new government of Turkey, the Bulgars declared their complete independence in the first week of October 1908, just before Austria annexed Bosnia and Herzegovina. The Young Turks threatened to go to war against Bulgaria, which had seized possession of the Ottoman-owned railroad through Eastern Rumelia. It was not until April 19, 1909, in the midst of the "Counterrevolution," that a Turko-Bulgarian Protocol was signed by which Turkey recognized Bulgarian independence.

When the news reached Crete that Bulgaria had declared its independence of Turkey, the Cretan Assembly promptly voted annexation to the Kingdom of Greece, decreed that all government officials should take an oath of allegiance to the Greek King George, and raised the Greek flag on public buildings. The representatives of the four occupying Powers—England, France, Italy, and Russia—looked on benignly and held their peace. The Greek government, which at the time was attempting to checkmate Bulgaria by arriving at an agreement with the Young Turks favorable to Greeks in Macedonia, cautiously stated that the future of Crete was a matter to be decided by the European Concert of Powers. In January Kiamil Pasha, the Grand Vizier, declared in Parliament that the settlement of the Cretan matter lay wholly in the hands of the Powers and mentioned the correctness of the position taken by the Greek government. Neither the Turkish cabinet nor the parliament, however, was determining the foreign policy of the Ottoman Empire. As G. F. Abbott in his book, *Turkey in Transition,* says with brutal frankness, policy-making had "to a large extent passed out of the control of responsible statesmen" into the hands of the C.U.P. which had "small regard for facts." Smarting under the loss of Bosnia and Herzegovina and the action of Bulgaria, the ardent young nationalists of the C.U.P. decided to take a stand on Crete, thinking it would raise their prestige at home and abroad. The press of the C.U.P. misrepresented the situation in Crete, where a Cretan Moslem population of only 30,000 out of a total population of 300,000 had had since 1897 equal political and civil rights with the Christian majority. The papers of the committee described the Moslems as living in Crete under an unbearable oppression, wrote of the loss of Crete as a national catastrophe, and said that the committee were determined to go to war if necessary rather than to surrender the island.

Confronted with this impasse, the occupying Powers withdrew their military forces from Crete, but kept their naval forces in the Cretan harbor at Suda Bay in order to see that the Turkish flag continued to fly there. E. C. Helmreich in his very thorough book on *The Diplomacy of the Balkan Wars, 1912–1913,* remarks that "it was clear that neither Turkey nor the Powers would ever permit Crete to join Greece until forced to do so." This situation resulted in a revolutionary uprising in Crete, led by Venizelos, which was suppressed by the four Powers. Venizelos promptly left for Athens, where he became a member of the Greek Parliament over protests to the Greek government by the Porte. The actions of the Young Turks drove to the Greek mainland a Cretan revolutionist who was to become premier of Greece in 1910 and one of the principal architects of the Balkan Alliance against Turkey, which forced the Turks not only to relinquish Crete but to surrender

Macedonia and part of Thrace. Blindly following their nationalistic policy, the Committee of Union and Progress instituted an economic boycott not only of Greece but of all the Ottoman Greeks and fanned Turkish hatred of Greeks in general. This policy alienated the Ottoman Greeks, who now turned against the Young Turks, and drove the Greeks into the arms of Bulgaria, resulting by 1912 in a Graeco-Bulgarian alliance and a joint military convention, and eventually into war against Turkey.

Egyptian and Arab Nationalists.—Some of the Young Turks tried to raise the issue of Egypt while Egyptian Nationalists approached the Sultan with the idea of getting rid of the British. The C.U.P., which during the first two years after the Revolution of 1908 was strongly pro-English and anti-German, since they considered Germany to be the principal foreign protagonist of the Hamidian regime, did not allow the question of Egypt to arise and practically prevented any public discussion of it.

The Arab intellectuals and liberals who at first welcomed the Turkish Revolution, some of the leading Arabs being associated with the Young Turk revolutionists, were soon to be disillusioned. Arab nationalism was to find itself incompatible with that of the members of the Committee of Union and Progress. Like the Arabs, the Zionists whose leaders eventually turned to the British during World War I found themselves in serious difficulties with the new Turkish government.

CHAPTER XII

The Italian and the Balkan Wars

The foreign difficulties of the Young Turks continued to increase as their domestic problems grew more serious. The Italian government, not having profited from the changes in the Balkans, decided that the time was ripe to seize Tripoli, the sole remaining Turkish possession in North Africa. Italy had prepared for this move long in advance.

THE WAR WITH ITALY

Italian ambitions in North Africa.—In the first half of the nineteenth century, more than twenty years before the Kingdom of Italy came into existence, the Italian Nationalists looked upon North Africa as a future Italian possession. Mazzini, the founder of the Young Italy nationalist movement, is reputed to have said: "North Africa belongs to Italy." Like other liberal nationalists of the last century, as well as of this, Italian patriots were dreaming of imposing Italian rule over non-Italian peoples even before they had thrown off the alien yoke of the Austrian Habsburgs. Among nationalists, sauce for the goose is never sauce for the gander. In the minds of liberal nationalists, imperialism imposed by autocratic monarchy was despotism, while imperialism imposed by a representative constitutional democracy was the fulfillment of a humanitarian mission.

When the Third French Republic seized Tunis in 1881, there was much indignation in Italy because the French had secured a territory of strategic importance to Italy where there were some 50,000 Italian colonists. Napoleon III had encouraged the House of Savoy in 1857, then reigning over Sardinia, to take Tunis. In 1878, Austria and Russia had offered Italy a free hand in Tunis, and even England and Germany gave the Italians encouragement. The establishment of the French protectorate in 1881 inevitably ended all Italian hope of obtaining

Tunis. The Italians then became determined that no other Power should establish itself in Tripoli.

The Great Powers agree to Italian expansion in North Africa.—Having joined the Triple Alliance in 1882, in part for the purpose of blocking further French expansion in North Africa, Italy in a treaty with Germany in 1887 succeeded in getting the Germans to agree to support Italy in her efforts to get Tripoli if and when France changed the status quo in North Africa. In 1890 and again in 1895, Italy contemplated occupying Tripoli, but did not dare to do so without the consent of France and England. The Franco-Italian *rapprochement* in 1901–2 resulted in an exchange of letters between the French and Italian governments by which France agreed to allow Italy a free hand in Tripoli in exchange for a free hand in Morocco. England gave her blessing to this blank check France had given Italy. Austria signified her consent to Italian desires in Tripoli when the Triple Alliance was renewed in 1902. After the Young Turk Revolution of 1908 and Austria's annexation of Bosnia and Herzegovina, Russia and Italy in 1909, by the Racconigi Agreement concerning the Balkans, came to an understanding whereby Italy would support Russia's demands for the opening of the Straits and Russia would grant Italy a free hand in Tripoli.

The steps to war.—By 1909 the Italian government had obtained the backing of the five major European Powers for eventual seizure of the Turkish provinces of Tripoli and Cyrenaica, called Libya by the Italians. In view of the long existing plans of the Italian government to annex Libya in due course of events at a favorable movement, it is somewhat astonishing to find Sir Harry Luke stating in his book, *The Making of Modern Turkey,* that "in September 1911, the Italian Government surprised not only Turkey but the world by declaring on the Ottoman Government a war that ended in the loss of Turkey's last direct possession in Africa." [1] (Actually, of course, Egypt remained a nominal possession of the Ottoman Sultan until England proclaimed it to be a British Protectorate in December 1914.) In Libya Turkish rule in 1908 did not extend much beyond the coastal towns except for a few military outposts in the interior.

The people of the world who have little time to keep themselves posted on foreign affairs and who were not informed by their governments of the secret political and military treaties, conventions, and agreements made by the diplomats and military men, naturally were taken by surprise when Italy, seemingly for no reason whatsoever, declared war on Turkey. There was far less excuse for the Turkish rulers or those of any of the other countries to be taken by surprise at Italy's ultimatum to the Ottoman government.

The Committee of Union and Progress showed as great ineptitude in dealing with the affair of Tripoli as it had in handling the Cretan problem. In both cases the C.U.P. pursued a policy which led to war and to the loss not only of Libya and Crete but of other territories. Catering to public opinion, sentiments, and prejudices, the C.U.P. deliberately misled the Turkish people about the actual situation in Libya and in Crete and about the international aspects of the Libyan question.

The Turkish people were led to believe that the Turkish forces in North Africa were much larger than was actually the case and that hundreds of thousands of Moslems there would rush to arms and overwhelm any Italian force which attempted to land in Libya. The Turkish people were not told that Tripoli was of neither economic nor strategic value to Turkey, that with the preponderant naval strength of Italy it would be impossible to send troops to Libya or to maintain adequate supply lines, and that Turkish ports and Turkish held islands in the Aegean would be helpless against Italian naval attacks.

Having been obliged to submit to the loss of Bosnia and Herzegovina, as well as of Bulgaria, the C.U.P. would not and probably could not have supinely accepted the loss of a North African possession whose inhabitants were overwhelmingly Moslem without losing its position of political power in Turkey. It handled the situation, however, so maladroitly that the Italian government was given the opportunity to whip their people into a war mood and to create a situation which eliminated any possibility of any or all of the other great Powers from restraining Italy.

The C.U.P. did not realize that Austria and Germany, both very friendly to the Young Turks, could not risk losing Italy as an ally by opposing Italian policy with respect to Libya. Even if the C.U.P. leaders were not aware of the commitments to Italy by all the great Powers, they might have known had they not been blinded by national pride and passion that the Teutonic Allies would not restrain Italy.[2]

When France in 1911 by her action in Morocco changed the status quo in North Africa, Italy decided to take Tripoli, knowing that the members of neither the Triple Entente nor the Triple Alliance would oppose her action. An ultimatum was sent to Turkey, and war was declared on September 29, 1911.

Libya had been practically independent of the Ottoman sultanate from 1714 until 1835, when Turkey regained a control which had been not much more than nominal since the organization in 1843 of the

Senussi Brotherhood, whose Grand Sheik was the real ruler. This profoundly religious organization had little use for the Young Turks who were considered not much better than infidels. Nevertheless, the Senussi gave full support to the Turks in the defense of Libya against the hated Italians. A leading Young Turk, who was soon to become one of the triumvirate who ruled Turkey until 1918, Enver Bey, managed to reach Libya and, preaching a Holy War (Jihad) against the giaours, organized the resistance to the Italians, who at first made little progress after landing their forces in North Africa. While the struggle dragged on in Libya, the Italians seized Rhodes and the Dodecanese Islands in the Aegean, attacked Turkish ports and blockaded the Dardanelles. The Turks continued this hopeless war in Tripoli until 1912 when they were threatened with war by the Balkan States.

The Treaty of Lausanne, 1912.—The Treaty of Lausanne of October 18, 1912, brought to an end the Turco-Italian War. Turkey recognized Italian sovereignty in Libya, and Italy agreed to restore the Dodecanese Islands to Turkey when the Turks fulfilled the terms of the treaty. Libya was lost in 1911, and the Turks never recovered the Dodecanese Islands which Italy held on one pretext or another. Following the losses in the Balkans and that of Crete the third step in the liquidation of the Ottoman Empire under the Young Turks had taken place at the time when the fourth was beginning. Although it is probable that the inexperience and political incompetence of the C.U.P. hastened the dissolution of the Ottoman Empire, the underlying causes of the failure of the Young Turks were much deeper than the lack of capacity of the leaders. The C.U.P. came to power at a time when the first great crisis in the twentieth century of the European political and social system was rapidly approaching. No Ottoman government could have remained unaffected by what Churchill called "The World Crisis," the Young Turk regime less than any other, because the revolution of 1908 created a situation in the Near East which precipitated action by the national minorities within the Ottoman Empire, by the Balkan States, and by the Great Powers. All three of these factors contributed to the causes of the Balkan Wars of 1912–13, and of World War I in 1914.[3]

THE BALKAN WARS

The honeymoon between the Young Turks and the Macedonian Christians did not long endure. Having lost any immediate chance of expansion to the west as a result of Austria's annexation of Bosnia and Herzegovina, the Serbs were more determined than ever to acquire control of western Macedonia. The Greeks, suffering a rebuff at the hands of the Young Turks, reached the conclusion that the time was approaching when the Macedonian as well as the Cretan question must be settled. The intensification of the policy of Ottomanization, which strangely enough was linked with a pro-Moslem, Turkish nationalistic program in Macedonia, antagonized Albanians, Serbs, Greeks, and Bulgars. The struggle for dominance in Macedonia recommenced shortly after the revolution of 1908.

The untenable situation in the Balkans.—The situation became untenable and intolerable. The Great Powers were not fully prepared for a general European war, so that neither the Triple Entente nor the Triple Alliance between 1908 and 1912 wished to precipitate it by intervention in the Balkans. Realizing the unwillingness of the European Powers to settle the Macedonian Question, the Balkan States most concerned decided upon united action and created the Balkan Alliance to carry out their plans.

The inability of the Turks to cope with the situation.—Among the many factors that led to the Balkan Wars of 1912–13 not the least in importance were the political conditions in the Ottoman Empire, and particularly the bitter political struggle among the Turks. At a time when the maladjustments in the Ottoman state had reached their apex, the differences between the Turks themselves were greatly intensified. There was no agreement among them either as to the causes of the maladjustments or as to the nature of the changes required. Elements of the Turkish ruling class were at complete odds with one another. In addition to the fundamental cleavage between the reactionaries and the Young Turks, profound differences developed between the "Turkish revolutionists" that led to bitter and ruthless political strife between the Liberal Unionists and the Young Turk Party, and even within the Young Turk Party and its controlling organization, the Committee of Union and Progress.

The divergences between the various minority groups—Albanians, Arabs, Armenians, Bulgars, Greeks, Kurds, and Serbs—and between all of these nationalities and the Turks made representative parliamentary government an impossibility. Constitutional government under the conditions prevailing in the Ottoman Near East between 1908 and 1918 could not function. The Turks remained the rulers. Lack of agreement among them resulted in government by a small Turkish oligarchy and then by a dictatorship.

From the *coup d'état* of July 1908 until February 1909, the Committee of Union and Progress ruled by indirection, as a secret organization controlling the armed forces and exerting hidden control of both the cabinet and the parliament. In February 1909 the C.U.P. took over more direct control, having discovered that since the meeting of the Chamber of Deputies in December of the preceding year their Turkish opponents, particularly the Liberal Unionists with the support of the non-Turkish minority groups, were undermining the power of the Committee of Union and Progress. Rising opposition to the C.U.P. resulted in the brief interlude of the "Counter Revolution" from April 13 to 25, 1909. Another *coup d'état* by the C.U.P. established the arbitrary government of the Committee until July 22, 1912. Disturbances in Syria, revolt in the Yemen, uprisings in Albania, and the futile war with Italy created discontent within the ranks of the C.U.P. and among the army officers that, coupled with that of the opposition groups, overthrew the C.U.P. ministry and gave the opponents of the C.U.P. control of the government until January 1913.

The acceptance by this anti-Committee ministry of peace terms proposed by the European Powers to end the first Balkan War brought about another *coup d'état* of the C.U.P. led by Enver Bey, a popular hero because of his spectacular activities in Tripoli during the Turco-Italian War. This *coup d'état* initiated a dictatorship of a factional group within the Committee of Union and Progress which the Russian historian and diplomat André Mandelstam, in his penetrating, if somewhat biased, book, *Le Sort de l'Empire Ottoman,* speaks of as "the period of Young Turk terror." [4] The dictatorship of Enver, Minister of War, Talaat, Minister of the Interior, and Jemal, Minister of Marine, with its secret police, its arbitrary arrests, its censorship, its harsh treatment of national minorities, and its pan-Islamic policy, differed little from that of Abdul Hamid. Whether this "Young Turk" dictatorship might have found a solution for the maladjustments in the Ottoman Empire if it had not been for World War I remains a futile academic question. World War I destroyed the Ottoman Empire and gave the Turkish Nationalists, who were the political, as well as logical, successors of the Young Turks, the opportunity to solve the "Turkish problem" within an area far more limited than the Ottoman Empire, in which the population was predominantly Turkish.

The Young Turks under C.U.P. leadership alienated all the non-Turkish minority groups, Christian and Moslem, and even provoked to insurrection and revolution the Albanian Moslems who for centuries had been staunch supporters of the Ottoman sultans. The Turkish government under C.U.P. domination pursued domestic and foreign policies that led to the war with Italy, the two Balkan wars and eventually to Turkey's entrance into World War I on the side of Germany and

Austria. The Committee of Union and Progress, contrary to its aims and intentions, prepared the way for the partition and liquidation of the Ottoman Empire. The Turks were, however, by no means the only ruling class in the twentieth century who were unable to resolve the maladjustments inherent in imperialism and the social order which gave rise to it.

The responsibility of the Great Powers.—The Great Powers of Europe, divided into two armed camps whose members had diverse policies based on their rival political and competitive economic interests, were in no small degree responsible for the conditions in the Balkans which gave rise to the Balkan Wars and which were the precipitating cause of World War I. By the Treaty of Paris of 1856, by the Treaty of Berlin of 1878, by their ceaseless intrigues, and by their failure to implement an effective policy of reforms, the European Powers helped to create the situation which caused the Balkan States to resort to arms in order to settle the issues.

The Turkish nationalistic and pro-Moslem policy of the C.U.P. and the settlement in Macedonia of Moslem *émigrés* from Bosnia and Herzegovina after the Austrian annexation convinced the Bulgarian Macedonians, whose revolutionary organization, the IMRO (*International Macedonia Revolutionary Organization*), established in 1893, had acquired very considerable political and popular influence in Bulgaria, that the time had come in 1911 for action against Turkey. Strong supporters of the war party in Sofia, the members of the IMRO urged the Bulgarian government to reach an agreement with Serbia. A similar development was occurring in Belgrade. The Serbians had organized in 1908 the *Narodna Odbrana* ("National Defense") to carry on nationalistic propaganda in Serbia and in both the Austrian and Ottoman empires. The leadership of this organization was taken over by the society of "Union or Death," known as the *Black Hand,* which had been organized in 1911 to carry on a more effective nationalist movement in Bosnia-Herzegovina and in Macedonia using terroristic methods. Control of both the *Black Hand* and the *Narodna Odbrana* centered largely in the Serbian army. In 1911 Colonel Apis, a leader of the *Black Hand,* informed the Serbian Minister of Foreign Affairs that his organization favored common action by Bulgaria and Serbia with respect to Macedonia. The outbreak of the Turco-Italian War in September 1911 increased agitation for a Bulgar-Serbian alliance in the formation of which Russia became actively interested. Negotiations between Bulgars and Serbs dragged on until March 1912, when an alliance and military convention were signed between Bulgaria and

Serbia, with Tsar Nicholas II of Russia acting as a sort of political midwife in helping the painful diplomatic labors of Serbian and Bulgarian statesmen.

Bulgars, Serbs, and Greeks plan for war and the division of spoils.— By this alliance Bulgars and Serbs came to an agreement as to a division of the spoils in case of victory over the Turks, for the treaty was, as Raymond Poincaré of France rightly remarked on learning of its terms, a *convention de guerre.* While Russia's interest in encouraging this alignment of Bulgaria and Serbia was mainly directed toward blocking Austrian and German control of the Balkans, that of both the Bulgars and the Serbs was the achievement of national irredentist aims in European Turkey.

Since their interests had long been in conflict in Macedonia, very definite territorial arrangements were stipulated in the treaty of alliance. The northwestern part of Macedonia was to go to Serbia, territory east of the Rhodope Mountains and the Struma River was to go to Bulgaria, an area in central Macedonia was to go to Bulgaria if an autonomous Macedonia was not created, and a "contested area" lying north and westward of this region was left to the decision of Russia as to whether it should be assigned to Bulgaria or Serbia. The treaty was vague with respect to the southern part of Macedonia where Greek and Bulgarian interests clashed.

Greek and Bulgarian conversations had been taking place concurrently with the Bulgar-Serbian negotiations in the autumn of 1911 and the winter of 1911 and 1912. The way had been prepared for a Graeco-Bulgar *rapprochement* by the advent into Greek political life of the Cretan rebel leader, a sworn enemy of the Turks, Venizelos. Before he became Premier of Greece on October 18, 1910, Venizelos talked with the correspondent of the London *Times,* J. D. Bourchier, whom he had known from his Cretan days, about an alliance with Bulgaria.

This policy he could not openly pursue until the Greek army was very considerably increased. In fact, Venizelos was obliged at first to feign a pro-Turkish policy. The friction between the Young Turks and the Greeks made such a policy impractical at a time when the C.U.P.'s activities in Macedonia were bringing about a reconciliation of Greeks and Bulgars.

With J. D. Bourchier and H. Wickham Steed of the London *Times* acting as marriage brokers, the Graeco-Bulgar exchange of views and negotiations, despite Russia's lack of encouragement, resulted in a treaty of alliance and a military convention signed on May 30, 1912. Though nominally a defensive treaty, it was actually an offensive one against

Turkey. Unlike the Bulgar-Serbian treaty, it did not contain any clauses dealing with the allocation of the anticipated spoils. So overlapping and opposed were Greek and Bulgarian claims to Macedonia that it had not been considered politic to deal with them in the treaty. The only concession Bulgaria made to Greek ambitions concerned Crete and the other Aegean Islands.

The First Balkan War 1912–13 and the Treaty of London.—The web around Turkey was being rapidly spun in 1912. A verbal understanding was reached by Greece with both Montenegro and Serbia. Montenegro made a written agreement with Bulgaria and signed an alliance with Serbia on October 6, 1912, two days before declaring war on Turkey. The Turks were entangled with the four Balkan Allies one day before the peace treaty of Lausanne with Italy was signed on October 18, 1912. The Balkan States ignored the advice of Austria and Russia. Turkey rejected the collective communication of the Five Great Powers. Both were attempts to prevent war by assuring the Balkan States that reforms would be made effective and by promising Turkey the maintenance of the status quo. This old and futile diplomacy of Europe in dealing with the "Eastern Question," as it was then called, was on the threshold of its nemesis for which the Balkan wars paved the way.

The Turks were unprepared for war. Military and political weakness made it impossible for them to cope with the Balkan allies. The Turkish forces were defeated by the armies of each of the four allies. Within a few weeks from the commencement of hostilities only the cities of Scutari in Albania, Janina in Epirus, and Adrianople and Constantinople remained in the hands of the Ottoman troops. The Bulgarians were near the gates of Constantinople at Tchalaldja and were besieging Adrianople. The Turkish cause appeared hopeless and an armistice was signed on December 3, 1912.

The Turks, however, were soon to profit from the disagreements of the Balkan allies and the interference with Balkan affairs by the European Powers. Russia gave notice that she would not tolerate an occupation of Constantinople. The Bulgars, realizing there was nothing more except Adrianople to be obtained by continuing the war with Turkey, were anxious to negotiate peace in order that they might have troops available to occupy the areas in Macedonia agreed to between Bulgaria and Serbia in their treaty of alliance. Although Greece refused to sign the terms of the armistice, these were accepted by Bulgaria, Montenegro, and Serbia, and peace negotiations began in London on December 13, 1912.

The European Powers had no intention of permitting the Balkan States to determine the peace terms. Austria had already notified the other Powers that she would not permit Serbia to acquire control of any part of Albania that would give the Serbs an outlet on the Adriatic. Italy was also unwilling to allow the Serbs access to the Adriatic Sea. Austria had mobilized considerable forces in Bosnia and threatened Serbia with military intervention if she attempted to reach the coast. Austria and Italy were likewise opposed to Montenegro taking over Scutari and part of northern Albania. Austria insisted that Albania should become an autonomous state within her historical frontiers. Russia was taking military precautions against Austria. The situation looked ominous. None of the Great Powers, however, was desirous in 1912 of precipitating a European war. Consequently, they all welcomed a conference of ambassadors at London, which foregathered on December 17, 1912.

With one eye on the Powers and the other on the political situation in Constantinople, the Turkish delegation was in no haste to conclude peace. The Turkish government knew how violent would be the reaction of the Committee of Union and Progress if the Aegean Islands and Adrianople were surrendered under the terms of peace. The Balkan Allies were insistent upon their surrender, but the Turks refused and peace negotiations were suspended on January 6, 1913. The Powers then forced the hand of the Turkish government by sending a collective note insisting upon Turkish acceptance of these terms. No sooner did the special council summoned by the Turkish Cabinet vote 65 to 1 to accept the peace terms offered than the government was overthrown by Enver Bey's *coup d'état* of January 23, 1913. The armistice was terminated and hostilities recommenced on February 3.

The C.U.P. dictatorship was no more able to cope with the military situation than the government it had replaced. The Greeks captured Janina and occupied southern Albania and the island of Samos. The Montenegrins took Scutari and the Bulgars captured Adrianople. As early as the end of February, the Turks were obliged to accept the mediation of the Powers, but it was not until the end of April 1913 that hostilities ceased. The First Balkan War was brought to a conclusion by the Treaty of London on May 30.

The Second Balkan War and the Treaty of Bucharest.—The international occupation of Albania and the decision to set up an autonomous principality of Albania forced Serbia to relinquish all hope of expansion westward. The Serbs were, as a result, determined to revise in their favor the territorial terms of their treaty with Bulgaria. The Bulgarians refused to do so. Urged by Austria to cede some territory to Romania, who up to this time had remained neutral, the Bulgarians again refused, depending ill-advisedly upon Russia to restrain the Romanians. Irritated by the treatment meted out to Bulgarian Macedonians in the areas occupied by the Serbian and Greek forces, the Bulgars attacked Greeks and Serbs. Greece and Serbia had made their preparations for war with Bulgaria a month earlier, on June 1, by a Graeco-Serbian Treaty and military convention, which, among other matters arranged for the partition of the greater part of Macedonia among themselves. The Second Balkan War had begun. Romania promptly joined in the hostilities and invaded Bulgaria. To meet this onslaught, the Bulgars withdrew their forces from Adrianople. Turkey renewed hostilities and on July 22, 1913, Enver Pasha rode triumphantly into Adrianople, the ancient Balkan capital of the Ottoman sultans prior to the fall of Constantinople in 1453.

There was great rejoicing in Turkey, the prestige of the Committee of Union and Progress was considerably enhanced, and the young Enver became for the second time a national hero. In this bloodless victory, due solely to the collapse of the Balkan Alliance and the avaricious war between the former allies, the Turks forgot temporarily the humiliating defeats and losses of the Turco-Italian and the First Balkan War.

Utterly defeated, the Bulgars accepted the dictated peace of Bucharest imposed upon them by the Christian Balkan states. Romania took Bulgarian territory between the lower Danube and the Black Sea. Serbia and Greece shared the major portion of Macedonia. Bulgaria was given an outlet on the Aegean at Dedeagatch (Alexandroupolis), which was of little commercial importance, since it lacked any harbor and was almost inaccessible during the winter months. This little Bulgarian village acquired, nevertheless, considerable importance during the early part of World War I, while Bulgaria was still neutral, because it was the only means of access to and an outlet from Constantinople.

Turkey was not permitted to take part in the peace conference at Bucharest, but signed a separate treaty with Bulgaria in September, and with the Greeks in November; it was not until March 1914 that the Turks signed a treaty with Serbia.

Between 1908 and 1913 the Young Turks had lost Libya and the Dodecanese Islands to Italy; Crete and most of the other Aegean Islands to Greece; Bosnia, Herzegovina, the autonomous principality of Bulgaria including Eastern Rumelia, Albania, Macedonia, and part of Thrace. Turkish territory in Europe had been reduced from 65,000 (c) to 11,000 (c) square miles and the population of European Turkey from over six millions to slightly less than two millions.

In addition to all their other difficulties, the Young Turks were confronted with an Arab nationalist movement which, in response to the aggressive nationalistic policy of the C.U.P., was developing into an underground revolutionary movement.

CHAPTER XIII

The Arab Renaissance and Nationalist Movement, 1866-1914

The Arab revolutionary movement and revolt of 1916 which confronted the Committee of Union and Progress were the outgrowth of an intellectual awakening in the nineteenth century that gave birth to a nationalist political movement shortly before the Turkish revolution. The Arabs were affected by forces similar to those which were arousing to national consciousness the other peoples of the Ottoman Empire. The closely associated triple phenomena of renaissance, liberalism, and nationalism were universal factors throughout the Near East during the nineteenth century. They were the determining elements in the historical development within recent times of Arabs, Armenians, the various Balkan peoples, and the Turks. In the case of each of these peoples, a great variety of variables created special aspects of their individual renaissance, liberal, and national movements.

❁ THE REBIRTH OF ANCIENT CULTURES

The renaissance of the Greeks was based on Byzantine Christian culture and that of pagan Greece; the renaissance of the Bulgars and Serbs was founded on a revival of ninth-century Orthodoxy and on memories of their respective medieval feudal empires; the Turkish renaissance turned backward to the periods of the Ottoman conquerors and of the earlier Turanian tribes; the Armenian renaissance was inspired by fourth-century Gregorian Christianity and the medieval Armenian culture; the Arab renaissance was founded on the culture of early Islam and the rich Arab heritage of the Middle Ages. Since each of these was inspired by and developed through contact with contemporary European culture, all of them were molded by nineteenth-century liberalism and nationalism.

The new and heady wines of the modern western world were being poured into ancient Near Eastern bottles of differing shapes and sizes. These were not empty containers, for each was partially filled with varying amounts of different age-old vintages. During the process, fermentation continued.

The peoples of the Arab world of western Asia, of Egypt, and of North Africa were all affected by their contacts with the West. The Arabic speaking people everywhere felt to a greater or lesser degree the Arab renaissance. Likewise, although local nationalist movements, such as that of the Egyptians, developed in various parts of the Arab world, most Arabs to some extent nursed the idea of Arab nationalism. It is, however, the renaissance which took place among Arabs of western Asia and the nationalist movements which sprang up there that are of most concern to the historical evolution of the Near East.

THE ARABS OF WESTERN ASIA

These developments among the Arabic-speaking peoples of western Asia were shaped by the geography of the Arab lands and by the characteristics of the various Arab groups who inhabited them. Although the Arab lands of western Asia have a certain clearly defined geographic unity, nevertheless the unity is considerably disrupted by their topographical features. This Asiatic Arab world lies roughly within the following boundaries, which do not conform with contemporary political frontiers: in the north from Alexandretta through Aleppo to Mosul; in the east by the present frontier of Iraq and Iran and by the western shore of the Persian Gulf; in the south by the Indian Ocean; and in the west by the Red Sea, the Gulf of Suez, the Suez Canal, and the eastern shore of the Mediterranean from Port Said to Alexandretta. In this area the overwhelming majority of people are Arabs by language and by culture, however mixed they may be biologically. Since the Arab conquest of this whole area in the seventh century, it has been the Arab world of Asia irrespective of who ruled over it. The former civilizations were in part assimilated and in part superseded by the Arabic culture. Although important minorities remained Christian, Arabic became the language of all. Irrespective of their previous culture and of their religion and creed the people became Arabs. Fundamentally, this situation in no way changed until the great migration of Jews to Palestine in the twentieth century created a Jewish enclave alien in language and culture.

The unity created by Arab culture and language persisted although the Arab lands of Asia are widely separated by vast semiarid and arid deserts. Like a great inland sea with its shores and islands, the deserts both divide and link together the Arab people living in fertile oases and along the fringes of the deserts. The connecting links between the Arabs of the cities and cultivated regions of the various Arab lands are the nomads of the desert, the Bedouins.

The meaning of ibn Arab.—In earlier times these pastoral nomads were called Arabs and were looked upon with contempt and even hatred by townsmen and peasants. The term Arab has, now, taken on a different meaning. Today all those who are Arabic by language and culture speak of themselves as Arabs, be they Iraqians, Syrians, Lebanese, Palestinians, Yemenites, Hejazi, or others in the Arab lands of Asia. Among a people who are exceedingly conscious of the importance of geneaology and who speak of themselves as "the son of—" or "the father of—," the expression *ibn Arab,* "son of an Arab," is significant. It is doubtful, however, whether this expression carries the same connotations as the jargon of western nationalists and racialists. It is only in most recent years that a nationalistic and racial meaning has been given to the expression *ibn Arab.*

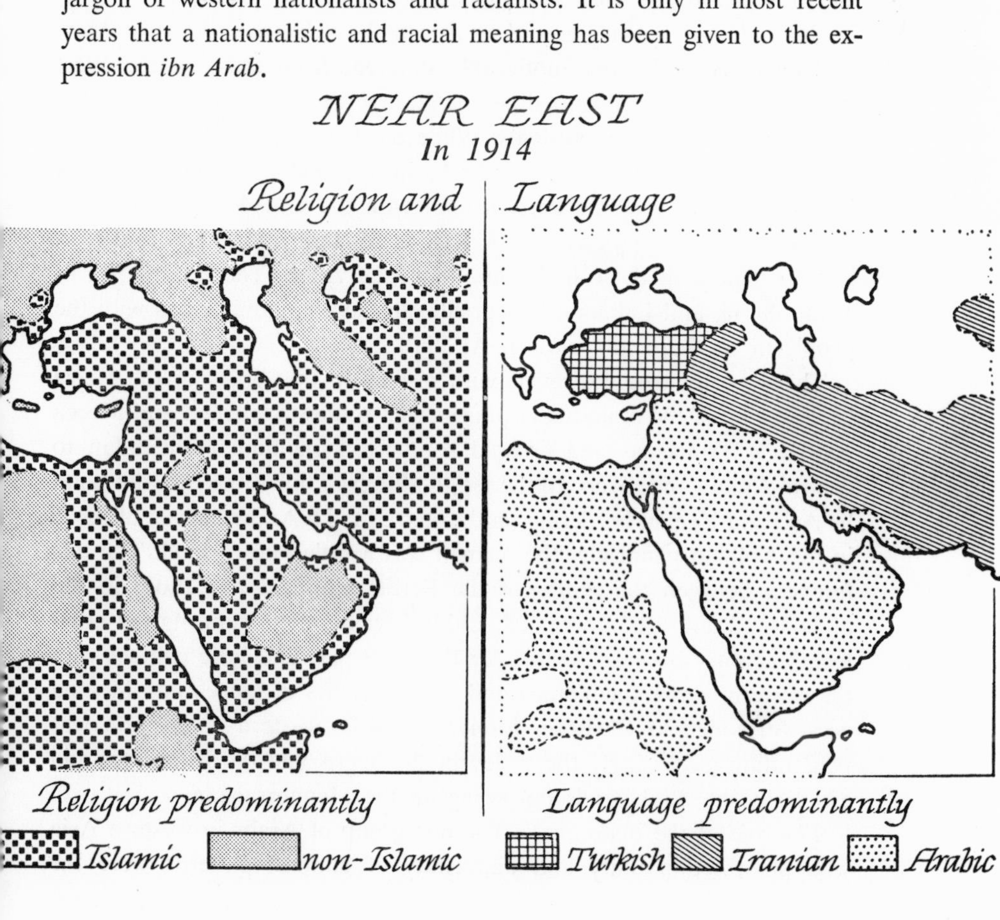

So diversified and varied are the various parts of the Asiatic Arab world and the people thereof that caution must be observed in using the terms renaissance and nationalism with respect to the Arabs of western Asia. Even at the beginning of the twentieth century an Arab was known by his tribe or by the village or the town he lived in. Even though he would speak of himself as an *ibn Arab,* he would identify himself with his tribe, region, town, or village. Except for the pilgrimage to Mecca and Medina and the seasonal movements of the Bedouins to their grazing grounds, few Arabs traveled far from their usual habitat. Consequently there was little communication between Arabs in different parts of western Asia.

Diversity and uniformity among the Arabs.—The Arabs in the western horn of the Fertile Crescent, that is, in Palestine, Transjordan, Lebanon, and Syria, were more closely related to one another than to Arabs elsewhere. Even among these Arabs there were very distinct differences and little uniformity. The Arabs in the eastern horn of the Fertile Crescent, in the valley of the Tigris and Euphrates between the rivers, in Mesopotamia, not only were noticeably different from those in the West but they were divided into different groups, the most important being the Sunnite and Shiite Moslems. While the Syrian desert separated the western Arabs from the eastern Arabs in Mesopotamia, the latter were in contact by way of the Persian Gulf with the settled communities of Arabs on the eastern coast of Arabia in el-Hasa and Oman and to a lesser extent with those in Hadhramaut and Aden. The Arabs of Palestine, Syria, and Lebanon had practically no communications with the people in southern and eastern Arabia.

This was not true, however, with respect to the Arabs in the Hejaz because one of the main hadj (pilgrimage) routes to Medina and Mecca started at Damascus and crossed southern Syria and Transjordan to central Arabia and thence to the Hejaz. South of this Moslem Holy Land lie Asir and Yemen bordering on the Red Sea. To Arabs outside of those in the Arabian peninsula, the Yemen was a little known land. The differences between the Arabs of the Fertile Crescent and those in the agricultural and urban areas of Arabia became greater during the nineteenth century because Arabia for the most part had little contact with the western world; the Yemen and the holy cities of Mecca and Medina were forbidden to Christian foreigners, while western civilization was penetrating increasingly the valley of the Tigris and the Euphrates and especially the Arab lands bordering on the Mediterranean.

The role of the Bedouins.—The one group of Arabs in western Asia who possessed a unity and uniformity of cultural patterns were the

Bedouins. Despite their division into rival tribes and their unending tribal wars, these pastoral nomads lived the same kind of life and had similar social organizations while their divergences were of a minor nature. All of the settled Arabs, whether in the north or south in the east or west of the Arab lands in Asia, were in contact with the Bedouins. The Arab nomads were a connecting tie with all other Arabs. The deserts were also breeding grounds which continually replenished the agrarian and urban populations of the Arab lands. The extraordinary capacity of the Arabs to absorb and assimilate the hordes of invaders who throughout history have seized control, for a longer or shorter period, of the settled parts of the Arab lands seems due in a considerable degree to the Bedouins. This unfailing source of Arab blood, language, and customs overflowing the lands bordering on the deserts counteracted the effect of the alien invaders and conquerors. It is due to the Bedouins that the inhabitants of these lands today call themselves Arabs.

Nationalism and the Arabs.—The western concept of nationalism, which Arab nationalists have and still are attempting to make synonymous with the expression *ibn Arab,* made slow progress among most of the Arabs previous to World War I. In fact it is still a question as to what Arab groups even today think in terms of Arab nationalism. There is nothing startlingly new in the statement that words lead to misunderstanding and false comprehension. Among the most tyrannous of modern words are nationalism and nationalistic. The phenomenon of nationalism is not easy to define or describe. In recent and modern times it has shown itself to be a very powerful social force with its roots deep in the political, economic, and psychological life of our period of history. It operates upon groups and individuals in a variety of ways, some of which have been closely analyzed.

In periods of great stress and strain typical of the crises in the modern world, nationalism becomes a very potent force. During World War I the author noted three striking manifestations of nationalism as it acted upon three different individuals. One was a Moslem Ottoman subject of Bosnian Slavic origin, another was a French Jew, and still another an American of Welsh extraction.

In Beersheba during 1915 a young Ottoman officer, to whom I had a letter of introduction from a mutual friend, talked as any patriotic Young Turk would, expressing his loyalty to Turkey and to Islam. In 1917 this same young officer at some risk to himself speaking with passion said, "What do I care about Turks or Moslems, I am a Slav, I come from Bosnia."

In Paris in 1919 during an interview, André Spire, the French poet, who had become a Zionist, said, "What other choice has a Jew? My family has lived in France for many generations each of which has made a contribution to France and to French culture. It is my culture. I am thoroughly French and yet before I was a grown man I fought a duel with a fellow student because in utter contempt he called me a *Yahudi*. What choice has a Jew other than to become a Zionist?"

As special agent of the Department of State at Cairo in 1917, the author was having continually dinned in his ears by British political intelligence officers Anglo-Saxon solidarity. Though his ancestors in the seventeenth century had come to New Haven from Wales, he had taken no interest in or knew nothing of Welsh culture. Nevertheless, one day "fed up" with this form of British propaganda he said with passion to an English colleague, "What do I care about Anglo-Saxon solidarity, I am a Celt."

The stress and strains to which Arabs were subjected during Abdul Hamid's regime and that of the Committee of Union and Progress after the Young Turk Revolution, and finally the suffering and oppression endured by the Arabs during World War I, intensified and gave wider spread to Arab nationalism. The Arab expression *anna ibn Arab* ("I am the son of an Arab") began to have connotations which gave it a meaning somewhat similar to western nationalism.

The strength and influence of a movement such as nationalism might be accurately assessed if there were means by which it were possible to measure the intensity of emotional reaction, individual and social, and the number of individuals who were stirred by nationalistic ideas. Because it is utterly impossible so to measure the degree and spread of nationalism among the Arabs of western Asia during any period of the nineteenth century and the first half of this century, judgments with respect to Arab nationalism are subjective in nature whether they be by George Antonius, Hans Kohn, or H. I. Katibah, all of whom write with some authority on the Arab nationalist movement.

Nationalism as an ideology and as a political movement arose in Europe as a product of the middle class in their struggles first against the feudal nobility and later against absolutism. The bourgeoisie formulated the cultural and ideological forms of nationalism and won to its support the peasantry. With the French Revolution modern nationalism began to take shape and for a while joined hands with liberalism and political democracy. Nationalism in the Near East, as in Italy from 1815 to 1859, developed out of the struggle against imperialism rather than against feudalism. Because of this fact the evolution of nationalism in the Near East differs considerably from the earlier evolution of European nationalism, which was largely the product of the rising capitalist class during the period of commercial capitalism.

Nationalism among the Balkan peoples, the Armenians, and the Arabs developed as a movement against Ottoman imperialism, while the nationalism of the Turks developed as a movement against the imperialism of the European states. These nationalist movements in the Ottoman Near East were not so definitely the product of the middle classes as the nationalist movements in Europe had been. The clergy played an important role as did also many of the secular feudal landowning class and to a lesser degree the tribal leaders. Although forms of the social struggle were not absent from the national movements of the Near East, they were not essentially in the nature of a class struggle. In fact the nationalists endeavored to unite all of the divergent groups in a struggle against the "alien" imperialists.

These political movements grew out of renaissance movements. Arab nationalism developed from the intellectual awakening which began in the first half of the nineteenth century. Political movements in the Arab lands of Asia previous to the flowering of the Arab renaissance cannot rightly, it would seem, be classified as nationalist movements although they took the form of revolts against the Ottoman government.

It is misleading to speak of the Wahhabi religious movement in the eighteenth and nineteenth centuries as being a nationalist movement. The Wahhabis were not against the Turks because they were Turks, but because they were considered to be false to Islam. The Wahhabis were as bitter enemies of the Shiite Arabs of Mesopotamia and the Sunnite Arabs of Mecca and Medina as they were of the Turks and of Mohammed Ali. The ruler of Egypt and his son Ibrahim Pasha attempted to arouse the support of the Arabs in a national movement against the Turks. Their efforts were a complete failure. Egyptian rule in Palestine, Lebanon, and Syria intensified the bitterness between Christian, Druze, and Moslem groups. Ibrahim Pasha failed to obtain the support of any significant segment of the Arabs in his war with the Turks. Arab nationalism was for all practical purposes nonexistent as a political and psychological force. The ideas and emotions typical of modern nationalism seemingly had no significance to the Arabs of western Asia in the 1830's and the 1840's. The innovations of Ibrahim Pasha, however, opened the door of the western horn of the Fertile Crescent, often called the Levant, to western influences.

۞ THE ARAB AWAKENING

Rival foreign religionists flowed in, bent upon bringing to the Arabs their respective ideologies, and fostered an intellectual revolution that began the process of undermining the political and social structure of the Ottoman regime in the Arab countries of western Asia. In the seventeenth century French Catholic institutions and schools had existed in the Levant. In the forefront of this missionary movement were the Jesuits and the Lazarists. Although the Catholic schools did nothing until the nineteenth century to revive the Arab language and literature, they did create a small educated class who learned French and so gained access to western culture. The American Protestant missionary work began in 1820 at Beirut.

The impact of schools—Egyptian, French, American.—The first real stimulus to education of the Arabs in the Levant was due to Ibrahim Pasha, who between 1834 and 1840 established a secular public school system based on the educational system introduced into Egypt by his father, Mohammed Ali. In this connection it is interesting to note that during World War I, after General Allenby's capture of the Holy City, the British Military Governor Ronald Storrs in 1918 considered reorganizing the municipal schools of Jerusalem on the basis of the Cairo school system.

After intervention by the European Powers brought an end to the Egyptian rule in Syria, Lebanon, and Palestine, public education practically ceased while on the contrary Christian missionary educational activities greatly increased. Moslems and Christians of all creeds, mostly of the well-to-do classes, began to recognize the necessity of education for their children and for the most part turned to foreign schools. Schools for girls as well as boys were founded by the missionaries, both Catholic and Protestant, French and American. Teacher preparation schools and institutions of higher learning soon followed. The development of foreign missionary schools tended to spur the clergy of the various indigenous sects to increase their educational activities.

The impact of French culture, French political and social philosophy, and French language and literature throughout the Near East and among the Arabs of the Levant was very great indeed. The Moslems and Christians were both profoundly affected by the rich stream of French culture. The French Catholic institutions in the Arab countries contributed considerably to the spread of French culture and were a potent factor in the intellectual awakening of the Arabs. The renaissance, however, of the

Arabic language and literature owed its original impetus to the American Protestant missionaries.

The advent of the printing press.—The reasons for this are quite apparent. Unlike the French Catholic missionaries, who worked principally among the large native Arab Catholic population, the American Protestant missionaries had no clientele on their arrival in the Levant. Following a Protestant tradition that goes back to Martin Luther, John Calvin, and the English Protestants, the American missionaries translated the Bible into Arabic. An Arabic Protestant Bible was an essential educational tool of the American missionaries. To secure wider circulation of the Protestant Bible and Protestant religious tracts it was necessary to have a printing press. With the first real printing press in the Levant, the Americans had a powerful instrument by which to augment their influence. In a type which came to be known as American Arabic, the American missionary press not only printed an Arabic Bible and Protestant missionary tracts but, perhaps of even more importance to the Arab Renaissance, printed textbooks and other educational materials in Arabic for use in their schools.

The Arab renaissance.—The Syrian Protestant College, opened in Beirut during the year 1866, became an intellectual center of attraction for Arab Moslems and Christians. Two rather remarkable Arabs, who were early leaders of the Arab renaissance, were encouraged by and worked with the early American missionaries.

Like Petrarch and other leaders of the Italian Renaissance, Nasif Yazeji in his passion for the literature of the classical period of Arabic culture ransacked the monastic libraries in search of manuscripts. His driving interest in the Arabic language and literature together with the books he wrote made him a central figure among those who began to interest themselves in Arabic culture. Butrus Bustani, an Arab of wider knowledge and broader education, did for Arabic and the Arab renaissance, in the preparation of a voluminous and an abridged Arab dictionary and of an Arab encyclopedia, what the Turkish writer Ebu-z Ziya did for the Turkish renaissance.

By the middle of the past century the Arab renaissance had been launched, and it continued to flourish in the Arab provinces of the Ottoman Empire until the regime of Abdul Hamid spread its blight among the Arabs as it did among the Turks. Before his accession to the sultanate Arabic political and literary periodicals were being published and cultural and scientific societies were founded. Antonius maintains that it was at a secret meeting of the *Syrian Scientific Society* "that the Arab national movement may be said to have uttered its first cry" in a poem by Ibrahim Yazeji appealing to the Arabs as a people and as a nation to revolt against their oppressors, the Turks.[1]

During this era Hamidian darkness was unable to extinguish the flickering light of the Arab renaissance in the Levant because it was being replenished from sources beyond the control of Abdul Hamid and his spies. Egypt under the imperial aegis of Great Britain was a place of refuge for Arab nationalists. Immigrants from Syria flocked to the Valley of the Nile where they became a small but important minority. Active in many fields, these Arab refugees continued their intellectual and political activities, and the Syrian colony in Cairo became an important nationalist center. France and Switzerland also became for the Arabs of the Levant, as they had been for the Young Turks, centers for their activities. Many Syrian Arabs had migrated to the United States and to Latin America. In these transatlantic Arab colonies, in spite of the powerful forces working for assimilation, Arabic newspapers and periodicals were published and Arab writers and Arabic societies contributed to the Arab awakening and to the Arab nationalist movement.

Under the rays emanating from these varied and widely scattered intellectual centers, the fog of ignorance and obscurantism, which for several centuries had so dimmed as almost to obliterate Arabic culture, was being dissolved. The sun of enlightenment first dispelled the mist over Lebanon and Syria before it reached the valley of the Tigris and the Euphrates, while most of Arabia still remained in utter darkness.

۞ NATIONALIST AND REVOLUTIONARY MOVEMENTS

Paralleling the development of the Young Turk underground revolutionary movement during the last two decades of Abdul Hamid's reign, an Arab underground revolutionary movement came into existence. An Arab revolutionary movement could not develop until leaders of the Arab Moslem majority turned to nationalism. The ferment of ideas resulting from the rapidly increasing encroachment of the Christian West upon the Moslem Near East as well as upon the rest of the Mohammedan world gave rise to the Pan-Islamic movement. The Old Turks under Abdul Hamid's direction cultivated pan-Islamism as an instrument of political power and of diplomacy. The Committee of Union and Progress of the Young Turks did likewise. So also the Moslem Arabs turned to pan-Islamism before they accepted nationalism. Christian Arabs educated in foreign religious schools gave the first impetus to the Arab renaissance and were the first to formulate the ideology of modern Arab nationalism. Although the Christian Arabs' contribution to the

Arab awakening and the Arab nationalist movement is undeniable, Christian Arabs could not become the leaders of movements which would embrace the Arabs as a whole. Christian Arabs could not be the leaders of an intellectual revolution against Moslem ecclesiastical obscurantism. Nor could Christian Arabs in the Moslem Ottoman Empire become the leaders of an Arab revolutionary movement, the aim of which was to free the Arabs from the rule of a Moslem Turkish sultan who was likewise caliph.

It was not until Moslem Arabs at the turn of the century became active leaders of the Arab revolutionary movement that it began to have real political significance. Furthermore, many among the Christian Arabs looked to one or another of the European Powers to deliver them not only from Turkish rule but from Moslem domination. For the most part Christian Arabs with memories of the long years of subjection to Moslems, both Arab and Turk, were fearful of Arab independence. The European imperialist powers sought to capture the Arab nationalist movement to use it for their own ends. In doing so they tended to compromise the Arab nationalists, particularly the Christians. Nevertheless, it was the Arab Christian nationalists who first formulated the objectives of the Arab nationalists. Shortly after the Syrian Moslem pan-Arabist, Abdul-Rahman Kawakebi published his attack upon despotism in his book, *The Attributes of Tyranny,* a Christian Arab from Palestine, Negib Azoury, published at Paris in 1905 his *Le reveil de la nation arabe dans l'Asie Turque* ("The Awakening of the Arab Nation in Asiatic Turkey"). Azoury, who had been assistant to the Turkish governor at Jerusalem, was obliged to flee from Turkey because of his revolutionary activities. He organized the "League of the Arab Homeland" (*Ligue de la Patrie Arabe*) which issued two proclamations: one in the name of the Arab National Committee addressed to the European Powers and the United States and the other in the name of the Arab National Superior Committee addressed to all the citizens of the Arab homeland subject to the Turks.[2]

Although there is no available evidence that Negib Azoury and the League of the Arab Homeland ever had any wide political significance or support among the Arabs, Azoury's "Awakening of the Arab Nation" and the proclamations of the League of the Arab Homeland are of importance because of events which have transpired between 1919 and 1949. The program formulated by the league founded by Azoury resembled closely that of the Syrian Congress at Damascus in 1919 which was presented to the American Section of the International Commission on Mandates in Turkey, better known as the King-Crane Commission. Azoury, who seems to have swallowed whole the thoroughly discredited "Protocols of the Elders of Zion" and who announced the publication of a book entitled *Le péril juif,* did nevertheless clearly foresee the dangers of a conflict between Arab nationalism and Zionism. In 1905 Azoury wrote as follows:

> Two important phenomena, of the same nature though opposed, to which nobody has drawn attention, manifest themselves at this moment in Asiatic Turkey; they are, the awakening of the Arab nation and the hidden efforts of the Jews to reconstruct on a very large scale the ancient monarchy of Israel. These two movements are destined to combat each other continually until one of them takes it [Palestine] from the other.
>
> . . . how favorable present circumstances are to the projects of the Zionists in the country which was the dream of their ancestors and which, even today, excites their cupidity.[3]

Azoury and his French commentator wrote nine and eight years respectively before the outbreak of World War I. Eugene Jung, putting the cart before the horse, wrote, "The awakening of the Arab nation will provoke the opening of a great world crisis"; actually, the "world crisis" aroused the Arabs to revolt against the Turks. The foundations upon which this revolt was built were laid during the five years between 1909 and 1914.

Arab liberals and the Young Turks.—The Arab liberals and nationalists were in sympathy with the Young Turks previous to the Revolution of 1908 and up to the *coup d'état* of the C.U.P. in 1909, although few Arabs participated in the Young Turk Party's activities. Shortly after the collapse of the Hamidian despotic regime, the Arabs, like other non-Turkish groups, rejoiced in the establishment of the constitutional regime. With hopes similar to those of the Armenians, the Arab nationalists expected the new regime in Turkey would lead to a large measure of autonomy and local government for the Arabs. Like the Turkish Liberal Unionists, many of the Arab nationalists favored decentralization within the framework of the Ottoman Empire. In the autumn of 1908 the Arabs in Constantinople organized, with the warm approval of leaders of the Committee of Union and Progress, the Ottoman Arab Brotherhood for the purpose of forwarding the interests of the Arab liberal nationalists. Between then and the dismissal of Parliament in 1912 and the establishment of the C.U.P. dictatorship, the Arab Nationalists discovered that continued co-operation with the Young Turks was impossible.

It is a curious, if somewhat obvious, fact that nationalists of one species have little understanding of or capacity to deal with nationalists of another. Underlying this incapacity of the nationalist is the incompatibility of exclusive competitive national groups. The Committee of Union and Progress which had successfully organized a secret revolutionary society and effectively carried out its objectives, showed no capacity to deal with non-Turkish national groups. For the problem of nationalism, the only solution the C.U.P. had was subjection, repression, and exploitation. In this the Young Turk leaders were neither more nor less unenlightened than the Tsarist Russians with their policy of Russification, than the Austrian-Hungarian government in dealing with its Slavic subjects, than the German Empire with respect to its non-Teutonic minorities and than the British government in its treatment of the Irish.

Although there was really little possibility of the Young Turks' finding an enduring *modus vivendi* with the Armenians and Balkan Christian national groups, there was a real possibility of reaching a compromise with the Arabs, the great majority of whom were Moslems who had no desire to seek the aid of foreign Christian Powers against their sultan and caliph. It was the policy adopted by the C.U.P. toward the Arabs between autumn of 1908 and the outbreak of World War I which drove the Arab Nationalists into subversive underground revolutionary activities and eventually into alliance with Great Britian and her Allies.

Arab clubs and parties.—The idea of a political separation of the Arabs from the Turks did not receive wide support among Moslem Arabs until after 1909, although it was promulgated as early as the 1870's. The Arab leaders were thinking, previous to that year, in terms of a large measure of local self-government under a system of decentralization. To the C.U.P., decentralization, which was part of the program of the Committee's political opponent, the Turkish Liberal Union Party, was abhorrent. After the C.U.P. *coup d'état* which broke the power of the Liberal Union Party in the spring of 1909, the Committee banned the recently organized Ottoman Arab Brotherhood. Arab reaction to this act was swift.

In the summer of 1909 leading Arabs at Constantinople organized an Arab literary club, which as a cultural institution the C.U.P. thought it unwise to interfere with. This "Literary Club" became a center in the Turkish capital for Arab nationalists. Soon after the founding of this Arab society, an officer in the Ottoman army, Aziz Ali, the Egyptian, was instrumental in organizing a secret Arab nationalist society known as Al Qahtaniya, the aim of which was to force the Turks to reorganize the Ottoman Empire as a dual monarchy under an Ottoman sultan but with complete equality of Arabs and Turks. A little over a year later a small group of Moslem Arabs in Paris organized during 1911 the most secret of the Arab revolutionary groups, known as *The Young Arab Society,* called briefly *Al Fatat.* Its members had abandoned all idea of co-operation with the Turks and devoted themselves to the attainment of complete Arab independence and the creation of an Arab sovereign state within the cultural and linguistic boundaries of the Arab lands in western Asia.

At Cairo, Arabs from Syria and Lebanon organized the Ottoman Decentralization Party which advocated co-operation with the Turks on the basis of equality and autonomy for the Arab provinces in the Ottoman Empire. A Beirut Committee of Reform was constituted to forward the objectives of the Arab party of Ottoman decentralization in Turkey. In February 1913 the eighty-six members of the Beirut Committee, which was comprised of Moslems and Christians in almost equal numbers, decided to give wide public circulation to their plan of Arab autonomy. Popular reaction to this proposal by the Arabs in Syria and in Lebanon was enthusiastic. Meetings and demonstrations favoring it were held. The excitement engendered by these activities resulted by April in suppression of the meetings by order of the C.U.P.

Even the moderate liberals among the Arabs were now coming to realize that co-operation with the Young Turks was not possible. When, on the initiative of *Al Fatat,* an Arab Congress was held at Paris in June 1913, representatives of all the Arab national groups and parties participated. This, the first Arab Congress, drafted a platform known as the Paris Agreement that proposed a scheme based on the plan of the Beirut Committee of Reform.

The emerging conflict with the Turks.—The C.U.P. dictatorship responded to this action in a manner completely typical of Abdul Hamid. Certain members of the Congress were invited to Constantinople and following lengthy discussion, the Turkish government agreed to accept the Paris Agreement. In August the Sultan issued an imperial decree purporting to carry out its provisions. Careful reading of the decree, however, made it quite clear to the Arabs that the C.U.P. had no intention of carrying out the agreement. Aziz Ali, the Egyptian, then set about organizing a new secret Arab revolutionary society among Arab officers in the Turkish armies. The members of this society, the Covenant, in Arabic *Al Ahd,* took an oath to devote their lives to becoming proficient officers in order that they might be fully prepared to be military leaders of the Arab revolution.

Whether or not the Turks knew of Aziz Ali's new activities is not known; they were, however, aware of the fact that he was one of the leading Arab nationalists. He had won great popularity as a military leader in Tripoli during the war against the Italians. To undermine his reputation and popularity among the Arabs, the Turks arrested him and brought him to trial on the charge of venality and treason in having accepted bribes from the Italians. The Turkish court found him guilty in April 1914 and condemned him to death. Only intervention by the British, who prevailed upon the Egyptian government to protest against the execution, saved Aziz Ali, the Egyptian. The indignation in the Arab world was intense. Weakly, the C.U.P. pardoned Aziz Ali. This sop to Arab feeling was to no avail. The Arab nationalists now understood that a complete break with the Ottoman Empire and the Turks was inevitable. The Committee of Union and Progress had prepared the way for the Arab Revolution which began in 1916.

Syria and Lebanon were the main centers of the Arab renaissance and nationalist movement in western Asia. Mesopotamia (Iraq) was intellectually and politically less advanced than the Levant where contact with Europe was of much longer duration and of a much more intimate nature. The urban centers of Mosul and Bagdad remained more medieval than Aleppo, Damascus, Jerusalem, Haifa, and Beirut. In Arabia the Arab renaissance and the modern form of Arab nationalism by 1914 had made little headway except among a few individual leaders.

Nationalism in Arabia?—There seems no justification for the assumption that Ibn Saud's conflicts with the Turks and the revolt in the Yemen were the result of the Arab awakening among the Syrians and Lebanese. The families of Saud and of Rashid had for generations fought for the control of the oases and of the tribes in central Arabia. The rise of the fanatical and reactionary Wahhabi sect in the last half of the eighteenth century gave the Saudi family control by 1800 of most of Arabia. The Wahhabite challenge to Turkish sovereignty in Arabia and attacks on Syria and Mesopotamia made the Saudi family the enemy of the Turks. Turkish support of the Rashid family was a means of holding in check the Wahhabites, under the leadership of the Saudi family, after their defeat by Mohammed Ali.

The late king of Saudi Arabia, Abdul Aziz Ibn Saud, by the beginning of the present century had defeated Rashid and regained control of central Arabia. Turkish forces sent to aid Rashid were defeated and Ibn Saud seized control of the coastal principality of al-Hasa on the Persian Gulf. The old tribal families of Rashid and Saud were again struggling for mastery, with the House of Rashid being backed by the Turks. The struggle between the Turks and the Saudi Wahhabites originated long before the Arab renaissance and before there was any Arab nationalist movement. In view of the long history of tribal warfare in Arabia, it seems a justifiable assumption that war would have continued between the Saudi family and the Ottoman Turks whether or not there had been an Arab awakening.

From early historical times down to the present the Arabian peninsula has been, because of its geographical location, a strategic area. Under certain conditions non-Arabian states could obtain the security thought requisite by a control of the coastal areas and strategic ports; under another set of conditions security of important trade routes made necessary attempts to control the hinterland of Arabia.

The Turks had never been able to maintain full control over the Arabian peninsula. During the nineteenth century, acting through the government of India, the British had obtained quasi-protectorates over the Arab principalities and sultanates on the islands of the Persian Gulf and along the eastern and southern coasts of Arabia to the port of Aden. Turkish suzerainty in these areas ceased to exist for all practical purposes. Central Arabia was never much more than a nominal possession of the Ottoman sultans, where one tribal family was used to hold another in check. The Hejaz, stretching from the head of the Gulf of Akaba in the north to Asir in the south, with its two sacred cities of Mecca and Medina, was of significant importance to the Ottoman sultan and caliph. Consequently, the Turks were obliged to control it. This they were largely able to do after the defeat of the Wahhabites by the forces of Mohammed Ali down to the revolt of the Sherif of Mecca in 1916, which began the Arab revolution. The Ottoman government maintained a governor (vali) of the Hejaz in Mecca, but its real ruler was the sherif of Mecca who, though appointed by the sultan, was always a direct descendant of Mohammed, the Prophet. At the suggestion of the First Dragoman of the British Embassy at Constantinople, Mr. Fitzmaurice, the Young Turks had had Hussein Ibn Ali, whom Abdul Hamid had forced to live in Constantinople as a hostage since 1893, appointed the Grand Sherif of Mecca. By so doing the C.U.P. prepared the way for the Arab Revolution because Hussein, who became king of the Hejaz, and his four sons—Ali, Abdullah who until his death was king of Jordan, Faisal who until his death was king of Iraq, and Zeid—were Arab nationalists. Abdullah even became a member of one of the secret Arab Revolutionary societies before the outbreak of World War I, while Faisal was initiated as a member of *al Fatat* in 1915. The position of the Turks in the Hejaz was in 1914 a precarious one, as it was also in Asir and the Yemen.

Asir was a borderland state on the west coast of Arabia between the Hejaz and Yemen. A primitive backward country of small extent, its ruler Mohammed Ibn Ali, the descendant of the Moslem Moroccan family of Idrisi, could hardly be classified as a modern liberal or nationalist. Closely associated with the Senussi brotherhood in North Africa, he was looked upon as a heretic by the orthodox Moslems of Arabia. Nevertheless, Sayyed Mohammed unsuccessfully challenged the Turks in 1909 and consequently is considered by some as one of the Arab revolutionary nationalists.

In the Yemen the Turks with great difficulty and at a considerable cost in money and men had been able to maintain a very uncertain foothold. The Yemen, despite its fertility and natural resources, was in 1900 and still is one of the most backward of the Arab countries in Asia. It was a theocracy ruled by an oligarchy controlled by the Yemenite sovereign, Imam Yahya Ibn Yahya. The Young Turks had inherited from the Hamidian regime a difficult revolutionary situation in the Yemen. After military successes and defeats the C.U.P. in 1911 came to a compromise with the Imam which made the Turkish position there slightly more secure. While the Yemen had intermittently waged war against the Turks for many years, nevertheless one's definition of nationalism would have to be extremely elastic to include Imam Yahya among the Arab nationalists. Needless to say, in the religious medieval state of the Yemen the seeds of the Arab renaissance found little, if any, fertile ground in which to germinate during the nineteenth century.

CHAPTER XIV

Turkey Enters World War I

❁ FOREIGN POLICY OF THE OTTOMAN EMPIRE

When the Young Turks seized power in 1908 there was a temporary reversal of foreign policy with respect to the Great Powers. The pro-German orientation of the Ottoman Empire under Abdul Hamid was changed to pro-British. The liberal revolutionists, who were familiar with British and French political philosophies, looked to England and France for friendly support of the new regime. For two years this attitude was maintained by the Ottoman government. Then Turkish policy became increasingly pro-German, with the result that in 1914 a Turco-German Alliance was signed at the outbreak of World War I when Turkey became a full-fledged member of the Triple Alliance and remained with the Central Powers until 1918. This diplomatic revolution was the result of a combination of factors.

All Turks, literate or illiterate, recognized Russia as the hereditary enemy of the Ottomans. It was well understood in Turkey that one of the main objectives of Russian policy was to capture Constantinople and control the Straits. Even when the exigencies of the situation demanded a pro-Russian policy on the part of the Porte, the Turkish people continued to view Russia as a potential enemy. The other traditional foe was Austria. Fear of Austria never became an obsession with the Turks as did fear of Russia. Furthermore, Austria generally acted as a counterbalance to Russia because the interests of both conflicted in the Balkans. For almost a century England had pursued an anti-Russian policy and had consistently opposed the partition of the Ottoman Empire. England, even though she had pocketed Cyprus and Egypt and had established control over the Arab sheikdoms on the islands in the Persian Gulf and along the east coast of Arabia, was the traditional friend of the Turks. France, too, was looked upon as an old and historic friend whose language and culture were known to educated Turks. For almost half a century France, like England, had opposed Russian encroachment on the Ottoman Empire.

Abdul Hamid's policy of balance.—The advent of the German Empire and the close alliance between the Austrians and the Germans after 1872 created a new alignment of the European Powers, which was well noted by Turkish policymakers. Turkish statesmen, like those of any other state, in formulating the foreign policy of their country, were obliged to take into consideration the policies of and relations between the other nations, particularly, the European Powers. Abdul Hamid had seized upon the new situation which had arisen after the Franco-Prussian War of 1870–71 to play one group of Powers off against another. Even though the results proved, in the long run futile, nevertheless Abdul Hamid pursued with considerable skill his policy of the balancing of the Powers. Although this policy after the accession to the throne of Germany of Kaiser Wilhelm became more pro-German and anti-English, the wily Sultan never allowed Turkey to become a pawn of the Teutons as did the Young Turks.

Liberal Turks, pro-British and French.—The year preceding the Young Turk Revolution, the Triple Entente had come into existence when the Anglo-Russian agreement with respect to Persia was signed in 1907. Turkish statesmen soon had to weigh the significance of this new alignment between her ancient enemy and her traditional friends. At first, the Young Turks oriented their foreign policy by sentiment rather than by reason. The Kaiser had been the supporter of Abdul Hamid, the English and French were the protagonists of liberalism and democracy, consequently the Young Turk revolutionists were pro-English and pro-French.

Reasons for reversal of a pro-Entente policy.—Circumstances were soon to reverse this policy. There were several elements among the Turkish revolutionists. Those who had long been in exile in France and England tended to follow the western pattern of liberalism and were favorable to a policy of alignment with the Triple Entente. The dynamic force of the revolution, however, sprang rather from the army officers, particularly from younger men to whom the Tanzimat liberal ideals meant little and from that group of young intellectuals who were turning to extreme nationalistic and racial doctrines. They were nationalists and Pan-Turanians with only a veneer of liberalism. In the Germanies, between 1848 and 1871, liberalism had been sacrificed to nationalism, so also in Turkey the same process was taking place. Turkish nationalism and Turanian racialism became the motivating forces of those who dominated the Committee of Union and Progress. It was in accordance with these ideals that the C.U.P. after the *coup d'état* of April 1909, and that of January 1913, shaped the domestic and foreign policy of the Ottoman government.

The former, it has been noted, alienated the Christian and non-Turkish Moslem peoples of the empire. The domestic policy of centralization and Turkification with resultant conflicts, repression, and ruthlessness convinced influential British and French groups that the Young Turks were "no better" than the old Turks. A discerning young correspondent of the London *Times* at Constantinople, Philip Graves, a nephew of the English author, Robert Graves, wrote on February 25, 1911, in a letter to Noel Buxton: "What I blame the Turks for is their persistence in attempting the impossible. *Ottomanization* under Turkish auspices is an impossibility . . . I object to the Young Turk policy first and foremost because it makes for political disturbance and weakens the Turks."[1] The adoption of Pan-Turanianism and Pan-Islamism as the basis of both domestic and foreign policies made attempts of the Young Turks to reform the Ottoman Empire even more impossible. Pan-Turanianism, which was an excrescence of nationalism, quite irrationally, but not altogether illogically, was coupled with Pan-Islamism. The agnostic freemasons among the members of the Committee of Union and Progress found it useful to adopt, without religious convictions, Pan-Islamism as a policy to win domestic support from devout Moslems. These could without offense to their religious ideas subscribe to the policy of Pan-Turanianism.

Under the domination of the C.U.P. the Young Turks not only became chauvinists, but practically abandoned the idea of a lay state. Bowing to the power of the religious element in order to gain their support for the Committee's domestic and foreign policies, the C.U.P. lost the support of the British and French. Its Pan-Turanian and Pan-Islamic ideals could be realized only at the expense of Russia, France, and England, and only with the aid of Germany.

In spite of the fact that the Germans had acquiesced in Austria's annexation of Bosnia and Herzegovina and had taken no steps to restrain Italian imperial ambitions in Tripoli and the Dodecanese Islands, nevertheless, it was Germany's policy to maintain the independence and territorial integrity of the Ottoman Empire. Of this the C.U.P. Young Turks felt convinced. They were uncertain what the attitude of England and France, as allies of Russia, would be with respect to Russian expansion toward the Mediterranean at the expense of Turkey. The few men who soon came to control Turkey after the *coup d'état* of January 1913 convinced themselves that the Triple Entente Powers were bent on the partition of the Ottoman Empire, that Turkish ambitions could only be achieved by the acquisition of the Moslem parts of the Russian, French, and British empires, and that the only hope of survival lay in an alliance with Germany and the other members of the Triple Alliance.

No doubt these were rationalizations used to support and justify a foreign policy which was opposed by the Liberal Unionists and those many elements among the Turks who were pro-English and pro-French. The fact is that the confused and conflicting philosophies which dominated the minds of the leaders of the C.U.P. led to domestic and foreign policies which antagonized the Triple Entente and which came to be directed against its interests. Eventually, these policies resulted in the C.U.P. seeking an alliance with Germany. Enver Pasha's close association with the Germans was incidental to, rather than causative of, the Turco-German alliance of August 2, 1914. Granted the alignment of the Great Powers after 1907 and the geographical situation of the Ottoman Empire, Turkish statesmen would have been obliged to seek alliance with either the Triple Alliance or the Triple Entente. When the nationalists, Pan-Turanians and Pan-Islamists gained the reins of power in Turkey, alliance with the Teutonic Powers was inevitable.

❁ THE TURCO-GERMAN ALLIANCE OF 1914–18

The Turkish government found itself in a position of complete isolation when Italy declared war in 1911 because the members of both the Triple Entente and the Triple Alliance were committed to a "hands off" policy with respect to an Italian seizure of Tripoli and Cyrenaica. This unsatisfactory international position in relation to the Great Powers became in Turkish eyes untenable when the Balkan War broke out in 1912.

The initial steps.—Divisions among the Turkish political groups concerning the question of a *rapprochement* with either the Triple Entente or the Triple Alliance made for a vacillating foreign policy until one of the Turkish political cliques obtained unchallenged power over the government. The *coup d'état* of January 1913 which brought the C.U.P. back into power did not immediately result in absolute control by the Committee. During the next six months resistance to the new government mounted despite the moderation of the Grand Vizier, Shevket Pasha. The assassination in January during the seizure of power by the C.U.P. of Minister of War Nazim Pasha had created a bitter feud among the officers of the army. The supporters and friends of Nazim never forgave the leaders of the C.U.P. who were responsible for the murder. A plot was hatched among some of these officers to assassinate Shevket Pasha and other leaders of the C.U.P. The murder of the Grand Vizier on June 28, 1913, enabled, if it did not actually force as a matter of self-defense, Enver, Talaat, and Jemal with the support of a few other top rankers in the C.U.P. to establish a dictatorship which became a triumvirate of Enver, Talaat, and Jemal by August 1914. With ruthless thoroughness the opposition groups were smashed and under a pliant new Grand Vizier, Prince Said Halim, it then became possible to adopt in secret a policy directed at securing an alliance with Germany.

Liman von Sanders' mission.—Before the death of Shevket Pasha discussions between the German government and the Porte concerning a German military mission to train the Turkish army had reached the point where the German Military Cabinet asked General Liman von Sanders on June 15, 1913, whether he was prepared and willing to become chief of a German military mission to Turkey.[2] After prolonged negotiations a contract was signed early in November 1913 and on December 14 of the same year, von Sanders and his staff arrived at Constantinople. There has been some confusion among American and English readers with regard to von Sanders' mission because the historian Winston S. Churchill in his book, *The Unknown War,* published in 1931, eleven years after the publication of the Berlin edition and four years after the publication of the Annapolis edition of von Sanders' book, stated that the German General Staff "were confident of Turkish successes"[3] in the first Balkan War, which began in October 1912 and came to an end in May 1913, because "the German Liman von Sanders at the head of a military mission was actually reorganizing the Turkish army." General von Sanders had never been in Turkey before his arrival there in the middle of December 1913!

The decision of the Turkish government to arrange for a German military mission to train the Ottoman army following their unsuccessful war with the Balkan States was in accordance with historical precedent. Five years after Turkey's defeat by Russia, Abdul Hamid's government had made arrangements for a German military mission under General von der Goltz in 1883. Military missions to train foreign armies have economic and political implications as well as purely military ones. A successful military mission results in the purchase of armament, munitions, equipment, and even uniforms in the country sending the mission, and it tends to the development of close professional and personal relations between the officers of the two nations and close collaboration between diplomats and officials. It was, therefore, quite logical for the Porte under the influence of the Young Turks to seek military aid from Germany in 1913.

The international situation in 1913, however, was very different from that of 1883. Thirty years earlier, France was completely isolated and so remained until 1893–94; England was strong enough to play a lone hand and followed an isolationalist policy by choice; Russia, Austria-Hungary, and Italy were in alliance with Germany. A German military mission to Turkey had minor political implications in the 1880's. In 1913 when Europe was divided into two armed camps and when any shift in military power was of vital importance to the members of both the Triple Entente and the Triple Alliance, a German military mission to Turkey had very considerable political significance. It is impossible to ascertain how many of the Young Turk leaders understood the full implications of such a mission. There is no doubt that a few of the leaders looked upon it as a step toward joining the Triple Alliance.

When in December 1913 von Sanders, shortly after his arrival at Constantinople, took command of the Turkish First Army Corps, the Russians were loud in their protests and were shortly joined by the British and French. The First Army Corps' Headquarters was at Constantinople and in the Corps' area were the Straits, the defense of which was its first responsibility. A German commander of the Turkish First Army Corps was in a position, in case of a crisis, to control the capital of Turkey and the much disputed waterway from the Black Sea to the Mediterranean. Liman von Sanders claimed that it was for strictly professional reasons pertaining to his job of training and reorganizing the Turkish army that he had insisted upon being appointed commander of the First Army Corps. He stated that he had not given a thought to the political consequences of his new command. It would seem, however, that he and the German General Staff must have understood its military implications.

The German Secretary of Foreign Affairs, Gottlieb von Jagow, was obliged by protests from the Entente Powers to recognize the political and international aspects of von Sanders' command over a Turkish army corps in so strategic an area. Rather than risk either a termination of the German military mission or possibly war von Jagow urged von Sanders to resign his command while remaining the head of the mission. Liman von Sanders said he would resign rather than give up his command under political pressure. The dilemma was solved by action on the highest levels. His Majesty, the Kaiser, promoted von Sanders to a rank which under the contract with Turkey made him a Turkish field marshal, a rank which made it impossible for him to retain command of an army corps. A Turkish officer took over the First Army Corps. The protests of the Entente Powers ceased and the international crisis over the German military mission subsided.

Jemal Pasha, one of the triumvirate of the C.U.P. leaders during World War I, in his book, *The Memoirs of a Turkish Statesman,* somewhat naively argues that the opposition of Great Britain and France to the von Sanders mission was an unfriendly action toward Turkey. This leader of the C.U.P. considered the protest of Russia and the other Entente Powers against von Sanders' command of the First Army Corps as unwarranted intervention in Turkish affairs. Theoretically, of course, as an independent sovereign state, Turkey had the "right" to appoint a foreign officer as the commander of a Turkish army corps; to exert that "right" would entail paying the price thereof. In the old language of common-sense deductions, the Young Turks carried a chip on their shoulders, and in the new language of psychology they had an inferiority complex which obscured their vision and weakened their judgment. Unfortunately, people have to suffer for the stupidities of their leaders.

The Turkish bid for an alliance.—By the time von Sanders arrived at Constantinople a group of three to five men controlled Turkey and began to shape its foreign policy in conformity with their own ideas and purposes. Feeble attempts to achieve an alignment with the Entente Powers having failed, the Porte through the Grand Vizier, Prince Said Halim, sought an alliance with Germany and membership in the Triple Alliance. Neither German nor Austrian statesmen wished in the latter part of 1913 and the first six months of 1914 to assume the liabilities of an alliance with Turkey. Even as late as July 18, 1914, only two weeks before the outbreak of World War I, the German Ambassador at Constantinople, von Wangenheim, despite Austria's desire for an alliance with Turkey, telegraphed the German Foreign Office that "Turkey is today without any question a worthless ally." The international situation was then a rapidly changing one and different ideas soon prevailed at Berlin.

Post-Sarajevo negotiations.—As tension increased in the European chancelleries after the assassination of the heir to the Austrian throne and his wife at Sarajevo on June 24, 1914, each of the Powers sought to improve its situation in the Balkans. The Austrians wanted to make sure of Bulgaria and Romania. They feared a *rapprochement* between Turkey and Greece lest Bulgaria turn towards Russia and Serbia. Germany encouraged a Graeco-Turkish alliance. In the midst of intrigue and counter intrigue, Enver Bey thought it an opportune time to press for an alliance with Germany.

On July 22, 1914, Enver told the German Ambassador that the Grand Vizier, Talaat and Halil, the inner circle of the Cabinet and key members of the C.U.P., earnestly favored a close connection with Germany. The following day Prince Said Halim informed von Wagenheim that the Turkish government wished to join the Triple Alliance. At this time Jemal Pasha had just returned from Paris where he had been invited as Turkish Minister of the Marine to attend a review of the French fleet. Jemal spoke French fluently, was fond of French literature, and was considered pro-French. Whether or not he favored at this time an alignment with the Triple Entente is not clear, but it is certain that Enver and Talaat did not feel sure he would endorse their policy of an alliance with Germany. Shortly after his return to Turkey, Talaat Bey asked him what he would say if Germany should propose an alliance. At about the same time Ambassador Wangenheim on July 23 told Jemal that Germany would be happy to have as an ally a country with so fine an army as that of Turkey.

The alliance signed.—Jemal Pasha was being conditioned to accept without protest a Turko-German alliance which was secretly being negotiated. On July 28 Turkey definitely asked Germany for an alliance and on the same day the Kaiser signified his approval. Negotiations in regard to terms continued until an offensive-defensive alliance was signed on August 2, 1914, the day following the commencement of World War I. After its signature Jemal Pasha was informed of it and still later another Cabinet Minister, Javid Bey. Actually, only three to five Turks were privy to a treaty which at the time it was signed obligated Turkey to go to war. The fate of the Ottoman Empire was sealed by the treaty. A decision which affected the lives of some thirty million people in the Near East was decided by a few men who kept any knowledge of what they were doing even from their closest colleagues in the Cabinet. The Turkish government was committed to a war that it was ill-prepared to wage and to which most of its articulate leaders were opposed.

THE ROAD TO WAR

Obligations under the treaty.—By article two of the Turko-German Alliance, which was virtually a military convention signed on August 2, 1914, "if Russia intervenes and takes active military measures and the necessity arises for Germany to carry out her pledges of alliance to Austria, Turkey is under obligation in such a case, to carry out her pledges made to Germany." Jemal Pasha stated that when Germany declared war on Russia "we saw ourselves bound by our treaty the ink of which was not yet dry, to intervene in the struggle at once." Actually, the treaty was signed a day after war began between Germany and Russia. It is obvious that Enver, Talaat, and Jemal knew that the treaty committed them to war. Prince Said Halim, the Grand Vizier who negotiated the alliance, claimed this was not so. Javid Bey when shown a draft of the alliance thought it was only a proposal for an alliance. The triumvirate was in no position to live up to the terms of the pledges by an immediate declaration of war against Russia.

From a military point of view it was considered dangerous to enter the war until the Turkish forces were fully mobilized and Turkey in a position to defend her most vulnerable frontiers: Constantinople and the Straits, Armenia and eastern Anatolia, Mesopotamia and Palestine. Jemal Pasha wanted a delay of six months at least. The Grand Vizier and Javid were opposed to entering the war at all, or until it became clear who would be the victor. Politically and psychologically, it would have been inadvisable to plunge suddenly into the war on the side of Germany and Austria when so considerable a percentage of the Turkish people were pro-English and pro-French. A series of incidents soon created a more favorable atmosphere for the plans of the pro-Teutonic group who controlled the Turkish government.

All were agreed that it was only good judgment to mobilize and to close the Straits. It was easy to present these measures as essential to the maintenance of Turkish neutrality and security, while in fact Enver Pasha and his associates were taking those steps which they considered essential to the fulfillment of their pledges to Germany. Mobilization played directly into the hands of the warmongers while at the same time arousing excitement in all parts of the Empire at a time widespread indignation among the Turkish people had been aroused by the British seizure of two warships being built for the Turkish government under contract. Three pairs of warships played a dramatic part in Turkey's entering hostilities at the end of October 1914.

The story of six warships.—In days when the United States gives hundreds of millions of dollars in military equipment to Turkey, not to mention military aid to Greece and Iran, it is difficult to realize that the sale of two warships to the Greek Government early in 1914 could have had any particular bearing upon international affairs. The Greek Government negotiated the purchase of the U.S.S. "Idaho" and U.S.S. "Mississippi" because it feared that Turkey would resume the war with Greece to regain possession of the Aegean Islands, taken over by the

Greeks as a result of the Balkan Wars. The Young Turks were determined to redress the unbalance of naval power in the Aegean as a preparatory step to regaining possession of the islands. As early as 1911 the Turkish government had ordered in England, previous to the Turko-Italian War, the battleship "Reschadier" and later contracted for the battleship, "Sultan Osman" which were to be paid for by popular public subscription throughout the Ottoman Empire. One of these new powerful ships was to be ready for delivery in 1914 the other in 1915.

Venizelos and his military and naval advisers considered the building of these two Turkish warships as a serious menace to Greece. In order to counteract the prospective increase in Turkish naval power, the Greek government promptly bought the American battleships, "Idaho" and "Mississippi." Whereas Greece obtained immediate delivery of the "Idaho" and the "Mississippi," Turkey failed to get possession of the "Reschadier" and the "Sultan Osman." The British had commandeered these Turkish ships on July 21, 1914, just a day before Enver informed the German Ambassador that he and his colleagues earnestly desired collaboration with Germany. It was in July 1914 that Greece received the "Idaho" and the "Mississippi"! It is doubtful whether Britain's action had any real influence on the decision of Enver, Talaat, and Prince Halim with regard to an alliance with Germany, but it is certain that popular anger against the British prepared the Turkish people for acceptance three months later of war against the Entente Powers. Before that occurred, two German warships were to play a considerable role in catapulting Turkey into the war.

When World War I began on August 1, 1914, the powerful German warships "Goeben" and "Breslau" were cruising in the Mediterranean. For a day or two there was uncertainty in Berlin as to how they might most profitably be employed. At Constantinople Wangenheim, on August 1, asked Berlin to send the "Goeben" to the Bosporus because a Russian naval attack was rumored. The German Foreign Office replied on August 3 that the "Goeben" could not be spared, but on the same day, which was the day Berlin learned that the Turco-German Alliance had been officially signed, von Tirpitz, head of the German Admiralty, ordered the two ships to proceed to Constantinople. The following day Enver Pasha in his capacity of Minister of War gave orders to the military authorities at the Dardanelles to admit German and Austrian warships.

Jemal Pasha learned four days later from the German naval attaché that the "Goeben," pursued by the British and short on coal, was moving toward the Dardanelles and would require fuel. On August 11 Enver jestingly remarked to the members of the inner cabinet that "unto us a son is born," as he informed them that he had given permission to the "Goeben" and the "Breslau" to pass through the Dardanelles where they had arrived that very morning.[4]

The "Goeben" *and the* "Breslau" *anchor in the Bosporus.*—Proceeding to the Bosporus these two powerful German warships had the capital of the Ottoman Empire at their mercy. It was not, however, their purpose to menace the Turks in Constantinople. The first use made of these ships was a psychological one. Under international law Turkey, having declared its neutrality, was obligated to demand that the German warships leave Turkish waters within twenty-four hours and should they fail to do so to disarm and intern them for the duration of the war. Should the Porte refuse to do so the Entente Powers would be justified in declaring war against Turkey. The inner cabinet was still divided on the question of joining Germany in the war. The impasse between the German Ambassador and Enver, who supported him, and the other ministers was resolved by a brilliant diplomatic stroke. The German government authorized the Turks to announce that the "Goeben" and the "Breslau" had been sold to Turkey. The Cabinet promptly gave wide publicity to the generosity of the Germans who had provided Turkey with two splendid ships to replace those "stolen" from Turkey by England.

Secretly, of course, strings were tied to this fictitious sale. Admiral Souchon was to replace the British Admiral Limpus as the commander-in-chief of the Turkish fleet and both German naval officers and sailors were to remain on and in control of the "Goeben" and "Breslau."

The Allies were at a loss to know what to do. If they refused to accept the fiction of the sale to the Turks of the German warships, they would be forced into the position of going to war with Turkey, which was contrary to their interests. Ignorant of the secret Turco-German Alliance, they continued to accept at face value the assurances given on August 9 by the Grand Vizier and the Minister of War with regard to Turkey's neutrality. Prince Said Halim stated emphatically that nothing would induce Turkey to join Germany and Austria as long as he remained Grand Vizier, while Enver Pasha lyingly assured the Russian Ambassador that Turkey had not become, as yet, a member of the Triple Alliance.

As the Germans were persuaded not to press for immediate action by Turkey, it was possible to proceed with military preparations and mobilization without precipitating a political crisis between the protagonists of war and of peace. The farsighted Rifaat Pasha, Turkish Ambassador to France, warned his government on September 4, before the issue of the Battle of the Marne was certain, that hostility to the Entente might endanger the very existence of the Ottoman Empire, and he urged the Turkish Cabinet to observe an honest and absolute neutrality which, he insisted, was the only sane policy to follow. By September 28, 1914, Rifaat declared that the Turkish government was pursuing a policy which would lead to dismemberment and annihilation. A few years later, the Ottoman Empire was partitioned by the victorious Allies and Jemal, Enver, and Talaat were dead at the hands of assassins.

The Turkish Cabinet increased its prestige among the Turkish people by abolishing on September 9, 1914, the Capitulations, the termination of which was one of the objectives of the Young Turks and part of their program to free the Ottoman Empire from foreign intervention.

The Germans began exerting increasing pressure on the Porte to declare war against the Allies. The von Schlieffen Plan of the German General Staff had failed. The German defeat at the Marne in September, followed by the withdrawal to the Aisne River of the German armies, brought to an end the German hopes of crushing France in six weeks and then marshaling all their forces against Russia. The Germans had been checked and thrown back in the west, and despite the German victory in the east at Tannenberg the Austrians were being hard pressed by the Russians in Galicia.

After a consultation at the German Embassy on October 11, 1914, at which the German Ambassador tried to persuade the Turks to enter the war, a meeting of the inner cabinet—a euphemism used to describe the clique who ruled Turkey—discussed the question of whether to intervene immediately in the war or to persuade the Germans of the necessity of remaining neutral for six months more. Despite German pressure and Enver Pasha's statement that he was unable further to oppose Admiral Souchon's insistent demand that the "Goeben" and the "Breslau" be sent to the Black Sea, the Porte refused to declare war.

Nevertheless, the will to peace in Turkey was being undermined at a time when military events in no way favored Turkey's entrance into the war. In the west the German armies had been driven back in both France and Belgium, in the east the German counteroffensive following the Battle of Tannenberg had been halted just within the Russian frontier, and the German-Austrian offensive in Galicia had collapsed. The Teutonic forces were retreating at the rate of ten miles a day, and by the end of October the Russians had regained the territory from which the German advance, begun on September 28, 1914, had driven them.

The naval attack on Russia.—With the Central Powers checked on both the western and eastern fronts at the end of October, the Kaiser, in order to force Turkey into the war, ordered Admiral Souchon to sail into the Black Sea with the "Goeben" and "Breslau." On October 28 units of the Turkish fleet accompanying the two German warships, all under Souchon's command, attacked the Russian fleet and then bombarded Russian ports in the Crimea.

Confronted with this arbitrary act the Turkish Cabinet met at once. The majority of the ministers were opposed to war and urged that the treaty with Germany be repudiated, Admiral Souchon and the German naval officers and sailors sent back to Germany and complete satisfaction given to the Allies. The prowar members of the Cabinet prevailed upon the peace bloc to accept a compromise which was unacceptable to the Allies. The pseudoneutrality of Turkey came to an end on November 4, when Russia declared war. Her action was followed the next day by that of both England and France, who promptly declared war on Turkey.

Judgment was passed on the action of the members of the Turkish government who precipitated war with the Allies by the postwar Turkish Republic. Ahmed Emin in his history of *Turkey in the World War* quotes as follows from an indictment drawn up by the Turkish attorney general on August 22, 1926:

> Turkey entered the War at a moment when the German offensive was halted on the Marne and the future issue of the conflict had become clear. The whole Turkish nation was dragged into the War as a result of a *fait accompli,* the work of a German admiral who received his orders from the Kaiser. In other words, a great and historic Empire had become a toy of this German admiral whose very name was unknown to the Turkish people. Turkish ministers who submitted to such steps look more like obedient, submissive servants of the Kaiser than ministers responsible for the welfare of Turkey. Could not these so-called Turkish patriots punish the folly of a German officer who had played with the self-respect of the Turkish state? [5]

Although this indictment was in the nature of a partisan document against political opponents who were accused by the government of the Turkish Republic of contemporary political conspiracy and of earlier war offenses, it does state succinctly, though not objectively nor altogether accurately, the immediate precipitating causes of Turkey's entrance into the war on the side of the Central Powers.

CHAPTER XV

Turkey at War—The First Two Years

IMPORTANCE OF THE WAR AND ITS CAMPAIGNS TO NEAR EASTERN HISTORY

The military history of a war is of very considerable interest to those who have lived through and participated in it. There are, however, far more important reasons for an account of the course of the war and of its principal military campaigns. The defeat of the Turks brought to an end the Ottoman Empire, which despite all its weaknesses had maintained the political unity of the Near East for more than four hundred years. It resulted in the political fragmentation of the Near Eastern area which now makes its unification impossible within any foreseeable time.

The developments during the war created those situations which have determined the course of the Near East since 1918. The Armenian massacres, the Arab revolt, and the Balfour Declaration promising the Jews a national home in Palestine were products of wartime policies of future import. The sending of large numbers of European troops to the Near East by both the Central Powers and the Allies brought the peoples of the Near East into contact with Europeans on a scale unexperienced since the Crusades. The waging of modern war introduced into the Near East on a wholesale basis new weapons, new means of transportation by motorcar, truck, and aeroplane, and further extended the building of roads and railroads. The war hastened the process of the destruction of medievalism which was already in an advanced state of deliquescence.

The defeat of the Turks and the untold misery and suffering of the Near Eastern peoples caused by the war coupled with the overweening power of the British and French in the Near East at the conclusion of hostilities created the illusion that the West had triumphed over the East.

In the light of subsequent events it appears as if the peoples of the Near East were the actual gainers and those of Europe the losers. Russia failed to attain her objects and even lost a strategic area in eastern Anatolia to the Turks. Germany lost her grip on the Near East and the Austrian-Hungarian Empire collapsed. Within less than three decades after the victory over the Ottoman Empire, France lost all her wartime gains in the Near East and even much of the prestige and influence of the prewar period while Great Britain was obliged to relinquish Palestine, and give up her postwar dominance in Iraq and Egypt.

MILITARY CAMPAIGNS OF 1914–15

The various military campaigns in the Near East take on added importance because they were undertaken for political reasons as much as for military ones and because they in a large measure determined the nature of those postwar developments which have created the present situation in the Near East.

Strategic plans.—The defence of the Ottoman Empire in the main determined Turkish military strategy and resulted in four principal theaters of war: the Dardanelles, Sinai-Palestine, Mesopotamia, and Eastern Anatolia. A strategy of defence was in part modified by Turko-German offensive plans which led to the attack on Egypt, military operations in Persia (Iran), and the invasion of Russian Transcaucasia. Churchillian strategy resulted in the Dardanelles campaign, the necessity of protecting the Persian (Iranian) oil fields caused the British to invade Mesopotamia, and Lloyd George's determination in 1917 to end the war in the Near East resulted in General Allenby's brilliant campaigns in Palestine and Syria. Inevitably, the military plans and operations of Turkey and Germany in the Near East as well as those of the Allies were conditioned by those of their enemies and by the course of the war in Europe.

The military campaigns in the Near East are of particular interest for political as well as military reasons. When Turkey entered the war at the end of October 1914, the Russians were not prepared to launch a large scale winter offensive against the eastern vilayets of Turkey. A covering force of only 100,000 men had been kept on the Turkish front to protect a frontier of nearly 500 miles in extent. The situation on the Russian fronts in Europe had been stabilized temporarily with the successful Russian counteroffensives in the north, bordering on East Prussia, and in Eastern Poland and Galicia. Under these conditions Russian interests centered on her European campaigns while the Germans, checkmated on both the western and eastern fronts, urged upon the Turks a vigorous campaign against the Russians. This corresponded with the ideas and ambitions of Enver Pasha, Minister of War. Minimum success in such a campaign would make Anatolia secure from invasion and protect northern Mesopotamia from attack, thus affording security to Turkish forces operating there against the Anglo-Indian invasion. Maximum success of the Caucasus campaign would help to achieve some of the idealistic objectives of the pan-Turanians and pan-Islamists and would result in the very materialistic advantage of obtaining control over the rich petroleum properties—oil wells, pipe lines, and refineries—in the Baku-Batum area.

Defeat in eastern Anatolia.—After minor encounters during November 1914 in which the Turkish troops numbering some 150,000 showed noticeable improvement over their condition during the recent Balkan wars, Enver Pasha, with fantastic ideas of invading India after defeating the Russians, assumed, in December, supreme command of the Turkish forces on the Caucasus front. The Russians began the campaign with a tactical offensive. Very shortly thereafter, on January 3, 1915, Enver's forces were overwhelmed and the Turkish Third Army was practically annihilated, being reduced to some 12,000 men. So crushing was the defeat, and so injurious to the reputation of Enver, that nobody was allowed to speak of this disaster under penalty of arrest and punishment. The failure of the Caucasus campaign, which was shortly followed by that of the attack on Egypt, began to undermine the prestige of the C.U.P. dictators, to create a defeatist attitude, and to foster increasing unrest among the non-Turkish subjects of the sultan.

Attack on Suez Canal and the situation in Egypt.—The Palestine-Sinai campaign of 1914–15 was in no way a military disaster. If tactically it was a defeat, strategically, on a wide scale, it had considerable success because it resulted in the British maintaining large forces in Egypt which might otherwise have been used to advantage at the Dardanelles throughout 1915.

A Turkish attack on the Suez Canal was desired by the German strategists, who considered an assault upon one of the most vulnerable points on Britain's lines of communication as a means of hindering, if not preventing, the flow of men, war materials, and other resources from Middle Asia and the Pacific area to the European front. German desires in this respect coincided with Turkish strategic concepts and the imperialistic ambitions of the Turkish rulers. An attack upon the Suez Canal, it was thought, would pin down British forces in Egypt which might otherwise be used for the reinforcement of the British invasion of Mesopotamia, or for British landings at Beirut, Alexandretta, Smyrna, or Gallipoli. Furthermore, there was the vain hope that Egyptian nationalism wedded to pan-Islamism would bring about a revolution against the British when Turkish troops reached the Suez Canal. Whether or not Jemal Pasha, who took over command of the Fourth Army, thought that he could conquer Egypt with 16,000 men when England already had assembled over 100,000 there remains a moot question. In his memoirs Jemal said that he had hoped that "Egyptian patriots, encouraged by the capture of Ismailia by the Turkish army, would rise *en masse,* and Egypt would be freed in an unexpectedly short time . . ." but he likewise stated that this first attack on the Suez Canal was to him "nothing but a demonstration in force." [1]

On the Palestine-Sinai front, as on that of the Caucasus, the Young Turk commanders, intoxicated by the hashish-like effect of almost absolute power, allowed "ambition's tiger to devour the sheep of contentment" in the form of the lives of the troops under their command.

Early in November 1914 Jemal Pasha, Minister of the Marine, was asked by Enver Pasha, Minister of War, to take command of the Fourth Army and the operations against the Suez Canal, for which preliminary preparations and plans had already been set on foot. This appointment had political aspects that for the next two years were to have considerable importance. Jemal seems never to have been taken fully into the confidence of Enver and Talaat, nor does he appear to have completely trusted them. Jemal's new assignment rather nicely resolved the differences between the members of the triumvirate which ruled Turkey. As commander-in-chief of the Fourth Army, Jemal became virtual dictator of Mesopotamia, Syria, Lebanon, and Palestine as well as of whatever part of Arabia he could control. In the Arab lands of western Asia he was the "big boss" as far as Turkish power extended.

During the period of Turkish neutrality, the Turks with some aid from the Germans were building a railroad from Afuleh, a station on the Haifa-Deraa-Damascus line, across the Plain of Esdraelon, through the Samarian hills and along the plains of Sharon and Philistia to Bir es Saba, and constructing military highways leading to the south in preparation for an attack on Egypt. As early as September 1914 Colonel von Kress of the von Sanders mission had been sent to Syria to assist as chief of staff of the Eighth Army Corps in its military preparations. It was not until November, after Turkey had entered the war, that orders were issued to form an army in Syria which, among other responsibilities, was to prepare a military attack on the Suez Canal. It was after these steps had been taken that Jemal Pasha was appointed commander of the Fourth Army.

To the hopeful the situation in Egypt seemed ripe for revolution. The Khedive Abbas Hilmi, who bitterly hated the English, had toyed with the pan-Islamic policy of Abdul Hamid and later with that of the C.U.P., and had flirted with the Egyptian nationalists, was on vacation in Europe when World War I broke out. He refused to return to Egypt and threw in his lot with the Turks. When Turkey entered the war the British, after negotiations with other members of the khedivial family and leading Egyptians, decided to declare all connections with the Turkish sultan at an end, to announce a British protectorate, to depose Abbas Hilmi, and to proclaim his uncle, Hussein Kemal, Sultan of Egypt.

The British anticipated that the deposition of the viceroy of the Turkish sultan, who as caliph had summoned on November 15 all Moslems to a jihad, a Holy War, against England and her Allies, would result in demonstrations and violence which might assume the nature of a revolution. The British authorities, in consequence, took extreme precautions. This they were well able to do on December 17, 1914, when there was not as yet a military threat on the Turkish Palestine frontier, because they had approximately 100,000 troops in Egypt, a large portion of whom were Australians upon whom pan-Islamic propaganda was of no use, as it might have been with Anglo-Indian Moslem troops. The show of force on December 17, 1914, when the British protectorate was announced, was dramatic and imposing. Through the narrow and tortuous streets of the old city of Cairo, Australians in full battle array accompanied by their light artillery marched from sunrise to sunset. Many of the byways of old Cairo were so narrow that those in the streets were pressed against the walls of the buildings by the flood of armed men. This exhibition of military power was impressive. If Turkish espionage had adequately informed Jemal Pasha in December, when he first took command of the Fourth Army, of events in Cairo he might not have had any wishful dreams about Egyptian patriots rising in revolt against the English.

While Jemal Pasha and von Kress were preparing the invasion force to cross the Sinai Peninsula, the British in December 1914 were organizing in Egypt the defenses of the Suez Canal. Strangely enough, they prepared no defense on the east bank of the Canal, not even providing a covering force with advanced bases in Sinai to give warning in due time of a Turkish attack. The British defense consisted of armored trains on the railroad from Port Said to Suez, warships in the Canal, and troops with artillery on the west bank. The defenses proved sufficient to throw back the Turkish attack after the Turkish forces had reached the Canal.

The Turkish expedition, although unsuccessful, was a notable achievement. From their advanced headquarters at Gaza and Bir es Saba in southern Palestine, the Turkish forces in a brief period of two weeks' time crossed an almost waterless desert of sand and rocks covering one hundred and fifty miles in seven marches during the night. Of a force of 22,000, Jemal was able to assault the Canal with almost 16,000 on February 2, 1915. Under British fire with no adequate artillery protection only a few score of Turks were able to cross the Canal before their pontoons were blown to bits. As the Turks had only a few days' supply of water, food, and ammunition, the attack had to be broken off on February 3. Because the British were unprepared for pursuit in the desert, the Turkish forces were able to withdraw successfully without serious losses and to establish outposts at oases in the Sinai Peninsula.

The Turks were never able again to threaten seriously the Suez Canal. The first attack alerted the British, and although it caused them to keep large forces in Egypt, these prevented any possibility of a successful Turkish offensive on the Sinai-Palestine front and provided a force which later invaded Palestine. British strategists became convinced that possession of Palestine was essential to the security of the Suez Canal and of Egypt. This idea had a very definite effect on British policy in the Near East during the next thirty-odd years and had considerable influence on the course of events in Palestine up to the time of the British withdrawal.

British invade Mesopotamia (Iraq).—Whereas the Turks had taken the offensive against the British in Egypt, the latter prepared for military operations in Mesopotamia shortly after the European war commenced. From the head of the Persian Gulf, where on the island of Abadan a refinery was located, a pipeline ran to the oil fields in southern Persia (Iran). This was a vital supply line, essential to the British navy, which must be protected. Sixty miles north of the head of the Persian Gulf the Tigris and the Euphrates join forces at Qurna, from which point to the mouth, the two rivers are known as the Shatt-al-Arab. In its lower reaches the island of Abadan formed the left bank of the Shatt-al-Arab. To gain access to the refinery British ships had to pass through the Shatt-al-Arab for a distance of forty miles. For British security an occupation of the southern part of Mesopotamia was essential to the protection of the refinery at Abadan and the pipeline to Ahwaz in the Persian oil fields.

The Government of India prepared an expeditionary force for operations at the head of the Persian Gulf which was sent there on October 16. 1914, three weeks before England declared war on Turkey. Bahrein

Island was occupied on October 23 and a military base prepared for the expedition against the Turks. As soon as war was declared the British forces moved to the mouth of the Shatt-al-Arab, occupied Abadan and then advanced, driving back a Turkish military force through Basra to Al Qurna where they arrived on December 8, 1914. For the time being the oil fields were secure but still remained vulnerable to attack by the Turks until the British made a deeper penetration into Mesopotamia, which they attempted in the following year. In the meanwhile the British attempt to force the Dardanelles resulted in the main military efforts of the Turks being concentrated on defending Gallipoli.

Successful defense of the Dardanelles.—The famous campaign of the Dardanelles was foreshadowed by a bombardment on November 3, 1914, of the forts at their entrance two days before England declared war on the Turks. By some subtle form of reasoning, the British thought that such bombardment would "frighten the Turks into remaining neutral." [2]

Having given the Turks due notice of what they might expect ultimately if they entered the war, the English waited until February 19, 1915, a total of 119 days, or seventeen weeks, before they launched their naval attack on the Dardanelles. This gave the Turks, with the assistance of German advisers, time to improve the defenses of the Straits from the entrance of the Dardanelles to the Bosporus. Liman von Sanders said that even if the Franco-British fleet managed to get through the Dardanelles and then should defeat the Turkish navy supported by the "Goeben" and the "Breslau" in the Sea of Marmora, the numerous batteries placed on the Princes Islands, and on both the Asiatic and European sides of the passageway from the Marmora to the Bosporus, would have made a "prolonged stay off Constantinople very difficult" for an Allied fleet.[3] The American military attaché at Constantinople, who was at Gallipoli when the British began their naval attack, said on his return from the Dardanelles after observing operations there that in his judgment the Allies' fleet would not be able to get through the Dardanelles.[4]

After a month of futile efforts the naval operation was abandoned when Admiral de Robeck gave up the attack on March 18, 1915, having suffered a loss of three capital ships sunk and three more disabled.

France and England had come to an agreement as early as February 18, 1915, to support the naval attack with a military force, but it was not until April 25 that the first landing took place. Again, this long delay gave the Turks time to make preparations and to perfect a strategic plan of defense against the military invasion the British were known to be planning in the near future. When the British had assembled 78,000 troops, 18,000 of whom were French colonials, the Turks under von Sanders had 90,000 men with which to oppose them.

The British succeeded in landing forces on the beaches at the southern end of the Gallipoli Peninsula and were able to maintain them there. They were unable, however, to gain the heights which dominated the passageway of the Dardanelles. On the first day of the landing a brilliant counterattack by Mustafa Kemal, who later played so important a role in the history of Turkey and the Near East, kept the Anzac Corps from holding positions which would have made it impossible for the Turks to remain in the fortresses and at the gun positions dominating the Dardanelles Narrows. The landing had been successful, but the operations had failed.

A bitter and ruthless struggle which imposed heavy losses and much suffering from heat, lack of water, and disease upon both Turks and British continued throughout May, June, and July. Finding themselves hopelessly tied down to their position on the beaches and in the foothills of the southern part of the Gallipoli Peninsula, the British decided to send reinforcements and make another attempt to drive out the Turks.

The second landing took place during August 6 to 10, 1915. In the meanwhile, of course, the Turks also had received reinforcements so that balance of forces was about the same as in April—110,000 Turks faced 99,000 British.

The second landing was a flat failure due in no small measure to the inadequacies of an antiquated British general, who recalled from retirement, was placed in command of the important land and sea operations at Suvla Bay. Instead of pressing forward with his troops after the landing had been successfully accomplished, he rested his troops for a whole day while other British forces who had driven the Turks from the commanding heights only needed as reinforcements to hold the position so hardly won those troops who then were bathing with carefree abandon on the beaches. Turkish officers, then at the Dardanelles, expressed astonishment more than a year later at Jerusalem that the British attack had not been pressed at a moment when the Turks were practically out of ammunition and could not have withstood another attack by fresh troops.

In August the moment of golden opportunity for the Allies passed. The heavy attacks failed to gain the commanding heights. In the autumn the British position became more and more hopeless. Although Italy had joined the Allies in May 1915 and declared war on the Turks in order that she might share in the partition of the Ottoman Empire, this was of little aid to the Allied forces on Gallipoli. When, however, Bulgaria threw in her lot with the Central Powers and declared war on Serbia, October 14, 1915, the fate of the Allied expedition to the Dardanelles was sealed. It was essential for the Allies to attempt to get aid to the Serbs when King Constantine of Greece refused to honor the treaty of alliance with Serbia of June 1913. A French and a British division was landed at Salonika on October 9, 1915. The Allies were not in a position to maintain a front in the Balkans and on Gallipoli. Furthermore, the entrance of Bulgaria into the war opened direct rail communications for supplies and munitions from Germany to Turkey. It was evident that the Turks could now bring up replacements even more rapidly than the Allies. Lord Kitchener came to Gallipoli to look the situation over. Shortly thereafter, on November 23, 1915, evacuation was approved. Beginning on December 10, 1915, it was completed by January 9, 1916. It was an amazingly able operation carried out with a minimum loss of men and materials. It has been spoken of as a military masterpiece.

The Dardanelles campaign had been costly to both the Turks and the British. It is estimated that during the military operations at the Dardanelles, which extended over a period of ten months, 1,200,000 men were employed, the Turkish casualties amounting to over 200,000 and the British to 120,000.

The Allies' plans for the dismemberment of the Ottoman Empire.—The British, whose century-old policy of "containing" Russia had prevented the Russians from securing control of the Straits, had not only agreed on March 12, 1915, to the Russians acquiring possession of Constantinople and the Straits but had spent ten crucial months and expended men and materials lavishly in a futile effort to open a route to her ally Russia. The Turkish victory in the Dardanelles campaign was one of portentous significance to the Allies, to all Europe and to the world. The collapse of tsarist Russia, the disintegrating Russian front in Europe, and the triumph of the Bolsheviks are not unrelated to the fact that the Turks at the Dardanelles effectively barred the door to southern Russia until October 31, 1918. By the time the French and British were able to send troops and armaments through the Straits and the Black Sea to Russia, the Bolsheviks had been in power for more than a year. Then England and France, under an agreement between Lloyd George and Clemenceau of December 1917 [5] regarding areas of occupation and economic spheres of influence, launched a losing war against the Bolshevik Soviet Russian government which was soon to give aid to the Turkish nationalists who had repudiated the Treaty of Sèvres imposed upon the Turks by the victorious Allies in August 1920.

The Anglo-French attack on the Dardanelles promptly resulted in the tsar's government insisting upon agreements between the Allies in regard to the division of the possessions of the "Sick Man of Europe," who at last was in his death agony. On March 4, 1915, two weeks after the naval attack on the Dardanelles began, Russia demanded that France and Great Britain should recognize her rights to Constantinople and the Straits. Both of Russia's allies grudgingly agreed on condition that their respective aspirations to territories in the Near East be recognized. The British had hoped that this concession to Russia would result in the Russians agreeing to accept the offer of the Greek Premier Venizelos to send a large expeditionary force to Gallipoli. The British having already annexed Cyprus and declared a protectorate over Egypt were hardly in a position, taking into consideration the military situation, to refuse the demand of the Russians or to force them to accept the Greek offer. Russia, well aware of the designs of Greek nationalists and imperialists with respect to Constantinople, insisted upon a refusal of Venizelos' proposal.

While the members of the Triple Entente were beginning to make arrangements for the division of spoils in the Near East, negotiations were being carried on with Italy who had declared her neutrality at the outbreak of the war. The decision of the Italian government to enter the war was based upon what it considered to be the vital interests of Italy. Foreign Minister Sidney Sonnino was well aware of the stakes of the war and his mind was not befogged by Allied propaganda. He bargained with the Allies for those territories so ardently desired by Italian nationalists and imperialists. In view of the fact that the great imperial powers, England and France, had not as much to offer Italy in the way of colonies as would a victorious Germany, Italian imperialistic demands were modest. In the Near East Sonnino insisted upon a recognition of Italy's right to the Dodecanese Islands, which she still occupied, and to Adalia in Asia Minor in case of the partition of Turkey. England and France willingly agreed, Russia somewhat reluctantly. England, France and Russia, having come to an understanding that all previous agreements among themselves concerning a peace settlement would remain unaffected by Italy's joining them in the war, signed the Treaty of London with Italy on April 26, 1915, which among other matters dealt with Italian claims in the Near East.

The attack on the Dardanelles forced the Allies to clarify their respective imperialistic plans for the disposition of Near Eastern peoples and territories. As Harry Howard very aptly said about Russia's insistence in February and March 1915 ". . . her demand for Constantinople and the Straits. . . . opened up the entire question of the future of Turkey—a fact which was to lead to the secret treaties and understandings of 1915–1917, which partitioned the sultan's heritage among the members of the Entente." [6]

Campaigns of 1915 end in a stalemate.—The piecemeal strategy in the Near East of both the Turks and their opponents, the Allies, resulted in neither side winning until four years later when the Turks were exhausted and the military power of the Allies had become predominant. Neither side was able to co-ordinate its offensives. Through most of the year 1915 when the Turks were obliged to concentrate the major part of their forces at the Dardanelles, the Russians on the Caucasus front did not follow up their victory over the Turks in the first week of January 1915, when the Third Turkish Army under Enver Pasha had practically been destroyed. Operations on Turkey's northeastern front were of a minor nature throughout the year. The British in Egypt, obsessed with the fear of further Turkish attacks on the Suez Canal, were quite content to establish outposts on its east bank and leisurely prepare for a campaign in 1916. Except for the Gallipoli campaign the British undertook aggressive action in the Near East only in Mesopotamia. There the British advance at first was essentially defensive in nature. The oil fields in Persia could not be considered safe from Turkish attack as long as the Turks held 'Amara on the Tigris 175 miles north of Basra and ninety miles north of the British advanced base at Qurna. In the spring of 1915 when the British were considering a further advance to the north, the Turks launched an attack on the main British base at Basra in April while another Turkish force held besieged at Ahwaz in the Persian oil field area a small British detachment. Action by the British was imperative. The Turks were driven back from Basra to An Nasiriya on the Euphrates, which was captured on July 24, 1915, the Turks retiring to Kut-el-Amara on the Tigris. This operation cleared the left flank of General Charles Townshend's force which meanwhile had driven the Turks up the Tigris and captured 'Amara on June 3, 1915, while other British forces drove the Turks out of southern Persia. Incidentally, during the war in the Near East neither Russians, Turks, nor British showed any compunctions about invading the small and helpless neutral country of Persia (Iran).

Having so easily occupied the southern part of the valley of the Tigris and the Euphrates, the Anglo-Indian government decided upon the risky venture of an attack on Bagdad some 150 odd miles north of 'Amara despite the fact that the London government was unwilling to supply an adequate force for such a far-flung advance. The ambitious General

Townshend continued to advance up the Tigris without having sufficient troops to hold more than the river and its immediate banks. The Turks, however, in no better position, were driven out of Kut-el-Amara on September 28, 1915, and fell back to a fortified position at Ctesiphon about twenty miles down the river from Bagdad. It was almost two months later when the British slowly moving up the Tigris attacked a Turkish force covering the approaches to Bagdad. The Turks were now in a position to bring up reinforcements more rapidly than the British, who were not able to dislodge the enemy from its entrenched positions at Ctesiphon. General Townshend, consequently, had no other choice than to retire to Kut-el-Amara, where the Turks promptly besieged his forces cutting him off from communication with main British bases at Al Qurna and Basra. As a defensive operation to protect the vital oil supplies the British invasion of Mesopotamia in 1915 was fully successful, but as an offensive to capture Bagdad and destroy Turkish military power in central Mesopotamia it was a "flop."

THE TRAGEDY OF THE ARMENIAN PEOPLE

The main line of communications from Anatolia to the Arab provinces crossed the Cilicia plain and the Amanus (Alma Dag) Mountain range, areas where there was a considerable Armenian population, the remnants of the Little Armenia of Crusader days. This entire region, like the Armenian vilayets of eastern Anatolia, was a highly strategic and vulnerable one. The ruthless rulers of Turkey used the excuse of ridding these areas of what they considered the disloyal Armenian population to carry out a plan to exterminate the Armenian people. The brutal Talaat Pasha is accused of being the foremost proponent of this cruel policy.

The forced migrations and wholesale massacres of Armenians initiated in 1915 by the Turkish government under the triumvirate of Enver, Talaat, and Jemal are known as the "Armenian atrocities." They were used by the Allies as propaganda against the Germans, and wide publicity was given to them during World War I when it was thought helpful to the Allied cause. Nothing effective in the political sphere was done for the Armenians except by the Russians, who permitted the organization of a Soviet Socialist Republic of Armenia within the framework of the U.S.S.R. Previously, however, the Bolshevik Russian government had ceded to Turkey part of the Armenian Transcaucasia in the region of Ardahan, Kars, and Erivan.

The emotional reaction in the western world to the Armenian atrocities was profound though only of a temporary nature. In 1915 and 1916 people had not yet accepted mass slaughter as a legitimate means of warfare. The emotions stirred by forced migrations and mass massacres tend, by awakening hatred of their instigators, to obscure the deeper tragedy of our times which lies in man's inability to rid himself without violence of those social institutions and inculcated ideas which are the underlying causes of modern genocide and mass destruction. Indignation and condemnation of such wholesale brutality and cruelty do not of themselves offer any security against such activities in the future.

The ideas which governed the minds and determined the actions of Enver, Talaat, Jemal, and company were of western vintage and origin. It was western thinkers who promulgated and exalted the ideas of nationalism, racial superiority, and the political survival of the fittest. The Turks applied them to achieve their survival at the expense of the Armenians.

Those who find in their collection of ideas justification for Buchenwald or Hiroshima should find no difficulty in discovering similar justification for the atrocious treatment of the Armenians by the Turks during World War I.

The inhumanity of man to man.—In the Ottoman Near East humanitarianism had become compartmentalized. Sympathy and compassion beyond the boundaries of religious and national groups were unusual phenomena. Striking examples of the inhumanity of the members of one group to those of another were constantly in evidence in Turkey during World War I.

During 1915, at a railroad station in Cilicia on the Berlin-Bagdad line, the confused secretary of the Turkish Senate, temporarily in the employ of the Standard Oil Company of New York, was looking for a porter among the forlorn mass of Armenian refugees who crowded the platform. Having found a porter to whom he talked volubly in Turkish, the secretary turned to his American traveling companion and remarked, "What a pitiful shame it was." Thinking that the Turk was talking about the Armenians, the American inquired why the Turkish government so treated the Armenians. With some haughtiness the secretary replied that he was speaking of the porter, a Turk who had been a wealthy landowner in European Turkey before the Balkan Wars but who had been forced to flee from Macedonia and, having lost all his property, was obliged to earn a meager living as a porter. To the secretary here was a refugee worthy of pity and a good tip.

A year later on the road from Jericho to Jerusalem two Armenian doctors in the uniforms of Turkish officers passed on their way to the Holy City some Armenian young girls, derelicts of the migrations and massacres, under the escort of a few Turkish soldiers. The doctors stopped to talk with the girls in Armenian and gave them money and food. A few miles farther on the Armenian military doctors halted for a rest at a *han,* where an old Arab had stopped to water his donkey heavily laden with oranges destined for Jericho. Because this Moslem peddler refused to sell his oranges at the Jerusalem instead of the Jericho price, the Armenians cursed him in Arabic and struck him with their riding crops. This harmless old Arab was beyond the pale of their compassion.

Deportations and massacres.—The ancient Armenian communities of Asia Minor were broken up and practically destroyed. Thousands were brutally murdered, thousands more died of hunger, exhaustion, and disease on the long migrations or in the concentration camps. Rape, forced conversion to Islam, and slavery were inevitable concomitants of the migrations. At the end of the war only a remnant of the Armenian population of Asia Minor remained alive in camps and orphan asylums. Turkish Armenia was at an end. The Turks thought they had rid themselves forever of their Armenian Question. They did not foresee that thirty years later a prosperous Soviet Socialist Armenia would develop irredentist tendencies toward the old Armenian lands in Turkey's possession that would for strategic reasons receive some encouragement from the Kremlin.

There appears to be no doubt that the little group who ruled Turkey deliberately planned to rid the country of the Armenians by a policy of forced migration and wholesale slaughter. It is to the credit of the Turkish people that many Turks opposed this policy. Some Turkish officials refused to carry out orders from Constantinople. Some Turkish families at considerable risk attempted to save their Armenian friends. Such efforts proved futile, except in western Anatolia.

It was the tragic misfortune of half a million Armenians who, it has been estimated, died or were slaughtered during the war, and of those uprooted and displaced Armenians who survived, that the bulk of the Armenian population lived in vulnerable areas of the Ottoman Empire, in eastern Anatolia on the Russian frontier, in Cilicia, and in northern Syria. For the most part pro-Ally, used by Russians in their war with Turkey, considered in the strategic plans of the British when contemplating a landing at Alexandretta, the Armenians were without doubt a military liability if not an actual menace to the Turks. Armenian revolutionary societies were active and their agents useful in a variety of ways to the Allies. Armenian revolutionary bands wreaked their vengeance on innocent Moslems as Turks and Kurds did on innocent Armenians.

The Turks were fighting a war for survival. The Armenians were a large minority group who favored the enemy and hoped for the defeat of the Turks. Among the Armenians a small but not unimportant group was actively engaged in treasonous activities and in armed resistance to the Turks. The Turks somewhat apologetically tried to justify the policy of forced migration of Armenians on ideological grounds similar to those used by warring governments in dealing with minorities considered as a potential threat to security.

In the winter of 1916 and 1917 the Turkish soldiers, in the eastern vilayets from which the Armenians had been driven, paid by death from starvation and disease for the stupidity and ruthlessness of their rulers who had destroyed in 1915 those Armenian peasants and craftsmen who otherwise would have fed and serviced the Turkish armies. Two of the three men most responsible for the Armenian policy of the government were assassinated; Talaat at Berlin in 1921, Jemal at Tiflis in 1922. Enver was killed in 1922 during a battle in Turkestan. "Let he who is without sin cast the first stone."

MILITARY EVENTS OF 1915–16

Declining power of the Turks.—By the end of 1915 neither group of belligerents was any nearer a decisive victory. Actually, the Turks had reached the peak of their power in November 1915. During the next year, although the Allies could chalk up only one important victory in the Near East, that of the Russians in eastern Anatolia, Turkish military power declined at a very rapid rate. Commandant M. Larcher in his technical but most useful book, *The Turkish War in the World War,* estimates that the Turkish fighting forces trained and armed amounted to 800,000 in November 1915, to only 400,000 in March 1917, and to only 200,000 in March 1918.[7]

The growing weakness of the Turkish armies cannot be judged solely by the loss of effective fighting men. The decline in morale, the increasingly large number of deserters, the lack of arms and equipment, malnutrition and sickness, these were the real indices of declining military strength. These weaknesses were not discernible to many in 1916. Liman von Sanders reveals the real situation and the blindness of those who refused to recognize the realities in Turkey. In his recollections of his five years in Turkey as chief of the German mission and commander of a Turkish army, he tells of two high-ranking German officers who had been sent by the German G.H.Q. to the Caucasus front in the spring of 1916 at the time of the great Russian victory and just previous to the disasters which overtook the Turkish Second Army and Third Army in the summer of 1916 and who reported to Hindenburg and Ludendorff that "the military situation of Turkey never had been better than now" and described the resources of Turkey as "inexhaustible." General von Sanders was then reporting that on an inspection he found 8000 soldiers in one depot with a miscellaneous lot of only 1050 rifles, and without cartridge boxes, side arms, and bayonets. Sanitary conditions in the Turkish army were in a deplorable state, a large percentage of the troops were sick and worn out, food supplies were low, and by the end of 1916 a division commander reported that many of his soldiers in mid-winter were still dressed in summer clothes without overcoats or boots and that all of his men were badly undernourished.[8]

Enver Pasha for reasons best known to himself sapped the strength of the forces remaining in Turkey in order to raise seven divisions of men in tiptop condition adequately equipped and well-officered for the European theater on the Macedonian, Galician, and Rumanian fronts. von Sanders observes that a grave mistake was made by the Turks and acquiesced in by the Germans when, against the interests of both Germany and Turkey, Turkish troops were sent to the European theater despite the fact that Turkey did not have sufficient forces to cope with the military situation on the Turkish fronts.

Among the many other reasons for thinking that the triumvirate and their supporters who governed Turkey during World War I were grossly incompetent is the evidence of their professional incompetency in purely military matters. The onus of blame rests most heavily on Minister of War Enver Pasha, who proved to be incompetent as a military commander and as chief administrator of the war effort.

At a time when Grand Duke Nicholas was preparing a Russian offensive on the Caucasus front and when forces no longer needed to defend the Dardanelles should have been promptly sent to the eastern Anatolian vilayets, three of the Turkish armies remained in European Turkey where there was no front and no enemy!

Russian victories in eastern Anatolia.—On the Caucasus front the Russians launched their attack on the Turkish Third Army on January 17, 1916, and in ten days despite the severe winter conditions in Armenia forced the Turks back on a seventy-mile front. Erzurum was taken within a month's time. Before, however, attempting a further advance along the center toward Sivas, the Russian Commander Yudenitch, who later was to play a counterrevolutionary role against the Bolsheviks in the Baltic states backed by the British in an attack on Petrograd (Leningrad), extended his right flank by capturing the important Turkish Black Sea port of Trebizond and his left flank by occupying Mush and Bitlis west of Lake Van. To parry a possible Turkish attack from northern Mesopotamia flying Russian columns were sent through northern Persia (Iran) to Ruwandiz sixty miles northeast of Mosul. Yudenitch then began a slow advance to Erzincan on the road to Sivas.

To counter this Russian offensive, the Turkish Second Army was eventually sent from Thrace but it was not until August 1916 that this force was in a position to come to the aid of the Turkish Third Army, which by that time had been decisively defeated by the Russians. Inadequately equipped with mountain artillery and pack animals the Second Army failed in its offensive mission and was defeated by the Russians. In full retreat it was overtaken by panic and suffered a loss of a very considerable percentage of its effectives. Deserters were numbered in the tens of thousands. Had it not been for the Russian collapse and revolution in the spring of 1917 the loss of Trebizond, Erzurum, Mush, and Bitlis in 1916 might have proved fatal to the Turks in 1917. As it was, the results of the defeats of the Second and Third Turkish armies greatly weakened the Turkish military power and left the Turks in a poor condition to deal with the British on the Palestine-Sinai and the Mesopotamian fronts.

British advance toward Palestine.—Owing to a stupid bureaucratic act at Constantinople by the Turkish government in the summer of 1914 before Turkey entered the war, the British in Egypt received a delayed windfall in 1916. In their mobilization of materials in preparation for war, the Turks seized at Constantinople two automobile trucks consigned to the Standard Oil Company of New York. Promptly this company had a ship in the Mediterranean bound for Jaffa, with a full cargo of oil-drilling equipment including pumps and miles of pipe and fittings, diverted to Alexandria where the goods were temporarily stored in bonded warehouses. The exchange was hardly in the Turks' favor. They gained two trucks while the British got pipe and pumps indispensable to their invasion of Palestine via the Sinai desert route.

While the British were organizing their defenses on the east bank of the Suez Canal, the German headquarters, wishing to prevent further withdrawals of British troops from Egypt, ordered an attack on the Suez Canal in February 1916. The Turkish high command obligingly agreed although the expedition could not be gotten ready until July, and it was inadequately trained and supplied. It was recognized in advance that this second onslaught against the Canal was futile. Not only were the Turks defeated, but they lost a third of their effectives, thus opening the way for a British offensive.

During the second half of 1916 the British in a most thorough but unhurried manner, waged a successful campaign in the Sinai Peninsula driving the Turks back to the Egyptian-Palestine frontiers. In the northeastern corner of the peninsula the British established by the end of the year an advanced base at El 'Arish some fifty to sixty miles southwest of Gaza and Bir es Saba. Having built a railroad and laid a water pipeline from the Suez Canal as they advanced, the British outpost at El 'Arish had superb communications by land with the plentifully supplied base in Egypt in addition to the sea route available to them because of Allied naval supremacy in the Mediterranean.

The British position at the doors of southern Palestine at the beginning of 1917 was in striking contrast with that of the Turks on the bank of the Suez Canal in February 1915. The Turks at that time had only a few days' supply of water, food, and munitions which could not be replenished rapidly because of the lack of adequate supply lines. When their attack on the Canal failed the Turks were obliged to withdraw immediately. The British on the contrary with excellent supply lines were able to establish themselves firmly at El 'Arish and to prepare with tortoise-like slowness their unsuccessful attacks on Gaza in March and April 1917.

Turkish victory in Mesopotamia.—In Mesopotamia, at Kut-el-Amara on April 29, 1916, the Turks forced the surrender of General Townshend and his troops whom the British had been unable to relieve after long and costly operations. The British had lost 8000 prisoners at Kut-el-Amara and suffered 22,000 casualties in attempts to rescue Townshend's forces. The Turks did not profit from their victory and from the British losses in men and prestige. Again egged on by the policy of the Germans, this time emanating from the Foreign Office, Enver Pasha, intoxicated with his imperialistic and pan-Islamic projects, weakened Turkish forces in Mesopotamia by an expedition into Persia (Iran), where Germans and Turks by bribery and other means were ineptly attempting to raise Persian forces to drive out the Russians and British. The failure of the Turks with German aid to develop in 1916 a strong national uprising in the Moslem country of Persia (Iran) against the Allies is in notable contrast to the success of the British in securing the backing of Arab nationalists who began their revolt against the Turks on June 5, 1916, under the leadership of the Grand Sherif of Mecca, Hussein Ali.

While the Turks were dissipating their military resources in Mesopotamia the British were making plans for the recapture of Kut-el-Amara in preparation for an advance on Bagdad. The British War Office at

London took over from the Indian Government the direction of British military operations in Mesopotamia and energetically prepared for a future offensive. Reinforcements were provided, Basra was transformed into a modern port, and lines of communication by river boats and light railroads were greatly improved. By the middle of November the British advance up the Tigris began, and by the end of the year they had started their attack on Kut-el-Amara. Enver Pasha's Persian policy had permitted the British to pursue unmolested their preparations throughout the summer and autumn of 1916 for a campaign which early in 1917 led to the fall of Bagdad.

CHAPTER XVI

Turkey at War— The Last Two Years

✿ DEPLORABLE CONDITIONS IN TURKEY— REVOLUTION IN RUSSIA

At the beginning of the third year of the war Turkey was in a deplorable condition. Starvation, privation, and disease were rampant among the civil population in large areas of the Empire. Turkish military power was in a state of rapid decline with effective troops numbering half of those available in January 1916. Furthermore, Arabia was in revolt and powerful offensives were being prepared by the British on the frontiers of Palestine and in Mesopotamia, while the Russians held a goodly slice of eastern Anatolia and were also preparing for an offensive in 1917.

The Russian Revolution—which began in March 1917, continued throughout the year, and was followed by civil wars—brought about a temporary disintegration of the military power of Russia until the Red Army grew powerful enough to cope with domestic and foreign enemies. In the interim there existed a condition bordering on political anarchy. In the Caucasus area the Russian Empire was undergoing a process of dissolution which was not checked until the Bolsheviks gained control many months after the end of World War I, when the Allied forces and the White Russian counterrevolutionists were obliged to withdraw.

✿ CAMPAIGNS OF 1917–18 IN TRANSCAUCASIA, PALESTINE, AND MESOPOTAMIA

In the interim the area south of the Caucasus Mountains between the Black and Caspian seas and stretching to the frontiers of Turkey and Persia (Iran) became the center of an exceedingly complex struggle in which the Turks took part. This area, known as Transcaucasia, has been and still is of importance to the peoples of the Near East and of significance to its historical evolution.

Transcaucasia, its strategic importance.—Transcaucasia is today a strategic frontier area of great concern to Russia, to Turkey, to Iraq, and to Iran (Persia) also, because of their far-flung political and economic interests, to Great Britain and the United States. Transcaucasia's strategic importance lies in the fact that geographically it is so located that it is a passageway from the Persian Gulf to the Eurasian plain. Crossing the Caucasus Mountains this passageway gives access to the steppes along the north shore of the Black Sea that extend through the Ukraine to Poland and Hungary, and to the routes of the Volga, Don, and Dnieper rivers which lead through the heart of western Russia to the Baltic. Transcaucasia from earliest historic times has been a highway along which have traveled Indo-European and Asiatic nomads. This was the highway used by the Tatar, Turanian, and Turkish tribes in their invasion of the western Eurasian plains.

The peoples of Transcaucasia.—The ebb and flow of invasions and conquests have left in Transcaucasia a variety of races and religious sects whose animosities made political integration possible only when imposed by some exterior power; lacking such power Transcaucasia split up into rival warring communities. Before the nineteenth century Turks and Persians, who at different times had controlled directly or indirectly Transcaucasia, had ceased to dominate it. In the nineteenth century it was brought under the rule of the Russian tsars. The Russians began a development of the natural resources, agricultural and mineral as well as industrial, which by the twentieth century, after the discovery of oil and the development of a vast petroleum industry, brought the urban and settled areas of Transcaucasia within the fold of the modern world.

In spite of the policy of Russification and the migration of nearly half a million Russians to the Caucasus, the old historical cleavages continued to exist and were augmented by the advent of the Russians.

The estimated population of Transcaucasia at the time of World War I was approximately 7,000,000. Of these over 2,500,000 were Moslem divided into Shiites and Sunnites, and over 4,000,000 were Christians. Most of the Moslems were Persians, Tatars, Turcomen, and Turks although there were also over 100,000 Kurds and nearly 140,000 Moslem Georgians. Among the Christians the Russians numbered nearly 500,000, the Georgians over 1,500,000, and the Armenians 1,750,000. Though these groups were intermingled to a considerable degree, the Georgians for the most part inhabited the western part of Transcaucasia, the Armenians the south central section, and the Persians, Tatars and Turanian Turks, and Turcomen the eastern part. Exclusive of the Russians, who had only recently settled in Transcaucasia, there were only two groups deeply conscious of their nationality and having a distinctive national culture. These were the Georgians and the Armenians. The Tatars, Turks, and Turcomen had no distinctive national culture, they had never formed a national state. They were the residue of tribal invasions and conquests. Their social organization was partly feudal and partly tribal. Most of them were peasant herdsmen.

The Georgians and Armenians while opposed to tsarism were pro-Russian except for the Moslem Georgians of the educated classes, who were pro-Turkish. The feudal Georgians and tribal leaders of the Tatars and Turanians, whose former power over and exploitation of their peasants and herdsmen to some degree had been curbed by the Russian government, toyed with pan-Islamic and pan-Turanian ideas disseminated by the Turks of the Ottoman Empire. These Moslem Tatar-Turanian leaders were not averse to using the Ottoman Turks in order to free themselves from Russia and to extend their control over wider territories with populations which could be exploited by them.

The confused political situation in Transcaucasia.—The situation in Transcaucasia was rendered even more complex by the fact that Marxian socialism had spread widely among certain elements of the population. Some of the most important leaders of the Russian Revolution of 1917 were Georgians, who were prominent in both the Bolshevik and Menshevik factions of the Social Democratic Party. Other Russian revolutionary parties had adherents among the peoples of Transcaucasia. When civil war raged between the Whites and the Reds throughout Russia and within that greater struggle a conflict between the Bolsheviks (Communists), the Mensheviks (Socialists), and the Social Revolutionists (the socialistic agrarians), partisans of these various revolutionists and counterrevolutionists in Transcaucasia took part. Consequently, the political confusion, bordering on chaos, created a situation favorable to intervention and invasion by British, German, and Turkish armed forces.

Enver's ambitious plans.—It was in this seething tumultuous sea that Enver Pasha decided to fish for imperialistic loot. The seizure of power by the Bolsheviks in November 1917, with their determination to end the war, opened in Enver's judgment limitless possibilities to exploit the pan-Islamic and pan-Turanian ideas which had become popular among various Turkish groups. Enver's Transcaucasian policy had an effect upon the Palestine and Mesopotamian fronts during the last year of the War.

On their northeastern front the Turks were spared a Russian offensive in the spring of 1917 as a result of the Russian Revolution. Although the successive revolutionary governments until the Bolshevik *coup d'état* of November 1917, favored the continuation of the war against the Central Powers, they were unable to wage offensive warfare or even to continue military operations. The tsarist armies were in a state of progressive disintegration, less so, however, on the Turkish front than in the European theater.

Behind their advanced line in Turkey running from Trebizond on the Black Sea through Erzincan on the road to Sivas and to Lake Van, the Russians had been improving their lines of communication by building roads and light railroads in preparation for an offensive in 1917. The outbreak of the revolution in Petrograd of March 9–12, 1917, effectively checked the carrying out of the ambitious plans of Grand Duke Nicholas for an attack upon the Turks. The Turkish forces on the Caucasus front were in a debilitated condition. The forced migration of the Armenian population left depopulated the area occupied by the Second and Third Turkish armies. It was an empty devastated land, and Turkish communications and skilled manpower were inadequate to supply troops with the food and technical labor that would have been available if the Armenians had not been driven out. As a result thousands of Turkish soldiers died from starvation and disease during the winter of 1916–17. The exhausted and weakened Turks were spared the onslaught of a Russian offensive because of the effect of the Russian Revolution on the soldiers of the tsar. They had lost the will to fight. Nevertheless, the Turks were unable to profit from the disintegration of the Russian forces for the manpower of the two Turkish armies amounted to only 20,000 rifles. After November 7, 1917, when the Bolsheviks became the rulers of Russia the Russian forces on the Caucasus front began to break up. In December the troops, no longer obedient to their tsarist officers, abandoned the front and an immense amount of war materials and animals. Still the Turks remained inactive except for the reoccupation of the Lake Van area from which the Russians had retired. In mid-December the Bolshevik Soviet government signed an armistice with the Central Powers including Turkey which, followed by the demobilization of the Russian forces in Transcaucasia, paved the way for a Turkish advance in 1918 not only to the pre-World War I frontiers but to those previous to the Russian-Turkish War of 1877–78.

Although the prodigious events in Russia had an effect on the Caucasus front favorable to the Turks, they had to meet two powerful offensives during 1917, one resulting in the capture of Bagdad and the other of Jerusalem.

Development in Mesopotamia.—In Mesopotamia the Turks on February 24, 1917, were forced to withdraw from Kut-el-Amara and to retreat to Bagdad, which they reached on March 8. Vigorously pursued by the British, the Turkish forces were driven out of Bagdad three days later. The fall of Bagdad had wide repercussions in Germany as well as in the Near East. British prestige, which had been at a low ebb after their failure at the Dardanelles and the fall of Kut-el-Amara to the Turks, was greatly enhanced among the Arab population. In Germany it was decided that the recapture of Bagdad was essential. Without consulting von Sanders and the German military mission who were fairly accurately informed of conditions civil and military in Turkey, the German High Command with Enver's approval decided to organize a new and completely independent force under German command to drive the British out of Bagdad. The Russian Revolution made it possible to withdraw Turkish troops from the European theater for their new striking force.

German plans and Yilderim.—At this period of the war the German General Staff decided to break the deadlock of trench warfare by adopting open methods of warfare which were later so effectively employed on the Italian front at Caporetto and still later in Ludendorff's great offensives in France during the spring of 1918. Their idea in Turkey was to create a powerful striking force which could move with great rapidity. While the Germans gave this new force the prosaic title of Army Group F, the Turks called it dramatically *Yilderim,* meaning lightning, borrowing a term first used during Napoleon's campaign in Egypt.

Not having availed themselves of the knowledge of von Sanders and his staff, the German High Command did not realize that under existing conditions in Turkey lightning-like operations, not to mention rapid transportation, were completely impossible. General von Falkenhayn arrived in Constantinople early in May 1917 and a month later preliminary preparations were begun in Mesopotamia, although on the spot investigations began to expose the impracticability of the plans made in Germany. Transportation was a major problem. German units required nearly triple the transportation facilities necessary for a Turkish unit. German supplies and equipment along the extended lines of communication from Constantinople to Aleppo were only safe from theft and pillage when guarded by German troops. In consequence of this condition of affairs, the larger part of the highly trained German technical and combat troops had to be employed in guarding the lines of communication from the soldiers and civilian population of their Turkish ally. Furthermore, the transportation of Turkish troops presented a problem because of the high percentage of deserters. It has been estimated that by the summer of 1917 the number of Turkish deserters equaled, if it did not actually exceed, the number of Turkish soldiers under arms.

Morgenthau's Special Mission.—Such were the delays that in November 1917 one of the important units of the Yilderim, the Asia Corps, was still encamped at Haidar Pasha in sight of the minarets of Constantinople! In the meanwhile the British who had long since learned of the much-touted Yilderim had decided to strike a crushing blow on the Palestine front following their failures in March and April. As a result the Yilderim was ordered to Palestine and the attack on Bagdad abandoned. In connection with these matters it is interesting to note that Henry Morgenthau, Sr., and Felix Frankfurter were persuaded at Gibraltar early in July by Dr. Chaim Weizmann, the Zionist leader, who was at the time negotiating with the British government for a declaration promising the Jews a National Home in Palestine, to abandon the Special Mission confided to them by President Wilson of negotiating a separate peace with Turkey. One of the arguments used by Dr. Weizmann was that the Turks would not be disposed to make a separate peace because of the Yilderim plan to recapture Bagdad and because of the weakness of the British position there.

Weizmann and his associate the French Zionist, Monsieur Weyl, were successful in persuading Morgenthau and Frankfurter from carrying out their scheme of going to Palestine via Egypt to open negotiations with Jemal Pasha at a most inopportune time for both the Zionists and British. Balfour, the British foreign secretary, in close collaboration with British and American Zionists had by July 1917 already well prepared the ground in England and the United States for the historic Balfour Declaration of November promising the Jews a national home in Palestine. The British War Cabinet in June appointed General Edmund H. Allenby Commander-in-chief of the Egyptian Expeditionary Force with instructions to prepare and execute a vigorous offensive against the Turks with the capture of Jerusalem as a prime objective. Both the British and the Zionists, anticipating the realization of their hopes of securing possession of Palestine by military means, were opposed to the special mission of Mr. Morgenthau.[1]

The Palestine front.—The British government did not decide to employ troops in Egypt for offensive operations against the Turks in Palestine until the early part of 1917. Operations in Sinai during 1916 were considered as defensive measures to protect the Suez Canal and Egypt from threat of Turkish attacks. Their advance across the Sinai Peninsula had brought the British force to El 'Arish from which they made a further advance on January 8 to the Palestine frontier at Rafa, the Turks retiring to Gaza and Bir es Saba. The Sinai Peninsula had been cleared and the British held a position from which Palestine could be invaded.

The time was most favorable for the British. The Turkish forces in Palestine were at a minimum. The morale of the troops was very poor and munitions and supplies were low. It would take several weeks to reinforce the Turks in southern Palestine. Fortunately for the Turks they were not the only ones who moved leisurely. Two months passed before General Murray was authorizd to execute a limited offensive.

In Jerusalem after the capture of Rafa on January 8 everyone felt certain the British would rapidly overrun Palestine. Turkish officers said that they had no force capable of withstanding a British attack. The British, however, waited until the last week in March to launch an offensive against the Turks at Gaza. During this delay of nearly three months after reaching the Palestine frontier, the British gave the Turks ample time to fortify the strong position between Gaza and Bir es Saba and to bring reinforcements, munitions, supplies, and equipment from the north. Along the Syrian and Bagdad railroads in the latter part of February and the early part of March there was a steady stream of military traffic moving southward.[2]

General Archibald Murray's two attempts to capture Gaza in March and April failed with rather heavy losses estimated to have been nine to ten thousand men. The initial down payment for dilatoriness was a heavy one, particularly for those whose lives were uselessly expended.

Allenby arrives in the Near East.—After the failure of these two attacks General Archibald Murray was recalled in June 1917 and Allenby sent to Egypt to replace him. General Allenby is said to have informed Lloyd George that he would accept the command only if he were given the necessary troops and equipment to carry out successfully the offensive operations desired by the British War Cabinet. Allenby was not unaware of the fact that British failures at the

Dardanelles, in Mesopotamia, and on the Palestine front were in some measure due to the lack of troops and materials necessary to success.

After a survey of the situation on the Palestine front General Allenby informed London of his requirements and began preparations for an offensive in the autumn. It was during this period that the military activities of the Arab revolutionary forces in Arabia were being organized with British help by the sons of Sherif Hussein Ali of Mecca. This resulted in the development of a subsidiary Turkish front in Arabia that was to play an increasingly important role in the Palestine campaigns of General Allenby.

The Arab revolt.—The unrest among the Arabs previous to the war was very greatly increased and became far more widespread in the Arab lands of western Asia during 1915 and the first half of 1916, despite the appeal which at first the Jihad made to the uneducated and the more fanatical of the Arabs. The incapacity of Jemal Pasha to deal with the problems arising from the war, of depreciating paper currency, rising prices, gross racketeering in foodstuffs and other essential products connived at and shared in by Turkish officials along with Arab speculators, widespread epidemics of typhus and cholera, and the development of famine conditions was one of the causes of sullen discontent and growing hatred of the Turks by the Arabs. The harsh and unimaginative policy of Jemal toward the Arabs and the Abdul Hamid-like spy system he employed created a burning indignation tempered with fear among the Arab people of Palestine, Syria, and Lebanon. The contempt of the Arabs for the C.U.P. was startling. In 1916 on a return trip from Es Salt to Jerusalem, an Arab from Transjordan on passing the putrefying body of a dead camel being torn to bits by snarling hungry dogs said to his companions, who needless to say were not Turks, "Look at the Committee of Union and Progress at work."

Conditions in the Arab lands of western Asia were, however, only one factor in bringing about the Arab revolt. Hussein Ali, Grand Sherif of Mecca and his sons, one of whom was a member of a secret Arab revolutionary society, had in the year previous to the war been contemplating a revolt against the Turks with British support. Correspondence had been exchanged with Kitchener, then Consul General and British High Commissioner in Egypt. After the outbreak of World War I, these diplomatic feelers were renewed and continued until a somewhat nebulous agreement was reached in the much discussed Hussein-McMahon correspondence. These arrangements were concluded at a time when events in Syria, Lebanon, and Palestine forced the cautious Emir Hussein Ali and his sons to reach the conclusion that the time was ripe for revolt.

The Turks had sent a Turko-German force to the Yemen which was considered by the British as a possible menace to Aden and by Hussein Ali as a threat to his position in Mecca. Consequently, the commencement of the Arab revolt was timed to check the march of this expedition through Arabia. Emir Faisal and Emir Abdullah proclaimed their revolt at Medina on June 5, 1916, and four days later the forces of Sherif Hussein attacked the Turkish garrison in Mecca. By the end of the year Hussein and his sons were in control of all of the Hejaz with the exception of Medina which was strongly held by the Turks.

This revolution forced upon the Turkish government another active front. Failing to drive the Arabs out of Mecca, Taif, and Jidda, the Turks were placed on the defensive in Medina and along the Hejaz railroad from there to Ma'an and later to Deraa. Ma'an was an important railroad station because it was in the wheatlands of southern Transjordan and because it controlled the route from the port of Akaba. Deraa was of greater importance because it was a junction on the Hejaz railroad from which ran the railway lines to Haifa, Tulkarm, and Jerusalem.

As a result of the Arab uprising in 1916 the Turks were obliged to maintain more forces in Medina and on the Hejaz railroad than were needed to contain the British forces of General Murray on the Palestine front. Nevertheless, the English commander of the Egyptian Expeditionary Force tended to belittle the Arab military effort. The British attitude toward the Arab force changed very definitely in the summer of 1917. In July the Arabs captured Akaba, to which Emir Faisal moved his headquarters. This port at the head of the Gulf of Akaba provided a base from which an offensive against the Turks in Transjordan and Syria could be launched and from which in the meantime raids could be made, interrupting Turkish lines of communication and obliging the Turks to retain considerable forces east of the Jordan. General Allenby was quick to perceive the very real advantages to his projected offensive in Palestine of Arab operations when these were presented to him by so persuasive a person as T. E. Lawrence. From the autumn of 1917 until the end of the war, the Arab military operations became a part of the Palestine front and an important factor in the victories of Allenby's forces in Palestine and Syria.

Allenby's first campaign.—General Allenby opened his offensive against the Turks by a bombardment of Gaza by land and sea designed to deceive the Turks with respect to the main attack on October 31 on the Bir es Saba position. The British forces greatly outnumbered the Turks in infantry, cavalry, and artillery. Under able leadership British victory was assured. The Turks who were reinforced by the Yilderim were able, after being driven out of Bir es Saba and Gaza, to establish a line from the coast a short way north of Jaffa across Palestine to the Jordan and thence to the Hejaz railway. The Turks had lost Jerusalem and Jaffa, but what was of great importance to their enemies, the Turks had lost control of the main line of lateral communications across Palestine from the Mediterranean to the Jordan Valley. This gave the British a definite advantage in the campaign of 1918, which did not commence until September because of the situation in France resulting from the German offensive in the spring of that year.

Allenby's victory in the autumn of 1917 had not destroyed Turkish military power in Palestine. In fact Turkish forces in strongly defensive positions in March 1918 were practically double those that had successfully defeated General Murray in March and April 1917.

There is no doubt that the Turks would have been compelled to surrender to the Allies by the end of 1918 even though they had not been defeated in Palestine, Syria, and Mesopotamia. The retirement from the war of Bulgaria, the defeat of Austria-Hungary on the Italian frontier, the defeat of the Germans in France and Belgium would have left Turkey as the sole remaining belligerent if Allenby's offensive had failed in Palestine and General Marshall's in Mesopotamia. Had this been the case conditions in the Near East would have been very different at the end of hostilities. The failure of the Turks in Palestine and Mesopotamia and the armistice of October 31, 1918, ended Ottoman power in the Arab lands of western Asia from the Persian Gulf and the Red Sea to the Taurus Mountains. The Arabs were not free, but they were freed from Turkish rule. The military victories which brought this about were in some measure due to Enver's decision to send Turkish military forces to Transcaucasia.

Mesopotamia and Transcaucasia.—General von Sanders, who had been placed in command of the Turko-German forces in Palestine in February 1918, distressed at the sending of Turkish troops to Transcaucasia wrote in June to the German ambassador at Constantinople that in 1917 the Turkish advance into Persia had been the cause of the loss of Bagdad and that now by their advance into Transcaucasia the Turks were going to lose the rest of the Arab lands. Edmund Dane, the British military correspondent of the *Westminster Gazette,* also was convinced that the Turkish expedition to Baku was most disadvantageous to the Turks. His judgment ran counter to that of the British military leaders at Bagdad. In his book on the *British Campaigns in the Near East* Dane claims that the Turkish military expedition to Transcaucasia was of advantage to the British. He also considered the British push to Baku indefensible from a military point of view. It is evident, however, that the British as well as Enver Pasha believed there was something of importance to be gained by occupying Russian territory in Transcaucasia.

After the Treaty of Brest-Litovsk of March 1918 which officially ended the war but not hostilities between Bolshevik Russia and the Central Powers, the Turks proceeded to occupy those territories in Transcaucasia which had been ceded to them: Kars, Ardahan, and Batum. The Armenians were determined to resist the Turks. Before the Bolsheviks came into power the peoples of Transcaucasia had formed the "United Russian Federated Democratic Republic." Its Diet, controlled largely by Marxist Social Democrats (Mensheviks), refused to recognize the peace treaty signed by the Bolshevik government and decided to act independently. As a result the Diet opened separate negotiations with the Turks at Trebizond. The Turks insisted that the Transcaucasian Republic should either recognize the Treaty of Brest-Litovsk or declare its independence of Russia. When the Diet in April 1918 declared the independence of Transcaucasia Turkey felt no further obligation to observe the terms of the treaty signed with the Bolsheviks. Thus, the way for Enver's ambitious plans in Transcaucasia was opened.

This new situation brought about dissension among the three principal peoples in the Transcaucasian Republic.[3] The Tatars, Turks, Turkomen, Persians, and miscellaneous Moslem groups which for convenience sake will hereinafter be called Azerbaijani, were pro-Turkish; the Georgians were pro-Russian but anti-Bolshevik and were interested in retaining control of Batum; the Armenians were determined to fight for their independence.

The political condition in Transcaucasia in the spring of 1918 was one of extreme confusion. In March by the Treaty of Brest-Litovsk the Bolsheviks had agreed to the immediate evacuation of the Turkish provinces in eastern Anatolia and to evacuate promptly the districts of Ardahan, Kars, and Batum ceded to Turkey by the treaty. Enver Pasha and his clique wished to exploit the situation to the uttermost. The Germans intended to do the same and likewise the British. The Georgians and Azerbaijani also desired to extend their territories largely at the expense of the Armenians. On May 26, 1918, Georgia declared its independence, thus breaking up the Transcaucasian Republic. Two days later the Republic of Azerbaijan was proclaimed. Batum was saved for the Georgians by the arrival of German troops. The Armenians were left to defend themselves from the Turks who occupied Russian Armenia. As the Armenians dominated the situation at Baku, Enver Pasha had an excuse to send Turkish forces there. This the British attempted to forestall and were able to do so for a few weeks.

The menace to Britain's imperial possessions in the East by the spread of communism, the old fear of an open door to India via Transcaucasia, and the oil fields of Baku were some of the factors in the decision to send a British force through northern Persia to Transcaucasia, where General Lionel C. Dunsterville's force arrived in July and took over the defense of Baku against the Turks. The narrow country of Transcaucasia, much coveted for its petroleum resources and its strategic location, was occupied by the troops of three competitors for this imperial prize: the Germans, the Turks, the British. By mid-September just previous to Allenby's offensive which drove the Turks out of Palestine, Lebanon, and Syria, the Turks forced the British out of Baku, which they did not reoccupy until November 17, 1918. For a few months in the autumn of 1918 the Republic of Azerbaijan was practically a Turkish province. Temporarily, Enver Pasha had achieved his goal in Transcaucasia but at a price which von Sanders had foreseen in June would mean defeat on the Palestinian and Mesopotamian fronts.

The activities of the British forces in Mesopotamia during most of 1918 were for the purpose of improving their position at Bagdad and along the Euphrates and the Tigris and the tributaries of the latter, which were important to the irrigation of the Bagdad area. In contrast to the Turks who neglected the economic welfare of the provinces in which their military forces were located, the British gave great attention to improving economic conditions in occupied enemy's territory. The training of the Turkish and British imperial administrators was quite different. For centuries the Ottoman bureaucrats exploited the wealth of the provinces without doing much of anything to increase the production of wealth. Consequently, as the wealth of the periphery was sucked to the center, the Ottoman provinces became progressively impoverished. The British bureaucrats did much to encourage increased production, leaving to the British capitalists, who themselves invested much capital, the economic exploitation of British possessions. Ottoman administration was wealth destroying; British administration, wealth producing. The British consequently took pains to improve the economic conditions behind their front lines as part of the preparation for their next offensive. It was not until October 1918 that General Marshall began his main attack on Mosul in northern Mesopotamia. This was after General Allenby's great victories in Palestine and the destruction of the Turko-German forces in Palestine and Syria.

Allenby's last campaign.—Allenby had spent the winter of 1918 in improving the position of his forces in Palestine. West of the Jordan in the highlands of Judea British attacks were met with stubborn resistance. Two British attempts in March and May to drive across the Jordan to Es Salt and Amman in Transjordan in order to link up the British with the Arab front operating from Faisal's base at Akaba were frustrated by the Turks. The Turkish defensive operations were a real achievement in view of the great superiority of the British forces in numbers, in equipment, in lines of communication, and in morale. Even in the early spring of 1918 the German officers were convinced that at any point on the front at any time they chose to, the British could break through the Turkish defenses.

Allenby was taking no chances. His highly integrated force of 1917 had been disrupted by withdrawal of troops needed in France to meet the Ludendorff offensives. Until the new troops assigned to him were thoroughly fitted into the Egyptian Expeditionary Force, Allenby was unwilling to risk an offensive which was being planned to destroy the Turkish forces in Palestine.

Looked at from the British point of view, Allenby's Palestine and Syrian campaign was a brilliant victory. Thoroughly and carefully planned operations were carried out with remarkable precision. Within a few days' time the greater part of the Turkish troops in Palestine were surrounded and destroyed as a fighting force. The remnants that escaped were dramatically pursued by lightning-like forces of cavalry and armored cars through northern Palestine to Damascus and thence to Aleppo. From the point of view of the Turkish soldiers it was stark tragedy. Underfed, poorly equipped, ragged Turks greatly outnumbered were surrounded, trapped along the mountain highways and in the passes blocked by transport trains, bombed and machine-gunned from the air. Those who escaped destruction and were taken prisoner by the thousands were well cared for after a gruelling march across the plains of Sharon and Philistia. Those who saw these exhausted patient Anatolians stumbling along four abreast under the guard of well-groomed Indian troopers, who could not stop to bother with those prisoners who collapsed and fell by the wayside to die of exhaustion or hunger, will not forget them. Their contrast with the sturdy, rugged

Anatolian infantry that arrived in Palestine in 1914–15 is an epitome of the history of the fighting men, whose lesson is learned fruitlessly over and over again by countless generations of men.

While British mobile forces of cavalry and armored cars were driving north to Aleppo and while British infantry were plodding slowly up the coast from Haifa to Beirut and Tripoli, Mustafa Kemal was gathering a striking force which might well have driven the British and Arab advanced forces out of northern Syria had it not been for the signing of the Anglo-Turkish Armistice at Mudros on October 31, 1918.

The Ottoman Empire was on its deathbed, the wars of the Ottomans under their sultans were at an end; the war of the Turkish nationalists was soon to begin. There was to be no peace in Asia Minor till the Turkish nationalist armies under the dynamic leadership of Mustafa Kemal (Ataturk) drove the Greeks out of Smyrna (Izmir) and forced the European Powers to annul the Treaty of Sèvres imposed upon the Ottoman sultan's government and to replace it by the Treaty of Lausanne with nationalist Turkey.

CHAPTER XVII

The Arab Revolt

❁ THE PROSPECTIVE HEIRS TO THE ARAB LANDS

The war hastened a process in the Arab lands of western Asia which had been under way for several decades. The modernization of the Near East coupled with the renaissance movements among the Near Eastern peoples was incompatible with the maintenance of the Ottoman Empire. When Turkey took sides in the war between the European Powers, it became evident that the defeat of Turkey and her allies would result in the partition of the Ottoman Empire. Therefore, during the war the question arose of what disposition would be made of its various parts. There were four principal claimants to Arab territories: the British, the French, the Jews, and the Arabs.

These claimants endeavored by a variety of means to attain their objectives in the Arab lands of western Asia and sought to justify their claims and their actions, frequently by misrepresentation and by biased interpretation of the facts. Not one of the four was in a position to achieve its goals without let or hindrance. England could not ignore the desires of the French, to whom open opposition was impossible and against whom secret intrigue proved unsuccessful. In the Near East France did not hold the military cards necessary to call the play, but politically she was in a position to oblige the English in large measure to accede to French wishes. The Zionists, by propaganda, by persuasion, by means of political pressure on legislative bodies and on administrative officials, strove to gain the backing of the Allies and the United States for the attainment of Jewish claims to Arab lands. The Arabs at first tried to protect themselves from British and French imperialism by seeking an understanding with the British and later from both imperialism and Zionism by appeals to President Wilson. They did not realize that his Calvinist philosophy was such as to enable him to reconcile self-determination with the promise of a national home for the Jewish people in Palestine as a fulfillment of Jehovah's will.

Claims of the Arab nationalists.—Before and during World War I the Arab nationalist leaders had set forth definitely their territorial claims to what they called the Arab countries.[1] Within these boundaries the people were in 1914 overwhelmingly Arab in culture and language with minor exceptions. When it became clear to the Arab nationalists that the Young Turks would not grant autonomy under the form of Ottoman decentralization to the Arabs, they began to organize secret revolutionary parties.

Unity of purpose and action was difficult of attainment by the Arabs of western Asia because they were scattered over so wide an area, divided into antagonistic religious sects Moslem as well as Christian, and were ardent partisans of rival feudal, tribal and political leaders. Under such circumstances it seemed doubtful whether national union could be achieved and freedom from Ottoman rule attained without the support of one of the Great Powers. The Arab leaders saw at the outbreak of World War I, as Cavour had in the 1850's with respect to Italy, that unification and independence might be realized through co-operation with the Allies through an understanding with Great Britain.

Hussein Ali of Mecca.—This idea fitted in with the fears and hopes of Hussein Ali and his sons. Hussein was aware that Enver and Talaat early in 1914 had secretly planned to send troops to forcibly remove the Grand Sherif. His son Abdullah, a member of a secret Arab revolutionary society, had been in treasonous correspondence with Lord Kitchener previous to the war. After the proclamation in December 1914 of the Jihad, Sherif Hussein's unwillingness to give the support of his high office to the Holy War made his position more precarious. The danger threatening him and his family was further increased in 1915 when his son, Emir Faisal, carried on negotiations with the revolutionary Arab leaders in Syria and was initiated into both of the Arab secret revolutionary societies, al-Ahd and al-Fatat.[2]

Faisal, early in 1915, had been sent to Constantinople on a mission by his father with instructions to consult with the Arab revolutionary leaders at Damascus in order to ascertain what their reactions would be to a proposal secretly made to Hussein Ali by the British. After tarrying a month in Damascus, Faisal went to the Turkish capital and returned to Damascus on May 23, 1915. On the return trip from Constantinople Emir Faisal's private railway car was attached to the train upon which the author was traveling. At each railroad station the Arab Emir was given an official reception by the Turkish authorities and was welcomed by hosts of enthusiastic Arabs. The author's companion, the Secretary of the Turkish Senate, was greatly impressed and remarked that the Turks were most fortunate that so popular an Arab leader was loyal to them! [3]

Emir Faisal and the Damascus Protocol.—Emir Faisal knew that the Turks were plotting to assassinate his father. He knew that he and his father and brothers were in a very dangerous position. He was anxious to find out on what terms the leaders of the Arab revolutionary al-Fatat and al-Ahd were willing to work with the British against the Turks. The Arab revolutionists drafted at Damascus a protocol setting forth their demand for a recognition of the independence of the Arabs within specified boundaries which, of course, included Palestine. Emir Faisal was given a copy of the Damascus Protocol of May 1915 to take to his father in Mecca. Thus, the leading Arabs in Iraq and Syria became engaged in a plot against the Ottoman government and through the Hashemite family began negotiations with the most potent enemy of the Turks.

All politically literate people in the Near East previous to the war knew of the imperialistic aims of the members of the Triple Entente. Consequently, when Turkey joined the Central Powers in the war, Near Eastern people were convinced that the British and the French would divide between them the Arab lands of western Asia. The Turks understood well what defeat would mean for them. The Arabs were convinced that if they did not receive assurances of their independence from one or more of the Allies the Arab countries would be divided as spoils of war between the British and the French. The Damascus Protocol and the negotiations with the British through the mediation of Sherif Hussein were designed to protect Arab national interests in the event of an Allied victory to which the Arab revolutionists were prepared to contribute.

Planning the partition of the Ottoman Empire.—The Arabs were not alone in taking steps to attain their aims in case of the defeat of the Central Powers and the partition of the Ottoman Empire. By March 1915, England, France, and Russia had made preliminary secret agreements concerning their interests in the Near East. The Italians before entering the war endeavored to insure that they would get a slice of the Near Eastern pie by the Treaty of London of April 26, 1915. France and England had not at that time come to any definite agreement as to a division of the Arab lands.

With the British playing a major role in the Turkish war at the Dardanelles, on the Sinai front and in Mesopotamia, the French were uneasy about their interests in the Near East. They were justified in being uncertain what the British might do. Many British officials and officers were anti-French and would have been glad to see the French out of the Near East. T. E. Lawrence in 1915, then a young second lieutenant in the British intelligence service, wrote from Cairo to David G. Hogarth on March 18, 1915, that Alexandretta in French possession would be a secure base for naval operations against Egypt and urged him to remember that with France in possession of Syria she could place 100,000 troops on the Suez Canal "in 12 days from the declaration of war." On March 22, four days later, Lawrence again wrote Hogarth about his somewhat ridiculous plan to overwhelm the Turks in conjunction with the Arab forces of Idrisi from Asir saying "we can rush right up to Damascus, and biff the French out of all hope of Syria." [4]

Of course, in 1915 Lawrence was a young man in his middle twenties without any political training and experience whose political and social thinking was adolescent-like and immature. His anti-French attitude was typical of many Britishers in the Near East during World War I. Needless to say, the Arabs were not slow in understanding how these British officers and officials felt toward the French, who, of course, also became aware that certain British representatives in the Near East wished to eliminate the French from all share in the spoils of the war against Turkey.

Mark Sykes and Georges Picot.—The British government, nevertheless, realized that their ally's claims in the Near East would have to be given due consideration. Consequently, as British negotiations and commitments to the Arabs progressed, an understanding with the French became imperative. Russia's adherence to any agreement also was essential to the unity of the Allies. The understanding reached between these three Allies in the spring of 1916 was known as the Sykes-Picot Agreement. Mark Sykes was a famous English traveler whose books on the Ottoman Empire and Persia (Iran) were widely known. He was a man of great independence, an individualist who spoke and acted very much as he pleased. Georges Picot, who had been French consul-general at Beirut in Syria when war broke out, was a French Foreign Office bureaucrat. When later the Sykes-Picot Agreement became known to the Arabs after it had been published by the Bolshevik government of Russia, Picot's name added fuel to the Arabs' indignation.

On leaving Damascus and Beirut after Turkey's entrance into the war, the French consuls had not destroyed their secret documents, several of which contained correspondence with, from, and concerning the leading personalities and organizations of the Arab nationalists. Picot, under instructions from Paris, had turned over the French consulate to the American consul at Beirut, who placed the official American seals on the doors of the French consulate without first transferring French official documents to the American consulate despite the fact that his vice-consul, Ralph Chesborough, had warned him that the Turks intended to seize them. The Turks broke the United States seals and took possession of documents which incriminated many Arab leaders. Picot, of course, was blamed by the Arabs.

JEMAL PASHA AND THE ARABS

Jemal Pasha when he reached Damascus to take over command of the Fourth Army was shown these documents.[5] It was a shocking revelation to him when he discovered that so many leading Arabs in Syria, Moslems and Druzes as well as Christians, were engaged in treasonable activities. Jemal differed greatly from his two associates, Enver and Talaat. He was deeply religious. For him the Holy War was not solely a political instrument with which to play upon the ideas and emotions of devout Moslems. Jemal found it hard to believe that leading Moslems would plot against the caliph. Furthermore, Jemal was not himself a nationalist, he was an Osmanli who believed in the Ottoman Empire. Loyalty to the caliph, to Islam, and to the empire were the principal motives which guided him. These loyalties were subordinated only to his vanity and drive for power.

On reading these incriminating documents, Jemal decided for the time being, not to use them in bringing the traitors to justice. In his memoirs he said he did not do so because he felt convinced that these Arab leaders could be won to the Turkish cause. He may have thought that on the eve of the attack upon Egypt when the propaganda of the Jihad was being energetically spread in the Arab lands and among Moslems of the French and British empires, it would have been unwise to expose the treasonous activities of leading Arab Moslems. No word nor sign of having obtained this damning evidence was given the Arab leaders by Jemal. On the contrary he proceeded to cultivate them and went out of his way to convince them that he was in sympathy with the aims of the Arabs for local autonomy and self-government within the Ottoman Empire.

Jemal Pasha was a man of many inner contradictions. His devotion to Islam and his devout religious attitude did not interfere with his being a modernist. He was an admirer of French culture and literature and had a social veneer which was patterned on French models. He was a patron of education and in Jerusalem opened a school in which French was taught by a Frenchman, chosen by Jemal, who with the connivance of the Spanish consul passed himself off as a citizen of Switzerland. When the German secret service ferreted out the Frenchman's real nationality, Jemal Pasha exiled both him and his mistress, the French wife of a Russian officer, to Aleppo. There, for some time, the couple lived in a condition of great poverty, until at a soirée given Jemal Pasha by the Arab ladies of high Aleppine society, Madam Bauran read aloud her lover's poetry. The Turkish viceroy of the Arab lands was so charmed with it that he gave orders that the couple should be given a suitable house and supplied with food and wines. In fact this French couple continued to enjoy until 1918 Jemal Pasha's favor, despite the fact that the poet refused to write a justification of Jemal's ruthless prosecution and treatment of the Arab nationalist leaders.

At a time when it was becoming increasingly difficult to get supplies for the Turkish forces, fuel for their railroads, and food for the civilian population, Jemal Pasha inaugurated civic improvements, tearing down buildings in order to construct boulevards and parks, in several of the Syrian and Palestinian cities.

Jemal, who while he was military commander of Constantinople, organized an espionage system which bears comparison with that of Abdul Hamid's reign and who flooded Syria and Palestine with his spies, unwittingly permitted Emir Faisal to continue, throughout most of the year 1915, plotting with the heads of the Arab revolutionary societies. In many ways Jemal was extraordinarily naive.

When starvation stalked the land and the noncombat troops died of hunger and exhaustion by the thousands Jemal Pasha with the aid of Halidé Edib Adivar, the Turkish feminist and author, opened orphan asylums and hospitals for the destitute Armenian children.

Jemal Pasha had a great deal of personal charm and those upon whom he showered favors spoke well of him. He was, nevertheless, feared and hated by most of the people from Bir es Saba to Aleppo.

In the spring of 1915 following hard on the heels of his unsuccessful attack on Egypt, Jemal became convinced that the Arab nationalists were in communication with the British and French through the Syrians in Egypt and were planning an uprising against the Turks to synchronize with an Allied landing on the Syrian coast. He grew annoyed with Sherif Hussein's failure to give his endorsement to the Jihad and to live up to his promises to supply fighting men for the attacks on the Suez Canal. His benevolent policy toward the Arabs changed. Arab leaders in Syria and the Lebanon were arrested and brought to trial before a court martial at Aley in Lebanon. A hundred leading Arabs were condemned to death, fifty-six *in absentia* according to the report of Jemal Pasha, although Antonius states that only fifty-eight in all were sentenced to death of whom forty-five, *in absentia.* The confused condition of affairs in Jemal Pasha's bailiwick may be gleaned from the account by Antonius of the amazing good fortune of one of the Arabs condemned *in absentia.* Hasan Hammad, a petty official in the Palestinian city of Nablus, received after much delay the summons to appear before the court at Aley. On his arrival there he picked up a newspaper and read his name among those condemned to death. He very promptly seized his bag and caught the next train to Damascus where he remained safely in hiding till the capture of the city by the British in 1918.

Several of the Arab leaders were hung, others with their families were deported to the interior or to Anatolia. Fear, anger, and indignation spread among all the Arab people of Palestine, Syria, and Lebanon whether Moslem, Christian, or Druze.

Deep misery intensified the hatred of the Arabs for the Turks. The blockade of the coast by the Allies cut off food supplies, and the locusts in 1915 devastated the crops from the Sinai Desert to the Taurus Mountains. Paper money was rapidly depreciating. Arab speculators and corrupt Turkish officials battened on the starving population. Cholera, typhoid, and typhus were widespread. Jemal Pasha was utterly unable to cope with the situation. Life for the many had become unbearable and intolerable. The time seemed ripe for action.

SHERIF HUSSEIN COMES TO AN AGREEMENT WITH THE BRITISH

Hussein came to an agreement with the British, which though far from satisfactory from an Arab nationalist point of view, did assure British aid. Then he telegraphed demands to the Grand Vizier at Constantinople that the Turks could not and would not accept. Faisal, who was at Damascus, with considerable risk to himself interceded with Jemal for the condemned Arab leaders. Jemal, who was in a furious temper on learning from Enver of Hussein's demands agreed to allow Faisal to go to the Hejaz, on the pretense of persuading his father to change his policy. Jemal claims he knew Faisal was lying, but thought that he must be allowed to proceed to Medina.

Hussein and his sons were so deeply embroiled with the British by the spring of 1916 that a break with the Turks became imperative for their own safety no matter how unsatisfactory were the nebulous prom-

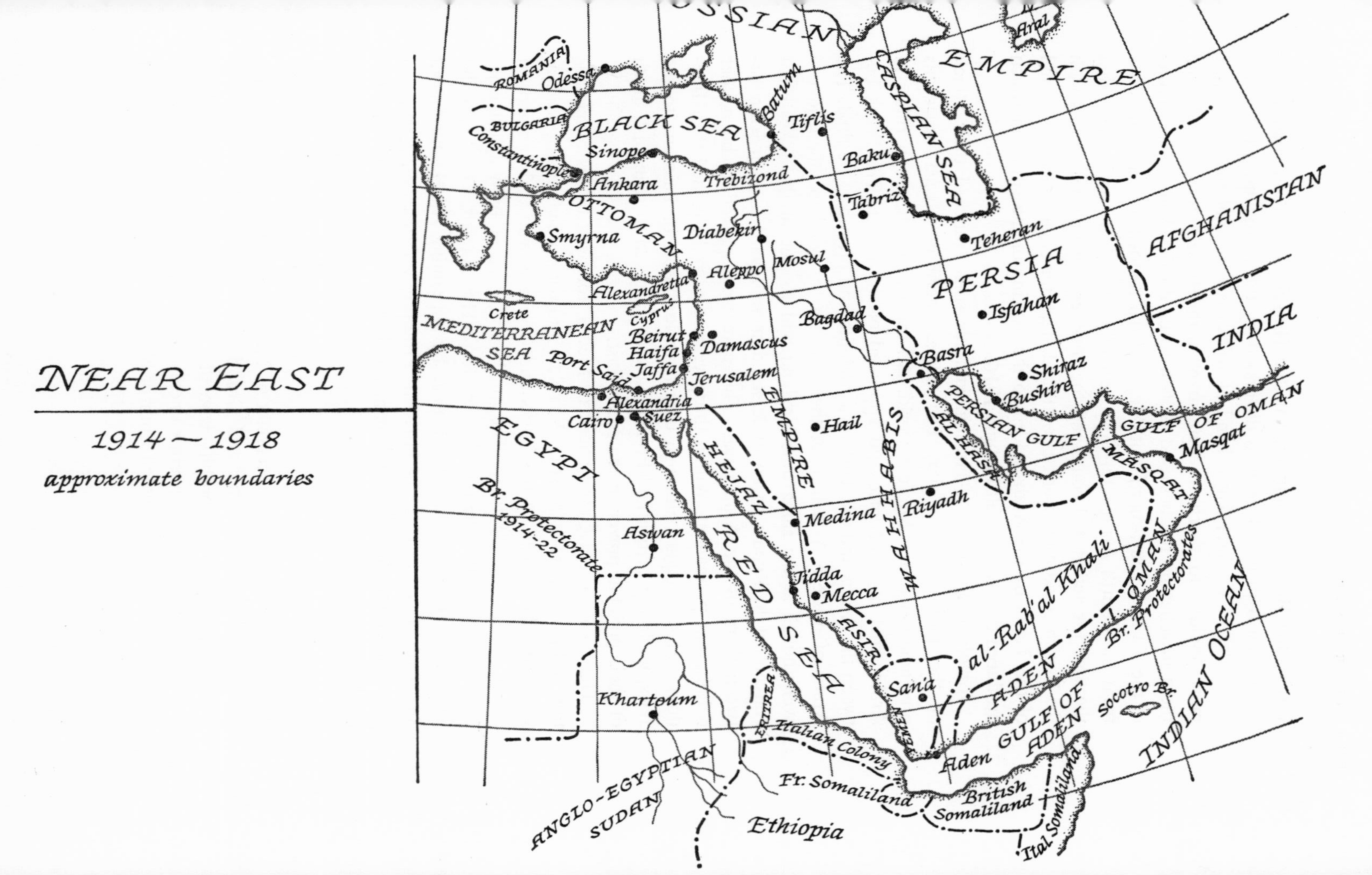

NEAR EAST

1914 — 1918

approximate boundaries

ises of the British as contained in the Hussein-McMahon correspondence. The British had been so distressed by the imminent threat of the surrender of General Townshend at Kut-el-Amara that they also were most anxious to reach an agreement with Hussein which might aid them in relieving the besieged British force on the Tigris. The verdict of the Turkish court-martial at Aley and the removal of Arab divisions from the Fourth Army's territory convinced the Arab nationalists that the time for action had come and that further haggling over terms with the British could no longer be continued. The universal anger and hatred of the Turks by the Arabs added to the making of the situation which produced the Arab revolt in June 1916.

Revolt in the Hejaz.—Hussein and his sons launched their attack on the Turks in the Hejaz. The Grand Sherif of Mecca issued his proclamation to the Moslem world. All but two of the Arab rulers in Arabia met in conference and approved of the revolt. The break between the Arabs and the Turks was definite and proved to be final. The Arabs of western Asia had set their feet on the road to independence even though at the same time England and France in the Sykes-Picot Agreement had come to an understanding in regard to a division between them of the Arab lands. This agreement proved to be neither definite nor permanent. Within thirty years the Arabs gained their freedom and sovereignty although they have lost most of Palestine to the Jews, while the British and French have been forced to relinquish much of their political power in the Near East.

The revolt of the Grand Sherif of Mecca, followed by his proclamation and its support by most of the rulers and tribal chieftains in Arabia, was like a bombshell to the Turks and Germans who had counted on great results from the Jihad. The much-advertised Holy War lost what potency it had after the defection of Emir Hussein Ali. The Turks did what they could to repair the damage by appointing Ali Haidar Grand Sherif of Mecca in place of Hussein. Promptly on June 19, 1916, two weeks after the Arab revolt began, Ali Haidar and his four sons left for Medina.

❀ ALI HAIDAR

Ali Haidar was a direct descendant of Mohammed, and had by heritage a greater claim to be Emir and Grand Sherif of Mecca than Hussein Ali. He was a man of probity who did not intrigue and bribe to forward his claims when Hussein's uncle Aoun-er-Refik died in 1905 and his nephew Ali was appointed Emir of Mecca by Abdul Hamid. Nor did

Ali Haidar resort to such methods to obtain the appointment from the government of the Young Turks when Emir Ali fled to Egypt and was replaced by Hussein Ali.

While Ali Haidar had friends among the Young Turks and among the members of the Committee of Union and Progress, he had not joined the party; neither had he become a member of any of the Arab reform and revolutionary societies, although it is claimed that he had been informed about even the most secret of the Arab revolutionary parties.

Ali Haidar was a supporter of the Ottoman Empire and felt that legitimate Arab aspirations could be realized within its framework and under the sultan-caliph. He was a liberal in religion and politics, though a devout Moslem he was opposed to religious fanaticism and obscurantism. His four sons were brought up with a liberal education and were far more Europeanized than their cousins, the four sons of Hussein Ali. Ali Haidar was a great admirer of the British Empire and believed that its principles could be applied to the Ottoman Empire. Moreover, he had married an English woman who became Princess Fatma.[6]

Although Ali Haidar's loyalty to the Ottoman government was above question, he nevertheless found himself under suspicion from Jemal Pasha whose experience with the Arabs had embittered him. The commander of the Fourth Army had lost confidence in all Arabs, which, after the way in which he had been bamboozled by Emir Faisal, is not to be wondered at. Ali Haidar found the same suspicious attitude toward him at Medina on the part of its courageous Turkish military commander, Fakhri Pasha.

Ali Haidar finally won Fakhri's confidence when he opposed with success Enver's and Jemal's proposal to abandon Medina. With respect to Medina military opinion differed and continues to differ. The German, von Sanders, thought Medina should be abandoned after the Turks had lost Sinai as he considered it a costly military liability. T. E. Lawrence was certain that it was more advantageous to let the Turks retain possession of Medina than to capture it.[7] Major N. N. E. Bray of the Anglo-Indian Army considered Medina as offering "a clear and imperative objective" after the Arabs had captured Wejh in January 1917 and thought that the strategy of Lawrence was at the expense of the British forces attacking the Turks in southern Palestine.[8] However that may be, Ali Haidar was in some measure responsible for the Turks' decision to hold Medina for political and psychological rather than purely military reasons.

After eighteen months in Medina Ali Haidar requested permission to return to and abide in Lebanon. He had become disheartened with the failure of the Turks to support his policy in regaining the Arab tribes for the sultan and caliph. Without food, arms and above all money, Ali Haidar could not win and hold the tribesmen. His inability to do so and his consequent retirement to Aley in the Lebanon were more in the nature of a defeat for the Turks than a failure on the part of Ali Haidar. He was unwilling to become a leader of the Arab revolutionists, and consequently he became a cipher in the Arab world at a time when Jemal's policy and that of the Ottoman government continued to alienate the Arabs.

DOUBLE-CROSSING THE ARAB

The bitterness engendered among the Arabs by Jemal's policy and treatment of them in 1915 and 1916 was too great to be overcome by the opportunities for reconciliation which came in 1917. During that year the Arabs felt themselves doubly double-crossed by the Sykes-Picot Agreement of 1916 and by the Balfour Declaration of November 1917. Revolutionary Russia's renunciation of all imperialistic agreements with England and France did not lessen the appetites of the British and French imperialists but rather increased their desire to profit from the collapse of the Russian as well as from that of the Ottoman Empire.

So indignant were the Arabs that they put out feelers to see whether satisfactory terms could be arranged with the Turks. Of course, the United States, which was not at war with Turkey, also had made an attempt in July 1917 to arrange a peace between Turkey and the Allies. This had been skillfully aborted by the Zionists at Gibraltar with the connivance of the British.[9] The British, also, according to T. E. Lawrence, in 1918 had been exploring through exchanges of views with Talaat, the Turkish Grand Vizier, the possibility of a separate peace.[10] Turko-Arab conversations came to nought. Arab distrust and hatred of the Turks were too great and British power was too evident. Furthermore, the United States had entered the war and in January 1918 President Wilson's Fourteen Points awakened new hope among Arab leaders, except for the politically more sophisticated and disillusioned. Few stopped to consider that the United States government had entered the war without exacting a statement from the Allies that all secret treaties of an imperialistic nature be scrapped as a condition of American aid. Arabs, even as late as 1945, found it difficult to realize that American idealistic aims, officially endorsed by the United States government as major war objectives, frequently did not correspond with political realities in the United States and with the realities of international relations. The Arabs were not alone, however, in believing in the Fourteen Points which proved to be excellent wartime propaganda but impractical formulae for peacemaking at Paris in 1919.

CHAPTER XVIII

Zionism Achieves Its First Objective

EFFECT OF WAR ON THE ZIONIST MOVEMENT

While the Arab nationalists were endeavoring to get recognition and acknowledgment of their territorial claims and their rights to independence, the Zionist leaders were striving to obtain the right to lay the foundations of a Jewish state in Palestine. The first effect of World War I on the World Zionist organization and the Zionist movement was disruptive. The division of Europe into two warring groups made travel and communication difficult for the members of an international organization of a people who were citizens or subjects of many different nations. Furthermore, patriotic Jews became as absorbed by and devoted to the wartime activities of their various countries as their fellow countrymen of different religious beliefs. Although these factors tended at first to lessen the movement among Jews toward Zionism and to hamper Zionist activities, other factors had an exactly opposite effect.

Intensification of Jewish nationalism.—For reasons which have never been adequately analyzed World War I made people far more conscious of their nationality as distinguished from their citizenship. This was as true of the Jews as it was of other people. Jewish self-consciousness tended to be intensified by the war.[1] The importance of this among American Jewry was rather significant in the first years of the war because the United States was the one great neutral Power and later because of the important role played by the United States in winning the war. During the period of its neutrality the United States became a center from which assistance to Jews suffering from hostilities and other effects of the war could be most efficiently organized. This was particularly true of the Jews in Palestine, whose existence depended upon outside help.

THE JEWS IN THE UNITED STATES

The Jews in the United States might be classified as Jewish Americans and American Jews. One might use the term Jewish Americans to refer to those who are Jews by religion but do not think of themselves as members of a Jewish nationality, and one might employ the term American Jews to apply to those who consider themselves Jews both by religion and nationality.

The Jewish community in the United States which was made up of both Jewish Americans and American Jews was the wealthiest of all the Jewish communities in the world and after that of Russia, which then included much of Poland, it was the second largest in numbers. Because of heavy Jewish immigration during the twenty-five years preceding the war, a considerable percentage of American Jews had close personal and business ties with the Jews of Germany and Austria and with those of Russia. American Jews from central and eastern Europe until the United States entered the war and until the Russian Revolution had little reason to be anti-German or anti-Austrian and very strong reasons for being anti-Russian, or rather anti-tsarist Russia.

In the top circles of financial power the Kuhn-Loeb and Company, New York Jewish bankers, were the rivals of J. P. Morgan and Company, New York Protestant bankers. Competitors in the United States, these two banking groups were associated with competitive groups in Europe. Kuhn-Loeb and Company's foreign interests were closely associated with Central Europe; J. P. Morgan and Company with France and England. During the war the latter became the general financial and purchasing agent of the Allies in the United States while as a result of the Allied blockade of the Central Powers, the foreign activities of Kuhn-Loeb and Company dwindled. The demands of the Allies for American credit increased so enormously by the autumn of 1916 that J. P. Morgan and Company were no longer able to meet them. Consequently, there was serious danger of a financial collapse of the Allies at the end of 1916. The entrance into the war of the United States saved the Allies in 1917 from financial disaster and in 1918 from military defeat.

The war and national minorities.—The declaration of war on the Central Powers by the United States, following, as it did, rapidly on the heels of the Russian Revolution, proved to be an important factor with respect to the achievement of Zionist aims. The attitude and action of the United States as a neutral Power from 1914 to 1917 was of vast importance to the belligerents. Minority groups became, therefore, important pawns to be used by the warring nations. The attitudes of French Canadian, Hungarian, Irish, Italian, Jewish, Polish, Rumanian, and other national minority groups among the American population were matters of very considerable concern to the Allies. Wherever it was thought advisable and possible, propaganda methods were used by the Allies to win the support of such minority groups in the United States.

This was a particularly important factor with respect to American Jewry because of the large Jewish populations in Germany and in Austria-Hungary as well as in Russia. If wholehearted support of the cause of the Allies by American Jews could be gained, a lessening of the support by German and Austrian Jews of the cause of the Central Powers might be anticipated. It is usual to think of minority groups as taking the initiative in attempting to influence the course of international affairs. Although this frequently is the case, there are times when foreign governments purposely use a minority group in the United States to forward their own aims. In such cases minority groups become instruments in the hands of those who play the game of power politics on an international scale.

Under circumstances of this nature nationalist organizations among American minority groups may find favorable conditions for the advancement of their interests. This becomes definitely the case when such nationalist interests are not opposed to the policies of the United States government and can be associated with its interests. World War I provided just such conditions for the growth of Jewish nationalism in the United States and for the expansion of Zionism.

Zionism in the United States.—Before 1914 members of Zionist organizations and societies in the United States came mostly from Jewish immigrants from eastern Europe.[2] At the outbreak of World War I dues-paying Zionists numbered only about 20,000 out of an American Jewish population of over 3,000,000. Jewish immigration to the United States between 1880 and 1913 amounted to more than 2,250,000. A large part of these migrants came from eastern Europe. It was among these "quite backward" [3] Orthodox Jewish elements that Zionists for the most part were recruited previous to 1914.

Before the meeting of the first World Zionist Congress at Basle a few Jews in the United States organized a *Hoveve Zion* society, similar to the Hoveve Zion societies in Russia. These were the organizational beginnings of the Zionist movement in America. After the Basle Congress in 1897 a national organization known as the Federation of American Zionists came into being. Its financial support was precarious until after the founding of the Jewish Colonial Trust. Even then support came mostly from the Jewish immigrants and not from the long-established well-to-do Jewish Americans.

Although by active organizational work Zionism began to spread in the American Jewish community previous to World War I, the rapid growth of Zionism took place after 1914 and as a direct result of the war. Soon after Turkey became a belligerent the burden of supporting and supplying the Jews in Palestine was assumed by American Jewry whose many organizations became interested in the relief and protection of Palestinian Jews. This interest in Palestine and Zionism was further stimulated, ironically for the Turks, by the forced exodus from the Holy Land of Russian Zionists. Some of the outstanding Zionist leaders of Palestine came to the United States, and became active in the American Zionist movement. As a result of a situation created by the war Zionism spread to wider circles among American Jews and won the support of prominent Jews who had attained wide recognition among non-Jewish Americans. Of these, some of the more notable were Justice Louis Brandeis, Judge Julian W. Mack, Felix Frankfurter, and Rabbi Stephen S. Wise.

BRITISH INTEREST IN JEWISH MINORITIES AND IN ZIONISM

The growth of Zionism in the United States during 1915 and 1916 did not go unnoticed in England. English Zionists kept in close touch with the American Zionist movement, while cultivating important members of the British Cabinet including Lloyd George and Balfour.

The Russian Revolution introduced a new factor into the situation. Tsardom collapsed. Under its provisional government which lasted, with important changes in its Cabinet of Ministers, from March until November 1917, revolutionary Russia was hailed by the Allies as a new accession of strength to the cause of democracy. Russian Jews had played an important role in various Russian revolutionary movements and several of the leading revolutionists were Jews. Among the Russian revolutionary parties were the Social Democratic Mensheviks and Bolsheviks. The Social Democratic Party in Russia, which had close affiliations with the Social Democratic parties in the other countries of Europe had split into right and left wings. The right wing had given their support to their respective governments and considered the war as one of self-defense and national security; while the left wing contended that the war was an imperialistic conflict of the ruling capitalist classes and should be used to bring about a social revolution.

The Allies were deeply concerned lest the left wingers, the Bolsheviks, should gain control of Russia and attempt to end the war by world revolution. There were Jewish leaders among both the right wing and the left wing of the Social Democratic parties. In Russia a large percentage of the Jewish population numbering over 6,000,000 were members of a Marxist organization, known as the Jewish Bund. It was important to the Allies to gain the support of the Russian Jews lest they join the ranks of the Bolsheviks. In this, Zionism was a factor.

Zionism had a strong following among Russian Jews although it was condemned by Marxist leaders as a bourgeois movement. It was a matter of high political import that many of the outstanding leaders of the Zionist movement in England and in the United States were of Russian origin and that a very considerable percentage of the Jews in America were also of Russian origin. Indeed, British statesmen in the spring of 1917 had, other than the reason of personal conviction, very real political grounds for a sympathetic view of Zionist aims. The British government by 1917 was so receptive to Zionist proposals that the British Zionist leader, Dr. Chaim Weizmann, Russian by birth, was able to say as the chairman of an English Zionist conference held on May 20, 1917: "I am entitled to state in this assembly that His Majesty's Government is ready to support our plans." [4]

To achieve their ends the Zionists, like the Arab nationalists, realized the necessity of securing the official support of one or more of the Great Powers. At the beginning of the war there was disagreement among Zionist leaders as to which side would win. Many of the important Russian Zionists were convinced that Germany would defeat the Allies. They admired German efficiency and thought that a victorious Germany would co-operate with the Zionists in the achievement of their aims in Palestine. Other Zionist leaders were convinced that Zionism should remain strictly neutral in the war so as not to jeopardize the Jewish populations in any of the belligerent countries nor run the risk of betting on the wrong horse. On the contrary, Dr. Chaim Weizmann and his collaborators in England believed the Allies would win and that Zionism should actively support the Allied cause.

Zionism gains support in Britain.—Basing their plans on the assumption that the Allies would be victorious and that the official backing of the British government was essential to the attainment of their aims, the Zionists in England set about winning British support for Zionism. This the English Zionists successfully did by the end of 1916. It was an amazing achievement which required great skill, unfaltering energy, and determination. The methods by which the conquest of the British government was made were diverse and of necessity in some cases devious.

There were those among British statesmen and leaders who could be won to the Zionist cause by being persuaded that Zionism was a fulfillment of Old and New Testament prophecies and was a solution of the age-old world problem of anti-Semitism and an atonement by Christian Europe for its long persecution of the Jews. In fact there were a variety of reasons why Zionism made a strong appeal to the idealisms of many Britishers. Their idealisms obscured the fact that Jewish nationalism was as ruthlessly egoistic as that of other nationalist movements and that its leaders had few inhibitions with respect to the means employed to achieve their objectives.

In Britain's wartime officialdom there were those whose principal concern was winning the war and those who thought first of strengthening and extending the British Empire. To such men aid to Zionism was considered on the basis of what it could contribute to the defeat of the Central Powers and to the security of Britain's empire after the war.

The Zionists in England well understood that British leaders would have to be approached on the basis of their interests and ideas. The job of the Zionists was to win British leaders to the support of Zionism. The means used were adapted admirably to the personal outlook and characteristics of the men to be influenced.

Men like Balfour, Robert Cecil, Lord Milner, Mark Sykes, and to some extent Lloyd George had to be persuaded that Zionism was a noble and righteous cause of significance to the welfare of the world as well as to that of the Jewish people. Other Britishers had to be persuaded that by backing Zionism world-wide enthusiastic Jewish support for the Allied cause could be assured and British imperial interests in the Near East greatly aided.

In 1916 the Allied cause was far from bright. The stalemate on the western front remained unbroken; although Rumania had joined the Allies in August she was thoroughly defeated by the end of the year, when it was evident that Russia was on the verge of collapse. In the United States President Wilson was advocating peace by negotiation and his presidential campaign was waged on the slogan, "he kept us out of war." In addition the Allies were faced with financial and economic collapse.

British officials were deeply concerned about the situation in general and particularly in the United States, where the attitude of the Irish and Jewish groups was unfavorable to the British. Sir Cecil Spring-

Rice, the British Ambassador to the United States, was convinced that American Jews had considerable political power. In January 1914 he wrote to Tyrrell of how "a Jewish deputation came down from New York and in two days 'fixed' the two houses so that the President had to renounce the idea of making a new treaty with Russia." [5] Later in November 1914 he wrote to both Sir Valentine Chirol and to Sir Edward Grey, then Foreign Minister, of the New York German Jewish bankers who, Sir Cecil said, "were getting hold of the principal New York papers" and "bringing them over as much as they dare to the German side" and "toiling in a solid phalanx to compass our destruction."

Efforts of the British and French at Washington and New York through wealthy American Jews to overcome this anti-British attitude proved futile. A Britisher of Armenian ancestry, James A. Malcolm (who had become deeply interested in Zionism) and some of the Zionist leaders pointed out to British officials that the wealthy Jews in the United States, as in England, did not represent the Jewish masses. Malcolm, Weizmann, and others explained that Zionism was a movement of the people not of the upper classes and that only through the Zionists could American Jewry be influenced. Lloyd George, who became Prime Minister in the latter part of December 1916, had been won over to Zionism by Weizmann with whom he had had frequent contacts while Minister of Munitions. Consequently, the new Prime Minister had absorbed very definite ideas with regard to the influence of the Jewish community in the United States. Lloyd George has said that "as soon as I became prime minister I talked the whole matter over with Mr. Balfour who was then Foreign Secretary. We were anxious at that time to gather Jewish support in neutral countries." [6]

British and French consider offering Palestine to the Jews.—An English Zionist, Samuel Landman, who was shifted to the British Ministry of Propaganda in accordance with the wishes of Dr. Weizmann and who became in 1917 Solicitor and Secretary to the World Zionist Organization, wrote in March 1936 that Mark Sykes, Under-Secretary to the British War Cabinet, Georges Picot, and Jean Gout of the French Foreign Office were convinced by 1916 "that the best and perhaps the only way (which proved so to be) to induce the American President to come into the war was to secure the co-operation of Zionist Jews by promising them Palestine, and thus enlist and mobilise the hitherto unsuspectedly powerful forces of Zionist Jews in America and elsewhere in favor of the Allies on a *quid pro quo* contract basis. Thus, as will be seen, the Zionists, having carried out their part, and greatly helped to bring America in, the Balfour Declaration of 1917 was but the public confirmation of the necessarily secret 'gentlemen's' agreement of 1916. . . ." [7] A contrary explanation of the reasons for British support of Zionism is given by Mrs. Dugdale, the niece of Mr. Balfour, who naturally felt repugnance at the idea that the Balfour Declaration was in the nature of a bargain. She quotes her uncle as saying in the House of Lords in June 1922: "But we have never pretended—certainly I have never pretended—that it was purely from these materialistic considerations that the Declaration of November 1917 originally sprung. I regard this not as a solution, but as a partial solution, of the great and abiding Jewish problem. . . ." [8]

Howbeit, by the autumn of 1916 the British Zionists were working hand in glove with various branches of the British Government. Exceptional privileges were granted to Zionist leaders, whose travels were facilitated and who were permitted to communicate with one another by the use of the diplomatic pouch and of the secret codes through the British embassies and consulates. When inner circles of the British government had been captured by the Zionists, the next task was that of gaining French and Italian acquiescence to a Jewish National Home in Palestine. Following these successful diplomatic moves, the next and all-important step was to secure American consent to the Zionist programme. This was a joint Anglo-Zionist maneuver undertaken shortly after the United States entered the war on April 6, 1917.

Role played by Balfour and Brandeis.—Mr. Balfour at the head of a British Mission arrived in Washington on April 22 and the next day he had his first interview with President Wilson. It was during his short stay of a month in the United States that Balfour met Justice Brandeis, who was then the leading figure in the American Zionist movement. Mrs. Dugdale reports that in his conversations with Brandeis the British Foreign Minister pledged his support to Zionism. When Balfour broached his idea of a joint British-American protectorate over Palestine, Justice Brandeis pointed out that most Americans were still against participation in the war and would be unwilling to assume foreign obligations beyond American frontiers. Of more importance, however, to the British government and its Zionist collaborators was Justice Brandeis' assurance that President Wilson was actively sympathetic to a Jewish Home in Palestine, for it was well known in England that Justice Brandeis was a trusted adviser to the President.

The Balfour Declaration.—With the certainty that President Wilson was favorably disposed towards Zionism, the Zionists and those in the British government backing a national home for the Jews in Palestine found the road was clear for the preparation of a statement and for securing its adoption by the Cabinet. Even before Balfour's return to England the British government was practically committed to Zionism. With serious opposition developing, it took, however, from May to November to secure the acceptance of the final draft of a declaration of policy by the British War Cabinet. Because this policy was made public by a letter dated November 2, 1917, of the Foreign Secretary to Lord Rothschild it came to be known as the Balfour Declaration.

The timing of the Balfour Declaration was nicely synchronized with the launching of Allenby's attack on Bir es Saba which was captured on November 2. The famous Biblical city of Jaffa was taken by the British two weeks later, and on December 11, 1917, the Holy City of Jerusalem was occupied by the British. This was exciting news for Christians, Jews, and Moslems all over the world.

FOUNDATIONS LAID IN PALESTINE

The Zionists were not slow in preparing the way for taking possession of the national home which now had been promised them. The British government was persuaded to send a Zionist Commission to Palestine under the chairmanship of Dr. Weizmann. By an announcement of Foreign Secretary Balfour the commission was designated as the representative of the Zionist organization and authorized to act in an advisory capacity to the British authorities in Palestine with respect to all Jewish affairs and to all matters pertaining to the creation of a Jewish National Home.

The arrival in Egypt on March 1918 of the Zionist Commission and the subsequent activities of its members in Palestine aroused increasing opposition and bitterness among the Arabs in Palestine and the Syrians in Egypt.

The still unsettled struggle for Palestine between Arabs and Jews began when the Commission arrived in the Near East and proceeded to lay the foundations of a Jewish state forty years ago.

CHAPTER XIX

Partition of the Ottoman Empire

The surrender of the Turks in 1918 brought about the final partition of the Ottoman Empire, which officially ceased to exist on October 29, 1923, when the Grand National Assembly declared Turkey to be a Republic. The partition and demise of the Ottoman Empire mark a significant change in the history of the Near East. An empire which had been in existence for nearly five hundred years had ceased to exist and the old dynasty of the Ottomans had come to an end as had those of the Habsburgs and the Romanovs.

THE FALL OF THE OTTOMANS AND FRAGMENTATION OF THE NEAR EAST

The fall of an ancient dynasty and state quickens the imagination and tends to assume more importance in men's minds than the termination of the functions they had performed. Superficially, there appears to be a certain similarity between the fall of the Byzantine Empire in 1453 and that of the Ottoman Empire in 1923. In both cases a decadent imperial state, which had once ruled over the Near East, had ceased to exist. The significant difference lies in the fact that when Constantinople was captured by the Ottoman Turks the Byzantine Empire existed in name only. It had lost control over western Asia and most of the Balkans. The political unity that Byzantines had failed to maintain was re-established by the Ottomans, who for nearly half a millennium had more or less successfully ruled over it and had prevented other states from encroaching upon it and other people from overrunning it. The really notable change which took place after the fall of the Ottomans was the breaking up of the political unity and the fragmentation of the Near East by the establishment of small competing and rival political units.

Whether this fragmentation of the Near East is only a temporary interlude raises a question as to whether such small political units will prove to be more politically and economically viable in modern times than in the past. The answer may well reside in the ability of the governments of succession states to find adequate solutions of their pressing social and economic problems. It is quite clear that by the nineteenth century the Ottoman Empire proved its incapacity to perform those functions inherent in political control of the Near East. The interplay of forces within the Near East and outside of it were such as to destroy the unity long maintained by the Ottoman Turks and to prevent any other people from re-establishing a unified political control of this strategic area. Now, as so frequently in its long history, two great Powers with dominion over wide territories confront one another in the Near East, the fate of whose people depends more on the struggle between alien states than upon their own efforts and resources. The *mise-en-scène* for the struggle for control, direct or indirect, of the Near East between the U.S.A. and the U.S.S.R. was being assembled during the precarious truce in the years between 1918 and 1933.

THE LAST YEARS OF THE OTTOMANS

The state of affairs in Turkey during 1918 could not be hidden from the people by the most rigorous censorship of the C.U.P. dictatorship. Wholesale desertion from the army, widespread famine conditions in many parts of the empire, devastating inflation, and the deepening misery of the masses and middle classes were known to all. The Arab revolt revealed the fact that Moslem as well as Christian subjects of the sultan were against the rule of the Ottomans. This was a shock to the old Turks but a stimulus to the Turkish nationalists.

The Russian Revolution and the denunciation of the secret treaties with the Allies regarding the partition of the Ottoman Empire and the renunciation of all imperialistic objectives in the Near East by the Russian revolutionaries made a deep impression upon the Turks. The Brest-Litovsk Treaty in March 1918 ending the war with Russia removed the main reason for the support by the Turkish people of the unpopular war policy of the Committee of Union and Progress. The ancient enemy was *hors de combat* and in the hands of a new revolutionary regime which was bitterly opposed to the imperialism of the former rulers of Russia, so in the minds of many Turks the *raison d'être* for continuing the war no longer existed.

The collapse of the C.U.P.—Ottoman autocracy revived.—The government of Enver and Talaat was hated and the C.U.P. discredited.

So general was the opposition that the Cabinet ceased attempts to suppress it and during the summer of 1918 censorship of the press was removed. Nevertheless, among the Turks there was no revolution. Apathy and resignation rather than revolt dominated the Turks, who anticipated defeat and awaited the end of the war for surcease from their suffering and for a solution of their problems. This passivity did not long survive under Allied control after the armistice of Mudros.

The Turkish military situation became hopeless as a result of Allenby's crushing victories in Palestine during September and of Bulgaria's surrender on September 29, 1918, which not only cut the supply line from the Central Powers but also freed the Allied forces in the Balkans for an advance on Constantinople. Bolshevik Russia abrogated on October 5 the treaty with Turkey. Two days later the C.U.P. Cabinet resigned; a new government was formed by Izzet Pasha with only two C.U.P. members. The Committee of Union and Progress was in such disrepute that in a party convention it confessed its failure and disbanded. Enver and Talaat Pasha fled. Upon Izzet Pasha fell the burden of negotiating on October 30, 1918, the armistice of Mudros with the Allies.

The Sultan, Mehmed VI, Vahid ed Din reasserting the power of the sultanate, strangely enough on the eve of its abolition, demanded the resignation of those members of the Cabinet who were considered to be C.U.P. sympathizers. Indignant at this interference with constitutional government, the whole Cabinet resigned. The Ottoman Empire at the culminating crucial moment of its history fell under the control of a government subservient to a sultan whose greatest concern was the preservation of his throne rather than his empire and who, consequently, became an obliging puppet of the Allies, particularly of the British.

The dissolution of the Committee of Union and Progress left the Turks without any defense against the old-guard reactionaries supported by the sultan. The ineffectively organized Liberal Unionists were unable to create a rallying point for the Young Turks, the reformists, revolutionists, and nationalists who had long been struggling against the old order. The Allies supported the sultan and the old regime in Turkey. The democracies of the West in order to forward their own aims were attempting to use in Turkey the reactionary rulers and classes who no longer could marshal the support of their people. This ill-conceived policy resulted in the Allied victory over the Turks of 1918 being transformed into the Turkish victory over the Allies in 1923. The road from Mudros to Mudania was strewn with the corpses of Greeks and Turks whose lives were added to the general cost in human suffering of the international struggle for control of the Near East.

The Allied occupation of Constantinople.—When, shortly after the armistice of Mudros, the warships of the Allied and Associate Powers sailed through the Dardanelles, and the Sea of Marmora to the Bosporus and anchored off Galata and Stamboul, the Ottoman Empire ceased to exist as an independent sovereign state. Ottoman government and authority already had been brought to an end in Arabia and the former Arab provinces, and within a few months the Ottoman sultan was to lose control over most of Asia Minor to the Turkish nationalists while his authority over the restricted area of Constantinople and its environment was limited under the close supervision and dicta of the Allies. The partition of the Ottoman Empire began before the Treaty of Sèvres was signed. Actually, the Ottoman Empire ceased to exist before it was pronounced dead officially by the decree of the Turkish Grand National Assembly at Ankara.

During the period of Allied domination at Constantinople from the autumn of 1918 until its reoccupation by Turkish troops in October 1923, the political details of the partition of the Ottoman Near East were decided upon by the Allies and finally embodied in the Treaty of Sèvres of 1920. In the course of these years the Turks recovered from the shock of their defeat and challenged the victors' plans for Anatolia and European Turkey.

The immediate reaction of the Turks to their defeat was not unfavorable to the Allies with whom they were prepared to co-operate. Their ancient enemy Russia no longer menaced them. They were glad to be rid of the Germans whom they had come to dislike bitterly. Their old friends the British and the French were in control. The loss of the Arab provinces the Turks were willing to accept with little reluctance. They somewhat naively believed that the Allies together with the United States would live up to the ideals of liberalism, democracy, the rights of small nations and the right of self-determination. The war-time propaganda of the Allied and Associate Powers was accepted at its face value by the Turks as it had been by millions of other idealistic and hopeful people. Events following the armistice of Mudros were soon to disillusion the Turkish people.

It was a bitter experience for the Turks to witness the jubilation of the Christian population who hailed with mad joy and rejoicing the arrival in the Bosporus of the Allies' warships. War-weary Turks, who only three years before had defeated all attempts by the Allies to force their way through the Dardanelles, now had to bear grimly the humiliation of final defeat and of the manifest disloyalty of their Greek and Armenian compatriots. The fact that the inordinate rejoicing of these Christian subjects of the sultan was dramatic evidence of the tragic failure of the Ottomans was of little solace to those Turks who long had striven to reform the Ottoman government.

The Turks were not at first aware that the Allies were planning to partition the Turkish territories in Europe and Anatolia. It was not long, however, before they were forced to realize that the Allied Powers were motivated solely by their national and imperialist interests in utter disregard of the wishes of the Turkish people.

The policies of the Allies.—The history of the Near East gives testimony to the unintelligent manner in which the statesmen of England, France, and Greece pursued their own interests in the years immediately following the war. Failing to understand the situation the Allied statesmen followed policies which led to the tragic conflict between the Greeks and the Turks and to revolts in Iraq and Syria.

At the end of World War I the British Empire was at the height of its prestige, influence, and power. Early in 1919 its military might and political authority appeared unchallengeable from the Sudan to the Caucasus, from Constantinople to Tehran. Nevertheless, within four years the British government was forced by a nationalist uprising in Egypt to abandon its protectorate, by a revolution in Iraq to revise its colonial policy in Mesopotamia, by Ibn Saud's attack on the kingdom of the Hejaz to give up its support of King Hussein, and by resurgent Turkish nationalism to accept Turkey's repudiation of the Treaty of Sèvres. These reactions in the 1920's to Britain's postwar policies foreshadowed the decline of Great Britain's power in the Near East during the forty years since the signing of the armistice of Mudros in 1918.

British statesmen misgauging the new revolutionary forces emerging in the Near East failed to realize that Great Britain could not retain its position of dominance by backing the former ruling classes. Western penetration had destroyed the validity of a social order which the western nations sought futilely to maintain so as to serve their own ends.

For a hundred years the statesmen of Europe had talked about the collapse of the Ottoman Empire and had considered the question of its partition. During World War I the Allies made their arrangements for the division of the Ottoman heritage. The exigencies of the war forced various changes and modifications of their original plans. When the time came for putting them into effect the statesmen, overwhelmed by domestic problems and by the complexities of peacemaking, did not grasp the significance of the profound changes which had occurred during the war and as a result of the defeat of the Central Powers.

The driving forces of revolutionary nationalism among the Arabs, the Turks, and the Jews were not adequately understood. Nor did the political leaders of the Allies realize the temporary nature of the eclipse of Germany's and Russia's power.[1] Somewhat intoxicated as well as exhausted by the vast powers which they wielded both during the war and at its close, the statesmen of the West assumed a Jehovah-like omnipotence and omniscience which rendered them blind to the realities of the new world beginning to take shape in the second and third decades of the twentieth century. Instead of moving along with the currents of the times, European statesmen by opposing them dammed up the troubled waters of social discontent until the torrents burst the futile restraints in Turkey and, later, in the Arab lands of western Asia.

British postwar policy with respect to Greece goes back to the proposal made by Sir Edward Grey, Britain's Minister of Foreign Affairs, to Venizelos in March 1915 that the Greeks be given Turkish territory in Asia Minor. This offer was made with the hope of bringing Greece into the war following Russia's refusal of the Greek Premier's offer to participate in an attack on the Dardanelles.[2] The British offer lapsed when the Cabinet of Venizelos fell and King Constantine insisted on the neutrality of Greece.

Two years later after Britain, France, and Russia had arranged for their respective shares in a future partition of the Ottoman Empire, these allies felt it advisable to accede to Italian demands for parts of Anatolia. Thus, by the Treaty of St. Jean de Maurienne of April 1917 the Italians thought they were assured of acquiring Smyrna and a part of the Aidin vilayet. By the end of the war the situation had changed to the disadvantage of Italy, and British statesmen thought Britain's interest would be served best by compensating Greece for her participation in the war and by allowing the Greeks to acquire Smyrna. The opportunity to do this at the expense of Italy arose at the Paris Peace Conference in 1919 when the Italians left the conference as a protest over the Fiume settlement. Fearful lest the frustrated Italians might extend their military occupation of Adalia to Smyrna, Clemenceau, Lloyd George, and Wilson decided upon its occupation by Greek troops in May 1919.

Some Turks by this time began to realize that the Allies, not content with the Arab portions of the Ottoman Empire, were planning to partition Asia Minor, the Turkish homeland. Clearly something had to be done if the Turkish nation was not to be destroyed.

❁ THE REVIVAL OF THE TURKS

The will to live was reborn among the Turks when they awoke to a realization of what the surrender of October 1918 would mean if effective resistance to the policies of the Allies was not forthcoming. The armistice, the arrival of the fleets of the victors at Constantinople, numbed the Turks who did not realize yet the threat to their existence as a nation. The awakening began after the Greek patriarch renounced his allegiance to the sultan, after Italian troops were landed at Adalia in southwest Anatolia, and when the Big Three at Paris on May 6, 1919, authorized a Greek occupation of Smyrna.

The landing of Greek forces and the slaughter which followed, electrified the Turks, even the most supine members of the sultan's government. The will to fight for their national existence was revived. In western Anatolia under the leadership of Rauf Bey Turks began to organize in preparation for military resistance against the Greeks, while in eastern Anatolia Mustafa Kemal capitalizing on this wave of indignation among the Turks took steps which eventually led to the creation of the Turkish Republic.

Mustafa Kemal.—This remarkable Turkish leader as a young cadet in the Turkish military schools had rebelled against the Hamidian regime and joined at an early stage the Committee of Union and Progress. His revolt was not just against the tyranny of Abdul Hamid but against the old Ottoman order. He was a man molded by the liberal and nationalistic ideas of his times.

After the revolution of 1908 Mustafa Kemal quarreled with Enver Pasha and the C.U.P. clique that ruled Turkey until 1918. Although his independent and somewhat overbearing spirit aroused the ire of Enver and his associates, his military competency won him an unassailable position in the Turkish army. His masterly defence of the Dardanelles had made him a national hero.

In 1919 on his return from Syria, the spineless Ottoman Cabinet to rid themselves of this intractable officer sent him as inspector general of the skeleton Turkish military forces in eastern Anatolia. On his arrival at Samsun he saw British ships disembarking Greeks and heard of a plan to revive the ancient Greek kingdom of the Pontus on the southern shores of the Black Sea. Soon afterward he learned from Rauf Bey, who had fled from the Greeks at Smyrna, of the conditions in the Smyrna area and of the preparations being made to resist Greek occupation.

As the news spread throughout Turkey of Greek activities, Turkish patriots flocked to Kemal's headquarters at Erzerum. Turkish deserters and peasants as well as the upper classes were fired with a passion to defend their homeland from the Greeks. Mustafa Kemal invited the civilian and religious leaders of the eastern Anatolian provinces to a meeting at Erzerum to discuss measures of national defense. This gathering, which came to be called the Congress of Erzerum, met in July 1919, drafted a series of resolutions, and organized the "Anatolian and Rumelian League for the Defense of National Rights." This congress marked the beginning of Turkish determination to resist the partition of Asiatic Turkey by the victorious Allies.

Anglo-French differences aid the nationalists.—Resistance to the seemingly all-powerful Allies appeared like a fantastic lost hope. Several complex and interrelated factors, however, made its realization possible. Among these the rival ambitions of the victors was one of the most important. The lack of trust in one another and the ill-will existing between the French and the British in the Near East seemed at the time astonishing.

Investments in Turkey had their bearing upon the divergence between French and British policies. French investments in the Ottoman Empire far exceeded those of the British. Of the Ottoman public debt French investors held over 60 per cent, the British less than 15 per cent. Because of the Bolshevik repudiation of the loans made to tsarist Russia and to the pre-Soviet revolutionary Russian government, French bondholders were fearful lest they should also lose their investments in Turkey. In "The Turkish Question" the French writer Maurice Pernot states the matter with trenchant frankness. Writing of an Anglo-French meeting in London to settle financial and economic questions concerning the Turkish peace treaty, Pernot says: "The French financial representatives endeavor to bring about the best possible administration of a patrimony which is the surety of French bondholders; the English delegates definitely subordinate financial to political interests and do not scruple about precipitating a failure which in their design would serve to make legitimate the seizure by the occupying powers of all the resources of the Empire." [3]

Obsessed with fears regarding Russian expansion and seeking some nation which would replace the Ottoman Empire as a buffer state against the Russians, the British backed the Greeks rather than the Turks, when it became evident that the puppet government of the sultan at Constantinople was losing the control over Anatolia to the Turkish nationalists. Politically and economically the Greeks were looked upon as British satellites. Consequently, the substitution of a Greek Orthodox empire controlling Constantinople, the Straits, and a large section of Asia Minor was not acceptable to the French. The Greek Orthodox Church which enjoyed the support of the Church of England was the rival of the Catholic Church which had long been under French protection in the Ottoman Near East. The rise of the Turkish resistance movement in Anatolia provided France with the opportunity to assume the diplomatic initiative in the Near East and break the monopoly Great Britain had acquired as a result of the predominant role she had played in military operations from 1914 to 1918. In the postwar years the divergent interests of England and France gave the Turkish nationalists the opportunity of playing upon the rivalry and jealousy of the European Powers. In this diplomatic game Turkish statesmen for generations had had much experience.

In dealing with the British and French the Turks were aided by the Bolsheviks, who not only had renounced all imperialist aims but were themselves engaged in a struggle to free Russia from the British, French, and other imperialistic interventionists. Consequently, the Russian Bolsheviks and the Turkish nationalists were able to come to a mutually advantageous settlement of their differences in Transcaucasia.

Count Sforza on Turkish nationalism.—The Turks were helped by the attitude of the Italians, who having been done out of what they considered their justified claims to Fiume and to territories in Africa and Anatolia, were opposed to Britain's pro-Greek policy. Count Carlo Sforza, the Italian High Commissioner at Constantinople, who was an experienced diplomat, understood clearly the power and significance of the Turkish nationalist movement in Anatolia. To this farseeing Italian statesman Philip Graves applied the adjectives "urbane and untruthful" [4] and A. Pallis "able and crafty," [5] qualifications which since the time of Machiavelli have been considered the hallmarks of competent diplomats. Actually, Count Sforza in dealing with the question of allowing the Greeks to occupy Smyrna showed the highest qualities of statesmanship. With a frankness that is a tribute to his courage and honesty, at the risk of his dismissal he informed the Italian Premier and Foreign Minister that he intended to follow a policy of "an early and honourable peace" which excluded "any idea of Turkish partition." [6] Sforza was in the fortunate position of being a diplomat whose opinions and judgments were given due weight by his government, whereas Lloyd George's Cabinet paid no attention to the warnings received from three competent British intelligence officers that a landing of the Greeks at Smyrna would precipitate a new war.

While feeling obliged to "go along" with British pro-Greek anti-Turk policy both the French and the Italians began to explore the possibility of dealing with the Turkish nationalists. Mustafa Kemal and his associates developed this chance to divide the Allies and to secure at crucial moments in the Graeco-Turkish war aid from France and Italy as well as from Russia.

So limited are our historical horizons and so parochial our interests that most people in Europe and the United States think of World War I of 1914–18 as being all important. In Russia and in Turkey where hostilities went on until 1921 and 1922, the added years of war had as great if not greater significance than the first four. In 1919 the Turks unofficially renewed their struggle against their victorious enemies and succeeded in winning the war and dictating the terms of peace. The years between 1919 and 1923 are of momentous significance to the Turks and of vital importance to the entire Near East. It was during these years of struggle that the new Turkey was conceived and born.

Anatolia rallies to Mustafa Kemal.—Early in July 1919 the puppet government of the sultan under pressure from the Allies declared Mustafa Kemal an outlaw and endeavored to undermine his leadership in the army and among the civilian provincial officials. Nevertheless, in both eastern and western Anatolia the Turkish nationalists with popular support were able to hold the first Congress of Erzerum on July 23 and that of Balikhissar on July 26, 1919. The resolutions passed by the first Congress of Erzerum proclaimed the right of the Turks to resist every territorial occupation and all intervention designed to establish Greek or Armenian control over any part of Anatolia. It stated that in the event of the Ottoman government's being constrained by the Allied Powers to surrender any of these Turkish territories the Congress would determine what political and military measures should be taken. In these resolutions provision was made for an organization called the Committee for the Defense of the Rights of Eastern Asia Minor with subordinate committees in the villages, the counties, and the provinces and for the election of county, provincial, and general congresses, thus laying the foundations of national political power in eastern Anatolia. The Congress of Balikhissar was called to resist the Greek occupation of western Asia Minor. It provided for the mobilization and maintenance of troops to fight the Greeks until they were driven out of Turkey. The Turks of eastern and western Anatolia were being rapidly organized during the summer of 1919 to resist the partition of Turkish lands in Asia Minor and in Europe.

In August the nationalists called the second Congress of Erzerum which issued a proclamation setting forth again its decision to resist, on the principle of self-determination, any foreign occupation or intervention designed to partition Turkey and demanding that the government at Constantinople submit to a national assembly all matters related to the fate and security of the nation.

Despite the threats of the Allies at Constantinople and of the attempts by the sultan's government to check the growth of the resistance movement among the Turks of Asia Minor, the nationalists held another Congress at Sivas early in September 1919. Its larger membership was even more determined than that of the Erzerum congresses, and more impatient with the government at Constantinople. However, in an effort to prevent a break between the nationalist organization in Anatolia and the Imperial Ottoman government, a Committee of the Sivas Congress sent a long telegram to the sultan. In this extraordinary communication the nationalists reaffirmed their determination to resist partition; they accused the Allies of having broken the terms of the armistice of Mudros; they expressed their loyalty to the sultan-caliph, but stated their lack of confidence in the Damad ministry and demanded that general elections to Parliament be held immediately.

On October 5, 1919, a month after the Sivas Congress met, the Cabinet of Damad Ferid fell. The sultan appointed Ali Riza Grand Vizier and authorized a general election. The growing differences between the British and the French were beginning to create a more favorable situation for the Turks. It was rumored that in September the British had made a secret agreement with the Grand Vizier Damad Pasha about Constantinople and the Straits. The French in the meanwhile had sent the ubiquitous Georges Picot to Sivas to see whether a deal could be negotiated with Mustafa Kemal on the basis of exclusive economic privileges for the French who were then planning to replace the British forces in Cilicia. These first conversations between the French and the Turkish Nationalists came to nought, but their importance lies in that they were the prelude to further negotiations in London during the winter of 1921 and at Ankara in October of the same year. Following these tentative moves toward a Franco-Kemalist agreement and the French occupation of Cilicia with military forces which included an Armenian contingent, hostilities began between the Turkish nationalists and the French.

The elections to the Ottoman Parliament during the autumn of 1919 resulted in a majority of the deputies being supporters of Mustafa Kemal and the nationalists. To those who were not blind to political realities the Turkish elections were clear evidence of the popular support back of the Turkish nationalist movement. Before proceeding to Constantinople the newly elected nationalist deputies met at Ankara, where Mustafa Kemal had established his headquarters, and formulated the basis for a declaration which later became the Turkish National Pact when on January 28, 1920, the Ottoman Parliament voted its adoption.

The Turks challenge the Allies.—This declaration accepted the loss of the Arab provinces, but rejected the partition of Anatolia and insisted upon complete sovereignty without foreign intervention with the exception of Thrace, where results of plebiscites were acceptable to the Turks. This was a direct challenge to the Allies, which the British decided to accept. On March 16, 1920, British military forces occupied Constantinople. The Turkish nationalist leaders who were not able to escape the British dragnet were arrested and exiled to Malta. Under British pressure Sultan Mehmed VI acting in his capacity of Caliph and in accordance with a fetva of the Sheik-ul-Islam condemned the Turkish nationalist movement as contrary to Islam. He then dissolved the last Ottoman Parliament.

By these acts, which were in the tradition of the old Ottoman order, the sultan unwittingly sealed his own fate and that of his dynasty. In response to these actions the Kemalists acted with vigor and promptness. An assembly of muftis, cadis, and ulemas, which foregathered from all parts of Anatolia, issued a counter-fetva condemning the sultan-caliph. In answer to the dissolution of the Ottoman Parliament they summoned a meeting of the Turkish Grand National Assembly which immediately claimed it was the only official body representative of the Turkish nation. It proceeded to draft a constitution called the Law of Fundamental Organization and to form a government. The break with Constantinople and the Allies was complete. The new Turkish nationalist government of Ankara promptly negotiated on April 24, 1920, a military convention with the Russian Socialist Federation of Soviet Republics.

Shortly thereafter, an Ottoman Peace Delegation representing the sultan's government arrived at Paris on May 6 and was given the draft peace treaty prepared by the Allies. While the Ottoman government was considering the peace terms which were utterly unacceptable to the nationalists, the Allies were considering what should be done about the Ankara government. Britain agreed that the Greeks should undertake military action against Mustafa Kemal. At the Allied Conference at Boulogne in the latter part of June 1920 Greek military operations in Anatolia were authorized by England and France and reluctantly supported by Italy. Count Sforza, the Italian representative, unsuccessfully opposed the use of Greek forces and declared that it would be a serious blunder to do so since it would greatly strengthen Turkish nationalism and lead to stronger resistance by Kemalist forces. Lloyd George in his vast ignorance of conditions in the Near East ridiculed Sforza's analysis of the situation as a gross exaggeration of the potency of the Turkish nationalist movement. The British prime minister forced the decision on the Allies for a Greek offensive against the Turkish Kemalists which began on June 22, 1920.[7]

❁ THE GRAECO-TURKISH WAR

This war was a struggle in the Near East between Turkish nationalism and Greek imperialism backed by Great Britain. The final victory of the Kemalist forces marked the first significant defeat of European imperialism in the Near East. The first round in this conflict proved inconclusive. After driving north to the Marmora Sea and capturing Panderma, Brusa, Mudanya and Ismid, Greek forces crossed over to the European shore at Rodosto and drove the Turks out of eastern Thrace, occupying Adrianople in July. Other Greek troops advanced eastward into Anatolia along the railroad from Smyrna toward Afiun Karahissar on the Bagdad railroad line occupying Ushak on the western edge of the central Anatolian plateau in August. The Turkish troops retired without major losses and still held the main railroad lines of central Asia Minor.

During the midsummer the authority of the Ankara government was augmented by the Ottoman government's acceptance on August 10 of the Treaty of Sèvres because its terms left no Turk in doubt as to the fate of the Turkish people and nation if resistance to the Allies was not continued. By this treaty the sultan's government accepted the loss of the Arab lands of western Asia in which Cilicia was included, a Greek mandate over Smyrna and its hinterland for a period of five years, the ceding of eastern Thrace as far as Chatalja as well as the Aegean islands to Greece, the creation of an independent state of Armenia in eastern Anatolia, and the granting of autonomy or independence to the Kurds. Furthermore, the Straits were to be internationalized and Turkey placed under an Allied Financial Commission with powers which implied almost complete control by foreigners of Turkish finances and economic life. Acceptance by the Turkish people of this treaty signed by their sultan's government would have been the death knell of the Turkish nation. Under such conditions the Turks chose to fight.

In September to make secure their eastern frontiers, the Turks invaded the Armenian Republic of Erivan and in October launched an attack in Cilicia, where again Armenians were slaughtered as victims of the conflict between Turkish nationalism and western imperialism. In Transcaucasia an ultimatum from Bolshevik Russia brought an end to the Turko-Armenian War and resulted in a treaty between the Bolshevik government at Moscow and the Kemalist government at Ankara.

The crisis in Greece.—In the meanwhile a political crisis was precipitated in Greece by the death of King Alexander. Venizelos called for general elections on November 11, 1920, and was overwhelmingly defeated by the supporters of Constantine who was recalled to the throne by a plebiscite on December 5.

The restoration of Constantine during a crucial period of the Graeco-Turkish War proved politically and militarily disadvantageous to the Greeks. The French had no use for Constantine, who was the brother-in-law of the former Kaiser Wilhelm II and who had opposed Greece's entrance into the war on the side of the Allies until his deposition. His return to the throne gave the French another excuse to reach an understanding with Mustafa Kemal. Constantine's return also resulted in the appointment of incompetent royalist officers to important commands in Asia Minor.

While Greeks were becoming badly divided by the quarrels between the supporters of Venizelos and of Constantine, attempts were being made to bring about co-operation between Ankara and Constantinople with a view to a modification of the Treaty of Sèvres. The sultan's Cabinet sent Izzet Pasha to Ankara to persuade the Turkish Grand National Assembly to send a joint delegation to discuss with the Allies a modification of the Treaty of Sèvres. Two weeks after Izzet's arrival at Ankara, Mustafa Kemal on January 30 notified Constantinople that the Ankara government alone had the authority to speak in the name of the Turkish nation. On February 8, 1921, the Ankara government sent a separate mission to the London Conference at which there appeared two Turkish delegations, that of Ankara and that of Constantinople.

The modifications of the Treaty of Sèvres offered by the Allies were unacceptable to the Ankara delegation, which, however, used the visit to London quite profitably. In contrast to the Allied statesmen the Kemalists were playing the diplomatic game with great skill. At Moscow under Bolshevik auspices a Turko-Afghan treaty was signed on March 1 and a Turko-Soviet treaty on March 16. At London a secret Franco-Kemal agreement (later not ratified) was signed on March 9, and a Turko-Italian agreement (not ratified later) on March 12. By these maneuvers of the Turkish nationalists the British in the Near East were being isolated. Furthermore, these negotiations with France and Italy foreshadowed abandonment by the Allies of the Greeks, who on March 23, 1921, launched their second great offensive.

The Allies leave the Greeks in the lurch.—Uncertain of the outcome the Allies, in order to protect their position at the Straits and at Constantinople, issued a proclamation of neutrality and established a neutral zone on May 18, two days after the Ankara government had ratified the Treaty of Moscow negotiated in March. This action of the Allies was due to the fact that they were in no position to face a general war developing out of the Graeco-Turkish conflict. In June the president of the Foreign Relations Committee of the French Senate, Franklin-Bouillon, went to Ankara ostensibly on a private mission which four months later resulted in his signing an official Franco-Turkish agreement.

As the Greeks by the middle of June had not attained their first objective, the control of the Anatolian railroad from Ismid to Afiun Karahissar, the Allies offered the Greek government their mediation. This was refused. The Italians then promptly withdrew from Adalia while the Greeks continued their offensive. In July the Greek forces had captured Kiutaya, Afiun Karahissar, and Eskishehr, key points on the Anatolian railroad. From the Eskishehr junction a branch railroad ran to Ankara which now became the main objective of the Greeks who by mid-July reached the Sakarya River.

To meet the Greek thrust toward Ankara Mustafa Kemal, President of the Turkish Grand National Assembly, was elected Commander-in-chief of the military forces of the Ankara government. A few days later the Supreme War Council of the Allies declared that the Greeks and the Turkish nationalists were engaged in waging a "private war" and proclaimed the neutrality of England, France, Italy, and Japan. Greece thus was unceremoniously abandoned at a time when she sorely needed help.

Greek military forces were far from their bases on the coast, their lines of communication were long, and to reach Ankara they would have had to advance across difficult terrain. The Turks were actually in a stronger position as a result of their retreat, and they were receiving supplies from the Russians and the Italians. Along the Sakarya for a full month from August 24 to September 23, 1921, a decisive battle raged. The Greeks were beaten and forced to retire to Afiun Karahissar in a general retreat.

The defeat of the Greeks at Sakarya and the French evacuation of Cilicia which freed some 80,000 Turkish troops for the next spring's campaign against the Greeks perturbed the Allies who called a conference at Paris. While Mustafa Kemal was preparing for his offensive of 1922 a Graeco-Turkish armistice was agreed to with some reservations by both the Ottoman and the Ankara governments. But before the three months' armistice ended, it was evident that hostilities soon would be resumed because the Allies were unwilling to accept Ankara's demands based on the National Pact.

In July the Greek high commissioner at Smyrna received orders from Athens to organize the autonomous state of Ionia in western Anatolia. The Greeks in order to confront the Turks with a *fait accompli* planned to seize Constantinople but were forestalled by the Allies. During the last week in August the Ankara representative in London, Fethi Bey, came to the conclusion that further discussion with the British over peace terms would be futile and advised his government to recommence military operations. Five days later, on August 28, Mustafa Kemal launched a long delayed but well-prepared offensive against the Greeks. The Greek front crumbled. On September 2 the Greek army headquarters was taken in a surprise attack and the Greek commander-in-chief captured.

Smyrna reoccupied—Britain's untenable position.—On September 9, 1922, the Turkish troops entered Smyrna without further opposition from the completely demoralized Greek forces. At the time of the Turkish reoccupation a conflagration, the origins of which have never been ascertained, swept Smyrna and destroyed the Greek quarter of the city.

Having freed Smyrna the next objective of the Turkish forces was to drive the Greeks out of eastern Thrace. The route to Europe, however, was blocked by the Allied forces who held both sides of the Straits. The British General Charles Harington, commanding the Allied forces at Chanak on the Asiatic side of the Dardanelles, refused passage to the Kemalist forces. Mustafa Kemal wisely avoided a conflict and had the patience to await the results of a division of opinion among the Allies. Events played into the hands of the Turks, for both the French and the Italians withdrew their troops from the Asiatic side of the Dardanelles to the Gallipoli Peninsula, leaving the British to hold the line alone against the Turks. Caught in the network of an untenable policy which it had followed since 1919 the coalition government of Lloyd George made a somewhat hysterical appeal to the British Dominions for their support in what might have developed into another Anglo-Turkish struggle at the Dardanelles.

The refusal of the Dominions to back the London Cabinet in a war against Turkey rendered the already critical position of the British untenable. The Near Eastern policy of the British government was unpopular at home; the French and Italian allies of Great Britain had very definitely shown their unwillingness to co-operate further with the British in their anti-Turkish policy. The Ankara government had negotiated treaties with the Russian Socialist Federative Soviet Republic, with the Socialist Soviet Republic of the Ukraine, with the socialist soviet republics of Transcaucasia and with Afghanistan, it had also been recognized by Persia. The military forces of Britain's Hellenic satellite had been overwhelmingly defeated, and, finally, the British Dominions refused to join Britain in a war against the Turkish nationalists.

British policy had proved to be a complete failure, and the British government was obliged to agree to armistice negotiations with the Ankara government. On September 23, 1922, Franklin-Bouillon was sent as special emissary of England, France, and Italy to request an armistice which was signed at Mudania on October 11, a little less than four years after the signing of the armistice of Mudros. Turkey was saved from partition. The European imperialists had met with a prophetic set back to their power in the Near East. The beginning of the recession of British and French predominance in the Near East may be dated as of October 11, 1922.

CHAPTER XX

Turkey—The Road to Modernization

The more rapid pace of modernization of the Turks and the Turkish areas of the Near East was made possible under the leadership of Mustafa Kemal when, after the victory over the Greeks, relations with Great Britain and her Allies were eventually restored by the Treaty of Lausanne of July 24, 1923.

THE TREATY OF LAUSANNE

The peace negotiations begun at Lausanne on November 20, 1922, continued over a period of eight months due in part to the fact that George N. Curzon, the British secretary for foreign affairs, found it difficult to adjust himself to the realities of the changed situation whereby the Turks were in a position to dictate the major terms of the settlement. After six weeks of inconclusive discussions the conference broke down when Lord Curzon left Lausanne. Negotiations, resumed again in the latter part of April 1923, moved more smoothly in the absence of the somewhat difficult Curzon.

By inviting representatives of the Sublime Porte as well as of the Turkish Grand National Assembly to the Lausanne conference, the Allies sealed the fate of the Ottoman dynasty as a result of the reaction to the invitation by Tewfik Pasha, the last Grand Vizier of the Ottoman Empire. On his receipt of the Allies' invitation Tewfik telegraphed Mustafa Kemal and the president of the Council of Ministers at Ankara in terms which precipitated a violent discussion in the Turkish Grand National Assembly over the question of the deposition of the sultan and the abolition of the sultanate. Against vigorous protests Mustafa Kemal, who would brook no opposition to his decisions, forced through the Assembly a bill which deposed Sultan Mehmed VI, abolished the sultanate, and provided for the election by the Grand National Assembly of a new caliph to be chosen from the House of Osman.[1]

Having taken this historically significant action the National Assembly, fearing the intrigues of the deposed sultan and his supporters, ordered the arrest and trial of the deposed sultan and the members of his Cabinet. By his flight from Constantinople on a British warship Mehmed VI played into the hands of the Kemalists by discrediting himself among all Turks both as sultan and as caliph. It is somewhat ironical that the "Terrible Turk," against whom William Ewart Gladstone had thundered at the time of the Bulgarian massacres, was transported to Malta "bag and baggage" as an honored refugee aboard His Britannic Majesty's dreadnought "Malaya" on November 16, 1922. Thus, being rid of an unwanted ex-sultan, the deputies at Ankara elected Abdul Medjid Effendi of the House of Osman and titular heir to the Ottoman throne supreme caliph of Islam.

Terms of the treaty.—The Treaty of Lausanne, which superceded that of Sèvres annulled by the Lausanne Conference, is of particular significance to the modernization of Turkey because by its terms the Turks were freed from the fetters imposed upon the Ottoman government by the western Powers. The Lausanne Treaty and subsidiary documents, which form a part of the Turkish peace settlement, determined to a considerable degree the political framework within which the course of history of the Near East and its component parts was to develop. The settlement with respect to the Turks is important because of its bearing on the evolution of the Turkish Republic.

Territorially, the Turks renounced all claims to the Asiatic Arab provinces of the former Ottoman Empire and also to Egypt, the Sudan, and Libya. They agreed to the annexation of Cyprus by Great Britain, recognized Italy's acquisition of Rhodes and the Dodecanese Islands, and accepted Greek sovereignty over all other islands of the Aegean with the exception of Imbros, Tenedos, and the Rabbit Islands, which the Turks were able to retain because these islands are near the Dardanelles and control the southern entrance to the Straits. None of the Great Powers was willing to have any state but Turkey control these strategic islands. In Asia, Africa, and Europe the Turks lost every vestige of territory that had made the Ottoman state an empire. The Turks reclaimed only those former Ottoman territories that were predominantly Turkish and they agreed to a plebiscite in Thrace and to defer a decision with respect to northern Mesopotamia where the population of the petroleum-bearing area of Mosul is largely Kurdish.

The Straits' settlement.—With the exception of the Straits, for which a special convention was signed, the Turks had regained full sovereignty and at long last had become the untrammeled masters in their own

BULGARIA
GREECE
B L A C K
Sinope
Zonguldak
Kastamonu
Istanbul
Sea of MARMORA
Bolu
Canakkale
Brusa
Bilecik
Ankara
Yozgat
Balikesir
Eskisehir
Kütahya
T U R
Manisa
Afyon
Ismir
L. Egridir
L. Tuz
Aydin
Denizli
Burdur
Isparta
L. Beysehir
Konya
Nigde
Mūgta
Antalya
Adana
Mersin
CYPRUS
MEDITERRANEAN SEA

Bosporus
Istanbul
SEA OF MARMORA
DARDANELLES
Canakkale

S E A
U. S. S. R.
Artvin
Samsun
Trabzon
Rize
Kars
Amasya
Gümüsane
Erzurum
Karakose
Sivas
K E Y
I R A N
Cemiskezek
Capakcur
L. Van
Mus
Kayseri
Elazid
Van
Bitlis
Malatya
Süirt
Diyarbakir
Cölemerik
Tigris R.
Euphrates R.
Maras
Mardin
Urfa
Gaziantep
Iskenderun
Antakya
S Y R I A
I R A Q

TURKEY

country, the great Powers having agreed to the abolition of the Capitulations. All the principal objectives set forth in the National Pact of January 1920 had been attained. The restrictions with respect to complete sovereignty over the Straits were done away with in 1936 by the Montreux Convention.

Regulations concerning passage through and control of the Straits have long been and still are matters of international concern. The special convention of 1923 set up an international commission to enforce the new regulations. The Turks considered the convention an infringement of their sovereign rights and the Soviet Union looked upon it as a direct threat to the security of the U.S.S.R. With a change in the international situation following the rise of Nazism in Germany and the menacing gestures of Fascist Italy in the Mediterranean, England and France were glad to accede to Turkish demands for a revision of the Straits' convention agreed to at Lausanne. The Montreux Convention of 1936 gave the Turks control of the vital waterway from the Aegean to the Black Sea. It was not until after World War II that this convention was challenged by the Soviets.

The transfer of populations.—The almost fanatical emphasis on nationalism to which World War I and its aftermath gave rise was further intensified among Turks and Greeks by the Graeco-Turkish War. The Turks attributed the misfortunes which befell the Ottomans to the fact that the Ottoman Empire was a multi-national state. Their insistence upon a purely Turkish state was one of the determining factors which led to the Graeco-Turkish agreement of January 30, 1923, regarding the transfer of populations stipulated in the general statement at Lausanne. By mutual agreement there was a planned exchange whereby Greek citizens of Turkey were transferred to Greece, and Moslem Turkish subjects of Greece to Turkey. It is to be noted that the Greek Orthodox inhabitants of Constantinople and of the three Aegean Islands under Turkish sovereignty were not included in this wholesale migration which was carried out under conditions as humane as such an uprooting of human beings could be.

This attempt to solve the problem of national minorities is of special interest to those who concern themselves with recent and contemporary history because the problems of multi-national states became of prime political importance in the nineteenth and twentieth centuries. Of the three large multi-national states of the prewar period—Austria-Hungary, the Ottoman Empire and Russia—only one has survived World War I. The Soviet Union alone was able to achieve a reintegration of the former Russian state with its many diverse national groups. The unsolved problems of national minorities were resolved in the Habsburg Dual Monarchy by its dissolution; in the Soviet Union by the creation of major and subordinate political divisions based upon cultural and national grouping; and in the Ottoman Empire by the deportation and massacre of the Armenians, by partition under compulsion, and finally by the planned transfer of Greeks.

During and since World War II genocide and forced migrations have been used as means to obtain national unity. The Germans employed genocide and forced migrations in dealing with Jews and Slavs. The Soviet Union, Poland, Czechoslovakia, and Bulgaria used compulsory migration. Israel used terrorization and exclusion of wartime Arab migrants.

REVOLUTIONARY CHANGES

Contrary to the usual connotation of the word revolution, it is herein employed to mean basic change irrespective of whether it was brought about legally or illegally, rapidly or slowly, peacefully or through violence. Revolution is not thought of as the opposite of evolution but as a part of the process of social evolution which may be likened to a flowing stream with its still waters, its rapids, and its falls, which may flow in a straight line, with gently curving bends, or with abrupt changes of direction.

Many of the basic changes brought about by the new rulers of Turkey were the result of the revolutionary thinking and ideologies which began to take shape in the minds of the Tanzimat reformers and their Young Turk successors. Other changes were determined by the events which transpired during the closing year of the war and the period of Allied occupation. In so far as its social changes may be attributed to one individual, it may be said that the ideas of Tekin Alp had a preponderant influence on the making of the new Turkey. A potent member of the C.U.P. for many years, M. Tekin had long been a strong opponent of Ottoman autocracy and Islamic theocracy. His well-turned phrase "theocracy has always been a faithful ally of autocracy" was widely known among progressive Turks. Alp as a passionate Turkish nationalist and for a time the leading protagonist of Pan-Turanianism, was bitterly opposed to Ottomanism and Pan-Islamism. This leading Turkish sociologist as a vigorous advocate of western liberalism was determined to free the Turks from the domination of the ulemas, the Islamic brotherhoods, and the religious schools of the softas. He advocated the elimination of the Sheriat and the ecclesiastical courts of the cadis and their replacement by a civil code and lay courts.

The political associations and the writings of Tekin Alp had done much to shape the ideas of that generation of Turkish young men and women who played a leading role in founding the Turkish Republic. Many of the changes brought about by them between 1919 and 1925 were based upon the ideas promulgated by Tekin Alp. The revolutionary measures enacted by the Turkish Grand National Assembly under the goad of Mustafa Kemal's dominating personality and persuasive oratory were the offspring of the intellectual revolution which had been developing in Turkey throughout most of the nineteenth century. In the beginning was the idea which in due course of time became a social reality.

Political changes.—The most revolutionary changes made by the Turkish Grand National Assembly were political. Outstanding among them were the abolition of the sultanate and its replacement by a republican and representative form of government in 1922, the doing away with the ancient institution of the Ottoman caliphate, the secularization of the government by the separation of Church and State, the suppression of the Sheriat courts, and the adoption of a civil code. The breaking up of the Islamic brotherhoods with the closing of their tekkes and the expropriation of their property undermined the influence and power of the Turkish Islamic "ecclesiastics" which were further weakened by making education a function of the state.

Cultural changes.—A cultural break with the Arabs and to some extent with Islam was fostered by a series of acts of the National Assembly which weakened the historic bonds of more than six hundred years' duration. The Arabic script was replaced by Latin characters and the Turkish language was purged of Arabic words. In their daily call to prayers from the minarets of Turkish mosques, the muezzins were obliged to use the Turkish instead of the Arabic language. A Turkish Koran replaced the traditional Arabic Koran. This had a significance somewhat similar to that in Christian Europe when during the Reformation, the Protestants substituted for the Latin Vulgate Bible, bibles in the national vernacular languages. Throughout the history of the Islamic people among the potent bonds between Moslems of all races and tongues were the Arabic language, the Arabic Koran, and the Islamic prayers in Arabic. For centuries in all Islamic countries the Islamic prayer and creed was known and used by all Moslems—*La illah ila Allah waa Mohammed rassoul Allah* ("There is no God but Allah and Mohammed is His Prophet"). How far some of the Turkish revolutionists carried their nationalism is evident in their attempt to substitute the Turanian word for God, Tanri, for the Arabic Allah.

Social changes.—The giving up of the fez, or tarbush as it was called in the Near East, and the passing of the veil, as part of the emancipation of Turkish women, are conspicuously noticeable and in some respects notable. This was not the first time in Turkish history that a dramatic change of male headgear took place. The ancient turban of the Arabs gave way to the Turkish fez, which by the way was manufactured for the most part in Austria, when Turkish officialdom adopted this new-fangled headgear. This earlier revolution was confined largely to the upper and urban classes. The fez was not worn by the Turkish and Arabic peasants nor by the nomads. The emancipation of Turkish women was an important revolutionary change as was also the making of polygamy illegal. The doing away with the veil, however, was a more dramatic change for urban women than for the peasants and nomads.

Even as late as 1913, five years after the Young Turk revolution, Turkish women in Constantinople as in other Ottoman cities were veiled in public places. They were segregated in curtained compartments of the tramcars. If a Turkish woman ventured to speak to a man in a public place she might be subject to arrest and exile to Anatolia. The end of woman's seclusion, the discarding of the veil, and the freedom to attend mixed social functions were exciting forms of this transition for women of the upper class. Princess Musbar Haidar Sherifa,[2] the daughter of Ali Haidar, Sherif of Mecca, and of his English wife, and Selma Ekrem,[3] who were young girls when World War I ended have given interesting and entertaining accounts of this transition in the mores of the Turks which began somewhat surreptitiously before World War I for some of the more daring young women of Turkey.

For the time being at least, these changes, so thrilling for the urban women, had little effect upon the peasant woman except when she came into contact with and was shocked by the behavior of the emancipated women of the city. At times history is somewhat distorted because of the illiteracy of the inarticulate masses and because the views and judgments of the articulate few whose experiences are more often than not limited to the class of which they are members. This distortion is true to some extent of the memoirs of Halidé Edib,[4] but more especially of those of Princess Haidar and Selma Ekrem.

Dictatorship under constitutional representative government.—The Kemalists, following the liberal tradition, drafted a constitution which provided for a representative form of government with a legislative assembly and organized the People's Party. Though the foundations had been laid for a democratic republic, actually the new Turkey in its formative years was under the dictatorship of Mustafa Kemal as the head of the People's Party. In the historical Hellenic meaning of the word, the ruler of the Turkish Republic till his death in 1936 was a tyrant, that is a usurper. He had taken over the reins of government "illegally" and replaced the former ruler.

The significance of events in Turkey following World War I may be better understood if they are examined with the historical perspective of former periods of revolutionary change. In Athens during the time of transition from a feudal agrarian city state to a commercial and industrial democracy, power was seized by the usurper Pisistratus who performed an important function. After the Roman Republic had conquered the Mediterranean the usurper, Octavius Caesar, fulfilled the necessary function of laying the foundation of an autocratic government capable of ruling a far-flung empire. In the various countries of Europe absolute monarchy, with some outstanding rulers, made it possible for the middle class to break the power of the feudal nobility. In twentieth-century Turkey Mustafa Kemal performed a similar function for the Turks.

Modernization and autocracy.—The Kemalists set about destroying or eliminating many of the political, social, and cultural institutions and patterns of the old Ottoman order which stood in the way of modernization. Thus, under the dictatorship the road to modernization was cleared of some of the obstacles which hindered the process. Destruction was accompanied by the construction of a new order. Such a process could not take place without opposition from those whose interests were threatened or appeared to be threatened by the changes. Old tribal, feudal, and ecclesiastical privileged classes rarely submit docilely to changes which menace their power, their wealth, their ways of living and ways of thinking. Nor do the masses, as represented by peasants and nomads, submit eagerly to changes in the patterns of their ways of life. Hence the political *raison d'être* throughout history of the usurpers, the tyrants, the autocrats among whom Mustafa Kemal holds an honorable place.

۞ CONCERNING ECONOMIC PROBLEMS

The heritage of the new leaders of Turkey created many problems that are common throughout most of the Near East wherever governments now are attempting to modernize rapidly their countries. Part of this heritage was the fact that the Turkish middle class was for the most part composed of former officers and officials of the Ottoman government. The bankers, the businessmen, and the industrialists in the Ottoman Empire were largely non-Turks. Few Turks had had any practical modern business experience. There did not exist in the Ottoman state a modern capitalistic Turkish middle class skilled and experienced in the techniques of modern commerce, industry, and finance. Consequently, there was no well-trained group of Turks to take over the functions formerly performed by Armenians, Greeks, Jews, and foreigners. The revolutionary leaders in Turkey as in most of the Near East during the past hundred years had concerned themselves largely with political and social studies rather than with economics. They had shown very little interest in the complexities of the western economic system although they were keenly conscious of the fact that European domination of the Ottoman Empire had been based upon economic controls. The Kemalists were determined that the Turkish Republic should not be controlled by European governments and western capitalists. With little knowledge of Marxian philosophy and no inclination toward Soviet Communism, they turned toward what is commonly spoken of as state socialism, but more correctly called *étatism,* which is a modernized form of seventeenth- and eighteenth-century European mercantilism.

Etatism and mercantilism.—State capitalism, or *étatism,* did not develop in the Turkish Republic under the same conditions and for the same reasons that it evolved in the highly industrialized and urbanized countries of the West. In western societies a complex variety of factors have led to state capitalism, to the welfare state and in some cases to the socialized states. Among some of the causes of these developments in the West the following are notably in contrast with the causes of the mercantilistic government of the Turkish Republic: the increasing complexities of modern industrial societies made it necessary for government to assume wider powers in both economic and social matters, the increasing centralization of power in the hands of vast corporations and the increasing dangers of economic anarchy resulting from the cycle of boom and depression, the spread of socialistic ideas coupled with the growth of political democracy, and finally in recent times during two World Wars the inescapable necessity for government to bring wide segments of commerce, industry, transportation, and finance under control.

"State Socialism" in Turkey was established not to restrain and control powerfully organized capitalists but rather to encourage capitalists and assist in the development of those capitalistic organizations and institutions considered essential to the economic growth and exploitation of Turkey's natural resources. It was not the result of the demands and political pressure either of a large and highly organized industrial wage-earning class or of a numerous "white collared" urban middle class. It was not a product of socialistic philosophies such as those of Christian, Utopian, and Marxist socialism which have so profoundly affected the West. In Turkey the new ruling class of officers and officials was motivated by a passionate nationalism seeking means by which to modernize an economically and socially backward society whose members for the most part were illiterate peasants.

The economic policies and methods of the Turkish government more nearly resembled those of the mercantilist states of Europe during the pre-industrial era rather than those of contemporary Europe whether capitalist or socialist. In Ankara a governmental bureaucracy with little previous experience in the field of economics attempted to modernize agriculture and industry, expand the system of transportation and communication, and exploit the mineral resources. After nearly eleven years of almost continuous warfare (1911–22) the Kemalist Turks took over the Turkish portion of the Ottoman Empire and set about to raise it by its bootstraps free from foreign economic and financial control. It is not surprising that during the first period of its history until after World War II the economic results were rather meager, for during those years the Turkish Republic functioned without either the fructifying free-enterprise capitalism of the West or the driving force of planned socialism of the U.S.S.R., with their tremendously productive forces.

Turkish mercantilism developed slowly the latent economic resources of the Turkish people and territory. One of the ways the Turkish government used to provide the financial means to carry out the economic policies without dependence on western capitalists was the creation of four state financial institutions. In order to provide and control the currency the Central Bank of the Turkish Republic was set up as a bank of emission. To finance and handle commercial transactions, the Commercial Bank of Turkey was organized. To meet the needs of agriculture and industry the Turkish government organized two special financial institutions, an agricultural bank and an industrial bank. In addition to these four banks which provided credit for the major economic activities of both the government and private enterprise, the Turkish government arranged for the founding of a *Credit Foncier* to provide loans on land and real estate and for the creation of savings banks and municipal banks to finance public works. The government of the Turkish Republic by these means not only supplied the immediate financial needs for expansion of the Turkish economy but encouraged the accumulation of capital for future investment.

Transportation problems.—One of the most pressing problems which confronted the Turkish government was that of transportation. The railroad system was quite inadequate to meet the needs of a modernized Turkey and the system of roads was even more inadequate. The greater part of Anatolia, with the exception of the coastal areas, had no commercially satisfactory outlets to the Black Sea, the Aegean, and the Mediterranean. In large areas of Asiatic Turkey agriculture could not rise above the subsistence level and minerals could not be developed profitably because the cost of transportation to Turkish and foreign markets was prohibitive.

An article by Robert W. Kerwin entitled "The Turkish Road Program" in the *Middle East Journal* of April 1950 throws much light on the relationship between the cost of ancient and modern systems of transportation and its bearing on the problems of economic modernization in Turkey and other Near Eastern countries. Caravan transportation whether on the backs of animals or in oxcart is exceedingly costly and time consuming. Perishable agricultural products and most bulk farm produce cannot profitably be transported any considerable distance. In many parts of Anatolia pack animals and oxcarts are still an essential part of the Turkish transportation system. Kerwin states in his article that an oxcart driver at a daily wage of $1.25 transports 500 pounds of freight a distance of five miles a day at a labor cost alone of $1.00 per ton mile, whereas a highly paid American truck driver can transport goods in the United States over modern highways at a high rate of speed and at an approximate cost of three cents per ton mile.[5] Motor transportation in the United States handles without difficulty bulk and perishable merchandise. Commercial farming and a standard of living above that of subsistence farming for a considerable portion of the rural population of Turkey depend upon the construction of modern highways and motorized transportation.

Turkey is predominantly an agrarian society and its exports are mainly agricultural produce. It is estimated that in 1936 over 80 per cent of all Turkish exports were agricultural in origin. Until outside capital is made available the modernization of Turkish agriculture, industry, and the transportation system will have to be financed from the agricultural exports which provide foreign credits.

Economic planning.—It is the fashion of our times to talk rather glibly about raising the living standards of the hundreds of millions of peasants in Asia by the process of modernization without realizing its complexities and all of its interrelated factors. The immense difficulties with which the Soviet government has been confronted in its attempt to modernize the vast and sprawling Soviet state and the huge problems that confront the Chinese Communists should alert us to the problems with which the governments of Turkey and of the other Near Eastern countries are faced in their endeavors to modernize their countries rapidly. The transformation of the Near East cannot be accomplished by wishfully polishing the modern Aladdin's lamp of economic planning in governmental bureaus at Washington and in United Nations committees at New York any more than it can be done by Congress voting billions for foreign aid.

Resistance to change.—Undoubtedly, the process of modernization is taking place in Turkey as well as in other Near Eastern countries, but it takes time before these revolutionary changes will be able to raise the standard of living of the urban masses, the peasants, and the nomads. It is naively utopian to believe that such changes can be brought about without considerable resistance from deeply entrenched vested interests whose power, wealth, and privileges are dependent on the maintenance of the old order and by the resistance of the illiterate masses, especially in the rural and tribal areas, who as yet are but dimly aware of what modernization could mean to them and who stubbornly cling to their way of life.

This process of change requires a strong government capable of efficient and effective action which it tends to produce in the form of dictatorships by individuals or oligarchies. It would seem that political democracy, as it is known in the West, is unlikely to function adequately until conditions favorable to its developments become a reality. It is therefore understandable that Mustafa Kemal and the People's Party governed the Turkish Republic in an arbitrary manner. And yet it does not seem unduly sanguine to think that the foundations of political democracy in Turkey are in the process of being laid.

We of the West, and this is especially so of Americans living in a dynamically revolutionary society in which the basic ways of living have been fundamentally changed in less than fifty years, resist the full implications with respect to changes in our patterns of beliefs and of thinking which modernization is forcing upon us. We seek to retain patterns which hardly conform to modern ways of living. The tenacity with which people cling to the well-worn ways is brilliantly depicted by J. B. Priestley in his novel *Daylight on Saturday*. The story centers around the lives of the workers in an English wartime airplane factory. The author describes those housewives who had taken jobs in the factory. He shows how little their new way of living changed the pattern of their thinking, their attitudes, their conversation, and their interests. Though they had become industrial workers they remained essentially family women.

An understanding of our own reluctance to give up the past and of our clinging to it should help us to understand the resistance of the masses of the Near East. The urban workers and more particularly the peasants and the nomads, whose ways of living as yet have not been greatly changed, have received few if any benefits from the process of change which is being forced upon them by the contact with the West and by their own rulers.

The basic patterns of life in the Near East for the majority of its peoples will not change significantly until the urban craftsmen become industrial workers, subsistence peasants become modern farmers, and pastoral tribesmen cease to be nomads. Until the patterns of life change, little change is to be anticipated in the psychology and ideologies of the peoples of the Near East. It is not surprising therefore that Lilo Linke, a young German writer who traveled widely through rural Anatolia in 1936, depicts in her very readable book *Allah Dethroned* village and provincial life differing only in minor unessentials from such as it was previous to 1914.[6] Revolutionary changes have only begun to affect the hinterland. Of course, the shift of the Turkish capital from the old city of Constantinople, officially renamed Istanbul, to the heart of the Anatolian plateau to ancient Ankara (formerly Angora) brought startling changes in its immediate vicinity with the construction of a modern city.

FROM CONSTANTINOPLE TO ANKARA

The transfer of the Turkish capital to Ankara was a dramatic historical event the future longtime significance of which it is impossible to determine. At the time the decision was made to establish permanently the seat of government in central Anatolia instead of on the shores of the Bosporus, recent and contemporary events weighed heavily on the minds of the Turkish nationalists. They were rebels against the old Ottoman regime, they hated the Byzantine and Levantine atmosphere of Constantinople, they thought in terms of Turanianism and wanted the capital to be a wholly Turkish city, which Constantinople had never been. Its non-Moslem, non-Turkish population had been too large, too wealthy, too important for the Ottomans to dominate it fully. The Kemalists wished to free themselves from the trammels of their non-Turkish past and to launch the new Turkish government in a less cosmopolitan and "tainted" environment. They fled from the fleshpots of Constantinople to the soon to be created fleshpots of Ankara.

The founding of the new capital poses some interesting questions to which no categorical answers should be given. The shifting of the site of the Turkish capital from a great economic center of trade, industry, and finance located on one of the great commercial highways to an inland provincial town resulted in a flow of wealth to the heart of Anatolia and brought to Ankara a governing class which otherwise would have remained in Istanbul. A Turkish bureaucracy at Ankara cannot so readily ignore conditions in Anatolia and the needs of the Turkish peasantry as the Ottoman bureaucracy had for centuries. The Ottoman government, however, was located at the economic center of the empire and was in close contact with those who held the reins of economic power and who controlled the economic life of the Ottoman state. The Turkish government at Ankara is distant from the great centers of commerce and industry, and its economic power and contacts with economic forces are due very largely to the Turkish Republic being a mercantilist state. With the increasing movement since 1945 in the direction of *laissez faire* capitalism there might be a shift of economic power from Ankara to Istanbul.

In a state organized on the basis of totalitarian "state capitalism" or "state socialism," the political center, wherever it may be located, becomes a great economic center also. Nobody has attempted to determine the significance of the location of the political capital far from the great economic centers of the state. Until the founding of the city of Washington, D.C., on the Potomac, the political capitals of the western world generally have been at centers where the vital functions of production, distribution, and finance were at least as important as those of government.

Psychologically and socially as well as economically there are important differences between a city whose function is primarily economic and one whose functions are essentially political. In a great economic center the population is enormously diversified in its social structure and in its activities with the result that the interplay between the great variety of occupational groups is vastly stimulating. In such a complex society hierarchical stratification is difficult to maintain and the individual can escape from the stultifying and oppressive feeling of being classified, whereby individual initiative is restricted to the highest ranks of a hierarchy and conformity is a vice imposed on the many.

In a purely governmental center where the population is largely made up of government employees, officials, legislators, and career bureaucrats, stratification seems inescapable, and a depressing consciousness of hierarchy is so omnipresent that even a high consumption of alcohol in leisure time cannot obliterate it. It may be that in Ankara there exist forces which make for the isolation of the new ruling class and a bureaucracy removed from the pulsing centers of economic life.

Up to the present time, however, the rulers of the Turkish Republic have been too preoccupied with the drive to modernize their country, with the problem of not becoming involved in World War II, and, since 1945, with their own involvement in the "Cold War" to have the leisure time in which to develop political arteriosclerosis.

CHAPTER XXI

The Kingdom of Iraq

The Arab lands of western Asia are now divided into several political units. Those of the Arabian Peninsula are the independent kingdoms of Saudi Arabia and the Yemen, the sultanates of Kuwait, Oman, and Hadhramaut in treaty relationship with Great Britain, the British Colony of Aden, and the Aden Protectorate. West of Arabia is the peninsula of Sinai now a part of the United Arab State. Northwest of Arabia are the republic of Israel, the Arab kingdom of Jordan, and the Arab republics of Lebanon and Syria. To the northeast of Arabia is the kingdom of Iraq, the land of the two rivers.

The kingdom of Iraq has no historical traditions as a national state. Its boundaries were determined by the European powers in accordance with their rival interests. Its frontiers conform to no principle of nationality. It lacks a homogeneous population with a common culture and a historical sense of unity. Its name stems from the time of the Arab conquest, when the Arabs called Mesopotamia, Iraq. The valley of the Tigris and the Euphrates, because of its long history and of the many states and peoples who have shaped its destiny throughout six thousand years, has had many different names some of which, like Mesopotamia and Iraq, are descriptive geographic terms with respect to the two rivers.

THE TWO GREAT RIVERS

Speaking geographically, practically all of modern Iraq lies within the watershed of the Tigris and Euphrates rivers and their principal tributaries. A considerable part of the watershed of the Euphrates and a lesser part of that of the Tigris, however, lie beyond the frontiers of Iraq. The headwaters of both rivers are in that part of the Turkish Republic previously known since classical times as Armenia. Rising northeast of Lake Van not far from Mt. Ararat near the frontier of the Soviet Socialist

Republic of Armenia the Euphrates flows in a westerly direction to Kharput, which is not far from the source of the Tigris. A short distance west of Kharput the Euphrates turns sharply to the south past Turkish Birijik and crosses the Turko-Syrian frontier and the Bagdad Railroad at Carchemish. Continuing southward for a way, some distance east of Aleppo it turns and flows to the southeast through Syria past Deir-ez-Zor, crosses the Syria-Iraq frontier at Abu Kemal, and passes Ramadi and Lake Habbaniya fifty miles west of Bagdad, where it again approaches the Tigris that it ultimately joins at Qurna about one hundred miles north of the Persian Gulf and half that distance north of Basra. The Tigris, rising in the mountains between Kharput and Malatya, flows through Turkey in a southeasterly direction to the Turko-Syrian-Iraq frontier at Faish Khabur and thence in a southerly direction past Mosul and Bagdad to its junction with the Euphrates, from where the two rivers are jointly known as the Shatt-al-Arab.

The Euphrates crosses the great Syrian Desert which extends from Jordan and Syria across southwestern Iraq. The Tigris skirts the foothills of southern Kurdistan which is the upland and highland part of northeastern Iraq. The land between the two rivers is like a sack tied two-thirds of the way down. The larger and upper part is bounded in the south by a line from Bagdad on the Tigris to Al Falluja on the Euphrates and in the north by a line from Abu Kemal to Faish Khabur. The smaller and southern part lies between Bagdad and Al Falluja in the north, and Qurna in the south.

Historical terminology.—In the time of the Sumerians and Akkadians the southern part of the valley was first known as the Land of Sumer and Akkad. When it was overrun by the Amorites, who built their capital in the southern lowlands on the Euphrates it came to be called Babylonia. Under Hammurabi, however, the empire of Babylonia extended far to the north and west. In the northern part of the valley along the Tigris, the Assyrian kingdom developed and eventually established its capital, Nineveh, near the site of the modern city of Mosul. Conquering the southern and northern parts of the Tigris and Euphrates Valley the Assyrians extended their conquests westward to Syria and Palestine, where the region of the Tigris and the Euphrates was spoken of as Assyria. Later, when the Assyrian dynasty was overthrown by the Chaldeans, this region was known as the land of the Chaldeans and Babylonians.

The Greeks called the upper part of the valley between the two rivers and north of the region of modern Bagdad and Al Falluja, Mesopotamia, which is a Greek compound of two words, "middle" and "rivers." The translation given to it in English, "between the rivers," misled modern writers and geographers into the error of using the term Mesopotamia to refer to the valley of the Tigris and the Euphrates from the Persian Gulf to eastern Anatolia. It is quite clear from the Greek geographer and historian Strabo that the Greeks used the word Mesopotamia to refer to the land between the two rivers northward from the region where they approach one another near modern Bagdad.[1] It is interesting to note that this region enclosed by the Tigris and Euphrates north of Bagdad is still called by the Arabs al-Jazirah, which may be translated as "the island" but more accurately refers to a land area encompassed by water. In modern times the entire valley came to be called Mesopotamia.

The Arab word Iraq means the banks of a great river "for the whole length thereof" and consequently is a more accurate term than Mesopotamia for this new Arab kingdom in the Tigris and Euphrates Valley. In earlier times Arab writers [2] used the terms Iraq-ul-Arabi and Iraq-ul-Ajami in referring to the part of the valley controlled respectively by Arabs and Persians. During the period of the Abbassid Caliphate the Tigris and Euphrates Valley area was divided into two administrative districts, the northern part of the valley being called, as it is today, al-Jazirah, and the southern part Iraq.

MODERN IRAQ

Geographical features.—The modern state of Iraq may be divided into five principal geographic areas. The land on the banks of and between the two rivers from Al Falluja and Bagdad south to Qurna is really the delta of the Tigris and Euphrates. It is called the lowlands. Part of the delta is comprised of land with a rich alluvial soil requiring, because of a maximum annual rainfall of only six inches, irrigation to make it cultivable; the remainder of the delta is made up of lagoons, lakes, and swamps. The average altitude of the delta is only one hundred and fifty feet. The land to the north of Al Falluja and Bagdad between the two rivers is a rolling semiarid plain where, for the most part, cultivation is impossible at any considerable distance from the banks of the rivers. This area, which in the northwest attains an altitude of 1000 feet, is really a northern extension of the Syrian Desert, the greater part of which lies south of the Euphrates. These desert uplands stretch down almost to the northwest corner of the Persian Gulf at Kuwait. The east bank of the Tigris north of Bagdad differs greatly from al-Jazirah and the Syrian Desert. Between the Tigris and the frontiers of Turkey and of Iran lies a land of upland plains, foothills, and high mountain ranges. It is crossed by tributaries of the Tigris flowing from the mountain ranges along the Turkish and Persian frontiers. To the north is the

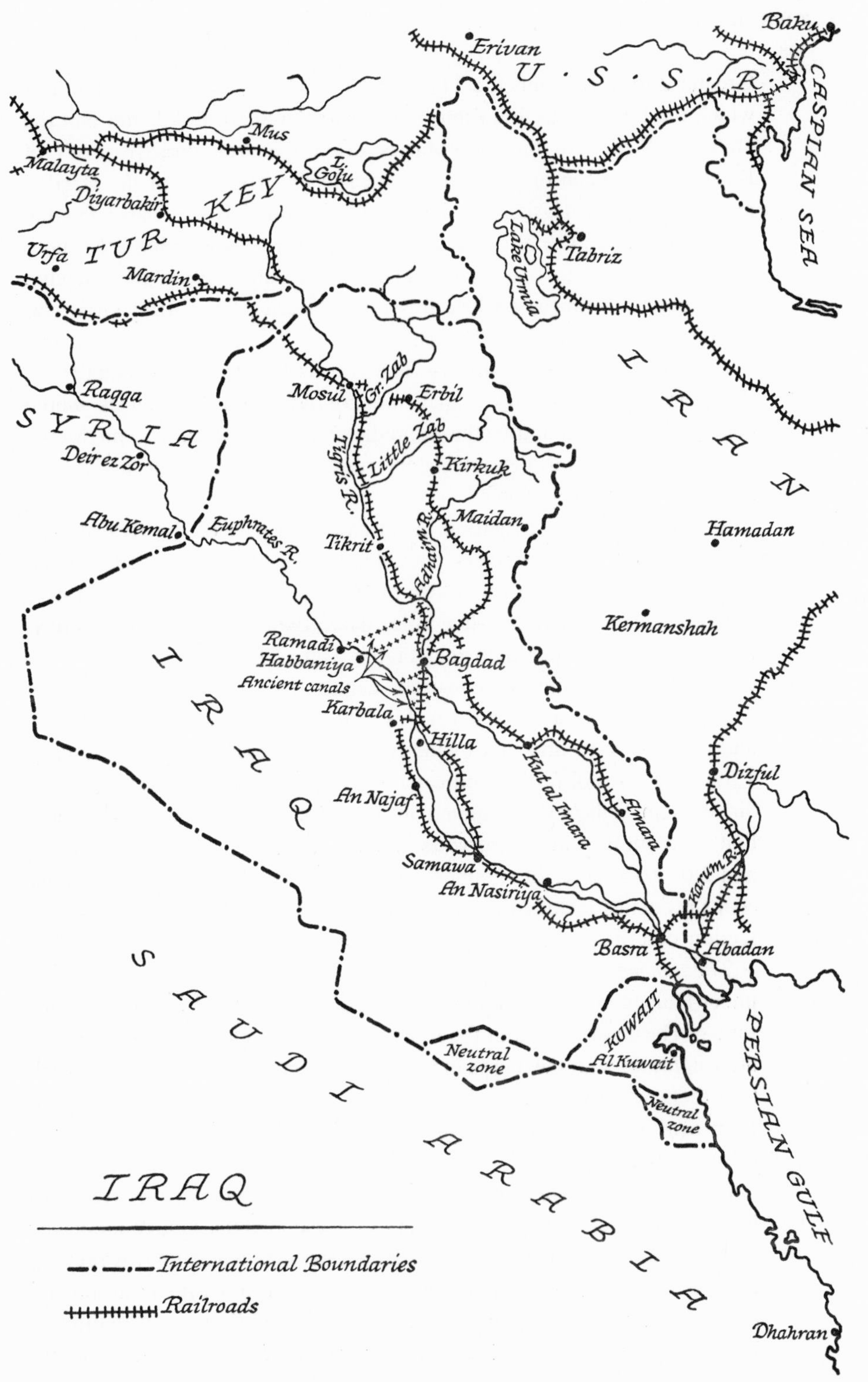

IRAQ
Baku
Erivan
U. S. S. R.
CASPIAN SEA
Mus
L. Golu
Malayta
Diyarbakir
TURKEY
Urfa
Mardin
Lake Urmia
Tabriz
IRAN
Mosul
Gr. Zab
Erbil
Raqqa
SYRIA
Tigris R.
Little Zab
Kirkuk
Deir ez Zor
Maidan
Abu Kemal
Euphrates R.
Tikrit
Adhaim R.
Hamadan
Kermanshah
Ramadi
Habbaniya
Ancient canals
Bagdad
IRAQ
Karbala
Hilla
Kut al Imara
Dizful
An Najaf
Amara
Samawa
Karun R.
An Nasiriya
Basra
Abadan
KUWAIT
Neutral zone
Al Kuwait
Neutral zone
SAUDI ARABIA
PERSIAN GULF
International Boundaries
Railroads
Dhahran

Greater Zab which joins the Tigris south of Mosul, eighty miles south of which the Lesser Zab flows into the Tigris; the Shatt al-Adhaim and the Diyala, which with their tributaries drain the area directly north of Bagdad, have been of great importance in the irrigation of the Bagdad area east of the Tigris. The Diyala River supplied the water for the famous Nahrwan Canal which extended from a point one hundred miles north of Bagdad to one on the Tigris ninety miles south of that city. High mountain ranges enclose this northeastern part of Iraq known as Kurdistan, the land of the Kurds.

Irrigation and flood control.—The rise and decline of civilization in the Tigris and Euphrates Valley are not unrelated to changes in the course of the rivers and to the unpredictable high floods. The prosperity of the valley has throughout history rested on a flourishing agriculture dependent upon irrigation.

Two factors made irrigation of an extensive part of the rich alluvial plain between the two rivers possible. In the region just south of Al Falluja and Bagdad the Euphrates and the Tigris approach one another within a distance of twenty-five miles. Here the level of the Euphrates is twenty-five feet higher than that of the Tigris. These geographical features made it possible to construct canals from the Euphrates to the Tigris across an area which is roughly 100 miles long from north to south and twenty-five to fifty miles wide from west to east, an area of roughly 1,500,000 acres of fertile land capable of being brought under irrigation. Sir William Willcocks estimated in 1909 for the Ottoman government that "without the aid of reservoirs. . . . 6,000,000 acres of winter crops and 3,000,000 acres of summer crops" could be counted on.[3] The Willcocks estimates included a far larger area than the limited region in the section described above.

The ancient canals.—Before the canals were destroyed by Tatars under Hulagu in 1258 A.D. at the height of the Abbassid Caliphate in the time of Harun al Rashid in the ninth century, five main canals connected the Euphrates with the Tigris in the Bagdad section of the valley. In addition there was the great Nahrwan Canal on the left bank of the Tigris from near Tekrit north of Bagdad almost to Kut-el-Amara south of the caliph's famed capital.

Floods and shifting river beds.—Erratic floods and shifting river beds have had their effect upon the history of Mesopotamia. Unlike the valley of the Nile, that of the Tigris and Euphrates has never known security from devastating floods. The annual inundation of Egypt is as regular as the cosmic system. Such is not the case in Iraq. So great was the first historically recorded flood that generations of children in the western world have played with Noah's Arks. The floods of the Tigris and Euphrates Valley are caused by the melting of the snow on the mountains and high plateaus of eastern Anatolia. Normally, during the springtime floods the Tigris rises some twenty-five feet, the Euphrates sixteen. For the people in the lower part of the valley even the normal floods are a serious problem because the river beds are above the general level of the land. Consequently, every year there is the danger of villages being engulfed by the floods and rich lands being ruined. The great floods, which occur from time to time, wipe out entire towns and cities, destroy extensive sections of the intricate system of irrigation canals and even change the course of the rivers.

When there was a wide shift in the course of a river, cities and towns no matter how great and rich nor how well or poorly governed had to be abandoned and soon fell into ruins. Twice within a thousand years the Tigris has shifted its course. In the seventh century about the time of the Arab conquest the Tigris shifted its bed from what approximately is now its present course to the Hai Branch, a distance of some fifty miles. Early in the sixteenth century near the time of the Ottoman conquest of Mesopotamia the Tigris shifted back again to its more eastern course.

In a land wholly dependent upon systems of irrigation and where, other than costly caravans, the principal transportation facilities are by river, one does not have to be a seer to understand that so significant a geographic change would affect the economic, political, and social life of the people of the valley. Such changes could result in much arable land becoming uncultivable for lack of water; they could disrupt transportation both by land and river; they could make uninhabitable populous cities and towns where industry and commerce flourished; and they could render useless extensive irrigation systems.

Another difficult problem confronting the people of the Tigris and Euphrates Valley is the fact that the waters of both rivers carry in solution a considerable amount of salts. As a result irrigated land which is not properly drained and "washed" becomes, sooner or later, uncultivable. Once fertile land supporting prosperous villages and towns may thus become barren wastelands. Irrigation and flood control are intricate matters which may be disrupted by a variety of factors. The result may bring disaster to wide areas. Unusually high waters, invasion and war, graft by government officials and sabotage by exploited serfs and slaves, and even mere carelessness may under certain conditions become catastrophic in their results. Those who know the Black River Valley in New York are familiar with the fact that for years local contractors, teamsters, and saloonkeepers, when other work was slack, deliberately cut trenches in the dikes of the Black River feeder of the Erie Canal near Forestport, and those who have lived in rural New Hampshire know that at times subsistence farmers have purposely set forest fires in order to obtain wage-paying jobs in periods of economic depression. It should not be surprising, therefore, if people in the valley of the Tigris and Euphrates sometimes may have changed the course of history out of either greed or need.

GEOPOLITICAL ASPECTS OF THE TIGRIS AND EUPHRATES VALLEY

As civilization spread from the southern end of the delta northward, those in the south became aware that their prosperity and even the possibility of their existence might depend upon what the people to the north did. Eventually, as population increased, a unified regulation of the rivers became essential, in fact indispensable, to the people who inhabited the river valley and depended upon the waters thereof. These are categorical imperatives of riverain people whether it be those of the Colorado, the Tennessee, the Rhine, the Danube, the Nile, or the Tigris and Euphrates. The wars between the Sumerian city states, the struggles to secure control of the Tigris and Euphrates Valley from north to south, are not unrelated to the physical factors concerning floods and irrigation and to the fact that the main highways north and south were the rivers and that the east-west roads were connecting links of the great caravan highways to and from the Mediterranean across Central Asia to China and India as well as to the northern steppes via the Caspian Sea and the Volga River.

Difficulties of political unification.—When the political unity of the Tigris and Euphrates Valley was achieved by the Babylonians and then by the Assyrians, the rulers sought to gain possession of the important highways across the Syrian Desert to the Mediterranean and to Anatolia. This made them a menace to their neighbors. The valley eventually became a battleground between powerful empires to both east and west. Likewise, in the twentieth century it was the interplay of the imperial interests of foreign powers which shaped the course of history in the Tigris and Euphrates Valley by creating conditions which gave birth to the kingdom of Iraq. Of these Great Britain long had considered the control, direct or indirect, of the valley of the Tigris and Euphrates essential to her imperial lines of communication. The discovery of petroleum in Iraq and in Iran only augmented British interests there.

Minorities—sectarian and national.—Internal factors, as well as external ones, make a strong unified government of Iraq exceedingly difficult. The population of the new Arab kingdom has many sharp divisions. Approximately five-sixths of the population, which is somewhat over 5,000,000, are Moslems, but of these half a million are Kurds who have their own language and somewhat primitive culture and very little in common with their fellow Arab Moslems. The Iraqi Kurds, for the most part, inhabit northeastern Iraq and have more or less close relations with the Kurds in Turkey and Iran. The Kurds are an upland and mountain people both pastoral and agricultural, who are dominated and exploited by their tribal and feudal chieftains. A certain degree of Kurdish nationalism has spread among the Kurds causing anxiety in Ankara, Tehran, and Bagdad.

With some two-thirds of the population Arabic, it would, at first glance, seem as if so large a cultural group would have little difficulty in dominating the minorities. This might have been the case were it not for the fact that the Arab Moslems are sharply divided into two bitterly antagonistic sects, the Sunnites and the Shiites. These two Islamic groups are separated geographically as well as religiously. For the most part the Shiites inhabit and predominate in the southern part of the valley. In addition to these major divisions there are minor ones due to religious and national affiliations. The 90,000 Assyrian Christians have been persecuted by Turks and Arabs and have been a rather serious problem. Until recent years the 100,000 Jews have been no trouble to the rulers, but since the rise of Zionism and particularly since the war between Israel and Iraq, the position of the Jews has become somewhat precarious. In 1950 it was reported in the *New York Times* that by a secret deal between the Iraqi and Israeli governments the Jews of Iraq were being transported to Palestine by air via Cyprus. This arrangement places the Iraqi government in a somewhat anomalous situation with respect to the other Arab states because it is abetting the immigration of Jews into Palestine.

The nomads.—A most serious population problem arises from the fact that such a large percentage of the population are nomads and seminomads control of whom is difficult for a government composed principally of urbanites. Most of the region south of the Euphrates to the borders of Saudi Arabia, Jordan, and Syria as well as a considerable part of upper Iraq, between the two rivers, is inhabited by Arab nomadic tribes known as Beduins, or Badawi. These Iraqi Beduins are part of the much larger Arab nomad world of the Arabian and Syrian deserts. Tribal activities, affairs, and movements in Saudi Arabia, Jordan, and Syria frequently have an effect upon the Iraqi Beduin tribes. The way of life, the patriarchal organization, and the tribal law of these Arab nomads lie outside the whole social and political structure of an organized urban society, and consequently special administrative institutions are required by the Iraqi government in dealing with the affairs of the Beduins. A different type of Iraqi Arab nomad is that of the shepherds of the Euphrates. They do not raise or own camels, they do not engage in raids, they are tenders of large herds of sheep which move from pasture to pasture but cannot roam far from assured supplies of water. Unlike the Beduins who frequently raid them, the Iraqi shepherds are not people of the desert. Their social organization, however, is patriarchal and tribal. Another important nomadic group is composed of the Kurdish tribes of northeastern Iraq who move annually from winter pastures in the upland plains to summer pasture lands in the mountains. To these people frontiers between Iraq and both Turkey and Iran are quite meaningless.

Considerable portions of the rural population of Iraq are seminomadic, but they are largely agricultural workers on the estates of the large landowners. These *fellaheen* retain a patriarchal and semitribal organization. Their tribal and village sheiks are dominant and powerful local potentates without whose support and collaboration effective government over the regions they control is difficult, if not impossible. In the latter days of Ottoman rule government officials dared not enter much of the rural area in the southern part of the Tigris and Euphrates Valley. In the swamps and lagoons of the lower part of the delta live people who are not Arabs, but are called the Marsh Arabs. Governmental administration of their affairs likewise presents difficulties. In the cities of Iraq the bulk of the population is made up of workers, from unskilled to highly skilled craftsmen, slowly giving way to an industrial proletariat increasing with the introduction of modern factories. The dominant urban classes are government officials, wealthy landowners, moneylenders, merchants, and the men of religion, ulemas, hodjas, muftis, cadis, and theological students.

OTTOMAN HERITAGE OF MODERN IRAQ

Economic stagnation.—Iraq became an independent state under an Arab ruler in 1932 three hundred and ninety-eight years after its partial conquest and annexation by the Ottoman Turks in 1534. For a period of a hundred years the Turks and Persians ruled parts of the Tigris and Euphrates Valley, but eventually it became an Ottoman possession in 1638 and so remained until 1918. When the Ottomans conquered the valley it had not recovered the prosperity of the years before Mongol and Tatar invasions and devastations of the thirteenth and fourteenth centuries. The intricate irrigation system had been largely destroyed. The Tatars had disrupted and changed much of the East-West nexus of ancient commerce and trade routes. The destruction of life and property by these Asiatic nomads was by no means the only factor affecting the economic life of the Tigris and Euphrates Valley.

The Mongol Empire linking China with Europe via the northern grasslands changed the situation in the Tigris and Euphrates Valley very considerably. In the great days of the Abbassids the Arabs pushed their commercial and financial activities northward across the Caucasus and via the Caspian Sea to the Volga River route of Russia. The great merchants and bankers of Bagdad carried on extensive operations with Kievan Russia and had in their control the trade routes leading across Central Asia to India and China from the Tigris and Euphrates Valley and also from the Volga-Caspian area. The Mongol Empire completely changed this advantageous position of the Bagdadi Arabs. Kievan Russia was annihilated. The Golden Horde with its headquarters on the Volga was in possession of the overland route to central Europe and the river routes to the north. The Tatar leaders of the Golden Horde also, through their relations with the Mongols in Mongolia and China, controlled the trade routes overland to central and eastern Asia. The Arab world in the Tigris and Euphrates Valley was in ruins, its commercial supremacy ended.

After the Turkish conquest of a country which had not recovered from the disasters that had overwhelmed it, another serious blow to its prosperity developed. The western Europeans who had discovered the all-water route to India and China, a route with which the caravan roads could not compete, broke the Italian-Arab monopoly of the trade between Europe and southern Asia. In addition to these political and economic upheavals, the valley underwent a geographic revolution—the Tigris shifted its course.

Ottoman administrative divisions.—This Arab addition to the Ottoman Empire was divided into the three administrative districts of the Mosul, Bagdad, and Basra vilayets. The Ottoman government at Constantinople gave little attention to the administration of Mesopotamia. The Porte's principal concern was its protection against attack by the Persians and the revenues which it gave the Imperial Ottoman government. Administrative posts were farmed out to high Turkish officials and to local pashas, emirs, and sheiks. Little or no consideration was given to the people and little was done to restore the prosperity of the Tigris and Euphrates Valley and to reconstruct its canals and irrigation system. Consequently, this potentially wealthy land instead of recovering from the misfortunes it had undergone for over three hundred years sank deeper into economic decline and political anarchy. Such remained the case until the nineteenth century when both the Turks and the British began to take a more active interest in the affairs of the Tigris and Euphrates Valley.

British occupation ends Ottoman rule.—The British invasion and occupation between 1914 and 1918 during World War I of what was then called Mesopotamia had political and economic as well as military objectives. The British during the four years of the war brought about more progress in the Tigris and Euphrates Valley than had centuries of Turkish rule. The channel of the Shatt-al-Arab was dredged and made navigable for ocean-going vessels; Basra was provided with a modern port, docking, and warehouse facilities; roads, railroads, and Decauville lines were constructed; river transport facilities were greatly augmented by fleets of motor launches and river steamships. Furthermore, as the British armies advanced, an efficient modern system of civilian government was organized by the highly trained Anglo-Indian officials provided by the government of India. Much was done to increase agricultural production and to facilitate commercial activity in order that local supplies might be made available to the British military forces and that law, order, and security might prevail along the British lines of communications from Basra northward.

Locally, the British were laying the foundations of an imperial colonial government patterned on that of British India. The ideal of the conscientious British civil servants was a sort of benevolent despotism which would efficiently administer the country and encourage its development much to the advantage of local ruling classes and of British enterprisers. At the same time the British Foreign Office was taking the steps which would result in Mesopotamia becoming, in one form or another, a part of the British Empire. These measures were made more difficult and complex by the necessity of reaching an agreement with France in regard to British and French claims to the Arab provinces of the Ottoman Empire, by the promises made to Sherif Hussein of the Hejaz in the Hussein-McMahon correspondence, by the Balfour Declaration promising the Zionists the establishment of a Jewish National Home in that part of the Arab lands known as Palestine, and by propaganda pronouncements of the Allied and Associate Powers in regard to those idealistic aims concerning the rights of small nations and of self-determination of peoples.

At the end of World War I the British political and military position in the Arabic Near East appeared, superficially, impregnable. British forces occupied Egypt, Palestine, Syria, Lebanon, and Mesopotamia. The British had a treaty with Ibn Saud, while Hussein and his sons were little more than British clients, or vassals, on the payroll of the British government. It looked as if there would be no question but that Mesopotamia would remain under British control and become a part of Britain's Asiatic Empire. There was, of course, the delicate problem of getting the French to give up their claim to the Mosul area which Mark Sykes had agreed in the Sykes-Picot Treaty should go to France. Between 1918 and 1923 Britain's position in the Near East changed very rapidly from a position of power to one of weakness.

EMERGENCE OF MODERN IRAQ

Mesopotamia and the Paris Peace Conference.—At the Paris Peace Conference in the winter of 1919 the protagonists of the League of Nations under President Wilson's leadership succeeded in having the Covenant adopted with its provisions for mandates, Class A mandates for certain parts of the Ottoman Empire and Class B and C mandates for the German colonies. Article XXII of the Covenant of the League of Nations, reads in part as follows: "Certain communities formerly belonging to the Turkish Empire have reached a stage of development where their existence as independent nations can be provisionally recognized subject to the rendering of administrative advice and assistance by a Mandatory until such time as they are able to stand alone. The wishes of these communities must be a principal consideration in the selection of the Mandatory." This was to require some adroit diplomatic maneuvers by the British government if it were to retain that control of Mesopotamia gained by military conquest.

The King-Crane Commission.—President Wilson prevailed upon the Big Four at Paris to accept a plan to send to the Near East "an International Commission on Mandates in Turkey" in order to determine the wishes of the various communities upon whom mandates might be imposed. When the other three powers, England, France, and Italy, decided not to send their respective sections of the International Commission, President Wilson instructed the American Section, which came to be known as the King–Crane Commission, to proceed to the Near East to carry out the purposes of the International Commission. As technical adviser on the Arab parts of the Ottoman Empire the author was asked to plan the itinerary and work of the King–Crane Commission in Palestine, Syria, and Lebanon. On inquiring whether the American Section would go to Mesopotamia he was told by Mr. Crane that it was not considered necessary because it was well known that the people of Iraq wanted Great Britain as the mandatory. This statement I did not challenge nor did Dr. King, Dr. Lybyer, and Dr. Montgomery. It was clear that Mr. Crane had no intention of permitting the commission to go to Iraq. It seems likely that Mr. Crane got his idea that the Iraqi favored the British control of Mesopotamia from leading Britishers at Paris. He probably met Gertrude Bell, who was Oriental Secretary to the acting Civilian Commissioner in Bagdad, Colonel Arnold T. Wilson, who had prevailed upon British authority to call Gertrude Bell to London for consultation in the winter and spring of 1919. Before leaving Bagdad she wrote to her father Sir Hugh Bell on December 17, 1918, in regard to the wishes of the Iraqi as follows: "About Arab rule. In Mesopotamia they want us and no one else, because they know we'll govern in accordance with the customs of the country." [4] From Paris on March 16, 1919, she wrote to Frederick Bell telling him of her luncheon with Lord Robert Cecil and T. E. Lawrence and in the letter said "I am deep in propaganda though I don't know that it does much good, I don't feel as if I can neglect the chance of doing something." [5]

Sir Arnold T. Wilson on November 30, 1918, had received instructions from the India Office which contained the following statement: "In our opinion it is of great importance to get a genuine expression of local opinion on these points, and one of such a kind that could be announced to the world as the unbiassed pronouncement of the population of Mesopotamia." On the same day Sir Arnold telegraphed his political officers in all of the administrative districts "detailed instructions for the taking of a plebiscite." [6]

It is in the light of this plebiscite of December 1918 that the attitude of British statesmen at Paris in 1919 with respect to the desires of the peoples of Mesopotamia should be considered. The statement by Henry White,[7] one of the members of the American Delegation to Negotiate Peace, to Sir Arnold that although he believed Mesopotamia was ready for self-determination it was "only a matter of form" makes Mr. Crane's assumption that it was unnecessary for the King–Crane Commission to go to Mesopotamia understandable.

The American commissioners did not realize the interpretation the French and the Arabs would give to their decision not to go to Mesopotamia. The French were disposed to believe that the United States was in cahoots with the British and that the King–Crane Commission was sent for the purpose of disposing of French claims to Syria and Lebanon. The Arabs were left to think that the American government, which had just recognized the British Protectorate over Egypt and disregarded the demands of the Egyptian nationalists of "Egypt for the Egyptians," would not oppose British control of Iraq.

Just one year later the Iraqi rebellion against the British broke out in July 1920. It was many weeks before it was brought to an end. Some sixty-five thousand troops were required to break the power of the Iraqi rebels, and it cost the British government approximately $100,000,000. If Mr. Crane, instead of basing his decisions on impressions received from officials of a foreign government, had had the benefit of the judgment of an adequate American intelligence service, the King–Crane Commission might have gone to Mesopotamia. Whether or not this would have eliminated the conditions which led to the revolt is purely speculative because its causes were varied and complex.[8]

The uprising changed Anglo-Iraqi relations, modified British policy, and led eventually to the termination of the mandate and the independence of Iraq.

British policies.—British diplomacy in the Near East for more than a hundred and fifty years has had a certain rigidity in its objectives and considerable flexibility of the means used in obtaining them. This is well exemplified in British policy with respect to the valley of the Tigris and Euphrates between 1914 and 1932. Before World War I the Persian Gulf area was almost a private British preserve, and in the Ottoman province of Mesopotamia the British were predominant politically and commercially. As long as the Turks remained on friendly terms with Great Britain and aided her in maintaining her dominant position there, the British felt satisfied that this strategically located area on the route to Persia and India was reasonably secure from access to her competitors, particularly Russia and Germany. When, however, Turkey under the C.U.P. threw in its lot with the Germans the British were determined to make sure of their control. The first step was to occupy the lower part of the Tigris and Euphrates Valley in order to protect the Anglo-Persian pipeline and oilfields and to deny the Turks and their allies access to the Persian Gulf. The next step was that of coming to an agreement with Russia and later in the Sykes-Picot Treaty with France to insure recognition of Britain's claim to lower and central Mesopotamia. Then followed military conquest which gave the British actual possession.

The promise to the Arabs, the growth of the Arab nationalist movement, the general unrest in Asia, and the rising resistance to western imperialism augmented by the Russian Revolution and Bolshevik propaganda together with the mandate system provided for in the Covenant of the League of Nations caused the British to consider the advisability of changing their policies if they were to retain control over the Tigris and Euphrates Valley.[9]

Mesopotamia after the British occupation of Mosul on November 7, 1918, allegedly under the terms of the Armistice of Mudros, remained technically occupied enemy's territory awaiting final disposition by the Peace Conference. The ratification of the Covenant of the League of Nations on April 28, 1919, assured that Mesopotamia would be placed under a mandate. Decisions arrived at in May by the Supreme Council of the Allies indicated clearly that Britain would eventually get the mandate for Mesopotamia. In June the Treaty of Versailles about clinched the matter and by August 1919 the Allied Supreme Council definitely decided upon the allocation of territories to be placed under mandate. Nominally, however, since no treaty with Turkey had been signed, Mesopotamia remained Ottoman territory occupied by the British on behalf of the Allies. Nevertheless, on September 15, 1919, at San Remo by an Anglo-French agreement France surrendered her claims to Mosul on the understanding that she would have a share in the petroleum of Mesopotamia and that British troops would evacuate Syria.

Assured, as they thought, of uncontested possession of Mesopotamia the British replaced military government by a civil administration under Sir Arnold Wilson. British army officers as well as civilian officials in Mesopotamia were largely Anglo-Indian and were dominated by the ideals of the Anglo-Indian army and of the Anglo-Indian civil service, with complete faith in the rightness of a government by highly trained Britishers aided in the lower ranks by native officials backed by a British controlled and officered native military force, justified by its honesty and efficiency. These men believed in British imperial rule whether in a colony, a protectorate, or a mandated territory, and following a successful war they were not aware that the heyday of European imperialism was over and its rapid decline had begun.

The mental attitude of the Anglo-Indian officer in Iraq in 1920 may be surmised from a statement by Lieutenant-General Sir Aylmer L. Haldane G. C. M. G., K. C. B., D. S. O., who in writing of the insurrection of 1920 in Iraq said: "But, as I have shown earlier, stationary and movable columns continued to collect fines in many areas, and teach the insurgents the price they had to pay for throwing down the gauntlet to the British Empire." [10] Of course, he was speaking of those insurgents who survived, those who perished were according to Moslem ideas enjoying the delights of the Islamic paradise, having died in fighting for Allah.

The Anglo-Indians were more than critical of the Arabian policy of the Britishers in Cairo who manned the famous British intelligence group known as the Arab Bureau. The Anglo-Indian Iraqi officers and officials resented Cairo's activities in Arabia; they spoke of "those amateurs" who supported Sherif Hussein and his sons; they questioned the entire policy of the Arab Bureau and were openly skeptical of the military and political ability of Colonel T. E. Lawrence.

Under the conditions existing in the Near East in 1919 and 1920 the Anglo-Indian policies in Mesopotamia were not adapted to the situation. In face of the resistance movement led by Mustafa Kemal in Anatolia, the nationalist uprising in Egypt, the proclamation of the Syrian National Congress on March 11, 1920, at Damascus recognizing Emir Faisal as King, it was hardly to be expected that the Iraqi would accept without resistance the imposition of a British mandate.[11]

The mandate and the Iraqi revolt.—Soon after it became known in Mesopotamia that at San Remo on April 25, 1920, the French and British had come to an agreement as to the allocation of the Class A mandates in the Arab land of western Asia resistance to the British began in the Tigris and Euphrates Valley. In June when the British High Commissioner, Sir Arnold Wilson, announced officially that the mandate for Mesopotamia had been assigned to Great Britain, Iraqi nationalists who had served in the Arab Forces under Emir Faisal drove small British military units out of posts along the upper Euphrates. In July the Iraqi insurrection broke out in the lower and middle Euphrates. The insurrection continued until autumn before it was crushed by the British. The Anglo-Indian forces suffered about 1600 casualties, the Arabs over 8000. The Anglo-Indian officials and officers attributed the uprising to the Syrian and Iraqi nationalists who, it was claimed, fostered unrest in Mesopotamia with gold supplied Faisal by the British Government, to Turkish nationalist agents who used Turkish gold to fan religious fanaticism, and to the Shiite clergy who wanted no interference in their affairs by the British in the region of the holy shrines of Karbala, Kufa, and Najaf. It would seem to an outside observer that the Anglo-Indian apologists confused the means used with the causes. Howbeit, the financial cost to the British of something near $100,000,000 and the threat to British control resulted in demands by the British public for the adoption of a new policy by the British government.

In Mesopotamia on October 17, 1920, the British High Commissioner, Sir Percy Cox, stated at Bagdad that it was the British government's intention to aid the Iraqi in establishing national government.[12] By November he had secured the co-operation of some of the leading Iraqi and had organized a Provisional Council and a Ministry. The next move in this political game was to secure an Arab prince who, while being acceptable to the Iraqi, would conform to British wishes. Several possible candidates were considered. The logical course was to choose Emir Faisal who had been forced out of Syria by the French in July 1920 after the French occupation of Damascus.

The British were most certainly under obligation to Faisal who had led the Arab forces against the Turks. The choice of Faisal was in some measure due to T. E. Lawrence, who was indignant at the deal meted out to the Arabs by the British and French imperialists. Churchill and Lloyd George because of the Iraqi insurrection were disposed to give ear to Lawrence's proposals. After affairs in the Near and Middle East were placed under the Colonial Office, in which a Middle East section was organized, Churchill shifted his position in the Cabinet, taking over the Colonial Office. With Lawrence in tow this ebullient British statesman went to Cairo in March 1920 to win Egyptian acceptance of the British offer of independence limited by a treaty granting specific rights to Great Britain and to find a solution of the Mesopotamian problem. As a young politician in England shortly after the conquest of the Sudan by Lord Kitchener in 1898 Churchill had said during an election campaign: "We are in the Valley of the Nile forever, and forever."

The Cairo conference decided that security could be maintained in Iraq by placing the main responsibility on the Royal Air Force and by so doing reduce both the number and cost of military personnel.[13] The conference of British Middle East civilian and military representatives also decided at Cairo to offer the throne of Iraq to Emir Faisal. Sir Percy Cox was officially informed of the decisions reached at Cairo and was instructed to make such arrangements as he deemed necessary for the choice of Emir Faisal as king. Churchill returned to London and told the House of Commons that British promises in regard to the creation of an Arab state would be fulfilled and that as for Emir Faisal his candidacy, which was progressing favorably, was a matter that rested with the British high commissioner in Bagdad. Emir Faisal, who at Cairo had given his assent to British plans for Iraq, proceeded to Basra, where he arrived on June 24, 1921.

Faisal chosen as king.—Percy Cox had no difficulty in obtaining a unanimous vote of the Provisional Council in favor of Faisal and a "rigged" plebiscite gave 96 per cent of the votes for the Hashimite emir who was proclaimed king of Iraq on August 23, 1921. With a satellite ruler in Iraq, the British thought their objectives could be achieved more effectively by a treaty than by a mandate, which implied restrictions by the new international organization. The British government therefore withdrew the proposed draft mandate it had submitted to the Council of the League of Nations in December 1920 and informed the Council that His Majesty's Government proposed to incorporate the principles of the mandate in a treaty with King Faisal of Iraq in place of a convention between Great Britain and the League.

Despite much opposition from Iraqi nationalists an Anglo-Iraqian Treaty was negotiated in October 1922, which left wide powers in the hands of the British high commissioner and British advisers attached to the Iraqi administration. British troops and air bases were maintained. Iraq, in fact, was practically a British protectorate and so remained until two years later when the Council of the League of Nations accepted the treaty and the subsidiary agreements, which by that time the Iraqi Assembly had ratified, in lieu of a mandate.

The Mosul settlement.—In the interim by the Treaty of Lausanne with Turkey signed in July 1923, the Ankara government renounced all claims to the Arab vilayets of the former Ottoman Empire with the exception of the Mosul district. By the terms of the treaty it was agreed that the boundary between Turkey and Iraq would be left for settlement after the signing of the treaty by negotiations between the Turks and the British. Since no agreement was reached by the two most interested parties within the nine-month period stipulated in Article 3 of the Treaty of Lausanne, the failure to agree was in accordance with treaty requirements placed by Great Britain on the agenda of the Council of the League of Nations in August 1924.

The Mosul Question was complicated by political and economic factors related to the fact that a very considerable proportion of the population of the Mosul area were neither Arabs nor Turks but Kurds, some of whom in their annual migrations went from the Mosul area into Turkey. The overwhelmingly important issue, however, was oil. The Turkish Petroleum Company organized before World War I had acquired rights to petroleum deposits in the Mosul area of northern Mesopotamia. It was well known that those oil resources were very great. During World War I the Germans lost their share in the Turkish Petroleum Company and it was taken over by the French in accordance with the Anglo-French Agreement of September 1919, by which they gave up their claim to Mosul.

The Arabs and the Turks were concerned about the Mosul oil as well as the British, the Dutch, and the French. American oil interests were also insistent that they should receive a share in the development of Mesopotamian petroleum deposits. The matter was not one which the League of Nations could decide lightly. Such a matter affecting populations of different nationality and race had to be decided in a manner which at least gave the appearance of concern for the rights of human beings rather than for the claims of vested interests. This, of course, required time.

The League of Nations appointed a Commission of Inquiry in September 1924. The British and Turks presented their memoranda and dubious statistical data to the commission which in July 1925 presented to the Council of the League of Nations a report which, as might well have been expected, was favorable to the British. The Turks then challenged the right of the League of Nations to fix the boundary, consequently the matter was referred to the Permanent Court of International Justice at The Hague, which august tribunal likewise gave a judgment favorable to Great Britain. Thus on December 16, 1925, the Council of the League of Nations awarded Mosul to Iraq, under the condition that the mandate be continued for twenty-five years in order to protect the non-Arab minorities in the Mosul area. In the Near East the League of Nations was doing splendidly. The great and powerful were obtaining what they wished under law without violence or threat of war.

Before the Mosul affair was brought to an end the Iraqi Assembly, realizing the potential financial importance of Mosul oil to the kingdom of Iraq and to its faithful officials, decided to ratify the Anglo-Iraqi Treaty of October 1922 and the four subsequent accords, which the Council of the League of Nations accepted in place of a mandate on September 27, 1924.

Iraq, with the major share of its oil, was safely in British hands, at least so it appeared. The people of Iraq nevertheless were far from satisfied. The ratification of the treaty had been obtained against the opposition of the Iraqi people by a British ultimatum that if it were not ratified by June 15, 1924, His Majesty's Government would ask the League of Nations to confirm the mandate instead of accepting the treaty.

Final steps toward independence.—Shortly after the Assembly had ratified the treaty with observations and reservations, it enacted with more satisfaction an organic statute and a new electoral law. Nevertheless, neither the British nor the Iraqi were satisfied with the arrangement. The British wished to be free from interference by the League of Nations and the Iraqi desired to rid themselves of the status of a people under a mandate. In conformity with a recommendation by the Council of the League of Nations a new Anglo-Iraqi treaty was drafted and approved by the League which was to run until 1950 unless Iraq became a member of the League of Nations previous to that time.

THE KINGDOM OF IRAQ, AN INDEPENDENT SOVEREIGN STATE

The British Colonial Office, aware of the dissatisfaction of the Iraqi with both the treaty and the mandate decided to make arrangements for the termination of the mandate under conditions favorable to Great Britain. A treaty which was to become effective when Iraq was admitted as a member of the League, was negotiated by the British with the Iraqi government. With this insurance policy in hand the British government requested the Council of the League of Nations in January 1930 to draft the conditions under which the mandate could be terminated. The matter was handed over to the Permanent Committee on Mandates, but it was not until the autumn of 1931 that the conditions recommended by the Committee were approved. The following year, on October 3, 1932, Iraq was admitted to the League.

The Anglo-Iraqian treaty of 1930.—Iraq was the first of the Class A mandates to be recognized as an independent state. Although its independence had been attained, the conditions under which Iraq was accepted as a member of the League of Nations placed restrictions on its absolute sovereignty. Furthermore, the Anglo-Iraqi treaty of 1930 also limited the sovereignty of Iraq. The British had evolved a diplomatic technique whereby under a bilateral treaty they attained such control as they considered necessary to the security of their imperial lines of communications and other imperialist interests without assuming the invidious burden of colonial rule which the people of Asia were determined to rid themselves of. The Anglo-Iraqi and the Anglo-Egyptian treaties have become models for those western nations that feel the need of extending their political and economic interests in the Near East. This less obvious form of imperialism, temporarily at least, was less objectionable to the Near Eastern countries concerned and escaped critical examination by the general public in the western political democracies. The ruling classes and the political leaders of the Near East were able under the treaty device to obtain the aid, diplomatic as well as economic and military, necessary to the maintenance of their power without risking a national outcry against western imperialism. In the Near East, however, it is somewhat more difficult to disguise imperialism under the cloak of treaty relationships than it is in the western nations. Despite their illiteracy, the people of the Near East, confronted by the realities of power, understand somewhat more clearly the significance of what they see in the world about them.

Because of the significance in the Near East of this modern streamlined method by which a great power controls a small power, the Anglo-Iraqi treaty of 1930 is of considerable interest. The elements of control lie largely in the field of foreign relations and military matters which are sometimes dealt with in annexes to such treaties. In Article 1 of the Anglo-Iraqi treaty both parties agreed to "full and frank consultation between them in all matters of foreign policy which may affect their common interests" and undertook "not to adopt in foreign countries an attitude which is inconsistent with the alliance or might create difficulties for the other party thereto." Article 1 gave the British effective control over the foreign affairs of Iraq. Article 4 contains the following sentence: "The aid of His Majesty the King of Iraq in the event of war or the imminent menace of war will consist in furnishing to His Britannic Majesty on Iraq territory all facilities and assistance in his power including the use of railways, rivers, ports, aerodromes and means of communication." In Article 5 although both parties recognized that the responsibility for maintaining internal order and defense against aggression rested on the King of Iraq, "nevertheless His Majesty the King of Iraq recognizes that the permanent maintenance and protection in all circumstances of the essential communications of His Britannic Majesty is in the common interest of the High Contracting Parties. For this purpose and in order to facilitate the discharge of the obligations of His Britannic Majesty under Article 4 above His Majesty the King of Iraq undertakes to grant to His Britannic Majesty for the duration of the Alliance sites for air bases to be selected by His Britannic Majesty at or in the vicinity of Basra and for an air base to be selected by His Britannic Majesty to the west of the Euphrates." In the annexure to the treaty, which was stipulated to be an integral part of it, all the military i's were dotted and the military t's crossed. Of particular interest to Americans are Articles 5 and 6 of the annexure, which have been adopted in modified form by the United States government in arrangements with countries far beyond the confines of the Near East. Articles 5 and 6 read as follows:

5

His Britannic Majesty undertakes to grant whenever they may be required by His Majesty the King of Iraq all possible facilities in the following matters, the cost of which shall be met by His Majesty the King of Iraq.

(1) Naval, military and aeronautical instruction of Iraqi officers in the United Kingdom.

(2) The provision of arms, ammunition, equipment, ships and aeroplanes of the latest available pattern for the forces of His Majesty the King of Iraq.

(3) The provision of British naval, military and air force officers to serve in an advisory capacity with the forces of His Majesty the King of Iraq.

6

In view of the desirability of identity in training and methods between the Iraq and British armies, His Majesty the King of Iraq undertakes that, should he deem it necessary to have recourse to foreign military instructors, these shall be chosen from among British subjects.

He further undertakes that any personnel of his forces that may be sent abroad for military training will be sent to military schools, colleges and training centres in the territories of His Britannic Majesty, provided that this shall not prevent him from sending to any other country such personnel as cannot be received in the said institutions and training centres.

He further undertakes that the armament and essential equipment of his forces shall not differ in type from those of the forces of His Britannic Majesty.

Whereas these military arrangements were highly satisfactory to the British War Office and to the British manufacturers and suppliers of ammunition and armament, there were those among the Iraqi who clearly understood the implications of them and resented the tutelage they implied. Even though Iraq was governed by an oligarchy under the façade of constitutional government, there was among the ruling classes a strongly anti-British faction, who despite the disastrous relationships between the Ottoman Turks and the Germans during World War I, looked to Germany after the rise of Hitler, as a means of freeing Iraq from British domination. Similarly, after 1945, there are those in the Arab states who look to Soviet Russia.

The fate of the Assyrian Christians.—The new independent kingdom of Iraq was faced with the problem of a Christian minority whose security and rights were of considerable concern to the western countries, where it was feared the Iraqi were going to pursue the old Ottoman policy of persecution of Christian minorities. A tiny remnant of the ancient Christian sect of the Assyrians had survived the vicissitudes of the centuries. Until World War I they lived in the mountainous Hakkiari country in the extreme southeastern part of the present Turkish Republic about one hundred miles north of Mosul. These hardy Christian mountaineers had joined the Russians in the war against Turkey and consequently found themselves in a most difficult position after the Russian collapse in 1917. To save themselves from the wrath of the Turks they sought refuge in Mesopotamia, where they became "displaced persons" under the protection of the British.

When the insurrection in Iraq broke out in 1920 the British organized levies of Assyrian Christians who made first class soldiers, as noted by Gertrude Bell in her *Letters,* against the untrained Arab Moslem revolutionists. British employment of this Christian minority to quell a popular and Islamic uprising bred, quite inevitably, ill-will against the Assyrians among the Arabs. When the League of Nations awarded the Hakkiari country to Turkey, the Turkish government refused to allow the Assyrians to resettle there. Wishing to retain their religious and historical identity the Assyrians asked the League of Nations to grant them the status of an autonomous national group in Iraq. When this was refused them, some of the Assyrian leaders decided to explore the possibility of settlement in Syria under the protection of the French. Armed bands of Assyrians leaving their women and children behind crossed over into Syria, but finding conditions there unsatisfactory they decided to return to Iraq. At its frontier they got into a row with the Iraqi border guards and killed them. This incident precipitated an armed conflict between the famed Assyrian fighters, who had been trained by the British, and troops of the new Iraqi army. Before the civilian government at Bagdad learned what was happening the Iraqi commander, General Bikr Sidky, who was reputed to be notoriously anti-Assyrian permitted a massacre of 400 unarmed Assyrians and invited Kurdish and Arab tribesmen to loot and pillage the Assyrian villages and encampments in a manner reminiscent of the days of Abdul Hamid's reign. When the civilian government regained control of the situation it took measures to supply relief to the destitute Assyrians.

These valiant stubborn people had come to the end of their long tempestuous history, victims of the hatreds engendered by the clash between western imperialism and the rising nationalism of Near Eastern peoples. A few thousand Assyrians were provided with refuge beyond the frontiers of Iraq and the remainder, numbering less than thirty thousand, remained scattered in northern Iraq.[14]

The new Arab state was soon caught up in World War II. Within twenty years after the Paris Peace Conference of 1919 the great competitive states of the western world again plunged into war as a result of their inability to solve the social, economic, and political problems of the modern world. During this brief breathing spell the valley of the Tigris and Euphrates was brought more fully into the swiftly whirling torrent of modernization. Those without historical perspective tend to be overcritical of the slow development of Iraq because they do not take into consideration that in 1919 life in Iraq in most all of its phases was preindustrial. The nomads lived as they had for centuries past. In 1930 approximately 56 per cent of the population were pastoral and agrarian tribes, 32 per cent were settled rural dwellers, and only 12 per cent were urban dwellers concentrated in the three large cities of Mosul, Bagdad, and Basra.[15]

Faisal I, 1921–33.—While comparatively little change took place in the way of living of the agrarian and pastoral inhabitants of Iraq during the twenty years between the two World Wars, the foundations for modernization were being laid. Land and river transportation was improved by the extension of rail, motorcar, and motorboat facilities. In the cities modernization was more rapid. Health and sanitary conditions were greatly improved, and a secular system of education began to modify social outlook and customs. Basra became a modern port and new construction in Bagdad forecast future development along modern lines.

Without the dynamic leadership of a Mustafa Kemal, King Faisal I, as a somewhat mild and benevolent despot, encouraged progress in Iraq, where he had acquired some prestige as the commander of the Arab military forces which had aided the British in driving the Turks out of Syria. During the war years he had gathered around him many of the young Iraqi nationalists who had been officers of the Ottoman army and members of a secret Arab revolutionary society, *Al Ahd.* With the support of these Iraqi officers, among whom the most notable was the youthful Nuri-es-Said many times since premier of Iraq, and buttressed by the British whose "client" he was, King Faisal I managed to maintain a considerable degree of political equilibrium until his death in 1933. Since then political life in Iraq has at times been more turbulent during the short reign of Faisal's son, King Ghazi I and during the early years of the reign of Ghazi's son King Faisal II who came to the throne at four years of age following the death of his father in 1939 as the result of an automobile accident.

Iraq, like all the other Near Eastern countries, became involved, directly or indirectly, in World War II. Its affairs, domestic as well as foreign, became interwoven with those of the other Arab lands and with world events which affected all the Near East. Consequently, some knowledge of what took place in Syria, Lebanon, Arabia, Palestine, and Transjordan between 1919 and 1939 is necessary before pursuing further the history of Iraq.

CHAPTER XXII

Syria and Lebanon Between Two World Wars

❁ FESTERING RIVALRIES

No sooner had the Turks been driven out of Syria and Lebanon by the Egyptian Expeditionary Force under General Allenby and the auxiliary forces of Emir Faisal than a three-cornered struggle began between the Arabs, the British, and the French. This was fostered in part by the military administrative organization which General Allenby, Commander-in-Chief of the occupation forces, set up. Occupied Turkish territory from the Egyptian frontier to the Amanus Mountains (Alma Dağ) was divided into three administrative districts known as O.E.T.S. (Occupied Enemy's Territory South), which was Palestine; O.E.T.W., which was the coastal strip from Ras en Nakura north of Haifa to Alexandretta; and O.E.T.E., which comprised the territory east of the Jordan and the hinterland of Syria from Damascus to Aleppo. All three of these areas were under the supreme command of General Allenby, with O.E.T.S. administered by a British military governor, O.E.T.W. by a French military governor, and O.E.T.E. by Emir Faisal, Commander-in-Chief of the Arab forces representing his father, the king of the Hejaz.

Military aspects 1917–18.—The military campaigns of 1917 and 1918 had a psychological impact upon the attitude of the Arabs, the British, and the French in the hectic period immediately following the end of World War I. Technically, the forces under Allenby's command were those of the Allies—the Arabs, the British, the French, and the Italians. Actually, the bulk of his command were British, Anglo-Indian, and Anzacs (Australians and New Zealanders). There was a small French cavalry contingent with the Egyptian Expeditionary Force in

Palestine and a French Moslem Algerian unit in the Hejaz which operated in conjunction with Faisal's Hejazi forces. The Italians had only a small token unit with Allenby's main forces. The Arabs composed a separate force commanded by Faisal under Allenby but not integrated with his troops.

The French were very much aware of the fact that their prestige suffered greatly because of the military predominance of the British in Egypt, in Mesopotamia, in Palestine, and in the Levant. To Arabs the French were a negligible factor in driving out the Turks. Furthermore, the Arabs attributed to the Hejazi forces of Faisal a far more important role than they actually played. All parties concerned knew that the British financed and equipped the Arab forces. These were factors which influenced the French who considered Faisal as a stooge of the British.

The Arabs played no part in the conquest of Palestine other than as a cover for Allenby's right flank east of the Jordan River. When, however, British forces late in September 1918 demolished the Turkish army in Palestine and swept northward through Syria and Lebanon, the political, if not the military role of the Arab forces took on much added significance. When the Turks fled from Damascus without attempting its defence, the British authorized the Arab forces to enter the great Syrian metropolis before their own forces. This helped to create the impression that the Hejazi troops under Faisal had driven out the Turks. The Arab forces occupied the city while British forces camped on its outskirts. Furthermore, Allenby authorized Emir Faisal to organize the military government of Damascus.

The French were indignant at the handing over of the city to the Arabs and at the political activities of the Arab military government. In fact during the first few days of the occupation an official and passionate protest was made by a French officer to the author, who was then American military observer attached to Allenby's G.H.Q.

After the fall of Damascus British and Arab troops rapidly overran the Syrian hinterland from Damascus northward through the Bekaa, Hollow Syria as it was called in classical times, that lovely valley lying between the Anti-Lebanon and the Lebanon mountain ranges and watered by the Leontes and Orontes rivers, which have their sources therein. Following the Orontes in its northern course the British and Arab cavalry dashed through the Syrian cities of Homs and Hama and thence on to Aleppo. To the inhabitants of the Syrian hinterland their deliverers from the Turks were the Arabs aided by the British.

Along the coast the situation was somewhat different. The Turks fled the ports of Syria and Lebanon before the arrival of the Allied forces. Ottoman officials on their departure turned over the administration to local Arab notables who immediately telegraphed the news to Emir Faisal at Damascus. Promptly, the Arab general Shukri Pasha Ayoubi, riding along trails across the mountains, went secretly to Beirut where he hoisted the Sherifian flag of the Arab forces and took over the government of the city. Having arrived there before the British forces reached Beirut, Shukri Pasha installed himself as military governor while a French warship lay at anchor in the harbor. The French admiral had to stand by helplessly and watch the Arabs take possession of a territory which by the Sykes-Picot Agreement was most definitely set aside as a part of the French spoils of war in the Near East. When the British troops arrived Shukri Pasha was ordered to haul down the Sherifian flag. This he refused to do, so it was cut down by British soldiers and Shukri returned to Damascus, his daring *coup d'état* having failed. Later, French troops of the D.F.P.S. (*Le Détachement Français en Palestine et Syrie*) were transported by sea to the coastal area and their French commander appointed military governor of O.E.T.W. by General Allenby. This was an inauspicious beginning for Franco-Arab relations in Syria and Lebanon during the next two decades.

This incident increased the tension between the French and the British and further convinced the French that the English were working to create a situation which would make it possible to eliminate France from the Arabic Near East. Without raising the question of the integrity of General Allenby or the honesty of the British Cabinet with respect to honoring their obligations to the French, it may be said categorically that there were among the British in the Near East those who were strongly anti-French, who felt that the French had done nothing to drive the Turks out of the Arab lands of western Asia, and who were not averse to creating situations which would make the position of the French there untenable.[1] There were Britishers who would have subscribed gladly to the statement which the French officer and author, Comte R. de Gontaut-Biron, attributed to a British agent in Syria: "Nous saurons bien dégouter la Syrie de la France, et la France de la Syrie" ("We well know how to disgust Syria with France and France with Syria").[2]

French handicaps.—The French were in a very weak position in the Near East and particularly so in the Arab lands. In military matters they were at a great disadvantage. The small French contingent with the Arab forces was composed of colonial troops from North Africa under the command of Colonel Bremond, a French officer who, although he had fought with Sherifian forces from the beginning of the campaign in the Hejaz to its close at Aleppo, is little known outside of France except in narrow military circles. He had no Lowell Thomas to make him world famous nor did he have millions of pounds sterling to distribute among the Arab tribes. The French detachment in Palestine and Syria, attached to the Egyptian Expeditionary Force, was so small that few people realized that France had any troops in the Levant. Instead of sending French soldiers to occupy enemy territory in Lebanon and Cilicia, the French War Office trained and equipped the Legion of the Orient composed of Armenians and Syrian volunteers, neither of whom had any support or backing among the Arab Moslems and Arab nationalists. Furthermore, the Armenian troops proved undisciplined and unreliable. The military prestige of France, although she had won a great victory over Germany, was at a very low ebb among the Arabs and throughout the Near East. The defeat of French forces by the Turkish troops of Mustafa Kemal north of Aleppo and in Cilicia did nothing to enhance the military reputation of the French.

The political position of the French likewise was far from strong. France, as a Catholic country, had long been the main supporter of the Catholic Maronites in the Lebanon as well as of all other Catholics. Among the other Christians, particularly the numerous and powerful Orthodox community, the French had comparatively few supporters. The Orthodox higher clergy were for the most part strongly anti-French and feared French rule in Syria and Lebanon as detrimental to their power and prestige. The Druzes of Lebanon as well as of Jebel Druze in Syria had long been pro-British and anti-French, generally speaking. Among the great majority of Sunnite Moslems in Syria there was a strong anti-French feeling which had been augmented by propaganda of the Arab nationalists and by Moslem religious leaders who feared the French as supporters and protectors of the Arab Christians. Nevertheless, there was a nucleus among the Moslems whose members were pro-French. In the main this group centered around the former Algerian family of Abdul Kader who, although exiled by the French, were devoted to France. The French had some influence among the Syrian Arab tribes certain of whom did not welcome the Sherifians from Mecca.

Most Christians and many of the enlightened Moslems were dubious about the role Hussein Ali, King of the Hejaz and Sherif of Mecca might play in Syria. Educated Syrians looked upon the Bedouin Arabs of Arabia as fanatical and uncivilized tribesmen. It was feared that Emir Faisal might become the instrument of imposing Mecca's rule upon Syria. This, however, did not cause many of the Moslem Syrians or non-

Catholic Christian Syrians and Lebanese to turn to France, although there were some who did.

The fact that the Emir Faisal and his Arab forces were subsidized by the British placed the French in an awkward position and convinced many of them that the anti-French attitude and propaganda of the Arabs were of English origin and at the suggestion of the British. In fact much of the opposition by the Arabs of Syria and Lebanon to a French mandate was attributed by the French to the influence and activities of British agents and of Dr. Bliss and his associates of the American Protestant University at Beirut.

Among the French as among the British, there were those who, looking upon the Near East as their private preserve, had no understanding of what was going on among the oppressed and exploited peoples of Asia and tsarist Russia. In 1918 and 1919 there were French and English leaders who thought that with a few hundred million dollars and a few tens of thousands of troops they could smash the Bolshevik revolution in Russia, divide up Turkey, partition the Arab lands, control Persia, keep Egypt and North Africa under control, refuse dominion status to India and self-government to French Indo-China. The awakening of the Arabs, the growing strength of Arab nationalism, the intensified opposition to imperialism and the determination to be free were not understood by either French or British colonials and imperialists or military men in the years following World War I.

It seems unfortunate for the French and more so for the Arabs who lost their lives in conflict with French troops between 1919 and 1939 that France did not send a man of larger caliber, broader vision and higher official status than Georges Picot to deal with an exceedingly difficult situation. A Foreign Office career man whose position had been the minor one of French consul general at Beirut was hardly in a position to cope with one of the great and dynamic captains of World War I. It would have required a much bigger man and one with much higher official status to have dealt with General Allenby on terms of equality. In his attempts to maintain French interests and prestige in the Levant Georges Picot only irked and irritated Allenby, whose irritation with and treatment of Picot were attributed to deliberate attempts by the British to humiliate the French. The British like all other people who believe they have a monopoly of power were difficult to deal with. There was all the more reason therefore to send a Frenchman with the highest qualifications to handle matters with Allenby.

Clemenceau forces the issue.—The French were very unhappy about the situation which confronted them in the Near East at the end of

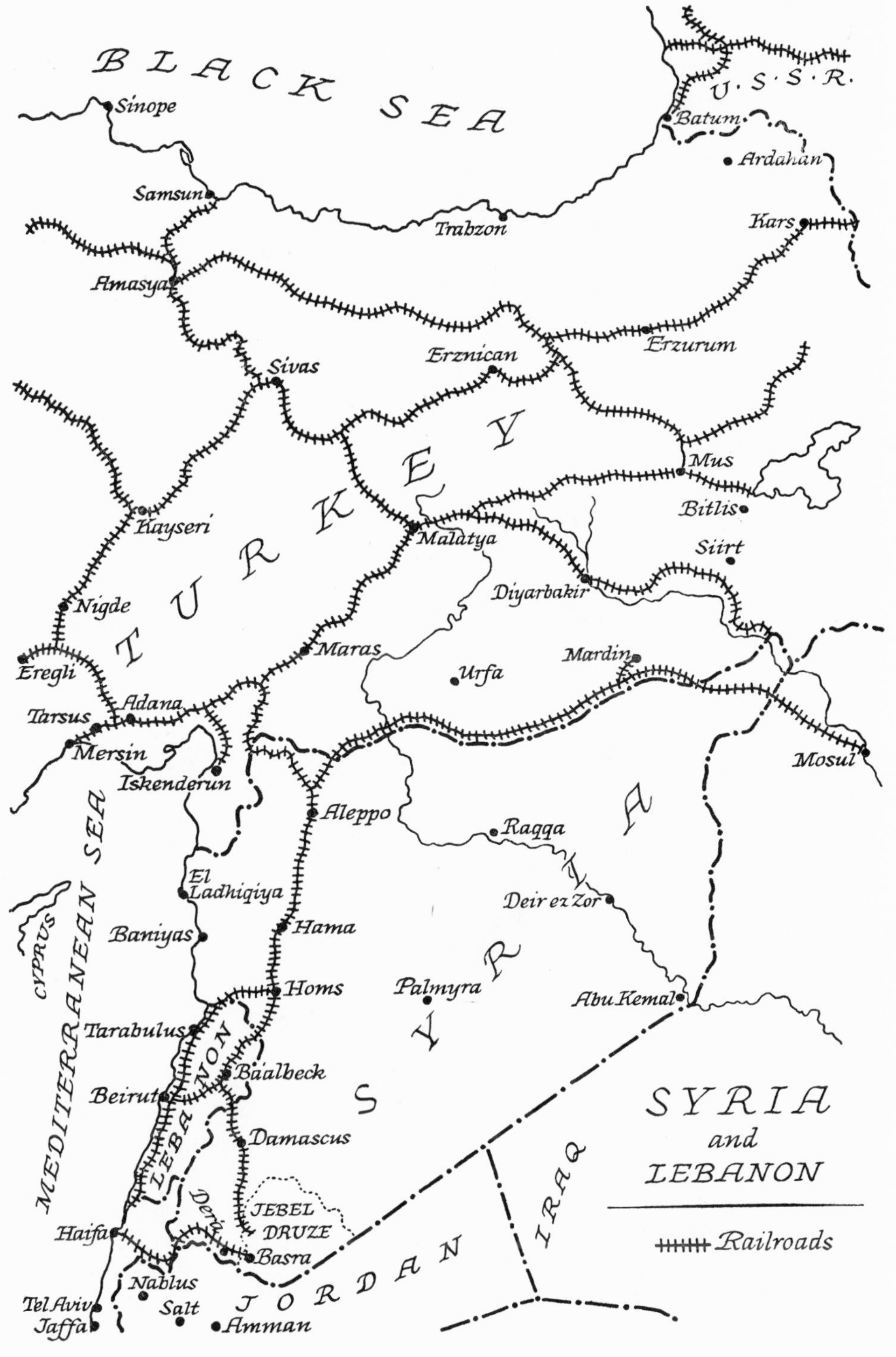

BLACK SEA
U.S.S.R.
Sinope
Batum
Ardahan
Samsun
Trabzon
Kars
Amasya
Erzurum
Erznican
Sivas
TURKEY
Mus
Bitlis
Kayseri
Malatya
Siirt
Diyarbakir
Nigde
Maras
Mardin
Urfa
Eregli
Adana
Tarsus
Mersin
Mosul
Iskenderun
Aleppo
Raqqa
MEDITERRANEAN SEA
CYPRUS
El Ladhiqiya
Deir ez Zor
Baniyas
Hama
Homs
Palmyra
Abu Kemal
SYRIA
Tarabulus
LEBANON
Baalbeck
Beirut
Damascus
SYRIA and LEBANON
IRAQ
Dera
JEBEL DRUZE
Haifa
Basra
Railroads
Nablus
JORDAN
Tel Aviv
Salt
Jaffa
Amman

1918 and on the eve of the Paris Peace Conference. The Arab lands of western Asia had been wrested from the Turks by armies under British command and largely composed of troops which were British, Australian, and Anglo-Indian. Mesopotamia, Palestine, Syria, and Lebanon were under the control of British military commanders. British commitments to Sherif Hussein, the Balfour Declaration, the proposals for a system of mandates, British exclusive control over the Mosul area of northern Mesopotamia which by the Sykes-Picot Agreement lay within the zone of French influence, known as Zone A, and the occupation of the rest of Zone A by the Arab forces under Emir Faisal appeared to the French as a serious menace to their ambitions and hopes in the Arabic Near East. Consequently, Premier Clemenceau at London in December 1919 decided to have a showdown with the British in order that a clear-cut understanding might be arrived at before the Peace Conference met at Paris so that the British and French could present a united front against any attempt by President Wilson to set aside the Anglo-French wartime secret treaties.

The French government, which during the war had come to realize the enormous significance of petroleum with respect to national security, was determined to obtain the German share of the Mesopotamian oil fields which the Deutsche Bank secured in 1914 through the Turkish Petroleum Company. By the Sykes-Picot Agreement Britain had made certain of exclusive control of Mosul oil when the Mosul area was included in the zone of French influence. Clemenceau was prepared to make territorial concessions to the British in order to secure petroleum rights in Mesopotamia. Lloyd George, the British Prime Minister, stated that his *quid pro quo* would be a British mandate in Palestine instead of international control, and the transfer of the vilayet of Mosul from the zone of French influence to that of British influence, a shift from Zone A to B. Clemenceau agreed to these changes in the Sykes-Picot Agreement if a satisfactory petroleum settlement should be reached, if Britain would give full support to France in opposing any changes the United States might propose with regard to the Sykes-Picot Agreement; and if in the event of a mandate system being adopted, Britain would support a French mandate over the Red Zone (direct French control) and over Zone A minus Mosul (Zone of French influence).[3]

Georges Clemenceau returned to Paris thinking he had everything well nailed down. The French Premier knew how to handle the seasoned lumber of nineteenth-century imperialistic diplomacy, but he had had no experience with the green timber of Wilsonian idealism in the construction of a "new world." England, in serious trouble with the nationalists in Egypt who were demanding representation at the Paris Peace Conference, wanted American recognition of the British protectorate so that the proposal of "Egypt for the Egyptians" would not be discussed by the "peace-makers." In addition to this the British were under obligations to the Arabs by the McMahon-Hussein correspondence. Having promised the Arab land of Palestine to the Jews, the British were also anxious to placate the Arabs by limiting French control to the coastal area of Syria. In February 1919 the British presented proposals accompanied by a map showing the French mandate limited to the coastal area of Syria. In April, as hoped, President Wilson recognized the British protectorate in Egypt. Even between allies the game of power politics tends to be ruthless and unscrupulous. As far as "log-rolling" goes, international politics differ little from domestic politics except for the fact that war may result from too much success.

President Wilson insists on self-determination.—Wilson, having made concessions contrary to his idealistic proposals for a new world order, temporarily was determined to see that the right of self-determination should be applied to the Ottoman Near East. Conveniently overlooking the fact that under the persuasion of his Jewish supporters in the United States he had completely disregarded the right of self-determination of the Arabs in Palestine when he gave his approval to the Balfour Declaration, Woodrow Wilson refused to recognize Anglo-French wartime commitments and insisted that an International Commission on Mandates in Turkey should be sent to the Near East to ascertain the wishes of the various peoples there with regard to their future political status and choice of a mandatory.

It was a result of Emir Faisal's protest to Colonel House against French obstruction to the sending of the International Commission on Mandates to Turkey that President Wilson was to send its American section, popularly known as the "King-Crane" Commission, to the Near East.[4] When Wilson made this decision Emir Faisal promptly dashed back to Damascus to make preparations for the coming of the Americans. Faisal and the Arab nationalists summoned Arab representatives to a Syrian Congress to be held at Damascus in June 1919 from all parts of what the Syrian nationalists called Syria; that is, Palestine, Lebanon, and the rest of the Arab lands west of Mesopotamia. The Arabs were not the only ones preparing to receive the King-Crane Commission. General Ronald Storrs, British Military Governor of Palestine, it was reported to the American Commission to Negotiate Peace at Paris, was boasting in Jerusalem that he would put the Americans in his pocket when they arrived in Palestine.[5] Georges Picot and his staff at Beirut were actively compiling lists of pro-French delegations to be received by the American commissioners.

Again, the King-Crane Commission.—Much criticism has been leveled at the King-Crane Commission by those whose ambitions and hopes seemed threatened by its work and its report. Its most virulent and bitter critics were the French and the Zionists, neither of whom have hesitated to use misrepresentation in order to discredit the commission and its report. Arabs and French would be quite justified in criticizing the commission for not having gone to Mesopotamia, which was the result of Mr. Charles R. Crane's ukase based on the assumption that the Arabs of Mesopotamia wanted Britain to have the mandate for Iraq. The work of the commission might justly be criticized as that of amateurs with no experience in the highly technical job of "self-determination." It can be said that the commission without ulterior motives private or political endeavored to do as thorough and unbiased a job as limitations of time and trained personnel made possible. Historical events since 1919 in Palestine, Syria, and Lebanon demonstrate conclusively that the investigation revealed with considerable accuracy the actual wishes of the principal religious and cultural groups in the area and that the commission's report, exclusive of its politically impractical recommendations, gave a reasonably accurate analysis of the situation as it existed in the summer of 1919.

It was quite inevitable, as foreseen by W. L. Westermann and his staff at Paris, that sending the King-Crane Commission would foster sectarian animosities, intensify antagonisms, and increase the friction between French and Arabs, and between French and British. The Arabs through the Syrian Congress used this opportunity to attack the Anglo-French policy of dividing the Arab lands which the nationalists called Syria, to protest against the Balfour Declaration and Jewish immigration, and to reject a French mandate. Of course, most of the Lebanese did not wish to be submerged in a Moslem Syria, almost all the Maronites and some elements of other Christian groups wanted a French mandate, the quarter of a million Nousariya inhabiting the coastal area north of Lebanon and south of Antioch disliked and feared the Sunnite Moslems who dominated the government of Emir Faisal at Damascus.

As Louis XVI discovered in 1789, the political device of consulting the people as to what they wish and what they think may be the prelude to revolution. Politicians, rulers, and ruling classes are accustomed to tell the people what they should want and what they should think; it was, therefore, quite a natural result that much political fermentation was caused by the King-Crane Commission's journey through Palestine, Syria, and Lebanon.

Astute Arabs quickly recognized that even the American commission had no intention of granting them their independence. The assembled sheiks of the Hebron district in Palestine when asked by Mr. Crane whom they wanted for a mandatory replied with considerable discretion and acumen that "all governments were evil," little realizing that Prince Kropotkin, Bakunin, and other leading European anarchists had long since come to the same conclusion. Nor did these village headmen know that most Americans had been conditioned by their newspapers to think of the anarchists as long-bearded Russians carrying a bomb with a sizzling fuse and so had confused the anarchists with the idealistic revolutionary nihilist youth of tsarist Russia. The sheiks, unaware of Mr. Crane's recent mission to Russia, thought that he was irritated by their insistence on their desire to rule themselves. Understanding the futility of further protest they departed with great dignity after informing the members of the King-Crane Commission that if the Peace Conference insisted upon imposing a ruler upon them would the commission please inform President Wilson that they preferred Allah!

By the time the King-Crane Commission reached Paris, President Wilson had returned to the United States, which was rapidly becoming isolationist. It would take more than one world war to convince the American people that their "manifest destiny" was that of assuming responsibilities and liabilities all over the world. Making the world "safe for democracy" did not have a strong appeal to Americans in 1919. With the United States rapidly vanishing from the stage of power politics, Britain and France found it necessary to come to an understanding with respect to the former Arab provinces of the Ottoman Empire.

The British and French come to terms.—On September 15, 1919, the French and British signed a military convention by which French military authorities would take over Cilicia and Occupied Enemy's Territory West and British troops would be withdrawn from these areas as well as from Occupied Enemy's Territory East. This left the Arab regime at Damascus, without American or British support, to deal with France. Faisal having returned to Europe was obliged to reach a tentative agreement with the French government. Shortly thereafter, General Henri J. E. Gouraud was appointed French High Commissioner in Syria and Lebanon and arrived at Beirut in November to assume his duties as Commander-in-Chief of the French military forces.

The Syrian nationalists were far from satisfied with Emir Faisal's dickering in Paris and London and opposition to him developed in the Committee of National Defense which found expression in the Syrian Congress which was still in session. Faisal was in a difficult position because political realities in Syria did not correspond with the realities of power politics. The United States had withdrawn from international affairs and Great Britain alone was no longer in a position to oppose the French. The Syrian nationalists wished to force Faisal to pursue a stronger policy toward France at a time when the exigencies of the international situation demanded a compromise with the French. Faisal found himself entangled with the inner contradictions of his position. He ordered the Syrian Congress to adjourn, but authorized military conscription and then in January returned to Paris to negotiate another compromise with the French.

Syrians defy the French.—The Syrian nationalists were stirred to further action by the defiance of the Allies by the Turkish nationalists under Mustafa Kemal. Discontent was seething in Syria as in Mesopotamia. Responding to this popular movement among the Syrians, Faisal provided for the election of a Syrian Congress which claimed that it represented Palestine and Lebanon as integral parts of Syria. In March 1920 two congresses foregathered in Damascus. The so-called Mesopotamian Congress which demanded the independence of Iraq and the Syrian Congress which proclaimed Faisal King of Syria. Promptly thereafter a Lebanese conference repudiated the Syrian Congress and at Baalbek proclaimed the independence of Lebanon. In April at San Remo the Allies definitely allocated the mandate for Syria and Lebanon to France, the British and the French having reached agreement with regard to Mosul oil, pipelines across the Syrian deserts, location of refineries, and oil ports.

European imperialism and Near Eastern nationalisms were moving toward a climax in their inescapable conflict. In defiance of the Turkish National Pact Allied troops occupied Constantinople; in complete disregard of the expressed opposition of the majority of the Arabs in Syria, Lebanon, and Palestine, the Allies at San Remo allocated Syria and Lebanon to France and to Great Britain Palestine under a mandate embodying the Balfour Declaration; and ignoring Iraqi opposition they awarded a mandate for Mesopotamia to the British.

French military occupation of Syria and Lebanon.—The results of these actions were the defiance of the Allies by the Ankara government of the Grand Turkish National Assembly, insurrection in Mesopotamia, and rejection of the French mandate by the Syrian government at Damascus. The Turks defeated the Greeks and forced the Allies to accept the terms of the Turkish National Assembly. The Iraqi Arab revolt was crushed by the British who, however, abandoned their "colonial" policy in Iraq and replaced it with a more subtle and less objectionable means of control. The Syrian Arabs were soon forced to submit to the French, who refused to recognize the ephemeral kingdom of Syria. General Gouraud, whose natural asperity and austerity were in no way lessened by the loss of an arm at the Dardanelles, did not hesitate to ignore Faisal's acceptance of his ultimatum of July 14 because he did not receive it within the time stipulated. After a brief brush with the Arab forces the French captured Damascus on July 25, Aleppo having been occupied previously without resistance.

Syria and Lebanon, as frequently occurs after a war, were governed by a succession of popularly known and successful generals whose victories in war had tended to increase their dominating attitude of men long habituated to wield arbitrary power. The idea that military leaders are the most appropriate men to guide conquered people in the ways of self-government and democracy prevailed among the masses who do not realize that men trained in the use of arbitrary powers may be most useful in laying the foundations for future arbitrary government.

The kingdom of Syria ceased to exist and the Syrian nationalist movement had met with temporary defeat. Emir Faisal was forced to flee, leaving the French masters of Syria and Lebanon, where they were to remain until World War II. Seemingly, French imperialism in the Levant, like British imperialism in Iraq, was triumphant. French rule, however, was not to remain unchallenged for long.

۞ UNDER FRENCH RULE AND MANDATE

The position of France in Syria and Lebanon was not a happy one. France had had little to do directly with freeing the Syrians and Lebanese from the Turks, but had made good its claim to these Arab lands only by a dicker with the British and by crushing the Syrian kingdom of the Arab hero, Emir Faisal. Although the Supreme Allied Council in April 1920 at the Conference of San Remo had awarded the mandate for Syria and Lebanon to France, the French were obliged to secure control of Syria by military operations against the Syrians. After the capture of Aleppo and Damascus in July 1920 the French ruled Syria and Lebanon quite arbitrarily for more than three years before the mandate of the League of Nations became effective legally on September 29, 1923.[6]

The military governors: General Gouraud's policies intensify Syrian opposition.—General Gouraud, who went to Beirut in the autumn of

1919, convinced that he knew what to do and how to do it, very shortly thereafter took two steps which intensified Arab opposition and eventually contributed to an insurrection which lasted for two years. This inept administrator, who thought of himself as another great French colonial administrator like Marshal Lyautey, enlarged the frontiers of Lebanon, nearly doubling its area and divided the mandated territory of Syria and Lebanon into five separate administrative divisions or autonomous states without self-government, namely: Greater Lebanon, Damascus, Aleppo, the Alawite territory of Latakia, and the emirate of Hauran. The Greater Lebanon included the city of Beirut, coastal territories north and south of the former provinces of Lebanon, and the much disputed Bekaa, through which the railroad and main highway from Damascus to Homs, Hama, and Aleppo run. The hinterland of southern and central Syria with their three principal cities was cut off from the coast. The enlarged Lebanon included a considerable Moslem Sunnite population and many Christians not in sympathy with the Maronites, whose desires and ambitions were achieved by the creation of the Greater Lebanon at the expense of non-Maronites. In 1860–61 the lesser Lebanon, overwhelmingly Christian and largely Maronite, had been placed under a special regime by pressure of the Great Powers largely as the result of French insistence. Early in World War I the Ottoman government brought to an end this special status of Lebanon. The French, whose most loyal supporters were the Maronites, rewarded them by extending the Lebanese frontiers. The new inhabitants of Greater Lebanon, particularly the Moslems, were bitterly opposed to being included in the Lebanese state with a Christian majority and proved to be a discordant and anti-French element. Greater Lebanon could not be depended upon by the French administration as the smaller Lebanon had been. Most Syrian Sunnite Moslems and all Syrian Nationalists were antagonized by this action of General Gouraud.

His division of the mandated territory into five separate states was in complete opposition to the wishes of the Syrian nationalists, who were convinced that the French government intended to frustrate any attempt to create a Syrian-national state.

The French mandatory government had a difficult task in governing the mandated territory of Syria and Lebanon. Its population was divided into numerous antagonistic religious groups and sects whose historical heritage was one of strife and bitterness which had engendered deep fears and hatreds that the religious leaders had sedulously cultivated for generations. There was, therefore, a logical basis for numerous administrative subdivisions. This logical action did not take into consideration the illogical aspects of nationalism.[7] Although Arab nationalism, and its subspecies Syrian nationalism, were not sufficiently strong to overcome the sectarian and other particularisms which divided the peoples of Syria and Lebanon, it was growing in strength and by attacking this policy of General Gouraud in their propaganda against the French mandate, the nationalists increased their appeal to their fellow Syrians. The old Roman adage about divided rule cannot be successfully applied if new factors entering the situation are not taken into consideration.

To recognize a Druze emirate in southern Syria for the Jebel Druze territory by an agreement with the feudal-tribal Druze chieftains in 1921 and, in accordance with its provisions, officially to proclaim Jebel Druze to be an independent state under the French mandate appeared to General Gouraud an effective way to deal with this proud and warlike group and to keep them apart from the Syrian nationalists in the newly created state of Damascus. This did not prove to be the case, however.

To set up a separate administration for the area inhabited by the ancient people called the Nousariya, members of a secret religious sect despised alike by Moslem and Christian Arabs who inhabited the mountainous region east of Latakia known as Jebel Ansariya, appeared, superficially at least, to be a reasonable thing to do. Under Ottoman administration Jebel Ansariya, the country of the Nousariya or Alaouites, was included in the sanjaq of Latakia. The French called it the Alaouite (Alawiya) Territory and later designated it as West Syria. Such an administrative division of course tended to perpetuate the isolation of the Nousariya and to maintain a hereditary feudal and religious caste whose members exploited the peasantry in a manner similar to that of the leading feudal and tribal families among the Druzes. To the Syrian nationalists and liberals General Gouraud's policy appeared to be one directed at preventing the spread of Syrian nationalism to all groups in Syria and at perpetuating an ancient and outmoded socio-economic order.

North of the Alaouite territory was the Ottoman sanjaq of Alexandretta in which 40 per cent of the population were Turkish-speaking people. It included Musa Dagh, an old Armenian center which has been made famous by Franz Werfel in his novel describing its heroic defense against the Turks during World War I.[8] Alexandretta is a port serving not only northern Syria but all the extensive area of southeastern Anatolia. Consequently this region was of particular significance to the Turks at Ankara. In an agreement with the Ankara government in 1921 France had promised to establish a special regime in the Alexandretta sanjaq that would protect Turkish cultural and economic interests there. It was, therefore, quite in order for General Gouraud to organize the Alexandretta area as an autonomous administrative unit in the state of Aleppo. This arrangement, however, strengthened the Turkish irredentist movement and consequently further antagonized the Syrian nationalists who correctly feared that it would eventually lead to the loss of Alexandretta to the Turks.

The creation of a state of Aleppo and a state of Damascus intensified the resentment against the French and General Gouraud among the Syrian nationalists whose principal center was Damascus. They felt that this action was designed to perpetuate and augment the old differences and rivalry between Damascenes and Aleppines.

Although General Gouraud faced no serious crisis in Syria and Lebanon after his occupation of Damascus, nevertheless his administration instead of allaying the resentment of the Syrians tended to augment it. Events in other parts of the Near East helped keep the Syrians in a ferment. The shah of Iran in June 1921 administered a blow to British imperialists by denouncing the Anglo-Persian Treaty of 1919 which had made Iran for all practical purposes a British protectorate. In August of the same year Emir Faisal became King of Iraq and in November the new king signed the Anglo-Iraqi treaty which gave Iraq a status somewhat different from that of the other Arab territories under Class A mandates. In 1922 the British protectorate in Egypt was terminated. In the autumn of this same year the Allies agreed to discuss at Lausanne peace terms with the new Turkish government at Ankara. To the Syrian nationalists it appeared as if the Egyptians, the Iranians, the Iraqi, and the Turks were making progress in ridding themselves of the shackles of British imperialism at a time when Gouraud was tightening the fetters of French colonialism upon Syria and Lebanon.

Under General Maxime Weygand, who succeeded General Gouraud as High Commissioner in April 1923, the Syrians were less restive. The practical, matter of fact, and objective manner in which General Weygand administered the mandated territories won support for him from among all groups. Although this French high commissioner did not remove the basic causes of Syrian opposition to the French mandate, his method of dealing with the Syrians lessened the tensions which had built up during the administration of General Gouraud.

General Sarrail precipitates a revolt.—In 1924 a change in the political situation in France brought about a very serious crisis in Syria and Lebanon following the replacement of General Weygand by General Maurice Sarrail. As a result of the French elections of 1924 the former liberal professor Edouard Herriot, as leader of the middle-class party known as the Radical Socialists, who were neither radicals nor socialists but rather conservative nineteenth-century liberals, became Premier of France. The anticlerical and antiroyalist attitudes of the Radical Socialists resulted in the recall of General Weygand and the appointment in November 1923 of the politically-minded General Sarrail as French High Commissioner to Syria and Lebanon. Imbued with the somewhat out-of-date ideas of the Radical Socialists Sarrail soon antagonized the powerful Maronite patriarch by attempts along anticlerical lines to weaken the power of the Maronite clergy. This policy of Sarrail instead of diminishing the influence of the Maronite patriarch tended rather to lessen Maronite enthusiasm for the French.

General Sarrail's arbitrary and contemptuous treatment of the leading Druze feudal and tribal chieftains precipitated a Druze uprising in July 1925 which soon developed into a widespread insurrection throughout the mandated territories that lasted for nearly two years and threatened to destroy the basis of French power in Syria and Lebanon.

The revolt of the Druze illustrates the complexities of social evolution in the Near East during this period of transition from a medieval-like to a modern society. The crisis in Jebel Druze developed out of a well-meant attempt of a French officer who as a liberal was honestly trying to better the condition of the Druze peasants. Captain Carbillet, who was acting French Governor of Jebel Druze, though supported by the Council of the Druze, antagonized the powerful Atrash family, whose leaders seemed to have understood that if Carbillet's policies were fully implemented they would undermine the feudal power of the Druze landowners.

Confronted with the rapidly developing crisis in Jebel Druze, General Sarrail relieved Captain Carbillet of his duties and then went out of his way to antagonize the Druze chieftains. In a manner reminiscent of Mohammed Ali's handling of the Mamelukes in Egypt, Sarrail invited the Druze leaders to a dinner party in Damascus at which all those who attended were arrested. Sultan Pasha Atrash, who anticipating this act of treachery had remained in Jebel Druze, immediately took up arms against the French. His call to the Druze clans made an appeal stronger than that of the class animosity between peasants and nobles. The Druze joined in a common struggle against an alien interloper. Soon the Syrian nationalists in Damascus, in Homs, Hama, Aleppo, and other parts of Syria joined in the uprising.

Sarrail's unannounced and ruthless bombardment of the crowded sections of Damascus, where Syrian insurgents had infiltrated, failed to crush the rebels, but it did arouse world-wide indignation and protest. The reaction in France was such that General Sarrail was recalled and a civilian, Henri de Jouvenel, was appointed French High Commissioner on October 30, 1925.

The insurrection took on a political aspect which threatened French control in Syria when the Syrian nationalist leader Dr. Abdurrahman Shahbandar, with several other leading nationalists, fled to Jebel Druze and there set up a provisional Arab government and raised the Syrian flag used by King Faisal during the brief life of the Syrian kingdom in 1919.

Civilian governors: De Jouvenel, Ponsot.—The new high commissioner before arriving at Beirut began to explore the possibilities of a compromise settlement. He consulted with a Lebanese Druze leader in Paris, and he had conferences at Cairo with members of the Syrian-Palestine Congress. After arriving at Beirut De Jouvenel received proposals from the various delegations to a conference at Beirut and became aware of the fact that there was a covenant between the rebel leaders in Syria and those of the Syrian-Palestine Congress in Cairo. There was considerable similarity in the proclamations and demands of the various Syrian groups and organizations.

The provisional Syrian government organized in Jebel Druze in August and September 1925 demanded the application of the principles of the French Revolution of 1789 and of the Declaration of the Rights of Man, complete independence of Arabic Syria one and indivisible, and the evacuation of the foreign army of occupation. The Lebanese Druze leader Shakib Arslan proposed to De Jouvenel at Paris in November the complete and integral independence of both Syria and Lebanon followed by their admission to the League of Nations and plebiscites in the Alawiya state and in the territories annexed to Lebanon during the administration of General Gouraud.

The Syrian-Palestinian Congress at Cairo in December 1925 demanded of De Jouvenel the termination of the French mandate and the admission of Syria to the League of Nations, the unification of Syria, and the reduction in size of Lebanon to its prewar frontiers.

These demands are interesting not only because they show the difficult problem which confronted the French government in 1925 and 1926 but also because twenty years later Syria and Lebanon gained their independence and as sovereign states became members of the United Nations.

The difficulties of De Jouvenel were complicated by the uncertainty of the action which the Turks might adopt with regard to the disturbances in northern Syria and along the Turkish frontier. The Turks were angered by the decision of the Council of the League of Nations with regard to the Mosul question which the Ankara government at first refused to recognize as valid. Nevertheless, to overcome opposition in the French Chamber of Deputies to the appropriation of eight million francs for Syria and Lebanon, De Jouvenel minimized the importance and dangers of the situation in Syria. On returning to France in June 1926 for discussion with the French government De Jouvenel was embarrassed by the renewal of heavy fighting in the Damascus area and sporadic hostilities in the Bekaa, the Hauran, and in the region around Tripoli. By August the situation was such that De Jouvenel was replaced by another civilian administrator, Henri Ponsot.

The new French high commissioner took his time and moved with great caution before announcing his policy. He listened without impatience to the demands of various Syrian delegations, but did not express any opinions of his own until July 1927, when the military situation was well in hand and the fires of insurrection were dying down. On July 26 M. Ponsot stated in an official declaration of policy that France had no intention of renouncing its mandate, but he softened this blow to the hopes of the nationalists by adding that France had received a "mission to assist the progressive development of Syria and the Lebanon as independent states" and that it would "not fail in its task."

The Ponsot declaration satisfied no one. Nevertheless, although opposition to the French mandate continued, armed resistance was soon terminated, and Ponsot was able to initiate a new policy which actually led eventually to the independence of Syria and Lebanon. The failure of French policy under the military high commissioners, Gouraud and Sarrail, resulted in the establishment of a civil administration and the adoption of a policy less offensive to the Syrian nationalists.

The dramatic episodes and events of this political conflict between indigenous nationalists and foreign imperialists tend to obscure the economic factors underlying the actions and reactions of both nationalists and imperialists. The economic problems of Syria and Lebanon were, during the period of the French mandate and have been since then, of primary importance to the social and political life of the populations of these two Levant states. Only by recourse to specialized works such as *The Economic Organization of Syria,* edited by Said B. Himadeh (published at Beirut in 1936), and *L'état actuel de l'economie syrienne,* by Salah Essaleh (published at Paris in 1944), can the general reader obtain some idea of the economic conditions in the Levant states.

Economic and social problems.—The two Levant states, which were formerly under a French mandate, are essentially agrarian and pastoral by occupation and by population. Approximately 62 per cent of the population in Syria and Lebanon is agricultural by occupation and 13 per cent pastoral nomads (Bedouins) forming 75 per cent of the entire population. In the 1930's over 80 per cent of the exports of native production in the Levant states consisted of agricultural and pastoral products. It is estimated that in 1932 more than 1,300,000 out of a total population of approximately 3,000,000 were actually engaged in tilling the soil.

Not including some 300,000 pastoral nomads, nearly two-thirds of the population of Syria and Lebanon have a very low purchasing power and live on a level not much above subsistence requirements. In Himadeh's *Economic Organization of Syria* the low standard of living of the Syrian peasantry is clearly set forth by two writers—Roger Widmer, who states that the peasants in Syria are unable to earn "an adequate living in agricultural pursuits either as laborers or proprietors," and Albert Khuri, who writes: "Syria under the present conditions is overpopulated agriculturally." [9] These statements are made in regard to a country which is estimated to have nearly 10,000,000 acres of cultivable land. Of this, however, only about 5,000,000 acres are cultivated, half of which lie fallow every other year. Agricultural production of the Syrian and Lebanese peasantry is low, consequently whether as owners or as hired workers the income of the peasants is also low. There are several factors which militate against the possibility of raising production per capita and raising the standard of living of the peasantry.

A fundamental cause of the sorry condition of the peasants is ignorance. The illiterate were estimated to be, in 1932, over 41 per cent of the total population. The land-owning system and the methods of farming are still quite primitive. The landowners lack the incentive to modernize farming methods. The peasantry lack the capital and knowledge necessary to the adaption of scientific and mechanized methods of agriculture. It is estimated that the agricultural production of the two Levant states could be more than doubled by bringing more land under cultivation and by employing modern methods. Agricultural progress made by the Jews in Palestine is evidence of what under more favorable social and political conditions might be accomplished in Syria and Lebanon.

Low agricultural production and limited industrial production have resulted in imports being largely in excess of exports. During the ten-year period from 1924 to 1933, inclusive, imports averaged in value 71 per cent of the total foreign trade. Remittances sent by Syrian and Lebanese emigrants, returning emigrants with capital, and other invisible imports have lessened the gap between imports and exports. Nevertheless, the Levant states tend to persist in having an unfavorable trade balance.

The owning and controlling classes, the tribal shieks, the semifeudal large landowners, the merchants, and moneylenders are not accustomed to invest capital in ways which tend to increase agricultural and industrial production or to develop natural resources. Commercial capitalism as it functioned in the Near East is extractive rather than productive. Conditions in the Ottoman Empire did not encourage the development of modern forms of capitalism. Those with capital for investment turned to the acquisition of foreign securities for investment rather than to the organization of a corporative and financial system for the development of the natural and labor resources of the Near East.

The currency situation during the period between World War I and World War II tended to discourage economic activity. World War I smashed the international monetary system of exchange based on a gold standard. During the early 1920's gold flowed in a stream from the Near East, eventually to the United States. European currencies were in a constant state of fluctuation in relationship to gold and to one another. The French based the Syrian currency on the French franc as the British based that of Palestine on the pound sterling and that of Iraq, first, on the Indian rupee and, later, on the English pound. One of the grievances of the Syrian and Lebanese was the French fiscal policy in the Levant states.

Political discontent was aggravated and augmented by economic distress and dissatisfaction. French administrators could not have alleviated the situation to any great degree even if they had bent all their efforts to improving the well being of the peoples of Syria and Lebanon. In the Levant states as elsewhere in the Near East economic modernization cannot be realized to its full extent until the masses of the people are educated and their inherent capacities released from the restraints of ancient outworn ways of thinking and from a social system that is incompatible with the modern world. A large proportion of the ruling classes, the tribal sheiks, the feudal landowners, the religious leaders, the merchants, and the money lenders tend to resist changes which appear to threaten the old order upon which their privileged position depends. Captain Carbillet discovered this to be the case in Jebel Druze in 1925 when he attempted to introduce liberal reforms as Mohammed Ali's son Ibrahim Pasha found out in the 1840's when he attempted to modernize Syrian and Lebanese institutions. The French required the support of these dominant classes in order to rule. Opposition to the indigenous privileged classes by alien rulers resulted in the peasants and urban craftsmen joining in a "crusade," as Miss Elizabeth P. MacCallum calls it, against the foreign intruders.

The crushing of the Syrian insurrection by the French in 1927 did not solve, or make possible, the elimination of the basic causes of discontent among the Lebanese and Syrians. Nevertheless, the French high commissioner set about meeting some of the political desiderata of the Syrian nationalists. He permitted in 1928 a group of less extreme Syrian leaders to draft a constitution, which he found not to his satisfaction so after dismissing the constituent assembly he promptly promulgated his own constitution for Syria in 1930 under which, two years later, elections to a Syrian chamber of deputies were held.

The Syrians were closely watching events in both Palestine and Iraq. The rising opposition to Jewish immigration among the Palestinian Arabs was arousing much feeling among Syrian and Lebanese Arabs, which kept them in a state of mental agitation and emotional excitement. The Anglo-Iraqi Treaty of 1930 and the consequent admission of Iraq as a member of the League of Nations in 1932 activated the Syrian political leaders who opened conversations with the French with regard to a Franco-Syrian Treaty similar to that of the British and Iraqi. The Syrians also brought up the question of the incorporation in the Syrian state of Jebel Druze and the Latakia territory of the Nousariya.

International complications.—The growing tension of international affairs following Hitler's rise to power was affecting French politics and policy and the situation in the Near East. Unrest in Syria led to the suspension of the Syrian Chamber of Deputies in the year 1934. The young Syrian nationalists, who had turned to the urban workers instead of to the landowners and peasants and to the sheiks with their nomadic tribesmen, were able to organize in a strike in 1936 and maintain it for seven weeks. The internal political crisis in France between 1934 and 1936 resulted in a French Cabinet of the Popular Front headed by the socialist Léon Blum which was sympathetic toward the aspirations of the Syrian nationalists. A Syrian delegation was then allowed to go to France where an agreement with the French was reached with respect to the incorporation of Jebel Druze and Jebel Ansariya in the Syrian state and to a Franco-Syrian Treaty somewhat similar to the British treaties with Egypt and Iraq. The Syrians were jubilant, anticipating their freedom from the French mandate and their admission by 1939 as an independent state to the League of Nations.

Their rejoicing did not long endure, and they had to await the demise of the League of Nations and the meeting of the United Nations Conference at San Francisco in 1945 before they could sit as "equals" in an international world organization. The world after 1936 was rushing towards its crisis and the French government increasingly anxious about the situation in the Mediterranean and the Near East after the Italian invasion of Ethiopia and the founding of the so-called Rome-Berlin Axis, began to backwater on its liberal policy in the Levant states, where indignation was mounting at the Franco-Turkish negotiations which led to the acquisition of the former Ottoman sanjaq of Alexandretta by Turkey. Although this had been foreshadowed by the French and Turkish Agreement of 1921 the cession of part of the mandated territory of Syria and Lebanon to Turkey by means of bilateral agreements which ignored the Syrians and by-passed the League of Nations aroused considerable feeling among the Syrians.

The Turks get Alexandretta.—Soon after the French government of Léon Blum had agreed upon a draft of the Franco-Syrian Treaty, the Turks protested against the incorporation of the Alexandretta territory in an independent Syrian state. When the League of Nations arranged for a commission to hold a plebiscite, the French and Turks promptly signed a treaty of friendship in June 1938 whereby Turkish troops entered the territory that then was declared to be "an autonomous territory under Franco-Turkish administration." Thus, without the authorization of the nearly defunct League of Nations the Alexandretta sanjaq which under Ottoman rule had been a political subdivision of the Vilayet of Aleppo ceased to be a part of the mandated territory of Syria and Lebanon. The following year on the very eve of World War II by a Franco-Turkish Declaration of Mutual Assistance, the transitory Republic of Hatay, named in memory of the ancient Hittites, became an administrative unit and an integral part of the Turkish Republic. Without raising the issue of the validity of this Turkish acquisition, it is interesting to note that just as the Japanese took over Manchuria in 1932–33, and the Italians took over Ethiopia in 1936, so the Turks without, however, bloodshed and violence, more gently and with the consent of France took over the Republic of Hatay conveniently created for that very purpose.

The situation on the eve of World War II.—The Syrians were to experience still another grievous disappointment. After much delay between the years 1936 and 1939, the French government early in 1939 stated that it did not intend to ask the French Chamber of Deputies to ratify the Franco-Syrian Treaty drafted in 1936. In July 1939 the French high commissioner suspended the Syrian constitution and then set up separate administrative machinery for Jebel Druze, for the Alawiya territory in the Latakia region, and for that part of the territory east of the Euphrates where a Kurdish minority exists.

To the Syrian nationalists it appeared as if they were back again in the years of the Gouraud administration: the Franco-Syrian treaty put on the shelf, their constitution inoperative for an indefinite period, and Syria once more divided into separate administrative units. Consequently, the Syrians at the outbreak of World War II were in a very unfriendly mood toward the French, which events between 1939 and 1945 did not appreciably ameliorate.

CHAPTER XXIII

Arabia

For centuries the Arabian peninsula has been a land little known to the peoples of the western world. Only a few ports along the coast were accessible to non-Moslem aliens. Travel in the interior was perilous and costly, only exceptional individuals ventured into these forbidding regions. Although thousands of Moslems from all over the world made annual pilgrimages to the sacred cities of Mecca and Medina of the Hejaz no Christians on pain of death were permitted to do so. Foreigners were rarely allowed to visit the Yemen. It was not until the nineteenth century that a few daring European travelers penetrated the interior of the peninsula. As the books written by these men were known only to a rather restricted circle of readers, Arabia remained a land of mystery to most Christians.

Until recent years information about Arabia was meager and comparatively little was known about its topography, its natural resources, its climate, and its inhabitants. Even today knowledge about Arabia is amazingly limited, but Arabia is no longer the mysterious nor, except in part, the forbidden.

❁ THE ARABIANS

It is customary to speak of the inhabitants of Arabia as the Arabs in the same way that one calls the inhabitants of the United States, Americans. It is more exact to speak of the people of Arabia as Arabians. Most of them are Arab by language, culture, and historical tradition, but the Arabs of Arabia are not all of the same stock. The nomads, especially those of the great central plateau, are probably more intensively inbred and have less "mixed blood" than those Arabians who live along the coast and more accessible areas. It is thought the Arabian hinterland was the place of origin of those Semitic speaking peoples who, at different times, overran the Valley of the Tigris and Euphrates, Syria, Lebanon, and Palestine. From the time when the Semitic Akkadians conquered the Sumerians in the delta of the Tigris and Euphrates and the Arameans, Phoenicians, and Canaanites dominated the Syrian hinterland and coastal plains and their southern extension in Palestine, Semitic languages and Semitic cultures have been predominant in the Fertile Crescent as in the Syrian Desert and in the Arabian Peninsula. It is probable that, despite innumerable invasions and conquests of the fertile Arab lands of western Asia by non-Semitic people Semitic culture persisted there throughout the centuries, because the Arabian Peninsula, uninviting to alien colonists, difficult to conquer and rule, and offering little to foreign invaders, remained thoroughly Semitic by language and culture and so was a source from which the people and culture of the Fertile Crescent were replenished.

The southern, eastern, and western peripheries of Arabia have always been in contact with the non-Arabic and non-Semitic worlds. The rich land of southwestern Arabia, the Yemen, is not a land of nomads and has been more free from their influence than any other part of the peninsula. Bordering on the southern end of the Red Sea it is separated from Africa by the narrow Strait of Bab el Mandeb. Before the rise of Islam, the Yemen was closely connected with northeast Africa. The Yemenite Arabs are very largely of Hamitic stock of African not Arabian origin. The western, southern, and eastern coasts of Arabia were an integral part of the ancient trade routes of the Red Sea, the Indian Ocean, and the Persian Gulf. Until recent centuries small sailing ships had to hug the coast and put in at frequent ports of call for water and food and for shelter in case of storms. For ages Arabian coastal cities flourished as service stations along the water routes of commerce as did the desert cities along the caravan routes. The many-storied skyscrapers of the cities of the Hadhramaut coast, so well described by Freya Stark,[1] remain as social fossils of a defunct transportation system. Until the decline of the age-old trade routes these coastal cities of Arabia were a part of a much wider world although, with the exception of the Yemenite ports, they were tied to the nomadic tribesmen of the interior and many of them also were dependent upon the trans-Arabian caravan trade. During the period of Arab domination of the land and sea routes from the Mediterranean eastward as far as Canton, Arabia was in close contact with most of the civilized world. After the all-water route from Europe to Asia was developed by the Portuguese who broke up the Arab commercial monopoly, Arabia entered a period of isolation which, with the exception of the annual Moslem hadj ("pilgrimage") to Mecca, endured almost to the twentieth century.

GEOGRAPHY—TOPOGRAPHY

Topographically, as well as climatically, there are many variations in the Arabian Peninsula: the coastal plains and mountain ranges of the west, the central plateau with its fertile oases encompassed by desert belts, in the southeast the great desert known as Rub' al Khali, and the eastern and southern coasts all present striking differences. The western coastal plain with its oases and swamps in the southern portion and its more arid lands to the north stretches from Sheikh Sa'id to Akaba. Flanking the plains of the western littoral are mountain ranges from the southern tip of Yemen to the northern part of the Hejaz. In the south both in Yemen and in Asir, now a part of Saudi Arabia, the mountains which reach elevations of 8000 to 10,000 feet have fertile valleys where sufficient rainfall makes cultivation possible for a numerous peasant population. In the Hejaz, with little precipitation, the mountains of igneous and metamorphized rocks are barren and desolate except for such occasional oases as Taif, Mecca, and Medina. East of the Yemen, stretching far across the peninsula almost to its eastern coast, lies the great sandy desert, Ar-Rimal, or as it is also called Rub' al Khali, the "Empty Quarter," which Bertram Thomas has well described as one of the most completely desert lands.[2] From the eastern highlands of Asir, Wadi Dawasir provides a route across southcentral Arabia to the oases of the hinterland plateau.

In the northern Hejaz, east of the mountain range that flanks the coast, are the areas of lava known as the Harra which makes access from the west to the northcentral plateau difficult. While the western slopes of the range are somewhat precipitous its eastern slopes towards the high central plateau are more gentle. This plateau dips gradually toward the east and south. Its mean elevation is about 2,500 feet above sea level.

The nature of the central plateau has had a significant effect upon the history and life of the people of most of Arabia. The heart of the plateau contains a group of oases that extends from Hail in the north to al Kharj, Jabrin, and Laila in the south. These oases, enclosed by belts of sand dunes are made possible by the mountains, Jebel Shammar in the north and Tuwaiq in the south. The rainfall on these limestone ranges provides an underground water supply for the oases of the central plateau which are enclosed on the east by a sandy belt known as Dahana. This belt extends from northeast of Hail to south of Riyadh, the capital of Saudi Arabia, separating it from the great Hofuf oases in

Hasa, and continues almost to the Jafura Desert that lies north of the Empty Quarter, Ar-Rimal. The oasis of Hail is separated from that of Jauf lying to the north by the sand dune desert area called Nefud.[3]

These oases of the central plateau enclosed by deserts and protected by them have ever been difficult of access to invaders. Hail, Buraida, Anaiza, and Riyadh have always been keys to the control of a large part of Arabia. Those who controlled these oases with their populous peasant villages and towns and the great trans-Arabian trade routes along which move the caravans from the Red Sea to the Persian Gulf, from Yemen, Asir, and the Hejaz to Kuwait, Basra, and Bagdad and from Oman and Hasa to Jerusalem and Damascus could dominate the nomads who lived meagerly on the steppes and on the fringes of the deserts.

While the great sheiks of the central oases were reasonably secure from invasion, they could raid and occasionally extend their control to the north, the west, and the east. Several large wadis give access to the periphery of Arabia. Wadi Sirhan running from the Jauf oasis north to al Azrak has often been a highway by which the Arabians invaded Syria. Wadi er Rumna, piercing the sand dune belts to the northeast and southwest of Buraida and Anaiza—cities of the central oases lying at a nexus of caravan routes and between Hail and Riyadh—provide a route from Medina to Basra. Wadi Dawasir offers a southern route to the west coast.

Because much of Arabia has little rainfall it is largely an arid or semi-arid land. Those areas with meager water supplies have been the homeland of the Arab nomads, the Bedouins. Although the Bedouins with their tribal organization of Arabian society have played a very important role in Arabian history, there exists in the various parts of the peninsula a numerous urban and also peasant population.

❁ POPULATION ESTIMATES

There are no exact data about the population of Arabia. The United Nations' *Demographic Year Book* of 1948 gives an estimate of 6,000,000 as the population of Saudi Arabia. *Webster's Geographical Dictionary* gives the population of the Hejaz as three and one-half millions and estimates the total population of Arabia to be 10,000,000, but the total of the populations of its various parts as given by *Webster*'s amounts to over twelve and a half millions. K. S. Twitchell in his book *Saudi Arabia* states his conclusion that a figure of 4,000,000 for Saudi Arabia would be a conservative estimate.[4] If the estimated population for Yemen, given variously as 3,500,000 to 4,000,000 and the population of other Arabian states be added to Twitchell's 4,000,000 for Saudi Arabia, a figure of

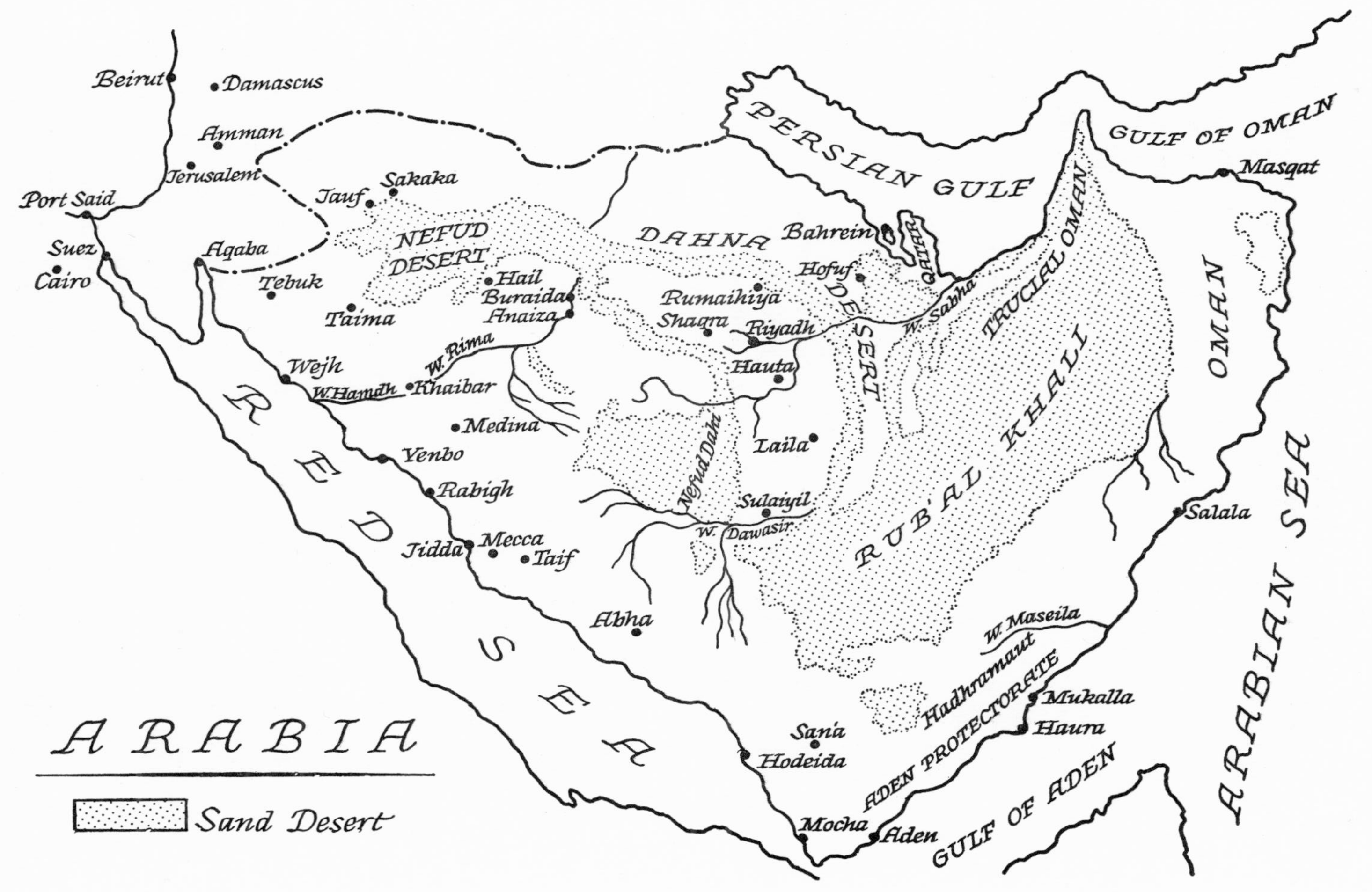
ARABIA
Sand Desert
Beirut
Damascus
Amman
Jerusalem
Port Said
Suez
Cairo
Aqaba
Tebuk
Jauf
Sakaka
NEFUD DESERT
Taima
Hail
Buraida
Anaiza
W. Rima
Wejh
W. Hamdh
Khaibar
Medina
Yenbo
Rabigh
Jidda
Mecca
Taif
Abha
RED SEA
DAHNA
Bahrein
QATAR
Hofuf
DESERT
Rumaihiya
Shaqra
Riyadh
Hauta
Laila
Nefud Dahi
Sulaiyil
W. Dawasir
W. Sabha
PERSIAN GULF
TRUCIAL OMAN
RUB' AL KHALI
GULF OF OMAN
Masqat
OMAN
Salala
ARABIAN SEA
W. Maseila
Hadhramaut
ADEN PROTECTORATE
Mukalla
Haura
San'a
Hodeida
Mocha
Aden
GULF OF ADEN

over 8,000,000 would be arrived at. Zwemer in his *Arabia, The Cradle of Islam* quotes A. H. Keane as giving in his *Geography of Asia* a figure of 11,000,000 for Arabia.[5]

The fact of the matter is that statistical population data are nonexistent and most population figures are based on rough estimates. A considerable portion of the Arabian population is composed of village, town, and city dwellers. The population of the Yemen is very largely settled, nonnomadic. "Field Notes on Saudi Arabia" made in 1935 and prepared by the British Air Ministry gives population data which show that about 42 per cent of the inhabitants of the Kingdom of Saudi Arabia is made up of settled, nonnomadic people. In Asir the settled population is as high as 62 per cent of its total population.

In Arabia there are many towns and cities of considerable size. In the Hejaz Mecca is estimated to have a population of 80,000, Medina and Jidda 30,000–50,000, Yenbo 10,000, and Taif 5000–8000. In Asir the capital of this province, Abha, has a population of 15,000 and the port of Kunfida 4000–5000. In the Nejd the capital Riyadh is estimated to have a population of 60,000, Hail 10,000–20,000, Buraida 20,000–30,000, Anaiza 15,000–25,000. This makes a considerable urban population from 105,000 to 135,000 in the very center of the Arabian plateau. In Hasa the city of Hofuf has an estimated population of 30,000. It is the center of an agricultural region with a population totaling about 150,000. In the Yemen, the capital San'a, has 25,000 inhabitants and the Yemenite port of Hodeida approximately 40,000. The city of Kuwait on the Persian Gulf has a population of 60,000, and Aden over 45,000. In addition to this urban population of from 423,000 to 450,000 must be added the population of towns in Hadhramaut, Oman and Trucial Oman for which data are not available. If the total population of Arabia be assumed to be 10,000,000, its urban population 500,000, and its village and small town (less than 5000) population 3,700,000, the nomadic population appears less formidable than has generally been assumed. Arabia as a whole is no more nomadic than Iraq, Syria, and Transjordan.

In North America the nomadic Indian population was, to use a most unpleasant and barbarous modern term, liquidated. It is doubtful whether the Bedouins will ever be so dealt with. It is possible that these Arab nomads will play a smaller role in the affairs of the Arab lands of western Asia, but as long as the steppes and deserts of Syria, Jordan, Iraq, and Arabia continue to provide pasturage for camels, sheep, and goats, it may be anticipated that the Bedouins will survive the modernization of the Near East. Prophecy, however, is a risky matter as may be seen from a statement in the handbook on Arabia published by H. M.

Stationery Office in 1920 and prepared under the direction of the historical section of the British Foreign Office. The authors of this volume advised by scholars, historians, and experts on the Near East and Moslem world wrote as follows: "So far as human foresight can tell, the peninsula is likely to remain parcelled out internally among a number of autonomous States as it is at this day" (1917).[6] Less than twenty years later the bulk of Arabia was brought under the political control of Ibn Saud, monarch of the Kingdom of Saudi Arabia comprised of the provinces of the Nejd, Hejaz, Asir, and Hasa and minor dependencies. Britain controls much of the southern coast known now as the Aden Protectorate, and the British have treaties with the Sultanate of Oman, the sheikdoms of Trucial Oman, and with Kuwait. Were it not for the British the balance of Arabia with the exception of the Yemen might well have become a part of the Kingdom of Saudi Arabia.

This process of unification and consolidation of power took place for the most part between 1919 and 1939. It is largely the story of the rise to power of Ibn Saud and the Wahhabis.

THE RISE OF IBN SAUD

The great princely families of the central Arabian oases, the er-Rashid sheiks of Hail and Jebel Shammar and the al Saud sheiks of Riyadh had long been rivals for the control of the Arabian plateau. In 1891 Prince (Emir) Muhammed ibn Rashid defeated the al Saud family which fled for refuge to Kuwait. On the death of Emir Muhammed ibn Rashid in 1897 the father of the present King ibn Saud, then a young man, aided by the sheik of Kuwait recaptured Riyadh and the old rivalry between the two ruling families recommenced. Between 1897 and 1904 there was almost constant war between the Rashids and the Sauds. In this struggle the Turks backed the Rashids. This fateful action was to determine Emir ibn Saud's relationship with the British during the next fifty years. Ibn Saud defeated his enemies and by 1910 was master of the Qasim oasis with its important cities and towns including Buraida.

Consolidation of his power in central Arabia.—In order to lessen the power of the nomad sheiks and to increase his control of the areas whose sheiks had acknowledged his leadership, Ibn Saud developed a novel system of agrarian settlement. In 1910 he organized the militant Wahhabite order of the Ikhwan ("brotherhood") and sent them to his newly conquered domains both as Wahhabi missionaries and as agricultural settlers. In this way he consolidated his power in the central oases. During the years 1913 and 1914 Ibn Saud sent his forces into Hasa, then a Turkish vilayet. His conquest of Hasa on the eve of World War I was of considerable significance because it brought him into contact with the British and particularly with the British government of India.

Although Ibn Saud remained neutral during World War I, while his rival ibn Rashid became an ally of the Turks, he entered into a treaty of friendship with the British in December 1915. By this Treaty of Qatif (a port of Hasa) Ibn Saud received British recognition as ruler of Nejd and Hasa. It is significant that this treaty was signed before the revolt of Sherif Hussein, and before the rival Arabian family of the Hashimites became the subsidized clients of Great Britain and the leaders of the Arab revolt against the Turks. Ibn Saud after 1915 had staunch supporters in that complex bureaucracy which determined British foreign policy in the Near East.

Sherif Hussein's bid for power and his assumption of the title of King of the Arabs, although the Allies recognized him only as King of the Hejaz, angered Ibn Saud who scorned the vast pretensions of the Sherif of Mecca. Emir Faisal Ibn Hussein, as the representative of his father at the Paris Peace Conference of 1919 succeeded in having the town of Khurma on the southern route from Mecca to Riyadh assigned to the King of the Hejaz. When Hejazi military forces proceeded to occupy Khurma, which was a direct threat to the ruler of Riyadh, Ibn Saud attacked with his devoted Ikhwan and defeated the enemy at the Battle of Turaba. Although war between Sherif Hussein and Ibn Saud was temporarily averted Emir Saud proceeded to consolidate his power in those parts of Arabia where he would not anatagonize the British.

Defeat of the Hashimites.—In 1919 he captured Abha, the capital of Asir, and annexed this rich territory of the Idrissi family. He invaded Jebel Shammar and attacked Ibn Rashid who had lent his support to King Hussein. By 1921 and 1922 he was master of the northern oases of Hail and Jauf and advanced his frontiers to those of Transjordan and Iraq. Ibn Saud encompassed the Kingdom of the Hejaz on three sides. Britain's impotent Hashimite potentate weakened his position in Arabia by proclaiming himself Caliph in 1924 after the Turkish Republic had renounced the Ottoman claim to the caliphate. In that same year the British ended their subsidy to Ibn Saud, who refused to recognize Hussein's claim to the caliphate and in August invaded the Hejaz. Hussein abdicated in favor of his son Emir Ali who was unable to defend the Hejaz. Ibn Saud completed its conquest in 1925 and early in the next year was proclaimed King of the Hejaz.

The British promptly occupied Ma'an and Akaba which were then incorporated in Transjordan and Palestine, respectively. With their long experience in imperialistic control the British avoided wherever possible costly and unprofitable wars against Asiatic people. Their client Hussein having been overwhelmed, the British promptly came to terms with his conqueror. In May 1927 General Clayton, who had played an important role in directing British intelligence and political activities in the Arab Near East since 1914, negotiated with Ibn Saud the Treaty of Jidda by which the British government recognized him as King of the Hejaz, the Nejd, and its Dependencies.

By 1927 Ibn Saud had utterly defeated his two rivals, the Rashids and the Hashimites, and made himself master of approximately two-thirds of the Arabian Peninsula. He was then confronted with the problem of consolidating his power and organizing his possessions into a well-governed state.

The creation of the Kingdom of Saudi Arabia.—The task facing Ibn Saud was one which demanded political acumen and talent of the highest order. The real greatness of Ibn Saud lies in his accomplishments after the conquest of central and northern Arabia. Although historical analogies and comparisons are of dubious validity and are often misleading, it may be helpful to look upon the work of King Ibn Saud as in some ways similar to that of King Alfred of England and King Charlemagne of the Franks.

The ruling classes in Mecca and Medina were exceedingly dubious about Ibn Saud and his Wahhabites. It is putting it very mildly to say that the people of the Holy Cities are far from being puritans, and they had as little in common with the Wahhabites as the luxury-loving clergy of Rome and the nobles of Geneva had with Lutherans and Calvinists in the sixteenth century. On the other hand the Wahhabi religious leaders and the Ikhwan hated the Meccans and feared and disliked the modern innovations Ibn Saud began to introduce. Obscurantist bigots aroused the Ikhwan to a revolt which continued from 1926 to 1930 before Ibn Saud was able to crush this threat to his power. In 1931 and 1932 ibn Rifada led a revolt of the Billi tribes in the northern part of the Hejaz. No sooner was this put down, than Ibn Saud was embroiled with Imam Yahya ibn Yahya ruler of the Yemen over control of Asir. The war between Saudi Arabia and the Yemen was brought to an end in 1934 by the Treaty of Taif by which Ibn Saud became the unchallenged ruler of Asir. At last there was peace, both internal and external, so that Ibn Saud until the outbreak of World War II was able to devote his undivided attention to the economic and social problems of the Kingdom of Saudi Arabia of which he was the absolute and undisputed ruler. In his charming little book *Arabia Phoenix* with its vignette-like descriptions of his trip to Riyadh in 1935 Gerald de Gaury says: "The King has completed two-thirds of his task—the restoration of his dynasty, the revival of Islamic teaching, and a renewal of internal security; but he has hardly begun the latter part of his work: the planning of economic prosperity." [7]

After centuries of political anarchy and widespread insecurity from raids, pillage, and fruitless tribal warfare, Ibn Saud established political order and security throughout the greater part of Arabia. It was a notable achievement which may have very considerable historic significance if the successors of King ibn Saud are able to create the economic foundations which are essential to centralized government and which can alone remove the causes of tribal warfare.

SAUDI ARABIA AND ITS PROBLEMS

In the Arabian Peninsula the Bedouins have always been of economic importance to the Arab lands of western Asia as the producers of meat, hides, and wool and of the main instrument of transportation, the camel. Agricultural lands were too valuable and too limited in area to maintain herds of sheep, goats, and camels, their natural grazing grounds were the steppes and deserts of Arabia, Iraq, and Syria. The caravan cities, the agricultural centers, and the ports of Arabia provided the markets for the products of the Bedouins. When the Arabs lost control of the trade by land and by sea from east to west and south to north, when the sea routes shifted far from the shores of Arabia, trans-Arabian trade routes collapsed, the ports, the inland caravan cities, and eventually the agricultural centers declined. The settled areas no longer possessed the resources with which to control the nomads nor did the dwindling cities and towns continue to provide great markets for the Bedouins. Economic decline and increasing economic insecurity resulted in increasing political insecurity and eventually in the political anarchy of ceaseless tribal warfare.

Economic development and finances.—As early as 1910 Ibn Saud, realizing the necessity of increasing agricultural production, began to develop his system of agrarian settlements. He soon discovered that any considerable agricultural development would require financial resources which he did not possess and technical knowledge unavailable in Arabia. Although his conquests between 1919 and 1933 increased his revenues they also increased his expenses so that there was little surplus with which to finance an extensive plan for the development of the agricultural and other resources of his kingdom. Statistical data of the revenues and expenditures of the Saudi government for the period previous to and during World War II are practically nonexistent. Such figures as were used in estimating the budget of the government of Saudi Arabia in 1938 showed revenues totaling $11,000,000 ($3,000,000 from customs and miscellaneous taxes and $8,000,000 from pilgrim tariffs) and expenditures amounting to $11,000,000.[8] It was not a budget which could provide funds for agricultural experimental stations, irrigation projects, road building, and other public works. Foreign capital was needed to realize ibn Saud's somewhat nebulous ideas in regard to the economic development of Saudi Arabia.

Two formidable difficulties confronted Ibn Saud with respect to obtaining foreign financial assistance. One was the opposition to aliens and to non-Moslems entering Arabia and to modern machinery, apparatus, and so forth, by the Wahhabite religious leaders, who could exert a power of control over all actions of the Saudi government similar to that of the Sheik-ul-Islam in the Ottoman Empire, because the laws of Saudi Arabia were based on and had to conform with the Sheriat. The other difficulty was how to obtain foreign economic aid without falling under the political control of an alien and Christian Power. With some knowledge of what had befallen Egypt and the Ottoman Empire during the nineteenth century, Ibn Saud understood the dangers which confronted him in seeking foreign help.

Oil prospects.—Although agricultural development was the king's most cherished interest he was not unaware of the revenue-producing oil fields of Iran and Iraq and he knew that the Prophet Mohammed had given the ancient gold mines of King Solomon as a feudal possession to the sheik of one of the Hejaz tribes.[9] Soon after World War I the oil magnates of the West began scouting about the outskirts of Arabia for petroleum deposits. In 1922 Mr. Ely and R. A. McGovern, who with the author had explored Palestine in 1913–14 for the Standard Oil Company of New York, visited the Yemen and Ethiopia on behalf of the Standard Oil Company of New Jersey. The D'Arcy Exploration Company which carried on prospecting for the Anglo-Persian Oil Company became interested, together with an American company, in the prospective oil resources of Kuwait and by 1934 organized the Kuwait Oil Company. A British company acquired an oil concession for the Bahrein Island petroleum deposits in 1925 which was taken over three years later by the Standard Oil Company of California. Another American company, the Near East Development Corporation during 1927 obtained a share (23.75 per cent) of the Iraq Petroleum Company in the Mosul oil fields equal to that pried out of the British by Clemenceau early in 1919. It was quite natural, therefore, that Ibn Saud would seek to find someone interested in the petroleum and mineral resources of his kingdom.

It was through two rather unusual North Americans, whose names will ever be associated with the modernization of Arabia, that Ibn Saud was able to begin his program of development with aid of foreigners. One of these was Karl S. Twitchell of St. Albans, Vermont, who graduated in 1908 from Queen's College and University with the bachelor of science degree in mining; the other was Charles R. Crane, that dilettante diplomat and eccentric benefactor of the Yemen. Well known in the Arab world because of the King–Crane Commission of 1919, Mr. Crane paid a visit to Imam Yahya of the Yemen at San'a in 1926 and 1927. The imam a few years earlier had opened the doors of the Yemen to the mining engineer and oil prospector R. A. McGovern, and because there were no tangible results of his explorations, Imam Yahya was all the more delighted with Mr. Crane's astoundingly generous proposal to send at his own expense mining engineers to examine and report on the mineral resources of the Yemen. The imam gladly accepted this offer, and as a result Mr. Twitchell was employed by Mr. Crane to go to the Yemen in 1927.

Ibn Saud, who kept himself well informed of all that went on in the Yemen, invited this modern American Harun al Rashid to come to Saudi Arabia, with the hope that Mr. Crane might become interested in helping Ibn Saud's agricultural development plans. Generous Mr. Crane sent his engineer Twitchell to Saudi Arabia. This act had momentous consequences. So important are they that Mr. Twitchell's account of his relations with Ibn Saud in his book *Saudi Arabia* is a historical record of considerable value.

As a result of Mr. Twitchell's professional and personal interest in the development of the natural resources of Saudi Arabia and of Ibn Saud's persistent search for foreign assistance, the Standard Oil Company of California in 1933 received a concession for the oil deposits in Saudi Arabia, and a Canadian mining company, the Saudi Arabian Mining Syndicate, obtained in 1934 a concession to explore and develop the mineral resources of the Hejaz.

It seemed as if Ibn Saud was well on the way toward realizing his ambitious plans when gold mining operations began at the Mahad Dhahab mine southeast of Medina in the Hejaz and oil drilling had begun at Dhahran in Hasa. Before any considerable benefits from these concessions became available for agricultural development Saudi Arabia was caught up in the maelstrom of World War II, which made Arabia a focus of interest to both the British and American governments. Ibn Saud was rescued from the threat of economic disaster resulting from the war by aid from Great Britain and the United States.

During the war Arabia became an area of great strategical importance to both Britain and the United States, in consequence of which the American government became increasingly interested in Arabian affairs. Ibn Saud welcomed and cultivated closer relationships with Americans. It was as a result of these that in the postwar period he was able to see his hopes for the economic development of his kingdom fulfilled.

CHAPTER XXIV

Oil in the Near and Middle East[1]

The world-wide importance of the Near East throughout much of known history has been greatly enhanced by the development in the twentieth century of its vast petroleum resources. The ever-increasing and insatiable demand for petroleum products based upon the compelling needs of this highly industrialized and mechanized age makes the Near East economically a more strategic area than it has ever been in the past. The crucial significance of the Near East was made dramatically apparent during the Suez crisis of 1956–57 following the Anglo-French-Israeli attack upon Egypt when it was feared that all of non-Communist Europe might be threatened with industrial stagnation and rendered militarily powerless if Near East oil ceased to reach Europe.

The great wealth of oil coupled with its importance to the rest of the world has had profound effects upon the people and states of the Near East. Early in the twentieth century the prospect of finding oil in the Ottoman Empire began to interest the great oil companies of Europe and the United States and the governments of the Great Powers. Near Eastern and foreign concession hunters sought to secure control of Turkish petroleum deposits which became an added source of international rivalry.

The development of oil production, refining, and transportation has resulted in a great flow of capital to the Near East and considerable increase of income in the form of royalties and wages, which in some regions are bringing about astounding changes. In a variety of ways the future destiny of the Near East and of its people is being shaped by its one great mineral resource, petroleum.

The amazing, if not fantastic, impact of oil upon the Near East cannot be fully understood without some knowledge of the petroleum industry, of the international struggle of the oil companies to obtain control of oil deposits, and of the history of the exploration and development of petroleum in the Near East.

۞ THE PETROLEUM INDUSTRY

World-wide competition.—The competition to secure control of these oil resources was on a global basis between the titanic oil companies of the world. By the end of the nineteenth century the very nature of the petroleum business had made this competition one between giant corporations, trusts, cartels, and combines operating throughout the world. The petroleum business has four main segments: production, refining, transportation, and marketing. All four of these are intimately interrelated and interdependent, and each requires a large amount of capital investment before its specific operations can produce revenues.

The two historic figures in development of the petroleum industry, John D. Rockefeller and Henri Deterding, differed in regard to the means of controlling the industry and operating it most profitably. The Rockefeller interests believed that control of refining and transportation would give them a secure grip on the entire industry. Deterding and his associates were convinced that control of production would give them control over all other branches of the petroleum business. Eventually, both of the great petroleum rivals developed along vertical as well as horizontal lines, neither acquiring complete monopoly in any one of the four principal operations while both engaged in all four. An example of this diversity of investments is clearly shown in a recent annual report of the Standard Oil Company of New Jersey. This report indicates that of the total investment in property, plant, and equipment of over $2,000,000,000 approximately 47 per cent was in production, 22 per cent in refining, 16 per cent in transportation, and 12 per cent in marketing.

The reason for the growth toward vertical organization lies in the nature of the product and the means of its distribution. Because of the large investment, oil fields, insofar as it is possible under price and market conditions, must be maintained in continuous production, on which profits and security of investment depend. In the oil business storage and storage capacity which may be considered to be parts of production, refining, transportation, and marketing, though usually classified as part of the transportation segment only, are of vital importance. There must be in the oil fields, at the refineries, along the lines of transportation, and at marketing terminals sufficient storage to take care of the flow of oil from the wells. All along the line there must be a continuous and continual flow of oil on its way to the ultimate consumer.

Shutting down production at the well head means reducing the return on the total investment; inadequate supply of oil to the elements of the transportation system—pipelines, pumping stations, tankers—results in costly equipment being inadequately used. In fact the interruption of any one of the four segments of the petroleum industry tends toward disorganization of the entire process. These are some of the characteristics of the petroleum business which of necessity fostered the growth of horizontal and vertical trusts tending toward monopoly. It was these factors which led to the international competition to control the oil resources of the Near East.

In the United States the vast corporate structure of the Standard Oil Company was built up by John D. Rockefeller. Completely dominant in North America, the Standard Oil Company controlled the European and China markets. By 1890 it was in a position to establish a world monopoly. This it failed to do. The Russian oil fields, the enterprise of the Dutch capitalists, the financial acumen of the Rothschilds, and the imperious and imperial necessities of the British resulted in consolidation of non-American oil interests which effectively challenged the powerful Standard Oil Company in every part of the world, even eventually in the United States.

Rivalry in the Near East.—Because of its oil resources, the Near East became a factor in the vast struggle for control of the oil business of the world. Originally, the Near East began to be a focus of rival oil interests because of the discovery and exploitation of the oil deposits in both Transcaucasia and in the Caucasus. The early years of the Russian oil industry were even more hectic and far more colorful than those of the Pennsylvania oil fields. Before highly organized western capital entered the Russian oil business Moslems, Christians, and Jews, Tatars, Georgians, Armenians, and Russians grew rich in ruthless competition with one another that prevented any rational development of the Russian petroleum industry.

The Russian Caucasian oil fields soon attracted the attention of the bankers and the enterprisers of western Europe. The Nobels of Sweden were followed by the Rothschilds in the early 1880's. Large-scale operations made possible by mergers and consolidations brought Russian oil business more and more under European control and into the field of world petroleum competition. The ultimate integration of the Russian oil industry with the great international combines waited upon developments elsewhere in Persia (Iran), in the Dutch East Indies, and in Burma.

Oil in Persia.—The immense profits and fantastic expansion of the petroleum business excited men to action in many different parts of the world. Eager men sought for oil. A Devonshire man, William Knox D'Arcy, who migrated with his family to Australia, had made a fortune out of the Australian gold mines and had retired in his early fifties to England. There, through a former British minister at Teheran and his Persian friend General Paul Kétabji, W. K. D'Arcy became interested in the oil prospects of Persia. After a personal prospecting trip he became convinced of the potential value of Persian oil resources and in the spring of 1901 obtained a concession for the exploitation of petroleum in all but the five northern provinces of the shah's kingdom.

Although a company was organized in 1903 to operate the D'Arcy concessions in Persia little was accomplished for several years. Lacking sufficient capital the first Exploitation Company created by D'Arcy and his associates was in financial difficulties when the Burma Oil Company and the British Admiralty became interested in Persian oil. For years Admiral Fisher had been aggressively advocating the shift from coal to oil as fuel for the British navy. When in 1904 he became First Sea Lord he was in a position to force consideration of his opinions. Two years later when the dynamic Winston Churchill became head of the Admiralty, the British government began to be interested in the Persian oil fields. In May 1908 after unproductive results from drilling operations, a gusher was brought in just seven years after the granting of the concession. The very next year the Anglo-Persian Oil Company was incorporated.

The Persian Gulf area had long been a preserve of the British Empire. The Arabian sultanates on the west shore and at the head of the Gulf were by treaties under exclusive British protection; southern Persia by the Anglo-Russian Agreement of 1907 had become a British sphere of influence; the British navy was unchallenged in the Red Sea and the Indian Ocean. In consequence the Persian oil fields and the approaches to them by sea were reasonably secure for the British. Persian oil appeared to be a safe and dependable source of supply for the British navy in an area rather thoroughly under Britain's control. The negotiation of contracts with the Anglo-Persian Oil Company to supply the British navy led to the British government's acquiring a controlling share in this company.

Role of Henri Deterding.—British naval, military, and civilian consumption of oil far exceeded the production, refining, and transportation facilities of the Anglo-Persian Oil Company, and it is not surprising that British financial and business interests became intimately associated with those of the Royal Dutch Oil Company. In 1880 oil was discovered in Sumatra and the Royal Dutch Oil Company was organized to develop the petroleum business in the Dutch East Indies. A newcomer in the world of oil, the Royal Dutch had to compete with Russian oil and the vast power of the Standard Oil Company. The survival of the Dutch company was in large measure due to the ability, insight, and ruthlessness of a young Hollander, Henri Deterding, who joined the Royal Dutch when it was a weak and unimportant concern. This man, who became a more dominant figure in the petroleum business of the world than John D. Rockefeller, saw what steps had to be taken if the Royal Dutch Oil Company was to survive and be able to compete on terms of equality with the Standard Oil Company.

To gain access to and be able to supply the markets of the world it would be necessary to acquire control of oil fields in all parts of the world, to build adequate refining facilities, to construct great fleets of oil tankers, to build storage tanks at all main distributing points, and to create a vast sales agency. To achieve these ends it was essential to bring about a merger of the principal non-American oil interests, which eventually resulted in the creation of a British controlled petroleum combine able to challenge the Standard Oil Company throughout the world. Some of the more important units in this competitive struggle were the Anglo-Persian Oil Company, the Asiatic Petroleum Company, the Shell Transport and Trading Company, the Royal Dutch Oil Company, and the Turkish Petroleum Company.

Concession hunting in the Ottoman Empire.—The Ottoman Near East in Asia Minor and the Arab lands of Asia were drawn into the struggle between the international oil titans. In many parts of the Ottoman Empire there were visible evidences of petroleum in various forms. On the shores of the Dead Sea there are asphalt deposits, throughout certain sections of Palestine surface limestone had been so saturated by petroleum that with a slight blow from a hammer, it gives off a strong petroleum odor. In Syria similar conditions prevail. In widely scattered areas stretching from the hinterland south of Sinope to the region of Erzerum oil seepages exist. In Mesopotamia oil pits have been known and utilized in a primitive manner for thousands of years.

It was therefore quite natural that enterprising Arabs, Armenians, Greeks, Jews, Turks, and miscellaneous Levantines, scenting the possibilities of great wealth, attempt to interest European and American capitalists in Near Eastern oil deposits. There were innumerable agents to call Abdul Hamid's attention to this petrolific source of wealth. It is possible that nothing would have been done for some time about the oil resources of the Near East if it had not been for a combination of factors related to the petroleum industry and to the division of Europe into two hostile armed camps.

Ida Tarbell's exposé of the Rockefeller monopoly practices and the various trust-busting activities of the "reformers" led by irrepressible "Teddy" Roosevelt, which resulted in the ostensible breaking up of the Standard Oil monopoly, had an unexpected effect upon the Near East. The Standard Oil Company of New York, whose main function in the foreign field was the sale of petroleum products, particularly in the East—Far, Middle, and Near—was completely dependent upon other Standard Oil companies for its supply of petroleum. This company's energetic and imaginative Vice-President William E. Bemis, who had hit upon the brilliant idea of giving lamps to the Chinese in order to promote sales, became convinced that his company must acquire its own oil producing properties abroad. Socony's foreign managers, therefore, were instructed to investigate oil prospects within their respective territories. Among these Mr. Oscar Gunkel at Constantinople, head of Socony's operations in the Near East, began to make discreet inquiries regarding crude oil deposits in his bailiwick. Sniffing rich rewards various Ottoman concession hunters brought prospects to Mr. Gunkel's office which led to Socony's despatching exploration parties to various parts of the Ottoman Empire in 1913 and 1914.

Before this time, however, European oil interests had been alerted by Socony's first furtive investigations. Furthermore, the British petroleum group, who had successfully blocked the acquisition of oil producing properties by Germany and her ally Austria-Hungary, except in Galicia and Romania, were alarmed at the possibility of Germans acquiring oil fields in the Ottoman Empire as a result of the Bagdad railroad concession, which granted the exclusive right to the exploitation of mineral and other natural resources in a twelve-mile strip on either side of the Bagdad railroad line. This danger became more critical after a rectification of the Turko-Persian frontier, when areas which were originally included in the D'Arcy concession fell within the Ottoman Empire. Both the British and the Germans were interested in securing concessions for the oil deposits in the Mosul region of northern Mesopotamia. To Germany, Turkey seemed to offer an opportunity to obtain crude oil from petroleum fields under German ownership and control. Before this could be realized Germans had to contend with the two great competing oil groups, the American and the Anglo-Dutch interests.

Standard Oil scouts had long since reported that the Mesopotamian oil deposits were among the richest in the world. This was well known at 26 Broadway, the heart and controlling center of the Standard Oil group. Why the Standard Oil neglected to acquire control of these deposits before the British and the Germans did so remains a puzzling mystery, for the reasons are unknown. England's interest in the Mosul oil region became active in 1907.

To adjust English and German interests in Turkish oil deposits and to be in a position to counter any activity on the part of the Standard Oil, the Turkish Petroleum Company was organized with 75 per cent of the shares owned by British and Dutch interests and 25 per cent by the Deutsche Bank. The final arrangements were made in March 1914 after Socony exploration parties had been examining oil prospects in Palestine, Anatolia, and eastern Thrace along the Marmora Sea. On the eve of World War I, in the latter part of June 1914, the oil fields in Mesopotamia were leased to the Turkish Petroleum Company. By business, financial, and legal methods the British had limited German interests to only a quarter share in Mesopotamian oil. With the secret treaty of alliance with Turkey of July 1914, the Germans on the outbreak of war stood to gain by military means full ownership of Turkish oil. While the British were fighting the Germans and Turks in Mesopotamia, Socony under the benevolence of Jemal Pasha was pottering around fruitlessly obtaining preliminary rights to exploit a large part of Palestine. Germany's one-quarter interest in the Turkish Petroleum Company effectively shut the Standard Oil out of Mesopotamia during World War I, thus ultimately protecting British interests there. Since Standard Oil's geologists later found its Palestine areas of little or no value, it was not until after the war that American oil interests secured a share in the oil fields of Iraq (Mesopotamia) and later in Saudi Arabia.

In the Near East until recently this rich natural resource was looked upon as a source of wealth for sultans, shahs, sheiks, and concession hunters. Between the rival foreign profit-making interests and the foreign political interests on the one hand and the predatory Near Eastern rulers and Levant concessionaires on the other, the interests of the people received scant consideration. Not until the venal and predatory Ottoman state was destroyed and until national and social consciousness developed in the succession states did petroleum begin to serve the needs of the poverty-stricken masses in the Near East. The war and the increasing momentum of political and social revolution throughout Asia, as well as in Europe, between 1914 and 1918 were preparing the way for new attitudes toward the development of petroleum and the other natural resources of the Near East.

❁ DEVELOPMENTS SINCE 1919

With the exception of the Iranian oil field operated by the Anglo-Persian Oil Company (later known as the Anglo-Iranian Oil Company) the development of the oil resources of the Near East did not begin until after World War I. Actual drilling operations were preceded by diplomatic maneuvers in 1919 during the period of the Paris Peace Conference. The Standard Oil Company of New York urged upon the American Delegation to Negotiate Peace the necessity of protecting its acquired rights in Palestine and of assuring American oil companies of an equal opportunity to obtain oil concessions in the other Arab countries of western Asia. Clemenceau, the Premier of France reached a settlement with Lloyd George by which France gave up its claim to the Mosul area in exchange for the acquisition of Germany's share in the Turkish Petroleum Company. About the same time the Sinclair interests were dickering with the White Russian counter-revolutionary General Denikin with the hope of securing a foothold in the oil fields of the Russian Caucasus.

The real race to obtain petroleum concessions in the Near East did not begin until after World War I. The enormous consumption of oil during the war and the vast expansion of the production and use of automobiles stimulated several of the great oil companies to secure control of the Near Eastern petroleum deposits. The governments of France, Great Britain, and the United States became increasingly conscious of the vital role of oil in times of peace and war and consequently gave support to the private companies seeking concessions.

Development of petroleum deposits.—Major Near East oil fields are in Iraq, Kuwait, and Saudi Arabia, and minor fields are in Egypt, Bahrain, Qatar, the Saudi Arabia-Kuwait Neutral Zone, Turkey, Syria, and Israel. Near Eastern oil production did not begin to be of importance until the late 1940's. In 1950, 55 million long tons were produced (M.L.T.), which amounted to approximately 10.5 per cent of the world total of 518 M.L.T. In 1959 Near Eastern oil production had increased to 186 M.L.T., nearly 19.5 per cent of the total world production of 964 M.L.T. By 1965 oil production in the Near East amounted to 22 per cent of the world total. The significance of this increase becomes evident when one notes that during the same fifteen-year period the U.S.A., which in 1950 had produced 60 per cent, in 1965 produced only 25 per cent of the total world production.

During the years since 1940 petroleum has made available in the Near East an incredible amount of wealth, created a host of new problems, domestic and foreign, and aroused many hopes which remain unfulfilled. The results, however, far exceed those that greeted Pandora and Aladdin. The development of these vast petroleum resources is bringing about basic changes in the Near East within decades, which in Europe took centuries.

Exploration and development.—The discovery of oil and its development in tsarist Russia during the last quarter of the nineteenth century followed by similar developments in Persia (Iran) early in the twentieth century stimulated exploratory activities in the Ottoman Empire, notably in Iraq and Palestine. World War I (1914–18) temporarily brought these to an end. During the interlude of peace between 1918 and 1939 widespread sophisticated technological explorations were undertaken in various parts of the dismembered Ottoman Empire. These resulted in the discovery of oil in Iraq (1927), Bahrain (1934), Kuwait (1938), and Saudi Arabia (1939). During this period general basic patterns relative to granting concessions took shape. Near Eastern rulers learned how to protect the interests of themselves, their governments, and their people.

World War II (1939–45) retarded activities, and it was not until its termination that Near Eastern oil production began to be of increasing importance. Within two decades it became a significant factor in the petroleum industry and in world affairs. In 1965 the Near East was yielding approximately a third of the total world oil production. The main centers of production in the Near East are Saudi Arabia, Kuwait, Iraq, the Neutral Zone (Kuwait-Saudi Arabia), Abu Dhabi, Qatar, United Arab Republic (Egypt), and Bahrain. Iran in the Middle East and the recently developed oil fields in Libya and Algeria make this general area one of the largest oil-producing areas of the world.

Petroleum production in millions of barrels per day, 1966

Arab Moslem countries of Near East	7.0
Arab Moslem countries of No. Africa	2.2
Iran and Turkey (Moslem)	2.1
Total Near East, Middle East, N. Africa (Moslem)	11.3
United States	8.3
U.S.S.R.	5.2
Total U.S. and U.S.S.R.	13.5

Source: *Reader's Digest Almanac,* 1968, p. 516.

Within little more than a decade the world petroleum industry—production, refining, transportation and marketing—has undergone signifi-

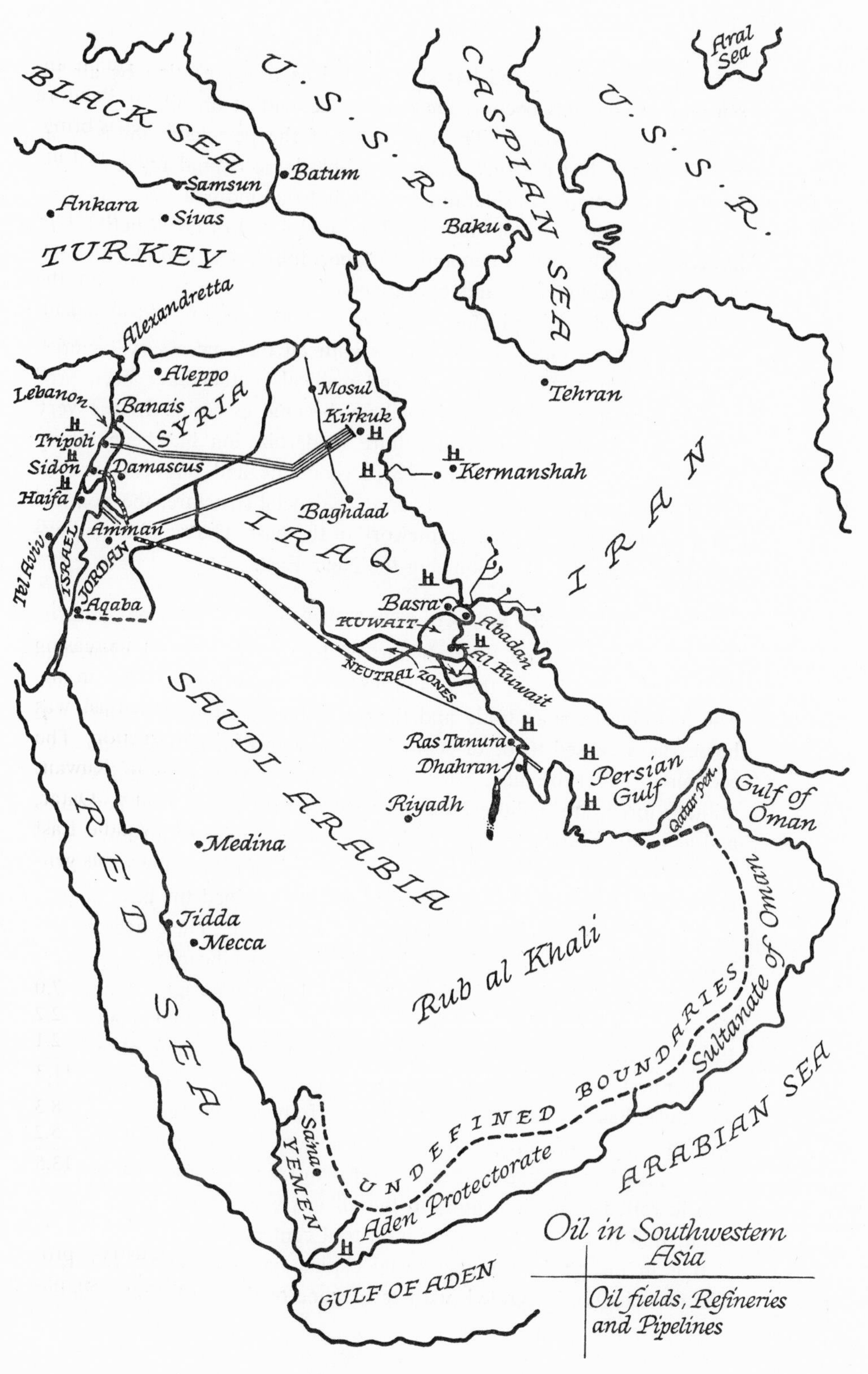

BLACK SEA
U.S.S.R.
CASPIAN SEA
U.S.S.R.
Aral Sea
Batum
Samsun
Ankara
Sivas
Baku
TURKEY
Alexandretta
Aleppo
Mosul
Tehran
Lebanon
Banais
SYRIA
Kirkuk
Tripoli
Sidon
Damascus
Kermanshah
Haifa
IRAN
Baghdad
Amman
IRAQ
Tel Aviv
ISRAEL
JORDAN
Aqaba
Basra
KUWAIT
Abadan
Al Kuwait
NEUTRAL ZONES
SAUDI ARABIA
Ras Tanura
Dhahran
Persian Gulf
Qatar Pen.
Gulf of Oman
Riyadh
RED SEA
Medina
Jidda
Mecca
Rub al Khali
Sultanate of Oman
UNDEFINED BOUNDARIES
Sa'na
YEMEN
Aden Protectorate
ARABIAN SEA
GULF OF ADEN
Oil in Southwestern Asia
Oil fields, Refineries and Pipelines

cant changes and demand has skyrocketed as transportation by air by sea and by land has become increasingly dependent on oil.

Subsidiary industries.—The expansion of the petroleum industry in the Near East has not only made available large capital resources for local investment of considerable variety but has more directly brought about the development of many local industries and of construction and has consequently created demands for labor, for clerical and office workers, and for technicians and executives.

Roads and airfields, pipelines and storage tanks, port facilities, camps, and larger urban and suburban areas with all their necessary facilities have been constructed. Hospitals and medical centers have been provided and modern educational facilities became essential. In the very heartlands of an old medieval culture modernization has been taking place with astounding rapidity. These economic and physical changes are inevitably having their effects upon the social structure, the political systems, and the ideological framework of the past. The rapidity and extent of change are revolutionizing the Near East.

THE CHANGING SOCIAL STRUCTURE

The tribal nomads and their sheikhs of Iraq, Syria, Transjordan, and Arabia have largely lost the wealth and power they formerly possessed. The lucrative caravan trade and the profitable breeding of camels and horses have ceased to be of economic significance in the oil-dominated economy. The tribesmen, who for centuries were a powerful mobile military force, are of little importance other than as pastoral herdsmen and as recruits for the modernized, mechanized armies of a central government. They are of little social significance in the contemporary Near East. The airplane and the motorcar have undermined the base of their wealth and made their desert fastnesses vulnerable. Their age-old historic role is at an end and with it their social significance.

The peasantry still retain their social and economic importance. The peasant village remains the basic social and economic unit of the Near East and the most obdurate obstacle to the development of modern, mechanized, scientific agriculture. Even the U.S.S.R., after nearly half a century, has not been able to modernize fully the peasant village. This ancient way of life upon which urban society has been dependent for thousands of years resists its extinction with tenacity. Slowly modernization in varied forms is coming to the village, while the surplus agrarian population seeks work in urban industrial centers.

It is in the cities that new social classes have come into existence. The most highly integrated of these in some of the Near East countries is the urban wage-earning industrial class. Learning rapidly the technics of labor organization and trade unionism they are beginning to make their power felt as a new political, social, and economic force to be reckoned with. The urban bourgeoisie is less unified. The old conservative mercantile bourgeoisie, which had a long-established modus vivendi with the land-owning class and with the religious hierarchy, are being pushed aside by various elements of the new bourgeoisie. The diversity of these new elements tends toward fragmentation—socially, politically, and ideologically—of the new bourgeoisie. Whereas "liberalism" of nineteenth century vintage remains the philosophy of some middle-class elements, "socialism" has made great progress among other and more numerous sectors. In the predominantly Arab countries middle-class socialism tends to be closely allied with Arab nationalism. While communistic ideas have spread to some extent, communism as an ideology and an organized political force is confronted by strong resistance throughout all social strata of the Moslem Near East, where atheism is anathema. On the other hand socialism tends to be looked upon more favorably by some as a fulfillment of the teachings of the Prophet.

The International implications.—Since the discovery of petroleum in the Near East oil has had an increasing impact upon international as well as domestic affairs. It is now one of the important factors in the domestic and foreign affairs not only of the nations of the Near East but also of the whole international community. So rapid are the changes in all sectors of the petroleum industry that no one can foresee what the future may hold. Nevertheless, policymakers have to take into consideration not only the present situation but future developments. With respect to the Mediterranean, the Near East, and Middle East, the foreign policies of the two superpowers, the U.S.A. and the U.S.S.R., are compelled to take into consideration the petroleum situation as of now and as it may be in the future. It is of similar concern to governments and peoples of the Near East.

POLITICAL CHANGE

The political structure of the Near Eastern states is undergoing significant changes. The formerly potent theocratic class is losing its political power, and the laity is increasing its political influence. Centralization of economic and political power coupled with modernized military power is rapidly eroding the strength of the tribal and sectional elements. Central government with its expanding bureaucracies is a result of the process of modernization forced by oil wealth.

New groups and classes are developing the means to exert power.

Industrial developments have created a wage-earning industrial class which has learned the technics of trade unionism and the means to exert both economic and political power that cannot safely be ignored. A varied and growing bourgeois class composed of elements quite different from those of the old commercial and banking oligarchies has come into existence. Its leaders are active politically. Although communism has made slight progress, it is significant that revolutionary movements in the Arab countries of the Near East are led by socialists, whereas during the nineteenth century Turkish revolutionaries were led by liberals. Turkish liberalism ultimately fell victim to Turkish nationalism, which brought disaster to the Ottoman Empire. The spread of socialistic and communistic ideologies to the Near East has been an increasingly important factor in the foreign affairs of the Near Eastern states.

CHAPTER XXV

Stormy Years in Palestine, 1919-39

The volume of literature on Palestine during the twenty-year period between 1919 and 1939 is so vast that one hesitates to add even an iota to it. Although there is a considerable amount of authentic and valid written matter on Palestine much of the literature is colored by hopes and fears, by wishes and desires, by ignorance and prejudice, and no inconsiderable part of it is downright propaganda. Furthermore, few readers peruse a book or an article about Palestine without having already accepted certain unproven premises and without deep-seated emotional and ideological, including theological, attitudes. Most people approach the "Palestinian Question" from the point of view of right and wrong, frequently mixing moral right with historical and juridical right.

THE PROMISED LAND

The leaders of the Hebrew tribes who invaded Palestine some three thousand years ago convinced their fellow tribesmen that their tribal deity Yahweh had promised them the land if only they would conquer it, which they did. The idea of the *Promised Land* for the *Chosen People* was carefully preserved and nurtured through the centuries by the Jewish priesthood.

When other peoples, whose leaders had persuaded them that their gods would give them what land they conquered, took possession of Palestine the Jewish religious leaders rationalized their defeat and their exile to other lands as punishment for disobedience to their god Yahweh, who had in their minds in due course of time become the "universal god," Jehovah. The ancient idea of a Promised Land was so modified that the Jewish people throughout the centuries of their Diaspora came to believe that it was God's will that some day they would be restored to Palestine. So thoroughly did this become a part of Jewish thought, life, and worship that most Jews looked upon Palestine as their homeland, eventually to be returned to them by Jehovah. The Jewish idea of the Promised Land was accepted by many Christians who believed that God's word and promise to the Jews would, in good time, be fulfilled.

However one may explain the origin of the idea of the Promised Land, the fact remains that most Jews and a very considerable proportion of the Christians believe that the Balfour Declaration, the Palestine Mandate with its clauses providing for the establishment of a Jewish National Home in Palestine, and the creation of the Jewish State of Israel are fulfillments of God's promise. If it had not been for this belief by Jews and Christians there probably would be no Jewish State in Palestine today.

❁ WHAT'S RIGHT? WHAT'S WRONG?

That which was right and just in the minds of Jews and those Christians who supported them was all wrong and rank injustice in the minds of the Arabs. As between Arab and Jew, who shall say what is right and what is just? An interpretation of history based on religion does not give a satisfactory answer because there is no evidence to prove that the will of Jehovah is more just than that of Allah. The competitive priesthoods of rival gods are unlikely to agree upon an universal *Ethik* where their interests are deeply engaged. Unless he have recourse to a higher *Ethik* superseding that of the tribe, the nation, or the race, the observer of the Arab-Jewish struggle has the choice of two opposing concepts of right and wrong.

A. G. Keller, the great teacher of anthropology and sociology at Yale, has said that "might then does not make right; it makes both right and wrong." [1] In a world where it is thought that "right" can only be maintained by H- and A-bombs, rocket missiles, jet planes, and other horrifying types of destroyer goods, it is vain to search for an *Ethik* in the Palestine issue, unless one seeks a cloak to disguise one's aims and purposes in order to appeal to man's hunger after righteousness.

With respect to juridical right not even a United Nations' jurist, to say nothing of a Philadelphia lawyer, could determine whether the British promises to the Arabs in the McMahon-Hussein correspondence and in Anglo-French declarations had greater validity than British promises to the Jews in the Balfour Declaration. Who shall say whether Wilson's Fourteen Points and the Covenant of the League of Nations proclaim a higher right than Congressional resolutions favoring a Jewish state in Palestine? The real difference lies in the fact that the Jews had the means with which to compel the Great Powers to live up to their commitments to the Jewish people and the Arabs lacked the means to do so. During the first thirty years of the Arab-Jewish conflict the Jews have had their way. It would be a bold prophet who would predict future developments in this relentless struggle. Another *might* may make a different *right*. In the world as it is now organized, an international juridical right is a utopian concept whose validity endures as long as there exists the power to enforce it.

✿ PALESTINE: AN IDEA OR A REALITY

Until the boundaries were determined with the awarding of a mandate to Great Britain, Palestine had no definite frontiers and existed as an idea rather than a reality. Its limits, conforming to the ideas of those who used the term, frequently were rather nebulous. Aegean refugees who fled from the invading Hellenic barbarian tribes and found a haven in the southern coastal plain of Palestine, were known as the Philistines. Their land was called Philistia, but eventually a much larger area than the Plain of Philistia came to be called Philistia or Palestine.

Hebrew nomadic tribes invaded Palestine, conquered the Canaanites and the Philistines, and created a national kingdom under David. His son Solomon, pursuing a vigorous imperialistic policy, extended his political and economic power and brought under his direct or indirect control areas which at present are parts of southern Syria and of Jordan, to the borders of Saudi Arabia. Some extreme Jewish nationalists claim most of the area which nearly three thousand years ago was ruled by Solomon. Somewhat less chauvinistic Jews lay claim only to Palestine and Transjordan, still others content themselves with calling Palestine that area which comprised the kingdoms of Judea and Israel west of the Jordan.

Christians, particularly those of the western world, generally speaking refer to the land where Jesus was born, lived, and died as Palestine, which they also call the Holy Land. Although its boundaries remained somewhat vague, roughly it extended from Gaza and Bir es Saba in the south to Acre, Nazareth and Galilee in the north, in Biblical terms from Dan to Beersheba. Here are the most important Christian shrines.

The Turks did not use the term Palestine which was neither an administrative nor a territorial division of the Ottoman Empire. Politically and officially Palestine was nonexistent.

Nevertheless, in millions of Bibles, in uncounted Sunday schools, and in innumerable geographies there are maps of Palestine so that throughout Christendom there has existed in the minds of most people a general idea of the geographic conformation and boundaries of the Holy Land. This corresponded approximately with the Palestine of the Mandate.

Henceforth in this book the term Palestine will be used to refer to that area, exclusive of Transjordan, under British Mandate until 1948. Despite the fact that Palestine is today partitioned, part of it incorporated in the Republic of Israel, part in the Republic of Egypt and part in Jordan, the author will continue to write of Palestine as a geographic area with the boundaries as of the period of the Mandate because in the English-speaking world this area is still rather widely thought of as Palestine.

THE EMERGENCE OF TRANSJORDAN

The boundaries of Palestine and Transjordan, which were placed under a British Mandate, were determined somewhat arbitrarily and as the result of various agreements and of certain historical events. The expression "trans Jordan" had been used solely as a geographic term until the British created the emirate of Transjordan with the consent of the League of Nations.

After the victories of General Allenby's forces in the autumn of 1918 the conquered Arab lands were divided into Occupied Enemy's Territory South, East, and West. Palestine was O.E.T.S., Transjordan was part of O.E.T.E. Technically, these areas remained O.E.T. until the conference of San Remo in April 1920 allocated territories to be mandated to Britain and France. Actually, however, the administration set-up in Damascus under Emir Faisal treated O.E.T.E., which included Transjordan, as if it were an independent Arab state. With the proclamation in March 1920 of Faisal as King of Syria, Transjordan became a part of the Kingdom of Syria. With its collapse in July when French forces under General Gouraud entered Damascus, Transjordan was left practically without a government and fell into a condition of anarchy. This political vacuum was filled in November 1920 by Emir Abdullah, Faisal's older brother. From Amman as a base Abdullah harassed the French in Syria. Realizing that the French would be obliged to put an end to this threat from the south, the British to forestall intervention by France promptly stepped in and began to dicker with Abdullah. In December 1920 the Anglo-French Convention defined the boundaries between French Syria and Lebanon and British Mesopotamia and Palestine (then including Transjordan). During March of the following year the British signed an agreement with Abdullah recognizing him as

Emir and in July provided him with an annual subsidy of 180,000 pounds sterling.

By these arrangements with the French and Abdullah, Transjordan came safely into British hands. The British were obliged, however, to regularize matters with the League of Nations. When the Supreme Council of the Allies at San Remo allocated the Mandate for Palestine to Great Britain not only was Transjordan included in the Palestine mandate but a rider was added "to the effect that the Mandatory Power should be responsible for giving effect to the Balfour Declaration." [2] The British well aware of the universal opposition by the Arabs to the establishment of a Jewish National Home in Palestine did not wish to have the Balfour Declaration apply to Transjordan, which under the Sykes-Picot Agreement of 1916 was in area B that was to become an independent Arab state. The decision of the British to exclude Transjordan from the terms of the Balfour Declaration was fortified by the disturbances in Palestine in 1920 and again in 1921 when it became necessary to establish martial law to restore order. The British government had little difficulty in persuading the Council of the League of Nations in September 1922 to assent to the exemption of Transjordan from the terms of the Palestine Mandate concerning a Jewish National Home, which led to Jordan's eventually becoming a separate state.

THE ARAB-JEWISH CONFLICT

Early in 1918 it was possible to foresee that the fulfillment of the Balfour promise to the Jews and the Zionists' plans to create a Jewish state would result in an Arab-Jewish conflict.

Warnings of the specialists disregarded.—There were in fact several official observers, specialists, and experts who in 1918 and 1919 very definitely informed their respective governments of the probability of such a conflict. Frequently, politicians disregard the information provided them by professional officers of the government, if their recommendations run counter to the desires of potent pressure groups. Many local, state, and national politicians in the United States during the years between 1917 and 1949 could not afford to oppose the wishes of the Zionists who were thought to be able to marshal in support of their program a considerable proportion of the Jewish voters in the critical states of New York, Pennsylvania, Ohio, Illinois, Massachusetts, New Jersey, and Connecticut, where in 1940, over 82 per cent of the Jewish population of the United States resided. The concentration of 68 per cent of the Jewish population of the United States in eleven great cities was considered to be a matter of political importance.[3]

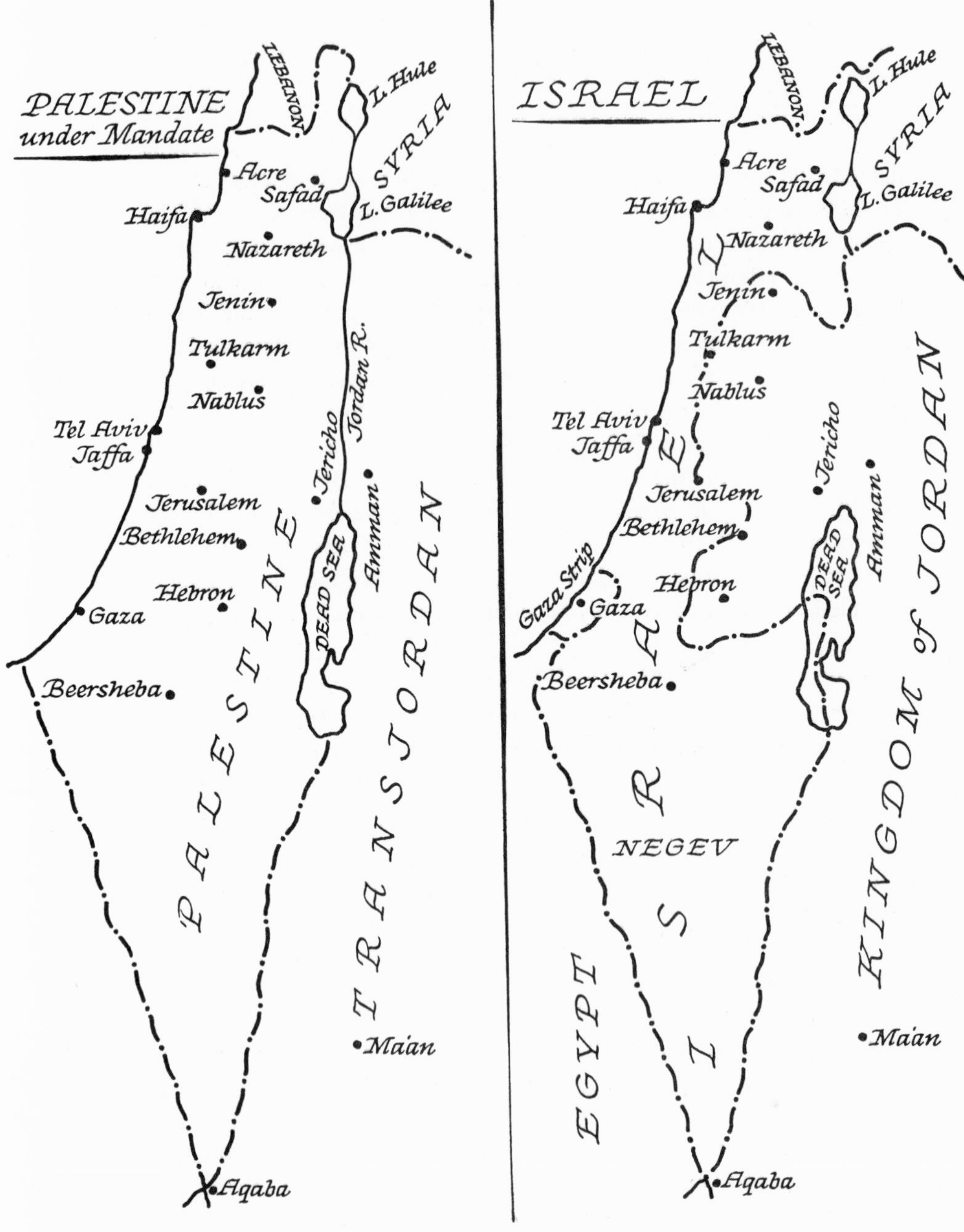
PALESTINE
under Mandate
LEBANON
L. Hule
SYRIA
Acre
Safad
L. Galilee
Haifa
Nazareth
Jenin
Tulkarm
Jordan R.
Nablus
Tel Aviv
Jaffa
Jericho
Jerusalem
Amman
Bethlehem
DEAD SEA
PALESTINE
TRANSJORDAN
Hebron
Gaza
Beersheba
Maan
Aqaba
ISRAEL
LEBANON
L. Hule
SYRIA
Acre
Safad
L. Galilee
Haifa
Nazareth
Jenin
Tulkarm
Nablus
Tel Aviv
Jaffa
Jericho
Jerusalem
Amman
Bethlehem
Gaza Strip
DEAD SEA
Hebron
Gaza
Beersheba
NEGEV
ISRAEL
KINGDOM of JORDAN
EGYPT
Maan
Aqaba

Neither the protests of the Arabs nor the judgments of official observers were heeded by the politicians of Great Britain and the United States. For weal or for woe the Balfour Declaration became an integral part of the Mandate for Palestine and the British government was committed to fulfillment of the obligations contained therein.

Zionist aims and Arab claims incompatible.—The Zionists were determined to use the Balfour Declaration as a means by which to make Palestine a Jewish land and create there an independent Jewish state. To accomplish these aims it would be necessary to increase the Jewish population by large-scale immigration, to acquire as much cultivable land as possible and settle Jewish immigrants on it, and to create Jewish industries in order to provide employment for the Jewish urban population. The Arabs, on the other hand, were determined that Palestine should remain an Arab land and that it should become either an independent Arab state or part of such a state. Arab and Jewish aims were incompatible. Unless both were prepared to modify their views and to arrive at a compromise an Arab-Jewish conflict was inevitable. In fact the victors in World War I by incorporating the Balfour Declaration in the peace settlement had set the stage in the Near East for a new national and religious conflict.

During the twenty years between 1919 and 1939 profound changes of a radically revolutionary nature took place in many phases of life in Palestine. So rapid and so startling were these changes that there would have been considerable maladjustment even if there had been no Arab-Jewish problem. Such maladjustment intensified the friction between Arabs and Jews over immigration, purchase of land by Jews, and economic matters.

FACTORS CONTRIBUTING TO THE CONFLICT

Palestine had begun to feel the impact of the modern world in the nineteenth century. World War I hastened the process of change and brought a much larger percentage of the people of Palestine in contact with modern ways of life. This acceleration, however, was of a minor nature in comparison with that which began in 1919 when the Zionists started to carry out their plans for a Jewish National Home. With the manpower, the trained minds well equipped with knowledge, with large financial resources, and with a passionate will to achieve their goals, the accomplishments of the Zionists during a short period of twenty years were, on a small scale, among the most striking achievements of the first half of the twentieth century. To some extent the Palestinian government and the Palestinian Arabs contributed to the fundamental changes taking place in Palestine between World War I and World War II, but the overwhelming contribution was made by the Jews.

Increasing population and immigration.—One of the most notable changes in Palestine which took place during those crucial years was the great increase in population from an estimated 750,000 in 1922 to about 1,500,000 in 1939. In fifteen years' time the population of Palestine had almost doubled. Of this increase approximately 40 per cent was the result of Jewish immigration, which amounted to 300,000. This number seems tragically small in comparison with the 6,000,000 Jews who perished in Nazi dominated Europe during World War II, whose lives might have been saved if they had been permitted to migrate to the United States and to other lands. In relationship, however, to the indigenous population and the resources of Palestine, this Jewish migration was colossal.

The supplying of land, dwellings, and employment for so many immigrants within such a short period of time—134,000 Jews arrived in Palestine during the three years between 1933 and 1935—was a major task. Its difficulties and problems may be more readily appreciated if one considered what the requirements would be if a state like New Hampshire which is comparable in size with Palestine were confronted with the necessity of absorbing 300,000 aliens within a period of a decade and a half. The economic expansion in industry and agriculture necessary to absorb such a large increase in population would require large investment of capital and much construction of farm buildings, factories, urban dwellings, school houses, and public works. The fact that the Zionist leaders and the Jewish people were able, in the main, to make provision for the growing Jewish population in Palestine is testimony to their ability and zeal.

The growth in population was due to natural increase as well as to immigration. Birth rates of Jews and Arabs were high, there was a decline in death rates and a very large decline in infant mortality rates, all of which contributed to the maintenance of a high rate of natural increase. A very thorough study of this problem was made at Princeton University by the Office of Population Research during World War II. The following chart shows graphs relative to the growth of the Palestinian population through natural increase.

The growth of population by natural increase created problems for the Arabs, whose numbers increased from 660,000 in 1922 to somewhat over 1,000,000 in 1938, an increase comparable to that of the Jews. Such large increases of population affected every aspect of the Palestine economy and caused serious economic dislocations especially during

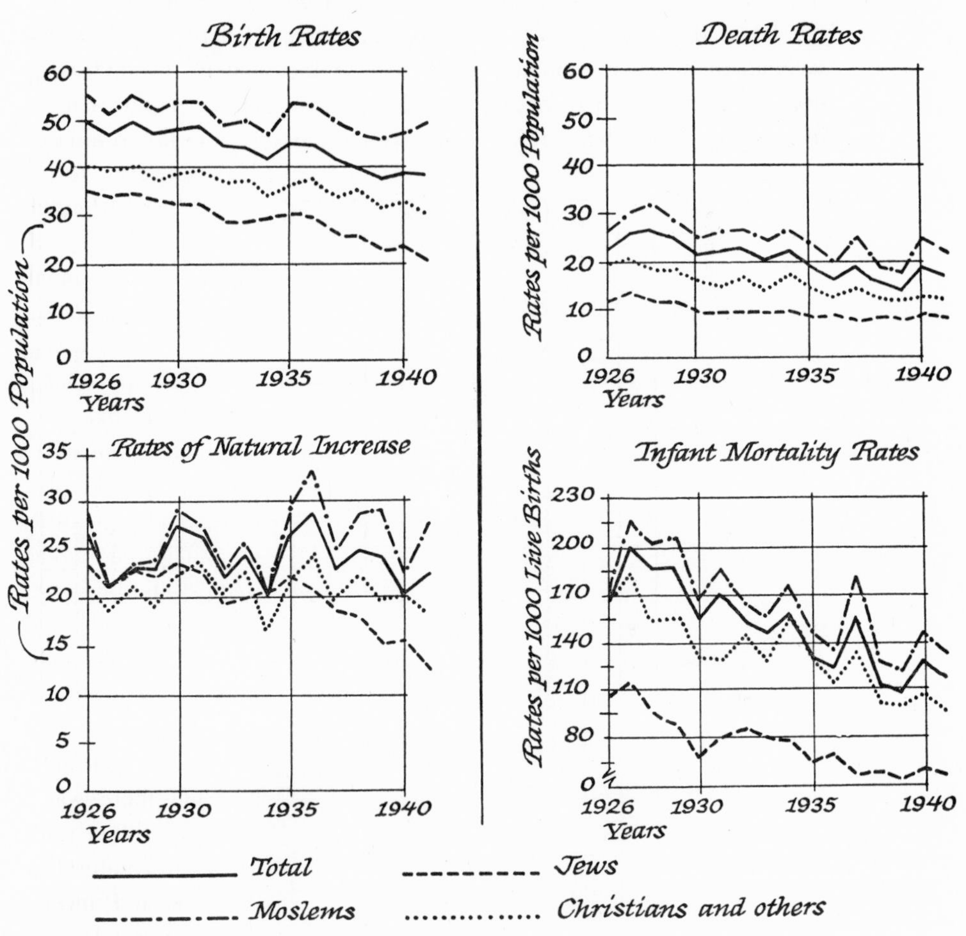
Birth and Death Rates in Palestine, 1926~1940
Birth Rates
Death Rates
Rates of Natural Increase
Infant Mortality Rates
Rates per 1000 Population
Rates per 1000 Live Births
Years
1926
1930
1935
1940
Total
Jews
Moslems
Christians and others

and following the years in which Jewish immigration reached its peaks —in 1925 when over 30,000 Jews entered Palestine and in 1935 when there were over 61,000 Jewish immigrants (see chart).

Economic crises resulted in widespread unemployment for both Arabs and Jews. Arab rural and urban workers, lacking experience in labor organization and in co-operative activities, were less able to protect themselves than the highly organized Jewish workers, familiar with all the latest developments of the labor movement. Friction rapidly developed in times of economic distress. The fact that on the extensive holdings of nationally owned Jewish land Arabs were not employed, that in many of the growing Jewish industries the employment of non-Jews

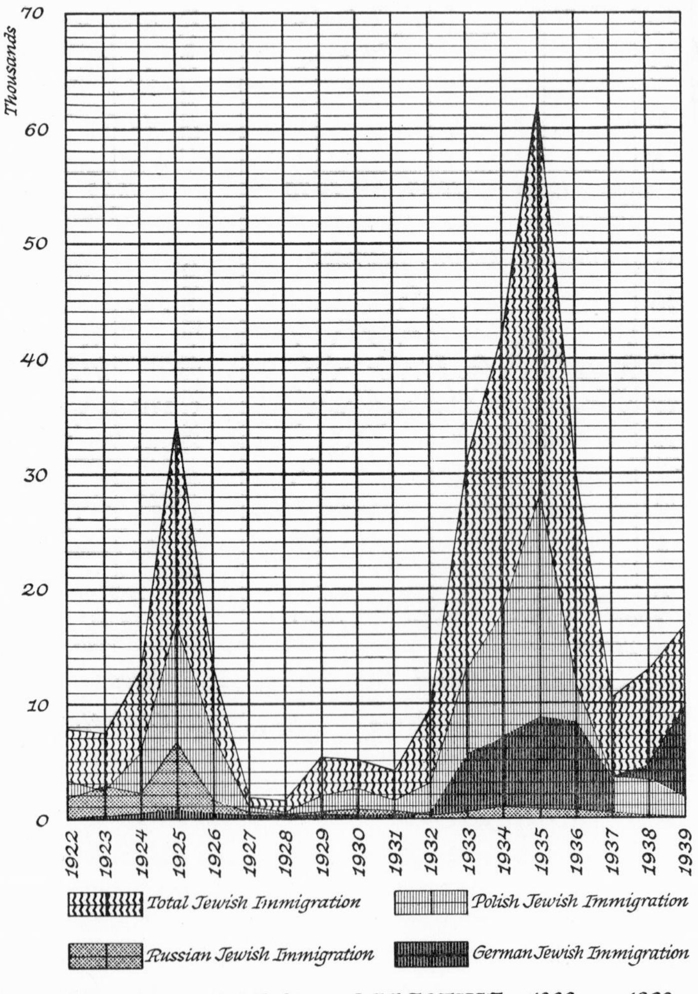

JEWISH IMMIGRATION to PALESTINE 1922 — 1939

was frowned upon, and that there was a considerable differential between Arab and Jewish wages intensified the growing discontent of the Arabs and their animosity towards the Jews. The years immediately following the great influx of Jewish immigrants coincided with the periods of maximum violence in Palestine.

The fear and dislike of the Jews by the Arabs was increased by the fact that not only were the Jews of a different religion, but they had no cultural ties in common with the Arabs. Few of the Jews spoke Arabic. Their social customs and way of living were very different from those of the Arabs. The clothes they wore were those of aliens. In a land where the majority of Arab women were still veiled, the scant modern clothing of Jewish women was deeply shocking to the Arabs. The realization that the Jews were coming not solely to establish a Jewish National Home but with the openly avowed purpose of making Palestine a Jewish country and creating a Jewish state further contributed to the rising tide of Arab opposition.

Immigration quite naturally became a major political issue between Arabs and Jews. Confronted with this tense situation the British government pursued a vacillating policy. Alternately, the British, under pressure from the Arabs and the Islamic world and from the Zionists and world Jewry, attempted to conciliate first one group and then the other. Internal conditions in Palestine and the critical international situation during the spring of 1939 finally forced the British to a drastic decision with regard to restricting Jewish immigration.[4]

The Arab peasant and "land transfers".—Another major issue between the Arabs and Jews was the all-important question of "land transfers"; that is, the purchase of Arab-owned agricultural land by the Jews. The Zionist leaders were convinced that the only sound basis for a Jewish National Home and a Jewish state was a large and prosperous Jewish rural and agrarian population. Consequently, the establishment of Jews on the land was one of their major objectives. The acquisition of land was essential to its achievement. The Jews were prepared to pay and did pay high prices for privately owned Arab lands. Furthermore, they did attempt to alleviate the effects of the resulting dispossession of the Arab peasantry. Because of the nature of the Arab agrarian economy and of the system of land-holding, a considerable part of the agricultural and grazing land in Palestine could not be transferred from Arab to Jewish ownership without social dislocations of serious import.

The economic and social unit of the Arab agricultural population was the village. The Arab peasant lived in his village, which in many instances was a crowded and unsanitary rural slum. Much of the Arab agricultural land belonged to a village even though an absentee landlord held title to it. Such landowners spoke in terms of their villages rather than their broad acres, because the village was the unit of agricultural production as well as a social unit. In a land with so scanty a supply of water as Palestine, each village was situated near springs or dependable wells. The spring or wells, the village itself, and the peasants who lived there were essential to the landowner.

The Zionists who bought the land, however, intended to replace Arab labor with Jewish labor and the ancient primitive Arab village with a modern Jewish agrarian settlement. When Jews bought Arab-owned land at high prices the Arab landowner profited, but in many instances the Arab peasant was dispossessed and no advantages accrued to him. Modern agricultural methods, and modern agrarian life as introduced by the Jews, were driving out of existence the age-old system of Near Eastern agrarian life with its bare subsistence level for the peasant and his exploitation by the landowner.

In other lands where industrialization changed the ancient agricultural system the rural population which was displaced found employment in new urban centers of industrial production. This was not the fact in Palestine. Ninety per cent of Palestinian industry was owned and operated by Jews. The Arab for the most part was not wanted in the Jewish-owned factory. He lacked the training and skills of the Jewish workers, and when he did find industrial employment his wages were low. On the fringes of Jaffa and Haifa ramshackle slums sprang up where unemployed and partly employed Arab workers lived.

As the Arab peasant watched the increasing purchases of land by the Jews his fear grew that the land he and his forebears had lived on and cultivated from time immemorial would pass into the hands of aliens who did not either need or want his labor. The Arab peasant's hatred of the Arab moneylenders and his grievances against the Arab landowners seemed of less importance than the threat of dispossession by the Jews. It did not require high-pressure propaganda by the semi-feudal Arab landowners and by their religious leader the Mufti of Jerusalem to arouse hatred against the Jews, to create in the Arab peasants and workers in the new urban slums a fierce hostility.

Because of the economic and social problems resulting from the purchase of land by the Jews, land transfers became, like Jewish immigration, a hot political issue. The Arabs were convinced that unless a check were placed on Jewish acquisition of agricultural lands they would be dispossessed. The Jews knew that limitations on their purchase of land would mean defeat of their hope to make Palestine a Jewish country.

On this issue, vital alike to Arab and Jewish nationalists, the British continued to temporize until 1939–40, when they felt compelled to impose severe restrictions on land transfers.

The gap between production and consumption.—Other fundamental problems arising from the whole process of creating the Jewish National Home in Palestine, which did not of themselves become acute political issues, intensified and aggravated the conditions which were the causes of the Arab-Jewish conflict. Among these were the increasing dependence on imported food and the continuing unfavorable trade balance.

In spite of the amazing progress made in agriculture by the Jews, with the application of the very latest scientific knowledge and the use of modern agricultural methods and equipment, Palestine became less self-sufficient in food production. Although Jewish agricultural achievements have aroused the admiration and won the praise of agricultural specialists in many parts of the world, Palestine was more dependent on food imports in 1938 than in 1924. While a very large increase took place in vegetable and fruit production, there was little gain in cereal, lentil, and other basic crops, and a decline in livestock. The rise in total food production did not keep abreast of increases in population. The widening gap between food consumption and food production may be observed by comparing the total and per capita value of Class I imports (Food, Drink, and Tobacco) in 1924 with those in 1938.

Class I Imports in L. P. (Palestinian Pounds)

	1924	*1938*
Total	1,400,000.00	3,000,000.00
Per capita	1.8	2.3

The increase in food imports was not unrelated to the increasingly unfavorable trade balance. In 1924 imports exceeded exports by more than L. P. 4,000,000, and in 1938 by over L. P. 9,000,000, while total foreign trade in those two years was respectively approximately L. P. 6,600,000 and L. P. 19,300,000. A basic factor in the economic situation in Palestine was the gap between production and consumption. It is estimated that per capita annual production, agricultural and industrial, for the year 1937, was between $66 and $73. Although the lowest of these two estimates represents a relatively high annual per capita production for several of the Arab countries in the Near East, the gross inequality in distribution reduced the living standard of the majority of the Palestinian Arabs to a level approximating that of the Arabs in neighboring lands.[5]

THE BRITISH DILEMMA

The British administration in Palestine was faced with increasing difficulties because under the Mandate British commitments to the Arabs and the Jews were as irreconcilable as the conflicting purposes of Arabs and Jews. The abnormalities of the Palestinian economy, together with other factors, created steadily mounting maladjustments for which the British found no solution. Recurrent disorders and violence, which first manifested themselves in 1920 and 1921, eventually culminated in the Arab insurrection just previous to the outbreak of World War II, and in a Jewish rebellion which, smoldering throughout the war, flared into open conflict with the British in 1945.

The frustrations of the Palestinian Arabs manifested themselves in violence from time to time between 1919 and 1939. This has been attributed to the Arab ruling classes, who were the indubitable leaders of the Arab resistance movement against the Jews and the British. It seems dubious reasoning, however, to conclude that the so-called Arab feudal landowners were the primary cause of the unrest and discontent of the Arab peasants and workers. Foreign invasion of Palestine by the Jews aroused the Palestine Arabs and tended to unite them, as foreign invasion of Syria by the French resulted in a national uprising.

The Churchill Memorandum of 1922.[6]—The early disturbances in Palestine prompted the British ministry to attempt to conciliate the Arabs by assuring them "that His Majesty's Government did not contemplate either the creation of a wholly Jewish Palestine or the disappearance or subordination of the Arab population, language, or culture in Palestine." [7] This was not a frank statement of what British statesmen had in mind in 1917 when the Balfour Declaration was made. The true facts are revealed by Lloyd George in his memoirs, where he states that the British Imperial War Cabinet expected that if the Jews availed themselves of the opportunities made possible by the Balfour Declaration, Palestine would become a Jewish Commonwealth.[8]

The Arabs were far from being mollified by the equivocal assurances of the British White Paper of 1922, and the Zionists were seriously distressed by it and by the severance of Transjordan from "Palestine." But the astute Vladimir Jabotinsky, who later founded the extreme nationalistic Revisionist Zionist party, realized that if the "Churchill Memorandum" were "carried out honestly and conscientiously" it would provide "a framework for building up a Jewish majority in Palestine and for the eventual emergence of a Jewish State." The policy of the British Government in its intent and in its application augmented the compulsions on the Zionists to increase Jewish immigration, while at the same time it made it imperative for the Arabs to prevent such immigration.

The immigration crisis.—The sudden increase in Jewish immigration in 1925 was very largely the result of new restrictive immigration laws, which cut down Jewish immigration to the United States from 50,000 in 1924 to 10,000 in 1925. Immigration to Palestine on so large a scale caused widespread unemployment and a serious economic depression which lasted until 1928. The conditions in Palestine and Britain's immigration policy based on the theory of "economic absorptive capacity" resulted in a marked decline in Jewish immigration. Thousands of Jews left Palestine between 1926 and 1931 during which period of six years the average annual net Jewish immigration was slightly less than 3200.

The second crisis over immigration arose in 1935 as a result of the great influx of Jews into Palestine in 1933, 1934, and 1935, which amounted to over 134,000. This new wave of immigration was precipitated by the action of the government of one of the Great Powers, for with the rise of Hitler to power in Germany, German and Polish Jews flocked to Palestine. This enormous influx of aliens frightened the Arabs and drove them into frantic resistance which did not need the added stimuli of Italian and German fascist propaganda to arouse hatred against the Zionists. The Arabs resorted to open rebellion in 1938 against the British and the Palestine government.

This uprising was the culmination of a series of events and developments from 1928 on, following the depression which had fostered increasing tension between Arabs and Jews. The illusion of peaceful relations between them was shattered by the violence which resulted from the dispute over the Wailing Wall in Jerusalem where for centuries Jews had lamented the destruction of Solomon's Temple. During 1929 and 1930 Arab and Jewish acts of violence occurred throughout Palestine. Under pressure to do something about the matter the British sent to Palestine in 1930 the first of several royal commissions to investigate the situation and to make recommendations.

British royal commissions.—The report of the Shaw Commission offered no solution to the problem of the Palestine mandate. It was unsatisfactory to both Arabs and Jews. And the Permanent Mandates Commission of the League of Nations severely criticized the manner in which the British government had administered Palestine. Under fire from all sides the British in May 1930 sent an experienced expert of the Anglo-Indian government to Palestine to report on land settlement.[9]

The report of Sir John Hope Simpson which resulted in another statement of British policy gave some encouragement to the Arabs but was immediately subject to penetrating and vigorous criticism by the Jews, which aroused a political storm in England that caused the somewhat timorous Ramsay MacDonald to write a letter to Dr. Weizmann which allayed Jewish fears only by arousing those of the Arabs, who became more and more convinced that Jewish pressure on the British government would always result in a policy unfavorable to the Arabs no matter what might be the findings of a royal commission.[10]

British plans for constitutional government received little encouragement from either Arabs or Jews. The increasing flow of Jewish immigrants which began in 1933 created a situation unfavorable to the adoption of a constitution. It appeared to the Jews as if the attainment of a Jewish majority was in sight and with it a Jewish state. The fear of this among the Arabs, created increasing unrest, which in 1936 began to find an outlet in renewed disturbances, disorders and widespread strikes throughout Palestine that culminated in a general strike. This critical situation brought reactions by the other Arab countries, by the Zionists, and eventually by the British government, which sent another royal commission to Palestine.

The report of the Peel Commission recommended the termination of the Mandate and the partition of Palestine, the royal commissioners having come to the conclusion that the terms of the Mandate were impossible of fulfillment.[11] In consequence of this recommendation the British government, which still was not aware of the fact that it was not its own master in matters pertaining to Palestine, futilely turned to partition as a solution. It requested on September 14, 1937, through its Foreign Office the approval by the League of Nations of the partition of Palestine. It also sent to Palestine a technical commission under Sir John Woodhead to work out the details for partition. This Palestine Partition Commission fulfilled its instruction with very great skill and shrewdness. It showed a variety of ways in which Palestine might be partitioned and in doing so convinced the British Cabinet that partition was impossible! [12] Whereupon the British repudiated partition.

The White Paper of 1939.[13]—Tension in Palestine was mounting as the world crisis approached its second great convulsion. The shillyshallying of the British government drove the Arabs into open rebellion in 1938. Confronted with an international crisis of major proportions and a stubborn insurrection in Palestine the British were compelled to use military force to crush the Arabs. After re-establishing order the British called an Anglo-Arab-Jewish congress at London. When, however, both Arabs and Jews refused to co-operate, the British in May 1939 made a unilateral declaration of policy known as the White Paper of 1939. This time the Arabs in view of the immediate threat of World War II were to be appeased.

The White Paper definitely stated that it was not the policy of the British government "that Palestine should become a Jewish State." It limited Jewish immigration during the next five years to a total of 75,000 and provided that thereafter Jewish immigration would be permitted only if the Arabs of Palestine were "prepared to acquiesce in it." That the Foreign Office had some reservations with respect to restricting further Jewish immigration may be surmised from the fact that an academic neophyte drafted for service in the British Foreign Office during World War II as a specialist on Arab affairs was initiated into the esoteric language of diplomatic documents by being informed that "to acquiesce in" had a very different meaning from "to consent to."

The 1939 White Paper provided for the placing of very definite limitations on the acquisition of land by Jews. It granted the High Commissioner authority to forbid the transfer of land and under this authority drastic Land Transfer Regulations were issued in 1940. The reasons given in the White Paper for the restriction of land transfers was based on the premise that in some regions in Palestine there should be no further acquisition of land by Jews.

The British White Paper of 1939 was of significant importance in shaping developments in Palestine from 1939 to 1949. Arab political leaders in Palestine and the other Arab countries of western Asia differed in their reaction to this new statement of policy by the British government. Some declared it unacceptable, others protested against it, and "only a minority of the Arab political leaders regarded the White Paper as an acceptable compromise." [14] On the whole, however, many of the Arab leaders came to realize how favorable the White Paper was to Palestine Arabs, and "eventually the Arabs became reconciled to" it.[15] The impression it made on the Arab people in western Asia tended to counteract in part the propaganda of the pro-Axis Arab groups in Palestine, Syria, and Iraq. On the contrary no Zionist could accept this White Paper. It aroused profound indignation throughout the Jewish world, and it was unremittingly opposed until Great Britain gave up the Mandate in 1948. It aroused such bitter feeling against the British that a dangerous Jewish subversive movement developed during World War II against the British, and it gave rise to a Jewish insurrection in Palestine in 1945. The Zionist leaders, however, in 1939 shortly before the outbreak of war showed great discretion and restraint.

The World Zionist Congress in August 1939, despite decided differences of opinion among its members, with real courage adopted resolutions which squarely faced the issues at a time when the security of the Jewish people might depend upon British victory. The Zionists took the stand that Great Britain should be given Jewish support, that the White Paper of 1939 should be rejected, but that everything possible should be done to convince the Arabs that its rejection was not directed against them.

THE SITUATION ON THE EVE OF WORLD WAR II

When World War II began in September 1939 Great Britain and her ally France faced a very critical situation in the Near East. The policy of the British and French governments in 1938 had alienated the Soviet Union whose agreement with Nazi Germany in 1939 created uncertainty as to the policy the U.S.S.R. might pursue in the Near East. Nazi and fascist propaganda had won some support among members of the ruling classes in Egypt and in several of the Arab countries of western Asia. The French had aroused antagonism in Syria and Lebanon by ceding Hatay to Turkey and by refusing to ratify the Franco-Syrian Treaty drafted in 1936. Dissident elements in Iraq were anti-British, and were prepared if occasion should arise to co-operate with the Germans. The Mufti of Jerusalem, who had taken refuge in Lebanon, and his followers were violently anti-British and were soon to seek aid from the Nazis. Palestinian Jews were embittered by the White Paper in 1939 and throughout world Jewry there was much ill-will toward the British government.

In Constantinople and Ankara, in Bagdad and Basra, in Aleppo and Damascus, in Beirut, in Jerusalem and Tel Aviv, in Amman, in Riyadh and Mecca the political leaders awaited uneasily the coming storm. The people of the Near East knew they could not escape untouched by war between the Gargantuans of the West, whose appetites, whether they were dictatorships or democracies, appeared insatiable. Once again the Near East had become the focus of rival imperialistic policies of the Great Powers, and the Near Eastern people pawns in their hands.

CHAPTER XXVI

The Arab Near East During World War II

The situation in the Near East at the commencement of World War II was fundamentally different from that at the outbreak of World War I. Nevertheless, this strategic area remained the crossroads where major interests of the Great Powers met in conflict, and consequently throughout World War II and during the uneasy truce which has followed it the history of the Near East has continued to be molded and shaped by forces and events far beyond its geographic limits. Shifts in the relationships between the Great Powers introduced variations on the old theme of imperialistic competition and nationalistic resistance to the imperialists, while the preliminary rumblings of social revolution were a prelude to the introduction of a new theme in the tumultuous twentieth-century Near Eastern symphony.

❁ ON THE FRINGES OF THE CONFLICT, 1939–41

The political fragmentation of the Near East which resulted from the defeat of the Ottoman Empire in World War I made it impossible for any clique like the Turkish C.U.P. to plunge the Near Eastern peoples into World War II in alliance with one of the Great Powers groups. The Turkish leaders warily avoided embroilment in the war until it was clear that the Axis would be defeated and Turkey would not become a battlefield.

Iraq became involved first in a conflict with Great Britain and then, following what was virtually a British military occupation, declared war against the Axis Powers in January 16, 1943, when Nuri as-Said, formerly a general in command of Arab forces under Emir Faisal in 1917 and 1918, was Prime Minister of a pro-British cabinet. Military operations in Iraq were of short duration and, except for their political and military significance, of a minor nature. Syria and Lebanon for a short time became the stage for a brief but sharp military campaign of British and De Gaullist Free French forces against those of the Vichy French mandatory government. Later, Syria and Lebanon declared war on the Axis Powers early in 1945 in order to receive recognition by the United Nations and to obtain invitations to the United Nations Conference at San Francisco.

Saudi Arabia, which remained neutral until February 1945 when it declared war on the Axis for reasons similar to those of Turkey, Syria, and Lebanon, became closely associated with Great Britain and the United States by matters of great urgency to the Kingdom of Saudi Arabia and of vital strategic significance to England and America. The mandated territories of Transjordan and Palestine were drawn into the global conflict because they were under British control and because of the dynastic ambitions of Emir Abdullah and of the compelling necessity for the Palestine Jews to help prevent the Axis Powers from gaining control of the Near East. Using Transjordan as a base, British-trained forces of Emir Abdullah played an important part in crushing the pro-Axis military clique in Iraq which had seized power by a *coup d'état* instigated by Rashid Ali al-Gailani in February 1941. Palestine was also the base for the operations in Lebanon against the Vichy French.

CAUGHT UP IN WAR

The Near East did not become deeply embroiled in World War II until 1941. Assured temporarily of a war on one front by the treaty with Soviet Russia in 1939, the Nazis did not wish to waste their resources in military operations in western Asia which would fall like ripe fruit into their hands as soon as France was overwhelmed and Great Britain forced to surrender. The Nazi failure to achieve the conquest of England after the collapse of France, which brought fascist Italy into the war, forced the Germans to operations in the Near East.

Italy's possession of Rhodes, and the Dodecanese Islands in the Aegean, of Cyrenaica in North Africa, and of Eritrea, Italian Somaliland, and Ethiopia brought hostilities close to western Asia. The impelling necessity for the Germans to cut vital communications of the British through the Near East coincided with the imperial ambitions of the Italians in the eastern Mediterranean and in the Nile Valley. Consequently, the Germans felt obliged to come to the aid of the Italians in Albania and northern Greece as well as in North Africa. As Germans advanced through the Balkans in preparation of the campaign against the Greeks, a new strategic factor entered the situation. The Soviet Union had forced one concession after another upon Germany from East Prussia and the Baltic states through Poland to Bulgaria. The German Military realized that it would be extremely dangerous to extend the Balkan front to the Aegean Islands and to the Arab Near East while leaving an exposed flank of a thousand miles from the Baltic to the Aegean to a potential enemy as powerful as the U.S.S.R. With Europe under their domination the German military leaders were no longer opposed to a war against Soviet Russia. The conflict between the General Staff, which had opposed war with Russia, and the Hitlerian ideas of conquest of the Slavs and the overthrow of Communism was resolved in 1941 and the Nazi forces invaded Russia.

Axis plans for conquest of the Near East.—War with Russia opened up new possibilities for conquest of the Near East. Stubborn Turkey, which refused to be dragged into the war, could be by-passed via the Ukraine and the Caucasus. A huge "pincer" movement operating from Transcaucasia and Italian North Africa might overwhelm the British in Egypt and throughout the Arab lands of western Asia. In 1942 this vast operation appeared to be on the road to success. General Rommel was at Al Alamein only seventy miles from Cairo, the German Sixth Army was pounding Stalingrad into rubble and German forces were advancing toward the Caucasus. The fate of the Near East trembled in the balance. The crushing defeat of the Germans by the Russians at Stalingrad and the retirement forced upon Rommel by General Montgomery spared the Near East the devastations incident to modern warfare, although it did not escape the economic distress and dislocations of the world conflict.

War-time problems.—During World War I disease and wholesale starvations as well as massacres and forced migrations decimated the peoples of the Near East. The situation in World War II was quite different. Whereas the Ottoman Turks had been utterly incapable of dealing with conditions created by the war and the Allied blockade, Britain, and later the United States, took effective measures to prevent economic collapse and social disasters, although much suffering resulted from inability to control inflation, rising prices, and depreciating currencies.

Because of the precarious lines of communications in the Mediterranean, the long supply lines around the Cape of Good Hope and across the Pacific, together with a limited number of cargo ships available for civilian needs, it was necessary for the British to organize what was known as MESC, the Middle East Supply Center, with headquarters at Cairo and branches in Iran and the principal Arab countries of western Asia. MESC successfully lessened pressure on the lines of communication by giving aid and encouragement to both agricultural and industrial production and reduced social distress caused by shortages of food, clothing, and other essential supplies.

❁ SAUDI ARABIA—A STRATEGIC AREA

Economic difficulties.—In the various parts of the Near East the problems which confronted the local governments and the British differed considerably. In Arabia, Ibn Saud was faced with grave difficulties arising in part from the war and in part from a series of annual droughts. The lack of sufficient rainfall during three years in succession had a devastating effect on both the Arabian peasants and the nomadic herdsmen. Much greater supplies of food had to be imported and distributed by a very primitively organized government whose revenues had been drastically cut by the decline in pilgrim traffic and whose expenditures were increased by rising prices. Furthermore, the controls imposed by the British on commerce, shipping, and currency throughout a wide area stretching from Egypt to India and the British Dominions and colonies in the Pacific region dried up the sources of Saudi Arabia's trade. As a result the patriarchal theocratic government of Saudi Arabia had to undertake the complex task of buying, importing, transporting, and distributing food, cloth, clothing, and other essentials of life for the tribes and the village people in the extensive domains of Ibn Saud.

Subsidies for Ibn Saud.—The Arabian American Oil Company aided the Saudi government by loans in the form of advanced oil royalties; the British government supplied an annual subsidy and facilitated Ibn Saud in obtaining food and supplies; the United States government through lend-lease and special presidential funds also came to the assistance of the Saudi government. Such aid to Ibn Saud was absolutely necessary if a state of great insecurity, which might have culminated in anarchy, was to be prevented in an area which had become of vital importance to the war effort of the "United Nations" not only because of oil but because of air routes of importance to and from the Near East and the Pacific War theater which crossed Arabia. The reasons for subsidies to Ibn Saud have been greatly distorted in some publications because of his bitter opposition to Zionism and because of the petroleum question.

In comparison with the astronomical sums which have been dispensed since 1945 to many nations, the aid given Ibn Saud was very small indeed, and both Britain and the United States obtained more than their money's worth in the security provided them by the Saudi government in Arabia and in the stabilizing effect of Ibn Saud's influence in the Arab and Moslem world. Important as oil is to the Arabians and to the development of Arabian agriculture and other resources, vital as its petroleum resources may be to American armed forces, and great as the profits may prove to be to the stockholders of the Arabian American Oil Company, the fact of the matter is that the Anglo-American aid to Saudi Arabia between 1939 and 1945 would have been a sound and reasonable investment solely with respect to the war needs of those years. Assistance given to Ibn Saud was for three main purposes: first, to protect American oil interests in Saudi Arabia both for the Arabian American Oil Company and for the future petroleum needs of the United States; second, to obtain military bases in Arabia; third, to retain the support of Ibn Saud and to make it possible for him to maintain law, order, and security in Arabia.

Ibn Saud meets FDR.—After the famous meeting of Ibn Saud and President Roosevelt in February 1945, when he "learned more of the whole problem" of the "Moslems and more about the Jewish problem, in 5 minutes than I could have learned by the exchange of a dozen letters," [1] the President wrote to Ibn Saud on April 5, 1945, that as "Chief of the Executive Branch of this Government" he would take no action which might prove hostile to the Arab people.

After his death when there was no more need of Ibn Saud's support in World War II, Harry Truman, President of the United States, vitiated this promise of a former President. Bartley C. Crum in *Behind the Silken Curtain* who deplores the "duplicity" of the Near Eastern policy of the United States, which he blames largely on the State Department, that favorite scapegoat of ill-intentioned or ill-informed persons, fails to understand that the contradictions of American society itself produce contradictions in the foreign policies of the United States government.[2] A nationalism bordering on jingoism demands vigorous protection of so-called "American interests" which cover a variety of matters; racial, religious, and minority national groups insist that their desires with respect to foreign affairs be the basis of foreign policy; and emotional idealists demand a noble and ethical justification of a foreign policy essentially based on unethical power politics.

The "duplicity" of the Near Eastern foreign policy of the United States government goes back to the contradiction between President Wilson's Fourteen Points and his endorsement of the Balfour Declaration. This contradiction was one of the underlying causes of the Arab-Jewish War of 1948–49. The contradictions of the policies of Mr. Roosevelt and Mr. Truman were among the immediate causes of that conflict.

PALESTINE: DIVIDED AND PARTITIONED

Although the people of Palestine were spared from hostilities between the Axis Powers and the United Nations, they suffered from the violence of Jewish terrorism, of the Anglo-Jewish conflict, and of the Arab-Jewish War. The years from 1939 to 1949 were another tragic decade largely due to the fact that the Arabs were unwilling to let the Jews have Palestine and the Zionists were determined to acquire it at any cost.

Arab and Jewish reactions to the war.—The Mufti of Jerusalem, the intransigent leader of the Hussaini nationalists, went over to the fascist enemies of both the British and the Jews, while the great majority of the Palestinian Arabs stoically awaited the outcome of World War II, unenthusiastic about the cause of the United Nations as they were skeptical about Britain's White Paper policy. They realized that the United Nations might have as little respect for the rights of the Arabs as the Allies in World War I had for their promises.

The Jews were in a different situation. German victory would not only bring to an end the Jewish National Home but very likely result in the brutal extermination of the half million Jews in Palestine. The Palestinian Jews to the number of about 30,000 volunteered for service in the British forces; they fought with but not for the British. During the war and at its close Jews fought against the British. In both cases they were fighting for the ultimate attainment of a Jewish state.

At the beginning of World War II an informal truce was arrived at between the Jews and the British. This did not last for long. The horror and ruthless policy of extermination pursued by the Nazis stirred the Palestinian Jews to their depths. This powerful emotional reaction reached a state bordering on frenzy when the British government resorted to violence in order to prevent illegal immigration of refugees who had managed to escape the hell of Nazi concentration camps and crematories. The Zionists claimed that the restrictions placed on immigration by the White Paper of 1939 were illegal and therefore illegal immigration was legal immigration. To rescue Jews from Europe and to carry out its policy of immigration despite the British, the Jewish Agency engaged in the dangerous business of smuggling Jews into Palestine. All sorts of vessels, some of them quite unseaworthy, were bought or chartered by the Zionists to bring Jews from the slaughterhouse of Europe to Palestine. To "Jews inside and outside" Palestine "to help *illegal* immigration had become the supreme ethical commandment." These "Little Death Ships" as Koestler calls them,[3] some of which sank while others were forcibly boarded by British armed forces and others compelled to return to Europe, brought home to the Palestinian Jews the frightful tragedy of European Jewry. The more extreme groups such as the Irgun Revisionists and the Stern Gang resorted to terrorism and assassination of British officers and officials as a form of reprisals.

The Jewish terrorists.—The Jewish terrorists had their organized supporters in the United States from whence they received funds. They carried on a bitter campaign in American newspapers with full-page advertisements attacking the British. They established themselves in Washington as representatives of the Jewish nation. Persons affiliated with them were granted visas to travel to the Near East under recommendations from highly placed officials in the United States government.

The Jewish Agency and its organized self-defense force called the Haganah, were so profoundly opposed to the methods of the Irgun and the Stern Gang that after the murder in Cairo during October 1944 of Lord Moyne, British Minister of State in the "Middle East," by a Jewish terrorist, they collaborated with the British in fighting the terrorists. This co-operation did not long endure after the end of World War II, when, in the summer of 1945, British Secretary for Foreign Affairs Ernest Bevin adopted his uncompromising policy with respect to Palestine.

Plans for the future.—During the war years four principal groups were making plans for the future of Palestine. Of these only one achieved its aims and then only in part. The Zionists, who succeeded in gaining the support of a very considerable percentage of the Jewish people, endorsed the Biltmore program adopted by a conference of American Zionists held in New York during 1942. The Biltmore program demanded unlimited Jewish immigration into Palestine and the establishment of a Jewish commonwealth there. These demands were the irreducible minimum of all Zionists and most Jews. The Arabs of Palestine insisted upon a cessation of immigration and the independence of Palestine as an Arab state. The Arabs of seven Arab states—Lebanon, Syria, Iraq, Transjordan, Saudi Arabia, Yemen, and Egypt—with British encouragement, organized the League of Arab States, one of the principal purposes of which was to maintain Palestine as an Arab country under Arab control. The members of the League, due to the rivalry of their rulers and ruling classes, could not agree as to the future of an Arab-ruled Palestine. Termination of the mandate, cessation of Jewish immigration, and independence were the minima of Arab demands.

The British wished to retain Palestine, secure the support of the Arabs throughout the Near East, and hold the good will of the Jews. It was an utterly unrealizable objective. The British minimum eventually

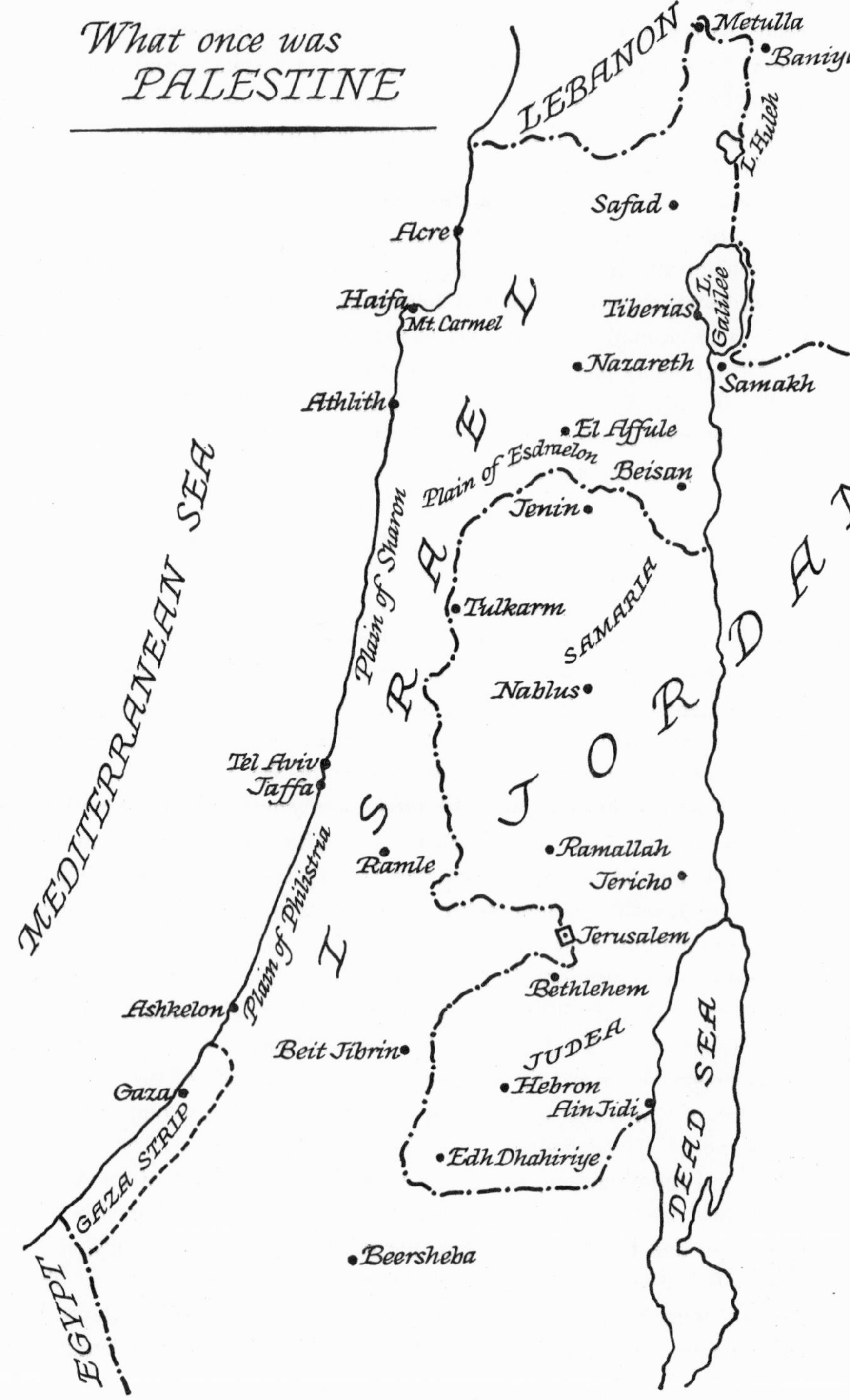

What once was
PALESTINE
LEBANON
Metulla
Baniyas
L. Huleh
Safad
Acre
Haifa
Mt. Carmel
Tiberias
L. Galilee
Nazareth
Samakh
Athlith
El Affule
Plain of Esdraelon
Beisan
Jenin
MEDITERRANEAN SEA
Plain of Sharon
ISRAEL
Tulkarm
SAMARIA
Nablus
JORDAN
Tel Aviv
Jaffa
Plain of Philistria
Ramle
Ramallah
Jericho
Jerusalem
Bethlehem
Ashkelon
Beit Jibrin
JUDEA
Gaza
Hebron
Ain Jidi
DEAD SEA
GAZA STRIP
Edh Dhahiriye
Beersheba
EGYPT

approached zero as the impracticability of their policy resulted in anarchy. The Department of State sought to have considered by the Secretary of State and the President as the basis for United States policy, a compromise plan which made provision for a national communal Jewish government, a national communal Arab government, for continued Jewish immigration, and for large-scale economic development of the water, land, and mineral resources of Palestine. The plan proved unrealistic because of the political influence of the Zionists and their supporters over the elected members of the executive and legislative branches of the government and because of the irreducible minima of both the Arabs and Jews.

The displaced Jews in Europe.—When, following the general election in the United Kingdom, a Labor government replaced the coalition cabinet of Winston Churchill late in July 1945, it was anticipated that the Laborites, who had vigorously attacked the White Paper policy and had come out categorically for unlimited immigration and a Jewish state, would pursue a policy favorable to the Zionists and in line with the Biltmore Program. The Zionists, however, had not calculated on the bullheaded intractable Bevin. An English labor "tsar" unaccustomed to being successfully challenged in labor circles in England, he proved far less flexible and much more arbitrary than Tory foreign secretaries. Bevin, the pseudo-Marxist Fabian labor boss, antagonized those Marxist Social Democrats who were the leaders of the Jewish labor organization in Palestine and who very largely controlled the Jewish Agency and the Haganah. Bevin was adamant in his refusal to open the gates of Palestine to Jewish immigrants. The desperate condition of the displaced Jews in Europe left the Jewish Agency no other choice than to join forces with the Irgun and Stern Gang terrorists in a war against the British.

The question of the future of Palestine became inextricably entangled with that of remnants of European Jewry. Out of an estimated pre-Nazi Jewish population in Europe, exclusive of the U.S.S.R., of 7,000,000 approximately 1,000,000 had survived the war years. Eighty-five per cent of the Jews of Europe had perished. Of those who had survived nearly three-quarters had been uprooted and were human flotsam and jetsam on the turbulent seas of postwar Europe. Some 100,000 were in detention camps for displaced persons. For a considerable percentage of these Jewish survivors only one social and human tie remained, that of being members of the persecuted Jewish people. Not more than a third of them wished to remain in Europe and to re-establish themselves there. The doors of those countries, particularly the United States, which might well have absorbed three-quarters of a million Jews were closed. Palestine became their goal and their only hope of refuge. As Richard Crossman, who was a member of the Anglo-American Committee of Inquiry, so keenly observed, "He (Hitler) created in central and eastern Europe a Jewish nation without a home. . . . , this nation must migrate." [4]

The 100,000.—The Zionists were determined that the tragic survivors of Hitler's terrorism should migrate to Palestine and that 100,000 should immediately be admitted to that country. In this the Zionists had the support of most Jews. The emotional drive back of the demands of the Zionists soon became politically explosive in the United States, where there was the largest Jewish community in the world and where there were over 950,000 shekel-paying Zionists out of a total number in the world of almost 2,200,000 as of 1946.[5]

Such pressure could not be resisted by American politicians, including President Truman who responded to the propaganda hue and cry, "Rescue the 100,000," by urging that 100,000 Jews be immediately admitted to Palestine. This action by Mr. Truman in the summer of 1945 jettisoned the compromise proposal of the Department of State which had been placed on Secretary of State Byrnes' desk just previous to the President's statement. The compromise proposal was based upon the hope of its acceptance by moderate Arabs and moderate Zionists. No moderate Arab could accept or dare to propose the acceptance of the Zionist demand for the immediate entrance of 100,000 Jews into Palestine.

The Anglo-American Commission.—Mr. Truman followed up his public statement by a letter to Prime Minister Attlee urging the British government to admit 100,000 Jews immediately. Another popular American politician, Mayor La Guardia of New York, shouted to an enthusiastic audience a warning to the British that "if Britain wants credit, the best way to get it is the indication that the borrower knows how to keep his word." [6] The British Labor government, which in 1945 had not yet come to realize fully that when Washington cracked the whip London had better respond to the reins, proposed the setting up of an Anglo-American Committee of Inquiry regarding the Problems of European Jewry and Palestine.

The report of the Anglo-American Committee, which was unanimous, was published on April 20, 1946. For the future of Palestine it had nothing constructive to offer. It recommended that 100,000 permits for entrance into Palestine be granted immediately and that restrictions on land purchases imposed by the Land Transfer Regulation of 1946 be removed. It rejected the proposal to create a Jewish state and suggested continuing the British Mandate in the form of a United Nations trusteeship. The British government refused to carry out the proposals of the Anglo-American Commission.

Civil war and terrorism.—From June 1946 until February 1947 terrorism and ruthless civil war by British and Jews continued while the British government diddled futilely with the so-called Morrison plan, which was a bastard combination of a British cantonization proposal and the compromise plan of the State Department, with a Palestine Round Table Conference rejected by both Jews and Arabs, and with the Bevin Plan, which the Zionists refused to consider.

Conditions in Palestine had so deteriorated that the Anglo-Jewish conflict had become a brutalizing series of reprisals. It was quite clear that against the determined opposition of the 600,000 Jews in Palestine the British were not able to maintain an effective government of the country.

Recognizing at long last his failure, Foreign Secretary Bevin informed the House of Commons on February 18, 1947, that as the mandate had proved unworkable the question of Palestine was being referred to the United Nations. Mr. Truman's subservience to the Zionists and Mr. Bevin's truculent inflexibility made any possibility of compromise out of the question, whether proposed by Arab or Jew, American or Britisher. Indeed, it is questionable whether any compromise could have been imposed by third parties until Arabs and Jews through armed conflict discovered the real limitations to their own desires.

U.N. enters the scene.—In May 1947 the General Assembly of the United Nations appointed a commission known as the United Nations Special Commission on Palestine to investigate and report. In November the Report of the U.N.S.C. on P. was adopted by the General Assembly of the United Nations. It declared the mandate to be unworkable and stated that partition was the only solution. The British government declared its unwillingness to carry out the proposals of the U.N.S.C. on P. and its intention of withdrawing from Palestine.

Partition—A U.N. Ukase precipitates war.—Under the dispensation of the new world organization the appointed representatives of thirty-three governments of countries whose people knew as much about the Palestine problem as they did about Einstein's theory of relativity arrived at a decision which will affect the destiny of Near Eastern people for an indefinite future. Of some fifty-six nations thirty-three voted for the partition of Palestine, thirteen voted against it, and ten abstained from voting. The fact that a majority of the U.N. Assembly at Lake Success voted that the will of a majority of the people in Palestine should be disregarded was considered a triumph in the application to world affairs of the nineteenth-century political ideal of majority rule. The Jews accepted the decision and made the most of it. The Arabs rejected the decision and resisted its implementation.

It soon became evident that the long predicted Arab-Jewish war for Palestine would begin as soon as the British left. The seven members of the League of Arab States met in Cairo in December 1947 and reached the decision to give armed support to the Palestinian Arabs in their resistance to partition. Both Arabs and Jews started to prepare for war. Soon after the British evacuated Palestine hostilities began in April 1948.

In short order the Jewish forces demonstrated their superiority in morale, in training, in organization, and in armament to the armies of

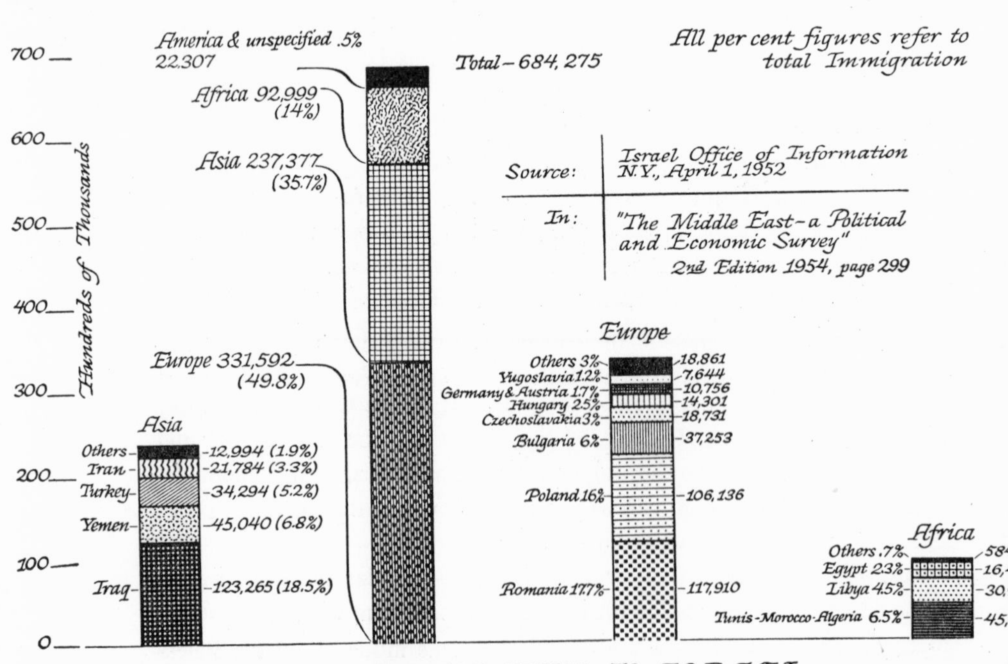

JEWISH IMMIGRATION TO ISRAEL
1948 – 1951

Egypt, Iraq, Syria, and Lebanon. The only Arab forces which were comparable to those of the Jews were those of the English-trained, equipped, and led Arab Legion of Transjordan. Concurrent with the open warfare between the Arab and Jewish military forces, were terroristic operations of the Irgun and the Stern Gang. The "blood bath" administered to the Arab peasants of Deir Yassim near Jerusalem by the Jewish terrorists created a panic among the Palestinian Arabs, who were persuaded by their leaders that the Jews were planning a wholesale massacre of the Arab population. This panic resulted in the flight of the Arabs from Palestine. Ninety-five per cent of the Arab population in Haifa and in Jaffa fled. Over 300,000 Arab refugees left those parts of Palestine held by the Jews. In a few weeks' time the Arabs by their flight eliminated one of the major problems of partition, an Arab majority in a Jewish state.

The birth of Israel.—Two days after the British troops left Jaffa, the Palestinian Jews on May 14, 1948, declared the independence of Israel and the Zionists achieved their goal of a Jewish state. On the same day the United States government with somewhat startling rapidity recognized the Provisional Jewish Government as the *de facto* authority of the new state of Israel.

The war in Palestine and the recognition of Israel by the U.S.A. nearly precipitated an international crisis. By treaties with Abdullah of Transjordan, with Egypt, and with Iraq, Great Britain was under obligation to supply armament and to give aid in case of invasion. The advance of Jewish forces in the southern part of Palestine known as the Negev had the possibility of a threat to Egypt in Sinai and more particularly to Transjordan at Akaba. A possible conflict in the Near East between the United States and Great Britain seemed ominous to those who were building an American and British united front against the Soviet Union from Trieste to Teheran. Action by the United Nations appeared as a way of ending hostilities.

The Bernadotte mission.—The United Nations sent the Bernadotte mission to Palestine in an endeavor to end the hostilities between Arabs and Jews. Although a precarious truce was arranged it collapsed after the assassination of Count Folke Bernadotte by Jewish terrorists. Hostilities recommenced in the autumn with military operations by the Israeli forces in the south against the Egyptians and in the north against the Lebanese and Syrians. The indefatigable Dr. Ralph Bunche of the United Nations, who had succeeded Count Bernadotte as United Nations mediator, with great patience continued to nurse the half-hearted armistice negotiations between Israel and the various Arab states.

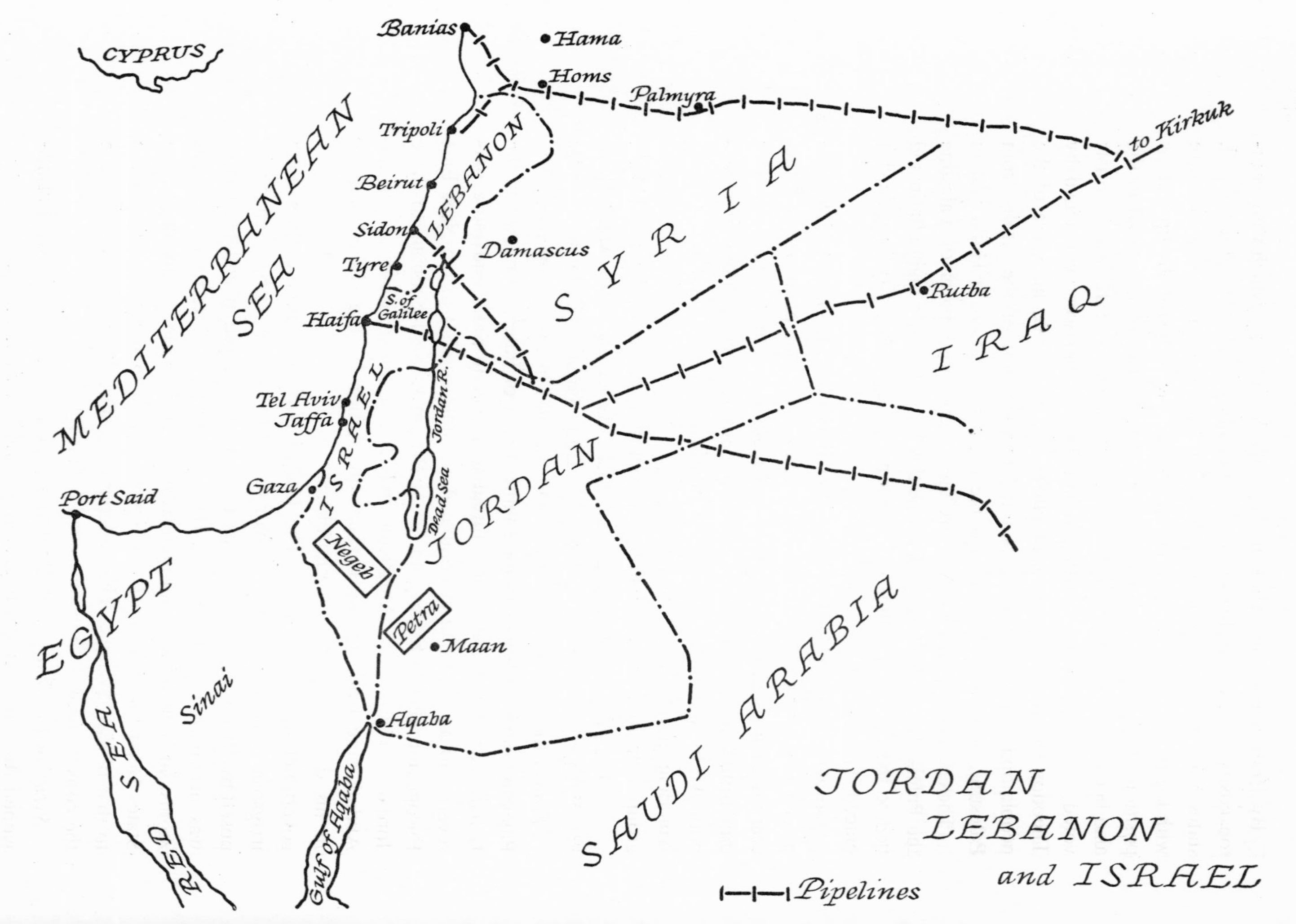

JORDAN
LEBANON
and ISRAEL

By 1949 it became obvious to Arabs and Jews that the war would be too costly and unprofitable to continue. The rivalry between the Arab states made it possible for Israel to reach separate armistice agreements with them. In the armistice negotiations of 1949 Israel was in a stronger position than previously not only because of its military victories but also because in March 1949 the Security Council of the United Nations voted 9 to 1 to admit Israel as a member of the U.N. The dream of Theodor Herzl and the early Zionists had been realized. The Jewish people had labored and produced a Jewish nation and a Jewish state in Palestine.

Those who paid the real human costs of the Arab-Jewish war were the Palestinian Arabs who lost their homes, their lands, and as refugees fled to the Arab states, where they still continue to be D.P.'s, the displaced Arabs of western Asia who have no "Promised Land." Truman's proposal to solve the problem of 100,000 Jews in the camps for displaced persons in Europe a few years later resulted in there being several hundred thousand Arab displaced persons in Asia. Perhaps in some dim future *Shalom aleihom* and *Aleikom salaam* may mean peace for both Arabs and Jews, but such is not likely to be the case as long as American politicians believe they can win votes by doing justice to one group at the expense of injustice to another.

❁ WAR AND THE OTHER ARAB LANDS OF WESTERN ASIA

Transjordan becomes Jordan.—Whereas a considerable portion of Palestine during the decade beginning with the outbreak of World War II had ceased to be an Arab land both politically and demographically, several of the other Arab lands achieved an increase of freedom from European tutelage. The emirate of Transjordan became the Kingdom of Jordan, so called because following the Arab-Jewish war of 1948–49 Abdullah acquired a considerable part of central Palestine, including in his domains territories west of the Jordan River. This places the government of Jordan in a strategical position with respect to large-scale irrigaton projects connected with the Jordan River, such as those proposed by Dr. Lowdermilk in his book, *Palestine, Land of Promise,* which was, according to a statement by Mrs. Lowdermilk, financed by a leading Zionist at a time when Dr. Lowdermilk was employed by the United States Department of Agriculture. A Jordan Valley development similar to that of the Tennessee Valley Administration (T.V.A.) would require the consent and co-operation of the government of Jordan.

Syria and Lebanon gain their independence.—Syria and Lebanon gained their independence and became members of the United Nations, both having participated in the United Nations Conference at San Francisco in 1945. French tutelage was brought to an end in these two Arab republics. In the Lebanon the old problem resulting from friction between the Maronites and the Moslems continues to cause difficulties both within the Lebanese Republic and between Lebanon and Syria. The two countries are inextricably bound together by geography and economics and perforce must find a *modus vivendi.* Their relations, however, probably will continue to remain strained until such time as modern culture modifies old Christian and Islamic cultures to an extent which eliminates the more marked differences in the ways of living of Moslems and Christians.

Iraq and the Yemen.—Iraq temporarily was subjected to what for all practical purposes was a British military occupation following the *coup d'état* of Rashid Ali during World War II. After 1945, however, the Iraqi government renegotiated its treaty with Great Britain, regained its full political independence, and became a member of the United Nations. In the Yemen modernism is beginning to undermine the feudal theocratic government of Imam Yahya, and the Yemen has emerged from centuries of isolation by becoming first a member of the Arab League and later a member of the United Nations.

Throughout all the Arab lands of western Asia the modern world is having an increasing impact, and changes are taking place at an accelerated pace. Nevertheless, in none of the Arab countries has any very real progress been made in finding solutions of its social and economic problems. Per capita production is extremely low. The living standards of the Arab masses are not much above subsistence levels. The older landowning classes and the moneylenders still very largely dominate these societies. The question arises as to whether solutions for these problems will be found before social revolution as in China and other parts of the Far East sweeps away the ancient social order under Communist leadership or before the United States and Soviet Russia meet in conflict in the Near and Middle East either indirectly as in Korea or in open warfare. The key to this unopened door of the future may lie in Iran or in Turkey.

CHAPTER XXVII

The Turks Resume Their Historic Role

۞ THE DILEMMA OF THE TURKS

The statesmen of the Turkish Republic during the first forty-five years of its existence have been confronted with the same dangerous situation that the Ottomans faced during the empire's long period of decline, which terminated in the catastrophe of 1918. Participation in World War I, as an ally of the Teutonic Powers, resulted in the partition of the empire and its end in 1922.

The precarious situation which has so long plagued the Turkish rulers arises when no one state within the Mediterranean basin is able to dominate the area and maintain security within it and when rival powers or groups of powers from without contend for control of it. Such a situation arose following the Russian Revolution of November, 1917, and the rapid emergence of the Soviet Union as a protagonist of social revolution. A new and more dangerous factor had been added to the foreign situation that the Turks had to deal with after 1923.

۞ TURKEY'S FOREIGN POLICY

Some of the victors in World War I pursued policies which resulted in the partition of the Ottoman Empire and threatened that of the Turkish Anatolian heartland. The Turks in their struggle to prevent the destruction of the Turkish nation sought assistance from Bolshevik Russia. It is significant that among all the varied peoples of the Ottoman Empire the Turks alone were able to resist successfully the imperialistic objectives of Great Britain, France, Italy, and Greece.

By 1923, having settled their differences with "the Allies" by the Treaty of Lausanne, the Turks were able for a time to pursue a policy of cautious friendship with both the Soviet Union and the Western Powers.

Turkey avoids alliance with either East or West.—The Turkish leaders were aware of the dangers inherent in their strategic position with respect to the new socio-economic order of the U.S.S.R. and the old capitalistic order of the West. The small Turkish ruling class was composed of neither capitalists nor socialists. The rulers were extreme nationalists—army officers, officials, intellectuals—who had no desire to fall under the control of the western nations through economic penetration by western capitalism. Nor did these ardent Turkish nationalists imbued with western ideologies wish to risk domination by Communists through dependence on Moscow. So, while observing friendly relations with both the Western Powers and with Soviet Russia, the Turks negotiated treaties of friendship with the Balkan states and with Iran and Afghanistan. This policy was based on a situation which was soon to be changed by political developments in Italy and in the German Weimar Republic.

The rise of totalitarian capitalism under the leadership of the Italian Fascists and the German Nazis confronted the Turks with a new international situation. Mussolini's aggressive policy in the Mediterranean and his attack on Ethiopia coupled with Hitler's Balkan policy were thought to contain a future menace to Turkey. The uncertainty during the middle 1930's as to whether the appeasement policy adopted by the British and the French would lead to a war between Nazi Germany and Soviet Russia tended to the adoption of a pro-Russian Turkish policy. When the Soviets signed a treaty of friendship with Nazi Germany in 1939 just previous to the outbreak of World War II, the Turks became somewhat dubious about Soviet Russia's future plans with respect to the Near East.

Nevertheless, the Turks were not entirely misled by the seeming contradiction in this new political alignment, as may be seen from the fact that when they signed a treaty of alliance with England and France in October 1939 they stipulated that nothing in the treaty would obligate Turkey to go to war against the Soviet Union. The rulers of Turkey had no intention of being dragged into another World War and risk Turkey's becoming a base for military operations against Russia. Nor did they wish to give the Russians any excuse for an attack on Turkey.

The international situation changed abruptly after the Germans invaded the Soviet Union, which joined Britain in the war against the Axis Powers, Germany and Italy. Henceforth, until after 1945, there were no contradictions in Turkey's relations with the U.S.S.R. and the western democracies.

The Turks adopt an anti-Russian policy.—After the defeat of the Nazis the Russian military occupation of Hungary, Romania, and Bulgaria followed by the establishment of Communist governments in all the Balkan states with the exception of Greece, where a Communist victory seemed probable, seriously weakened Turkey's military position with respect to the Soviet Union. Russia had emerged from the war as the predominant military power in Europe and by means of the Communist regimes in the Balkans the Russians had gained control of the major part of the Balkan Peninsula. Communism was at the gates of Istanbul and controlled the land route between Turkey and Central Europe. It was becoming evident that Turkey could no longer depend upon Great Britain's ability to check a Russian drive to the south. Nevertheless, until 1946 the Turks had no choice other than to turn to Britain as a counterweight against the powerful Soviet Union.

After World War II (1939–45) Great Power rivalry took on new aspects in the Near East, as in Europe and throughout the world, becoming a capitalist-communist conflict known as "the Cold War," with volcanic-like irruptions in widely scattered parts of the globe. These were accompanied by nationalistic movements against Western imperialism and colonialism. The British, unable to cope with the situation in Greece and in the Near and Middle East, sought support from the United States.

The policy of denying the Near and Middle East to the Russians could not be carried on effectively unless the United States could be persuaded to underwrite it. When Winston Churchill came to this conclusion, he set about the task of persuading the United States to assume the necessary economic, political, and military obligations inherent in the undertaking. His proposal at Fulton, Missouri, of an Anglo-American alliance against the Soviet Union met with approval in the United States.

American policy with respect to the Near and Middle East during the years after World War I was reversed after World War II. No longer did the State Department consider Palestine and other trouble spots in the Near and Middle East British responsibilities. The United States government and American private business had acquired vital interests in the area. Soon after Churchill's prodding in March, 1946, Loy W. Henderson of the Department of State, in an address at Los Angeles, stated the basis of the new Middle Eastern policy. He made it clear that an important element in the policy of the United States in the Near and Middle East was ". . . promoting American communication facilities to and through the Near and Middle East . . . I am referring here to aviation, tele-communication, and shipping." [1]

The Communist revolt in Greece and Joseph Stalin's demand that the Soviet Union be given military bases along the Straits and that Turkey return Kars and Ardahan to the U.S.S.R. precipitated announcement of the Truman Doctrine with respect to Greece and Turkey, to the spread of communism, and to Russian aggression in the Near East.

Turkey's alignment with the Western Powers.—The assumption by the United States of a major role in the Near East appeared to the Turks as adequate security against potential Soviet aggression and communism. Furthermore, alignment with "the West" offered in addition tempting financial and other economic advantages. Turkey became a member of the International Money Fund and the International Bank for Reconstruction and Development. Later, admission to NATO (North Atlantic Treaty Organization) appeared to insure further political and military protection against the northern neighbor.

The Turks were not, for some time, disappointed in these hopes. A certain degree of disillusionment developed later. The full implications of this political, economic, and military alliance with the West were not foreseen by the Turks. The rapid recovery of the Soviet Union from the destruction of World War II and its emergence as a superpower in possession of nuclear weapons created new complications for Turkey.

The construction of air bases by the United States extending from the Bosphorus to the eastern Turkish frontier was at first looked upon by the Turks as adequate defense against attack from the north. The offensive potentials of these bases were clearly revealed in 1948 by an American officer attached to the Air Force Group of the American Mission for Aid to Turkey. This officer boasted to Major Eliot that "we could operate American long-range bombers from it [the Anatolian plateau] on a large scale, we could tear the lights and liver out of the principal industrial area of European Russia: the Ukraine and the Donets Basin, to say nothing of the Baku oil fields. It's all within comfortable reach of Turkish air bases." [2] The publication of these remarks in American periodicals, though they probably did not convey any information unknown to the Soviet government, may have seemed somewhat indiscreet to Turkish diplomats. The establishment by the United States of missile bases in Turkey placed that country in the position of becoming a primary military target for the Russians in the advent of war. Alignment with the West was increasingly embroiling the Turks in what might become a mondial conflict. Other events revealed further implications of the increasing complications which the alignment entailed.

The Bagdad Pact (1955) between Turkey and Iraq (kingdom of

Iraq, 1932–58) became CENTRO, a defensive treaty including Turkey, the kingdom of Iraq, Iran, Pakistan, and the United Kingdom, with the U.S.A. participating. SEATO (South East Asia Treaty Organization, the members being Australia, France, New Zealand, Pakistan, Philippines, Thailand, the United Kingdom, and the United States) came into being in 1955. Turkey's alignment with the West had involved this small Near Eastern republic in a fantastical worldwide network of "power politics" designed not only to contain the Soviet Union and other Communist states but with the more nebulous objective of containing communism for the purpose of maintaining vast economic interests of the West.

Events in the Near East in the 1950's and 1960's left Turkey in a somewhat isolated position with respect to the other nations of the Near East. The second Israeli-Arab war of 1956–57 and the Israel, French, and British assault on Egypt brought forth a strong ultimatum from Soviet Russia; American intervention in Lebanon, the announcement that followed of the Eisenhower Doctrine of Intervention, the Iraqi revolution of 1958, and the republic of Iraq's withdrawal from CENTRO gave clear evidence to the Turks that they were confronted with a new state of affairs.

New factors in the situation.—The declining power of France and Great Britain throughout the Mediterranean and the Near and Middle East was placing Turkey in the position of becoming a satellite of the United States at a time when the increasing power of the Soviet Union and its influence in the Near East was becoming quite evident. Dulles' and Eisenhower's policy of containment was in a state of collapse. The new regimes in Syria and Iraq became somewhat less than cordial toward the United States and more amicable toward the Soviet Union, though not procommunist. Revolution in the Yemen and the successes of South Arabia Arab-Yemenite nationalists gave further indications of declining Western strength. The third Israeli-Arab war of June, 1967, resulted in a serious setback to American influence in the Near East and added to the prestige of the U.S.S.R., with its increasing display of naval power in the Mediterranean.

The situation in Cyprus became of increasing concern to the Turkish government. Acceptance by Turkey in the Treaty of Lausanne (1923) of Britain's annexation of Cyprus and of its becoming a Crown Colony in 1925 was accompanied by a feeling of assurance that the Turkish Moslem minority would enjoy security and equality of treatment. This was not to be the case. The rise of a nationalistic underground movement among the Greek Christian Cypriotes, known as EOKA, demanding union with Greece (*enosis*) during the 1930's, resulted in growing violence the British were unable to cope with. This anti-British, anti-independence, and anti-Turkish movement reached a state of terrorism in 1955.

Indignation in Turkey threatened to disrupt relations between the republic of Turkey and the kingdom of Greece, both members of NATO and associates in the world-wide policy of containment of Soviet Russia of which the United States was the center and Turkey a keystone in the Near East. The termination of the status of a British Crown Colony and the creation of the independent republic of Cyprus in 1959 did not end the conflict, which reached the proportions of a civil war by 1961. President Makarios confronted with Greece's demand for *enosis* and Turkey's demand for the partition of Cyprus went to Moscow and Cairo for support for total independence. Turkey prepared for invasion of Cyprus. A letter from President Johnson warned the Turks that the United States would not permit a Turkish attack on Cyprus. The publication of this letter in Turkey aroused some anti-American feeling among elements of the Turkish people. With the international situation in a state of flux, there are indications that the Turks are not averse to cultivating economic relations with the Soviet bloc.

COMMUNISM IN TURKEY

Comment on communism in Turkey calls for some clarification with respect to the word and its meaning to the Turkish people. Communism as Marxist social philosophy with its atheistic assumptions is utterly alien to the religion of Islam and to the bulk of the deeply religious Turkish Moslems, among some of whom there is still opposition to the secularizing policies of the Turkish government begun in 1923.

A Turkish Communist Party as a means of fostering revolution and as an instrument for seizing political power is another matter. The question is whether economic and social conditions are such as to give rise to maladjustments and discontents so widespread and intense among the Turkish people as to create a broad-based revolutionary movement, of which a highly disciplined Turkish Communist Party might seize the leadership. In the existing social structure of the Turkish people this appears highly unlikely. The bulk of the peasantry are just emerging from a peasant-village way of life and of thinking. An urban, modern, and industrial proletariat is of comparatively recent development and has not as yet acquired the political and economic power of organized labor in the West or even of that of some of the Arab urban workers.

There is a new and growing sector of the Turkish middle class—the businessmen, the entrepreneurs—some of whose leaders exert an increasing role in public affairs, challenging the power of the military and the governmental bureaucrats. The pseudosocialism of "etatism," which is comparable to seventeenth-century European mercantilism, is being questioned by this new bourgeois capitalist class. The drive to modernize Turkey, which proceeds at an accelerated pace, may give rise to conditions that could nurture revolutionary situations leading to the growth of communism. This seems far from likely at present.

CHAPTER XXVIII

The Near East—A Focus of World Attention

OBSERVATIONS

The historian approaches the problem of writing about recent and contemporary events with caution and reluctance whereas the political analyst and commentator does so with eagerness and zest. When both roles are assumed by a writer, which is the present situation, the reader should be informed of the fact. The historian seeks to consult all pertinent source material, knowing quite well that much of it will not become available for years hence. The analyst and commentator uses what data are available to him and by his analysis and interpretation adds to the source material which future historians will have to take into consideration. In dealing with recent and current history it is the function of the historian to set forth the frame of reference within the limits of which the analyst and the commentator formulates his observations. Henceforth the reader is cautioned to remember the age-old warning of the merchants, *caveat emptor*.

BETWIXT AND BETWEEN

As throughout much of its long history the Near East is now caught up in the struggle for power between two great antagonists and the people of this strategic area might again become the sacrificial victims of those nations which are more concerned with their own interests and security than with those of the hapless millions who live in the Near East.

No sooner had Germany and Italy been eliminated as contenders for control of the Near and Middle East than Great Britain renewed her former policy of preventing the Soviet Union from extending its influence to any part of the entire region. To the old cliché of the "bear who walks as a man" was added the bugbear of "Communist imperialism." As of old Britain considered that her vital imperial lines of communication were menaced by the Russians from the Balkans to Afghanistan. More threatening even was the possibility of communism engulfing not only the Near and Middle East but also Africa and southern Asia. Throughout English history since the time of Henry VIII British statesmen, when unable to protect fully their nation's interests, have sought to inveigle other states to come to their assistance.

After 1945 this was not difficult to do. Throughout most of World War II there had been close collaboration between American and British leaders, military, political, and economic. Although they did not see eye to eye on all matters they came to view the U.S.S.R. and communism as potential enemies. Russia had become a great military and industrial power functioning on a political and economic system thought to be inimical to the political and economic systems of the West. The ruling class in the U.S.S.R. subscribed to a philosophy which struck at the roots of Western capitalism. Furthermore, Americans had acquired a really enormous and vital economic stake in Near Eastern oil. Consequently, American leaders came to consider control of the Near East and the exclusion of Soviet Russia and communism in both the Near and Middle East as essential to the security of the United States and to the Western world and to what has come to be called the "free world," that is, those parts of the world not under Communist governments.

Beginning of the Cold War.—When the Soviet Union failed to remove its troops from northern Iran in accordance with the treaty of 1942 between Britain, Iran, and the U.S.S.R. and used their control there to carry on anti-Western propaganda and to give support to the Iranian Tudeh (Communist) Party in a rebellion against the Iranian government in the province of Azerbaijan in 1945, the United States became concerned about the maintenance of the territorial integrity of Iran and its freedom from complete domination by the U.S.S.R. and its possible communization. Here British and American interests and aims coincided.

Concomitant with the Iranian crisis were the demands of the Soviet government on Turkey for control of the Straits as well as for territorial secessions in eastern Anatolia, and the civil war in Greece pregnant with the possibility of a seizure of power by the Greek Communists. So when in February 1947 the British government informed the Americans that it could no longer continue to aid the anti-Communist government of Greece, the President with the support of Congress announced his policy of aid to Greece and Turkey known as the Truman Doctrine which

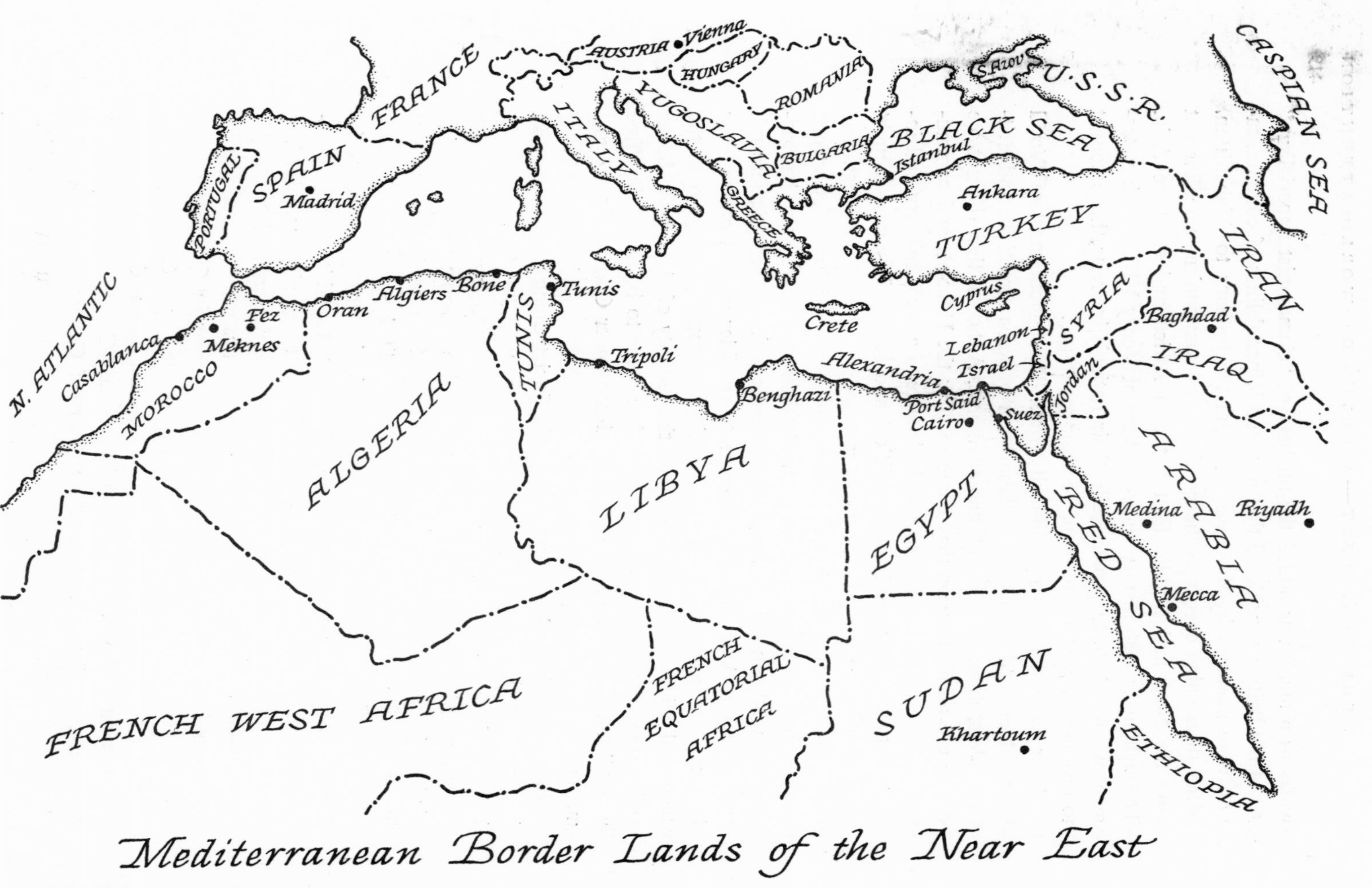

Mediterranean Border Lands of the Near East

was based on firm determination to "contain" the U.S.S.R. in the Near East as well as elsewhere.

The events between 1945 and 1947 produced a clash of interests between the Soviet Union and the United States which had as one of its most important foci the Near and Middle East. The division of the world into two antagonistic power groups, the Communist and the Western-led orbit, placed the peoples of the Near and Middle East between the hammer and the anvil. Because of the ideological conflict and because for the first time in history the United States had appeared on the stage as one of the two principal contenders for power, the contemporary struggle had certain new aspects. In general, however, the pattern was an ancient one and as the French say, *"plus ça change, plus ça c'est la même chose."*

The dynamic nucleus of each of these two great power groups is a vast continental state. One far distant and overseas but one whose economic, naval, and air resources make possible the extension of its power to every crack and corner of the Near and Middle East. The other, like a vast arctic icecap borders on the northern frontiers from Afghanistan to European Turkey. It also has formidable air resources and immense reservoirs of manpower. In a war between these two gigantic powers, which is thought by some to be inevitable, the Near and Middle East would probably become a major area of military conflict. Consequently, the winning of the Near and Middle East has become an objective of each of the opposing groups to whom these areas are of increasing strategic importance.

❁ PRINCIPAL FACTORS—FOCUSING WORLD ATTENTION

The factors which make the Near East a focus of world attention are not only complex but closely interrelated, to a degree of entanglement that tends to obscure the basic issues.

Strategic factors.—The geographic location of the Near East as a strategic factor is well known. Its importance has been increased in recent times by the importance of East-West airways which cross the area with airbase facilities, weather stations, and other essentials to transcontinental flight. Petroleum has made the Near East of vital importance. The vast deposits in the Near East and the adjacent areas of North Africa and Iran supply, together with the U.S.S.R., much of the oil required by Asia and Europe. As approximately 53 per cent of the total energy requirements of the world come from petroleum and natural gas (43 per cent from oil), the significance of the Near East is apparent. Its importance is enhanced by the fact that a variety of subsidiary industries

—shipbuilding, shipping, refineries—depend on oil from the Near East area. Capital investment in the Near East petroleum industry is immense, and the profits therefrom likewise. Much of this capital is of European and American origin.

Religion.—The Near East is the focal center of three religions which had their origin there. The oldest is Judaism. The State of Israel is a center of deep and passionate interest to all Jews, who number an estimated 16,000,000. Of these, more than 2,000,000 are in Israel, 6,500,000 in the United States, 3,900,000 in Europe, and more than 2,000,000 in the U.S.S.R. The others are widely scattered. The welfare and security of Israel are of utmost concern to all Jews, and consequently Jewish people pay close attention to events in the Near East.

The Arab Near East is the center of Islam to all Moslems, who are scattered throughout Asia and Africa and number some 406,000,000. To the holy cities of Mecca and Medina in Saudi Arabia a half million Moslems make an annual pilgrimage—the Hadj. Between 1947–48 and 1967–68 an estimated 10,000,000 Moslems made the Hadj to the Moslem and Arab heartland, where they heard of the Arab-Israel conflict in the Arab versions, of the woes of the Palestinian Arab refugees, and of the "New Order" that challenges the old way of life of Islam.

The Christians, who are estimated to number 1,000,000,000, though widely scattered throughout the world, are concentrated largely in Europe and the Americas. The Christian holy cities of Palestine—Jerusalem, Bethlehem, and Nazareth—have been the centers of pilgrimage for many centuries. Consequently, when violence, turmoil, and war occur in Palestine, Christians, who generally concern themselves far less than Jews and Moslems with events in the Near East, become more aware of the issues involved there: The "East-West" conflict, the internal conflicts of the "Old Order" and the "New," and the Arab-Israeli conflict.

The conflict between the "Old Order" and the "New Order."—As elsewhere in the world the rapidity and degree of change throughout the Near East is causing maladjustments in the entire social structure: among nomads and peasants, all elements of the middle class, and within the ruling classes. This condition of affairs in the Near East has its bearing on the "East-West" conflict, and more especially upon the rivalry between the U.S.A. and the U.S.S.R. for dominance in the Near East and adjacent areas in southeastern Europe and North Africa.

After a brief period of American dominance at the end of World War II, the revolutionary movements in Egypt, Syria, Iraq, the Yemen, and South Arabia opened the door to Soviet penetration and shattered the foundations of the Dulles-Eisenhower policy of containment. Astute lead-

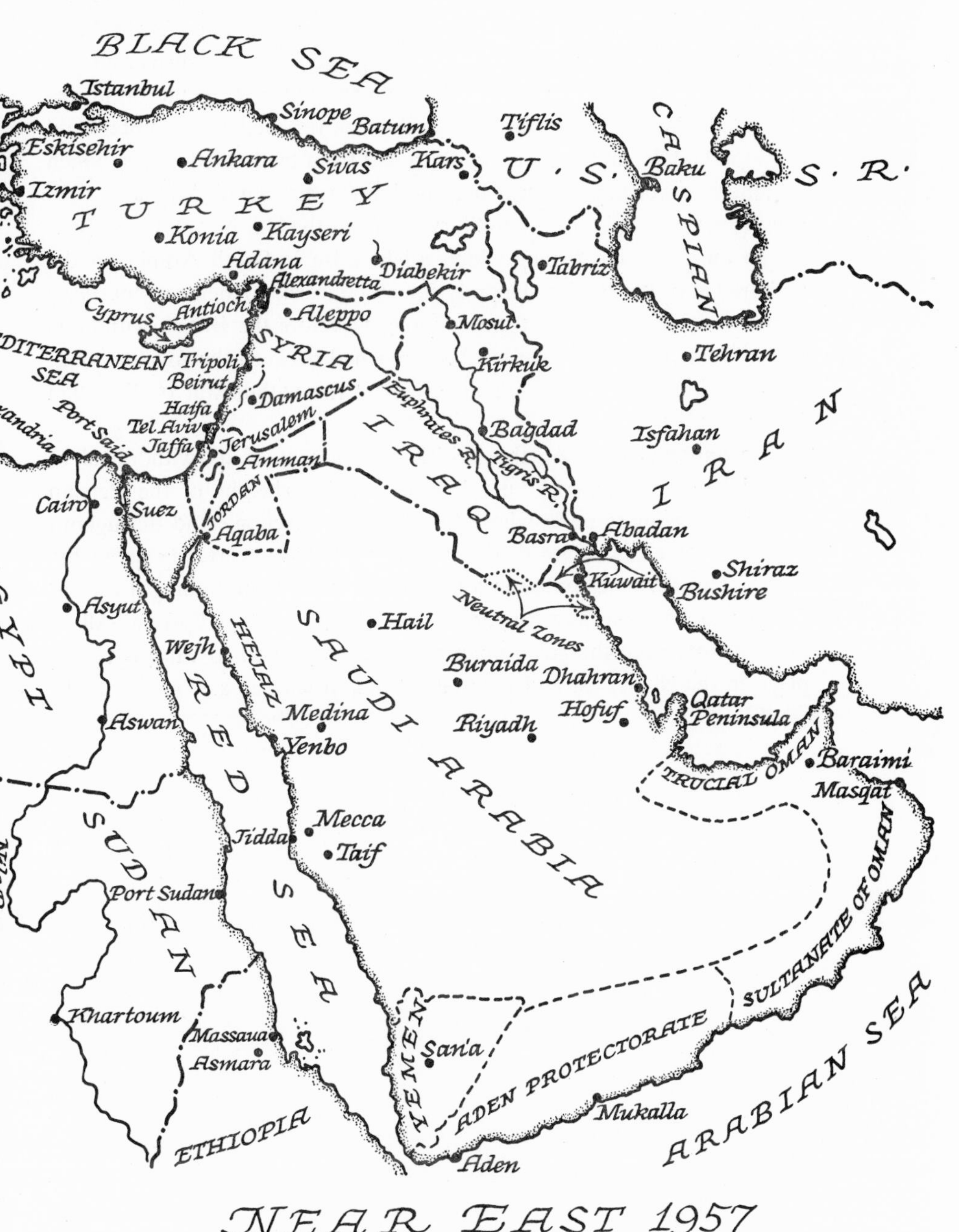

NEAR EAST 1957

ership in the U.A.R. (Egypt) firmly established under Nasser, played one rival against the other; he was uninterested in communism and satisfied to see neither the East nor the West obtain dominance in the Mediterranean. Revolutionary Syria and Iraq, incurring the displeasure of the United States, gladly sought aid from the U.S.S.R. to the disadvantage of the West. The Yemenite republicans received large military aid from the U.A.R. and some nonmilitary aid from the United States, which became less welcome when it became known that Saudi Arabia was receiving very special types of military aid from the U.S.A. and Great Britain to meet any emergency which might arise in South Arabia on the withdrawal of the British. Happily for all concerned Aden revolutionary elements took over without undue violence before the British withdrew. In the Yemen no settlement has been reached between the royalist counterrevolutionists and the republicans after the withdrawal of Egyptian forces.

The announcement by the British government of its withdrawal of imperial outposts east of Suez left the oil-rich sheikhs of the Persian Gulf in a quandary as to where to turn for protection. And throughout the Arab Near East there is increasing unrest and uncertainty about the future. The Turks, as noted in a preceding chapter, are finding it advantageous to do business with the Soviet bloc of Eastern Europe. All of these factors keep the governments of the world alert to what is taking place in the Near East and focused on that crucial area.

CHAPTER XXIX

Revolutionary Egypt

The overthrow of the Egyptian monarchy and the setting up of a republic under the leadership of Gamel Abdul Nasser by a group of revolutionary-minded army officers and their civilian collaborators were the result of a long historical process which began during the first quarter of the nineteenth century, a hundred and fifty years ago. It was then that Egypt started to regain the political and economic importance which it has had throughout most of its long history from the time of the ancient pharaohs.

For three centuries previous to 1800 Egypt had been in a state of decline. It was by-passed by European and world trade, neglected by the Ottomans, and pillaged by the Mamelukes. Culturally and commercially, Egypt had become a stagnant backwater. The country's resurgence began when the great powers of Europe, activated by the potent expansive forces of emerging industrial and finance capitalism, extended their political and economic competition to the Near East. Whereas the economic and political developments in Europe in the sixteenth century were in some measure the cause of retrogression in Egypt, those of the nineteenth century brought about its revival.

The profound and rapid changes which took place in Egypt became increasingly subversive of the old order with its medieval economic, social, and political institutions. Early in the nineteenth century during the reign of Mohammed Ali, the founder of the modern Egyptian dynasty recently ousted, Egypt became a center of revolutionary ideas which had their influence elsewhere in the Ottoman Near East.

Western statesmen and policy makers, deeply immersed in the rapid flow of recent and contemporary events and absorbed by the "cold war" in their preparations for another global war, viewed with alarm the regime of President Nasser and Egypt's appeal to the Arabs of Western

Asia and North Africa. The political and military leaders of the West regarded revolutionary movements, leaders, and regimes only with respect to the balance of power between the Communist Soviet and the Western capitalistic states. The West concerned itself, only incidentally, with revolution in the Near East, while on the other hand the leaders of the Soviet Union have given the closest study to its every aspect. The modernization of the Near East, which is so largely due to the West, particularly so in Egypt, entails social and political revolution. The forces underlying it are irresistible. It is inevitable. The seething unrest and the surging desires of the peoples of the Near East for a better way of life will not be denied.

Patronizing interference accompanied at times by high-faluting moralizing and occasionally by threatening displays of armed might undermines the influence of the more moderate and increases the prestige of the more radical leaders. The West antagonizes such leaders while the Russians encourage them.

There is also a tendency in the West to overstress nationalism and to ignore the significance of other potent forces generated by the extremely revolutionary economic and social changes which are taking place. Nationalism is a powerful psychological and political force to which Egyptian leaders, as those in other Near East countries, must respond whether they be conservative or revolutionary. The leaders like Nasser, responding to social demands of the masses, strive to marshal the ideological and emotional drive of nationalism to accomplish the social and economic changes they seek to bring about. In the struggle between the Soviet orbit and the Western orbit over control of the Near East, success may depend upon which of the two power groups pursues policies based upon an understanding of the historical processes now taking place there.

THE HISTORICAL EVOLUTION OF CONTEMPORARY EGYPT

The history of modern Egypt begins with the rule of Mohammed Ali, appointed governor in 1805 by Sultan Selim III, whose attempts at reform of the Ottoman Empire resulted in his dethronement and assassination by the Janissaries and their reactionary supporters. Mohammed Ali was determined to modernize Egypt and took no chances. He broke the power of the Mamelukes in 1811 by a massacre of their leaders. Four years later he crushed a revolt of his Albanian troops who objected to his military reforms. He thus cleared the way for his ambitious program.

During the first period from 1805 to 1882, the khedives were the actual rulers of Egypt. Throughout the second period from 1882 to 1936 during the British occupation the khedives were only puppet rulers. The changes which took place during these hundred and thirty years created conditions which fostered revolutionary movements.

The achievements and failures of the ruling khedives.—Mohammed Ali and his descendants between 1805 and 1879, with the exception of Khedive Abbas I (1848–54) who opposed further Western innovations, were strong advocates of modernization. They pursued policies which resulted in notable progress that brought to an end the medieval regime typical of Egypt since 1250. An intellectual awakening began which took various forms. The religious philosopher, Jamal-ud-Din al-Afghani, who attacked materialism and urged a return to Islamic orthodoxy and supported the Pan-Islamic movement as a defense against Western political and cultural encroachment on Dar-al-Islam,[1] nevertheless condemned autocracy as contrary to Islamic doctrines and advocated a form of Islamic nationalism. Despite his opposition to Western ideas he promulgated two of the most dynamic concepts of Western nineteenth-century thought—liberalism and nationalism, which he linked with his religious fundamentalism. Jamal-ud-Din al-Afghani is a notable figure in the evolution of modern Egypt because among those he inspired were great leaders of the Egyptian nationalist movement, Mustafa Kemal, Sheikh Abdul-Aziz Shawish and Saad Zaghlul.[2]

A brilliant student of Jamal-ud-Din al-Afghani, Mohammed Abduh (1849–1905), became an important religious and intellectual leader who recognized the necessity of liberalizing the rigidly orthodox interpretation of Islam and of reforming the old oppressive political system He molded the thinking of Moslem leaders during the second half of the nineteenth century. His influence significantly helped to prepare the Moslems of the Near East for the rapid process of modernization which was to overtake them in the twentieth century. Abduh's opposition to autocracy and his emphasis on the rights and welfare of the people foreshadowed the democratic and socialistic movements which have spread beyond Egypt to the Arabs of southwestern Asia. In some respects Abduh's political, economic, and social philosophy is comparable to the "Christian Socialism" of Saint-Simon (1760–1825). Abduh's "Islamic socialism" prepared the way for those socialistic elements introduced by Nasser and his association in the political and economic system of the United Arab Republic of Egypt.

The Boulak Press founded by Mohammed Ali played a significant role in the spreading of ideas not only in Egypt but in Arab and Turkish parts of the Near East. Mohammed Ali, his son Mohammed Said

(1854–63), and his grandson Ismail (1863–79) fostered education by opening schools, elementary and secondary, as well as specialized schools. In addition, intellectual life was stimulated by Egyptians who were sent to Europe to study and by foreign schools which were opened in Egypt, which became an intellectual center for much of the Near East. After the British Occupation, when the Ottoman connection became purely nominal, revolutionary leaders from the Turkish empire established themselves in Egypt, which became a center of enlightenment.

In material matters Egypt made very considerable progress under the early khedivial rulers. The cultivation of cotton, which revolutionized the agrarian economy of Egypt, was introduced. The modern irrigation system began during the reign of Mohammed Ali with the construction of the Barrage. The encouragement of foreign capital investment in Egypt made possible the building of the Suez Canal, the development and equipment of modern port facilities at Alexandria, Port Said, and Suez, the building of railroads, and the providing of modern municipal facilities, water works, sewers, street cars, lighting. European banking methods and institutions began changing the age-old commercial practices. Cotton-ginning and cigarette-making were entering wedges for the introduction of other modern industries.

These Albanian dynasts have to their credit some very substantial achievements. Future developments were based upon these khedivial accomplishments. Charles Issawi testifies to this in his statement that: "To a much greater extent than he would have cared to admit, Cromer merely carried on Ismail's work, often using the same methods." [3] The British built upon the foundations laid by Mohammed Ali and his successors to the khedivial throne. Their contributions to Egyptian progress are sometimes lost sight of because of their manifest weaknesses, which eventually led to the overthrow of the dynasty and the establishment of the Republic of Egypt.

One of the fundamental reasons for the failure of the monarchy lies in the fact that Mohammed Ali after destroying the exploiting class of Mameluke feudal landowners replaced it with another. He created a parasitical class of landowning pashas who dominated the political and economic life of Egypt for more than a century. Wealthy landowners, bureaucrats, and palace sycophants became increasingly parasitical and oppressive when the older agrarian exploitation was coupled with modern financial exploitation typical of nineteenth-century Europe. In Egypt such exploitation was not ameliorated by humanitarianism, which in Europe tempered the ruthlessness of classical economic theories and practices. The Egyptian peasants (fellaheen) and urban workers were not protected as in Europe by the broadening of the franchise, by trade unionism, and by social legislation. In Egypt those social and political institutions which in the West began to restrain the owning and controlling classes had not as yet come into existence. Furthermore, the khedives and their advisers were ignorant of the technical devices of European finance, and they also were fleeced by bankers and money lenders who catered to their extravagances. This was notably so in the case of Khedive Ismail who brought financial disaster to the Egyptian government, which led eventually to dual control by the British and French of governmental finances and finally to British occupation in 1882.

The failures of these Egyptian rulers were closely related to their achievements. Modernization had opened Egypt to Western exploitation before the Egyptian people had acquired the means by which to protect themselves from the economic and social ills which were concomitants of European penetration. This situation gave rise to maladjustments which created fertile ground for political revolutionary movements. The khedives and their subjects became victims of the rapidity of modernization.

The first crisis arising from this situation was precipitated by discontent among the Egyptian army officers with the discrimination against them by the higher ranking officers who were members of the ruling caste and who looked with contempt upon the native Egyptians. The leader of the movement was Ahmed Arabi, the son of a village sheikh, who was a veritable representative of the Arab-speaking Egyptian peasantry. Arabi's uprising contained the seeds of a genuine social revolution as well as of an Egyptian nationalist movement directed against foreign control of Egypt. The revolution of 1881 under his leadership had no parallel in Near Eastern history in modern times with the exception of the revolution in 1952 of Egyptian army officers led by General Mohammed Naguib and Colonel Gamal Abdul Nasser. Both revolutions had the support of the people because both gave expression to their hopes and voiced their discontents. This cannot be said to have been the case of the Young Turk revolution of 1908, which was distinctly an upper-class movement little understood by the Turkish peasantry. Arabi's revolt differs fundamentally from the so-called Arab Revolution of 1916–18 which had little social content and was essentially a revolt against Ottoman rule, or rather misrule.

It is somewhat futile to speculate on what might have been the course of Egyptian history and that of the Near East if this Egyptian revolution had not been snuffed out by the British. For the next seventy years the discontents of the Egyptian people found an outlet in the Egyptian nationalist movement to get rid of the British, with its slogan "Egypt for the Egyptians."

The British occupation of Egypt changed the direction and aims of the revolutionary movement. Foreign domination fostered a passionate Egyptian nationalism tinged in some segments of Egyptian society with anti-westernism and xenophobia, which have their counterparts today in the Moslem Brotherhood. The socio-economic revolution now taking place under the guidance of the government of the Egyptian Republic is colored in all its aspects by Arab nationalism, the successor of the nineteenth-century Egyptian nationalism.

The British occupation 1882–1936.—Under British administration the pace of modernization increased and the processes, which had already begun to undermine the old order, continued to prepare the way for revolution. Egypt was given an efficient government. Highly proficient British civil servants and administrators trained an Egyptian bureaucracy to handle much of the detailed work of government. The harsh treatment meted out to the lowly peasants and urban workers, such as the courbash and the bastinado, was abolished. The compulsory mass labor of the corvée was done away with. Much of the corruption and graft was eliminated. Law and order were maintained in the cities and villages. Health and sanitation were greatly improved. Egypt was well governed.

Governmental finances were put on a sound basis. Business flourished. Foreign capital flowed into Egypt, providing funds for extending irrigation, equipping cities with modern facilities, and expanding the production, ginning, and export of cotton. On the surface Egypt appeared prosperous, but prosperity was largely confined to the upper classes, the foreigners in Egypt, and the foreign bankers, investors, shipping companies, and their agents.

From the British point of view their occupation and administration of Egypt were eminently successful. One can but admire the zeal, ability, and integrity of the British administrators and officials in Egypt. Their devotion to their jobs, their very real interest in the welfare of the Egyptians, their loyalty and high standard of conduct were admirable. The British administration of Egypt, however, was not primarily in the interests of the Egyptian people but of the British, the foreigners, and the upper classes. British purpose was that of providing an efficient and honest government and of maintaining law and order. In the main, British administration was patterned on the theories of the laissez-faire economists of midnineteenth century. It created and maintained a state of affairs favorable to the large landowners among the Egyptians, to foreign financiers, enterprisers, investors, and business interests.

Lord Cromer and his successors did not conceive of their task as that of bringing about revolutionary changes in the social order but rather of maintaining it while purging it of its worse abuses. They might well be called reformers carrying out their reforms with the consent of the upper classes, who found British occupation and administration advantageous. The Egyptian upper classes, particularly the landowners and the pashas, prospered.

With keen insight and notable objectivity Charles Issawi in his book *Egypt at Mid-Century* has this to say about British rule in Egypt:

> In *Modern Egypt* Lord Cromer distinguished two kinds of reforms: those which could be carried out by administrative action and those which required a social revolution. British reforms will be found to belong exclusively to the former category: irrigation, sanitation, prison reform, substitution of paid for forced labor in canal clearance and upkeep of river banks (abolition of the corvée) etc. But no effort was made to reform such institutions as al-Azhar, the *Sharia* courts, village schools, wakfs, or to speed up the education and emancipation of women, or to attempt such a shaking up of the country as was carried out by Mustafa Kemal in Turkey. Nor is it to be expected that foreign rulers should make such an attempt, still less that it should be successful. Although its ultimate results are often extremely revolutionary, foreign rule is generally conservative in its aims. (pp. 44–45).

Issawi has placed his finger on the basic cause for the failure of Western colonialism. The imperialist government relies for its control on the existing ruling class, whose power and security are the products of a given socio-economic order and whose continued position of privilege depends upon its maintenance. The imperialist control accelerates processes of change that destroy the foundations of the old order. At the same time the relations between the imperialist overlord and the people of the colonial area result in their absorbing political and social ideas and ideals which are subversive of the ideas and ideals of the old ruling classes. Foreign rulers interested in maintaining the socio-political institutions of a colony or protectorate are inhibited from becoming leaders of a revolution which their rule makes imperative. Thus, inner contradictions lead to the nemesis of colonialism and imperialism.

In Egypt, whereas the British rulers limited themselves to administrative reforms, the British Occupation prepared the way for economic and social revolution which, now, is in the process of consummation under the republican regime of President Nasser. Throughout the last quarter of the nineteenth century and the first half of the twentieth increasing contact with the Western world and the growing interrelationship of the Egyptian economy with that of the West inevitably brought changes which spelt the end of the old regime. British textile industries became increasingly interested in cotton production in Egypt. The American Civil War shut off Britain's principal source of cotton and after the occupation of Egypt British textile manufacturers and importers of cotton looked upon Egypt as the logical place to develop cotton growing in an area under British control. Furthermore, Egyptian long staple cotton was superior to any except the limited amount of Sea Island cotton grown in the United States. Egyptian agriculture was transformed from a food-producing to a cotton-producing economy to meet the demands of the British textile industry. Egypt became dependent upon cotton export to pay for imports of grains, fuel, raw products, and manufactured goods.

Britain and other foreign countries established banks in Egypt, introducing modern financial institutions which took over the greater part of commercial financial transactions. Egypt became a part of the Western world's economic system of commerce, shipping, and finance. This basic change in the agricultural, commercial, and financial life of Egypt had repercussions on many aspects of the Egyptian social framework.

The British prepared the way for the overthrow of the old social order and the termination of their control of Egypt. In the cliché-like terms of dialectic materialism, the British administration in Egypt sowed the seeds of a new social order which within less than seventy years was to supersede the rule of the British, of the Egyptian monarchy, and of the pashas.

British occupation of Egypt gave rise to Egyptian nationalism, which is not to be confused with the Arab nationalism that now dominates to a considerable extent the Egyptian leaders and people. Nationalism is essentially a psychological phenomenon the component parts of which are a body of ideas and emotional responses to them. Modern nationalism developed in Europe as a product of the class struggle between the bourgeoisie and the aristocracy and later of the bourgeoisie, the peasantry, and urban workers against absolute monarchy. Essentially, it was a basic shift in loyalty from the feudal noble and from the king to the state or nation. In the Near East nationalism developed not as a result of class struggle but in the struggles against alien governments. The various subject peoples of the Ottoman Empire, including the Arabs and Egyptians, turned to nationalism in their fight for independence.

In Egypt the early phases of Egyptian nationalism appeared during the period of Arabi's revolt, which was directed against the ruling caste of Turkish pashas and officials. Later, during the British occupation of Egypt, the nationalist movement was directed principally against British rule. It leader, Mustafa Kemal, was a romantic liberal and a disciple of Jamal-ud-Din al-Afghani, who, although an opponent of autocracy, supported pan-Islamism. In a quite contradictory manner the autocrat of Turkey, Abdul Hamid, gave encouragement to Mustafa Kemal and to Egyptian nationalism. Such inner contradictions within Egyptian nationalism as liberalism, pan-Islamism, religious orthodoxy, and xenophobia are phenomena similar to contemporary contradictions within Europe, such as liberalism, nationalism, racialism, socialism, and fascism.

In 1900 the Egyptian nationalists under Mustafa Kemal's leadership organized an Egyptian nationalist party known as al Hizb al-Watani with the appealing and popular slogan "Egypt for the Egyptians" and a program demanding the absolute independence of Egypt and the Sudan. By 1914 at the outbreak of World War I the Egyptian nationalist movement had spread widely throughout urban and rural Egypt and had produced an articulate and popular leader, Saad Zaghlul, who although of peasant origin had become a high official in the Ministry of Education. Khedive Abbas Hilmi was bitterly anti-British and looked with sympathy on the nationalist movement and for support to the Ottoman sultan.

When the Ottoman Empire entered the war in November 1914, the British government was confronted with a difficult problem. Nominally, Egypt was under the suzerainty of the Turkish sultan. Foreigners in Egypt, including the Austrians and Germans, enjoyed a privileged position under the Capitulations. An attack on the Suez Canal by Achmed Jemal Pasha was launched shortly after Turkey entered the war. Egypt had become a staging ground, training camp, and a military and naval base for the British, Australian-New Zealand, and Anglo-Indian forces. The sultan of Turkey had proclaimed a Jihad. The British were threatened not only with invasion but with the possibility of an uprising of the Egyptians under the banners of nationalism and religion.

To meet this potential danger, the British with the support of the leaders of the ruling classes proclaimed a protectorate over Egypt, abolished the khediviate, and proclaimed the sultanate of Egypt, appointing a member of the reigning dynasty, Hussein Kamil, sultan. This collaboration of the owning and controlling class was obtained after verbal promises were made by the British with respect to a larger measure of self-government at the end of the war.

Although the Egyptian nationalists remained quiescent throughout the war, nevertheless their ardor was increased by the ideas and ideals proclaimed by the Allies throughout the Near East and by the hopes that the United States would see that the "rights of small nations" and of "self-determination" were enforced as well as endorsed. No sooner was the war over than the Egyptian nationalists organized a widely based political movement known as the Wafd al-Misri, or Egyptian Delegation, to present the demands of the Egyptian people to the British government and to the Paris Peace Conference. The Egyptians became thoroughly disillusioned when the British refused to allow an Egyptian delegation to leave Egypt. When this refusal was met with widespread demonstrations the British exiled Zaghlul Pasha and three other leading nationalists to Malta. Later, when it became known that President Wilson would not support the claims of the Egyptian nationalists, Zaghlul and his collaborators were permitted to go to Paris, where the leaders of the conference denied them recognition.

In 1919 the behavior of the victors makes one turn to biblical language: "They have eyes and they see not, they have ears and they hear not." The uprising in Egypt in early 1919, however, did force the British to attempt to arrive at a compromise settlement with the Egyptian nationalists. In December 1919 Lord Milner was sent to Egypt at the head of a mission to investigate the causes of violence and unrest in Egypt. From a British viewpoint generous concessions were proposed by the Milner Commission. These were embodied in the British Declaration of Policy of 1922. The British agreed to terminate the protectorate and to recognize Egypt as an "independent sovereign state" under conditions which in contemporary language would have made Egypt a British satellite state. These restrictions on full Egyptian sovereignty, particularly the retention of British troops in Egypt, were unacceptable to the Egyptian leaders. When negotiations in London failed, the British government seized and deported the leaders of the Wafd and promptly declared the protectorate at an end and without further ado, changed the title of Hussein Kamil's successor and brother, Fuad, from sultan to king.

These temporary expedients in no way solved the Egyptian problem. During the following year, 1923, Britain's puppet government in Egypt promulgated a constitution under which in the ensuing elections the nationalist Wafd Party won a smashing victory. Zaghlul Pasha became prime minister in January, 1924, and the differences between the British and the Egyptians over the Sudan and the maintenance of British troops in Egypt were again brought to an impasse.

The years between 1924 and 1936 were troublesome ones because no acceptable compromise was found. Sporadic violence in Egypt was met with sharp reprisals by the British. After the death of Saad Zaghlul in 1927, his successor as leader of the Wafd, Mustafa Nahas, became premier. It was not until 1936 after successive Egyptian cabinets, Wafdist and non-Wafdist, failed to reach a settlement with the British that

Nahas finally negotiated an agreement with the British government which was the basis for the Anglo-Egyptian Treaty of 1936 ratified by the Egyptian Parliament.

Under this twenty years' treaty of alliance, which was unilaterally abrogated in 1951 by the Egyptian Parliament at the instigation of Premier Nahas, Egypt was able to become a member of the League of Nations and to obtain abolition of the burdensome Capitulations, a heritage of the former Ottoman domination. Britain was granted the right to maintain a naval base at Alexandria for a period of eight years and a military force of 10,000 in an area restricted to the Suez Canal Zone. It is significant that this treaty was negotiated under the increasing threat of fascist aggression and only three years before the outbreak of World War II. Egyptian nationalists had been alerted to the danger by the Italian invasion in 1935 of Ethiopia and its annexation in the spring of 1936.

Superficially, it appeared as if the crisis was at an end and that the stress and storm of Anglo-Egyptian relations were over. Seemingly, Egypt was entering a period of tranquility under the then popular boy King Farouk, who at the age of sixteen succeeded to the throne of Fuad.

In his book *The Middle East in World Affairs* George Lenczowski paraphrases an observation of a French writer, Paul Morand: "England and Egypt are like an old married couple: they may quarrel but they never break their bond." [4] This is reminiscent of Chancellor Prince von Bulow's remark in the German Reichstag on January 8, 1902, in reference to the Franco-Italian *rapprochement* of 1900–1902: "In a happy marriage the husband must not get angry right off if his wife innocently takes an extra dance with another partner." [5] Such asides, which in American slang would be called "wisecracks," are considered in some diplomatic and other circles to be evidence of great shrewdness, insight, and wisdom. In reality old married couples do not always make up, and their disagreements, like extramarital flirtations in the ballroom, sometimes lead to divorce or even murder.

In 1914 Italy declared her neutrality and in 1915 joined the Entente Powers in war against her former allies, Germany and Austria-Hungary. Between 1951, when the Egyptian Parliament abrogated the Anglo-Egyptian Treaty, and 1956 when the British bombed the open city of Port Said, Anglo-Egyptian bonds were shattered as effectively as were the dwellings of the Egyptian inhabitants of Port Said. Aphorisms and adages are poor substitutes for accurate analysis. In this atomic age when statesmen and politicians—also scientists—glibly talk about the vital necessity of controlling interstellar space, policies based on "wise-cracks" appear somewhat like neolithic thinking, with all due apologies to Neolithic man.

THE REVOLUTION OF 1952

The political revolution in Egypt began on July 23, 1952, when a group of army officers, who five years earlier had organized a Committee of Free Officers, seized control of the Egyptian government by a sudden coup d'état. The underlying causes of this revolution grew out of the reactions among Egyptians to the process of modernization during the period of the British occupation and also to the effect of international developments, especially those during the years from 1914 to 1936. The more immediate and precipitating causes arose between 1936 and 1952.

The underlying causes.—The disintegration of the traditional Islamic social order created increasing unrest that found expression in the growth of a variety of diverse and antagonistic groups. In the field of religion the cleavages began to make their influence felt in the realm of politics. The conventional religious leaders of al-Azhar University with its associated ulama began to lose influence both on the masses and the classes.

There were those who had been greatly influenced by Western ideas. These modernists wished to bring about a separation of Church and State along the patterns of the West. They hoped to do for Egypt what Mustafa Kemal Ataturk had done for Turkey, where a secular state had been set up. They wanted to do away with the Sharia and the Sharia courts as the base of the legal and juridical system.

Another group, sometimes referred to as the reformers, who more appropriately might be called religious reactionaries, desired the re-establishment along traditional lines of an Islamic theocratic state based on the Koran and the Sharia. They advocated the application and enforcement of Islamic law as in the time of Mohammed and of the early caliphs.

A third group, who might be called the moderates, were content with the status quo and did not wish to see any significant change in the existing Islamic compromise with modern innovations.

The modernists and the religious reactionaries were ardently nationalistic and both favored social reforms and concerned themselves with the betterment of the living conditions of the masses. The modernists were favorable to Western and modern culture though opposed to foreign political domination and economic exploitation. The religious reactionaries were nationalists very largely because of their conviction that Western culture and domination were undermining the Islamic way of life and were corrupting Moslem youth. Until Egypt was freed from British control these two groups were able to co-operate in their efforts to achieve their strictly nationalistic aims. Later, after 1952, however, when Egypt became completely independent, their opposing ideas with respect to the nature of the state and to the type of government brought them into conflict with one another.

The moderates, both with respect to religion and politics, were for the most part members of those classes which had profited from the British occupation and administration. They were the landowners whose dominant position in Egyptian society was being challenged politically and economically by the new professional, business, and financial classes. Under the British regime and down to 1952 the interests of the landowners were protected by governments which controlled the army, the police, and the bureaucracy and had the support of the al-Azhar ulama. Generally speaking, the landowners did not concern themselves with social reforms which might take away their privileges and destroy the foundations of their wealth, their power, and their social position. The modernists and the religious reactionaries alike were a menace to them. This upper class sought compromise with the British and frowned on the extreme demands of the nationalists, but gave mild support, however, to nationalism, which tended to focus the emotional and ideological discontents of the peasantry and urban workers on the struggle for independence rather than on social and economic ills.

In course of time the mass support of nationalism began to isolate the landowning upper class and the al-Azhar theologians. As a consequence, some of them turned either toward the modernists or to the reactionaries who were gaining the backing of the masses.

During the period between World Wars I and II fascism and Marxism with their exciting ideas and ideologies added to the turbulence of political life in Egypt. The political atmosphere became more stormy due to the Palestine situation. The Arab-Jewish struggle during the period of the British mandate aroused the emotions of the Egyptians. From their point of view an Islamic people, thought of as brother Moslems and Arabs, were being threatened by Jews under the protection and with the support of the British and other Western Powers. The Egyptians thought of Palestine as another Moslem land fallen victim to Christian imperialism and being handed over to the Jews.

It is not surprising, therefore, that Egyptians had little enthusiasm for the cause of the British and, later, for the United Nations in the war against the Axis Powers. Even when Egypt was invaded by Italians and

Germans, the Egyptians did not look upon the Axis Powers as their enemies. Egypt, like Turkey, remained neutral until victory for the United Nations became certain and participation in the United Nations Conference at San Francisco of 1945 hinged upon a declaration of war against the Axis.

Immediate and precipitating causes.—During World War II both the monarchy and the Wafd Party were discredited in the eyes of a great many Egyptians. King Farouk's scandalous personal behavior alienated pious Egyptian Moslems. His flirtations with Italian fascists did not please others. His opposition to and treatment of the Wafd antagonized still others, and, finally, humiliation at the hands of the British further discredited both Farouk and the throne. The enthusiastic support he had received when he became king was replaced by a contemptuous unpopularity.

The Wafd Party also suffered a serious decline in its popularity. It had developed intrenched and vested interests which were little concerned with the welfare of the Egyptian people. Corruption and graft permeated the upper rank of the party. This condition of affairs was exposed by one of its leaders, Makram Ebeid Pasha, who disgusted and indignant resigned and published a documented exposé of Wafdist peculations in the widely circulated Black Book.

Between 1939 and 1945 Egypt was inundated with a human flood of foreign troops composed for the most part of Christians of European descent: Europeans, South Africans, Americans, Australians, and New Zealanders. For a second time within three decades Egypt became an armed camp and Egyptians were brought into intimate contact with foreign soldiers representing the mass product of Western civilization. In manners and conduct these foreigners differed greatly from the highly selected group of British civil servants and officers who had governed Egypt from 1882 to 1914 with the support of a small British garrison of disciplined professional soldiers. This experience with foreign troops in the two wars augmented the social and ideological unrest of the Egyptians which was increased by the inflationary effects of huge military purchases and expenditures in Egypt.

By 1945 a revolutionary situation had developed. A powerful organization of the "religious reactionaries" known as the Moslem Brotherhood, in Arabic el-Ikhwan el-Muslimin, had a mass following estimated to number over half a million members. The Ikhwan was founded by Hassan Banna in 1928. This rather amazing individual, with a talent for organizing, was the son of an Egyptian watchmaker and Islamic scholar and writer whose religious ideas had a deep influence on his son. Hassan Banna on the completion of his studies obtained a minor position as a schoolteacher at Ismailia on the Suez Canal.

Well grounded in Moslem theology Hassan Banna was distressed by what he considered to be the evil effects of Western culture and modern ways upon Moslems and upon the Islamic way of life. Like other dynamic political leaders of the first half of the twentieth century, he was a product of a profoundly maladjusted society seething with political, economic, and ideological discontents. Neither a fascist nor a Communist, he was driven on by religious zeal and a love of power. Beginning with a few followers in Ismailia he rapidly built up a quasi-religious organization which he developed into a political movement with a broad mass base. His ideas made a strong appeal to many elements among the discontented and somewhat bewildered Egyptian people. Using modern publicity methods Hassan Banna and his lieutenant organized branches throughout Egypt and in some of the neighboring lands. Money poured into the coffers of the Ikhwan, which under Hassan Banna's leadership became a political force to be reckoned with by all political leaders. The Ikhwan in the struggle against the British also developed a clandestine para-military organization with caches of arms and munitions.

The moderates of the upper classes in Egypt in their disgust with the growing condition of violence, fearing the unrest among peasants and workers and possible spread of Communism, attempted to use the Ikhwan in a way which was not altogether dissimilar to the ways in which the upper classes in Germany and Italy attempted to use the Nazis and fascist movements. Some of the political leaders among the moderates even became members of the Ikhwan.[5a]

The Ikhwan grew to be so powerful that its leaders might have taken over the government and become the rulers of Egypt. Faced with the increasing violences of the Ikhwan and the assassination of political leaders, the prerevolutionary government took stern measures against the Brotherhood in 1948 and in February 1949. Hassan Banna was assassinated by an unidentified assailant. Temporarily, the Ikhwan was set back on its heels, but the organization still continued to exist and had regained some of its political power when the military junta overthrew the government in 1952. Two years before the coup d'état J. Heyworth-Dunne wrote in his *Religious and Political Trends* . . . that: "Time is running out. Egyptian ruling classes must realise the urgency of their social problems." [6]

The monarchy and the ruling classes proved incapable of resolving the social crisis in Egypt, incompetent in conducting the war with Israel, and unable to arrive at terms with Britain in regard to the termination of the Treaty of 1936 and of the maintenance of British troops at Britain's great air base in the Suez Canal zone. The Egyptian nationalists with the support of the masses were demanding the termination of the Anglo-Egyptian Treaty and the complete withdrawal of British troops from Egyptian soil. The Communist revolt in Greece, Moscow's demands on Turkey, and Communist activities in Iran resulted in both Great Britain and the United States becoming deeply concerned with the defense of the Near and Middle East. After withdrawing from Palestine and Greece, the British became more determined to retain control of their Egyptian air base. Under the Truman Doctrine the United States, providing aid to Turkey and Greece in accordance with the American over-all policy of the containment of Russia, had extended its assumption of military obligations in the Near East. In order to resolve the problem of the maintenance of British troops in Egypt it was proposed that Egypt should join a Middle East Defense Command with joint air bases in Egypt. The Egyptian government's reply to this on November 20, 1950, was a refusal based on the opposition to the stationing of foreign troops in Egypt.

During this period the patience of the Egyptian masses and nationalists was rapidly coming to an end. Sniping at British troops in the Ismailia region began to develop into a sort of guerrilla warfare.

Demonstrations and violence in the Egyptian cities of Alexandria and Cairo continued sporadically throughout 1951 and the first half of 1952, indicating the increasing temper of Egyptian people against the continuation of British military occupation of the air fields in the Suez Canal zone. Mob violence broke out on August 26, 1951, the fifteenth anniversary of the Anglo-Egyptian Treaty of 1936. The Egyptian nationalists with the backing of the masses were demanding complete independence of the British. The international situation had changed fundamentally between 1936 and 1951 as well noted by Albert Hourani.[7] Whereas in 1936, confronted by the Fascist-Nazi menace, even the nationalists were willing to accept a compromise settlement with the British, by 1951 the political leaders of the large landowners favored complete independence of Britain. The victory of the United Nations in the war against the Axis Powers had changed basically the international situation. Germany and Italy had ceased to be, at least for the present, Great Powers, relatively the power of Great Britain and France had declined, while the United States and the Soviet Union had emerged as two super Powers. In the Near East the United States under the Truman Doctrine had with respect to the Western Powers assumed a dominant role.

From an Egyptian viewpoint continued subordination to the British had ceased to be necessary or advantageous. Albert Hourani describes the situation succinctly: "Britain had no alternative to withdrawal from Egypt except virtually to reoccupy the whole country; . . . ." [8] Under past World War II conditions in Great Britain and in view of the international situation as a result of the creation of the United Nations, the British were not in a position to reoccupy Egypt. This was clearly demonstrated in the Suez Canal crisis of 1956–57, although there were those in England who did not fully realize the significance of the fundamental changes in the world.

The long drawn out negotiations between the various Egyptian cabinets and the British government, first over the termination of the Treaty of 1936 and then over the withdrawal of British troops from the great British air base, exacerbated the Egyptian masses, who were stirred to increasing violence under the constant excitation of the nationalists, the Ikhwan, the pseudo-national socialists, and the Communists. Clashes during 1951 at Ismailia and throughout the Suez Canal zone between the British and the Egyptians precipitated violent disorders in Cairo on January 26, 1952. British property more particularly, but also that of other foreigners, was destroyed by the mob. The famous Shepeard's Hotel and the well-known British Turf Club were demolished.

Events in Egypt were rapidly moving toward a crisis and the time was approaching when the acute political situation would be resolved by a seizure of power. The death of Hassan Banna and the measures taken against the Ikhwan by the Egyptian government in 1948–49 appear to have eliminated the possibility of the Brotherhood's taking over the government in 1952 and so prepared the way for the coup d'état by the Committee of Free Officers on July 23, 1952, when Colonel Muhammad Naguib proclaimed himself army commander-in-chief. Under his orders the royal palace and the principal government buildings were surrounded by tanks and armored cars. The political revolution had begun.

THE REVOLUTIONARY GOVERNMENT

On the third day after the seizure of power, King Farouk abdicated in favor of his son, Crown Prince Ahmad Fuad, for whom a regency council was set up under the authority of the Officers' Revolutionary Council. During the first period of the revolutionary government Naguib as the leader of the Officers' Revolutionary Council maintained the monarchy and attempted to collaborate with former political leaders and parties and with a cabinet of civilian ministers. Before the end of 1952 it became clear that the carrying out of the revolutionary changes desired by the Revolutionary Council would require dictatorial power because of the opposition to them by various groups. The decree law No. 178 of September 9, known as the agrarian law,[9] and other decrees abolishing the Constitution of 1923, establishing a Permanent Council for the Development of National Production, announcing a Five Year Plan, and dissolving all political parties and prohibiting the creation of new ones inevitably led to the dictatorial power of Premier Naguib being extended for six months. This was followed on January 23, 1953, by the establishment of the Liberation Front, which appeared as a step toward the creation of a one-party system and which led to the termination of the monarchy and the proclamation creating the Republic of Egypt on June 18, 1953, with Naguib president and prime minister and Colonel Gamal Abdel Nasser, deputy prime minister and minister of the Interior.

Like many revolutionary regimes, that in Egypt was confronted by opponents who were determined either to prevent the changes being made or to bring about more radical changes. The large landowners and other privileged classes, the Wafd, the Ikhwan, and the Communists as well as some reactionary elements among the army officers sought the overthrow of the Revolutionary Council. Drastic action was taken against leading members of the Communist Party, and against the Wafd, whose aging leader Nahas was arrested. When street fighting took place between student members of the Ikhwan and the Liberation Rally on January 12, 1954, the Supreme Guide, Hasan el Hudaybi, and seventy-odd members of the Ikhwan were arrested and the Brotherhood was dissolved—being accused of having conspired with the British to overthrow Naguib.

During 1954 dissension arose within the ranks of the Revolutionary Council between the supporters of Naguib and Nasser; the former were advocates of a more moderate policy and of compromise, the latter were determined to carry out basic social changes and opposed to compromises which might jeopardize their revolutionary program of social and economic reform. On the last day of March student demonstrations against the military regime were openly harangued by Communists, socialists, and members of the Ikhwan el-Muslimin. It was evident that disagreement among the members of the military junta was encouraging both the counterrevolutionists and the more radical groups.

The differences between the supporters of Naguib and Nasser were temporarily solved by Nasser's becoming head of the Revolutionary Council and prime minister while Naguib retained the presidency with only nominal power. Colonel Nasser was on the way to becoming the dictator of Egypt. He consolidated his position during the next two years and on June 24, 1956, he succeeded in having himself elected president by the overwhelming vote of almost 5,500,000, more than 99 per cent of the total votes cast. Quite in the Napoleonic tradition!

Historians writing of contemporary times are handicapped by the unsifted mass of available data and by the fact that much information is now unavailable. Such historians have some responsibility to comment on what appears to them significant with respect to the future.

Throughout the long history of Egypt, peasant agriculture and the peasant village have been more enduring than its ancient monuments. The Egyptian fellah and his way of life have persisted for millenniums. How successful the revolutionary government will be in modernizing Egyptian agriculture, the Egyptian village, and the Egyptian fellah is uncertain. Modernized, mechanized farming has been driving the Negro population in the Southern sections of the United States into urban ghettoes. It is driving the small farmers of New England off the land while suburbanization and industrialization are changing the New England village and countryside. In contemporary Egypt the development of modern industrialization acts as a magnet drawing the surplus peasant population to the cities, creating problems which perhaps only more industrialization can solve. In the past Egypt's need for capital resulted in dependence on foreign private capital. Under the present partly socialized economy, the revolutionary government has become dependent upon loans and grants from foreign governments, notably the United States and the U.S.S.R. This has had certain temporary advantages and has prevented Egypt from becoming a satellite state. Actually, however, independence becomes precarious for a state which has to depend upon foreign capital to any large extent.

The U.A.R. with Nasser, the outstanding protagonist of Arab nationalism and of revolutionary modernization, as leader, became entangled in the struggle between the "new order" and the "old order" in Arabia, with a costly military engagement in the Yemen and in Syria—an abortive frustrating experience.

As the champion of Arab nationalism and Arab unity Nasser has found himself unable to come to any settlement with Israel. His policy of denying free passageway to Israel through the Suez Canal resulted, after June 1967, in the Suez Canal becoming unusable by anyone!

Like every country of the world, in fact like all mankind, Egypt is in the midst of revolutionary processes the dimensions of which are now immeasurable.

CHAPTER XXX

A Decade of Significant Change, 1958-68

The most significant factor in recent and contemporary history is the ever-increasing rapidity of change which confronts mankind. The impact of change is far more intense in the Near East than in the West, where the transition from medievalism began centuries ago. For most of the people in the Near East—peasants, nomads, and the inhabitants of inland towns and cities—the passage from medieval ways of life to those of the second half of the twentieth century has been a matter of decades. Consequently, there is no understanding of the events of the past ten years without some comprehension of the problems which modernization imposes upon the peoples and the leaders throughout the area.

The complexities of the problems confronting the leaders of the Arabs are greater than those with which the statesmen of Israel and Turkey have to deal because the Arab people are widely scattered geographically and are divided politically into independent states, petty amirates and sheikhdoms of the Persian Gulf area, and the South Arabian Federation, including the Arab Republic of South Yemen (formerly the British Crown Colony of Aden), which attained independence in 1968.

SAUDI ARABIA

The forbidding and long-forbidden land of central Arabia was opened to the dynamism of modern industry when its vast petroleum deposits began to be developed on a major scale after 1945. This could not have been possible under the chaotic political conditions which prevailed before Abdul Aziz ibn Saud * subdued the tribes and gained control of the Hejaz and Hasa, providing ports on the Red Sea and the Persian Gulf (now referred to as the Arab Gulf by the Arabs).

Abdul Aziz ibn Saud laid the foundations of a centralized state with the basic governmental apparatus for handling the complex problems arising from the development of the kingdom's petroleum resources. During his reign Abdul Aziz supplemented the traditional tribal system with a Royal Council, a Council of Ulama, and an administrative bureaucracy. As the king of an Islamic theocratic absolute monarchy he set a precedent for succession to the throne. Disregarding the principle of primogeniture he conferred upon his second son, Saud, the title of crown prince. On the death of his father in 1953 Saud became king and promptly named as crown prince his younger brother Faisal. Both acts were approved by the Council of the Saudi family, by the Council of Ulama, and by the Council of Ministers, all pledging allegiance to King Saud ibn Abdul Aziz. The transfer of power took place without protest or violence.

During the short reign of Saud (1953–64) two serious crises arose which might have brought disaster to the kingdom. The first was a financial one resulting from a fantastic squandering of the income from oil royalties. The extravagances of the royal family and the inadequacy of the Ministry of Finance plunged the Saudi government into debt and undermined the value of the currency. Alarmed by the situation King Saud conferred upon Crown Prince Faisal full power over the finances and the foreign affairs of the kingdom. Prince Faisal called upon Anwa Ali, a Pakistani Moslem member of the Board of Directors of the International Money Fund, to reorganize the Ministry of Finance and National Economy. In 1958 as governor of the Saudi Arabian Monetary Agency Anwa Ali was able to restore the finances of the kingdom, reestablish the value of the rial, and check the extravagances of the royal family.

The second crisis was of a political nature. The recurring illnesses of King Saud, which necessitated frequent and long absences from Arabia obliged him to confer full royal powers on Crown Prince Faisal. In March, 1964, King Saud demanded the restoration of his royal powers. This demand was refused by the Council of Ulama, the Saudi family council, and the Council of Ministers. A fetwa of the Council of Ulama

* Saud, a generic name of a central Arabian family, is also used as a surname. During Abdul Aziz's life he was called ibn Saud in the West. His son the second king was called Saud ibn Abdul Aziz.

deposed Saud and pledged allegiance to Faisal as king. The other councils accepted the fetwa and pledged allegiance to Faisal. In an orderly manner with the sanction of the religious leaders a king was deposed and a king enthroned.

The deposed king, Saud ibn Abdul Aziz, who soon fled to Cairo with one of his four wives, has under the protection of Nasser been denouncing the "reactionary regime" of the Saudi government and of King Faisal, demanding that he be dethroned as an enemy and oppressor of the "people." Saud also insisted that he be restored to his throne.

The Saudi government had shown a high degree of stability and a capacity to deal effectively with the challenging task of governing a state in which modernization was bringing about revolutionary social and economic changes. It seems rather significant that an Arab state under the leadership of an age-old tribal family, and within the framework of Islamic law and traditions, had shown surprising flexibility in meeting the challenge of the rapid and profound changes thrust upon it.

The foreign problems of Saudi Arabia are primarily in its relations with the other Arab states, with Britain over matters of conflicting and also mutual interests in Arabia, and with the United States, on matters which at times concern Israel.

One of the most significant factors in the Arab Near East is the growing conflict between "the old order" and "the new order." There are two phases of this struggle. One is taking place within all the Arab states, the other is taking place between the governments which are protagonists of "the old order" and those of "the new order." The two major antagonists are King Faisal of Saudi Arabia and President Gamal Abdel Nasser of the United Arab Republic. One of the focal centers of the struggles has been the Yemen, where Faisal supports the deposed ruler, Imam Muhammed al-Badr, in a counterrevolutionary movement against Abdullah al-Salal of the Yemenite Arab Republic, which has considerable military support from the United Arab Republic. Unable to persuade Nasser to withdraw his military forces from the Yemen Faisal broke off relations with the U.A.R.

The second most important focus of the struggle between the "old order" and the "new order" is that of the Arab proletariat of Aden against the local bourgeoisie of Aden and the sheikhs of South Arabia. Faisal in the mid-1960's began preparing specialized forces to support the South Arabian Federation in the event of an attempted seizure of power by the Arab workers, who were aided by the Yemenite Republic and the U.A.R. In the training and equipment of these forces Faisal has secured aid from both the United States and Britain.

Saudi Arabia has friendly relations with Kuwait and sent a military force there to prevent an attack on Kuwait by Iraq in 1962. Faisal's only ally among the Arab states is King Hussein of Jordan, who is menaced by the Republic of Syria. In the crisis of May, 1967, Hussein went to Cairo and in talks with Nasser prepared the basis for a military alliance coordinating the armed forces of the two states.

The only conflict of interest between the United States and Saudi Arabia has been over Israel. These differences have been of a minor nature. They date back to the historical meeting between President Roosevelt and King Abdul Aziz ibn Saud during World War II with respect to the future of Palestine. Since November, 1917, the Christian nations of the West have failed to realize that the Arab people of the Near East were adamant in their opposition to the creation of a Jewish state in Palestine and since 1948 irreconcilable to the loss of it. This is one of the realities of the situation in the Near East. The other is the existence of the state of Israel.

In matters of prime concern to both Saudi Arabia and the United States both countries have shown considerable discretion in dealing with one another. In April, 1961, when the Saudi government stated that the demand for the withdrawal of United States military forces from the Dhahran air base had been in consequence of a United States loan to Israel, the American government took it with good grace. When it protested discrimination against Americans visiting or working in Saudi Arabia for the Arabian American Oil Company, as claimed by American Jewish organizations, the Saudi government replied that as long as a state of war existed between the Arab states and Israel no Jews would be permitted to enter Saudi Arabia. After the unpleasant episode in New York during King Faisal's visit to the United States there was no interruption of friendly relations between the two countries. The United States did not demand that Saudi Arabia change its laws concerning the entrance of Jews in the country, and the Saudi government did not consider canceling Aramco's concessions because of the discourteous treatment the King had received at the hands of the mayor of New York City and the governor of the state of New York.

These episodes served a certain purpose in that they gave America the opportunity to learn of the bitter opposition of the Arabs to Israel, and it gave the Arabs an idea of the power of minority groups in America in shaping the foreign policy of the United States.

One of the strong bonds between Saudi Arabia and the United States is the successful manner in which the Saudi government and people and the Arabian American Oil Company have handled the many delicate relationships which have resulted from the construction and operation of vast industrial complexes, including exploration, drilling, transportation by pipelines, motor trucks, and airplanes, refining, and in addition all the minor industries contributory to the main operations. To these must be added the housing and other facilities and the essential services provided the workers and their families. The most delicate of all problems have been those of human relations in a country where for centuries no non-Moslems had been permitted to live or travel. The introduction of foreign labor was essential. Besides the skilled American workers, less skilled workers were brought from India and from the western Mediterranean countries, most of them Christians or non-Moslems.

The social and legal relations between the Aramco workers and Saudi Arabs were handled with great skill. One of the successful methods used by Aramco was that of educating young American lawyers, who studied the Arabic language, history, literature, and Islamic law and jurisprudence. These men were able to handle the affairs of non-Moslems in the Islamic courts and to win the respect and friendship of Saudi judges and jurists. Between Aramco and the Saudi government and the people of Saudi Arabia, there has been no trouble serious enough to disrupt their good relations.

❁ THE YEMEN

Since 1962 the Yemen has become the focal center of the conflict in the Arab Near East between "the new order" and "the old order." The civil war between the revolutionary government of the Arab Yemenite Republic and the deposed Imam Muhammed al-Badr has already brought about intervention in support of the republicans by the United Arab Republic of Egypt and in support of the royalists by the kingdom of Saudi Arabia. The critical situation in Aden, which has long been entangled in the affairs of the Yemen, has added to the wider international implications of the struggle.

Many facets of the situation in the Yemen have their origin in the history of that country since its conquest and conversion to Islam in the seventh century and the rise of Moslem sects following the death of Uthman, the third caliph, in 656. The Moslems of the Yemen are divided into two main sects, the Sunni, who for the most part inhabit the south and the coastal areas, and the Shiites, who dwell in the north and central regions. The Zeidis of the Shiite sect have for centuries been a ruling caste in the Yemen. They claim descent from Ali and Fatima, the daughter of the Prophet. In 897 A.D. the first imam of the Yemen, Yahya ibn al-Husain, a Shiite Zeidi, founded an Islamic theocratic state.

After the evacuation of the Yemen in 1918 by the Ottoman Turks, Yahya ibn Yahya of the Rassi family re-established the Rassid dynasty and the autocratic theocracy of the imamate. One of the ironic factors in the recent and contemporary history of the Yemen is that Imam Yahya, his son Ahmad, imam from 1948–62, and his grandson Muhammed al-Badr, the deposed imam, pursued policies which led to the overthrow of the imamate and the Zeidi monopoly of power by the establishment of the Arab Yemenite Republic on September 19, 1962.

Imam Yahya was determined to maintain the old order intact and to keep the Yemen and its people in a state of ignorance, immune from the subversive ideas of the modern world, but the rising power of Abdel Aziz ibn Saud by the conquest of the Hejaz and Asir forced Yahya to the conclusion that his army officers must learn the technics of modern warfare. He sent young boys abroad—and thus a Zeidi boy of fourteen, the son of a humble blacksmith, was chosen for training at the Military Academy of Bagdad in 1936. This was Abdullah al-Salal, who as a colonel in the Yemenite army seized power on September 18, 1962, and on the following day became the president of the Arab Yemenite Republic.

Yahya's obscurantist and ruthless policies gave rise to a revolutionary movement in the Yemen which received support from wealthy Yemenite merchants in the Crown Colony of Aden and from non-Zeidi elements in the Yemen. The revolutionists failed in their principal objective but succeeded in having Yahya assassinated in 1948.

His son, Prince Ahmad, who became imam, had previously visited Aden, where he had met leading Yemenite merchants who impressed upon him the necessity of developing the resources of the Yemen. To explore the possibilities of obtaining foreign aid he sent his son Muhammed al-Badr to Egypt, to Europe, and even to the Soviet Union. The doors of the Yemen, which had been kept tightly closed for more than a century, were at last being opened. Events in the Near East during the reign of Ahmad, which were causing an increasing ferment throughout the Arab Near East could not be prevented from affecting the people of the Yemen.

It is difficult for those who are not of the Near East to understand fully the impact upon the Arabs of the events which followed the end of World War II: the withdrawal of France and Great Britain from the Fertile Crescent, of the British from the Nile Valley, the creation of the State of Israel, the Arab-Israeli war of 1948–49, the overthrow of monarchy in Egypt, the rise of Nasser, the spread of a passionate Arab nationalism, the humiliation of Britain and France by the Suez fiasco, the vast wealth flowing into the coffers of Kuwait and Saudi Arabia. These and the increasing tempo of change could not be concealed from the people of Yemen.

The soliciting of aid from foreign countries in the development of the resources of the Yemen resulted in a threefold rivalry—economic, political, and ideological—between the capitalistic nations and the Communist states. Both Imam Ahmad and Crown Prince al-Badr showed considerable skill in playing upon the competitive nature of this neo-imperialism. There is a certain humorous irony in theocratic autocrats inviting Soviet Russia to build a modern port at Hodeida and Communist China to construct a modern highway from that city to Sana, the capital of Yemen.

During his father's absence in Italy, where he had gone for medical care, Crown Prince al-Badr attempted to introduce political and social reforms which antagonized supporters of the old regime and increased the activities of those who sought to destroy it. On his return Imam Ahmad restored his personal control by a ruthlessness which precipitated the revolution following his death on September 18 and resulted in the creation of the Arab Yemenite Republic.

The new republican government was promptly recognized by the United Arab Republic and by the Soviet Union and in November, 1962, by the United States. The republican government was not able to overcome the opposition of the deposed Imam al-Badr, who fled to the north with his supporters and secured the backing of the northern tribes and, soon thereafter, aid from King Faisal. President al-Salal was obliged to seek help from Nasser. A mutual treaty of defense between the U.A.R. and the Arab Yemenite Republic brought increasingly larger Egyptian forces into the Yemen. This brought increasing intervention by Saudi Arabia.

The Yemenites were being drawn into the wider conflict of the "old order" and the "new order" throughout the Arab Near East. The nexus between the Arabs of the Yemen and the Yemenite Arabs of the recently created South Arabian Federation further widened the implications of the civil war, for Nasser had long since encouraged Yemenite and Arab nationalist movements in Aden among the Arab workers, while King Faisal favored the sheikhs of the South Arabian Federation.

The United States and Great Britain both became involved in the affairs of the Yemen: at the request of King Faisal they trained and equipped special Saudi Arabian military forces that were to be used in the event of an attempted seizure of southwest Arabia and Aden by the Yemen republican government, supported by the Egyptians, on the British recognition of the independence of the South Arabian Federation.

THE SOUTH ARABIAN FEDERATION AND THE ARAB REPUBLIC OF SOUTH YEMEN

The crucial center of South Arabia is the port of Aden, the highly urbanized section of the former Crown Colony of Aden that became a member of the South Arabian Federation. After the construction in 1953–57 of a large refinery and port facilities for meeting the needs of the largest oil fueling port in the world, Aden became a densely populated urban area with a rapidly increasing proletariat. This created serious problems of housing, living conditions, educational facilities, wages, and political rights with which the British colonial government was unable to cope. The mounting discontents of the workers, for the most part Arabs, aroused by the rising tide of Arab nationalism and gusty blasts of anticolonialism from Cairo, gave rise to increasing disorder and violence.

Confronted with the increasing gravity of the situation by 1962 the British began to seek a way out. A ministerial form of government was set up in the Crown Colony, and the Legislative Council of Aden was enlarged to include a number of elected members. As the franchise was confined to a small percentage of the people, the bulk of the workers had no political rights. The amirs and sheikhs of the Western and Eastern Protectorates, which were not a part of the Crown Colony, were persuaded to organize the Federation of South Arabia, of which the Crown Colony became a member. A federal government was organized which it was thought would be able to maintain law, order, and security throughout South Arabia. As a precautionary measure the British announced that when the Federation of South Arabia became an independent state Great Britain would negotiate a treaty with the federation providing for the maintenance of a British garrison at Aden. Having successfully accomplished this political sleight-of-hand the British government in an official communique announced in 1964 that independence would be granted in 1968.

This political solution was unacceptable to the Arab nationalists and to the Yemenite inhabitants of Aden who sought the union of South Arabia with the Yemen. This settlement was also completely unsatisfactory to the workers, who would be left to the tender mercies of the Aden bourgeoisie and the feudalistic amirs and sheikhs.

Seemingly, in concocting such a plan the British colonialists failed to note that the trade union leaders of Aden had created a center of power typical of modern industrial societies. Labor could no longer be ignored and discriminated against with impunity. Its power had become stronger than that of the Aden bourgeoisie and the local sheikhs. Consequently, the indignation of the workers against the British proposal led to further labor trouble, violence, and terrorism.

The Aden trade union leaders had won the confidence of the workers and had shown skill in organizing trade unions and in directing their activities. Twice in recent years the Trade Union Congress of Aden had successfully organized and carried out general strikes which paralyzed all activities of the port for a period of twenty-four hours. The Aden Trade Union Congress fortified its position by becoming a member of the Trade Union Congress of the Arab states, by establishing relations with the International Conference of Free Trade Unions, and by keeping in touch with the activities of the Communist World Federation of Trade Unions.

The refusal of the Aden government to satisfy reasonable demands of the trade unionists played into the hands of the extremists, with the result that the workers became more receptive to propaganda from Cairo and to the agitators for violence. Denied political means by which they might legally improve their condition, the use of illegal means was inevitable. The denial of the right to those leaders who might use their power with moderation resulted in power passing into the hands of those who used it without restraint.

By the spring of 1967 the situation in Aden became so critical that the Assembly of the United Nations sent an investigating committee of three of its members to Aden to ascertain the facts and report to the United Nations, with the hope that a peaceful and acceptable solution might be worked out. The U.N. committee arrived at Aden in April, only to discover that its presence there augmented the disorder, that some organizations refused to meet with it, and that the British officials refused to cooperate with it adequately. After a few days of frustration the committee left without accomplishing its mission.

The complexities of the situation in Aden are related to the rapid growth and nature of the population. Between 1955 and 1963 Aden's population more than doubled. Of its inhabitants, numbering then about 220,000, 80 per cent were Arabs, 50 per cent of whom were recent immigrants from the Yemen. Most of the other Arabs are of Yemenite stock, born either in Aden or in its immediate hinterland. Geographically and historically Aden and much of its hinterland, formerly known as the Western Protectorate, may be considered a part of the Yemen, according to Dr. Gamal Heyworth-Dunne. Owing to these factors Arab nationalism and the movement for union with the Yemen appeal strongly to many of the Arabs of southwest Arabia. These ideas and desires are inherent in the people of the area and are not solely the result of foreign propaganda. The Aden bourgeoisie and the amirs and sheikhs favor an independent federated state of South Arabia, while most of the Yemenite Arab workers and peasants want reunion with the Yemen.

The future status of South Arabia is not only a matter of dispute between the people of that region but one of concern to the Yemenite Arab Republic, to the United Arab Republic, and to Saudi Arabia. In addition, because of the strategic importance of the port of Aden, it is a matter of international importance. Strife in that city is also a part of the struggle within the Arab Moslem world between the "old order" and the "new order." A statement made on March 23, 1967, by the permanent representative of the United Arab Republic at the United Nations about the situation in South Arabia makes this point clear. His government, he said, gave its support to "the people," who must overthrow the government of the Federation of South Arabia. He went on to say that the conflicts within and between Arab states were not of "socialism" against "monarchy" but of "progressives against conservatives."

The recent center of that conflict has been in the Yemen, where the deposed Imam al-Badr and his followers with aid from Saudi Arabia have been engaged in a civil war against the Yemenite Arab Republic, which had massive military support from the United Arab Republic. Both the United States and Britain have been indirect accessories to this intervention by supplying and training military forces of King Faisal. The republican government of the Yemen reportedly aided a small force of Aden Yemenite Arabs who were preparing for an invasion of the South Arabian Federation. (This force was said to have been stationed south of Taiz, where, in May, 1967, some Americans engaged in a United States aid program were accused of having blown up an ammunition dump.) In 1968 the Yemenite Arabs took control and proclaimed the Arab Republic of South Yemen.

THE AMIRATE OF KUWAIT

Kuwait in the northeast corner of the Arabian peninsula was, until a few years ago, a petty Arab sheikhdom, the impoverished relic of a past when it was noted for its shipbuilding industry, its sailors, and its pearl divers. Throughout most of the first half of the twentieth century its only importance was that of being a minor British outpost for control of the Persian Gulf. In the 1930's petroleum exploration led to the discovery of the vast oil deposits of the Burggan oil field. It was not, however, until the 1950's that oil production in Kuwait began to provide revenues large enough to make possible the transformation of Kuwait from a tribal society into a modern city state.

Under the astute leadership of Amir Sheikh Abdulla As Saba, Kuwait became a constitutional monarchy with a national legislative assembly, its members elected by universal manhood suffrage. The old squalid town of Kuwait was rebuilt, the slums replaced by modern quarters with homes for the workers as well as for those of higher income. Modern schools, hospitals, and clinics provided free education and free medical care for all. These basic and revolutionary changes were brought about without violence or civil strife. This is in striking contrast during the same period with the failure in Aden to provide for its rapid development and with resulting violence.

Kuwait became a fully independent state in 1961, when by mutual consent the Anglo-Kuwait treaty of 1899 was terminated. Shortly thereafter, Kuwait became a full member of the League of Arab States and of the United Nations.

The oil royalties, which paid the high cost of modernizing this welfare state, also provided large annual surpluses. Unlike the fantastic squandering and folly in the neighboring state of Saudi Arabia until 1958, when Crown Prince Faisal put a stop to them, the astute leaders of Kuwait quickly learned the technics of modern finance and investment. With so much surplus capital to invest Kuwait became a member of the World Bank and International Monetary Fund. And in 1962 the Kuwait government established the Kuwait Fund for Arab Economic Development which participates on a fifty-fifty basis in development projects in Arab countries of Africa and Asia.

Kuwait's role in the affairs of the Arab world, especially in the Near East, is of considerable importance in other than economic matters. In this period of profound and rapid change, which we call modernization, Kuwait has been a pacemaker. The emergence from medievalism in most of the Near East has been so recent that the innovations have greatly increased the difficulties in making suitable and effective adjustments. In most of the other Arab states the difficulties in adjustment have been more difficult because of the lack of adequate economic resources.

Kuwait has demonstrated in the Near East that within the framework of the "old order" of Arab Moslem culture the transition to modernity can be made where there is intelligent leadership and plenty of money. Under the leadership of an old Arabian tribal family Kuwait has achieved modernity without violence and without destroying the basic values of the "old order." The synthesis of the old and the new has made it possible for Kuwait to stand aside from conflicts taking place in the other Arab countries between the revolutionists and the counterrevolutionists, the monarchists and the republicans.

The geographic location of Kuwait between Iraq and Saudi Arabia obliges the Kuwait government to walk warily in its dealings with its neighbors, for it lacks the military power to defend itself and its great wealth. In 1962 when President Kassem of Iraq claimed sovereignty over Kuwait, the Kuwait government applied for help from the League of Arab States, but took the precaution while the League was discussing the matter to ask Britain to send forces to defend the amirate. The British promptly did so, but just as promptly withdrew when Saudi Arabia sent troops after reaching the conclusion that it was not advisable to allow Iraq to acquire Kuwait and its rights in the Neutral Zone.

Following the assassination of Kassem in February, 1963, Iraqi claims to Kuwait were given up after negotiation with the new Iraqi government and a loan to Iraq of 30,000,000 Kuwait dinars (a dinar equaled the British pound). Eight days later Iraq officially recognized the independence and sovereignty of the amirate of Kuwait.

The attitude of Kuwait toward Israel is of significance as revealing the depth of feeling even among Arabs who, previous to 1948, had few contacts with Palestinian Arabs. The loss of a part of Palestine became a matter of deep concern to the people of Kuwait. Some of the Arab refugees from Palestine secured employment in the amirate, where their skills and knowledge found a market. In November, 1964, the Kuwait government began to deduct 5 per cent from the pay checks of Palestinians employed in the amirate, to support the Palestine Liberation Organization, which was recruiting a Palestine Army of Liberation. Units of this force took part in the six-day war of 1967. In June, 1965, the Kuwait minister of Finance, Industry, and Commerce, Sheikh Jabir al Ahmad Al Salah, stated that "Kuwait will be the first to carry out a decision to cut off Arab oil from those states which support Israel, provided the other oil producing countries—Saudi Arabia, Iraq, Algeria, and Libya—agree to such measures." This was done at the time of the 1967 fighting.

THE REPUBLIC OF IRAQ

The coup d'état of 1958, which an undiscerning American columnist stigmatized by the headline "Catastrophe in Iraq," was an initial step in a many-faceted revolutionary process of significant importance. During a period of four and a half years under the presidency of Abdul

Kassem important revolutionary changes were brought about. July 14, 1958, marked the beginning of the "new order." The Hashimite dynasty, installed by the British in 1921, came to a tragic end, and British colonialism faded away. The overthrow of the "old order" prepared the way for the modernization of Iraq.

By the Agrarian Reform Law of 1958 the power of the large landowners was ended. The government of Kassem took the drastic step of confiscating and redistributing the cultivatable land of those landlords possessing more than 620 acres of irrigated land and 1,260 acres of rainfed lands. Over 3,000 landowners were affected by this expropriation. Within four years more than 5,250,000 acres were taken over by the Iraqi government, and of these 1,500,000 acres were distributed to small landholders, aproximately twenty-five acres to a family.

This beginning of an agrarian revolution was only a first step in the modernization of Iraqi agriculture. It created new major problems which Kassem's government was unable to cope with, problems which only later were dealt with more adequately. This initial revolutionary act aroused extravagant hopes among the peasants; it eliminated a managerial class that was replaced by government bureaucrats with meager technical knowledge, little practical experience, and woeful ignorance of the peasantry.[1]

Lacking education, the peasants were unable to handle effectively the complex problems of finance, marketing, and management. Without effective leadership, guidance, and management, modernization and mechanization of Iraqi agriculture could not take place. The immediate results of the reforms were a serious decline in agricultural production, costly importation of formerly exported agricultural food products, and growing unemployment, with a sixth of the working class seeking jobs and peasants flocking to the cities.

This situation and a costly war in the north against Kurdish insurgents produced a political crisis which was intensified by Kassem's dismissal of Colonel Abdel Salam Aref from the cabinet. The revolutionary and nationalistic army officers lost confidence in Kassem, and the urban middle class became increasingly fearful of the growing influence of the legalized Communist Party among the trade unions. The Iraqi Federation of Trade Unions had become affiliated with the Communist World Federation of Trade Unions.

By the end of 1962 Kassem's role as a revolutionary leader was drawing to a close. In 1958 his leadership had precipitated the revolution, but his inability to deal with the mounting problems of revolutionary changes resulted in his assassination on February 8, 1963. A coup d'état by army officers supported by the Ba'thist Party set up a new revolutionary government with the Ba'thists in control and Abdel Salam Aref as president.

The Ba'thist Party was divided over the question of union with the United Republic of Egypt. This was shortly after the United Arab Republic of Egypt and Syria had come to an end. The Iraqi Ba'thist group in control of the government opposed union with Egypt, while President Aref and his supporters among the army officers were ardent pan-Arabs who favored the union.

The rivalry of these two groups and the continued unrest resulted in another coup d'état in November. The Ba'thist government was ousted, and President Aref chose a premier and a cabinet in accord with his ideas and those of his backers. He remained in control until his accidental death in 1966, when he was succeeded in the presidency by his brother, Major General Rahman Aref, who was removed by a coup in 1968.

Salam Aref had set up a revolutionary dictatorship, and all political parties had been declared illegal. Following the example of Nasser, he drafted a temporary constitution that concentrated power in his hands while declaring Iraq to be a democratic socialist republic. Generally speaking, Aref had the support of the middle and upper classes, which had grown fearful of the increasing spread of communism among the workers and trade unionists, although some have assumed that the crest of the Communist movement in Iraq had been reached in 1958.

The Communist ideology, like other revolutionary ideologies, tends to gain wider support when basic economic and social problems affecting the welfare of large segments of the population are not adequately dealt with. Edicts, laws, and ruthless suppression do not end radical revolutionary movements if the conditions which give rise to them continue.

Iraq has the natural resources and the economic potentialities to modernize agriculture and to develop domestic industries that could eliminate many of the basic causes of poverty and discontent, but it is still lacking the technical skill, the administrative organizations, and the requisite experience to cope effectively with the difficult and complex problems of modernization. This is in no way surprising, because the revolution began less than ten years ago, and the Iraqi governments have not had time to train a sufficient number of leaders, to educate the people, and to create the necessary economic, social, political, and educational institutions.

Iraq is one of the most favored of the Arab states of the Near East. It has more cultivatable land per capita than any other Near Eastern state. It has an abundance of water and water power. It has plentiful petroleum for years to come. It has access to the seaways of the world. It does not have nearby enemies that threaten its existence and that require it to spend fabulous sums to maintain a military establishment.

It is too early to comment on the future of Iraq's foreign policies. Aref's policy of union with Egypt and Syria, which Salam Aref has pursued, may not be looked upon as favorably as it was earlier. The immediate reaction to the events of June, 1967, with respect to Great Britain and the United States conformed to that of the other Near Eastern Arab states. Iraq did not suffer military defeat nor loss of territory, and it is not directly threatened by the military power of Israel. Its suffering has been vicarious and psychological.

THE KINGDOM OF JORDAN

In the summer of 1967 the fate of the Kingdom of Jordan hung in the balance, with all of its territory west of the Jordan occupied by the military forces of Israel. Only Transjordan remained under the rule of King Hussein ibn Talal ibn Abdullah. Hussein's grandfather Abdullah became amir of Transjordania in 1921, king of Transjordan in 1940, and king of Jordan in 1949, following his occupation of part of Palestine during the first Arab-Israel war.

In June, 1967, Hussein in the fifteenth year of his reign appeared before the General Assembly of the United Nations and in a well-received speech demanded that Israel's forces be withdrawn from his territories west of the Jordan River. The demand was one of serious import with far wider significance than the fate of a small kingdom.

The kingdom of Jordan, since its creation in 1949, has acquired an importance in the Arab world and internationally in striking contrast to its size, its meager resources, and its population of less than 2,000,000. This small Arab kingdom, which lacks the historical heritage of a nation, is an independent constitutional state and a member of the United Nations. During its short history of less than two decades Jordan has had a significant political impact upon the history of the Near East.

Its importance is due to several factors. Among these is the geographic location of its eastern and western sectors. The Transjordan part of Hussein's kingdom is a highway from Syria to the port of Aqaba and the heart of Arabia. The western section contained part of the ancient city of Jerusalem and large segments of Palestine, both north and south of the Holy City. Another factor which increased the importance of Jordan was that nearly 75 per cent of the population of the kingdom were Palestinian Arabs who passionately looked forward to the time when Palestine would once more become an Arab land. This obsession with the recovery of Palestine has been a constantly irritating factor in the domestic and foreign policies of the government. It was a psychological as well as a political factor which the government could not ignore, and it embroiled the kingdom in the Palestine Liberation movement sponsored by the League of Arab States.

Previous to the revolution in Iraq and the creation of the Republic of Iraq in 1958, there were close relations between the Hashemite kings of Iraq and Jordan, but the relations of Hussein with the new republican government of Iraq, which was supported by the Ba'thist Socialist Party, became increasingly strained. Similar developments in Syria, which adopted a pro-Soviet policy, left Jordan isolated in the Arab Near East. Hussein consequently began to cultivate closer ties with Kuwait and Saudi Arabia. He thus became aligned with "the old order" as against "the new order" in Egypt, Syria, Iraq, and the Yemen.

The dependence of Hussein on Britain and the United States caused him to be looked upon as a tool of American and British imperialism. However, the compelling financial and economic realities made subsidies from Britain and the United States essential for the survival of his kingdom. Hussein, despite his dependence on the United Kingdom and the United States, has shown himself to be a man of courage and integrity.

The internal problems of Jordan have been more baffling than those of its foreign relations. The basic economic difficulty is the lack of adequate natural resources to meet the needs of its people and its government. Internal revenues were insufficient to meet governmental expenditures and to supply the capital with which to develop more fully the few resources of the country. The economic and financial situation of Jordan in 1961–62 reveals clearly the problem confronting King Hussein prior to the military debacle of 1967.

The gross national income in 1962 was estimated to be about $200,000,000. It was thought that a five-year development plan might by 1967 increase the total to $350,000,000 annually. In the financial year 1961–62 the government's revenue was approximately $87,000,000 of which $54,000,000 was in the form of foreign grants and loans. The government's expenditures totalled $93,000,000, of which about $50,000,000 was for defense needs. During that year in addition to direct military aid the United States gave Jordan $40,000,000.

Jordan's involvement in the third Arab-Israel war was inevitable. In the spring of 1967 Hussein could not risk refusing to coordinate the military plans of Jordan with those of the U.A.R. of Egypt because for both military and political reasons Jordan could not remain neutral. The major part of Hussein's kingdom was in Palestine, and the population of Jordan was largely Palestinian. They would not have tolerated a policy of neutrality, and Hussein might have been assassinated had he adopted a policy of noncooperation with the other Arab states. Nor could he have been certain of what Israel might do if Jordan had remained neutral.

The war and its aftermath resulted in the flight eastward across the Jordan of Palestinian refugees suffering a misery and nursing a hatred comparable to that of the Arab refugees of 1948–49. Those who had been rescued from the Nazi concentration camps in 1945 after years of misery and terror came seeking refuge in Palestine. Their coming brought terror and misery twice within fifteen years upon nearly 2,000,000 Arabs, mostly peasants whose ancestors for more than 1,300 years had tilled the plains and hills of Palestine, their homeland.

In 1919, when the Arabs of Hebron and the villages of the southern hill lands were asked by the King-Crane Commission, sent by President Wilson of the United States to inquire whom they wished to have rule over them, they replied: "We wish to rule ourselves." When the commissioners insisted that the Peace Conference had decided that Palestine should be placed under a mandate the sheikhs of Hebron with grave dignity said: "Tell the Peace Conference and your President we want Allah to rule over us." [2]

THE REPUBLIC OF LEBANON

This small Arab state has a uniquenes of its own. It was created by France in 1920 as the state of Greater Lebanon by adding to what was known as Jebel Lubnan territories whose Moslem population thought of themselves as Syrians. During the period of the mandate the state of Greater Lebanon in 1926 was proclaimed by the French to be the Republic of Lebanon. During World War II General Catroux, commander of the Free French Forces, proclaimed Lebanon to be an independent sovereign state. Although this made it possible for Lebanon to attend, as a full-fledged member, the United Nations Conference at San Francisco in 1945, the Lebanese were far from happy about continued control by the French. Their discontent resulted in an insurrection during which the Christians and the Moslems joined forces under an agreement known as the National Pact of 1943.

This agreement marks a turning point in the history of the Lebanon.

It became the basis for Christian-Moslem cooperation that made possible the survival of the republic after the French withdrew their troops when Lebanon attained full independence as a sovereign state in 1946.

The "confessional" form of government provided proportional representation in parliament for all the diverse sectarian religious groups. The constitution stipulated that the president always be a Christian and the premier a Moslem. This political compromise, which conformed with the National Pact, made it possible for Lebanon to survive two serious crises. The first, in 1949, following defeat in the first Arab-Israeli war, was precipitated by the influx of Palestine refugees, for the most part Moslems. This upset the ratio between Christian and Moslems. The far more serious crisis of 1957–58 after the second Arab-Israeli war and the Anglo-French attack on Port Said reached the proportions of an insurrection that threatened the destruction of the republic. The military intervention by the United States at the request of President Chamoun acted as a catalytic agent reuniting the Christians and the Moslems in support of the National Pact. Lebanese leaders recognized that intervention in the internal affairs of their country whether by Syrians, Egyptians, or Americans was a threat to Lebanese sovereignty.

The causes of both crises are too complex for detailed analysis, but some knowledge of the salient factors is essential to an understanding of the problems confronting the Lebanese in maintaining their independence. The initial opposition of the Moslems of a Greater Lebanon was intensified by the spread of Arab nationalism as a political force throughout the Arab Near East, which gave rise to the pan-Arab movement for a Federation of Arab States. The union of Egypt and Syria in February 1958, was a first step toward achieving an Arab unity. The existence of the United Arab Republic of Egypt and Syria created fears in Lebanon of intervention by the Egyptians and Syrians in support of the Lebanese insurrectionists.

The Anglo-French-Israeli plot against Egypt, resulting in the attack on the Suez Canal, and the Bagdad Pact policy of the British, so strongly backed by Secretary of State Dulles as a part of the American policy of containment of the U.S.S.R. in the Near East, created a ferment in Iraq, Syria, Egypt, and Lebanon.

The policies of the "West" had backfired. The Suez fiasco had brought the U.S.S.R. into the Near East in defense of Egypt in collaboration with the United States, which continued to support the Bagdad Pact policy though it was on the verge of collapse. The Iraqi revolution of 1958 and the emergence of revolutionary movements against the "old order" in other Arab states supported by the Western Powers caused the Arabs advocating the "new order" to turn for support to the U.S.S.R. The increasing influence of the Ba'thist socialist parties and of the less numerous Communists was due in some degree to American and British policies. These developments in Syria and Lebanon augmented the ferment which resulted in the Lebanese crisis of 1957–58.

The success of the Lebanese leaders in subduing the insurrection in 1958 was a result of the political experience they had acquired since 1943 under the "confessional" system, which lessened the forces of disunity. Furthermore, the Moslem feudal and commercial leaders were becoming dubious about union with Syria and of joining a pan-Arab federation. The instability of the Syrian government with its Soviet orientation, the revolution in Iraq, and the revolutionary movements gestating in Yemen and Aden further tended to convince Lebanese men of property that an independent Republic of Lebanon had more to offer them than did absorption in an Arab federation.

The government of Lebanon under the "confessional" system had proved viable at a time when revolutionary movements were spreading widely in the Arab Near East. Although a political revolution had been checkmated in Lebanon, nevertheless the people of Lebanon were undergoing significant social and ideological revolutions in the modernization of their ways of living and their ways of thinking. The old regime of feudalism and of "clerical" domination was being undermined, and loyalties were shifting to other social and political groups. The extensive construction of roads coupled with rapid motor transportation was ending the isolation of the village, the peasant, and the herdsman, and the contacts between the rural and the urban population were becoming more frequent. These changes and the expanding educational system that has raised the percentage of literacy in Lebanon above that of any of the other Near Eastern Arab states have increased the sense of Lebanese unity and hastened the process of modernization of Lebanese society.

It is becoming evident that political revolutions and coups d'état which do not result in the modernization of the economic structure of agriculture and industry nor provide the educational system upon which modernization depends are not really revolutionary. Lebanon, having successfully crushed political revolutionary movements, has been more successful than has Syria in the revolutionary modernization of its social and economic system.

Political stability and security in Lebanon have proved an added attraction to men of business and finance who fear expropriation of their wealth. Lebanese bankers have profited from depositors who prefer to use Lebanese banks with the expectation of more security for their funds. This expectation was, however, rudely shaken by the temporary banking breakdown in 1967. Under stable conditions tourism has flourished and the mountains of Lebanon have proved profitable as a resort for those seeking to escape from torrid Near Eastern summers and as a sports center in winter.

The Lebanese have in the past been called Levantines. It is a rather misleading term with various connotations. The people of Lebanon are Arabs, their language is Arabic, and their culture is Arabic. They are a part of the Arab community and their destiny is inescapably bound up with that of the other Arab peoples and states. Though the Lebanese have rejected union with or absorption in a pan-Arab Federation, they are not immune to the potent appeal of Arab nationalism. It is significant that without having participated in the third Arab-Israeli war of June, 1967, Lebanon aligned itself with the other Arab states in the dramatic meeting in July, 1967, of the General Assembly of the United Nations, summoned to deal with the Arab-Israeli conflict.

SYRIA: TROUBLOUS YEARS

During the years since 1918 when the Syrians were freed from Ottoman rule, they have had only a scant fifteen years of independent self-government. Previous to the twentieth century and throughout their long history Syrians had never achieved independence as a national state.

The ephemeral kingdom of Syria under Emir Faisal in 1920 lasted only a few weeks, and it was not until 1941 that France recognized the independence of the Syrian Republic. The Syrians, however, did not become fully masters in their homeland until 1946. Twelve years later by their own choice the Syrian Republic became a part of the United Arab Republic, of which Nasser was president and ruler. This marriage of Egypt and Syria proved to be incompatible and ended in "a shotgun divorce" as a result of a military coup d'état by Syrian officers in Damascus in September, 1961. The offspring of this short union was the Syrian Arab Republic, now in its seventh year.

The Syrians, who have had so short an experience in self-government and who have shown little aptitude in maintaining political stability, have been fertile in the realm of political ideas and their propagation. They have been outstanding leaders of Arab nationalism and in the movement for Arab political unity. They have been leading propagandists of radical social and economic ideologies and in organizing political parties.

The most important factor in the political instability of Syria is the shattering effects of modernization on the political power structure of the former ruling classes: the large landowners, the wealthy merchants, and the religious hierarchies. These still exist, but their power has been considerably weakened, much of it having passed into the hands of army officers and of the new middle classes.

During the decades following World War I, the Turkish Kemalist revolution, and the creation of the Soviet Union, new ideas of a radical and revolutionary nature spread among the younger generation in Syria and Lebanon. Students and graduates of the new secular educational institutions lost respect for the old customs and patterns of thought and behavior. These new elements in the Syrian social structure—army officers, doctors, lawyers, teachers, technicians, engineers, and members of the governmental bureaucracy—soon began to challenge the power of the old social and political order.

These new young Syrians also challenged nineteenth-century liberalism and the confidence of liberals in capitalistic political democracy. The fraud of the mandate system, the expanding imperialism of France and Great Britain in the Near East, and the implementation of the Balfour declaration fostered the growth of Arab nationalism, of socialism, and of communism. The turmoil of World War II, followed by the rise of the U.S.S.R. as a great power, the creation of the state of Israel, and the Arab-Israeli war of 1948 had a potent effect upon all Arabs of the Near East, giving rise to a passionate Arab nationalism and to movements for Arab political unity accompanied by the spread of revolutionary socialistic and communist ideologies.

The creation and maintenance of a Syrian army seemed indispensable to the existence of an independent Syrian state. A modern military establishment is enormously expensive, and the days have passed when a powerful military force could be supported by the economic resources of a Syria. The nomads no longer supply what in the past had been an essential element of military power, a skilled cavalry. The Syrian peasants with none of the technical skills essential to modern infantry are not a military asset. The skilled craftsmen of Syria who for centuries were noted for the fine weapons they produced cannot supply modern arms. With limited industrial resources the Syrians are obliged to acquire from the highly industrialized nations the weaponry of modern warfare.

There is no real independence for a nation which depends on other states for military supplies for which it is unable to pay. In a strategic area such as the Near East, where the rivalry of two or more great states is intense, a small country seeking to increase its military establishment beyond its economic resources inescapably becomes a pawn. The unfortunate results of this situation for Syria became startlingly evident during the third Arab-Israeli war of June, 1967.

The chaotic conditions in Syria and in most of the Arab states of the Near East gave rise to revolutionary ideas and movements which did not have a mass base. The revolutionary movements and ideologies arose among the younger intellectuals and the new middle class. In Syria neither socialism nor communism has any strong support among the peasantry or from the small industrial working class. The socialist party known as the Ba'thist Party has considerable following among the members of the new bourgeoisie and among certain elements of the army.

Socialistic and communist ideas undermined the somewhat synthetic and romantic idea of Syrian nationalism which was popularized in the 1930's by Antun Sa'ada, who organized the conservative pseudo-fascist group known as Parti Populaire Syrien (P.P.S.). The idea of Arab nationalism and of Arab unity was considered fully compatible with socialism by the Ba'thists and the Communists. The Moslem Brotherhood, which after being banned as subversive by the United Arab Republic moved its headquarters to Damascus, looks favorably upon Arab nationalism and Arab political unity as a step toward the revival of the Arab caliphates of Damascus and Bagdad. Socialism as a means of restoring the old Islamic theocratic state was not objectionable, for they considered social welfare to be one of the basic elements of Mohammed's religious teaching. Communism, of course, with its emphasis on atheism remains an anathema to the Brotherhood.

Although the Ba'thist Party has a strong following in Syria and Iraq, no political group has been able for long to establish and maintain political dominance in Syria. The effects of the crushing defeat of Syria, Jordan, and the United Arab Republic during June, 1967, upon the political situation in Syria have not seemed to change this situation.

EGYPT—THE UNITED ARAB REPUBLIC

The political evolution of Egypt during the past fifteen years began in July, 1952, when the Free Officers took over the government of the kingdom of Egypt which was established in 1914 by the British. A year after their coup d'état the revolutionists abolished the monarchy and established the Republic of Egypt. This was accomplished with a minimum of violence.

Five years later, by mutual agreement, the United Arab Republic of Egypt and Syria was created as a first step toward the realization of the

Pan-Arab hope of an eventual union of all the Arab states. It was a premature attempt because elements in Syria were unprepared for such a radical step. By a coup d'état they seized control of the government in Damascus, proclaiming Syria to be the independent Arab Republic of Syria. President Nasser promptly renounced all claims to Syria by the United Arab Republic of Egypt.

The numerous coups d'état in Syria, the three military coups in Iraq between 1957 and 1963, and the revolution in the Yemen have given rise to the impression of political instability in the Arab people and governments. In view of the profound impact of the rapid modernization throughout the Arab Near East political instability might well be expected. Actually, with the exception of Syria and Iraq, and possibly the Yemen, where the civil war continued, there was remarkable stability in Kuwait, Saudi Arabia, and revolutionary Egypt. In comparison with the revolutionary period of European history between 1789 and 1848 there has been a minimum of violence in the internal affairs of the Arab states. Since the revolution in Egypt of 1952 external violence was forced upon Egypt by Israel, France, and Great Britain in 1956–57 and by Israel in 1967. Egypt at the invitation of the president of the Arab Yemenite Republic participated in the Yemenite civil war.

The revolutionary significance of the policies of the government of the United Arab Republic is most clearly evident in three major spheres of activity: the domestic economic and social programs, the promotion of Arab socialism and Arab nationalism, and Nasser's foreign policies. There is a close relationship between these elements of the Egyptian revolution.

Domestic objectives and policies.—In 1952 the initial aim of the Egyptian revolutionaries was to establish a government which would remove the remaining elements of British control and would be capable of carrying out their social and economic program. After the coup d'état of July, 1952, the revolutionary officers abolished the monarchy, established a republic, and by November, 1953, rid themselves of conservative President Naguib; they then suppressed the antagonistic Moslem Brotherhood and arrested the leading Communists. The way was cleared to carry out the Arab socialist revolution. Only piecemeal measures were taken, however, previous to 1961. Land reform measures and the expropriation of the landlords, individual and corporate, did little to solve the problem of the fellaheen and their backward villages. The necessity of rational planning resulted, through an effective propaganda program, in a series of governmental decrees by 1961, based on the principles of Arab socialism with its avowed aims of increasing agricultural and industrial production and achieving economic prosperity and more equable distribution. These highly desirable objectives were to be attained in a mixed economy with a predominant public sector and a minor private sector. All economic enterprises above the level of small farmers, petty store owners, craftsmen, and other artisans were to be either owned or controlled by the state. The ultimate aim was a fully socialized state, its purpose and principles clearly set forth.

Governmental propaganda and information services show clearly that the Egyptian revolutionists had given considerable thought to various means by which economically retarded countries might achieve greater economic prosperity. The Egyptians rejected the Western capitalist system of "plundering capital resources," and both the Chinese and the earlier Soviet system of rapid economic development within one generation. The Egyptians believed in proceeding at a slower pace, considering the social welfare of the people as important as economic growth.

There were and still are serious obstacles to the achievements of these aims. It is proving to be a difficult matter to change the ways of living, of thinking, and of working which for unnumbered generations have been inherent in the fellaheen. Vast irrigation projects and electric power plants take time and large amounts of capital. The construction of industrial plants and the training of skilled workers, technicians, and administrators also require time and financial resources. The rapid increase in population and the delay in achieving sufficient agricultural and industrial production could become a menace to the success of the ambitious projects of the revolutionary leaders. The fact that Egypt does not produce enough food to meet the needs of both its urban and rural population and that imports exceed exports creates major financial problems. Ten years ago in his book *The Passing of the Traditional Society,* Daniel Lerner, in a chapter on the United Arab Republic entitled "Egypt, the Vicious Circle" wrote: "But already, it is clear, the Middle East will never be the same as it was before Nasser rose. He has shaped and diffused a new image of *self and society* in Egypt and the area. If he cannot satisfy its requirements, this image may prove his undoing. But the image will remain."

Foreign policy.—The foreign policy of the United Arab Republic cannot be understood in terms of the popular cliché of procommunism and anticommunism. International affairs have become so complex that a pseudo-moralistic dualism of good and evil forces is an inadequate and misleading approach. Clichés are the tools of politicians, not of statesmen.

Nasser of Egypt has become the outstanding leader of Arab nationalism. This is a new role for an Egyptian. During the prerepublican period Egyptian nationalism developed as a political and ideological movement against British imperialism and colonialism. It antedated the nationalist movement among the Arab subjects of the Ottoman Empire in western Asia. The only factors common to the two movements were their anti-imperialism and their Western origin.

The fusion of Arab and Egyptian nationalism took place after World War I. The postwar settlement of 1922 placed the Arabs of the Fertile Crescent under a disguised form of imperialism—the mandate system which liberals at the Paris Peace Conference in 1919 called "the mandate swindle." The Arabs and the Egyptians acquired a common enemy —Western imperialism. Unfortunately for all concerned, the implementation of the Balfour Declaration and the establishment of a Jewish National Home in Palestine under British auspices came to be looked upon by Arabs as an instrument of British imperialism. Seemingly unnoticed, Egyptian nationalism vanished.

It was not, however, until after World War II, when the struggle between the Palestinian Arabs and the Jews in Palestine resulted in the termination of the British mandate, the creation of the state of Israel, and the first Arab-Israel war of 1948–49, that Arab nationalism became an increasingly potent force in Egyptian politics and foreign affairs. The success of the Israelis and the failure of the Arabs were two of the factors which led to the revolutionary coup d'état of 1952 in Egypt and the rise of Nasser to power. In control of the Gaza Strip and both banks of the Suez Canal, Egypt became the leading Arab nation. With the Egyptian resources, including broadcasting stations capable of carrying his words and his image to all corners of the Arab world, President Nasser became the leader and spokesman of Arab nationalism and Arab socialism. This position of leadership of the Arab peoples placed limits on the flexibility of his foreign policy with respect to a settlement with the state of Israel. Palestinian refugees were scattered throughout the Arab countries of the Near East, and they acquired a considerable influence in those countries where they established themselves. An Arab political leader who attempted to reach an agreement with the government of Israel would run the risk of being discredited or assassinated.

Nasser's leadership of Arab nationalism and socialism has made it impossible for him as president of the United Arab Republic to pursue a foreign policy based exclusively on the domestic needs of Egypt and the Egyptian people. These goals have embroiled his country in the domestic affairs of other Arab states. This has been notably so with respect to Syria, Saudi Arabia, the Yemen, and South Arabia.

The first attempt at a union of the Arab states by the creation of the United Arab Republic of Egypt and Syria was a failure. Direct military intervention in the civil war of the Yemen at the invitation of President al-Salal of the Arab Yemenite Republic has been a heavy financial burden. In addition, it embroiled the United Arab Republic with Saudi Arabia, whose king had been aiding the counterrevolutionary forces of Imam al-Badr. In South Arabia, particularly in the port of Aden, Nasser has given support to Arab workers in their struggle against the British, the South Arabian sheikhs, and the Aden bourgeoisie. These activities have irritated both the British and the Saudi king, who feared a joint take-over of South Arabia by the Republic of Yemen and the United Arab Republic in the event of a revolt by the Aden Arabs, a large percentage of whom are Yemenites.

These activities have led to accusations in the West that under Nasser the Egyptian government is engaged in imperialistic activities rather than in efforts to bring about a federation of Arab states. In the West there are those who look upon Arab socialism and the support by Nasser of revolutionary movements in the Arab countries as a pro-Soviet or Communist policy.

In the "cold war" between the United States and the U.S.S.R. Nasser has endeavored to pursue a neutral position, as clearly made evident at the Bandung Conference of the unaligned nations. Until June, 1967, following the third Arab-Israeli war, the United Arab Republic sought and received aid from both the U.S.A. and the U.S.S.R. On the whole Nasser has played a skillful game of profiting from the rivalry between them in the Near East area. The containment policy of former Secretary of State Dulles played into the hands of the Egyptians due to Soviet unwillingness to be contained and eagerness to seize the opportunity to extend economic and military aid to the Egyptians.

On the whole the United Arab Republic, with the very significant exception of its policy toward Israel, has had reasonable success in dealing with the United States and the Soviet Union. In a world of competing political and economic units, the lesser states, dependent upon greater states, find it profitable to play upon the rivalry of the Great Powers.

THE STATE OF ISRAEL

The amazing achievements during the past two decades of the people and the government of Israel cannot be understood without a knowledge of the factors which have made them possible. Among these the psychological determinants are the most significant. Without, however, a series of historic events during the latter part of the nineteenth century and the early decades of the twentieth, the realization of the long-cherished hopes of the Jewish people could not have materialized.

Theocratic nationalism has been a dominating idea of the Jewish people throughout their entire history. They looked upon themselves as the Chosen People of Jehovah and upon Palestine as the divinely Promised Land. For nearly two thousand years they have cherished the idea that eventually in God's time they would return to their "Homeland" in Palestine and there re-establish a Jewish state. This belief was a factor in their keeping alive their history, their culture, their religious rites, and the traditional social patterns of their way of living.

In the latter part of the nineteenth century and during the first half of the twentieth various developments took place that created circumstances which prepared the way for the establishment of the state of Israel. The emancipation of the Jews of Western and Central Europe following the French Revolution brought the closely knit Jewish communities into the full flow of life's activities. This freedom in a highly competitive society gave rise to modern anti-Semitism, which produced political Zionism with its aim to re-establish a Jewish state in Palestine. In Eastern Europe and tsarist Russia two events proved eventually to be of vital importance in the creation of Israel. The deeply religious Zionism of the Eastern European Jews developed into a passionate political Zionism combined with Western Zionism under Theodor Herzl's leadership, thus creating a World Zionist Organization. During the same period millions of Eastern European Jews migrated to the United States, where freed from the trammels of oppressive governments they prospered. Within a few decades the Jewish immigrants made many significant contributions to life in the United States in a wide variety of activities. As a highly respected, economically prosperous, and politically influential group, the American Jews were able to win public and governmental support for a Jewish National Home in Palestine and, at a later date, for the state of Israel.

The Balfour Declaration of 1917 during a critical turning point in World War I opened the doors of Palestine for political Zionism, so that under the auspices of the British mandatory government between 1922 and 1948 the foundations of Israel were laid, and over 450,000 Jews migrated to Palestine between 1919 and May 15, 1948, previous to the founding of the Jewish state.

The incredible barbarism of the Nazis, with their purpose of exterminating the Jews of Europe, made the Jewish people all over the world—and millions of Christians—think that the Jews should have a land of their own in ancient Palestine where they might be secure. Thus, when the Nazis were defeated and over 100,000 Jews were found alive in concentration camps, President Truman used his great influence to gain permission from the British to allow these refugees to enter the Holy Land.

On becoming citizens of Israel, the Jewish "refugees" from Europe proved to be of vital importance in building the new Jewish nation. The flight of the Palestinian Arabs during the first Arab-Israeli war of 1948–49 left much of the land, the villages, and towns of that part of Palestine occupied by Israel military forces without inhabitants. The solution of the grievous problem of the Jewish refugees from Europe occurred at a time when tragedy befell hundreds of thousands of Palestinian Arabs, who, twenty years later, were still living with their offspring in refugee camps, where some 30,000 young men and women attain the age of twenty-one each year, with no place to go and little or no training or education to fit them for jobs in the modern world. The Jewish people and the government of Israel have shown the will and the ability to find a place for their refugees; the Arabs and their governments have shown neither the will nor the capacity to cope with the tragic problem of the Palestinian Arab refugees. Israel had acquired the requisite territory and the necessary human resources essential to its existence while at the same time incurring the enmity of the Arab peoples of the Near East and North Africa.[3]

Having gained political control of a viable portion of Palestine, the Israelis with impressive support from Jews in the Western sections of the Diaspora were by 1949 in a position to build a prosperous "Homeland." The newborn state of Israel had the manpower, the skills, the courage, and the will to cope with the difficult and complex problems which confronted them if Israel was to survive.

The domestic achievements have been astounding. The natural resources and the major sources of wealth in the Jewish state are meager. Nevertheless, Israel has successfully improved the methods of agriculture, developed all available water resources for irrigation and the production of electrical power, constructed an adequate system of main and subsidiary roads, and established profitable if minor industries to meet the needs of an increasing population. These were remarkable accomplishments when one considers the increase of population between 1948 and 1966.

In May, 1948, the inhabitants of Israel were estimated to number about 900,000; of these 780,000 were Jews over half of whom were immigrants who had arrived between 1919 and the founding of the state in May, 1948. During the following sixteen years over 1,100,000 more Jewish immigrants settled in Israel, half of them being refugees from the Arab states of the Near East and North Africa.

The Israeli government found the means to provide housing and occupations for these recent arrivals while at the same time creating an adequate educational system, modern social welfare and health services, and in addition a powerful military force. The major problems of Israel, other than those of economics and relations with the Arabs, are the result of profound differences among the Jewish citizens of Israel. In addition to the political and religious divergences ranging from the conservatives to the Communists and from the "Orthodox" to the "Reform" congregations, there has been the cultural gap separating the "Western" Jews and the "Oriental" Jews, most of whom are refugees from the Arab states. This cultural gulf represents five centuries of Western European culture.

The one outstanding weakness of the state of Israel is its inability to arrive at a modus vivendi with the Arabs. As Israel is in the center of the Arab Moslem world and at one of the focal points at which vital interests of the United States and the Soviet Union are in conflict, it has become entangled in the perilous game of power politics between the two nations in which the bulk of the Jewish people outside of Israel are located. On one of these, the United States, Israel is largely dependent for both economic and political support.

Israel's dependence upon American Jews creates considerable embarrassment for the American government with respect to its Near Eastern policies. For more than twenty years the United States has endeavored to prevent the expansion of Soviet influence in the Near and Middle East. This necessitated amicable relations with the Arab states of the Near East as well as with Israel. The conflict between Israelis and Arabs has resulted in a disturbing dichotomy in American Near Eastern policy, which creates complications in domestic American politics.

The rise of modern Jewish nationalism has been concurrent with that of Arab nationalism. The Balfour Declaration, the period of the mandate, and the creation of Israel brought these two movements into sharp conflict and resulted in three Arab-Israeli wars within a period of twenty years. In each of these Israel was victorious. The Arabs are further from achieving their goal of liquidating Israel and the Jews have attained no greater security. The impasse continues.

In the six-day war of June, 1967, Israel gave proof of its superiority over the military forces of Jordan, Syria, and Egypt. Unless an agreed-upon settlement between Israel and the Arab states is reached the war will have only increased the problems of Israel and its insecurity. The

Israeli government has insisted upon dealing directly with the Arab states without intermediaries. It has given the appearance of wishing to arrive at a settlement that would provide reasonable assurance that it will be free from future attacks. The initiative has passed from the United Nations and from the United States, and the Arab states at a conference in Khartoum discussed proposals suggested, it was alleged, by the president of the Communist state of Yugoslavia.

It is somewhat ironic to recall that following the capture of Khartoum by Kitchener the ebullient young Winston Churchill during a political campaign in England shouted: "We are in the Valley of the Nile forever and forever." With little certainty about the future of nations, one may with some assurance say that as long as human life continues to be possible in the Near East and in the Nile Valley the Arab peasants and tribesmen will continue to predominate throughout most of southwestern Asia and Egyptian peasants will still be in the Nile Delta.

THE REPUBLIC OF TURKEY

The Turkish Revolution began in the formal sense . . . in 1908. In another sense . . . it has been going on for nearly two centuries. . . .

The basic change in Turkey from an Islamic Empire to a national Turkish state, from a medieval theocracy to a constitutional state, from a bureaucratic feudalism to a modern capitalist economy was accomplished over a long period, by successive waves of reformers and radicals.—*The Emergence of Modern Turkey,* by Bernard Lewis (New York, 1961), pp. 473–74.

No one in so few words has written such a comprehensive account of the scope of the revolutionary processes by which the Turkish people have reached the threshold of a modernized society as Bernard Lewis has in the preceding statement.

Although the Tanzimat movement in the nineteenth century and the Young Turk Revolution of 1908–9 prepared the way, it was the Kemalist revolution of 1922–38 that created the foundations upon which successive governments of Turkey have striven to transform the social, economic, and ideological structure of their state into that of a twentieth-century nation. Only when this has been more fully achieved will it be seen whether it is to be a highly competitive capitalistic, a paternal socialistic, or an authoritarian Communist nation. In any case it is to be anticipated that the "new" Turkish state will be modernized.

The road to modernization has so far been arduous for the Turks during a period when the entire world and its inhabitants have been in the throes of the most tumultuous and rapid changes the human race has ever been subjected to.

The political history of the Turkish Republic since 1950 has been somewhat hectic. Previous to that, for a quarter of a century Mustafa Kemal and his immediate successors governed Turkey under a disguised form of dictatorship known as the one-party system. Lacking adequate knowledge and experience with respect to many of the complicated factors of modern industrialization these political revolutionists undertook a rapid program of industrialization under a system of governmental control known as etatism. Their difficulties were greatly increased during the years of World War II, which imposed additional burdens on the government and the people.

Unrest and mounting discontent made the continuation of a one-party form of government impossible. President Inönü felt compelled to announce the end of this system, with the result that numerous political parties were organized, and the recently formed Democratic Party became the principal opposition party following the elections of 1946. Four years later in the election of 1950 the Democratic Party won an overwhelming victory, and under President Bayar, with Adnan Mederes as premier, it held full control of the government until 1960.[4]

The Law of Associations uncorked the bottle releasing the genii of political democracy with the right of dissent. The elements of discontent ranged from the forces of clericalism and reactionary groups, which opposed many of the changes brought about by the Kemalist revolution, to the discontents of the new bourgeois class of businessmen and entrepreneurs, and to the few but articulate leftists. Increasing opposition to the Democratic Party government resulted in undemocratic measures against demonstrators and critics. Riots of university students in Istanbul and Ankara brought strong reaction from democratically minded army officers, who by a coup d'état overthrew the government and brought to an end the first Republic of Turkey.

A Committee of National Unity was set up by the military junta headed by General Gürsel in May, 1960. It announced that it would renounce its power when order was re-established, a new constitution promulgated, and elections held. In accordance with this promise a newly elected parliament voted for a civilian coalition Cabinet with Inönü as premier. The second Republic had an auspicious beginning.

The curse of Turkish politics has been the unremitting personal animosity of the leaders of the principal political parties. During the following five years, however, the rivalry of the new Justice Party and the old Republican Peoples Party created no serious threat to the republic. The Justice Party, with the support of the new middle class, favored economic development by "free enterprise," while Inönü of the Republican Peoples Party continued to support etatism.

Modernization of a nation requires far more than the modernization of its governmental apparatus. The role of political revolution may be primary or secondary. In the latter case revolutionary changes of a social, economic, and ideological nature may precipitate a revolution to overthrow an outmoded form of government. In Turkey, after the political revolution of Mustafa Kemal of 1922 to 1924, the revolutionary government of the first Republic of Turkey strove to bring about an economic, social, and ideological revolution of a people the majority of whom were peasants in isolated villages of Anatolia and whose ways of living and thinking were medieval. Only fundamental changes in their way of living could bring about new ways of thinking.

This process has been going on at an increasing rate. Industrialization, exploitation of natural resources, the construction of a network of highways and roads, the introduction of motorized as well as railroad transportation, wider employment of mechanized farm equipment, and an expanding educational system are eliminating the isolation of the peasantry. The penetration of the political parties into the villages, coupled with periodical national elections with a high percentage of the electorate participating, is bringing about revolutionary changes of increasing significance.

In the field of foreign affairs the Turks are becoming more sophisticated, having learned that it can be more profitable and possibly less dangerous to cultivate wider commercial intercourse with the U.S.S.R. and the Communist states of Eastern Europe than to remain politically and economically dependent upon the United States and Western Europe. The new and growing "free-enterprise" middle class may have acquired a keener understanding of the value of encouraging competition between the West and the East with respect to participation in the industrialization of Turkey.

It is of interest that radio and television are playing a significant part in breaking down the isolation of the Turkish peasants in ways similar to those, brought about by cheap Japanese transistors, of educating and enlightening the Indians of the high Andes of Bolivia.

NOTES

NOTE TO CHAPTER I

1. Mehemed Fuad Köprülü, *Les origines de l'empire ottoman* (Paris, 1935), l'étude III, pp. 35–37.

NOTES TO CHAPTER II

1. Köprülü, *Les origines*. This Turkish historian gives an interesting and informative account of the Seljuk empire.
2. Albert H. Lybyer, *The Government of the Ottoman Empire in the Time of Soleiman, the Magnificent* (Cambridge, Mass., 1913).
3. Sari Mehmed, Pasha, *Ottoman Statecraft, the Book of Counsel for Vezirs and Governors* (Nasoih ül-Vuzera ve l-ümera), Introduction by W. L. Wright (London and Princeton, 1935).

NOTES TO CHAPTER III

1. Ali Haydar Midhat, *The Life of Midhat Pasha* (London, 1903). This biography of Midhat Pasha by his son reveals the ideas of the Tanzimat reformer and portrays the personality and character of the outstanding leader of the nineteenth-century Turkish reformers.
2. Mehemed Fuad Köprülü, *History of Turkey* (Turkiye ta kihi).
3. Edwin Pears, *Turkey and Its People* (2d ed.; London, 1912), p. 7.
4. E. J. W. Gibb, *A History of Ottoman Poetry* (London, 1900–1909). This monumental work in six volumes is a revelation to those who think of the Ottoman Turks as uncultured barbarians.
5. Gibb, *A History of Ottoman Poetry*.
6. Ahmet Emin, *The Development of Modern Turkey as Measured by Its Press* (New York, 1914), pp. 57–58. Emin's doctor's dissertation is a mine of information.
7. Hidayette (pseudonym), *Abdul Hamid* (Zurich, 1896).

NOTE TO CHAPTER IV

1. W. L. Langer, *The Diplomacy of Imperialism 1890–1902* (New York and London: A. A. Knopf, 1935). Professor Langer's definition of imperialism expresses so closely the author's concept that he has adopted Dr. Langer's terminology, with modifications. The necessity of a precise and limited definition is essential if the author and his readers are to achieve a reasonable degree of objectivity in regard to "imperialism" in the Near East.

NOTES TO CHAPTER V

1. William Muir, *The Mameluke or Slave Dynasty of Egypt 1250–1517 A.D.* (London, 1896). This English authority on Islam gives an excellent account of the Mameluke rulers of Egypt.
2. Henry Dodwell, *The Founder of Modern Egypt; a Study of Muhammad Ali* (Cambridge: Cambridge University Press, 1931). This recent study of Egypt under Mohammed Ali makes clear the fundamental importance of Mohammed Ali's long reign to the evolution of modern and contemporary Egypt.
3. Frederick Jones Bliss, *The Religions of Modern Syria and Palestine* (New York, 1912). Frederick Bliss, whose father and brother were both presidents of the Syrian Protestant College of Beirut now the American University of Beirut, made a special study of the various religious sects among the Arabs of the Levant. His book is a help to an understanding of the factional feuds in Mount Lebanon which had much to do with its turbulent history.
4. Levfe de La Jonquière, *Histoire de l'empire ottomane depuis les origines jusqu' à nos jours* (Paris, 1914), I: 432. This is a revised edition of an earlier work by La Jonquière. His views reflect those of ardent French patriots who think of England as *perfide Albion.* His observations regarding British policies in the Near East aid in understanding the later antagonism between British and the French officials and officers in the Near East.
5. Edward S. Creasy, *Turkey* (rev. ed.; Philadelphia, 1906), p. 454. Creasy's first book on Turkey, *History of the Ottoman Turks,* was first published in 1854–56. Its importance is due largely to the fact that it provided English and American readers at the time of the Crimean War and the Congress of Paris with a history of the Ottoman Empire derived in no small measure from the voluminous writings of the German historian J. von Hammer-Purgstall, who published his ten volume history of the Ottomans, *Geschichte des osmanischen Reiches,* during 1827–35.
6. La Jonquière, *op. cit.,* I: 450. This quotation, freely translated, again reflects the anti-British attitude which to some degree affected British and French relations with respect to the Near East throughout the nineteenth century and during the first half of the twentieth.
7. Halil Ganem, *Etudes d'histoire orientale. Les sultans ottomans* (Paris, 1901), II: 236. This French writer of Lebanese origin influenced to some degree French opinion on matters pertaining to the Near East and especially to the Levant.
8. George J. S. Eversley, *The Turkish Empire, Its Growth and Decay* (London, 1917), p. 298. This limited edition was published during World War I. Its attitude toward Russia appears to be colored somewhat by the fact that Russia was an ally at the time of Britain and France. Eversley is frankly critical of Britain's nineteenth century policy toward the Ottoman Empire.

NOTES TO CHAPTER VI

1. David Harris, *A Diplomatic History of the Balkan Crisis of 1875–1878, The First Year* (Palo Alto, Calif.: Stanford University Press, 1936). This detailed account of the diplomatic background of the crisis which led to the Russian Turkish War 1877–78 and to the Congress of Berlin provides an insight to the complexities of the Balkan problems which confronted the Ottoman government in dealing with European imperialistic interests and the rampant nationalisms of the various Balkan peoples.
2. Mihailo D. Stojanovic, *The Great Powers and the Balkans, 1875–1878* (Cambridge: Cambridge University Press, 1939). This more generalized account by a Yugoslav scholar reveals how the conflicting interests of the Great Powers intensified tensions and rivalries in the Balkans.

NOTES TO CHAPTER VII

1. Alma Wittlin, *Abdul Hamid, The Shadow of God,* trans. by Norman Denny (London: John Lane, the Bodley Head, 1940). This delightful biography of the "Red Sultan" makes this much maligned ruler appear as a man of some integrity and intelligence who despite his upbringing and education attempted to live by those truths he "held to be self-evident."
2. Ali Yahbi Bey, *Pensées et souvenirs de l'ex-Sultan Abdul Hamid* (Paris, 1914), p. 211. This is a significantly revealing book. It uncovers the character and motives of a tyrant who, governed by his fears and motivated by his beliefs, caused untold suffering to his subjects and earned world-wide detestation.
3. Elbert E. Forman, *Egypt and Its Betrayal* (Grafton Press, 1908). U.S. Consul General Forman presents the opinions and judgment of an American official who was indignant at what he considered to be a falsification and misinterpretation of the events which led to the bombardment of the seaport by British warships and the occupation of Egypt by the British.
4. Wilfrid Scawen Blunt, *The Secret History of the English Occupation of Egypt* (London, 1907; New York, 1922). This extremely individualistic Britisher who was exceedingly critical of Britain's policy toward Egypt during the 1870's and 1880's knew intimately many of the British, Egyptian, and Turkish personalities connected with the British occupation and the events leading up to it. In his apologia, *Modern Egypt* (New York, 1908), Evelyn Baring Cromer, former British high commissioner, tends to challenge the views and assertions of Blunt and other critics of Britain's policy. Although Cromer's book cannot be considered fully objective it is, as a splendidly written book by one of the outstanding British proconsuls of the nineteenth century, a valuable part of the historical record.
5. Cromer, *Modern Egypt,* II: 372.

NOTES TO CHAPTER VIII

1. Richard Davey, *The Sultan and His Subjects* (London, 1897), II: 193–94. The author has an informative chapter on the Armenians with data not readily come by elsewhere.
2. Davey, *The Sultan and His Subjects,* II: 155–208.
3. B. J. Kidd, *A History of the Church* (Oxford, 1922), III: 425. This item of ecclesiastical history gives one an idea of how the religious sectarian disputes of the early Christian Church have affected the history of the Near East and the destinies of its people down to contemporary times.
4. Leon Arpee, *The Armenian Awakening* (Chicago, 1909). This objective study of the intellectual and political awakening of the Armenian people is an excellent antidote to the distress caused from reading the mass and the mess of propaganda books and pamphlets which appeared after the tragic massacres of Armenians in 1894, 1895, and 1909.
5. Simon Uratzian, "The Revolutionary Movement and Political Parties," a chapter in a propagandist book, *Armenia and the Armenian Question* (Boston: Hairenik Publishing Co., 1943). Uratzian is a somewhat naive and idealistic Armenian nationalist.
6. Pears, *Turkey and Its People.* Pears states that at least 250,000 Armenians perished during the massacres of 1894–97. In his *Life of Abdul Hamid* (London, 1917) his estimate of the number of Armenians killed is 350,000 and he writes that ". . . few observers put the number of victims lower than 100,000." Such is the lack of reliability of statistical data when recording "Turkish atrocities."

NOTES TO CHAPTER IX

1. Ahmed Softazade, *La Crète sous la domination et la suzeraineté ottomanes* (Paris, 1902). The writer presents a Turkish viewpoint which has the merit of not showing partiality toward any of the European Powers. It is less emotional, more analytical, and less biased than many contemporary accounts of recent and current insurrections.
2. David G. Hogarth, *The Nearer East* (London, 1902), see ethnographic chart on p. 176. This book by the renowned British scholar, an authority on the Near East deals with the geography, topography, and the peoples of the Near East.
3. J. Ivanoff, *La question macedonienne* (Paris, 1920). The author maintains that the bulk of the Macedonian population is Bulgar by language and culture. This Bulgarian professor marshals a formidable array of scholars to the support of his thesis.
4. P. D. Draganof, *Macedonia and the Reformers* (London, 1908), p. 5.
5. Harry F. B. Lynch, *Europe in Macedonia* (London, 1908).

NOTES TO CHAPTER X

1. David Philipson, *The Reform Movement in Judaism* (New York, 1907), pp. 488–89.
2. *Proceedings of the Zionist Congress* (New York, 1897).

NOTES TO CHAPTER XI

1. G. H. Fitzmaurice during the first decade of the twentieth century was considered one of the best informed officials of the British Foreign Office with regard to affairs of the Ottoman Empire. His official comments on the situation in Turkey during 1908 and 1909, which are to be found in *British Documents on the Origin of the War, 1898–1914,* Vol. 5, *The Near East 1903–09,* are shrewd interpretations and analyses of the events of the revolution and counter revolution of 1908–9.
2. E. F. Knight, *The Awakening of Turkey, A History of the Turkish Revolution* (London, 1909), pp. 111–12. Mr. Knight, himself a Mason, had close contacts with the Young Turks and friends among the prominent members of the Committee of Union and Progress.
3. Youssouf Fehmi, *La revolution ottomane* (Paris, 1911), pp. 24, 152–53. Despite his intense opposition to Freemasonry and to the C.U.P. Fehmi's description of the tight oligarchy that dominated the Committee of Union and Progress is confirmed by other writers and eventually by events.
4. Charles Roden Buxton, *Turkey in Revolution* (London, 1909). Another roving British writer who was an enthusiastic admirer of the Young Turks and of the members of the C.U.P.
5. Knight, *Awakening of Turkey.*
6. G. F. Abbott, *Turkey in Transition* (London, 1909). Abbott was not blinded by enthusiasm and idealism to the realities underlying the structure of the C.U.P.

NOTES TO CHAPTER XII

1. Harry Luke, *The Making of Modern Turkey from Byzantium to Angora* (London: Macmillan, 1936). Sir Harry, who is considered to be a competent writer, seemingly knew little of the diplomatic history behind Italy's war against Turkey. At the time Sir Harry wrote all the basic documents pertaining to Italy's intention of seizing Libya and Cyrenaica had been published.
2. Thomas Barday, *The Turco-Italian War and Its Problems* (London, 1912). William C. Askey, *Europe and Italy's Acquisition of Libya* (Durham, N.C.: Duke University Press, 1942). These are first-rate books on the Turko-Italian War.
3. E. C. Helmreich, *The Diplomacy of the Balkan Wars* (Cambridge, Mass.: Harvard University Press, 1938). After an exhaustive study of the vast amount of documentary materials and literature which

became available after World War I, Helmreich has written an authoritative book of utmost value and interest on the causes of the Balkan Wars.
4. André Mandelstam, *Le sort de l'Empire Ottoman* (Lausanne, 1917).

NOTES TO CHAPTER XIII

1. George Antonius, *The Arab Awakening* (New York: J. B. Lippincott and Co., 1939). George Antonius, a Christian Arab Nationalist wrote the first important book on the Arab Renaissance. With respect to political matters concerning the Arab Revolt and the British Commitments to the Arabs in the Hussein-McMahon correspondence Antonius had the advantage of first-hand information from Emir Faisal but he did not have access to materials since made available. See Elie Kedourie, *England and the Middle East* (London: Bowes and Bowes, 1956) and Jane Worth Harbaugh, *Origins of the Balfour Declaration* (unpublished Ph.D. dissertation, Fletcher School of International Law and Diplomacy, 1957).
2. These proclamations of the League of the Arab Homeland are to be found in Eugene Jung's *Les puissances devant la revolte arabe* (Paris, 1906), pp. 22–29.
3. Negib Azoury, *Le reveil de la nation arabe dans l'Asie Turque* (Paris, 1905), pp. 48–49.

NOTES TO CHAPTER XIV

1. Philip P. Graves, *Briton and Turk* (London: Hutchinson & Co., 1941). This English journalist shows intimate knowledge and sound judgment of the situation in Turkey between 1908 and 1914. In the author's preface, he frankly admits that like "many Western journalists [he] . . . did not make sufficient allowances between 1908 and 1914 for the difficulties of a nation which had endured such paralyzing misrule."
2. Liman von Sanders, *Five Years in Turkey* (Annapolis, 1927), pp. 1–3.
3. Winston S. Churchill, *The Unknown War* (New York: Charles Scribner's Sons, 1931), p. 43.
4. Ahmed Djemal Pasha, *Memoirs of a Turkish Statesman* (New York, 1922).
5. Ahmed Emin, *Turkey in the World War* (New Haven: Yale University Press, 1930).

NOTES TO CHAPTER XV

1. Jemal Pasha, *Memoirs of a Turkish Statesman,* pp. 154–55.
2. G. L. McEnlee, *Military History of the World War* (New York: Charles Scribner's Sons, 1937), p. 147.
3. Liman von Sanders, *Five Years in Turkey,* p. 47.
4. William Yale, "It Takes So Long" (unpublished memoirs).

5. References to this little known agreement may be found in an article by Leonid I. Strakhovsky in *Current History,* 33 (March, 1931): 839–41, in Winston S. Churchill's *The Aftermath* (London, 1929), pp. 167–68; in Louis Fischer's *The Soviet in World Affairs* (London: J. Cape, 1930), II: 710, 836; in *The Daily Herald* (London, Aug. 30, 1920).
6. Harry Howard, *The Partition of Turkey, A Diplomatic History 1913–1923* (Norman, Okla.: University of Oklahoma Press, 1931), p. 137.
7. M. Larcher, *La guerre turque dans la guerre mondiale* (Paris, 1926), p. 60.
8. von Sanders, *Five Years in Turkey,* p. 123.

NOTES TO CHAPTER XVI

1. William Yale, "Morganthau's Special Mission of 1917," *World Politics,* (1949), 1, No. 3: 308–20.
2. En route from Jerusalem to Constantinople in February/March 1917 the author passed a considerable movement of Turkish troops and military equipment going towards the southern fronts. William Yale, "It Takes So Long."
3. P. G. La Chesnais, *Les peuples de la Transcaucasie pendant la guerre et devant la paix* (Paris, 1921). This is a most useful little volume on the complex situation in Transcaucasia during 1917–19.

NOTES TO CHAPTER XVII

1. For definite geographical boundaries see page 188.
2. George Stitt, *A Prince of Arabia, The Emir Shereef Ali Haidar* (London: George Allen and Unwin, Ltd., 1948).
3. William Yale, "It Takes So Long."
4. *The Letters of T. E. Lawrence,* ed. by David Garnett (London: Jonathan Cape, 1938). See also T. E. Lawrence, *The Seven Pillars of Wisdom.*
5. Achmed Jemal Pasha, *La verité sur la question syrienne* (Stamboul, 1916). This interesting volume, a copy of which is in the Harvard Widener Library, contains photostatic copies of the documents seized by the Turks in the French consulates at Damascus and Beirut.
6. Stitt, *A Prince of Arabia.*
7. T. E. Lawrence, *Revolt in the Desert* (New York, 1927), pp. 66–67.
8. N. N. E. Bray, *Shifting Sands* (London: Unicorn Press, 1934).
9. Yale, *World Politics,* 1, No. 3.
10. *The Letters of T. E. Lawrence* (New York: Doubleday, Doran & Co., 1939), Letter 397, p. 670. Lawrence's letter to Yale was censored by the editor. A photostatic copy of the original is in Yale University Library. Also at Boston University C.L.A. Library.

NOTES TO CHAPTER XVIII

1. Nahum Sokolow, *The History of Zionism* (London, 1919), II: 4. "The first expression of this unity was an increase in self-consciousness."
2. Jessie E. Sampter, *A Guide to Zionism* (New York, 1920).
3. Karl Kautsky, *Are the Jews a Race?* (London, 1926).
4. Sokolow, *The History of Zionism,* II: 5.
5. Stephen Gwynn, ed., *Letters and Friendships of Sir Cecil Spring-Rice* (New York, 1929), II: 200–201.
6. David Lloyd George, *War Memoirs of Lloyd George* (London: I. Nicholson & Watson, 1933–36), II (1915–16): 50.
7. Samuel Landman, *Great Britain, the Jews and Palestine* (London: New Zionist Press, 1936).
8. Blanche E. C. Dugdale, *Arthur James Balfour* (New York: G. P. Putnam's Sons, 1937), II: 158.

NOTES TO CHAPTER XIX

1. Leonid I. Strakhovsky, see *supra* Chapter XV, note 5, p. 12. Strakhovsky wrote as follows: "The Murmansky Agreement of July 6, 1918, was far from pleasing to those leaders of British Foreign Policy who were responsible for striking the bargain with France for an economic dismemberment of Russia as embodied in the secret agreement of December 23, 1917."
2. A. H. Pallis, *Greece's Anatolian Venture and After* (London: Methuen and Co., 1937). A. F. Frangulis, *La Grèce et la crise mondiale* (Paris, 1926).
3. Maurice Pernot, *La question turque* (Paris, 1923), p. 240.
4. Philip Graves, *Briton and Turk,* p. 199.
5. Pallis, *Greece's Anatolian Venture,* p. 132.
6. Carlo Sforza, *The Makers of Modern Europe* (London: Mathews and Maurot, 1931). Sforza has a provocative chapter on Mustafa Kemal.
7. Sforza, *The Makers of Modern Europe,* pp. 358–61.

NOTES TO CHAPTER XX

1. Aziz Hanki, *Turcs et Ataturk* (Cairo: Noury et Fils, 1939). This fulsome and uncritical tribute to Mustafa Kemal Ataturk is useful principally in revealing the enthusiasm awakened in Arabs and Turks for this dynamic Turkish leader and in making more understandable the contemporary popularity among the Arabs of Ataturk's Egyptian counterpart, President Nasser.
2. Princess Musbar Haidar Sherifa, *Arabesque* (London: Hutchinson & Co., 1945). This modernistic daughter of Ali Haidar by his English wife gives an entertaining account of her childhood and upbringing.
3. Selma Ekrem, *Turkey, Old and New* (New York: Charles Scribner's

Sons, 1947). This prolific Turkish writer presents her view of the transformation of Turkey which began in her early youth.

4. Halidé Edib (Adib) Adivar, *Memoirs* (New York, 1926). Halidé Adivar was the outstanding feminine leader of the Young Turk intellectuals. Her *Memoirs* portray a vivid contrast between the life of the upper bureaucratic middle class under the Ottoman regime and during the emerging new Turkey.
5. Robert W. Kerwin, "The Turkish Road Program," *The Middle East Journal,* IV, No. 2 (1950): 198–99.
6. Lilo Linke, *Allah Dethroned* (London: Constable and Co., 1937). It is refreshing to read a book by an untrammeled reporter who traveled through Turkey in 1936 as an ordinary Turk would travel and who hobnobbed with all sorts of people instead of hanging around Ankara with the V.I.P. and retailing their views and press "handouts." Lilo Linke grew up in Berlin during World War I. During the early years of the Weimar Republic she joined the Youth Movement, met the young Marxist socialists and communists, but joined the liberal Democratic Party. She watched the growth of naziism and fled to England on Hitler's accession to power. When she went to Turkey as a correspondent she was a free agent—not the hired employee of powerful news and broadcasting agencies.

NOTES TO CHAPTER XXI

1. *The Geography of Strabo,* trans. by Horace L. Jones (London: Heinemann; New York: G. P. Putnam, 1917–32), II: 148–49, V: 329.
2. G. Le Strange, *The Lands of the Eastern Caliphate* (Cambridge, 1905).
3. William Willcocks, *Mesopotamia: Past, Present and Future* (Washington, D.C., 1909), p. 410.
4. Gertrude Bell, *Letters of Gertrude Bell* (New York, 1927), II: 464.
5. *Ibid.,* pp. 466–68.
6. Arnold T. Wilson, *Clash of Loyalties: Mesopotamia 1917–20* (London: Oxford University Press, 1931).
7. *Ibid.,* pp. 102–3.
8. Ernest Main, *Iraq from Mandate to Independence* (London: Allen & Unwin, 1935), p. 76.
9. Philip W. Ireland, *Iraq, A Study in Political Development* (New York: Macmillan Co., 1938), pp. 136–65.
10. James Aylmer L. Haldane, *The Insurrection in Mesopotamia, 1920* (Edinburgh and London, 1922).
11. Bell, *Letters,* p. 535. "It was extraordinary with what aversion the mandatory idea had always been regarded in Iraq."
12. Bell, *Letters,* pp. 526–27. On her arrival at London in July 1920 Miss Bell cautiously advised the British government with regard to establishing a national government in Iraq, saying "—that the risk was at any rate worth taking if regarded as the only alternative to evacuation."

13. Wilson, *Mesopotamia, 1917–1920,* pp. 238–39. Sir Arnold discusses the use of airplanes as a military means of controlling Iraq.
14. R. S. Stafford, *The Tragedy of the Assyrians* (London: Allen & Unwin, 1935).
15. Ernest Dowson, *An Inquiry into Land Tenure and Related Questions* (Bagdad: Iraqi Government Report, 1931).

NOTES TO CHAPTER XXII

1. The author as special agent of the Department of State in Egypt 1917–18 and later as American military observer with the Egyptian Expeditionary Force in Palestine and Syria was in a position to hear and observe the friction between the British and the French.
2. R. de Gontaut-Biron, *Comment la France s'est installée en Syrie* (Paris, 1922), p. 70. Comte de Gontaut-Biron writes as a passionate and indignant patriot about the propaganda of the British and Americans and the methods which he claims were used by them to undermine the French position in Syria. Although statements of the comte cannot always be depended upon (viz., p. 267, data regarding "le capitaine Yale" are contrary to fact) his distrust and suspicion of British and American motives reveal the attitude of French officials and officers in the Near East during the years 1918–19.
3. André Tardieu, "Mossoul et le petrole," *L'Illustration,* June 19, 1920, pp. 380–88. A revealing article on Anglo-French negotiations of 1919.
4. *Supra,* pp. 315–17.
5. Collection of Papers of William Yale, Yale University Library.
6. Elizabeth P. MacCallum, *The Nationalist Crusade in Syria* (New York, 1928), p. 31. This is a balanced and competent account of the causes and the events of the revolt in Syria and Lebanon against the French in 1925–27.
7. *Ibid.,* pp. 85–88.
8. Franz Werfel, *The Forty Days of Musa Dagh* (New York: Viking Press, 1934). This novel gives an account of the heroic struggle for survival of the Armenians in Musa Dagh.
9. S. B. Himadeh, *Economic Organization of Syria* (Beirut: American Press, 1936), p. 15.

NOTES TO CHAPTER XXIII

1. Freya Stark, *The Southern Gates of Arabia* (New York: E. P. Dutton Co., 1945). On the southern coastal area of Arabia; like all of Freya Stark's books on the Near East, it is delightful reading.
2. Bertram Thomas, *Arabia Felix* (New York: Charles Scribner's Sons, 1932). Contains a vivid description of Bertram Thomas' trip across the "Empty Quarter."
3. Great Britain Foreign Office, *Arabia* [London: H. M. Stationery Office, 1920].
4. K. S. Twitchell, *Saudi Arabia* (Princeton: Princeton University Press, 1947–).

5. Samuel M. Zwemer, *Arabia, the Cradle of Islam* (New York, 1900). A. H. Keane, *Asia* (London, 1882).
6. Great Britain Foreign Office, *Arabia.*
7. Gerald de Gaury, *Arabia Phoenix* (London: George G. Harrap & Co., 1946).
8. William Yale Papers, Cambridge, Mass., Harvard University, Houghton Library, Accession No. 50M188, restricted.
9. De Gaury, *Arabia Phoenix,* p. 24. Twitchell, *Saudi Arabia,* p. 161.

NOTE TO CHAPTER XXIV

1. The sources for material in this chapter are numerous and varied. The author herewith expresses his special obligation to *Reports of the Arabian American Oil Co.,* provided by former vice-president James Terry Duce; to *The Middle East, Oil and the Great Powers,* by Benjamin Shwadran (New York: Frederick A. Praeger, 1955); *Oil in the Middle East: Its Discovery and Development,* by Stephen H. Longrigg (London, New York; Oxford University Press, 1954); and *Arabian Oil America's Stake in the Middle East,* by Raymond F. Mikesell and Hollis B. Chenery (Chapel Hill, N.C.: University of North Carolina Press, 1949).

NOTES TO CHAPTER XXV

1. A. G. Keller, *Man's Rough Road* (New York: Frederick A. Stokes Co., 1932).
2. *Great Britain and Palestine 1915–1939* (London: Royal Institute of International Affairs, 1939), p. 13.
3. William Yale Papers, Houghton Library, accession 50M188, restricted.
4. For details see page 395 *infra* and the British *White Paper.* Palestine Statement of Policy Comd. 6019. 1939.
5. Herbert F. Rudd, "Some Facts and a Formula for Balanced Representation in World Government" (A privately circulated mimeographed paper, see William Yale Papers, Houghton Library).
6. British *White Paper* of 1922, Comd. 1700; the so-called Churchill Memorandum.
7. D. Lloyd George, *The Truth About the Peace Treaties* (London: Gollanez, 1938), p. 1139.
8. Chaim Weizmann, *Trial and Error* (New York: Harper and Brothers, 1949), p. 291.
9. *Great Britain and Palestine,* p. 38.
10. British *White Paper,* Palestine, Statement of Policy by H. M. Govt. Comd. 3692, 1930.
11. British *Blue Book,* Palestine Royal Commission, Comd. 5479, 1937.
12. British *Blue Book,* Palestine Partition Commission, Comd. 5854, 1938.
13. British *White Paper,* Palestine, Statement of Policy, Comd. 6019, 1939.
14. Esco Foundation for Palestine, *Palestine, A Study of Jewish, Arab and British Policies* (New Haven: Yale University Press, 1947), II: 909. Pro-Zionist useful reference work.

15. Frank C. Sakran, *Palestine Dilemma* (Washington, D.C.: Public Press, 1948), p. 159.

NOTES TO CHAPTER XXVI

1. *Congressional Record,* 91, Pt. 2 (79th Congress, 1st Session Feb. 26, 1945, March 26, 1945): 1662. Quotation from the address of President Roosevelt.
2. Bartley Crum, *Behind the Silken Curtain* (New York: Simon & Schuster, 1947).
3. Arthur Koestler, *Promise and Fulfillment, Palestine 1917–1949* (London: Macmillan, 1949), p. 56.
4. Richard Crossman, *Palestine Mission, A Personal Record* (New York and London: Harper & Brothers, 1947), p. 202.
5. *Supplement to the Survey of Palestine* (published by the Government of Palestine, June, 1947), pp. 131–33.
6. Quoted by Koestler, *Promise and Fulfillment.*

NOTES TO CHAPTER XXVII

1. Quoted from an address by Loy W. Henderson, at the time director of the Office of Near, Middle East, and African Affairs of the Department of State, published in *The Middle East Journal,* I, No. 1 (January 1947): 85–88.

NOTES TO CHAPTER XXIX

1. H. A. R. Gibb, *Modern Trends in Islam* (Chicago: University of Chicago Press, 1945), pp. 27–28.
2. J. Heyworth Dunne, *Religious and Political Trends in Modern Egypt* (Washington, D.C., published by the author, 1950), pp. 12, 17. This brief monograph is exceedingly helpful. The account of the growth and nature of the Moslem Brotherhood is almost essential reading for an understanding of its role in Egyptian politics.
3. Charles Issawi, *Egypt at Mid Century, an Economic Survey* (London, New York, Toronto: Oxford University Press, 1954).
4. George Lenczowski, *The Middle East in World Affairs* (Ithaca, New York: Cornell University Press, 1957, 2nd ed.), p. 414.
5. Sidney B. Fay, *The Origins of the World War* (New York: Macmillan Company, 1930), I: 146.

5a. C. Harris, *Nationalism and Revolution in Egypt* (Stanford: Hoover Institute Publications, 1964).

6. Dunne, *Religious and Political Trends in Modern Egypt,* p. 78. Although the author's remarks were concerned with the danger of the spread of Communism, they are just as applicable to the possibility of a seizure of power by the fanatically anti-foreign, anti-western religious reactionaries, the Ikhwan el-Muslimin.

7. Albert Hourani. "The Anglo-Egyptian Agreement: Some Causes and Implications," *Middle East Journal,* 9, No. 3 (1955): 248–49.
8. *Ibid.*
9. See *Middle East Journal,* 7, No. 1 (Winter 1953): 74–80.

NOTES TO CHAPTER XXX

1. John Simmons, "Agricultural Development in Iraq," *Middle East Journal,* 19, No. 2 (1965).
2. The author, as technical adviser to the King–Crane Commission, was present at this meeting of the American section of the International Commission on Mandates in Turkey.
3. The American people have become deeply involved with the problem of both Jewish and Palestinian Arab refugees. Previous to the entrance of the U.S. into World War II, President F. D. Roosevelt discussed with his close friend Justice Felix Frankfurter and other leading American Zionists whether some thousands of Jewish refugees in Western Europe should be admitted to the U.S.A. A negative decision was arrived at for the alleged reason that it would intensify the allegedly strong anti-Semitism in this country. The anguish of the Palestinian Arab refugees resulting from both the Arab-Israeli wars of 1948–49 and 1967 has given rise to such bitterness that a Palestinian Arab (a citizen of Jordan), accused assassin of Senator Robert Kennedy, had written in his diary that Kennedy should be assassinated on June 5, the anniversary of the second Arab-Israeli War.
4. Arslan Humbaraci's *Middle East Indictment* (London: Robert Hale, 1958) throws considerable light on the Cold War in the Near East. Humbaraci is a Turkish liberal whose treatment by his own government led to his becoming a Communist agent and whose treatment by the Soviet government led to his seeking asylum in Great Britain from both the Communists and the Turks.

SUGGESTED READINGS

It is the author's conviction that the proper place for an extensive bibliography is in specially prepared bibliographies. Readers wishing further bibliographical material are referred to: *A Selected and Annotated Bibliography of Books and Periodicals in Western Languages Dealing with the Near and Middle East with Special Emphasis on Medieval and Modern Times.* Edited by Richard Ettinghausen. Washington, D.C.: Middle East Institute, 1954.

Those interested in knowing about current research projects are referred to: *Current Research on the Middle East.* A series of annual surveys begun in 1955, published by the Middle East Institute, Washington, D.C.

Note

Students and others would find the books herewith listed both interesting and useful in extending their knowledge of the Near East, its peoples, and its problems.

GENERAL

Eliahu Ben-Horin. *The Middle East: Crossroads of History.* New York: Norton, 1943.

Alfred Bonné. *The Economic Development of the Middle East.* London: Kegan Paul, Trench, Trubner and Company, 1945.

William B. Fisher. *The Middle East, a Physical, Social and Regional Geography.* London: Methuen; New York: Dutton, 1950.

William H. Hocking. *The Spirit of World Politics, with Special Studies of the Near East.* London, 1932.

David G. Hogarth. *The Nearer East.* London, 1902.

George E. Kirk. *A Short History of the Middle East: From the Rise of Islam to Modern Times.* Rev. ed.; New York: Frederick A. Praeger, 1955.

George Lenczowski. *The Middle East in World Affairs.* 2d ed.; Ithaca, N.Y.: Cornell University Press, 1956.

William M. Ramsay. *The Historical Geography of Asia Minor.* London, 1890.

M. I. Rostovtsev. *Caravan Cities.* Oxford: The Clarendon Press, 1932.

The Royal Institute of International Affairs. *The Middle East, A Political and Economic Survey.* London, New York: Chatham House, 1951.

Stephen H. Longrigg. *The Middle East—A Social Geography.* Chicago: Ildine, 1963.

Walter Z. Laqueur. *Communism and Nationalism in the Middle East.* New York: Praeger. 1956 (See Review, *Middle East Journal,* Spring 1957, pp. 204–15, by Bernard Lewis)

THE OTTOMAN EMPIRE

Edward S. Creasy. *Turkey*. Rev. ed.; Philadelphia, 1908.

G. J. S. Eversley. *The Turkish Empire, Its Growth and Development.* London, 1917.

Herbert A. Gibbons. *The Foundations of the Ottoman Empire.* Oxford, 1916.

Mehemed Fuad Köprülü. *Les origines de l'empire ottoman.* Paris, 1935.

Harry C. J. Luke. *The Making of Modern Turkey from Byzantium to Angora.* London: Macmillan, 1936.

Paul Wittek. *The Rise of the Ottoman Empire.* London: Royal Asiatic Society, 1938.

TURKISH NATIONALISM AND THE TURKISH REPUBLIC

Halidé Edib Adivar. *Memoirs.* New York, London, 1926.

Kemal Atatürk. [Speech delivered October 15–20, 1927.] Leipzig, 1929.

Niyazi Beakes. *The Development of Secularism in Turkey.* Montreal: McGill University Press, 1964.

Frederick W. Frey. *The Turkish Political Elite.* Cambridge, Mass.: Mass. Inst. of Technology, 1965.

A. Haluk and Frank Jachav. "Turkish Politics. The Attempt to Reconcile Rapid Modernization with Democracy," *Middle East Journal,* 19 (1965) no. 2: 153–68.

Uriel Heyd. *The Foundations of Turkish Nationalism: The Life and Teachings of Ziya Gökalp.* London: Harvil Press, 1950.

Harry N. Howard. *The Partition of Turkey, a Diplomatic History 1913–1923.* Norman, Okla.: University of Oklahoma Press, 1931.

Kemal H. Korpat. *Turkey's Politics: Transition to a Multi-Party System.* Princeton: Princeton University Press, 1959.

ARABS—COUNTRIES AND HISTORY

Saudi Arabia

H. St. John B. Philby. *Saudi Arabia.* London: Ernest Benn, 1955; New York: Frederick A. Praeger, 1955.

K. S. Twitchell. *Saudi Arabia.* 2d ed. Princeton: Princeton University Press, 1953.

D. van der Meulen. *The Wells of Ibn Sa'ud,* New York: Frederick A. Praeger, 1957.

History

Philip K. Hitti. *History of the Arabs, A Short History.* Princeton: Princeton University Press, 1943.

Freya Stark. *The Arab Island.* New York: Knopf, 1945.

Nationalism

George Antonius. *The Arab Awakening.* London: Hamilton, 1938.

Nejla Izzeddin. *The Arab World Past and Present.* Chicago: Regnery, 1953.

Egypt

Evelyn B. Cromer. *Modern Egypt.* New York, 1916.

Charles Issawi. *Egypt at Mid-century, An Economic Survey.* New York: Oxford University Press, 1952.

Gamal Abdel Nasser. *Egypt's Liberation.* Washington, D.C.: Public Affairs Press, 1955.

Arnold T. Wilson. *The Suez Canal, Its Past, Present and Future.* 2d ed. London: Oxford University Press, 1939.

Iraq

Gertrude Bell. *Letters.* Ed. Lady Florence Bell. New York: Boni & Liveright, 1927. 2 vols.

Philip W. Ireland. *Iraq. A Study in Political Development.* London: J. Cape, 1937.

Majid Khadduri. *Independent Iraq. A Study in Iraqi Politics since 1932.* London: Oxford University Press, 1951.

Jordan

Philip Graves, ed. *Memoirs of King Abdullah of Transjordan.* London: Hodder and Stoughton, 1948.

Palestine

Paul L. Hanna. *British Policy in Palestine.* Washington, D.C.: American Council on Public Affairs, 1942.

J. C. Hurewitz. *The Struggle for Palestine.* New York: Norton, 1950.

Joseph M. N. Jeffries. *Palestine the Reality.* New York: Longmans, 1939.

Syria and Lebanon

Philip K. Hitti. *History of Syria Including Lebanon and Palestine.* New York: Macmillan, 1951.

Albert H. Hourani. *Syria and Lebanon, a Political Essay.* London; New York: Oxford University Press, 1946.

Elizabeth P. MacCallum. *The Nationalist Crusade in Syria.* New York: Foreign Policy Assn., 1928.

Z. K. Zeine. *The Struggle for Arab Independence.* Beirut, 1960.

Petroleum

Stephen H. Longrigg. *Oil in the Middle East.* New York: Oxford University Press, 1954.

R. F. Mikesell and H. B. Chenery. *Arabian Oil, America's Stake in the Middle East.* Chapel Hill, N.C.: University of North Carolina Press, 1949.

Benjamin Shwadran. *The Middle East, Oil and the Great Powers.* New York: Frederick A. Praeger, 1955.

THE ARAB WORLD—ADDITIONS

General

Charles D. Cremeans. *The Arabs and the World.* New York: Praeger, 1963.

Daniel Lerner. *The Passing of Traditional Society, Modernizing the Middle East.* New York and London, 1958.

"Transformation of Ideology in the Arab World," *Middle East Journal,* 19 (1965), no. 4.

Zeine N. Zein. *Arab-Turkish Relations and the Emergence of Arab Nationalism.* Beirut: Khayat's, 1958.

Egypt

Malcolm H. Kerr. *Islamic Reform. The Religious Theories of Muhammad Abduh and Rashid Rida.* Berkeley, Calif.: University of California Press, 1966.

Terence Robertson. *The Inside Story of the Suez Conspiracy.* New York: Atheneum, 1965. (See Review by Daniel Crecelius, *Middle East Journal,* 19, Autumn 1965.)

Robert L. Tignor. *Modernization and British Colonial Rule in Egypt 1882–1914.* Princeton, N.J.: Princeton University Press, 1965.

Iraq

John Simmons. "Agricultural Development in Iraq and Management Failures," *Middle East Journal,* 19 (1965), no. 2: 129–40.

Yemen

Gamal-Eddine Heyworth-Dunne. *Al-Yemen, A General Social, Political, and Economic Survey.* Cairo, 1952.

William Harold Ingrams. *The Yemen: Imams, Rulers, and Revolutions.* London: J. Murray, 1963.

Kuwait

Ragaeit-el-Mallakh. "Economic Development through Cooperation: The Kuwait Fund," *Middle East Journal,* 18 (1964), no. 4.

Elizabeth Monro. "Kuwait and Aden," *Middle East Journal,* 18 (1964): 63–64.

Lebanon

Charles Issawi. "Economic Development and Liberalism in Lebanon," *Middle East Journal,* 18 (1964), no. 3: 271–92.

Leonard Binder, Ed. *Politics in Lebanon.* New York: John Wiley & Sons, Inc., 1966.

South Arabia and Aden

Gillian King. *Imperial Outpost.* New York: Oxford University Press, 1965. (See Review by Elizabeth Monro, *Middle East Journal,* 19, Spring 1965, no. 2.)

ZIONISM, ISRAEL, AND THE ARAB-ISRAEL CONFLICT

Zionism

Ben Halpern. *The Idea of the Jewish State.* Cambridge, Mass.: Harvard University Press, 1961. (See Review by Elie Kedourie, *Commentary,* 33 (1962), no. 1: 82–84.

Samuel Halpern. *The Political World of American Zionism.* Detroit: Wayne State University Press, 1961.

Nahum Sokolov. *History of Zionism 1600–1918.* New York: Longman's, 1919. 2 vols.

Israel

David Ben Gurion. *Rebirth and Destiny of Israel.* New York: Philosophical Library, 1953.

Walter Eytan. *The First Ten Years: A Diplomatic History of Israel.* New York: Simon and Schuster, 1958. (A notable quotation: "It is a commonplace of our Foreign Service that every Envoy Extraordinary and Minister Plenipotentiary of Israel has a dual function. He is Minister Plenipotentiary to the country to which he is accredited and Envoy Extraordinary to its Jews," p. 192.)

Ronald Sandes. *The View from Masada.* New York: Harper & Row, 1966. (See Review by Edward Grossman, *Commentary,* Feb. 1967.)

Chaim Weizmann. *Trial and Error, Autobiography of Chaim Weizmann.* New York: Harpers, 1949.

Arab-Israeli Conflict

Earl Berger. *The Covenant and the Sword. Arab-Israeli Relations 1948–1956.* Toronto: University of Toronto Press, 1964. (See Review by J. C. Hurewitz, *Middle East Studies,* 3 (July 1967), no. 4: 427–29.

H. C. Hurewitz. *The Struggle for Palestine.* New York: W. W. Norton, 1953.

H. C. Hurewitz. "Recent Books on the Problem of Palestine," *Middle East Journal,* III (1949).

"How To Speak To The Arabs. MAARIV Round Table, Held in Tel Aviv, August 16, 1963," *Middle East Journal,* 18 (1964), no. 2: 143–62.

W. R. Polk, D. M. Stamler, E. Y. Affour. *Backdrop to Tragedy: The Struggle for Palestine.* Boston: Beacon Press, 1957.

INDEX